UPTON'S REGULARS

Upton's Regulars

The 121st New York Infantry

in the Civil War

SALVATORE G. CILELLA, JR.

 University Press of Kansas

© 2009 by the University Press of Kansas

Published by the University Press of Kansas (Lawrence, Kansas 66045), which was organized by the Kansas Board of Regents and is operated and funded by Emporia State University, Fort Hays State University, Kansas State University, Pittsburg State University, the University of Kansas, and Wichita State University

Library of Congress Cataloging-in-Publication Data
Cilella, Salvatore G.
Upton's Regulars : the 121st New York Infantry in the Civil War / Salvatore G. Cilella, Jr.
   p.   cm. — (Modern war studies)
   Includes bibliographical references and index.
   ISBN 978-0-7006-1645-9 (cloth : alk. paper)
   1. United States. Army. New York Infantry Regiment, 121st (1861–1865) 2. New York (State)—History—Civil War, 1861–1865—Regimental histories. 3. United States—History—Civil War, 1861–1865—Regimental histories. I. Title.
   E523.5121st .C55 2009
   973.7—dc22   2009011070

British Library Cataloguing-in-Publication Data is available.

Printed in the United States of America

10 9 8 7 6 5 4 3 2 1

Contents

Preface and Acknowledgments

The story behind the production of the 121st's original history is almost as interesting as the regiment's story itself. In 1996, I learned of a reprint of the *History of the 121st New York Infantry* by Isaac O. Best with a special introduction and new material and photographs by Joseph S. Covais. The news rekindled my interest. I had used the original 1921 edition for my thesis in the Cooperstown Graduate Programs. That volume had been a gift from upstate New York bookseller Roger Butterfield, who appreciated my interest in old books and my curiosity about the history of a local regiment. I was unable to act on my renewed interest until 2001, when I made a serious attempt to find Joe Covais. His publisher in Baltimore (Butternut and Blue) led me to his last known address in Middlebury, Vermont, and then, through an independent bookseller, I was able to track him to his current home in Burlington. We talked on the phone, exchanged emails, and agreed that a new history of the regiment was needed. Joe's eyesight had failed, and we came to an agreement that I would do the writing if he would share his research. His materials became the cornerstone of even more research neither of us contemplated when I began this venture. What follows is a labor of love on both of our parts.

This story of the 121st is a sixty-year common biography of a group of men from upstate New York who were subjected to the hellish experiences of separation, exposure, disease, deprivation, and death. In Oliver Wendell Holmes's words, they shared the "incommunicable experience of war." It is also a story of how they coped with it all well beyond the regiment's three years of combat. This book looks at these men as young recruits in their rural environment, where they went, and how they fared during and after the war.

This study is also concerned with the 121st's leadership. The regiment's three commanders—Richard Franchot, Emory Upton, and

Egbert Olcott—each brought to the position a completely different background and a special talent or skill, and each was responsible in a different way for what happened to the men he led. Each one's term of service was completely unlike the others, and each man was larger than life. Franchot was the stereotypical soldier-politician, who immediately left the stage after separating from the service. He was replaced by the career-minded, West Point–trained, straight-laced Emory Upton, a Regular Army combat veteran. When Upton's ambition moved him on, another combat veteran, the enigmatic Egbert Olcott, a native of Otsego County, took his place as the war went into its final, brutal phase. It was Olcott, the volunteer with hard-earned battlefield experience, who saw the regiment through to the end.

One strong theme runs through the history of the 121st, however. From the day that New York responded to Lincoln's call for 300,000 more men to the day the regiment was mustered out of federal service—and through its reincarnation as a reunion association—national, state, and local politics were never far from the front lines. Officers fought for promotion among themselves and with the politicians back home, and enlisted men railed against Copperheads and draft dodgers back home. As the administrations of President Lincoln and New York governor Horatio Seymour agreed to disagree, political decisions affected life and death on the battlefield. Officers postured for political gain; politicians meddled in war strategy. Northern governors tried to micromanage the war. They insisted on the states' right to appoint officers and control their volunteers as they had their militias. Officers who knew how to play the system with friends in high places were able to advance; those who did not were shut out. Either way, the common soldier who was not part of the system suffered. A few officers saw the need to protect their most vital resources—the men in the ranks—and went out of their way to ensure their comfort. Most did not.

Politics played a major role in the story of most units, but it was particularly prevalent in the 121st. At the local, state, and national levels alike, the major players' connections with the men and officers of the 121st were remarkable. And, ignoring the chain of command, some were not above taking advantage of their connections with men of influence back home. Although the battles and hardships that the men of the 121st endured are interesting in themselves, the interplay between officers and men and between these men and officers and the civilian establishment is revealing.

Members of the 121st were vocal to the end of the war about everything, including matters of duty, honor, courage, the Emancipation Proclamation, the Union, George McClellan, Abraham Lincoln, freed slaves, slavery, and incompetence at all levels. Recent historians have written extensively on soldiers' motivations in joining the fight. Most men of the 121st fought to preserve the Union and were markedly upset with the idea that the Lincoln administration's

Emancipation Proclamation was a reason for carrying on the war. Many clearly and precisely stated that they had gone to war to save the Union, not to free 4 million slaves. Yet they abhorred the Copperheads and all they stood for. As dire as the war became, especially in the summer of 1864, the boys of the 121st repeatedly told their families and friends that they would do it all again, that they would rather die on the battlefield than run in cowardice, and that they would have felt guilty staying home. The story of the 121st is one of hope and sometimes despair evinced by a group of young, sheltered men, most of whom would not survive the war. They expressed the hope that they would soon return home "when this cruel war was over"; some were philosophical about returning—"perhaps a cripple"—but they persevered with the thought that they would do their duty. And most concurred with the sentiment expressed by George Teel in a letter to his wife before Grant's Overland campaign in 1864: "If I fall, I fall in the best of causes, fighting for my country." Many of those who survived the war were either mentally disturbed or physically impaired as they returned to civilian life.[1]

Every writer eventually comes to a point where he or she acknowledges what the reader knew all along: writing is a solitary endeavor but impossible without collaborators. So it was with this book—from my first conversation with Joe Covais to the last revision. Because of the long gestation of this volume, many people who helped me originally have slipped from the scene and have been replaced by others. And small incidences and coincidences marked the journey of this book.

In the years between 1971 and the present, several new works of varying quality have been published that provide fresh insights into the 121st New York. Joseph Covais's update on Best's history in 1996 produced more photographs and information on the daily lives of the men of the regiment and a particularly messy court-martial after the battle of Rappahannock Station. In the early 1990s, James Greiner explored Daniel Holt's papers at the Herkimer County Historical Society and, with others, edited them into a valuable and accessible resource. Greiner went on to edit the letters and papers of Capt. John S. Kidder. His history of Kidder's Company I, entitled *Subdued by the Sword* (2003), is an extremely useful microhistory of one unit, based on the letters of an articulate company commander who saw the war from a ground-level perspective. Another compilation of original materials became available in 1997 when Ann Britton and Thomas Reed published the letters and diaries of Sgt. John Hartwell, a carpenter who joined Company C. Less valuable is an account of Henry Hilton Wood's experiences as a drummer boy in Company E, which was published by a family member in 1990 and entitled *Drummer Boy*. Wood's unvarnished accounts of his service are available through the U.S. Army Military History Institute in Carlisle, Pennsylvania. David P. Krutz's *Distant Drums:*

Herkimer County in the War of the Rebellion (1997) was useful in providing context from the home front in Herkimer County, relying heavily on single primary and secondary sources.

There have been several newer studies on the individual soldier since I first wrote about the 121st in 1970. At that time, the principal source on Civil War soldiers, their motivations for going to war, their feelings about home and hearth, and their reactions to war came from Bell Irvin Wiley, whose Billy Yank and Johnny Reb studies in the late 1940s and early 1950s informed our knowledge of the common soldier. Since then, scholarship such as that found in James M. McPherson's *For Cause and Comrades: Why Men Fought in the Civil War,* Gerald Linderman's *Embattled Courage: The Experience of Combat in the American Civil War,* and Michael Barton and Larry M. Logue's *Civil War Soldier: A Historical Reader* has illuminated our understanding of the emotions encountered by the men of the 121st.

The Internet has been invaluable in locating letters and diaries of participants from Herkimer and Otsego counties. Helpful leads from family members, archivists, librarians, historians, and museum professionals all over the country, along with the impersonal search engines on the Internet, proved that an overwhelming amount of original, fresh material was available nationwide. The librarians at the University of Arkansas were most solicitous in photocopying William Remmel's extensive letters, which found their way to Arkansas when his family moved there after the war. Further help came through Robert Bender of Eastern New Mexico University at Roswell, who was editing Remmel's letters when I discovered him through David Ward in Connecticut and the Internet. With Bob Bender's generous sharing of the transcripts of the letters, I was able to get a clearer and more accurate picture of Remmel's thoughts.

The most intriguing aspect of writing this book has been to hear in the voices of the descendants of the 121st's men the excitement and interest in their ancestors' stories and as a result to sense the connectedness of the living in a genuine pursuit of understanding the past. I am particularly indebted to many people who offered their letters and precious family memorabilia for study. A few of them went to extraordinary efforts to get material to me: Peggy McGuire of Bethel, CT, Patricia Mabie of Roseboom, and Bill and Marsha Mabie of Westford, New York—all descendants of Allen and John Lovejoy of Company G—were enjoyable to deal with. Peggy provided an entire archive of letters written by John and Allen as well as the responses from their mother and others—rarities all. Included with those manuscripts is a forty-three-page, pen-and-pencil "history" of the 121st written in 1887 by John Lovejoy on the blank backs of pages in the Tenth Annual Regimental Reunion pamphlet of the prior year. After the war, Lovejoy served in various capacities with the survivors of the 121st after they began holding their reunions in 1876. He was the group's secretary at the time, and the invitation for the picnic reunion to be held in Cooperstown in 1886 raised the hope "that some final action will be taken in regard to a 'Regimental History.'" Lovejoy's account began with Lincoln's call for troops in July 1862 but ended abruptly with the historic charge and battle at Rappahannock Station in November 1863.

Most useful, thanks to Delavan Bates's great-grandnephew William S. Saint Jr., were seventy-seven transcribed letters Bates wrote to his father, Alpheus, between September 5, 1862, and June 1867. Great-grandnephew Dr. John G. Saint of Springfield (William's brother), along with Ted and Carole Miller of Nebraska Webmasters, has posted the letters on the Nebraska Genealogical Web Project site. Another member of the family, Richard Bates Booth of Binghamton, New York, the uncle of John and William Saint, was most generous in sharing additional materials pertaining to Delavan Bates. The letters and articles have proven to be invaluable primary sources from a very intelligent and articulate officer who went on to win the Medal of Honor. Charlott Wells Jones was kind to share stories of her great-great-granduncle Nelson Wendell.

Jerry Reed of Whitesboro, New York, and his uncle, Harrie Kidder Washburn of Sharon Springs, New York, descendants of Capt. John S. Kidder of Company I, were most generous in sharing copies of original letters, documents, and photographs. Kidder's observations of other officers in his letters to his wife proved absolutely invaluable. The thoughts he expressed in his excruciatingly detailed letters concerning his fellow officers, his notions of loyalty, and army process and procedure were unlike anything found elsewhere. Kidder survived the war, and thanks to his descendants, his letters have been preserved for future scholarship and evaluation. I am grateful to Frank White of Florham, New Jersey, who graciously shared with me his research on Sailor's Creek and on the controversy surrounding the capture of George Washington Custis Lee by members of the 121st and the 37th Massachusetts. He was ably assisted by Joan Evans of West Winfield, New York, and the town historian, Steve Davis. All three were instrumental in digging out copies of the 1912–1913 editions of the *West Winfield Star* in which appeared a series of articles by Thomas Hassett, who was at Sailor's Creek and wrote his own version of the 121st for that paper.

I am also thankful to another "friend of the 121st"—Evelyn Edwards of Clinton, New York, a descendant of Francis Carran of Company B, who photocopied transcripts of letters from and to Francis. From Barbara Lucas of Latham, New York, I received copies of photographs of Andrew Davidson and Delavan Bates. Dan Fout of Burkettsville, Maryland, provided photocopies of letters by Elinas Hills, a private in Company G from Cherry Valley. I am grateful to David Ward of Lakeville, Connecticut, who shared leads with me from his research on the Sixth Corps and Upton. The good people at the Cherry

Valley Historical Society were helpful, and Susan Perkins at the Herkimer County Historical Society generously provided current information; also helpful were those from the society who allowed me access to Dr. Holt's original work thirty years ago. Susan provided me with Clinton Beckwith's obituary, which connected stories that defied understanding until the information it contained was in hand. I am especially grateful to James Greiner, not only for his books on Holt and Kidder but also for sharing some rare Regimental Association pamphlets for my research. These small printed programs were ephemeral and today are gems and extremely difficult to obtain.

Wayne Wright, Glenn Linsenbardt, Kathy Stocking, Beverly Olmsted, JoAnn Van Vranken, and Susan Deer at the New York State Historical Association provided immeasurable help either in finding new and old materials that I had missed years ago or with recent acquisitions. The association's acquisition in 1985 of Samuel Burdett Kelley's letters and diaries was central to this book. Thanks also to Jeanne Eichelberger in the Bartles Library at the State University of New York (SUNY) at Binghamton, who patiently provided new materials in process by the library. Robert Jones of Stanhope, New Jersey, gave me copies of Robert P. Wilson's wartime correspondence. Earl McElfresh of Olean, New York, shared the passion of finding Dewitt Clinton Beckwith's original memoirs. And Civil War author Stephen Sears, who put me in touch with Earl, provided fresh information on Richard Franchot. Martin Touhy of the National Archives in Chicago was helpful with leads in finding more information on James H. Smith and his Victor Specialty Shop in Chicago. Andy Turner, the owner of the *Gettysburg Magazine,* provided David Ward's article on Sedgwick's march to Gettysburg, which helped me understand that aspect of the saga.

Emory Upton is sorely in need of a thoughtful and rigorous new biography. In 1885, Professor Peter S. Michie at West Point, one of Upton's close friends, published the celebratory and sympathetic *Life and Letters of Emory Upton.* Stephen Ambrose relied heavily on Michie for his 1964 book, *Upton and the Army.* Several articles on Upton through the latter half of the nineteenth century until the present time cover his military theories and his suicide. The only full-length presentation on Upton is David Fitzpatrick's unpublished dissertation, "Emory Upton: The Misunderstood Reformer." That work and Fitzpatrick's article, "Emory Upton and the Citizen Soldier," were most useful in my research and understanding of Upton's contribution to American military policy. As Fitzgerald noted, not many of Upton's letters survive, and those that do are in the Library of Congress in William Sherman's, Philip Sheridan's, and James S. Wilson's letters and papers. The majority are in Michie's book or have been lost to researchers until recently. Patrick Weissend, the director of the Holland Land Office Museum in Batavia, New York, was most generous in providing scanned copies of letters recently donated to the museum by the Upton family. They contain blueline directions, probably by Michie, to the printers concerning the quotes he chose to use in his biography of Upton. Highlights of the collection are Upton's Gettysburg letter, describing the battle, and his last letter to his sister, expressing his despair over criticism of his theory of tactics. Comparing the original letters in Batavia with Michie's versions, it is obvious that Michie took liberties with Upton's words and in some cases distorted his original meaning. Upton's letters are, in Michie's book, heavily edited, with glaring omissions. Until the recent acquisitions by the Holland Land Office Museum, scholars had to rely heavily on Michie for their picture of Upton. In the future, the newly acquired letters will form the nucleus of research on Upton.

Susan Christoff, head of the Archives and Special Collections at West Point, guided me toward the Emory Upton materials there. In the early stages of this manuscript, Alan Nolan, a Hoosier historian who chronicled the exploits of the Iron Brigade many years ago, as well as Doris Kearns Goodwin and Harold Holzer all encouraged me to continue my writing. Mark Dunkelman was especially helpful in navigating the intricacies of publishing and Civil War writing after reading early drafts. John Hennessey, chief historian/chief interpreter, and Noel Harrison, park ranger, at Fredericksburg and Spotsylvania National Military Park read early drafts on Salem Church and Grant's Overland campaign. John particularly "got me through the Wilderness." Frank O'Reilly read and critiqued the Fredericksburg chapter. Steven Woodworth and Earl Hess read early drafts and made insightful suggestions that strengthened the manuscript immeasurably.

Suzanne Hahn, reference librarian at the Indiana Historical Society, obtained microfilms of upstate New York newspapers, books, and manuscripts via interlibrary loan—as did Ron Sharp at the Indiana State Library. Special thanks go to June Murray Wells, director of the Confederate Museum in Charleston, South Carolina, and the staff at the Charleston County Library, who tracked down information on the Sisters of Charity of Our Lady of Mercy and the Confederate prisons in Charleston where Samuel Burdett Kelley was held. Katherine Collet, Hamilton College archivist, located material on Dr. James P. Kimball, Charles Butts, and Isaac Best. My deepest gratitude goes to Joe Covais, whose reissuance of the history rekindled my interest; I also thank him for sharing his research materials.

In addition, each of the following individuals played a role in the quest for materials on the 121st. I am grateful to Wilda Austin, Herkimer County Historical Society, Herkimer, New York; Chris Beauregard, New York State Library Manuscripts and Special Collections, Albany, New York; Janet Bloom, Clements Library, University of Michigan, Ann Arbor; Virginia Bolen, librarian, Schenectady Historical Society, Schenectady, New York; Diane Cooter, Syracuse University, Syracuse, New York; Paul D'Ambrosio, chief curator, New York State Historical Association, Cooperstown, New York; Douglas Denne, archivist and curator of rare books, Hanover College, Madison, Indiana; Brian Dunnigan,

Clements Library, University of Michigan, Lansing; Leigh C. Eckmair, historian, Town of Butternuts, New York; Jim Gandy, New York State Military Museum and Veterans Research Center, Saratoga, New York; Bill Gorman, New York State Archives, Albany, New York; Sarah Hartwell, Dartmouth College, Dartmouth, New Hampshire; John Heiser, historian, Gettysburg National Battlefield Park; Tom Heitz, Otsego town historian, Fly Creek, New York; Nancy Horan, New York State Library Manuscripts and Special Collections; Ned Irwin, John Fain Anderson Collection, East Tennessee State University Archives, Johnson City, Tennessee; Sarah Kozma, Onondaga Historical Association, Syracuse, New York; Katherine Lerch, Park Tudor School, Indianapolis, Indiana; Dan Lorello, New York State Archives; Hugh MacDougall, official historian, Cooperstown, New York; Elaine McCurry, Renwick, Iowa; Michael Martin, Onondaga Historical Association; Elizabeth Matson and Bev Olmsted, New York State Historical Association; Michael Musick, National Archives, Washington, D.C.; Ted O'Reilly, Manuscript Division, New-York Historical Society, New York ; Don Pfanz, Fredericksburg-Spotsylvania Battlefield Park, Fredericksburg, Virginia; Anne Prichard, University of Arkansas Libraries, Fayetteville; Elaine Smith, Raymond H. Fogler Library, University of Maine, Orono; Don Sommers, U.S. Army Military Historical Institute, Carlisle, Pennsylvania; Kathy Stanley, New York State Library Manuscripts and Special Collections; Kathy Stocking, New York State Historical Association; Ed and Teddy Wiedemeier, Alameda, California; and Donald Wisnoski, Oneida, New York.

I am especially grateful to the great staff at the University Press of Kansas. Special thanks to editor in Chief, Mike Briggs, who took a flier on a first-time writer with his encouragement; editors Susan McRory and Larisa Martin, who caught all my most egregious errors and made me look better than I deserve. The remaining errors are mine alone.

I dedicate this book to my wife, Marifred, who has put up with the 121st and me since she typed my original manuscript into a thesis in 1971, and my two sons, Salvatore III and Peter Dominic, who share my interest in history but in a quiet, nonfanatical way.

Introduction

The roster of the old veterans is each year bearing thousands less than before. Tales of actual service in the field, the camp, the march, the picket line, the advance, the victory, the retreat, the hospital, will soon be told by other pens than of those who participated. Even the flowers that are strewn on Memorial Day—the festival of the dead—will soon be strewn by other hands than those of comrades who stood by their side when bosoms were bared to shot and shell and glittering steel. The results of what we did will never be forgotten in the history of the world, but as individuals the passing of a single century and the crumbling of the marble monuments that now mark their last resting place will wipe out the memories of those who fought in the civil war and leave a clean tablet on which to record the deeds of future heroes.

Delavan Bates, Company I, July 17, 1895

Steinwehr Avenue in Gettysburg, Pennsylvania, becomes U.S. Route 15 as it progresses south of town. It is the old Emmitsburg Pike, and as it slices diagonally through the most famous and historical battlefield in the United States, you can still imagine George Pickett, James Pettigrew, and Isaac Trimble marshaling their 15,000 Confederate troops in the wood line along Seminary Ridge—to your right—for their ill-fated assault on the opposite Cemetery Ridge on July 3, 1863. As you continue south, you pass the reconstructed rail fences on either side of the two-lane road that had to be negotiated by Pickett's men in order to reach the copse of trees on Cemetery Ridge that Robert E. Lee had personally selected as their ultimate objective. Toward the southern end of the battlefield park, you turn left at the Peach Orchard and pass the Wheatfield on your right. You wind through the rough rocks that make up the Valley of Death and Devil's Den—all landmarks that saw the punishing action on both sides during the second day of James Longstreet's assault on Daniel Sickles's forward positions,

July 2, 1863. You wind slowly up the south side of Little Round Top, where Joshua Chamberlain and his 20th Maine held the Union left flank that same day. At the top of this smaller hill, you encounter the dramatic sculpture of Gen. Gouverneur K. Warren with his binoculars in hand "discovering" the Round Top's undefended and exposed condition. Warren is credited with sounding the alarm that the left of the Union line, occupied by only a few signalmen watching the action below, was vulnerable to attack from Confederate forces and, if taken, could be used to roll up the entire line back into the town. Although that interpretation has recently come under close scholarly scrutiny, Warren continues to "watch" alertly over the Union's left flank.

Traveling a few yards north along the Union line, you encounter another monument—one of more than 1,300 monuments and sculptures that dot the Gettysburg National Battlefield Park. The 121st New York State Volunteer Regimental Association dedicated this one in 1889. The four-sided Quincy granite monument measures 6 feet square at the base and tapers up 7 feet, surmounted by a 7-foot figure of a soldier cast in bronze. The monument sits precisely in the center of the line held by the 121st on Little Round Top. The front face bears the inscription "121st N.Y. Infantry (Col. Emory Upton)/2d Brigade, 1st Division, 6th Corps/Held this position from evening of July 2d, 1863, until the close of battle," and in bronze are the cross of the Sixth Corps and the coat of arms of the state of New York. On the reverse side, facing Sykes Avenue along the crest of Cemetery Ridge, is a bronze bas-relief of Emory Upton, the regiment's most famous commander. On either side are two bronze tablets. One lists the names of the battles the 121st participated in—officially, twenty-five in all, from Crampton's Gap in 1862 to Appomattox in 1865. The other gives a brief history of the regiment in cold numbers, including the total number of men who mustered in on August 23, 1862; the number who joined by transfer; how many were killed, wounded, or struck down by disease; the number discharged due to wounds and illness; and how many transferred to other commands. You are struck not only by the disparity in numbers—940 officers and men mustered in during August 1862, 308 mustered out in 1865—but also by the realization that this is the only memorial to the 121st for its entire three years of service during the war.

Despite the regiment's participation in twenty-five officially recognized battles, no monument exists on any of the other battlefields where the men of the 121st saw combat. The irony of this particular monument's placement is that, although the 121st was present at Gettysburg, the regiment did not actually participate in the battle; it suffered no casualties (except for one or two slightly wounded men, depending on the sources). The Union command held the 121st in reserve the entire time, reducing its troops to observers of the action occurring below and to their left and right. The regiment's nonparticipation exemplified the randomness of war and combat. While Strong Vincent and his Fifth

Corps brigade, including Joshua Chamberlain and his 20th Maine, were "saving" the Union army and the United States, the 121st and other units that were never committed to the battle that day stood less than half a mile away.

The monument is a testament to the 121st's survivors, who saw the memory of the war being shaped in the last quarter of the nineteenth century. They recognized that they were engaged in a second battle. This time, they fought for the "history" of the war being molded by the victors who were destined to be permanently immortalized on the most popular battlefield of the Civil War. Because the Gettysburg Monuments Committee decided that this historic battlefield would be *the* permanent monument to the Union war effort and because multiple memorials were beyond the means of most members, the men of the 121st Reunion Association joined with the rest to stake their claim to immortality at Gettysburg rather than Fredericksburg, where they saw their first action, or Salem Church in the Chancellorsville campaign, where they incurred terrible losses. They did not choose to memorialize their courageous attack at the Mule Shoe at Spotsylvania or at Cedar Creek in the Shenandoah Valley, when they were part of Philip Sheridan's remarkable effort in snatching victory from defeat. They chose not to remember Petersburg during the siege or Rappahannock Station or Sailor's Creek, where in the latter two instances they captured battle flags from the retreating army of Robert E. Lee.

Although the monument remains a tribute to the regiment and provides a capsule history of its exploits, the real story of the 121st lies on other battlefields, on farms and in picturesque villages in upstate New York, in the capitals of Albany and Washington, and now in archives and libraries scattered throughout the country.

I

Congressman Franchot Recruits a Regiment

Such hills as those in old Otsego make men patriots despite themselves.

Douglas Campbell, Company E, July 4, 1876

I know how important to success it is, that a young man should choose his occupation in life and follow it steadily but the government wants me, and I could leave better than many others.

Samuel Burdett Kelley, Company F, 1862

Leatherstocking Country

July 1862—the heat of a languid summer lay on the land. In upstate New York, young, rosy-cheeked twenty-one-year-old James H. Clark toiled in his father's rye field near the village of Half Moon in Saratoga County. "In a deep study" over President Lincoln's recent call for 300,000 more troops, Clark believed that his farmwork had become insignificant. "It was with great difficulty that I restrained the fire of youthful impatience and patriotism," he wrote. As he tediously mowed the long rows of rye, he decided he had no alternative but to join the army. After all, he came from Revolutionary War stock; both sides of his family had fought against the British. He turned to his cousin, who was raking and binding the sheaves next to him, and asked if he would join him in enlisting. They decided on the spot to sign up. James spiked the rake into the ground, declaring that he had collected his last bundle of rye. His father, shocked that he would quit with a full harvest still in the field, did not think to ask him why he was leaving. Despite his mother's understanding and encouragement, James told neither of his parents about his plans. Without hesitation, he and his cousin harnessed a horse and wagon and made their way to Clifton Park, where they signed up to put down the rebellion. James became a private in the 115th New York State Volunteers.[1]

All across the Empire State, in small rural villages and hamlets, a similar scene was being reenacted. Seventy-five miles west of Half Moon, in the counties of Otsego and Herkimer, intense and immediate patriotic fever prevailed. There, as in Saratoga County, young men left farms, general stores, and mills to answer the government's call for new recruits. These two central New York counties, nestled between the Adirondacks on the north and the Catskills to the south, were by 1860 dotted with picturesque farms and timberlands and inhabited by a diverse population of northern European immigrants. Idyllic lakes, clear waterways, and rolling hills added to the region's charm and mystique. To the north, Herkimer's upper tip thrusts into the Adirondacks. The county is 80 miles long; its major geographic feature is the Mohawk River and Valley, which slices through it east to west in the southern part of the county.

To the south lies Otsego County, best known for its place in American literature as the home of Natty Bumppo in the Leatherstocking tales of James Fenimore Cooper. Its most prominent natural feature is Lake Otsego, a 10-mile-long narrow body of water that runs north and south in the northern part of the county; it was immortalized by Cooper as Glimmerglass. Cooper lyrically depicted the lake's mirrorlike surface as "smooth as glass, and as limpid as pure air, throwing back the mountains, clothed in dark pines, along the whole of its eastern boundary . . . the bays were seen glittering through an occasional arch beneath, left by a vault fretted with branches and leaves." The waters yielded up an abundance of aquatic life. "The water is cool and deep," Cooper noted, "and the fish are consequently firm and sweet."

At the southern end of the lake lie Cooperstown and the headwaters of the Susquehanna River. According to Cooper, the region lacked only "ruined castles and recollections, to raise it to the level of the scenery of the Rhine, or, indeed, to that of the minor Swiss views." An anonymous writer in the last quarter of the nineteenth century blamed his inability to "write soberly" about it on the mystic qualities and the "misty fascination" of the area. "An enchanter's wand has waved over these scenes, and this is hallowed ground." The winters in these upstate counties are long, dark, and harsh, which makes the short summers even sweeter. Autumn is always glorious, but in some years, spring never appears. Winters are so severe that the lake's surface may freeze 3 to 5 feet deep. In the spring, the thawing ice moans as Glimmerglass returns to its clear, deep blue summer glory.[2]

The region is rich in myth, legend, and romance rooted in Native American and colonial history. Douglas Campbell, an original member of the 121st New York, asked rhetorically: "Who would not love old Otsego? Who ever saw such verdure as that which clothes her hillsides? Who ever saw such lakes as those which nestle in her bosom?" He wondered how the original settlers could

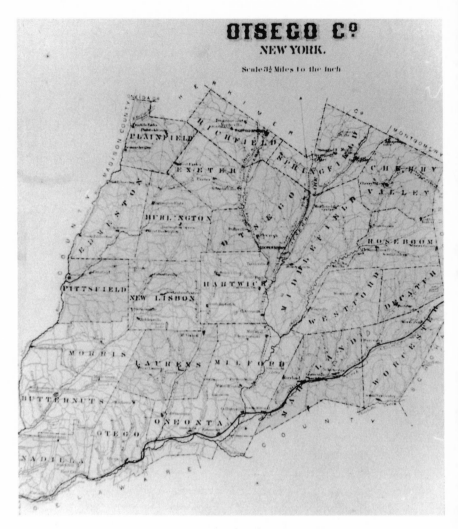

Otsego County in 1868. From F. W. Beers, *Atlas of Otsego County, N.Y., 1868*.

not have "hesitated for a moment" when they looked down on the rich valleys and the landscapes with their "ever changing panoramas." He affirmed the land's "magic" and its influence on the human mind. "Its beauty sinks into the soul, and breeds the love of home and the love of country," he continued. "Such hills as those in old Otsego make men patriots despite themselves."[3]

Before the Revolution and until the outbreak of the Civil War, immigrants from the German Palatine region settled in Herkimer County, where they established townships with names such as Manheim, Palatine, and German Flats. The county took its name from German Palatinate refugee Johan Jost Herchhcimer, who settled in German Flats below the present-day village of Herkimer.

His son Nicholas followed him in farming, trade, and transportation; he anglicized his name to the current spelling. At the time of the Revolution, Nicholas was a wealthy landowner who would become a hero and a martyr when he was mortally wounded at the battle of Oriskany on August 6, 1777.

Otsego County was the site of one of the most horrifying events of the Revolution. In November 1778, over a period of five days, 700 British and Native Americans massacred nearly 50 men, women, and children in Cherry Valley, a small village northeast of Cooperstown. They burned the village and scalped and mutilated the residents, leaving their remains for the dogs to feast on. The savageness and brutality of the attack and a similar atrocity in New York's Wyoming Valley mobilized George Washington to shift his troops to the interior and aroused the American armies and civilians against the British. Herkimer County suffered as well. The town of Ohio stood on land "upon which deeds the most foul were perpetrated by Tories and Indians" before and during the Revolution. The Civil War generation understood the region's bloody heritage.[4]

In the autumn of 1783, while awaiting the arrival of the final Treaty of Paris ending the war, George Washington toured upstate New York. "Struck with the immense diffusion and importance" of the inland waterways and the opportunities they offered to navigation and commerce, Washington urged the new nation to seek the "wisdom . . . to make good use of them." With the war's end, migration west began in earnest, and Indian lands were there for the taking. Following the Treaty of Paris, Judge William Cooper, a lawyer and native of Burlington, New Jersey, and the father of James Fenimore Cooper, immediately seized on the opportunity the new lands represented. He learned of tracts of land in upstate New York from fellow Quaker Richard Smith, who persuaded him to venture north. The timing could not have been more opportune, and with the fledgling government's help, Cooper immersed himself in questionable land dealing and ownership. Two years later, he moved to the southern end of Lake Otsego, and in 1790, he brought his family up from New Jersey. The next year, Otsego became a county and Cooperstown its principal village and county seat.[5]

Both Otsego and Herkimer counties lent themselves to farming, potash production, and, later, dairying. But Herkimer County, by virtue of its geographic attributes, became involved in manufacturing. The Mohawk River and Valley, the Erie Canal, and then the railroad became powerful east-west thoroughfares for people and goods moving in both directions. Although Cooper's patents claimed that upstate New York was virgin territory, settlers had moved into the interior of New York as early as 1624. A sprinkling of Dutch from Albany, Scots-Irish from New England, and Quakers who rode out the war in one of the many remote valleys that cut north and south through the two counties had settled the land during the mid-eighteenth century.

Some of the immigrants who were heading west with the intention of

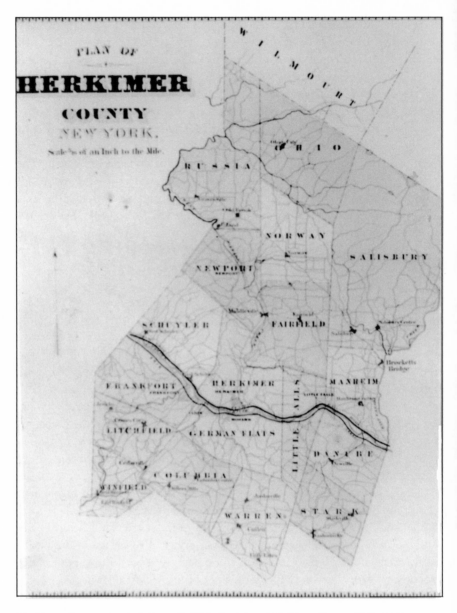

Herkimer County in 1868. From B. Nichols, *Atlas of Herkimer County, N. Y., 1868.*

inhabiting Buffalo, Rochester, and Syracuse passed through the lower end of Herkimer County and decided to settle there instead, in the manufacturing towns of Ilion, Herkimer, and Little Falls. As a result, Herkimer County developed an openness to worldly ideas and was less insular than Otsego County. The long, narrow mountainous section in the north of the county was ill suited to industry and agriculture, but its rich timberlands were harvested continually. The southern end of the county benefited from the Mohawk River, which it straddled on both the north and south banks.

When markets for milk were slow to develop, cheese dairying became a viable occupation, and it provided a steady source of income in southern Herkimer County until well after the war. New England immigrants brought with them the art of cheese making and quickly realized the importance of Herkimer's soil: its abundant minerals produced grasses that were consumed by the county's prolific cow herds—short-horned Durhams and "Dutch cows"—which, in turn, drank from plentiful, clean streams and produced cheeses of extraordinary quality. In 1861, Little Falls became a cheese farmer's market, entertaining buyers from the New York City, Baltimore, and Philadelphia cheese houses. Between 1864 and 1869, Herkimer County sold nearly 18 million pounds of cheese per year. Other industries provided a diverse economy. Eliphalet Remington founded the oldest Herkimer County enterprise—the Remington Arms Company in Ilion on the southern bank of the Mohawk River, established in 1816. The company would play a major role during the Civil War by supplying revolvers and some rifled muskets to Union troops.[6]

Otsego County's rural landscape enhanced its agricultural production. Hills and valleys running northeast to southwest sliced the county into ribbons of land that effectively blocked east-west migration. The land insulated the residents, and the county only rarely experienced new in-migration during the nineteenth century. Between 1820 and 1900, hops became the principal crop in Otsego County. The railroad promoted the establishment of villages and enabled development of the crop with access to downstate markets.

By the 1860s, population growth in both counties had peaked. In 1830, Otsego County had a population of 51,000, which leveled off at 50,000 in 1860. In contrast, Herkimer County shrank that year, to a total population of 40,500. William Cooper brought slaves to Cooperstown. Earlier, blacks had migrated to upstate New York during the French and Indian War. In 1860, 251 free blacks lived within Herkimer's borders; Otsego counted 217. According to the unofficial census of 1855, the two counties possessed a "free colored" population of 172 and 217, respectively. In the 1820s, prior to New York's abolition of slavery in 1827, slaveholding and slave trading existed in both counties. Abraham Roseboom, a prominent and wealthy early settler, released his slave Bob in 1818 when the Overseers of the Poor for the Town of Cherry Valley certified that Bob was under the age of forty-five and had worked for Roseboom for at least seven years. As late as 1818, the *Cherry Valley Gazette* ran an advertisement offering "a good healthy negro girl of 18" for sale. With emancipation, approximately "two dozen" blacks lived as free servants in the area. No evidence exists that slaveholding in Otsego was prevalent in the preemancipation period, but that does not necessarily indicate that it did not subsist there.[7]

Herkimer County comprised eighteen towns, several of them "fields"— Fairfield, Litchfield, Winfield, and the Village of West Winfield. Five of Otsego County's twenty-four towns were "fields" as well—Middlefield, Pittsfield, Plainfield, Richfield, and Springfield. Cities were led by mayors, towns by supervisors, and villages by presidents and trustees. Herkimer, Little Falls, and Ilion were the largest urban centers in Herkimer County. They competed with Otsego County's town centers of Oneonta, Cherry Valley, and Cooperstown.

Most families in the two counties called their villages "home." The men who eventually joined the 121st New York officially enlisted from towns, not villages, yet in their letters and diaries, they routinely referred to their *villages*. Most villages consisted of nothing more than a crossroads with a general store, a bank, a blacksmith, and modest homes along the two intersecting streets. From the center, farms radiated out through the valleys and hills, where they eventually melted into the next community. During the area's formative years, citizens of Cooperstown and Cherry Valley argued over the location of the seat of power, the organization of county structure, and the placement of buildings. Judge Cooper harbored no doubts in these matters. In his opinion, "The courthouse should be placed in Cooperstown, the jail in Middlefield, and the gallows in Cherry Valley."[8]

In the beginning, Judge Cooper held the county power at his seat in Cooperstown. But by the 1830s, he was gone and his family's influence with him. Cooper and his son, James Fenimore, hoped to build a utopian village in an idyllic setting where the lord of the manor would preside over a content and acquiescent populace. Instead, the Cooper family lost its influence to a bourgeois merchant, William Holt Averell, who replaced Cooper's wistful vision of a return to the colonial elite with a practical and cold business attitude that offended the first families of Cooperstown. In 1850, Susan Fenimore Cooper lamented the existence in the village of "many persons in want . . . who may be called regular beggars." Those on the top rung of power and wealth changed and coarsened as the inequality of the classes "endured and deepened."[9]

Herkimer and Otsego counties attracted powerful and prominent men and their families in the nineteenth century, providing a refuge from the crowded and noisy streets of New York City. The sulfur waters of Sharon Springs and Richfield offered wealthier travelers the ability to take advantage of the "waters" for their physical and spiritual well-being. Cherry Valley peaked in population in the late 1850s. During the previous decade, the village's 11,000 residents boasted of state officers, members of the state's board of regents,

Cooperstown, 1862. Lithograph by M. Dev. Martin, draughtsman and lithographer, printed by Lewis and Goodwin, Albany, N.Y. Author's collection.

senators, judges, and congressmen. The arrival of the Erie Canal and later the railroad to the north of the village crippled its further development, and over the next fifty years, it fell into decline. The Campbells, Morses, and Olcotts became leading families in the Presbyterian and Episcopal churches and in the fields of law and banking. Inventor and painter Samuel F. B. Morse established the telegraph in Cherry Valley in 1844, effectively connecting Albany to Syracuse. Morse also traveled to Cooperstown, where he painted the rich and famous of the prewar years. His brother Oliver Morse was elected to Congress for one term just before the war—from 1857 to 1859.[10]

In Cooperstown, as Averell's influence waned, the Clark family's rose. Edward Clark, a successful lawyer in Poughkeepsie in the 1830s and 1840s, bought Apple Hill in Cooperstown in 1854 from lawyer George A. Starkweather to use as his summer residence. The house, built in 1800 by Richard Fenimore Cooper, sat a few yards from the southern end of Lake Otsego, at the headwaters of the Susquehanna River. Over the years, it served as the home of U.S. Supreme Court justice Samuel Nelson; Maj. Gen. John A. Dix, the coauthor of the Dix-Hill cartel that aided prisoner exchanges early in the war; and Maj. Levi C. Turner, Secretary of War Edwin Stanton's associate judge advocate—all Cooperstown residents at one time.

Samuel Nelson was admitted to the New York Bar in 1817. In 1831, he became an associate justice on the state's supreme court, a position he held until

1845. He served the last four years of that period as chief justice. Nelson was on the Taney Court throughout the war. He defied an obstinate Roger Taney in the *Dred Scott* decision but was overruled when Taney substituted his own opinion, which provided one more link in the chain of events that led to the Civil War. In 1864, the Democrats offered up Nelson as a compromise presidential candidate, but George McClellan won the nomination. After the war, Nelson served on the Alabama Claims Commission in 1871. He died two years later at age eighty-one.

John Adams Dix moved to Cooperstown in 1828 to manage his new father-in-law's landholdings in town. He filled several state and national posts until the war broke out. As the secretary of the treasury, he became an instant hero in the North when his intercepted message to treasury agents in New Orleans—"If any man pulls down the American flag, shoot him on the spot"—was trumpeted by the press. During the war, he became a major general and was responsible for keeping peace in New York, particularly after the draft riots, a position that put him in direct conflict with Governor Horatio Seymour. After the war, he became minister to France (1866–1869) and governor of New York (1873–1875), and he ran unsuccessfully for mayor of New York City in 1876.[11]

In 1848, Edward Clark and his law partner Ambrose Jordan became acquainted with the young and eccentric inventor Isaac Singer. When Singer asked Clark to help him retain the patent rights on his new sewing machine, Clark wisely chose to be remunerated initially with a one-third interest in the new invention rather than taking cash. Eventually, Clark bought out a group of minority shareholders so that he and Singer became equal partners in their enterprise, thereby bringing into existence the Singer Sewing Machine Company. By the time the war broke out, there were seventy-four Singer factories making more than 100,000 machines for sale worldwide. The business, worth more than $10 million by the middle of the war, became a source of unlimited wealth for Edward Clark. The newly formed company donated 1,000 sewing machines to the Union army.

New York City may have been the center of the fiscal universe for the Lincoln administration, but Herkimer County and Otsego County held considerable capital—monetary and political—as the war progressed. The Remingtons, founders of the Remington Brothers Arms Company in Ilion, and the Clarks of Cooperstown were soon at the top of the new order in upstate New York.[12]

On the eve of the Civil War, the state of New York's population hovered around 338,000. Herkimer and Otsego counties, both predominantly Republican, supported Lincoln in the presidential election of 1860. In fact, he carried Herkimer County by 2,000 votes over Stephen Douglas. He also carried most of the villages but lost the towns of German Flats, Herkimer, and Little Falls. He won the state by 50,000 votes, and a new Republican governor, Edward

Morgan, was ushered into office at the same time. On the way to Washington for his inauguration, Lincoln traveled across New York State. On a cold Monday morning, February 18, 1861, he addressed the residents of Little Falls, a town that had gone to Douglas. There, for the first time, the people of the county and the Mohawk Valley were able to see their new president. A village cannon and bells signaled the arrival of his train from the west. As the Little Falls Citizen's Brass Band played "Hail Columbia," ladies waved handkerchiefs and strained to get a glimpse of the president. Little Falls village president Seth Richmond introduced him to the crowd, and Lincoln responded with the humble demurral he had used at every stop before. He may have been in Little Falls for no more than fifteen minutes. The *Herkimer County Journal* reported that he possessed a kind smile and a homely face but a "manly voice."[13]

The newspapers in both counties played a large role in shaping public opinion. Each paper was thoroughly loyal to its chosen political party and was considered by all to be nothing more than a party organ, expected to propagate the party line. Otsego County had five weekly newspapers, and Herkimer County enjoyed four. Among the loyal opposition to the new president was the *Herkimer Democrat,* which regularly and alternatively excoriated or lampooned the radical Republicans and Lincoln and his administration for the prosecution of the war. In its January 22, 1862, edition, in a piece entitled "What We Are Fighting For," the paper issued a clear warning that the country embraced the "ruinous abolition idea of changing this war for the 'integrity of the Union' into a fanatical crusade for the extirpation of slavery."

For many years, Cooperstown's small population of 2,500 supported two weekly newspapers, in circulation since James Fenimore Cooper's time. The *Freeman's Journal,* strongly Democratic, began its existence in 1818 as a Federalist organ. In the Civil War years, it supported the administration's goals of reuniting the Union and putting down the rebellion but frequently lashed out at the radical abolitionists in the state and on the national stage. The *Otsego Republican*—in Cooper's time "esteemed for a respectable literary taste" but much changed by the Civil War—toed the Lincoln administration's line. As Cooper remarked dryly, "In politics, as a matter of course, these papers are opposed to each other." During the war, the *Republican* accused the *Journal* of southern sympathies, and the *Journal* cited the abuse of power by the Lincoln administration.

In Herkimer County, both the *Herkimer County Journal,* which started life as a Whig paper in December 1837, and the *Mohawk Courier* were Republican and pro-Lincoln. In January 1864, the two papers merged into the *Little Falls Journal and Courier,* a move that the rival *Herkimer Democrat* applauded for its "efficiency and potential." The *Democrat's* editor applauded the Republicans for showing a "degree of wisdom in this matter." It was to their credit that they took this move to "strengthen and consolidate their party." According to the *Democrat,*

"Too many party organs is worse than none—a fact which even Democrats" might learn to their advantage. The *Democrat* expressed the opinion that the county could sustain only one paper per party. Any more would lead to a "weekly existence and be without influence . . . the weeding process continues."[14]

The Call for Volunteers

The original enlistees of the 121st New York State Volunteers witnessed the first eighteen months of the war from home, and the local papers brought them news of the roller-coaster progress of the fighting. The press focused on the individual stories of several towns and villages that supplied recruits to the first fresh troops in the field. The papers reported vivid details of each new battle, which produced equal measures of depression and elation for those on either side of the conflict.

With the fall of Fort Sumter in April 1861, both sides predicted a short war and little bloodshed. Southerners believed that 16,000 scattered federal troops fighting Indians in the West would never stand and fight a gritty rebel army. In addition, state militias were either nonexistent or engaged in weekend drinking orgies organized around minimal training. No draft existed. But using the threat of a draft and believing that the conflict would be short, the administration called for 75,000 volunteers to serve ninety days in their existing state militias.

Before South Carolina fired on Fort Sumter, the New York state legislature, led by a majority wishing to avoid conflict and bloodshed, was in a conciliatory mood. In fact, the state was ill prepared for war: "The military spirit of the state was almost dead and general apathy if not actual hostility, toward things military prevailed." Only 19,000 men were enlisted in New York's militia, and only 8,000 muskets were serviceable and in condition to be issued. Although the state provided Lincoln with a 50,000-vote plurality in the 1860 election, the vote was split between a Republican majority upstate and a pro-Douglas plurality in New York City. The city, in fact, threatened to secede before shots were fired; bigotry fueled by labor unrest became rampant; and even the National Bank Note Company of New York held contracts with the new Southern government to print Confederate money. Sympathetic New York bankers and shippers feared they would lose a large and lucrative trade in Southern cotton to England and other foreign countries.

But Sumter's fall changed everything. Before Lincoln's call for help, Robert Anderson's surrender prompted an emergency meeting in the governor's office in Albany, held on Sunday afternoon, April 14. Governor Morgan called his principals together to respond to the rebellion and to an anticipated call from the Lincoln administration for aid. State officials agreed to push through the legis-

Recruiting advertisement placed by Douglas Campbell to raise men for the 121st New York Infantry. *Freeman's Journal,* July 25, 1862.

lature a series of laws to raise 30,000 volunteers for the state militia, serving two-year terms, and to appropriate $3 million to fund the effort. The officials would establish a state military board that would be responsible for coordinating the state's diverse efforts at raising men to meet the threat.

The response to the immediate threat of war was marked by many false starts in Albany and in Washington. The authority and responsibility for arming the nation against the Southern insurrection remained elusive. Neither the Morgan administration in Albany nor the Lincoln administration was clear about where the constitutional authority lay for raising troops. The independent, voluntary organization of well-meaning citizens known as the Union Defense Committee in New York City complicated issues further. Organized in a patriotic frenzy in April 1861, it confused the governor's authority to raise troops with federal authority. Despite such problems, however, New York State responded immediately to the first call from Washington.[15]

Herkimer and Otsego counties answered promptly as well. Cooperstown began raising funds to pay for the formation of a military company and for a "home guard." By mid-June 1861, the women of Cooperstown furnished over 600 havelocks to the Union Defense Committee of New York City, which, in turn, presented them to the Anderson Zouave Regiment. The havelock was a "light cloth covering for a military cap, falling over the back of the neck for protection against the sun." The regiment's commanding officer, Col. J. Lafayette Rider, thanked the "Women of the village of Cooperstown" for their commonsense patriotic efforts, which would keep the soldiers' "heads cool for action" and their hearts "warmed by this evidence of interest in the comfort and happiness of the volunteers." In July, the news of Bull Run reached the upstate area, including the fact that nearly 1,000 wounded and sick were in hospitals in and around Washington, D.C. Otsego's women responded again, this time by holding an ice cream sale for the sick and wounded that raised nearly $300 in cash in addition to approximately $250 in usable gifts.[16]

Throughout the summer and fall of 1861, communities across the state responded to the initial call for volunteers. On April 20, Herkimer County set out to obtain $5,000 for the support of families whose men had gone off to war. Two days later, Mohawk hosted a "large and enthusiastic" meeting that raised $1,500 for families of volunteers from the towns of Ohio, Norway, and Russia and the villages of Mohawk and Herkimer. By August, the *Freeman's Journal* estimated that there were nearly 40,000 New Yorkers in uniform. At the war's outbreak, only one militia unit existed in Herkimer County—the undermanned 38th Regiment New York State Militia. Officers scrambled to fill it, "and by the first of May a number of companies were on their way to Albany to be mustered" into federal service. By June 15, the 34th New York Volunteers had also been mustered into federal service. Five companies came from Herkimer County. The 34th remained in service for two years and fought in the Seven Days Battles around Richmond. In the popular mind, it became Herkimer County's regiment. Before the first battle of Bull Run, nearly 1,000 men were serving from Herkimer County in the 34th, 14th, and 26th regiments. By autumn 1861, "Ellsworth's Avengers" (the 44th New York) had one company of men from Herkimer serving with it.[17]

From Otsego County, forty men recruited from Milford, Laurens, and Fly Creek left Cooperstown in the middle of June to join the Van Guard Regiment training on Staten Island. Capt. H. W. Lyon, a recruiter from New York City, set up offices in Cherry Valley and Cooperstown to solicit men for the Ira Harris Cavalry at $15 per month. A few volunteers went to Albany to join the Ellsworth Regiment. In October, the *Freeman's Journal* tallied 300 men from Otsego County in various regiments and other units, but the county had no regiment of its own, made up of "her hardy and intelligent yeomanry." The paper argued that the county never received proper credit for its war efforts, as others had. Richard Franchot, who represented Otsego and Herkimer counties in the U.S. Congress, assumed responsibility for mustering a regiment.[18]

Congressman Franchot

Richard Franchot was born in 1816 in Morris, New York, and attended public schools there and later the Hartwick and Cherry Valley academies in Otsego County. He came from one of the county's prominent pioneer families.

(Left) Samuel Burdett Kelley, who joined the 121st as an enlisted man, rose to the commissioned ranks, and was captured with Olcott and Paine at the Wilderness. He survived Confederate prisons in Macon, Georgia, and Charleston, South Carolina, only to die at home two months before the war's end. Author's collection. (Right) A native of Germany, William Remmel left Fairfield Academy in Herkimer County to join the 121st. He served admirably until the battle of Cedar Creek, when he disappeared. His family clung to the belief that he survived the battle and had been imprisoned at Andersonville. They persisted well into the twentieth century in efforts to determine his fate. Courtesy, University of Arkansas, William Remmel Papers (MC 597).

His father, Pascal, sired ten children before he died in 1855. His grandfather, Charles, had emigrated from Chamouilley, Department of the Upper Rhine, in France, where he conducted the family business in iron forging; he arrived in New York City in 1789. Traveling by riverboat and covered wagon, he took the family to Morris, where he formed a business partnership with Volckert Van Rensselaer.[19]

As an adult, Richard Franchot was an imposing figure in prime physical condition, standing 6 feet tall and weighing 200 pounds. He "carried himself very erect, and in his younger man-hood" became a "very powerful man." Franchot studied civil engineering at the Polytechnic Institute in Troy, New York. He became a prominent political leader by first becoming a town supervisor and later being elected as a Republican member of the Thirty-seventh Congress (from March 4, 1861, to March 3, 1863), representing the Nineteenth Congressional District.

Representative Franchot called a meeting in Morris on June 26, 1861, inviting William Davis, a lawyer from Buffalo, to speak. Davis appealed to the patriotic impulses of his audience, "gathered together from the valley of the Chenango, and from the high hills and pleasant vales of Otsego," and urged them to put aside political differences and rally to the president's call for troops. A central executive committee was formed, consisting of two representatives from Otsego and one each from Chenango and Delaware counties. Officials designated the fairgrounds at Cooperstown as the training camp for the new recruits.[20]

Two weeks later, Gen. S. S. Burnside reported that his New York Militia could muster 1,000 men within twenty-four hours and 5,000 in twenty days—he was taking the cream of the crop of all recruits and leaving nothing for Franchot. In Cherry Valley, an entire company of 100 men was raised in two weeks and offered to Governor Morgan. It became the first company formed in Otsego County, though "several persons" from the county "enlisted at other points." The *Freeman's Journal* expressed its satisfaction that "a full regiment can be had when needed." By mid-August, various units, none associated with Franchot, were enthusiastically recruited in and around the two-county area.

The Otsego Hotel opened for recruiting through the month of August. A Regular Army regiment recruited fifty men primarily from Oneonta, and thirty-four men from Schenevus and surrounding villages joined a new cavalry regiment being formed in Schoharie County. A month later, Col. Edward S. Serrell traveled through Otsego County to recruit a company of engineers; he was looking for "mechanics and laborers accustomed to handling the axe." Along with Capt. I. G. Atwood and a Captain Fellows, he set up an office in the Empire House and in George Story's saddlery shop, hoping to attract as many mechanics, artisans, and laborers as possible. All of this recruiting activity, particularly by outsiders, raised the anxiety of the local papers to have a "purely" Otsego regiment.[21]

At the beginning of October 1861, the *Freeman's Journal* gave voice to the anxiety. Many men had offered their services to regiments throughout the army, but there were no Otsego regiments for Otsego men. "Thus Otsego receives little or no credit for what she has done to uphold the government in this contest," the paper's editors complained. They held out hope that the neighboring counties of Chenango and Delaware would provide their sons for the war effort. Franchot appealed to the patriotism of all men in the immediate three-county area.

A confident Franchot predicted that he could raise a regiment in ten days, as he called on the residents' sense of pride to "place themselves on a par with other Counties of the state" and form eight companies of thirty-two men each. Officials in Albany assured him that once a regiment was formed, the state would establish a "Camp of Instruction at Cooperstown"; it would also provide uniforms, arms, subsistence, and camp equipment. "Several gentlemen" would help him recruit, and able officer material would be provided to train the new recruits. Franchot received assurances from state authorities that they would furnish "all necessary aid and encouragement" in speedily enlisting a regiment from Otsego and neighboring Chenango and Delaware counties. The state's adjutant general gave Franchot every indication that he would be in control of recruiting a new regiment. He left the choice of the grounds up to Franchot and even went to Otsego County to look over the situation, taking "certain initiatory steps in the matter."[22]

On October 11, 1861, the *Journal* reported that Lt. Col. John D. Shaul's 39th New York State Militia, which the *Journal* and the *Cherry Valley Gazette* quickly dubbed the Otsego Regiment, voted to go to war. Their training ground was to be in Cherry Valley, and the Cooperstown site was dropped. A native of Stark, in Herkimer County, Shaul had moved to the town of Springfield in 1839, where he became a farmer of considerable means. He had served with the 39th New York Militia since his election in 1850 as the regiment's commander. His grandfather had served in the Revolution and his father in the War of 1812. His recruiting in Cherry Valley met with little enthusiasm; few men seemed anxious to join.

By the end of November 1861, convinced that the war would soon end, local papers urged recruiters to "bestir themselves to avoid being 'consolidated' with some other skeleton regiment" or, worse yet, missing out on the fighting altogether. On the snowy evening of January 7, 1862, between 500 and 667 volunteers in five companies left Cherry Valley for Albany in seventy-five wagons, sleighs, and carriages, with family, friends, and relatives saying tearful good-byes. According to the *Gazette,* "The many idle and absurd rumors about the misconduct of the volunteers while here, were without a particle of foundation, and were fabricated by parties who desired to prevent enlistment." Shaul, who had been unable to attract more men to the 39th, expressed dismay about the . rumors that were circulating and about the poor response to his recruiting efforts. On reaching Albany, the regiment lost its identity when the state merged it with the 76th New York State Regiment, from Cortland.[23]

As a consolation, the state authorized Franchot to form another regiment at Unadilla "if the people of Delaware, Chenango and the southern part of Otsego" were interested in doing so. Enduring additional interminable meetings, Franchot pursued his dream of raising a regiment in the three counties—but without success. Otsego's hope for an all-county regiment and Franchot's dream of recruiting and leading a volunteer regiment would have to wait.[24]

Governor Morgan and President Lincoln

As the women of Cooperstown knitted mittens, conducted bake sales and ice cream sales, and provided blankets for the wounded and sick, healthy troops in the field were faring poorly in a number of ways. The American Civil War evolved through three distinct periods. The first, characterized by exuberant patriotism and passionate flag waving, occurred between the fall of Fort Sumter and the battle of Antietam in September 1862. The picnic atmosphere in this period epitomized the nation's naïveté attendant upon the first battle of Bull Run in July 1861. The brutality of the battle of Shiloh in Tennessee in the spring of 1862 and the severe losses that both armies sustained in the Seven Days Battles around Richmond and at second Bull Run in August were largely unknown by the general public. But when Mathew Brady circulated his photographs of the carnage after the battle of Antietam, the public realized that the country faced a dehumanizing event of massive proportions.

Between September 1862 and the spring of 1864, the nation came to understand the bloody nature of the war. The 121st experienced the taste of battle in this second phase as the country witnessed carnage on a large scale. Frontal assaults by both armies at Fredericksburg, Vicksburg, Gettysburg, and Chattanooga, across open fields and on entrenchments, resulted in unimaginable losses. Improvements in small arms, making them more accurate and more deadly, eroded the efficacy of "two-file" attacks by quick-stepping infantrymen and gave the advantage to defenders positioned behind earthworks.

By the spring of 1864, the war entered its third and most brutal phase. Lincoln made Ulysses S. Grant supreme commander of all Union armies. His comrade in arms, William Tecumseh Sherman, began his march to the sea through Atlanta, and Philip Sheridan waged war on the Confederacy's infrastructure in the Shenandoah Valley. Grant's hammering campaign attacked military supply lines and threw men at fortified positions in assaults at the Wilderness and Petersburg. Only unconditional surrender became acceptable. In Grant, Sherman, and Sheridan, the nation had found leaders who could prosecute the war to a successful conclusion.

Earlier, however, the summer of 1862 had brought alarm to the North and hope to the South. The war began its second year, and Lee was determined to take the fighting northward. He outmaneuvered and "outgeneraled" George B. McClellan, commander of the Union armies around Richmond, during the Peninsular campaign that summer. Maj. Gen. John Pope, in charge of the new federal Army of Virginia, began following Lee to the north and west after the Peninsular campaign. Pope ran into the Army of Northern Virginia at Manassas, where he lost a disastrous second battle of Bull Run to a constellation of outstanding Confederate generals—Thomas "Stonewall" Jackson, James Longstreet, and Lee. Once again, Lee imperiled Washington as he roamed north nearly unimpeded. He felt that freeing his troops from the defense of Richmond put the Union forces on their heels and that a large-scale maneuver into northern territory offered the best hope to seize the initiative and end the war favorably for the South. After second Bull Run, the Confederate army's movements forced McClellan to head north and remain between the Southern army and Washington. With continuing Union losses and the threat of invasion, Northern sentiment to prosecute the war began to flag in certain quarters.

Copperheads, Northern peace democrats led by former Ohio congressman Clement L. Vallandigham, advocated peace at any price. The original federal enlistees who had signed on for ninety days with the militia had long since departed the battlefield, having left the previous summer after first Bull Run. Over the 1861–1862 winter, Secretary of War Simon Cameron had directed Northern governors to cease their recruiting efforts: the federal government would assume that responsibility. Morgan and other governors in the North protested. With McClellan's spring offensive on the Peninsula and the inordinate need for more men, the new secretary of war, Edwin Stanton, reversed Cameron's order by suspending all federal volunteer recruiting in the North on April 3, 1862, relinquishing that authority to the governors with instructions to maintain existing regiments. But by summer, the editors at Cooperstown's *Freeman's Journal,* realizing that the state's militias were inadequate to the task, asked: "Volunteers are needed to reinforce our brave army in the field. How shall they be obtained fast enough, and in sufficient numbers?"[25]

That summer, the Lincoln administration, fearful of a public panic over rebel advances and wary of conscription and the appearance of demanding state participation, quietly urged seventeen Union governors to petition the president to ask them for additional volunteers. In a joint letter signed by all seventeen, dated June 28, 1862, the governors formally petitioned Lincoln, urging him to request that all the loyal states provide additional manpower. In addition to stressing the need for more troops to "garrison and hold all the numerous cities and military positions" already in federal hands, the governors argued that men were also needed as replacements for those units already engaged: supplying these new troops would hasten the end of the war. Carrying out his part in the scripted drama, the president wasted little time in replying to the petition. On July 1, he completed the performance by responding to the governors' request and "fully concurring" with their views. As a result, he "decided to call into the service an additional force of 300,000 men," mostly infantry. He alluded to all he could do with even half that amount; indeed, he argued, "if I had 50,000 additional troops here now, I believe I could substantially close the war in two weeks." The quota for New York State was set at 59,705. Prompted by Lee's march north and the governors' petitions, "a wave of meetings" rolled through New York during the summer of 1862. The meetings were intended to encourage enlistments, raise money for bounties, and reemphasize confidence in the Lincoln administration's prosecution of the war.[26]

Governor Morgan, a loyal Lincoln man, moved quickly. As the putative father of the Republican Party in New York State, Morgan had responded to the national emergency in 1861 by producing seventeen regiments. This time, with a much greater challenge, he produced 223,000 men for the Union cause. By war's end, the Empire State would send more than 448,850 volunteers into the field. Morgan issued a proclamation on July 2, 1862, calling for 50,000 more men to "quell the rebellion, restore the rightful authority of the government and give peace to the country." To underscore the urgency of the moment, he used Revolutionary War patriotism to convince his fellow citizens to respond to the call. The plea resonated well in Herkimer and Otsego counties. "Let not her [New York's] history be falsified, nor her position be lowered," he implored. Like many others, he believed that the Confederacy was in "her death throes."

Morgan ordered regiments to be formed from "contiguous counties or districts" that conformed to existing senatorial subdivisions, with a training camp to be established in each district. In a brilliant departure from past recruiting efforts, he placed responsibility for raising the new regiments on committees of leading citizens in each community. The *Herkimer County Journal* hoped that "one more great and impulsive movement . . . may be made by the people and thus the struggle promptly and forever ended." The *Otsego Republican* joined in the *Journal*'s initial enthusiasm, stating boldly: "Let the watchword be—an Otsego and Herkimer County regiment in the field in twenty days."[27]

Morgan's establishment of local committees and thirty-two regimental camps (one in each senatorial district), together with a $2 premium offered to new enlistees, spurred recruiting in the summer of 1862. His tactics were intended to create awareness in the local populace "of the dangers that threatened the country." His strategy allowed him to deal with rogue recruiting efforts by independently minded individuals who sought military glory; at the same time, it enabled him to comply with the federal government's request for new troops. Morgan's plan to recruit regiments from contiguous counties tapped into established networks of friends, extended families, and neighbors who joined together as a coherent force, with the sense that they were protecting their homes and those left behind. The state directed each county to establish a list or "enrollment of all persons liable to military duty." Only men between the ages of eighteen and forty-five were considered; the exceptions were "idiots and lunatics." The rolls contained the names, ages, and occupations of those subject to call. Exemptions were granted for medical reasons and for certain public servants, such as justices of the peace, sheriffs, and teachers in common schools.[28]

The commanding general of the Army of the Potomac, McClellan, appealed to the loyal governors, including Morgan, to fill existing regiments to their fully authorized strengths rather than recruiting new ones. He argued that "50,000 men in the old regiments will be worth 100,000 men under new officers. By far the best arrangements would be to fill up all the old companies; if that cannot be done, the next best thing is to consolidate the old companies and add new ones to each regiment." He emphasized the experience that had been gained in the first eighteen months of the war by the current officers, who should be "preferred to any new appointments." They deserved it: "Policy and gratitude alike demand that their claims should be recognized." His words went unheeded.[29]

The *New York Times* echoed McClellan's call with similar arguments, which the *Freeman's Journal* published. The *Journal* called for Otsego County to provide 400 men of the 50,000 required by the state, effectively asking for support of both strategies. On one hand, the paper asked why the government did not fill Colonel Shaul's 76th Regiment, which left Cherry Valley undermanned; on the other hand, it called for "at least one 'Otsego County Regiment' in the field which also doubtless needs as reinforcements all the additional men she can raise at the time." The paper urged that a $50 "donation" be given to each volunteer, paid for from a county bond issued in the amount of $20,000; the bond was to be paid back in four years and was to be used both to boost enlistments in the new regiments the president requested and to provide subsistence to the volunteers' families. The paper opined, "None of us [will] feel the poorer. Shall it be done?" In a rousing patriotic meeting in Frankfort, a committee of nineteen took on the responsibility of raising a company and the money to support it, which was to be divided equally among the recruits. When the bidding lagged, the band that was present struck up "Yankee Doodle," and the crowd finished the evening with $405 in hand. In Otsego County, Sheriff Andrew Adrian Mather, whose two sons would soon be members of the 121st, recorded a meeting at the house of a "General Brown" on the evening of July 10 to consider "the best course to raise volunteers."[30]

The Bounty System

At the war's inception, rampant patriotism was the only inducement needed to get young men to join and fight. The military scene consisted of pomp and circumstance writ large. Parades, socials, long lines of well-wishers, martial music, flags, ribbons, lengthy speeches, and colorful uniforms made war seem more like a picnic than a deadly serious business. Over the first eighteen months of the conflict, however, the news of battlefield casualties depressed enlistments and eventually forced both governments to introduce conscription. In April 1862, the Confederate Congress instituted the first draft in American history. And though the federal government did not authorize a federal draft until the next year, it used the threat of conscription to encourage voluntary enlistments. It found itself entangled in the principle of states' rights, as the Northern governors reminded Lincoln, since the administration desperately needed men from the Union states to respond to the national emergency. The long-held American fear of maintaining a standing army prevented the central federal government from raising arms in its own defense. Instead, tradition forced it to rely on the people's militia, a system that was embedded by law, custom, and political necessity in the states. The idea of a large standing army was well suited to the "monarchist whose ideas of empire are ever inseparably connected with large armies." It remained anathema to the American democratic ideal.

"Although Abraham Lincoln called for volunteers in the name of the Union, the people would answer only through their states." Despite the fact that the war reduced states' rights, when it ended, "the regiments in the field bore the names of the states from whence they came, and when they finally furled their battle-torn flags, they deposited them in the state capitals." Ironically, many of the dead were buried in federal cemeteries. On July 17, 1862, Congress passed the Militia Act, which drafted all white men between the ages of eighteen and forty-five into *state* service for up to nine months. The War Department followed with a mandate on August 4, 1862, ordering a draft for all states that did not meet their quotas in enlisting a total of 300,000 militiamen by the fifteenth of the month. This call has been confused with the president's call for 300,000 volunteers on July 1, 1862. In fact, it was in addition to that call. Governor Morgan saw it as a simple matter of arithmetic for New York counties. All troops raised since July 2 would be credited toward each county's totals. A draft would be used to make up the difference.[31]

The new regiment to be formed within the state's Twentieth Senatorial District—the 121st New York—would come from Otsego and Herkimer counties, and its headquarters were to be established at Richfield Springs, a small village in Otsego County situated almost halfway between Herkimer and Cooperstown. In compliance with the governor's order, fifty prominent citizens from both counties held an organizational meeting at Richfield Springs on July 17 to discuss raising a regiment from the district. The committee met to coordinate the efforts of the two counties to ensure that each district reached its quota. The Honorable George W. Ernst of Otsego, Lorenze Carryl of Herkimer, and S. S. Burnside of Otsego presided over the "Grand Union" meeting. The group included well-known men from each county. From Cooperstown came Levi Turner and James Hendryx, editors of the *Otsego Republican;* Hezekiah Sturges, a lawyer and longtime stalwart of the community, and William Averell also joined the committee. William Fields represented the town of Laurens, and Horatio Olcott, president of the Central National Bank, represented Cherry Valley. The Herkimer contingent included Samuel Remington; the Democratic Herkimer County supervisor and future commander of the 152nd New York, Leonard Boyer; and E. D. Beckwith, a distant cousin and later nemesis of Dewitt Clinton Beckwith, who became the face of the 121st New York.[32]

The group warned that a failure to meet the town quotas by enlistment would probably "be followed by an order from the president for a draft." The prospect of a draft on either the state or national level proved a powerful incentive to prospective enlistees. A smaller committee of sixteen men, eight from each county, accepted responsibility for selecting and recommending the new regiment's commander to the fifty-person committee and, ultimately, the governor. The larger committee determined a quota based on each county's total population. Otsego, with a population of 50,000, set a levy at 595, and Herkimer, with a smaller populace, aimed for 461. The committee delegated the authority to enroll men for the new regiment to another layer of committees at the town level. Any individual could raise and enroll an entire company of 100 men, provided he received the approval and recommendation of the town and county committees. The final step in the process required the commander's endorsement.[33]

Members of the commander selection committee from Otsego County were William Averell, John H. Gilbert, C. H. Crippen, H. H. Babcock, Richard Franchot, William C. Fields, Ezra Whipple, and Horatio J. Olcott. Herkimer representatives included M. W. Priest, H. P. Alexander, William I. Skinner, L. L. Lowell, George Hinckley, Dean Burgess, E. Graves, and William Gates. The general committee eventually passed eight high-minded resolutions pledging to stamp out the rebellion. Committee members quickly and unanimously appointed the Honorable Richard Franchot as commander of the yet-to-be-numbered regiment. The larger body accepted the committee's unanimous recommendation with "great enthusiasm and three hearty cheers. Col. Franchot eloquently and appropriately responded." Making it official, Governor Morgan "authorized Congressman Richard Franchot of Morris, Otsego County, New York to raise a regiment of Infantry."[34]

Every level of government, including that of individual towns, promptly moved into the bounty business, offering a crazy quilt of payments to enlistees. Because each town in Otsego County, from Burlington to Worcester, worked toward a specific quota (ranging from ten men in Decatur to fifty in Otsego), competition for recruits became fevered. The military committee in the town of Otsego adopted a resolution to pay a bounty of $25 to every man who responded to the call for 300,000 troops and to float a bond to that effect, authorizing the town supervisors to proceed with borrowing "on the credit of the town." The town of Middlefield passed a similar resolution three days later but without the line of credit or bonding authority. For twenty days, the total bonus to a resident of the town of Otsego in Otsego County reached a substantial $175; then, on August 29, the town raised its portion of the bounty again, this time to a handsome $100, which the *Journal* saw as "only equitable" and which was met with the "hearty acquiescence of all tax-payers."

In Cherry Valley, Horatio Olcott, Davis Bates, Edward Clark, Judge William W. Campbell, and the Reverend J. W. Mitchell voted for an additional $50 per recruit, with many of them pledging another $5 per recruit from their own purses. The *Cherry Valley Gazette* raised the specter of the 1778 massacre and burning of the town by reminding readers that the Reverend Mitchell was the grandson of the massacred Mitchell family, "whose child was butchered by Newberry the Tory." The paper drew a parallel between the events of 1775 and those of 1862: "The spirit of his forefathers still lives, and he is doing effective service in the noble cause." At the county courthouse in Cooperstown, Judge Campbell gave a fiery speech to the 200 to 300 people who had assembled for a patriotic war rally. He called on everyone in Otsego to "emulate the sacrifices made by her revolutionary fathers." Campbell, the grandson of Revolutionary War officer Col. Samuel Campbell, was a practicing lawyer and justice of the New York City Superior Court, and he had served as a representative in the Twenty-ninth Congress from 1849 to 1851. He also served as a supreme court justice for the Sixth District of New York from 1857 to 1865. His aged father and mother were still alive and strongly pro-Union: his father wanted to live long enough to see Jefferson Davis hanged. His three sons, Lewis, Douglas, and Cleaveland, would all serve during the war.[35]

The board of supervisors in Herkimer County voted to borrow $25,000 to "facilitate enlistments" under the president's call in order to provide $50 per volunteer. Like its counterpart in Cherry Valley, the *Herkimer County Journal* invoked the spirit of the Revolution: "Let not the emergency show that Old Herkimer of 1862 is less patriotic than Old Herkimer of 1776—nor less patriotic than she proved herself to be but twelve-months ago." The paper, however, editorialized against the bounty system as unfair and inequitable. It noted that the town of Fairfield offered a bounty of $500 and probably could have induced men to enlist at a lower price, whereas equally patriotic towns could not afford to raise the ante so high. The *Journal* characterized the bounty policy as a mistake that would "seriously effect the business of recruiting throughout the county."[36]

The adjutant general of New York deplored the system of random and competitive bounties being offered by counties, towns, and villages across the state. Although pleased with the recruitment efforts in response to the July 2 call for volunteers, state officials recognized that bounties offered by individual towns increased the number of bounty jumpers and deserters, which "reached an alarming extent and defied all ordinary means of prevention." Governor Morgan, responding to calls from all over the state for a special session of the state legislature to enact a uniform bounty, acted on his own, which only added to the confusion. Citing the emergency nature of the government's need for men, Morgan ignored the calls *and* the state legislature with the assurance that all would agree with his unilateral decision, and on July 17, he set the state bounty at $50; he reasoned that "the popular will [demands the] additional premium . . . to promote enlistments. The exigency clearly requires the promptest action."

Albany spelled out the terms of the bonus payment. One-half would go to the recruit upon enlistment, and he would receive the remaining $25 when the regiment officially mustered into service and took to the field. The bounty eventually enabled the state of New York to put 35,000 men under arms by October 1, 1862. Meanwhile, further complicating the issue, the federal government offered a bounty of $100, with $25 paid to the individual when his unit mustered into federal service and the remaining $75 payable at war's end. The larger recruiting committee in Richfield Springs endorsed Governor Morgan's end run around the legislature, establishing the $50 bounty for each enlistee. The committee felt "confident that this act will be sustained by the whole people of the state and sanctioned and legalized by the next Legislature at its regular session."[37]

In its instructions to recruiters, the state made clear just who they could enlist. Recruits under eighteen were barred from service, with the exception of two per company to serve as musicians if they obtained parental consent. Those under twenty-one also needed a parent or guardian to consent to their service. Men brought in by those having no authorization to recruit could be mustered, but they would have to be assigned to a company with official recruiters. An illiterate recruit signing with a mark was required to have his mark witnessed by another. Nearly all of the rules were ignored at one time or another.[38]

The surfeit of bounties became the recruiters' lure to attract able-bodied prospects. One successful recruiter, Judge Campbell's son Douglas, left his theological studies and opened a recruiting office in Cooperstown next door to the *Journal*, "in a room over J. A. Schroms Jewelry store, one door east of J. H. Story's store." He placed a large ad—headlined "To Arms, To Arms"—proclaiming that his company (which eventually became Company E and he its commanding officer) would be "the first Company of the regiment and have the post of honor." He announced that recruiting stations had been set up in Cherry Valley and in Springfield Center at the northern end of the lake. As an inducement, Campbell offered a total of $152 in bounties in addition to the monthly pay of between $13 and $23. He spelled out the terms in an advertisement in the *Freeman's Journal*, offering a man an additional $2 bounty from the county committee "if he enlists on his own." In total, the "pay" a private soldier might gain from enlisting immediately amounted to $13 per month, or $156, plus a federal bounty of $100, a state bounty of $50, and a $2 county bounty, for a grand total of $308. Campbell successfully raised two companies. Edward Clark helped raise the second company, and his reward was a commission as captain and commander of Company G. As the *Journal* and the *Republican* summed it up, "In all human probability, the Rebellion will be crushed out, and the war concluded within a year. There are few men, comparatively, that can secure a better income in any other way."[39]

The crazy quilt of financial inducements worked. Despite its cumbersome nature, the bounty system spurred recruiting and rewarded the recruiters with military commissions as officers leading the men they enlisted. Before the end of July, Henry Galpin recruited 85 men; Clinton Moon, 65; and Irving Holcomb,

60. Sackett Olin and Erastus C. Weaver of Otsego were busy putting together what would eventually become Company K, while Nelson O. Wendell of Cooperstown competed with Campbell for men. By August 1, Herkimer County had 400 enlistees waiting to go into camp. Villages and communities solicited contributions from wealthy citizens, including the Remington brothers in Ilion, who, in an act of enlightened self-interest, pledged $1,000 to the recruiting effort. The small town of Roseboom in Otsego County exceeded its quota. By the beginning of August, most towns had organized enlistment rallies or were scheduling enlistment meetings. Sheriff Mather attended a meeting on August 5, during which the large crowd listened to the virtues of patriotism as interpreted by Lyman J. Walworth of Cooperstown. Six men volunteered that night.[40]

Ingraham Smith, a native of Fulton County, New York, spent the summer of 1862 working in Middlefield in Otsego County. He mulled his options: should he enlist for the bounty or wait to be drafted? He suspected that if the authorities came into Otsego County looking for draftees, they would find "some balky ones." In the end, the combination of the county, state, and federal bounty incentives proved irresistible, and he enlisted in the 121st. His reasoning was quite simple: enlistees "will enjoy themselves better and be thought more of, while the drafted soldier does not get but $11 per month and no bounty."[41]

In the Schenevus Valley village of Worcester, Delavan Bates "headed the list of volunteers." Bates had tried to get into West Point in 1857, with the endorsement of S. S. Burnside of Oneonta, the commander of the 5th New York Militia. But because the congressman for the area at the time resided in a county other than Otsego, Henry B. Noble became a cadet instead of Bates. Noble went on to become an officer in the 8th Regular Infantry, whereas Bates "remained just a clerk in a country store until August, 1862." But serving under Col. John Shaul in the 39th New York Militia, Bates learned all the necessary moves and commands, and he was especially well suited to military life. After he received his enlistment papers, he canvassed the town for recruits rather than waiting for men to approach him. Armed with the town's funds for the $25 bounty, Bates signed up twenty-six men and boys. By August 16, the small band left Worcester for Camp Schuyler, where they were consolidated with recruits from the western part of the county who were recruited by John Kidder. Bates received his commission as a second lieutenant, outranked by Colonel Franchot's nephew John D. P. Douw.[42]

2

"The Nursery of Soldiers": The Men and Boys from Herkimer and Otsego Counties

Emmet and Elias left for Mohawk, enlisted to fight for their country.

Sherriff Andrew Mather, Otsego County, Diary Entry of August 14, 1862

The part of Otsego's history which interests me the most is her record in war; she is greatest as the nursery of soldiers.

Douglas Campbell, Company E, July 4, 1876

Boys and Men Join to Fight the Rebellion

Despite the lure of bounties and the fear of the draft, long lines began forming at doctors' offices, and the *Freeman's Journal* noted a sudden onset of sicknesses among many of Cooperstown's formerly healthy male residents. In one case, it published a small notice regarding an anonymous letter sent from Hartwick, whose author claimed to know a certain resident in that town who recently lost his trigger finger. And medical deferments were not the only means being used to evade military service. The paper reported that the postmaster of Edmeston in Otsego County, a town of no more than a dozen households, deputized his own sons as mailmen so they could avoid service. (The story was later retracted when a citizen of Exeter pointed out that although the town boasted three postmasters, they all had sons under the age of nine.) Meanwhile, however, many other young men of Otsego and Herkimer counties answered the urgent call for recruits and signed their enlistment papers.

In a move to stem the tide of desertion that would seriously affect the Union army over time, Secretary of War Stanton, in August, appointed Cooperstown resident and newspaper editor Levi C. Turner to be associate judge advocate for the army around Washington. Turner was born in Sullivan County, New Hampshire. He studied law at Dartmouth and Union colleges and eventually practiced with his father-in-law, Robert Campbell. In the 1840s, Turner became the owner and editor of the *Cincinnati Gazette*. He arrived in Cooperstown in 1855 as the associate editor of the *Otsego Republican*.

Turner's boundless energy allowed him to serve two terms as county judge of Otsego County while functioning as the paper's editor. A self-made man, he kept grueling work schedules; he once went a week without changing clothes, sleeping only when and where he could. His passion to succeed was balanced by his modest behavior, and his fierce streak of independence was coupled with a strong moral compass; he was firm, but cheerful. Turner counted as his friends many of the older statesmen who had helped shape the nation in its early years, among them Daniel Webster.

The men of the 121st regarded Turner as the man to help them with their political and military problems. He resigned his judgeship and editorship of the *Republican* and promptly accepted Stanton's invitation. In the new position, he held inordinate power, which increased exponentially when the Lincoln administration began to clamp down on dissidents and Copperheads. Turner's mandate to investigate and determine the fate of "all cases of State prisoners" placed him in a position to effect "military arrests in the District of Columbia and the adjacent counties of Virginia." Stanton further ordered the military governor of the District of Columbia and the provost marshal of Washington to report to Turner "cases wherein the action of a Judge Advocate may be required."

The *Republican* expressed its awe of Turner's role in the Lincoln administration, depicting his situation as "a most arduous, intricate and delicate office." Citing his daily visits to the Old Capitol and Fort Carroll prisons, the paper noted that the "developments which there came to his knowledge, from the South and from the North, would stagger a Christian mind." In the spring and summer of 1865, Turner played a major role in the prosecution of Lincoln's assassins.[1]

The *Freeman's Journal* congratulated its old nemesis at the *Republican,* claiming that it had promoted Turner's services and talents to the national government for more than a year. The paper pointed out that the framers of the Constitution had never contemplated the new office that Turner would occupy, and it warned him to be "an astute lawyer and upright, impartial judge." It reminded its readers of Turner's patriotic zeal when, on one occasion when he disagreed with the law, he appeared to advocate "mob law and violence," earning him a "stern remonstrance" from his own party as well as an "indignant rebuke" from the opposition. The paper concluded that Turner would be valuable to his party and country anywhere he could help in "putting down the rebellion."[2]

As recruiting gathered steam, a minor dustup occurred between powerful upstate figures. The state charged Timothy Herkimer of Exeter—a distant relation of General Nicholas Herkimer of Revolutionary War fame and an ardent Democrat—with "facilitating the escape of his son and another young man into Canada." Republican sheriff Andrew Mather arrested him "[for advising] a deserter from the army not to return to duty, and for uttering disloyal sentiments." Herkimer hired Hezekiah Sturges, Esq., to represent him in the matter. Sturges applied to Judge Samuel Nelson of the U.S. Supreme Court for a writ of habeas corpus ordering Mather to appear before him to "determine the legality of" Herkimer's "arrest and inquire into the nature of the charges" leading to his incarceration. Nelson granted the writ and served it on Mather. Mather retaliated with a telegram to the War Department asking for instructions. The reply came from Levi C. Turner. Siding with Mather, Turner told him to "resist the execution of the writ" and report anyone who would try to free Herkimer. When authorities were unable to find a federal marshal to arrest the sheriff, lawyer Sturges's application to Judge Nelson for an attachment against Mather became moot.

After a brief incarceration at Fort Lafayette, a prison for political detainees in New York City on an island in the Hudson River, Herkimer was released upon giving assurances that his son or a substitute would go into the army. The *Journal* gleefully reported that Herkimer did not have to "surrender the opinion he holds, that there are some very great scamps holding office under this Republican Administration, and that the people would be benefited by a speedy return to Democratic rule." Five months later, Herkimer sued Mather for arresting him illegally and petitioned the new, Democratic governor, Horatio Seymour, to remove Mather from office. Seymour served a copy of the complaint on Mather with an order to answer the charge within ten days. The case dragged on through the summer of 1863, at which point Herkimer subpoenaed Secretary Stanton, Levi Turner, Governor Morgan, and two others to testify on his behalf, turning the proceedings into a circus. When none of the "big lights and small" appeared in court, the judge postponed the hearing. With Mather's term due to expire in December, the prospect that any judicial decision would soon be issued became a long shot. The major players in the minidrama—Turner, Judge Nelson, Morgan, and Seymour—would reprise their roles many times during the next three years.[3]

Men who did not obtain a medical deferment or take flight to Canada were harassed by those opposed to the war and enlistments. Antiwar agitators employed outrageous and inflammatory arguments, stating, for instance, that the government teetered on the brink of bankruptcy and that the promised bonuses would never be delivered. They asserted that any new recruits lucky enough to escape alive would return home "naked and diseased, dependent on the charities of the world." The *Cherry Valley Gazette* called for all the home-grown traitors to be thrown in jail and claimed that there were some in Middlefield "who rejoice when rebels rejoice." The paper concluded, "We must either be *for* the Union or *against* it; and those who are not for it must conclusively be against it."[4]

Schoolboys and Farmboys

But most young men went into the service without complaining. The Lovejoy family of Roseboom sent three sons—John and Allen joined the 121st, and Jonathon enlisted in the 152nd but died one year later. On August 7, 1862, John had made the trip to South Valley, a few miles from his home, for a patriotic rally. His friends tried to persuade him not to enlist and then ridiculed him after he took the oath. Two years later in the field, he still smarted from memories of "that night and how some folks took on that night at the church." The Wood family of Middlefield in Otsego County sent three sons to enlist in Company E—Henry Hilton, aged eighteen, John T., nineteen, and James, twenty-six—and all survived. Sheriff Mather's two sons, Elias Cummings and Andrew Emmet, enlisted in the 121st, Elias joining at Albany and Andrew at Mohawk; thereafter, Elias personally recruited nearly forty men from New Lisbon for Company K. Both enjoyed distinguished careers with the regiment. The senior Mather, a man of few words, recorded in his diary on August 14, 1862, that he left for Garrattsville at 8 A.M. "to see the soldiers off. Emmet and Elias left for Mohawk, enlisted to fight for their country." Five days later, he traveled to Mohawk to say good-bye to his sons. He confided in his diary: "Felt as though it was the last time I should ever see them on earth, prayed to God that he would preserve them from all harm."[5]

In the little village of Cedar Lake, located within the town of Litchfield in Herkimer County, three cousins—twenty-year-old Francis "Frank" Carran, twenty-two-year-old William Henry Harrison Goodier (known as "Tip"), and twenty-two-year-old Richard Turner—signed up together at the end of July and were all assigned to Company B. Frank died of his wounds after the battle of Salem Church, but his cousins survived the war. The Huartson family of Danube in Herkimer County sent four sons into the army—William into the 34th New York and James, George, and Robinson into the 121st. George and Robinson were killed and William was wounded at Cold Harbor. James deserted on January 7, 1863, less than five months after the 121st joined the Army of the Potomac. The two Orvis brothers—Alvah, age eighteen, and Aaron, twenty-one—joined at Herkimer on August 5, survived the war, and were mustered out together with the rest of the regiment three years later. Joe Heath, from Little Falls, was twenty years old when he joined Company A. His grandfather Joseph had fought in the War of 1812, and his great-grandfather Hezekiah had served under Gen. Joseph Warren at Bunker Hill. Joe Heath survived the war. The Miner family suffered greatly. They gave two sons, eighteen-year-old George and nineteen-year-old Isaac, who enlisted together on August 2, 1862, and died on the same day, May 3, 1863, at Salem Church.[6]

Cherry Valley contributed mightily to the war cause. The Campbell family held the power in the village. Douglas Campbell's efforts to enlist a company enticed good friends from Cooperstown: Henry Walker, Andrew Clark Farr, James Clark, William Waffle, John Gates, Dewitt Wells, and Homer Graham all joined his Company E. They remained together throughout the war. Campbell, the descendant of Revolutionary War heroes who participated in the 1777 battle of Oriskany, resigned before war's end, in April 1863. He had interrupted his studies "in another state" in order to enlist and then rushed to Albany to receive his commission; once that was done, he began recruiting as soon as he reached Cherry Valley. His father, William, worked tirelessly in the war effort, recruiting, raising bounties, giving speeches, sitting on patriotic committees, and generally providing every means of support at his disposal to ensure Cherry Valley's representation wherever its men were needed.

The elder Campbell expressed pride in his three sons. He was the "model of a patriot," according to son Douglas, and remained hopeful even during the war's darkest hours, always "making light of rumors, standing by the government, encouraging the depressed," and reproving the naysayers "everywhere." Son Cleaveland initially joined the 152nd but later transferred to the 121st. The third son, Lewis, also became a member of the 152nd.[7]

The three Herdman boys—George, eighteen, Lyman, twenty-two, and Norman, thirty-two—enlisted together and suffered differing fates. George was captured at Salem Church in May 1863 and then wounded at Rappahannock Station on November 7, 1863, dying of his wounds three weeks later. Lyman received a disability discharge, and Norman survived the war. Recruiters initially rejected eighteen-year-old Charles Stockley because of his age and his height. He finally enlisted as a member of Company G with the help of a shoemaker who applied "an extra thickness of sole leather" to his heels to make him appear taller. Dorr Devendorf joined Company B at seventeen years of age. He cut the number 18 out of a newspaper and put it in his shoe. When the recruiter asked his age, he truthfully answered, "I am over 18." Before the presidential call for 300,000 more troops, tiny Cherry Valley provided 128 men, and the *Gazette* voiced its optimism that the new quota would be reached within ten days.[8]

On the day Fort Sumter fell, Dewitt Clinton Beckwith was attending school in Utica, New York. His family had moved west from his birthplace, Troy. As a fifteen-year-old, he kept busy after school as a general gofer in his father's general store, a community gathering place frequented by members of various New York militias in Utica. In the evenings, the young Beckwith sat on a barrel in the store, listening to stories about the war and the glories of combat related by the men gathered there. When war became reality, every youngster like Beckwith wondered what his role would be as a soldier: "many a deed of daring was enacted in imagination in that old store." Beckwith also stole away to the armory of the Washington Continentals to listen to embellished stories of a faraway war from overly stimulated young men. Although he was only fifteen, he began "to feel large." As Ellsworth's Avengers left for the front, he longed to be going with them. He pictured himself fighting the rebels; in later years, he explained that "as a consequence, I began to get *cerebral elephantiasis*." Beckwith's father raised a few companies, but his desire to enlist was dampened by Beckwith's stepmother and "the presence of a goodly number of small children."

The young Beckwith became obsessed with the news from the front. "Bull Run made me wild," he declared. "I was burning up with what is known as 'war fever.' My suggestion that I would make a soldier was treated with derision by my father, and I was told boys not dry behind the ears could not enlist, even as drummers." But his urge to enlist was overwhelming. After many sleepless nights, he decided to leave home and join the army. He began hoarding any money he earned to make his move. One Saturday night in October, he slipped away. He stood on a bridge on John Street in Utica, and when the first canal boat heading west passed below him, he dropped onto it. As he sat on the horse cabin on the bow of the boat, "the whole world opened up" before him, and he "formed a plan that [would] end the suppression of the rebellion." "I saw my home disappearing in the darkness without regret, and a feeling of exultation filled me," he revealed years later.

The boat captain roused him from his reveries to ask about his destination. Beckwith told him he wanted to reach Rome, New York, in order to enlist. The captain scoffed at the boy's dream but said he would do what he could to get him enlisted if Beckwith stayed on the boat all the way to Buffalo and served as the captain's assistant. The idea of working on the canal barge did not appeal to the young boy, but if it would get him in the army, the tribulations would be worth it.

At Buffalo, the recruiter rejected him as too young and too small, sending him away with the admonition to either wait a year or grow a mustache. Beckwith stood only 5 feet, 4 inches or 5 feet, 9 inches tall (the sources vary on this detail). The boat captain, sympathizing with the young Beckwith, offered to take him back across the state to Albany, with the assurance that he would certainly be enlisted there. Beckwith agreed. The trip across the state proved uneventful, and when they reached Albany, the captain paid him off. Then, true to his word, he went to the recruiting office with Beckwith and enlisted him on the spot in Company K of the 91st New York Volunteer Infantry.[9]

During the summer of 1862, William Remmel turned nineteen. An intelligent, sensitive boy who respected and loved his parents, Remmel was a devoted and hardworking student to whom learning came easily. He deeply valued his education, a trait he learned from his German-born parents, who had originally settled in Fulton County just east of Herkimer County. In 1854, when fire destroyed the family home, the Remmels moved west, just over the line into Herkimer County, to the village of Devereaux.

William and his four brothers were sent to Fairfield Academy (or Seminary) for their education. Founded in 1803 and located 10 miles from the village of Herkimer, the school, "noted for its beauty of scenery, and pleasantness as a Summer Residence," employed 10 teachers for its 389 students in 1859. Its administration managed an annual budget of $14,000 per year—the sixth-largest in the state, including the New York City schools. Fairfield received $600 per year from the New York Board of Regents from a pool of $40,000 in the Literature Fund in a statewide competition. The academy's courses ranged from Latin and the other classical languages to biology and oil painting. Unaffiliated with any particular religion, the school offered a business course and a college preparatory course for men and a five-year course for women comparable to a college degree program. It gave "special attention [to those] preparing for college. Peculiar advantages for music and oil painting," the school's brochure explained. Tuition for "Common English" was $4 per semester; "Higher English" cost a dollar more, and ancient languages were $6. In addition to the basic fees, school supplies were charged as needed. Room and board ran $4.75 per term.

As a student, William Remmel exploited every opportunity to help pay for his tuition and other expenses at school. The summer term ran from March 26 through July 2 in 1862. During that period, he busied himself with schoolwork, with the hope that improved writing skills would allow him to teach. He received no financial assistance from the school or from home: his schooling was funded solely by his own labor in summer and winter breaks. Very much on his own, William searched for work in the area around the school. In February 1862, he had a bout with the measles and missed classes, but he returned to make them up successfully. During the 1861–1862 winter, he earned $20, and the school promised to hire him during the coming semester. He told his parents that he would be home for only a week and needed to return to school to earn money for the next term.[10]

The progressive school catered to families of influential means and to boys such as Remmel regardless of a family's financial condition. The school ultimately contributed many men and boys to Herkimer County's manpower needs in the war, particularly to the 121st. Remmel rarely spoke of his schoolmates, but a number of former Fairfield students would find a home in the

121st, including Adam Clarke Rice, Fred Ford, Wilbur Lamberson, Thomas Arnold, and Angus Cameron. Rice, Ford, and Cameron were staunch antislavery men. All five men were mustered into Company C, and every one of them perished during the war.[11]

In the March–July term, Remmel returned to the academy to take geometry and trigonometry while "sweeping halls and splitting wood" and living frugally—"sometimes I do not have a penny in my purse," he told his parents. Occasionally, his family would send him a dollar or two along with a special medicinal "syrup" for his vague "anxiety attacks." That summer, he sought work in the Fairfield area with the hope of earning wages higher "than near home." On July 6, four days after school closed for the summer, he found a job with a farmer a mile from Fairfield; it offered the prospect of making $20 to $35, enough money for yet another fall term, beginning August 22. Remmel's parents, now back in Fulton County, fully expected William to return to school for the fall semester.

The next letter his parents received was dated August 31 and postmarked New York City. It came not from a student but from Pvt. William Remmel, a member of Company I of the 121st New York Volunteer Regiment. Remmel's letters implied that he was lured from his studies by the several bounties being offered and by the prospect of earning a soldier's pay. The previous spring, his father had refused his plea to answer Lincoln's first call for 75,000 men. Remmel threatened that if another call came, he would answer it. He traveled alone to Camp Schuyler. Unaware of his actions, his parents did not go to the camp to see him off.[12]

Remmel's most prominent schoolmate was Adam Clarke Rice. Born in 1840, the fourth son in a large family of five boys and three girls from Fairfield, Herkimer County, Adam assiduously avoided reading and the strict instruction common for boys his age. At sixteen, he joined his brother George in New York City in an unspecified business, which engendered his entrepreneurial spirit. Obstacles challenged him. After a year with his brother, he returned home and, for a second time, entered Fairfield Academy; however, "as before, being inclined to be wild, as some said, he made little progress in his studies." Again, he grew restless, and he decided to visit his sister Mary in Minnesota. When he arrived there, he found her in extremely poor health; she died soon afterward. As the only family member who was with her in her last days, he took on the responsibility of making her funeral arrangements. The experience had a maturing influence on the young, impetuous man from Fairfield. He astounded his parents on his return home by reentering the academy and throwing himself into his studies. He relished the activity of writing: his surviving works are heavy, melodramatic, and overwrought. A slow learner, he struggled to keep pace with his fellow students. When he graduated in 1862, the world opened to him, and he chose to go to college—until the war interfered. At that point, he enlisted as a private and reputedly rejected help from influential citizens to join at a higher rank.[13]

Samuel Burdett Kelley was born in 1842 in Schenevus, located in the town of Maryland, Otsego County. His village of no more than 600 people sat in the Schenevus Valley along the creek of the same name, nestled between South Hill on its southern side and Crumhorn Mountain to the north. His family consisted of his father and mother (Almond, who was forty-four in 1862, and Mary Anne, forty-two) and his two sisters, Sylvina and Jessie. His mother sang in their local church, and his father supported the family as a shoemaker. Sylvina was Sam's older sister, at twenty-two, and the 1860 census listed her as a milliner. Jessie was three. Samuel (or Burdett, as his friends and family called him) stood 5 feet, 8 inches tall and had piercing gray eyes and brown hair. His enlistment papers described him as a merchant. He had apprenticed as a clerk in Isaac Slingerland's store in Schenevus until he decided, early in 1860, that he would improve his lot in life and attempt to get a job in the big city—Cooperstown. He applied as a clerk in James Cockett and Harvey Marvin's dry goods store on Cooperstown's main street. Armed with several favorable references, Kelley secured the job in April and proved himself to be an honest, reliable, and hardworking clerk. Slingerland took credit for the "making of that boy" in his "career" move to Cooperstown. His employment was something of an apprenticeship and was intended to last three years, "if I suit and am suited," he noted. His pay was to be $75 the first year, $100 the second, and $150 the third, "if I am steady and do well. Making in all $325.00." Included in his pay were board and all his washing.[14]

At age eighteen, he settled in with the Cockett and Marvin partnership, which he described as "one of the nicest stores in Cooperstown." He enjoyed the picturesque village. The rector of Christ Church, the Reverend S. H. Synott, who kept up with him after he enlisted with the 121st, befriended Kelley. The young man spent his free time walking the quiet streets of town, visiting the Episcopal Christ Church, the Universalist Church, and the Cooper monument, which stood "some 30 feet high" at Lakewood Cemetery and had the figure of Leatherstocking at its peak. Inheriting his mother's penchant for music, he was drawn to recitals and sang in the choir of Christ Church as a tenor. When the deep snows came and were of the right consistency, he could be persuaded to embark on a sleigh ride. But sometimes, the snow could be "so gol-darned poor that there was not much fun in it." He did not go home except on holidays and for special events, but he wrote often to his family. Kelley described the devastating Cooperstown fires that ravaged the town in the spring of 1862. His employer James Cockett survived the fires because he lived in a stone house down the street, a structure that remains today.[15]

National events intrigued Kelley as they spiraled out of control. He watched the November 1860 elections closely. "My nerves were rather unsettled before Lincoln's election but now as he has got through Splitting Rails you see that I have concluded to settle down." He told his parents a convoluted story about a Republican father who frightened his young son with the peculiar mock threat that if the Democrats elected "their president," he would take the boy down south and sell him, for all he was good for "was to eat bread and butter." At the next meal, the story went, the child burst into tears as the bread was passed around the table. He eagerly asked to eat "taters" so that he would not have to be sold down south. Kelley concluded: "Lincoln is elected; the boy eats bread as usual."

The influx of recruiters into Otsego County at the end of 1861, all veterans of the first battle of Bull Run, energized Burdett Kelley. Their exotic Zouave uniforms impressed him, making him eager to enlist, and he begged his father for permission to do so. The returning regiments whose terms of enlistment had expired were allowed to bring their weapons home with them. This strategy, according to one politician, had a positive effect "among young men," inflaming their patriotic fervor and inciting their desire to get to the front. To that point, youthful civilians were ignorant of the trials of those returning soldiers who were "spectators to the perils and toils" of the battlefield.[16]

"I have a heart that is beating warmer and warmer for the cause of my country," Kelley wrote to his parents. "Knowing that it is my duty in this trying time I appeal to you for the word GO. There is no time for talking about situations when our rights and interests are about to be snatched from us by Rebel Foes." He pleaded for a positive response. "You will please write immediately and if you have any objections you will name them." He would not be deterred. "I have thought the matter over earnestly and carefully and am willing to do the duty which would devolve upon me." His father let his sister Sylvina deliver the answer. She begged him not to enlist, and initially he acquiesced. Eventually, however, he asked no one's counsel and joined the army. As he saw it, enlisting was his duty. He told the *Otsego Republican*, "I know how important to success it is, that a young man should choose his occupation in life and follow it steadily; and I went to Cockett and Marvin's with that view, but the government wants me, and I could leave better than many others."[17]

Meanwhile, in the Deep South, Clinton Beckwith was living the life of a young soldier in Key West, Florida. In December 1861, the bored and freezing men of the 91st had been on Governor's Island in the Hudson. Then they boarded the steamer *Ericson,* bound for Florida, for what would be an unbearable trip for upstate landlubbers: the recruits were soon on their knees, "paying their respects to Neptune." Soon, however, the seas calmed, and the air warmed; the landscape changed to palm trees, seaweed, and tropical birds as they reached land. Once the boat had docked and the officers had dismissed the regiment from its formation, a thousand men raced liked schoolchildren to the beach and the cool waters.

Teaming with "wreckers, slavers and smugglers," Key West was about as exotic a place as one could find without leaving the United States. As a "fresh fish," Beckwith was quickly initiated into the life of the soldier, including being tossed in a blanket. Cuban cigars and commissary whiskey were everywhere, and the authorities did little to discourage their use. Beckwith enjoyed a good cigar and quickly became a connoisseur of cool, sweet Cubans, but the whiskey did not set well on his young stomach. When he awoke in the guardhouse with a hangover, he remembered nothing of the riot he had participated in the night before.

All was not well in paradise, however. The soldiers soon learned the difference between benign insects and reptiles and those that could bring pain and sickness. Occasionally, a "darting chameleon lizard would slip up your trouser legs, and then you took your pants off without ceremony," Beckwith wrote years later. Brackish water, tarantulas, centipedes, and borer crabs were all new and potentially deadly wonders to the men of the 91st. Eventually, the young Beckwith became disillusioned with the lifestyle in the Keys, and he fell ill with dysentery. He "longed for the cool North wind," as well as the flags, pomp, and circumstance of the military life of which he had dreamed. "The grind of preparation appalled me, the food of camp sickened me, and I found myself growing feebler as the days dragged on." On Washington's birthday in 1862, he collapsed while marching. After a few rounds with the regimental doctor, who pronounced him unfit for duty, Clinton Beckwith was placed on the next steamer to New York City. Again, the rough passage made him seasick, and at one point, he nearly fell overboard.

The beginning of March found Beckwith in New York City and recovered enough to make his way back to Albany. By May, he had returned to his father's store in Utica and once again was listening to the stories of war and glory from the customers. But the desire to reenlist still burned brightly in his psyche. Indeed, the elder Beckwith thought his son was mad; he called him "a sap head" for wanting to rejoin the army. On the Fourth of July in 1862, Clinton Beckwith marched in the parade as part of the "Seymour Artillery." That convinced him that he would try to sign up again. Gathering together his latest savings and in collusion with a friend, Beckwith hopped a canal barge to Ilion, where the two bought train tickets to Albany to pick out a regiment they liked. His friend soon decided that military life was not for him and returned home. Beckwith did not like any of the regiments either, and so he made his way back to Herkimer County, getting off the train in Little Falls. There, he visited two recruiting stations before moving on to Mohawk, where he concluded that the 121st New York Volunteer Infantry Regiment suited him. He enlisted on the spot. A mutual friend spotted him in uniform and informed his father where he was. And as a result, the day after Beckwith mustered into the U.S. Army, his father "appeared upon the scene," and the two enjoyed a long walk during which they reached an accord that was satisfactory to both of them. "This talk did me a world of good," Beckwith recalled in later life. "I felt more confident in myself. I was entirely familiar with the ordinary duties of a soldier and young as I was, the nettle ambition was in my brain."[18]

The Regiment Is Raised

Those who answered the call to join the 121st New York State Volunteer Infantry Regiment came from all walks of life. William Remmel and Samuel Kelley were representative of the recruits of the 121st; Beckwith was unusual. The majority were farmers and tradesmen who worked the land or produced goods for those who did. They were blacksmiths, coopers, carpenters, and shopkeepers, and there were some professional men as well; like Remmel, Beckwith, and Kelley, most were very young and unmarried. Some of the farmers—including James Clark in Saratoga County, who was working in his father's rye field—literally dropped their pitchforks and haying equipment and, "Cincinnatus-like," signed up. In Otsego, the farmboys were working the hop fields to bring the summer's crop in to market when Lincoln's call came. The choice they faced was stark: either answer the siren call of the "glamour" of the military or remain at the repetitious work on the land. Many asked their parents for permission to join; others merely ignored parental advice and informed them after enlisting.

The boys attended war meetings held in local churches or other community assembling places. In a routine fairly uniform throughout the state, the pastor or the recruiting officer passed around a simple list, and those willing to join signed the paper. Few people asked if the boys were of age or had obtained parental permission. At an assembly, the crowd would squeeze inside the flag-covered walls to hear stirring speeches by prominent local businessmen or political leaders. A glee club would render patriotic songs, and a stirring band would whip the audience into a state of frenzy. At one church, a participant reported, the pastor "kissed the flag draped behind the pulpit, pledging himself as a volunteer in the company and his congregation to eternal fidelity to the union. There was wild enthusiasm, and the scene was indescribable." When community leaders stepped forward to enlist, it "had a powerful influence" on those who wavered in making their decisions.[19]

Charlie Butts, a native of Sheffield, Lorraine County, Ohio, was in his junior year at Hamilton College in the picturesque town of Clinton, New York, when war broke out. He left a comfortable college environment and the leisurely life of a student and member of Delta Kappa Epsilon fraternity. Having been promised a commission, he went to Otsego County to recruit a company, "obtaining a number of men." When the promised commission never materialized, he joined the 121st in July as a corporal in Company K. He desperately wanted a commission, but "he had no powerful friends" in Albany.

A year later, he and six other Hamilton students received their diplomas "in consideration of good service in the army." According to one of his teachers, Charlie Butts's "real life began when he took up the musket in that war."[20]

By the time they mustered out of the service in Virginia in 1865, thirty "Smiths" had served in the 121st, including five "John Smiths." Many of their names were from another time and place: Abel, Asabel, Asa, Alonzo, Abner, Aaron, Aurelius, Cassius, Delos, Elias, Elijah, Erastus, Ezra, Hiram, Isaac, Jacob, Jeremiah, Josiah, Levi, Lucius, Silas, Shadrack, Uzel, Zebulon, Zephariah, and Zachariah. Few had traveled outside either county—their birthplaces and homes. The handful who were Europeans—such as the German-born Remmel; Andrew Davidson, a native of Roxborough, Scotland, but a resident of Middlefield, Otsego County; and Remmel's company commander, John Swain Kidder, a resident of Laurens who was of English birth—contributed to the war effort and the success of the 121st.

John Kidder was born in 1830 in Charing County, Kent, England. In 1842, when he was twelve, his family left England for the United States. His father, a tea dealer and grocer who provided his customers a "good assortment of Teas, Coffee and spices from the East India Company's warehouses," joined his brothers George and Thomas in upstate New York. John Kidder apprenticed to a wagon maker six years later, and wagon making became his life in Laurens until the war came. He lived with his wife, Harriet, whom he had married in 1853, and continued his apprenticeship while living with his sponsor, a Morris resident and businessman named James Kenyon. Kidder learned everything he could from Kenyon, applying his talents to all areas of carriage manufacturing. He left Kenyon the year after he married Harriet. The newlyweds then moved to Laurens, where John partnered with Elisha Fisher and set up shop in the carriage-making business.

In that same year, 1854, Kidder, an old-line Whig, became one of the founding fathers of the Republican Party in Otsego County. During the course of his work, he became acquainted with manufacturing moguls such as fellow Republican William C. Fields of Laurens (to whom Kidder would appeal for help during the war). But money became a constant concern, and the depression of 1857 nearly sank Kidder and Fisher's company. Wagon orders slowed, and Kidder did not respond quickly. By the summer of 1862, the wagon-making business in Laurens was in dire straits. The call to serve and the prospect of receiving steady pay from the federal government promised the relief Kidder needed to provide for his family, even if it meant supporting them from the hazards of battlefields many miles away. He attacked the business of recruiting with a passion, and by the end of August, he had raised a company.[21]

The governor of the state of New York was the commander in chief of the state militia. In 1860, the state's military consisted of 220 infantry companies, 126 artillery batteries, 41 cavalry troops, and 37 rifle companies, for a grand total of 18,000 officers and men under arms. Males between eighteen and forty-five were eligible for military duty. With the exception of major generals and the commissary general, militia officers were chosen by election, an old military tradition. During the Black Hawk War, Abraham Lincoln was voted captain of his militia unit by his men. The New York State Constitution of 1822 provided for the election of all militia officers below the grade of major general. But on May 4, 1861, the federal Adjutant General's Office in Washington, ignoring the militia model, laid out the ground rules for the new volunteer army. The Lincoln administration called for a minimum of 34,000 and a maximum of 42,000 new officers for all the new regiments that would be needed to put down the rebellion. The new mandate allowed the governors to appoint all commissioned and field and staff officers in the rapidly forming volunteer units. Governor Morgan interpreted General Order No. 15 as his authority to sweep away the old militia election process by setting specific recruitment totals for the new volunteer regiments. When an individual met the requirement for forming a company—recruiting a minimum of 83 officers and men up to a maximum of 101— he became the company commander.

Morgan set the new rules down clearly and forcefully: "The person who enlisted the necessary number of recruits received their votes for the office. The second lieutenant gets his commission when he recruits 30 men, the first [lieutenant] when he recruits 40 men, a Captain upon completion of the company." Once the troops were in the field, Morgan insisted that he alone would promote those "who have gone through the battles, and have proved themselves worthy." He turned to his business and political friends to recruit regiments, and he rewarded them with commands. In July 1861, the War Department further mandated competency examinations for all officers, but many regiments ignored the rule and continued to elect their officers. Few made the connection between the successful recruitment of a full regiment and the necessary skills for successful leadership under combat conditions. Having recruited a full regiment of 1,040 men, Congressman Franchot became Colonel Franchot.[22]

Caught between the old ways and the new, those who were successful recruiters led the 121st; its officers were rewarded for their efforts in recruiting able-bodied men "apportioned according to the number each had enlisted." The *Herkimer Democrat* refused to let go of the democratic notion of officer elections. It cleverly insisted that the enlisted men did indeed have a voice in choosing who led them: "An impression has obtained some currency that the selection of company officers has been taken out of the hands of the rank and file. This is not so," it continued knowingly. "Every man's commission does depend upon his securing a certain number of men." Echoing Morgan's proclamation, the paper pointed out that any man filling an entire company could be named a captain. "Nothing can be fairer," it proclaimed happily, "making as it does, efficiency the test of promotion."

James Cronkite remembered that the officers of the 121st were assigned to their ranks and commands because they mutually agreed to the plan: "By a partial agreement among the officers, each was to take his rank in the company according to the number enlisted, and the understanding was so closely adhered to that very little dissatisfaction occurred." But Cronkite's description missed the essential elements of the process. The enlisted men of the 121st did not vote for their commanders as militia units before them had done. Rather, they in essence picked their leaders by agreeing to enlist in the company.[23]

Although Morgan retained the authority to appoint staff officers and replacements throughout the war, Franchot was allowed to handpick his own staff—specifically, his adjutant and his quartermaster. As early as July 23, 1862, the *Democrat* reported that Franchot had chosen as his quartermaster Albert Story, the son of one of the members of the local committee formed to stimulate recruitment (A. G. Story of Little Falls). Otsego resident Alonzo Ferguson was selected to be his adjutant. Ferguson, an Oneonta merchant, had previous service in Kentucky and Tennessee. "Beyond these," the paper reported, "the staff appointments are all open, and their disposition will depend upon the energy and ability shown by aspirants in getting up the Regiment."[24]

General Order No. 15 contained a provision that would haunt the regiment throughout the war. It called for a minimum of 830 men in the ten companies plus 36 staff (including 24 musicians in the band), for a total of 866 men. The maximum ranged between 1,010 and 1,046. By extension, the order authorized one colonel, one lieutenant colonel, and one major for every regiment with a minimum number of men. Although the order contained no specific language about regimental strength, the commanding officers of the 121st remained concerned about that issue throughout the war. They feared losing the regiment's identity through merger into a larger, healthier regiment *and* the inability of state volunteer officers commissioned at a higher rank but refused that rank at the federal level because their troop strength fell below that mandated by the general order. Troop strength was also misleading. The number of men could and almost always did include not only those present for duty but also those on sick leave and on furlough as well as those captured, wounded, or detailed to another command. A regiment might be at full strength but have only 480 "rifles"—that is, only 480 men and officers fit for combat.

The Adjutant General's Office in Albany issued Special Order No. 463, dated August 21, 1862, which officially recognized and numbered the unit as the 121st Regiment of New York Volunteers. This paperwork merely caught up with the reality on the ground. An earlier order, dated August 11, named the regiment and instructed it to move from Camp Schuyler to Washington on August 25. All infantry regiments were to consist of 1,000 men organized in ten companies of 100 troops each. Military tradition dictated that each company of the 121st would be lettered A through K (but with no Company J). Each company was authorized to have three officers: a captain, a first lieutenant, and a second lieutenant. The original commissioned staff officers consisted of the regiment's organizer, Col. Richard Franchot, age forty-six; Lt. Col. Charles H. Clark, twenty-eight, who had recently served with the 43rd New York Regiment; and Maj. Egbert Olcott, son of Horatio Olcott (president of the Cherry Valley Bank) and one of the few men with prior military experience.

Three doctors were assigned to the 121st as it assembled at Camp Schuyler: Surgeon William Bassett, First Assistant Surgeon Stephen B. Valentine, and Second Assistant Surgeon Daniel M. Holt. The unit's first chaplain, John R. Sage, had enlisted as a private "with no expectation of [attaining] the position" of chaplain, and he put forth "no effort to obtain it." Adjutant Alonzo Ferguson and Quartermaster Albert Story rounded out the commissioned officers on the staff.[25]

Ferguson was forty-two when he enrolled at Albany for three years. He accepted a commission as a first lieutenant and an appointment as the regiment's adjutant immediately afterward. His organizational prowess greatly expedited the process of getting the 121st into the field. With the urging of Franchot and the local war committee, he later accepted Governor Morgan's charge to organize the 152nd New York State Infantry. That regiment, also from Otsego and Herkimer counties, mustered in the fall of 1862 soon after the 121st left the state for the front lines. Henry Roback, official chronicler of the 152nd, complained of slow recruiting in October because the 121st had snapped up "the choice of the material," forcing the 152nd "to accept a few old men."

Completing the staff of the 121st were the noncommissioned officers: Sgt. Maj. Charles M. Bradt; Quartermaster Samuel J. Cooke; Commissary Sergeant George H. Snell; hospital steward Oscar A. Chatfield; Roselle A. Jackson, drum major; and thirty-seven-year-old native of Newport Napoleon B. Barney, fife major. Snell, a post office clerk from Little Falls, held the distinction of being the first man to enlist in the new regiment.[26]

The men of the 121st came from each town of the state's Twentieth Senatorial District and were led by the officers who had recruited them. The enlisted men came from the laboring classes, and most were farmers, mechanics, and mill hands; the officers, by contrast, were predominantly community leaders in their towns and villages and usually held influential positions as lawyers, merchants, municipal officials, ministers, doctors, and the like. Students fell into both groups. Some were older and mature enough to lead men in combat. The first four companies, A through D, were from Herkimer County. Men from Manheim, Little Falls, Salisbury, and Danube filled Company A, which took the post of honor. The state relied on the lettering to designate the earliest date of muster for the entire company and in combat. Traditionally, Company A held the honor of leading the regiment. Since Greek times, the first company was posted on the "right" of the regiment's battle line because most commanders interpreted the upcoming battle as a series of right maneuvers to flank the enemy's left, or "weak," flank. Capt. Henry Galpin, a merchant from Little Falls, commanded Company A. He had led the recruiting derby from the beginning. 1st Lt. Jonathon Burrell and 2nd Lt. George W. Davis filled his command positions.[27]

Galpin originally joined the 44th New York, known as Ellsworth's Avengers. He was in the field when Lincoln's call came. His friends in Albany asked him to return to the state capital, where he received permission to recruit for the new regiment being formed in the Twentieth Senatorial District. He returned to Little Falls on a Monday night and attended a recruiting rally in Richfield Springs the next day. On Wednesday, with his brother S. J., Galpin turned his family's stove store into a recruiting office. The two men bought a fife and drum, hung a flag at the store's front door, and set up shop as recruiters. Both brothers were pleasantly surprised at the enthusiasm expressed by the young men who came in to enlist, and word spread quickly as the new recruits returned home to rally others to the cause. Galpin and his brother spent $140 on rented livery wagons to bring the boys in from the farms and return them home. Competition quickly ensued between Little Falls and Frankfort over who should get the credit for forming Company A. Galpin won the recruiting sweepstakes, enabling him to march off within thirty days with a full complement of men.[28]

B Company hailed from the Herkimer towns of Winfield, Plainfield, Litchfield, German Flats, Columbia, and Stark, and its officers were Capt. Irving Holcomb, 1st Lt. Henry C. Keith, and 2nd Lt. George A. May. Clinton Beckwith became a corporal in Company B. Holcomb, Keith, and May returned home within months of taking the field after resigning their commissions in a purge instigated by Emory Upton.

The men in Company C came from the northern Herkimer County towns of Fairfield, Russia, Herkimer, and Newport. Capt. Clinton A. Moon, a practicing lawyer and the district attorney of Herkimer, led the company. He was assisted by 1st Lt. Thomas S. Arnold, who was also a lawyer and was the excise commissioner for the Herkimer County Board of Supervisors, and by 2nd Lt. Angus Cameron. The *Oneonta Herald* described Moon and Arnold as "sterling citizens, energetic, and justly popular who enlisted from a sense of duty." Moon had run unsuccessfully for county judge in 1855 as a Republican, and when the village of Newport was incorporated in 1857, he became the first county clerk. He held numerous town offices—county supervisor and school commissioner—before and after the war. Before the war, he consolidated two school districts with the goal of establishing a graded school in the new district. Arnold, one of seven children, came from a prominent Herkimer County family that had lived in Fairfield since 1799.

D Company, commanded by Capt. John D. Fish, 1st Lt. Delos M. Kenyon, and 2nd Lt. Charles E. Staring, consisted of a blend of recruits from Frankfort, Warren, Manheim, Schuyler, Columbia, and Salisbury. Fish came from the town of Frankfort. Kenyon joined the regiment in August, and Staring, a carpenter from Schuyler, joined the regiment as a private and accepted a commission as an officer less than ten days later. When the war ended, all three were no longer in the 121st. Salisbury raised 147 men in the earlier calls by the federal government, and by August 6, the town met the quota assigned to it.[29]

Companies E, F, and G were from Otsego County. Recruiter Capt. Douglas Campbell speedily and efficiently assembled Company E from the immediate Cooperstown area: Middlefield, Milford, Cherry Valley, Hartwick, Springfield, Otsego, and Roseboom. Campbell's confidence increased when he got to Cooperstown; he would raise two companies. He gave up one of the companies to another man—probably Company G to Edwin Park—and he retained command of Company E. The townspeople of Roseboom were relentless in their attempts to fill their quota. They were able to beat all others in exceeding their goals and were therefore christened the "banner town" in the current round of recruitments by the *Freeman's Journal*. Campbell's first and second lieutenants were Theodore Sternburg and Harrison Van Horn. The *Otsego Republican* characterized the men of Company E, all recruited from the immediate vicinity, as the "finest assortment of muscular machinery displayed in one lot." Years later, Campbell would maintain that he got the best material Otsego County could offer. "These were the brawn and muscle of our land," he declared. Other regiments may have enlisted men who needed the bonus or a steady paycheck or those who were unemployed. He boasted that every man who joined his company successfully answered one question: "Your country is in peril; will you help save her?"[30]

The men in F Company came from the outer fringe of the county—Edmeston, Exeter, Unadilla, Otsego, and Maryland—and were commanded by Capt. Nelson Orville Wendell assisted by 1st Lt. Byron T. Peck and 2nd Lt. Frank G. Bolles. Sam Kelley began military life in Company F as a corporal. Nelson Wendell became a large figure in the regiment. He, too, had joined the famed 44th New York one year before at twenty-nine years of age. He had attended Hanover College in Madison, Indiana, for his sophomore year in 1856. Originally a small Presbyterian school on the Ohio River founded in 1827, Hanover was similar to Fairfield Academy. Wendell was one of three New Yorkers in a class of fourteen: two were from New York City; he listed his residence as Oneonta. He took courses in ancient and modern history, Bible studies, and the classics. After college, he returned to Cooperstown to accept an appointment as school commissioner of Otsego County before the war and then moved on to become a professor at West Winfield Academy, the position he occupied when the war broke out. His unshakable assurance that the Union cause was in the right led him to enlist. He declared a love for the flag and his country, with all of its faults. "I am not my own," he declared, "my life is my country's." He expressed "happiness . . . in defending the flag I venerate and serving the country I love."[31]

The towns of Cherry Valley, Roseboom, Decatur, Middlefield, Westford, Worcester, and Herkimer were represented in Company G. Capt. Edwin Park accepted command of the company, and its first and second lieutenants were Charles T. Ferguson and J. D. Clyde. Capt. John Ramsey commanded Company H, a Herkimer County–Otsego County mixture. Its troops were from Little Falls, Richfield, Salisbury, and Otsego. 1st Lt. Ulysses F. Doubleday and 2nd Lt. Marcus R. Casler assisted Ramsey. Doubleday came from perhaps the most famous Otsego County family. His great-grandfather Abner was the reputed inventor of baseball, and his cousin—also named Abner—was a West Point graduate and a veteran of the Mexican War. Cousin Abner was serving at Fort Sumter with Maj. Robert Anderson when the Confederates fired the war's opening shots. Company I, also a mixture, consisted of citizens from the Otsego towns of Milford, Laurens, Morris, Worcester, Pittsfield, and Hartwick and the Herkimer town of German Flats. William Remmel found himself in Company I. Most of the men were recruited and led by Capt. John S. Kidder, a Laurens native and wagon maker; 1st Lt. John de Peyster Douw, a nephew of Colonel Franchot; and 2nd Lt. Delavan Bates.[32]

The last unit, K Company, featured a representative sample of personnel from all over Otsego County—Laurens, New Lisbon, Oneonta, Burlington, Otsego, Butternuts, and Pittsfield—as well as Plainfield in Herkimer County. They were commanded by Capt. Sackett M. Olin; 1st Lt. Andrew E. Mather, the son of Sheriff Mather; and 2nd Lt. Frank Gorton from Mohawk. Olin blossomed relatively late in life. He attended school in Laurens and married at thirty-three. He had two years of prior experience as a captain of the Burnside Guards, and he and Mather recruited most of the men of K Company. Olin remained with the regiment through Fredericksburg—barely three months—before resigning his commission because of ill health. Upon his return to Otsego County, he dabbled in running a general store and later became involved in real estate and eventually politics. As a strict prohibitionist, he served a term as a justice of the peace. Single-handedly, Mather signed up seventeen men from the tiny village of Garrattsville, population 192. When it was fielded at the end of August 1862, the regiment fairly represented the Twentieth New York Senatorial District.[33]

Generally, the first four companies were considered Herkimer County companies and the next six Otsego County companies, even though the last two had a mix of recruits from both counties. Ultimately, Herkimer County supplied men to nine infantry regiments, five cavalry units, and five artillery groups between 1861 and 1865. Otsego County men joined ten infantry regiments, six cavalry troops, five artillery batteries, and one engineer regiment. The *Freeman's Journal* voiced its pleasure with the results once the 152nd filled up. "Two regiments in three months from Herkimer and Otsego," it trumpeted. "Who says the 'Hop District' is not loyal, patriotic and wide awake?"[34]

Camp Schuyler

State authorities originally intended that the gathering point and training camp for the new regiment would be located in Richfield Springs in Otsego County. But given the existence of rail and river access farther north, Mohawk was chosen "as a matter of convenience, and to save a heavy expense in transportation of camp equipage and supplies." Just south of the Mohawk River and a short distance from the village of Herkimer in the town of German Flats, Herkimer entrepreneur Henry J. Schuyler owned a large tract of land. On July 25, Quartermaster Albert Story, acting on behalf of the state of New York, entered into a formal contract with Schuyler to use the land as a training camp. The contract allowed the state to take as much land as it needed for $10 an acre. It could erect as many buildings as it deemed necessary. It could remove fences only if it later replaced them or reimbursed Schuyler for the cost to replace them when the state no longer needed them.[35]

The camp's preparations were complete by the end of July. The regiment remained at Schuyler only a short time. No physical archaeological evidence of the camp's actual size remains, but contemporary descriptions and a rare lithograph indicate that it could accommodate more than 1,000 men. It consisted of four main components: a large tented area for sheltered sleeping; two large, wooden framed buildings used for mess and meetings and officers; and a large open field for drilling and maneuvers. The newly formed 152nd New York used Schuyler immediately after the 121st departed. The state moved to put up temporary shelter for the 121st once it signed the contract.

Silas W. Burt, assistant inspector general of the New York Militia, wielded the authority and responsibility for selecting and developing campsites throughout the state. He visited Camp Schuyler on August 14 and found the completed buildings sound and suitable for occupancy. Although he noted the camp's well-sited position on hills with good drainage, he discovered that the water supply was too far removed from the camp. John H. Starin solved the problem. Starin, a private citizen of Herkimer, generously provided an entire water supply system at his own expense.

The state let a separate contract for board and lodging for the new regiment "to Messrs. Lowell, Prescott & Snell, at forty cents per day per soldier." The buildings for the enlisted personnel were uniform throughout the state's camps. They were "flimsy and insubstantial, but they subserved their purpose at a very trifling cost," since the lumber they were built with could be used later. The main quarters were 96 feet long, 20 feet wide, and 13 feet high at the walls. In each, the roof rose to a peak of 19.5 feet at the center of the building, and both

Camp Schuyler, 1862. Lithographed and published by B. F. Smith, Jr., and Stanley Fox, Albany, N.Y. Courtesy of the Herkimer County Historical Society, Herkimer, New York.

ends of the structure featured large doors and gable windows. Each large building could hold four rows of bunks, three tiers high, extending the entire length of the facility—enough to accommodate 180 men. Officers were quartered in wall tents, both shared and individual.[36]

The camp's central location prompted the enlistees' families to visit during the short time the regiment occupied Camp Schuyler. This, in turn, led to a picniclike, family reunion atmosphere that the *Herkimer County Journal* captured. Editor Jean R. Stebbins—"J. R." to his intimates—described the informality of breakfast with the soldiers, commenting on the food, sanitation, order, discipline, and general appearance of the new tent city. He pronounced it fit and the men ready to take on the role of soldiers. Isaac Best, in his official *History of the 121st*, dismissed the camp and the regiment's experience there because nothing of the "physical characteristics or structural features" suggested "beauty or interest, and the stay of the 121st in it was so short after their muster in, that nothing worth remembering by the men seems to have occurred there."[37]

The local papers nonetheless poetically described the picturesque camp to their readers. Located on a plateau high above the Mohawk, it offered a breathtaking view of the valley below, running east and west as far as the eye could see. "The camp is on one of the most beautiful localities ever visited," wrote one reporter. The West Canada Creek, "like a streak of silver, winding, and sparkling in the sunlight," came out of the Adirondacks and cut across the plain as it emptied into the Mohawk River. Part of the creek formed the boundary between Herkimer and Fulton counties. It flowed through the picturesque village of Brockett's Bridge: "The farm houses, the several villages, the canal with its ever moving burthens, the lovely emerald of the fields, and the forest and the shade trees, all combine to render the scene one of charming beauty." By mid-August, there were approximately 600 men in camp, where neat rows of white tents and broad company streets were set into the hillside and surrounded by a forest. "The men now in camp are uniformly splendid fellows physically, and in all other respects are among the very best youth our county affords." The *Cherry Valley Gazette* contributed to the portrayal of the idyllic scene when its correspondent wrote of "some [men] playing ball, some taking afternoon naps, some doing one thing or some another, but all enjoying themselves." Horseplay was inevitable. When Allen Lovejoy of Company G accidentally discharged a pistol into Pvt. David Finch's leg, Franchot immediately ordered every pistol "found in the hands of a private after 24 hours . . . confiscated." Franchot sent Finch home to recuperate for thirty days.[38]

The local papers outdid themselves in praise for Franchot, Assistant Surgeon Valentine, and Alonzo Ferguson: "These gentlemen seem to work with system, and are *making* progress as rapidly as the occasion requires," opined the *Democrat*. The *Gazette* found "Col. Franchot and his aides busily at work; a smile and a word for each, but with little time to spare to any." The *Otsego Republican* claimed that Franchot needed "only the experience . . . of actual service to make him every inch a Colonel. His fine figure is set off to advantage by the military uniform, and his bearing is calculated to inspire his men with confidence in his ability to command" and serve faithfully. Dr. Valentine and Adjutant Ferguson were pressed into service for at least a week mustering in the new recruits. The *Chenango Telegraph* congratulated Franchot for his ability "to respond to his country's call with so fine a regiment. Whether in Congress or in military life, Col. F. *always* honors the draft made upon him."[39]

Recruiting did not end on August 23, the day the regiment mustered into federal service. New recruits slowly made their way into camp on every known form of conveyance, with enrollment continuing throughout the month. The newspapers dutifully recorded the many hastily called "war meetings" and allowed recruiting officers free space in their columns to garner recruits.

By the summer of 1862, Henry Wood had grown "tall and strong." In the preceding spring, Ogden Beach in Springfield had hired him as a laborer, and all that summer, Wood saved his money without missing a day of work. In early August, Wood's father and his two brothers came to speak with him, and they agreed that the three boys should "go together." The Wood brothers left Middlefield on August 13, the day after they had enlisted. They found it difficult to say good-bye to their family and the "old home" where they had grown up. They walked the 3 miles to Cooperstown, where they boarded a large wagon pulled by four horses to make the 22-mile trip to Mohawk. It and several other wagons were loaded with other recruits, and "with flags flying [they] started on the journey to the camp." Henry Wood remembered, "All along the road there were people gathered in large throngs, waving flags, cheering us and wishing us God-speed." They arrived in camp late in the afternoon, where they received medical examinations before being fed and directed to a temporary city of eight-man tents. They slept on beds of straw with one blanket per person. The next morning, they bathed in the canal.

Samuel Kelley arrived at Herkimer too late, and the guards refused him admittance into camp. He found a room at the Railroad Hotel, and the next morning, he walked the mile into camp. There, he met Capt. Nelson Wendell, who helped him get his gear, and settled into one of the "long buildings, with many tables arranged by company," where he got a solid breakfast. His articulate manner and ability to write thrust him into the role of filling out "blank receipts for a part of the State bounty" from morning until nightfall. That night, he slept in his overcoat, as the supply of blankets was exhausted.[40]

As long as the regiment remained on New York soil, it fell under the jurisdiction and control of state authorities. Once in the field, the regiments were under federal control, but the governor retained the authority to promote and appoint officers. He appointed one second lieutenant in each company of each regiment to be the "official mustering officer." The health and well-being of each recruit were in the hands of the regimental surgeon. The federal government provided quartermaster, medical, and ordinance support to the states, including the reimbursement of travel expenses to recruiting officers.[41]

Assistant Inspector General Silas Burt, Governor Morgan's man in the field, arrived in Camp Schuyler on August 22 and paid the men of the 121st the state bounty—despite bureaucratic delays as well as the confusion attendant on assembling so large a body of men and preparing them to travel to the front. Muster rolls, documenting who had enlisted where and which company they were assigned to, became "confusing and misleading particularly where there had been a contemporaneous equalization of companies." Many men were uncertain where they belonged. At the same time Burt paid the state bounties, the federal paymaster distributed advance federal bounties and a month's pay to the men. Some New York troops left immediately for the field after being paid, leaving no chance for corrections to be made. The money counting was done outside in the elements, even when it rained, and because he used new money, Burt was constantly washing his hands of the fresh green ink. He disbursed a total of $47,150 to the men of the 121st; 935 men received $50 each, and 16 were paid $25.[42]

Sgt. George Teel, of Company I, wrote home that he would receive "enough to make one hundred dollars, if it is paid according to agreement." Teel also commented that they would soon be issued uniforms and a Bible and that he had had his picture taken in camp. William Remmel found the heat that withered many did not bother him. He told his parents that he actually enjoyed himself at Herkimer and could not wait to get "to the seat of war." He, too, sat for "embrotypes," which he sent home with friends. On August 23, Delavan Bates remembered a "Lieutenant Cranston" from the U.S. Army examining the adjutant's rolls for accuracy, and he recalled the regiment being formed in line as "each right hand was lifted toward heaven and each one swore" his allegiance to the United States. Thus, in the week between August 23 and August 30 at Camp Schuyler, preparations were devoted to filling out forms, outfitting troops with equipment, and paying the men.[43]

The confusion and turmoil in camp were but a small part of the drama being played out on the national scene. Union losses in the field and increasing Confederate threats placed more pressure on the Lincoln administration to get as many fighting men as possible into action as soon as possible. As early as July 28, the president queried the loyal governors on their progress in recruiting. Governor Morgan assured the president that he could get men into the field in two weeks, twenty days on the outside, and surely no later than sixty days. He added gratuitously that recruiting for the old regiments was "not rapid." Edwin Stanton pushed hard on Morgan in mid-August. During the month of August 1862, communiqués flew between Washington and the loyal state capitals concerning the threat posed by the Confederate armies and the need for help.

When Morgan told Stanton that at least one regiment was headed for the front, Stanton rejoiced—"For Heaven's sake, keep them moving." Again, Stanton queried Morgan on August 12: "How soon will the New York troops begin to move to Washington? Can you send any to-day?" Two days later, Morgan reported that he had nearly completed the quotas for New York. He listed four important reasons for the quick enrollment of nearly 60,000 men—the bounties, the "efforts and zeal of local committees, a fear of the draft, and the apprehension of unfavorable intelligence at any moment." A day later, Stanton revealed his concern and apprehension when he telegraphed Morgan and urged him to move the troops the next day: "Hours are pressing." If the railroads would move the troops on Sunday, Stanton would "make the arrangement if the troops can be ready. Please answer."

Three days later, Stanton again implored Morgan to move quickly: "I cannot tell you how precious time is now. Every man is needed at once. Do not wait to pay them the bonuses; send them to Washington and the government would pay them there." Again on August 19, he told Morgan, "The emergency for troops here is far more pressing than you know or than I dare tell. Put all your steam on and hurry them up." And on August 22, Stanton praised Morgan: "I am rejoiced to see the energy with which you are pushing forward your troops." Fulfilling Stanton's and Morgan's fears, Lee pressed northward. In one of the most celebrated tactical movements of the war, Stonewall Jackson seized the Federal Supply Depot at Manassas Junction after a stunning 50-mile march over August 25 and 26. In the week that the 121st was preparing to leave upstate New York, Lee and Jackson outmaneuvered the Union army at the second battle of Manassas, August 28 to 30. Lee was now positioned to invade Maryland.[44]

The pressure exerted by unfolding events and by the Lincoln administration eventually pushed the new regiment into the field with little or no training or drill. On the day the 121st left Camp Schuyler, Morgan promised the secretary ten more regiments would arrive within the week. Stanton expressed gratitude and relief: "They are much needed, for the exigency is pressing." A *Cherry Valley Gazette* reporter noted their leaving with more romance than reality. These were men "fresh from the farm, the shop, the office and the counting room; strong, healthy, and athletic, going cheerfully forth with a determination manfully to perform the highest duty they owe to their God and their country. They are entitled to the warmest commendations, and will be remembered by their country, which rarely fails to reward her sons who merit it." Years later, Clinton Beckwith remembered the period at Camp Schuyler fondly as a time he thoroughly enjoyed, and he remarked that whenever he passed the site after the war, it engendered "recollections of a pleasant nature to my memory."[45]

The Trip to the Front

The 121st left camp at 11 A.M., August 30, 1862, after only one week of drill. Untrained in the school of the soldier, unable to properly defend themselves in combat, and against the backdrop of a hypercritical national emergency caused by Lee's invading army, the men departed for the unknown. The 121st was originally scheduled to leave Mohawk on August 25, but its departure was postponed by five days because bureaucratic and organizational ineptness delayed the payment of bounties. The *Republican* noted that the 121st needed only one week to instill in it the necessary discipline and that the regiment would "not be excelled in physical or moral force by any regiment in the field." The first general order from Colonel Franchot's headquarters at Camp Schuyler, dated August 26, ordered two days' cooked rations for each man. All canteens were to be filled with fresh water at Albany, Jersey City, Philadelphia, and Baltimore. Meals would be supplied along the route. Leaving behind 117 men who had been discharged for disability, 30 officers and 946 enlisted men departed Herkimer for Albany with orders to travel to Washington via New York City.[46]

At their departure, county representatives presented the 121st with a regimental flag purchased from the firm of Storrs and Company in Utica but made possible by the fund-raising of two recent female graduates of Fairfield Seminary who traversed Herkimer County and ultimately collected $110. The officers and men of Company A presented Captain Galpin with a sword and sash as Colonel Franchot made a speech, to which Galpin "appropriately responded."

On behalf of Company H, Captain Ramsey accepted a "beautiful flag" presented by the grateful citizens of Herkimer. The grateful citizens of Litchfield and "other towns where his splendid company was recruited" presented Captain Holcomb of Company B with a flag. The equally proud citizens of Herkimer County gave Colonel Franchot a sword, belt, pistols, sash, shoulder straps, spurs, and gauntlets, costing $130. They expressed their appreciation to Franchot for leaving his seat in Congress to answer the call in the national emergency and for his willingness to protect the Constitution and the Union. Franchot responded that the time he spent at Camp Schuyler would be among the most pleasant of memories as long as he lived.

When the ceremonies ended, the regiment, consisting of 1,000 men standing 4 abreast, marched to twenty waiting railcars. They were accompanied by the Frankfort Band, engaged for the occasion by Capt. Clinton A. Moon, Company C. The enlisted men filled the forward cars; the staff and line officers occupied the last car. Moon's wife and Capt. Edwin Clark's wife accompanied their husbands. Thousands lined the tracks to bid farewell to the "boys" from Otsego and Herkimer counties. The train stopped for a few minutes to allow last handshakes, hugs, cheers, tears, and words of farewell. Babies to be kissed were raised to the soldiers as they leaned from the cars as families said goodbye. "There were few dry eyes in that assemblage, and though the majority attempted to conceal the anguish felt, it was a solemn and impressive parting."[47]

William Remmel's parents did not make the trip from Fairfield to see him off. The boy who had worked on a farm in upstate New York a few months earlier and had been a serious student before that wrote them to describe the scene at the Mohawk train station once he arrived in New York—"I am writing to you from the largest city in America," he began. "Many were the tears shed by relatives and friends at our parting and there could be seen in the faces of all an expression of deep sorrow at the moment of our departure." All along the route, well-wishers waved handkerchiefs and flags. As they passed through Schenectady, residents threw apples into the open car windows. In Albany, the crowds lining the streets and the tracks into town greeted the troops' arrival with similar enthusiasm. The ladies of Albany provided them with "suitable refreshments"—a handsome dinner at the Delavan House. Samuel D. French, a twenty-year-old farmer from Warren, Otsego County, and now a private in Company F, naively expressed his delight with the flattery lavished on the 121st by the people of Albany, who called the regiment the "best behaved and most intelligent lot of men that had passed through."[48]

When the entire regiment finished its meal in Albany, it marched down to the banks of the Hudson River opposite Merchants Hotel. There, "midst the cheers and greetings of thousands of people both male and female," the men boarded the river steamer *New World*—the "largest river steamer in the world." Once again, the residents of Albany lined the streets to wish them well and shake their hands. "I shook hands with many a fine 'gal,'" Delavan Hills rejoiced in his first letter. At 10 P.M., they began their journey to New York City with a celebratory cannonade. Hills called the steamer "a magnificent boat, a perfect floating palace." In a letter signed by all the officers of the regiment to the captain of the *New World*, Col. J. W. Harcourt, the 121st offered its official thanks. The *Albany Journal* published both the thank-you letter and Harcourt's response. The colonel expressed "pride and pleasure to witness so noble a body of young men comfortably taken care of while on their way to those stirring scenes now enacting near our National Capital. Judging from the vigor and soldierly deportment of your command, you will certainly be closely identified therewith." George Teel "slept on a box of guns and slept very well." The rest settled down wrapped in blankets. They slept until around three in the morning.[49]

For the schoolboys and farmboys of upstate New York, the trip on the river was a wondrous adventure. On a starlit night, they passed the quiet villages along the river and, farther downriver, West Point and the Palisades. For the young Delavan Hills, the view along the river "was the most beautiful sight I ever beheld." Twelve hours later, the regiment reached Park Barracks in New York City on Sunday morning, August 31. There, they "marched to the barns," where they finally got breakfast at 12:30 P.M. The barracks were in the business district directly across the road from Barnum's Museum and the Astor House and behind City Hall with its magnificent fountain and surrounding fence.

The men of the 121st left New York City and their native state the next morning, September 1, at around 8 A.M., not knowing, of course, that the regiment would return three years later with only one-fourth its original number. The regiment passed through New Jersey by rail and reached Philadelphia, where the men took a "first rate supper by the citizens" at the Cooper Shop Volunteer Refreshment Saloon—a stark contrast to the meager rations they had received in New York. Once again, the men enjoyed their meal so highly that many wrote home about it. They feasted on bread and butter, beef, "first rate coffee," cheeses, and beets. After dinner, they marched to the depot accompanied by cheers and handkerchiefs waving on all sides. Many of the local women, young and old, came out of their houses to shake the men's hands as they went past. The regiment stayed but a short time in Philadelphia. As the men waited for the train to Baltimore, a raid on a watermelon patch broke the tedium. More than half the regiment participated in the raid. Led by an unnamed officer along with other officers who encouraged the enlisted men to vault the fence, "like a swarm of bees . . . they stripped that field in a hurry," and each "raider" returned with a melon.[50]

Just before midnight, they left Philadelphia in freight cars for an all-night ride to Baltimore. En route, they passed two dead soldiers from another regiment who had been riding on the top of the cars and fallen off; one man was decapitated. There were rumors that several other soldiers had died in a similar manner. In Maryland, the boys from upstate saw their first free blacks and slaves. "Negroes are as thick as hops in the south," Delavan Hills told his friends. They arrived in Baltimore at 8 A.M. and spent the entire day in the city.

The soldiers' reactions to the new experiences and places they encountered revealed their naïveté. Andrew Mather eagerly took in all the compliments they received along the route, as when they were called the "best behaved and the finest looking regiment that had passed." By contrast, James Cronkite perceived their reception in New York as one of "cold indifference" and in Baltimore "positive contempt." John J. Ingraham, a private from Brockett's Bridge, remarked that they "marched through the streets where disloyal residents attacked the Massachusetts Regiment the year before. We did not see anything looked like Secesh there. The Union Flags were flying all over although they told us they were about two thirds of them Secesh but they dare not say so." Delavan Hills agreed and expressed surprise that the residents were so friendly. Because rumors circulated that Union troops had recently been poisoned on their way through the city, Franchot forbade them from buying any food. All the rail lines were closely guarded by Union troops.

Baltimore struck Sam Kelley as the "meanest, nastiest place I ever saw." Adelbert Reed, an eighteen-year-old on his first trip outside his village of Edmeston, heard rumors that the 121st would be attacked by Southern sympathizers. The regiment waited in the streets until one in the morning, when it "was once more seated in passenger cars" for the trip to Washington. The men arrived in the nation's capital at 6 A.M. on Wednesday, September 3. John Lovejoy found Washington a "very dirty town" full of "wounded soldiers" and "stragglers from Pope's army and the Army of the Potomac direct from Bull Run." The men were ordered to assemble in front of the capitol after arriving, where they lay for two hours in the hot sun until ordered to move to Fort Lincoln.[51]

The lack of training and discipline caused officials and officers to institute elaborate precautions to ensure that the entire regiment would arrive at the front unscathed. All noncommissioned officers, musicians, and privates were prohibited from carrying personal weapons. No weapons or ammunition were issued to the men. Commanding officers were made responsible for the conduct of their men and had instructions to prevent straggling. Commanders selected one guard and one commissioned officer for each railcar. Individuals were not allowed to leave the train without the commanding officer's permission, and commanders were tasked with taking roll at Camp Schuyler and again upon arrival in Washington. Absentees were to be reported immediately, and medical personnel were ordered to keep a close eye on sick and malingering recruits and report them to the staff officers. The quartermaster assumed responsibility for all the enlistees' personal baggage in an effort to discourage desertions, based on the theory that a disillusioned private would think twice about "skedaddling" without his baggage.[52]

As the new recruits left the security of upstate New York for the unknown perils of war at the front, one newly minted soldier presciently remarked as he surveyed the green troops: "There's a great many holes in the skimmer."[53]

3

Stumbling into War

I believe we are in Gen. Bartlett's brigade and Gen. Slocum's division.

Daniel French, Company F, September 11, 1862

I thought I would drop you a few lines to let you know that I was not dead yet.

James F. Hall, Company I, October 21, 1862

Washington and Fort Lincoln

When the regiment reached Washington, Maj. Egbert Olcott moved ahead to headquarters for further orders. The new regiment, with fresh uniforms and at full strength, drew long looks and comments from the older regiments and the residents of Washington. Veteran officers asked Olcott if the men in his command were good "choppers," meaning good axe men and therefore eligible to fell trees in order to fortify the Union positions in the Washington vicinity. Olcott explained that his men were farmers and dairymen and not suited to cutting timber and building fortifications. Meanwhile, the troops were discovering the full meaning of the term *foot soldier*.[1]

The regiment's assignment placed it in a provisional brigade before reporting to Fort Lincoln—only 5 miles from the train depot but, according to Pvt. Daniel French, a "pretty tiresome march." Situated northeast of Washington, Fort Lincoln sat on a hill on the Bladensburg Pike near Hyattsville, Maryland, just one of a string of forts hastily constructed for the defense of Washington. A year earlier, Brig. Gen. Joseph Hooker had invited the president to the fort's inaugural ceremony and festivities. The president promptly accepted, and the army christened the fort on October 22, 1861, naming it in his honor. From

Fort Lincoln, Washington D.C. Courtesy of the Library of Congress.

Fort Lincoln, the regiment could see camps "in almost every direction," including Arlington Heights across the Potomac.

The 121st set up camp a hundred feet below the fort and positioned its large guns on an open, empty plain. Sergeant Teel said the fort was as "tough a looking place as I ever saw" and located on a "rebel farm." Delavan Bates liked the location but lamented the fact that soldiers were "fast ruining the place" that once consisted of "splendid orchards and everything nice around." Through binoculars, the men of the regiment caught sight of their first rebel flag nearby. The "boys" were reportedly "very anxious to go down and destroy the village" where it flew. The fort boasted fifteen artillery pieces—"twelve 32 pounders, one howitzer, one rifled cannon, and one Parrot Gun"—with a garrison of about 1,500, including the artillery company and two infantry companies as well as the 121st. Lovejoy thought it a "nice camp . . . [with] a full compliment of 'A' tents for the men and wall tents for the officers," which would be the "first and last 'A' or wall tents the regiment [would ever see]." Because the enlisted men did not have enough tents, as many as sixteen slept in each.[2]

At Fort Lincoln, the 121st began to drill seriously as infantrymen in company and battalion movements. The new soldiers tried on their uniforms, drilled, and performed the army routine in endless repetition. Slowly, the 121st received its equipment. Each soldier was given a greatcoat, a frock coat, a pair of trousers, a shirt, a fatigue cap, company letters, a blanket, a pair of shoes, a knapsack, a haversack, a canteen, a mess kit with all the utensils, two under-shirts, and two pairs of shorts and socks. Sergeants and corporals received chevrons denoting their ranks. Officers got inches of blue and red lace. The regiment carried one regimental flag but no national colors. It also received 7 fifes, 3 bugles, 28 wall tents, 315 common tents, 1 hospital tent, 96 axes and handles, 108 hatchets, 96 pickaxes, 136 spades, 136 camp kettles, 340 mess pans, 11 sets of company ledger books, and 1 regimental ledger book. Weapons and ammunition had been issued on July 25 and August 30 to officers and noncommissioned officers at Camp Schuyler. Six sergeants' swords, waist belts and plates, and frogs for sword bayonet scabbards were also issued on July 25. On August 30, as the 121st prepared to leave camp, the commissary general of New York State, Brig. Gen. Benjamin Welch, issued full field gear and weapons to the regiment.

The men of the 121st did not actually receive their weapons until the regiment reached Fort Lincoln, however, for the officers had recommended that the weapons be shipped to Washington and issued there. Thus, "it was here that the regiment received its arms and accoutrements. Enfield Rifled Muskets." Colonel Gibson, Fort Lincoln's commandant, fearing an imminent attack, ordered the unpacked muskets to be loaded at once, and as a consequence, the muskets were distributed to some men who had never even held a gun before. The enlisted men were issued 950 English-made Enfields—in the dark—"causing much trouble in the ordnance accounts of the officers." Each man received one cartridge box and plate, a cartridge box sling and plate, an enlisted man's waist belt and plate, a cap pouch and pick, a gun sling, and a bayonet scabbard and frog. In keeping with the official army position that recruits wasted ammunition, only 5,000 cartridges and 6,000 percussion caps were issued—which meant that although each man received a weapon comparable to the American Springfield, he received only enough ammunition for five shots.[3]

The figure of 950 weapons per regiment was only a theoretical number. According to the War Department, as conveyed in a tutorial given to Governor Morgan by P. H. Watson, only 900 weapons were actually authorized per regiment. The department arrived at that number on the basis that not all men were always present for duty. Many were on sick leave or detailed as cooks, wagoners, and teamsters, thereby reducing the number of "musket bearers." And throughout the war, few regiments reached their fully authorized strength of 950 men. "Overarmed" regiments discovered that some of the 950 weapons they had been issued were "superfluous," and they were thus "commonly sold for a trifle to grogshop keepers or pawnbrokers, or . . . given away." Watson wanted to ensure New York instituted "measures [that would] prevent an over issue of arms."[4]

As both sides scrambled to supply the arms needed in 1861–1862, each turned to the importation of foreign arms. Initially, Albany and Washington flirted with Austrian arms that were destined for Ohio and Indiana. But the arms eventually proved inferior to the Springfield and the Enfield. New York City arms and accoutrement supplier Solomon Dingee had a contract with the federal government to provide 53,500 Austrian muskets in the spring of 1862. In a dispute over the price of $19 per arm and the uneven quality of the arms to be supplied, Edwin Stanton reached an agreement with Dingee on June 25 that allowed the supplier to substitute English Enfields for the Austrian models. The contract called for delivery in ninety days, which was within the time of the 121st's mobilization to the front. Morgan specifically asked Stanton for Springfields, but Stanton issued them to other states. Instead, the War Department told Morgan that he could buy his own Enfields and the federal government would pay for them and their accoutrements. In a twist, when the 152nd New York took the field immediately after the 121st, Albany reissued Austrian weapons that a sister regiment, the 153rd New York, had rejected earlier because they were deemed "entirely worthless."[5]

The British Enfield closely resembled the U.S. Springfield, with the only differences being a .577-caliber bore and a 39-inch rifled barrel. Despite those variations, the Enfield could fire the .58-caliber U.S. cartridge. Commercial contractors in Birmingham and London, not British government arsenals, made the imported Enfields. They featured a long-range rear sight graduated to 900 yards, which was effective at much greater range than smoothbores. Between 1861 and 1865, the United States imported almost 1 million Enfields. The 121st carried the Enfields until the troops exchanged them in late 1863 and early 1864 for Springfields. In the end, the Springfield proved more reliable than all the foreign imports.[6]

Doctor Holt Joins the Regiment

When Dr. Daniel M. Holt, a native of Newport in Herkimer County, wanted to serve, New York State surgeon general S. Oakley Vanderpoel suggested that he take the medical board examination for all potential army surgeons in Albany, which Holt did on July 20. He received notice a few days later that he had passed the exam. Although he qualified as a chief surgeon, he received his commission on August 27 as an assistant surgeon, and Holt never forgave this slight; throughout the war, he reminded his wife how it annoyed him.

He joined the 121st, his first choice, in Albany on September 2. He stayed at the Gibson House in the state capital until he assured himself that he had all the required field gear, including blankets and the "necessities of camp life." The next day found him in Washington, luxuriously ensconced in Brown's Hotel, next door to Willard's. Holt sent his trunk ahead to Fort Lincoln "by a negro," and as he walked the 5 miles to the fort, his new regimental commander, Richard Franchot, overtook him and offered the footsore doctor a ride in a carriage. Holt eventually caught up with his trunk and moved into a tent occupied by his new colleagues, Chief Surgeon William Bassett and First Assistant Surgeon Stephen Valentine. During his short stay in camp at Fort Lincoln, Holt made his bed in a gun box that resembled a coffin.[7]

At Fort Lincoln, rumors circulated of Confederate spies, of pickets that Union troops fired on, and of impending attacks on the fort from a nearby rebel camp that was "about three hundred strong." The capital bustled with energy and activity. Troops moved in every direction and responded to each rumor of Confederate movement. The men of the 121st spent the first day "lounging" and then proceeded to pitch their tents when they should have retired for the day. They crawled into their tents with one loaf of bread for five men and no weapons or ammunition (yet) "and dreamed of friends and home." On September 5, Dr. Holt reported a near revolt that was attributed to hunger. According to the doctor, the men had not drawn a ration for three days. Holt himself survived the temporary setback with cakes supplied by his wife, packed before he left for the front. Samuel French wrote less dramatically than Dr. Holt. When the regiment reached Washington at daybreak on September 3, he reported that he ate "dry bread, cold meat and coffee without milk" for breakfast but had "nothing more to eat" until evening, when he feasted on a "slice of bread and one piece of meat." The next morning, he ate nothing until his replacement released him from special duty. Sam Kelley ate pork in camp and "paid dearly for it." The meal plagued him most of the day until bread and water "restored him." Kelley never mentioned the food riot.[8]

The following two days were filled with tedium, ultimately broken in dramatic fashion with some real information. "We were astonished by news that McClellan had fallen back from Harrison's Landing, Pope was falling back from Culpepper Court House, Jackson was on Pope's flank, and Lee was partially between Pope and McClellan, and Washington. Everything was magnified in the most outrageous manner," Beckwith realized. Andrew Mather, on duty as officer of the guard one night when the commander of the fort expected an attack, reported that nothing happened but that "some of the boys saw ghosts, others heard strange noises. One ordered a stump to halt. And one sentinel shot a cow." The men were restless and wanted to get on with the fighting. Fort Lincoln proved to be merely a rest stop for the untrained and uninitiated men and boys from upstate New York.[9]

The leadership of the 121st throughout its three-year existence mirrored the larger Union leadership in a very real way. Just as Lincoln moved from one commanding general to the next, the 121st started out with a politician who lasted just one month and was followed by Emory Upton, fresh from West Point. Upton used the 121st for personal advancement in the army as he built a résumé that would qualify him for higher rank. His ambition and reputation grew as he climbed the ladder of command. The volunteers and the generals who were appointed without benefit of a West Point education did not impress him. Yet a succession of Otsego County–Herkimer County volunteers followed him in the command position.

These men took turns commanding the 121st from mid-1864 until the war's conclusion. Cherry Valley native Egbert Olcott followed Upton, and others, such as Andrew Mather, James Cronkite, Henry Galpin, and John Kidder, rotated in and out of the commanding officer's role during the war. By the time these officers led the regiment, it was significantly smaller, but those soldiers who had survived were experienced veterans. Their ascendancy to command begged the question of whether it really mattered who led the regiment. In the end, Upton used his professional military training to prepare the commanders who succeeded him. Forgotten by most accounts is Charles H. Clark, who filled in between Franchot and Upton for one month in 1862. He played a larger role than he has been given credit for in shaping the men of the 121st into a disciplined and valuable component of the Sixth Corps.[10]

In his defense, Franchot worked with inexperienced and tentative leadership material. On the staff level, Olcott and Clark had prior military service. Both served in the 25th New York Militia with the outbreak of war, Clark as a sergeant and Olcott as an officer. Clark saw service with the 43rd Infantry Regiment until he received a commission with the 121st. Olcott served with the famous 44th New York—Ellsworth's Avengers—as a private. He and Henry M. Galpin of Little Falls joined the 44th in Albany. Galpin had been wounded in the head as a sergeant at Malvern Hill on July 1, 1862. James Johnston from Frankfort served previously as a private in Company D of the 53rd New York and later joined the 121st as a sergeant in Company D. Capt. Nelson O. Wendell of Company F joined Ellsworth's Avengers, enlisting in Mohawk in August 1861 as a private and rising to the rank of sergeant. Most of the other line officers had no military experience, not even minimal militia training. They were volunteers who had recruited enough men to gain commissions, but they lacked leadership skills. Within nine months, most were gone—some died, some were discharged, and some deserted. In less than a year, the officer corps bore no resemblance to the original group that had left Camp Schuyler.

Politics and family were never far from personnel decisions. John Kidder recruited James Cronkite of Milford, who became Company I's first sergeant. Cronkite's father, Louis, had established a carriage-making shop in Portlandville in 1833 and was a strong Whig. Kidder practiced his trade as a carriage maker in Laurens, Otsego County. James Cronkite had never showed an interest in political office, but Congressman Franchot engineered Louis Cronkite's appointment as doorkeeper of the House of Representatives in Washington. In Company I, Sgt. George Teel married James Cronkite's cousin Mary, making him Cronkite's cousin-in-law. Unlike certain other situations that involved close relatives working closely together, Cronkite proved himself to be a very good

(left) Richard Hansen Franchot, who raised the regiment and soon discovered that he had no stomach for military leadership and returned to his seat in Congress. Courtesy of James Greiner. (right) Egbert Olcott. Fond of wine and the good life, he commanded the regiment after Upton was promoted to brigade commander. He was wounded and captured in the Wilderness and died in a New York insane asylum after the war. From Isaac O. Best, *History of the 121st.*

leader and advanced rapidly on his merits, not his connections. His fellow officer Delavan Bates remembered Cronkite as "young, ambitious, intelligent, and full of vim . . . a model soldier" and "one of Colonel Upton's first promotions." When Bates became a first lieutenant, "Cronkite was made a Captain." Bates recalled that the only criticism he ever heard of Cronkite reflected on "his methods of discipline [which] were a little too severe for the volunteer service, but in Colonel Upton's eye that was a point worthy of praise rather than censure."[11]

Kidder also earned a reputation for being extremely hard on his men. But he exhibited another trait once the army became engaged in the business of fighting. His letters revealed that he was a "mother hen" who worried constantly about his charges. Desertions bothered him; the men who fell ill or died were always mentioned in his letters because Kidder and his wife knew most of them intimately. Twenty-seven-year-old Charles Dean of Laurens was one of Kidder's star recruits. His enlistment papers described him as a merchant. At only 5 feet, 2 inches tall, Dean had a head for numbers and details. Kidder quickly realized Dean's value in filling out the myriad military records, forms, and paperwork with which he dealt on a daily basis. Kidder gave Charlie Dean the job of company clerk and bragged about him as one of the best men in the company, if not in the regiment. Kidder boasted of Dean's robust health and an even more robust mustache that the young man cultivated as he enjoyed the camp life of a soldier and his position of importance: he affected the mustache because it made him look more military. But in September the following year, Dean became ill, and over the next two years, he became the mystery man of the regiment. By the end of 1863, Kidder had reported Dean as a deserter.[12]

Joining the Sixth Corps

Colonel Franchot received orders to join Maj. Gen. Fitz John Porter's Fifth Corps along with the 68th, 114th, 118th, 119th, and 142nd Pennsylvania volunteer regiments. His quick reaction to get his men into the field as he tried to comply with the order nearly ruined the raw regiment. Quitting Fort Lincoln at 2:30 A.M. on Sunday, September 7, 1862, Franchot ordered the regiment to leave "everything not absolutely necessary" behind—including "nearly all its baggage." Four days later, the regiment halted in Darnestown, Maryland. "Company commanders left their clothing and descriptive books, in fact all their company [records]." It is hard to imagine an entire regiment leaving behind its equipment but even harder to understand how it marched without its fife and drums. Blankets, an absolute necessity in each private's gear, were left behind, and the cold Maryland nights coupled with the lack of blankets contributed directly to an immediate increase in sickness among the raw recruits.

William Remmel described very warm days and cold nights without blankets. The differences in temperature made marching uncomfortable, and the abandonment of knapsacks at Fort Lincoln deprived the men of the 121st of a "great many comforts." Sam Kelley lamented, "You can imagine the predicament we are in"—little food, no shelter, everything left behind. Marshall Dye apologized for the dirty sheet of paper he used to write home, explaining, "We all left our writing paper in our knapsacks at Fort Lincoln." Yet despite the hardships, Remmel optimistically wrote: "I like a soldier's life as well as I expected. It is very hard and dangerous work, yet—I think that I can stand it and have high hopes of coming out safe."[13]

Franchot had told Dr. Holt that the regiment planned only to go "out for a fight and would be back in two days." Holt bitterly told his diary: "But no return for us in two days or two years." John Lovejoy remembered the march as "the worst the regiment ever was called upon to make" and recalled that it sowed "the seeds of disease . . . that brought such an abundant harvest during the next two months." Samuel French, although "[vomiting his] stomach up," stayed in his column until the march ended around two in the afternoon. Hundreds of men fell out of the ranks "from fatigue and sunstroke."

Rumors were that four men had died along the way. To ward off sunstroke, many, including French, put green leaves in their caps for shade. Except for the ingenuity of the individual soldier, shelter did not exist. During extended stops, some men constructed lean-tos of brush, boughs, and pole frames. Samuel French reported that he had not "been inside of a house, nor slept under a tent in a month," and he expressed surprise that he remained well. Albert Bailey, a private in Company E, slept for six weeks on the ground with no more protection than his "coat of blue." However, by October 21, he reported receiving a shelter tent and dress coat, and he expected his overcoat soon. The Reverend Sage pointed to "the trash" that soldiers were eating as the root of the health problems—"apple-plexy and pie eaty." When the regiment left Maryland on October 31, Sgt. Edward Wales, a native of Cherry Valley in Company G, recorded in his diary: "Leaving about 10 men dead from disease on the soil of Md. from out of our regiment."[14]

The differing versions of how the 121st Regiment of New York Infantry joined the Sixth Corps instead of the Fifth are amusing, if not slapstick. As Corporal Beckwith remembered it years later, a funny thing happened to the 121st on its way to join the Army of the Potomac. The regiment was ordered on September 6 to join Fitz John Porter's Fifth Corps along with five other new regiments from Pennsylvania. In its attempt to catch up to the Fifth Corps, the regiment bumped into Maj. Gen. Henry W. Slocum's First Division of the Sixth Corps. Slocum and Franchot were old chums, and Franchot blurted out to Slocum that he had with him "a thousand of the best boys that had joined the army"; further, he admitted that he "knew nothing about military matters himself" and that he "wished personal directions from General Slocum and a proper commander at an early day for his regiment." Slocum sent an orderly to McClellan's headquarters to countermand Franchot's prior orders and asked to have the 121st placed in his command. He put the regiment in a support position, with the admonition to "fire on any men in grey who might come near enough." At the same time, he recommended the appointment of Lieutenant Upton to command the 121st.

The regiment was ordered to march south to Hall's Hill, Virginia, to join the rest of the army. But Franchot misunderstood the order and "being rather raw and green for so fair and plump a looking personage 'kept on going'" until Maj. Gen. William B. Franklin, commander of the Sixth Corps, "picked up" the regiment near Hallstown, Maryland, wrote Dr. Holt. Beckwith was sure that the fix was in before the regiment left the fort because the prospect of being put "in one of the choicest brigades of the army, and that Colonel Franchot had secured this as a great favor" struck him as exciting and worthy. Samuel French epitomized the confusion of the common soldier: "I believe we are in Gen. Bartlett's brigade, and Gen. Slocum's division."[15]

French was correct. The 121st was assigned to General Franklin's Sixth Corps, in Maj. Gen. Henry Warner Slocum's 1st Division. That division comprised three brigades: New Jersey regiments composed the 1st Brigade. The 3rd Brigade was a mix of three New York regiments and the 95th Pennsylvania. The

121st joined the 2nd Brigade commanded by Col. Joseph Jackson Bartlett. It was made up of the 5th Maine, 16th New York, 27th New York, and 96th Pennsylvania regiments. The 121st remained with the 2nd Brigade, 1st Division, Sixth Corps throughout the war.

That Slocum and Bartlett were both from upstate New York proved beneficial to the new regiment. Slocum was born in Delphi in Onondaga County, once a part of Herkimer County and best known for its growing city of Syracuse. He had graduated from West Point, a roommate of Philip Sheridan. His prior military experience occurred after leaving the academy in 1852 but before the Civil War erupted. In the early 1850s, he was stationed at Fort Moultrie near Charleston, South Carolina. That posting gave him spare time, which he used to read the law, and by 1856, he was admitted to the bar. He eventually resigned his commission and moved his growing young family back to Syracuse, where he practiced law while holding several public offices. In 1859, he represented his district in the lower house of the state legislature. When war broke out, he was a colonel of instruction in the militia, and he offered his services to the state. Initially rebuffed by the authorities in Albany because they were convinced that the war would be short-lived, he went on to become the colonel of the 27th New York Volunteers. His second in command was Maj. Joe Bartlett. By the time Franchot caught up with Slocum, Slocum had fought through first and second Bull Run and the Peninsular campaign and was headed toward Antietam. Both Slocum and Bartlett were singled out for honors at first Bull Run for holding fast while all hell broke out around the newly formed federal army.[16]

Bartlett was a trained lawyer who enlisted at the war's outbreak and rose quickly through the ranks. He was born in Binghamton, Broome County, just south of Otsego County. Soldiers elected him captain of one of the companies of the 27th New York, and when "the regiment chose its field officers," it chose Slocum as colonel and Bartlett as major. He distinguished himself repeatedly at the first battle of Bull Run, at Gaines Mill on the Peninsula, and at Crampton's Gap. He possessed a classical military bearing, standing 6 feet tall with a powerful build and a posture "straight as an arrow," and had black eyes and black hair. He "sat in his saddle as though horse and man were one." Bartlett wore tightly fitting, tailored uniforms and a "low cap with straight visor . . . and rode a fine black horse," projecting the image of a man who understood his role.

Attached to the 1st Division was an artillery brigade composed of four batteries commanded by a youthful captain of artillery and West Point graduate named Emory Upton. He caught the eye of Slocum and Bartlett, who were soon most impressed with him. Although brigade, division, and corps commanders changed throughout the war and the composition of the 2nd Brigade changed, the 121st remained with the 2nd Brigade, 1st Division, Sixth Corps of the Army of the Potomac until it mustered out in 1865. Thus, the fate of the 121st became forever linked with Slocum, Bartlett, Franchot, and Upton.[17]

The veterans in the 2nd Brigade did not warmly greet the new regiment—an attitude that seemed "excessively annoying" to Corporal Beckwith. The older troops showered the green regiment with epithets (such as "Fresh Fish," "Bandbox Soldiers," "Paid Hirelings," and "Two Hundred Dollar Men"—in reference to the bounty system—and "Sons of Mars") and the various comments seasoned troops typically direct toward new recruits, "a lot of stuff too foolish to speak of." Beckwith was more than annoyed; he was offended. He conjured up the image of the yeoman Yankee farmer nurtured by the fertile land, rich history, and beautiful landscape of Herkimer and Otsego counties. These men were "the worthy sons of an ancestry who had turned back the dark hordes of British, Indians, Tories and Mercenaries in the darkest days of the struggling colonists and brought victory to the flag." John Lovejoy expressed alarm when he saw the diminished size of the veteran regiments and wondered if the 121st, with nearly 1,000 men at full strength, would look the same after a year of battle. Indeed, the new regiment looked so large at full strength that veterans whose ranks had been diminished by eighteen months of hard campaigning asked the biting question: "What Brigade is this?" Adelbert Reed admitted, "We are not sharp as the old regiments are. They say we do not know anything about it [war] yet but will learn by the time we have been in the service as long as they have. (*I think we learn very fast.*)"

Nevertheless, the new regiment bonded with the 5th Maine. The relationship grew over time and would be fondly recalled in reunions long after the war and all because the 5th, unlike the other three regiments in the brigade, welcomed the 121st to service. The 5th Maine provided advice, encouragement, and support to the new regiment as opposed to the abuse heaped on it by the others. As Beckwith said, "Over and above all the other regiments in the brigade the 5th Maine filled our ideas of what perfect soldiers should be." The 121st so liked and respected the 5th's chaplain, John Ripley Adams, that the men of the regiment asked for Adams as their chaplain when the enlistments of the 5th Maine expired. When he first encountered the new regiment, Adams remarked to his wife on the unit's "greenness" and told her "the marching comes hard for them." But the new men were determined not to let the abuse piled on them by the older regiments drag them down.[18]

As Delavan Bates remembered years later, "When the 121st Regiment joined the Army of the Potomac, on the night of September 7th, 1862, we knew little of the ways of war, nothing of camp life in the field, not the care of clothing, arms, army discipline, guard duties, the picket line of the battlefield." That changed quickly. At the brigade level, Colonel Bartlett wasted no time in familiarizing the 121st with the rigors of army life and incorporating them as an integral part of his command. On September 9, in order to render the 121st "efficient for immediate service," he ordered one captain, two lieutenants, two sergeants, and three corporals to be detailed from throughout the brigade to immediately begin instruction with their counterparts in the 121st. The drill included instruction in the *Manual of Arms* and in "how to divide their messes, cook their rations, and all other information which it is necessary for them to learn immediately." Bartlett took the exercise one step further. He also ordered an identical "number of commissioned and non-commissioned officers from the 121st" assigned to various seasoned regiments for instruction. The "cross-training" orders were effective immediately, and all men involved were to report the next morning at 9 A.M. to brigade headquarters.[19]

The reasoning was sound—train fresh troops with seasoned veterans. But the exercise did not work. Fred Ford spent three days of instruction with the coterie of officers to the 96th Pennsylvania. and ended up convinced "that an old regiment is not a model for a new one. Their spirit is gone, and both officers and men seemed to have no higher desire than that of getting home again."[20]

At the Front

By September 18, after days of hard marching and the deprivations of the recent comforts of hearth and home, the regiment witnessed but did not participate in the conflicts of Antietam, South Mountain, and Crampton's Gap, Maryland. Marshall Dye, a private in Company B, doubted the war would last very long: "The war is of short duration, & you may believe it to be true." "[General] Slocum himself has said that our winter quarters will be at home," and Dye convinced himself that the 121st would "never be engaged in any battle." John Ingraham had it on no less than Maj. Gen. George McClellan's authority that everybody could go home "in about two months." If the army took it to the rebels with a good fight, "we can clean them out by that time." Charles Staring went so far as to ask his brother to prepare his carpentry tools when the war ended in "a week or two."[21]

Near the village of Burkittsville, Maryland, the 121st experienced, for the first time, men firing weapons in an effort to kill each other. William Remmel wrote to his parents while minié balls were "whistling over his head." For a while, the regiment came under cannon fire from the mountain passes before Crampton's Gap. Franchot longed for his regiment to engage the enemy, but Slocum prevailed in keeping the 121st in reserve because of its inexperience. "It was a desperate fight till darkness closed the contest," Lt. George Davis told his wife. Here, "under a Colonel who had never seen a battle, with men one-half of whom had never fired a gun," Delavan Bates remembered years later, they waited and watched the battle below them. "Perhaps some of our hearts did palpitate just a little when the firing began at Crampton's Gap," he wrote. The brigade commander, Joe Bartlett, chose the 96th Pennsylvania, the 27th New York, the 5th Maine, and the 16th New York to attack the rebel positions. The

16th, heavily involved in the charge, succeeded in driving the rebels from their positions but at a terrible cost to the regiment.[22]

As the 121st watched the whole affair, the weathered veterans marched past them to the front. "[They] had been on the Peninsula Campaign and they looked pretty rough; a blanket rolled and thrown over the shoulder, a haversack with rations, their cartridge boxes tightly buckled on, their guns at trail, and with a swinging step, the line was formed as coolly as if they were on dress parade," recalled Delavan Bates. Charley Shockley tried to determine the cause of all the commotion he was hearing and inadvertently exposed himself to Union batteries playing on the Confederate forces in the gap near South Mountain. Supposedly, Colonel Franchot saved him when he yelled: "Come back, you little devil, you'll get hurt. What in hell are you going out in front for?" Shockley, who had never witnessed such a demonstration of brute artillery force, meekly replied that he merely wanted to see them "work those big guns on the rebels." Bates remembered the Shockley incident and characterized Franchot's warning as "[the only order] he ever gave while with the regiment."

Lester Murdock of Hartwick, hit in the left groin by a shell fragment, spent the next six days unattended in a barn. After another four weeks recuperating in Jefferson, Maryland, he returned to the regiment. The raw troops wanted to join the battle, but the commanders wisely chose a different course. Adam Clarke Rice correctly gauged the decision to hold back the new troops: "Owing to our inexperience, we were ordered to stay behind . . . though all were willing, if not anxious, to go forth and try their chances." Egbert Olcott heaped unwarranted praise on his commanding officer. Even though the regiment never faced the enemy, its training and discipline served it well, he said, because "Colonel Franchot has shown himself to be a man more capable of command than many who have seen years of service." Olcott gushed that he had never seen an officer "in the volunteer service who so readily adapted himself to his position." He praised Franchot for his decisiveness, firmness in dealing with others, and "a quick perception of his own duties and the duties of those under him. Otsego may congratulate herself upon such a representative in the field." Olcott's fawning sentiments, purely for public consumption and undoubtedly uttered for personal gain, were not shared by anyone else in the regiment.[23]

The seasoned troops held the gap, and eventually, the rebels were forced to retreat. Federal troops marched columns of captured Confederates to the rear of the Union lines, giving members of the regiment their first up-close view of the enemy. Lt. George Davis led a contingent of men from the 121st to Frederick, accompanying more than 350 rebel prisoners who were to be sent on to Baltimore. From there, he proudly wrote his wife of his experiences. Pinned to the letter was a small piece of blue cloth that Davis told his wife came from the "1st secesh flag that hoisted in Virginia." Within a month, Davis was dead from diarrhea.

Several rebels were wounded. One officer, tall and dignified in his gray uniform with gold braid, opened his coat and revealed his wounded torso. Union surgeons attended to him. The enlisted men were more poorly clothed, and they were wearing the slouch hats of "Cobb's Legion," from Georgia. The curious new troops of the 121st struck up conversations with their enemies. Clinton Beckwith and Adelbert Reed asked them why they had invaded Maryland and why they fought. The rebels responded that they "were starved out" and "made to fight." Reed's rebels told him they were prepared to fight it out six months or six years but admitted they were "sick of fighting" and did not know "what they were fighting for" at Antietam. Beckwith was told that they were proud soldiers of Lee's army and "that Lee would wipe us off the face of the earth on the morrow; that he would not have been taken prisoner except that 'we uns' had got around behind 'they uns' and there was six of 'we uns' to 'they uns' one." "Oh, they are a hard looking set," John Ingraham said of the rebel survivors, "dirty and ragged, some without shoes and caps."[24]

Although the regiment did not participate in either the battle of Crampton's Gap or the battle of Antietam, it policed the debris from both battlefields and collected and buried the Confederate dead, which men from the regiment clambered over as "bundles of grain after binding." At Antietam, "the regiment had its first view of a Battlefield . . . a truly sickening and harrowing sight showing plainly that there had in many instances been a hand to hand encounter," according to John Lovejoy. The Confederate dead "lay in rows of 50 and 60" all over the field. Dye observed that the rebels were emaciated and ill equipped, and he added ghoulishly, "One thing I cannot account for is that the Rebs . . . will turn black and smell bad in six hours, while our men will remain fresh for at least 24 hours." "It is a bloody, ghastly scene upon which I am looking now," Clarke Rice wrote. Henry Wood became sickened by the sight of the dead, but after a while, he "became so accustomed to it" that he could "lay down and sleep with them all around me." Despite his earlier experience, the young regimental commander, Emory Upton, confessed that he "heard of the dead lying in heaps, but never saw it until this battle. Whole ranks fell together. The trials of some of the wounded were horrible."[25]

Clinton Beckwith observed that the dead at Crampton's Gap were not "changed much from life, but they lay in all shapes and positions. Many were shot through the head." He witnessed the mass burials with corpses laid side by side, one row on top of another. On the Antietam battlefield, he stumbled on a dead rebel soldier whose body was propped up against a tree, with a daguerreotype of his wife and child in his hand. He thought of taking the photograph but left it and upon his return discovered it gone. He regretted that he had not taken it "because some day it might have gotten to the wife and child." At another spot, he came upon "mounted officers . . . under their horses, both dead." Capt. Edwin Clark in Company E observed that going onto the battlefield "takes away a great deal of the 'poetry of war.' You see human beings lying in every conceivable shape." The "sight and stench" repulsed Lyman Herdman. In one area, an entire brigade lay where it had been slaughtered, a scene that horrified him. He described the soldiers as lying "in a perfect winrow. God forbid that I should ever witness another such scene." Dr. Holt commented on the transformation of the men of the 121st within two weeks, from the peaceful home front to bloody war, as "strange and awful." He coldly told his wife that he could pass "over the putrefying bodies of the dead and feel as little unconcerned as though they were two hundred pigs. Their protruding bowels, glassy eyes, open mouths, ejecting blood and gases, the last wild expression of despair."[26]

George Teel eloquently described the backwash of war: "We were marched over a road that 150 thousand men had marched three days [before]," strewn with baggage, arms, and "everything that could be thought of." The reality of war was unfathomable; the imagination was not great enough to capture the horror. "Just think," he wrote, "of forty miles lined with wagons, batteries, soldiers, ambulances and everything" one can imagine and "you can form some little idea of what is going on in this country of ours." Lyman Herdman realized how little the home folks knew "of the stern realities of war," and he appreciated that his beloved Cherry Valley was spared the "devastating hand of war." One soldier of the 121st told the *Herkimer Democrat* of his thoughts of home when, "a few weeks before," the men of the regiment "were sitting quietly at their own firesides. My soul rebelled," he said, "when I thought of the cause of this horrible war, and as I saw the Negroes flaunting along with their Sunday clothes, I despised them from the depths of my soul."[27]

Sgt. Joe Heath and John M. Smith of Company A and the commissary sergeant, George Snell, found the war a lark in its first weeks. Most of the men of the Company A were among the more upbeat of the entire regiment during the early months in the field. As the troops encamped at Bakersville, Maryland, they built cabins of rather large cornstalks, complete with doors and windows. As one of them wrote: "Oh, we live gay here, you can bet! We had a 'bully' dinner today" that consisted of fresh meat, potatoes, and soft bread.

A few short days after Antietam, the hard march from Fort Lincoln faded in memory. The men proclaimed it "a jaunt for green troops; but the boys don't grumble, and are happy as clams." They dismissed the horror around them— "the rebels lay in piles for miles around"—and reveled in the "foraging" they were able to accomplish and the ability to cook up a gourmet feast. "We have good living here as a general thing." The daily life of the soldier made the regiment "healthy and tough." They ended their letters to the editors of their hometown newspapers with lines such as "Bully for our side, and down with the rebellion, and hoop-de-doodle for Company A and Captain Galpin, for he is the finest Captain in the 121st regiment." Galpin's soon-to-be competitor, Andrew Mather, walked away from the battlefield with "a nice coat which was taken from a rebel 2nd Lieutenant and a few balls. I would have collected a great many trophies if I could have carried them," he boasted.[28]

Albert Bailey also bragged about his battlefield souvenirs. He picked up a dead rebel's handkerchief and a bayonet. After the long and arduous march from Washington, as well as the distasteful cleanup duties following the battles, Bailey slept among the dead for two nights just as comfortably on a solid rock as he would have at home safe in his bed.[29]

But the battle and horror of Crampton's Gap and Antietam were responsible for Clinton Beckwith's conversion. The "war fever" he had experienced as a teen just a few months earlier was replaced with an introspective analysis of war. He came to the realization that the recent traumatic occurrences he had witnessed were quite "wrong." Beckwith revealed that at the time, he felt like a tiny "atom" in a sea of soldiers and "the magnitude of battles." If he "took off," what would it matter? "Everything seemed quite different to me from what it did when hearing the war speeches and the deeds of valor" in the comfort of home and hearth, he recalled years later. "The romance of war had departed forever, its glory was overshadowed by its terrible realities and its terrible duties became the question of the hour." He questioned his ability in real combat to shoot or stab others to death and his own reactions to being shot and left on the battlefield to die unattended, "dead and perhaps rotting." He wondered aloud: "Shall I have the courage to do this? I was filled with a feeling of dread," and he wished he were a commissioned officer and could resign and confess himself "not up to the heroic standard." The dead and the wounded weighed heavily in his self-analysis. "And, as I thought of the vast number of dead I had seen lying unburied on the field and the myriads of wounded men, I felt the awful horror of war upon me." He felt "grateful" that he had seen the aftermath of battle "in order to . . . know what we are coming to." The abandoned dead seemed horrible to him; leaving their bodies to rot on the field bordered on the obscene, and he hoped that if he fell in battle, "his comrades" would give him a "decent burial." He made no distinction for his enemies, showing equal empathy for those killed at Crampton's Gap: "I expect a proper inscription upon their tombstone would read: 'Here lies some men from Georgia who were killed in battle.'"[30]

The horror of the battlefield had not reached Hamilton College in upstate New York. Nearly a third of enrolled students at the Clinton, New York, school had "gone to war." But as sophomore James Kimball wrote to his sister at the beginning of October 1862, "those at the seat of war say they have no desire to be back at college. Shouldn't be surprised if owls and bats should hold their carnivals in these classic halls at the beginning of another year. I don't know but we shall all go yet."[31]

Franchot Resigns

Congressman Richard Franchot's talents and prowess as a recruiting salesman made the 121st a reality, but he was not a military leader. Although he held command of the regiment for only a month, the unit suffered irreparably from his poor leadership. Forced marches, severely cold nights without blankets or tents, and a lack of experience crippled the 121st physically and psychologically. The nation's critical military situation dictated the need for immediate replacements, no matter how raw and unskilled they were, and although the 121st never saw combat under Franchot, it lost nearly 300 men in the first month in the field due to disease and desertion.

His inexperience was immediately apparent. Soldiering proved relatively easy from Camp Schuyler to Fort Lincoln: most men suffered only from lack of sleep. But once the regiment reached the fort, the atmosphere changed radically, and Franchot suddenly found himself in uncharted waters. With no military experience or skills, he found events quickly moved beyond him. The pressure to push inexperienced troops into the field to ward off the rebel masses, the blazing sun, and the unrelenting forced marches began to take their toll on the untrained troops.[32]

The regiment's dislike of Franchot built quickly. He deserved some of the criticism but not all of it. The suffering men directed their anger toward him. They were uncomfortable for the first time in their young lives, and with that, combined with Franchot's genuine shortcomings as a commander, their anger boiled over. Holt's criticism continued unabated. He called Franchot the worst commander ever imposed on a regiment. The fact that the regiment had left all the necessary equipment behind as it quit Fort Lincoln had infuriated the doctor, who complained that the situation occurred "because of the consummate, ignorant folly of a man, whose brains were anywhere but in his head." Holt railed against the forced marches, "with no enemy in sight," and about how the unrelenting rigorous physical demands harmed the untrained troops. Franchot's name "became a reproach and stench among the men of his command."

Overall, Teel thought that the regiment attracted a "good set of officers except our 1st Lieutenant [John D. P. Douw] and Colonel [Franchot], and they are as mean as they can possibly be." Teel showed no respect for Franchot and his nephew and who had jumped over more qualified men, including Delavan Bates. Beckwith recognized Franchot's weakness immediately and saw that "he was as inexperienced as any of us"; he observed that the "hardships of the march" sapped the colonel's physical and emotional strength and added that "somehow we got to feel that he was not cast in the same mould as we believed Colonels and commanding officers ought to [be]. We soon ceased looking in his direction for advice and consolation." Lovejoy remembered that Franchot caught "cannon fever" at Crampton's Gap, where he incurred the enmity of his men when he ordered them to lie down for no other reason than that they had entered the "enemy's country."[33]

Franchot's legacy was recruitment and organization. During the regiment's days in Camp Schuyler, the *Herkimer County Journal* praised his industrious labor, and the grateful citizens presented him with those accoutrements befitting a commanding officer prepared to do battle in the field. But on September 23, 1862, a month to the day from the 121st's formation, Franchot resigned his commission, "greatly to the relief of the regiment." Captain Kidder refused to say how he felt about Franchot, but the tone of his correspondence indicated he was not distressed with the resignation and, further, that most of the men felt the same way. In fact, Franchot had confided in Kidder: "Franchot told me the reason why he resigned. It was for the best interest of the regiment. *I thought so myself* as he had no taste for it [command]." Kidder's sidekick, James Cronkite, felt that Franchot's desire to be back in Congress trumped his "taste for active field service." John Lovejoy echoed the sentiment when he noted sarcastically that Franchot was "thoroughly convinced that he preferred a seat in Congress . . . to one in the saddle." In Franchot's defense, it should be noted that he did no more than respond to the Lincoln administration's urgent call for fighting men on the front, no matter how ill prepared they were. He responded in a clumsy and inept manner to the pressure placed on New York and other states to expedite men to the front. He was swept up in a larger frenzy that proved disastrous to the raw troops under him.[34]

The 152nd New York Infantry, also from Otsego and Herkimer counties and recruited a few months after the 121st, faced a similar situation. That unit's organizer and leader, Col. Leonard Boyer of Little Falls, refused to admit that he was not a military man and also refused to resign immediately. The *Freeman's Journal* actually called for his dismissal. As early as August 1, citing a speech by Franchot wherein he admitted his military shortcomings, the paper hinted: "We wish all civilians would act in the same manner." The paper pointed out that the district committees picked both Boyer and Franchot because they could exert influence "in procuring enlistments and organizing the regiments." In a strongly worded statement, the Cooperstown paper said: "It was admitted that they had no knowledge of military matters, and hence—whatever might be their other qualifications—they should not hold command longer than the good of the men and the service might demand."

The *Journal* called on Boyer to follow Franchot, who "fulfilled the wishes and expectations of his friends, and placed the 121st under command of a regular army officer." But Boyer clung to his appointment. As late as January 1863, he blamed the 121st's troubles in the battle of Fredericksburg and the disastrous Mud March on Franchot. In the *Herkimer County Journal*, he wrote: "Your own officers are ambitionless; therefore you are where you are, enjoying the luxuries of peace, or as others think, ingloriously stuck in the mud." Fred Ford defended the honor of the 121st, arguing that everyone including Franchot knew that he, Franchot, would leave and return to Congress as soon as his friend General Slocum found a suitable replacement for him. According to Ford, Slocum assured Franchot he would have the services of Emory Upton. Further, Ford reminded Boyer that the 121st fared better than the 152nd, which was relegated to guarding forts around Washington while the 121st struggled with heavy campaigning. The 121st also benefited from the experienced services of Lt. Col. Charles Clark, Capt. Henry Galpin, and Maj. Egbert Olcott, veterans of the Peninsular campaign.[35]

Franchot's official discharge came through on September 25, 1862, and he soon returned to Congress to finish out his term. The *Cherry Valley Gazette* praised the man who had attracted 1,000 men to the cause and took them into the field. In an egalitarian farewell, the paper assured readers of his officers' universal respect and love for Franchot: "He retires with their good wishes for his health and happiness." Yet the truth is that the first two months in the field were devastating for the men of the 121st. Disease, desertion, death, officers' resignations, and the lack of discipline reduced the original unit number of around 1,000 men to approximately 800 able-bodied members of the regiment within the first month.[36]

Charles H. Clark, the Forgotten Commander

By the end of September, another month had passed and McClellan had allowed Lee to slip back across the Potomac. It sickened Dr. Holt "to see such parleying with rebels when we have the power to do differently." He likened the lack of action to "treason upon the part of our officers to let the bars down" and enable the enemy to easily escape. The Union army followed Lee back into Virginia.[37]

Between the time of Upton's promotion (his commissioning) on September 25 and colonel commanding (his mustering into federal service) on October 23, the 121st fell under the temporary command of twenty-eight-year-old Charles H. Clark, formerly a captain in the 43rd New York. In the month before Emory Upton reported for duty, Clark attempted to reverse the destructive direction the regiment had taken to that point. According to James Cronkite, Franchot found Clark "unsuited for the position" and wanted "to leave his command with a competent officer." Upton was his choice, and the irony that Clark made an immediate mark on the command has been lost in the story of the 121st. In fact, the enlisted men "universally appreciated [Clark] as a thorough drill master." But the men preferred Upton, and early on, Egbert Olcott remained much of an unknown. Jonathon Burrell's early judgment of Olcott erroneously made him a "favorite with all the officers and men of the regiment, but [Clark] is just as far the other way with all." According to Burrell, some of the lieutenants blamed Clark for many of the problems plaguing the regiment, a position Burrell did not share—"he [Clark] always treated me well," he testified. Beckwith never mentioned Clark, giving Upton all the credit for the regiment's turnaround. But it was the combined efforts of Clark and Olcott that brought the regiment up to minimum military requirements. Olcott proved to have the meaner disposition of the two men when he took command of the regiment later in the war. Delavan Bates remembered that when the two were drilling the troops and would "get things mixed," Olcott would pull his copy of military tactics from his pocket and "study out a solution of the proper move." But generally, he observed, the two officers were well rehearsed before drill time.[38]

Because of his previous "experience and courage—having been in all the battles from Williamsburg to Harrison's Landing"—Clark mustered in at Camp Schuyler on August 23 as a lieutenant colonel. He had originally enlisted at age twenty-seven in Albany on April 19, 1861, for a three-month stint with the 25th New York Militia and mustered in as a sergeant in Company A. He remained with that unit from May until August, when he finished his ninety days of service. He immediately reenlisted in Albany for three years with the 43rd, and this time, he served as a captain in Company D. Discharged a year later, in July 1862, he enlisted for a third time and joined the 121st in August. Although he commanded the regiment only a month, he remained with it for seven months. When he enrolled in Herkimer, he had originally committed to serve three years, but for personal reasons (including a pending civil case in Albany), he resigned his commission and received his discharge on March 23, 1863.[39]

Clark's primary responsibility was to hold the 121st together until Upton assumed command on October 23. His leadership brought the regiment into fighting form. Although Emory Upton got most of the credit for molding the 121st into an effective regiment, it was Clark who issued the first drill and training orders, moved to clean up the camps in order to improve sanitation and therefore the regiment's health, and attempted to stop the rampant desertions plaguing the regiment. Clark set up a primitive but fixed schedule of drills. Immediately, he ordered three specific basic and practical drill movements to be practiced by the regiment: (1) wheeling on a fixed pivot and movable point, (2) forming from the flank into line by companies and platoons, and (3) forming line of battle on right and left by file into line.[40]

For the first time since Camp Schuyler, the 121st began learning the art of combat, the tedium of discipline, and the boredom of drill. Clark ordered daily company drills at 9:30 in the morning, battalion drills (which involved two or more companies but fewer than five) at 2:30 in the afternoon, and a formal dress parade at 5:00 P.M. The orders applied only when the regiment was in camp and "until further order(s)" were received. While the regiment encamped at Dam No. 4 on the Potomac, Clark devoted most of the time to drilling the men. The stress of drill ground on the new recruits, but he intended to forge them into fighting men. During dress parade drill, Clinton Beckwith fondly remembered Clark barking out, "'Hands down in B company, it's disgraceful,' as the regiment stood at parade rest when some of ours would make a rap at a fly or mosquito on his face."[41]

The men of the 121st tried out their new drill skills when President Lincoln came to the field and reviewed the troops on October 3, 1862. (The short stop in Little Falls that the president had made on his way to Washington had not allowed any of the men to see him.) Clark ordered all companies to be "minutely inspected." The men were "required to have on their best uniforms, coats buttoned," with all buckles and other belt plates "neatly polished." Company commanders were authorized to punish anyone whose "arms and accoutrements [were] out of order at inspection previous to dress parade." Inspections in camp were held once a week or more often if the situation demanded it, and arms and accoutrements as well as the men were closely scrutinized. On October 3, the men were called out for the president's visit five hours before he arrived. They milled around before standing at attention when the inspecting party finally appeared.

John Hartwell did not let the formal occasion ruffle him. He told his wife: "Old Abe rode past my door, bowed very respectfully. I told him 'that's a good boy, now run right back to the white house and don't get away so far again.'" John Ingraham enjoyed seeing both Lincoln and McClellan. "You could not of told Abraham from a farmer. He looked comical. I tell you he had on a tall hat and it set on the back part of his head. He looked like some green farmer. He was dressed in black clothes, very common. You could not told McClellan from any Major General. We saluted them and they returned it with much pleasure." The president stood out above McClellan, although Henry Walker "did not get a first rate sight of them."[42]

Clark also addressed the issue of discipline and familiarity between enlisted men and commissioned officers. The 121st differed little from all the other volunteer regiments, which were recruited among friends and neighbors by friends and neighbors. During the war, men who had been raised in the same small villages and attended the same small schools were thrust together into a rigid system of social stratification, and they found it difficult to discard first names for "sir," "sergeant," and "lieutenant." Familiarity between men who, one month before, were lifelong companions and now were placed into a hierarchy reflected an unresolved, age-old conflict between military and civilian attitudes to status and rank. "For the Civil War generation, a regimental designation was not merely a military convenience. The regiment was the primary object of identification for the men who fought the war. A unit meant neighbors, friends, and in many cases blood relatives. To speak the name of a unit was often to summon up a host of associations within a particular state and community."

The 121st was no exception. In the Cherry Valley town cemetery, there is a tombstone marking the final resting place of a woman who died in 1900. Her name, Grace Olcott Morse Campbell, encapsulates the interconnectedness of the small village community. Sergeant Cronkite and his cousin-in-law, George Teel, served in Captain Kidder's Company I. Adelbert Reed, a private in Company F, sold his revolver to Captain Kidder, an unheard-of transaction in modern times. Brothers such as the Lovejoys and Huartsons were often in the same company although unequal in rank. Both of the Rices from Fairfield, Herkimer County, served in Company C. The two of them started out as enlisted men, but Adam Clarke Rice became an officer in January 1863. His cousin, Ward, joined the regiment as a sergeant and later left to become an officer in the 32nd U.S. Colored Troops.[43]

Colonel Clark immediately recognized the situation, and he deeply regretted "the great degree of familiarity existing between the officers and men" of the regiment. In deploring "such a course" as "greatly prejudicial to military discipline and good order," he ordered it to "cease immediately. Officers must maintain the dignity of their rank. No excuse will be entertained for any violation of this order." Major Olcott questioned whether sergeants and commissioned officers ought to eat together, but George Teel liked that arrangement. "Our mess mates are as follows, Captain John Kidder, Lt. Bates, Orderly Sergeant James Cronkite, and Sergeant George Teel, private Samuel Fenton of West Laurens and Charles Nichols of the same place. I do the cooking and they pay the bills and we all mess together and we all enjoy it very much." Teel bunked with his commanding officer, Captain Kidder, his in-law Sergeant Cronkite, and Lieutenant Bates. On one occasion, near Bakersville, Teel, Bates, Cronkite, and Nichols took off on an unauthorized "tramp" 1.5 miles along the Potomac to Dam No. 4. They discovered a tavern, where they were served dinner by "three white females" and accepted "the honor to be fanned by a nice white girl while eating." Cronkite thought the fanning alone was worth the price of the dinner. Upon their return, they described the outing to their roommate and company commander, Kidder, who instead of reprimanding them for taking off, "started out with some of the boys to see what they could find." On their return, they pronounced the trip worthwhile, but they had missed the fan treatment enjoyed by the first contingent. It seems that old habits were hard to break. It is to Clark's credit that he recognized a problem and dealt with it.[44]

Clark also established the regimental mail system—and he placed the task of handling the mail in the chaplain's hands. The chaplain separated the officers' and enlisted men's correspondence when it arrived at the 121st's headquarters. From there, he delivered the officers' mail directly to their quarters; the first sergeant passed out the private soldiers' mail at mail call. Any mail that came in for deserters went back to the chaplain, who returned it to headquarters. Despite his attempts to manage everything, Clark could not control the various conditions encountered in wartime that delayed or interrupted the delivery of army mail, including poor roads, faulty supply wagons, troop movements, battle, weather, and more.

During his tenure as interim commander, Clark also reduced soldiers in rank for insubordination, inefficiencies, and ineptitude, and he rewarded meritorious conduct with promotions. He ordered any soldier absent without authority arrested.[45]

Clark recognized the connection between the rampant diseases that plagued the troops and the unsanitary conditions in the camp, and he immediately took steps to remedy the situation. Near a "pretentious house" used by General Slocum, a barn was employed as the regimental hospital. Beckwith learned that many new recruits died in the barn or were shipped to Frederick for further care. Those who remained healthy were the subject of his rigid new sanitary rules. The men were "required to keep the camp clean," and quarters were now regularly inspected. Clark ordered an extra tour of duty for those who needed advanced lessons in hygiene, and according to Beckwith, "one such dose was usually sufficient to cure the most careless offender." Clark complained to the assistant adjutant general of the 2nd Brigade, Robert Wilson, that other regiments of that brigade "refused to dig [refuse] sinks," which led not only to an unpleasant surrounding but also "to disease and evils too numerous to mention." He complained directly to Colonel Bartlett that exposure and lack of attention to "several cases of a feverish nature" were reducing his command.

Clark's calls for assistance went unheeded. Unable to receive any help or consolation from brigade headquarters, he began to fix what he could. He ordered the officer of the day to see that the camp area was policed daily. He concerned himself with the cleanliness around headquarters, the hospital tents, and the commissary department. He ordered the "Pioneer" corps to lay a "coating of dirt" every day over the "accumulation" in the officers' and men's latrines and, where necessary, to dig new sinks. Garbage barrels were issued to each cook of the 121st, and Clark ordered refuse to be emptied and buried every morning "or oftener if necessary." He also ordered the officer of the guard to arrest "any private soldier for committing a nuisance" (that is, relieving himself) within the camp's perimeter. Clark pointed out that sinks were dug for that purpose, and he sternly warned the officers and noncommissioned officers that they would be reported to headquarters if found committing the same violation. He directed that "all offal what may have accumulated" in company streets or near tents be removed "a suitable distance from camp and buried." Sick soldiers encountered out of their quarters during battalion drill, "except to obey the call of nature," and any soldier found committing "a nuisance" in or near the camp became subject to arrest. Anyone absent from drill without permission and those excused for health reasons were required to produce a written excuse from the regimental surgeon.[46]

At some point, Maj. Egbert Olcott and the drummer boys returned to Washington to retrieve all the tents, blankets, and company books that Colonel Franchot had abandoned at Fort Lincoln. Unfortunately, when Olcott and the others returned with knapsacks and personal belongings on Sunday and Monday, October 19 and 20, members of the regiment found most of their items were missing. Stockings, gloves, toothbrushes, and personal trinkets were gone. The next day, the regiment received overcoats—and none too soon, for the weather turned bitter cold with high winds a day later. Many of the men had brought gloves or mittens with them, since none were issued by the government. "I guess the old soldiers at Fort Lincoln had a pretty good time overhauling them after we left," Frank Carran complained to his brother in a letter. Henry Walker valued his lost clothing and other personal belongings at $35 to $50.[47]

In the end, Clark lost out to his rival Egbert Olcott. The two men were not compatible, and ultimately, Upton forced Clark out. As soon as Upton took command at the end of October 1862, Clark absented himself on detached service to the headquarters of the Left Grand Division during the month of November. Then he rejoined the regiment for just two and a half months. On February 15, he received a ten-day leave of absence to take care of personal business in Albany. He stayed on another month and finally resigned his commission on March 23, 1863. He turned over to Upton a far more disciplined, soldierly regiment that was at least partially prepared for the rigors awaiting it. Upton never acknowledged Clark's service.[48]

The individual's spiritual needs were lost in the army's hurry to train, to impose discipline, and to race to the front. Most of the soldiers were God-fearing, churchgoing men. The military assigned a chaplain to each regiment. But it was not until the end of September that the regiment heard preaching—the "first Sunday we have had for two months," Fred Ford reported to the *Journal*'s readers. In many respects, Sunday was no different than any other day of the week for the troops. William Remmel complained that chaplains had preached only two sermons since the regiment left Camp Schuyler—and those seemed "more like lectures than sermons." Samuel French confessed that he "had almost forgotten" to observe Sunday because of the paucity of services. He remembered only the one mentioned by Fred Ford after leaving New York.

The Reverend John R. Sage, former minister of the Universalist Church in Little Falls, had enlisted as a private at the age of twenty-nine and immediately became the regiment's chaplain. He refused the enlistment bounty, a move that the *Herkimer County Journal* called "patriotic." But Sage made little impact on the regiment during the ten months he served before being honorably discharged. He was a "favorite of Captain Galpin" and some of the other officers, but he never connected with the enlisted men. A majority of the men disliked him more than he probably knew. James Cronkite disliked Sage intensely and scathingly grumbled after the war that "it was the misfortune of our regiment to get a miserable chaplain at the time of its organization, and when he left, during the Gettysburg campaign, no one was grieved,—not even the officers who had contributed ten dollars each to provide him a horse with which to carry our mail." Delavan Bates sniffed: "Our chaplain has resigned and gone home, got tired of the business, I suppose." After the war, Sage eventually gave up the ministry and became the head of the Iowa State Weather Bureau in Des Moines. But he never forgot his service with the 121st. He often wrote from Iowa to the Reunion Association, sending a dollar or two as a contribution to the group's treasury. Despite his experience with the regiment, Sage's departure from the service was a "source of keen regret" for him, and he later stated that had it not been for his "ailment" (pleurisy)—a "deep seated and painful" malady—he would have maintained his position with the 121st. But alas, he said, the condition made him incapable of rendering "efficient service."[49]

Samuel French described Sage's one attempt at holding a "short service" and assumed the regiment would have a prayer meeting that Sunday. By Sergeant Wales's count, Chaplain Sage held only three "discourses" as of Sunday, November 23. The men spent Thanksgiving 1862 in drill and the usual duties. That evening, Sage "read a few lines from the hymn book." The following Sunday, the men were occupied with clothing and weapons inspection in the morning, another "discourse" from Sage in the afternoon, and a dress parade in the evening. "This is the way we spent our Sabbath," Wales told his diary.

By the spring of 1863, little had changed. On March 1, Capt. Douglas Campbell held a prayer meeting in his tent, the first since those held in the fall at Bakersville. Eight men from the regiment drew together without benefit of the chaplain and spent an hour in prayer, pledging to meet two or three times a week thereafter. "We have had so little Sunday and outside religious influence of any kind," Henry Walker complained. "There seems to be almost a universal thoughtlessness and neglect of religion among all in the army, and indifference among those that professed Christ at home." Some of the men went off on their own to hold private services, greatly displeasing Chaplain Sage. Sage insisted that he would hold services only on two conditions: if he received a direct order from the commanding officer or if common sense warranted doing so. He maintained that he "did not want to bring the men out when they would feel more like swearing than praying."[50]

If the majority of the regiment prayed for Franchot's resignation and for him to be replaced by a professional soldier, their prayers were answered. Franchot used his friendship with General Slocum to gain the services of Emory Upton as his successor—a move that turned out to be his most important contribution to the regiment. Before he left Camp Schuyler, Franchot had remarked in a speech that he would refuse to "leave these men until [they were] under the control of one thoroughly competent to fit them for the field, and to lead them ably in battle." When Charles Clark relinquished his post to Upton in October, he left a regiment that was better prepared than when he accepted his assignment, even though it had not experienced battle. Clinton Beckwith took a Darwinian approach in his assessment of the noncombat losses and Upton's appointment. He considered the 121st "stronger and better for its recent experience—the weeding out of unfit men, the retiring of incompetent officers, and the acquiring of a young, intrepid, and skilled officer for its commander" who would lead it to victory. He echoed the thoughts of many of his comrades.[51]

4

Emory Upton Takes Command

He is a man, every inch of him.

John Ingraham, Company D, December 9, 1862

Upton is all I represented him to be, brave and gentlemanly. He seems to consider that, although we are slaves through necessity, we were once freemen by right. You may believe any good of him. The people may be assured that their sons will be dealt justly with so long as Upton commands.

Fred Ford, Company C, November 27, 1862

Emory Upton: Boy Commander

Emory Upton descended from a family of devout Methodists in an area in western New York called the Burned Over District. The name derived from the fact that the region had experienced so many religious revivals that, it was said, the soil could no longer support new religious conversions. In Upton's early years, beliefs then current rejected Calvinism, placing more responsibility on the individual for his or her own salvation. The rejection of predestination produced a heady mix of religious and patriotic fervor that fostered the idea religion could affect social issues—such as slavery. Believers increasingly viewed abolition as divinely inspired and a moral imperative. The prevailing religious atmosphere greatly affected the young Upton, shaping his thinking and behavior.

Upton was born on a farm west of Batavia, on August 27, 1839. After spending the 1855–1856 school year at Oberlin College, he received an appointment to West Point. He reported on July 1, 1856, and graduated on May 6, 1861, eighth in his class of forty-five. Mentor and teacher Peter Michie called him a "quiet, peaceful, negative fellow," who came east as a "raw country youth." Because he applied himself to his studies, he improved "his standing year by year." Michie proudly boasted that his student eventually "developed into a magnificent leader of assaulting columns and a fighting general of the first magnitude."[1]

The young Upton unwaveringly embraced pro-Union and antislavery stances. His strict military training at West Point and the austere religious and family atmosphere of his earlier years forged the attitudes and character of the young man who eventually led others through the flames of war. He firmly believed that slavery was the cause of the conflict. His opposition to human bondage manifested itself "in every form, viewed in any light—political, social, or moral." He harbored no subtleties in his opinions about states' rights or regional custom or cultural distinction. There were no gray areas. "God's providence" would see that slavery would be overthrown. In April 1861, he asked his sister to buy and send him an imported English, five-shot Adams and Deans revolver, which she could purchase in Batavia. His request carried a sense of urgency—he needed "to be ready for orders any moment. No other kind is wanted." When word reached West Point that fighting had broken out in Baltimore, Upton hoped "to be ordered away immediately." Rumors swirled around the campus that the students' orders were already at the academy. He welcomed the challenge presented by the gathering clouds of war. "How glad I shall be when the order comes," he wrote.

Three weeks later, at twenty-two years of age, Emory Upton received his commission as a second lieutenant and his assignment to the 4th Artillery, Regular Army, and was stationed in Washington, D.C. By late May, he had been promoted to first lieutenant, and within a year, he became a captain of artillery, in charge of four batteries with twenty-six guns in the Sixth Corps's 1st Division. He fought on the Peninsula and at Bull Run, where he was wounded. That was his position when Franchot chose him as the new commander of the 121st. By age twenty-five, he received a promotion to major general.

After a month's leave, he assumed command of the 121st on October 25, 1862. During his first day with the regiment, he gathered his officers together and made a short speech outlining what he expected of them and the regiment. No one recorded his exact words, but Capt. Douglas Campbell, commanding Company E, remembered that he went away from that meeting "feeling that we had indeed found a man. How the regiment was affected is shown by its subsequent record."[2]

Silas Burt believed that Franchot had always intended to have Upton take command when he resigned and that he had merely hung on until the young officer could step in. Little evidence for that interpretation exists. As the regiment gathered at Camp Schuyler, Franchot admitted his ignorance of military matters but affirmed his determination to go "only so far in the matter as the best interests of the proposed regiment [dictated]." Both Upton and Franchot were silent on Upton's appointment, but the men received him "with cheers." Upton came highly recommended for his "gallantry and good judgment" by Gen. Henry Slocum and others in the chain of command under which he had served on the Peninsula and at Antietam. His accelerated promotion and accession to the command of the 121st New York Volunteers can be attributed to one man, General Slocum.[3]

Handsome, well trained, bright, and ambitious, Upton made an immediate and favorable impression on his new command. At the end of May 1861, no longer a cadet, he had assumed the role of a full-fledged officer. He was his own master, and though his future may have been unknown, he hoped that he would have a "prosperous and useful career" as an officer. He revealed his ambition in his communication with the Left Grand Division's assistant adjutant general, E. R. Platt, inquiring about his date of rank—he wanted to know whether the date of rank was his date of commissioning, September 25, or his date of muster into the federal service, October 23, 1862. The young colonel understood the importance of the date because seniority would play a large role in the selection of officers when future promotions were handed out. The service confirmed his date of rank as October 23, 1862.[4]

Upton's physical appearance and stoic military bearing were assets as he assumed his new assignment. He possessed deep-set blue eyes below a full brow, and his dark-complexioned face featured well-chiseled and prominent cheekbones, sunken cheeks, a strong jaw, and a small mouth. Occasionally, he embellished his appearance with a mustache and goatee. His picture as a freckle-faced West Point cadet with a healthy head of dark brown hair looked like a Hollywood publicity photograph for a period movie filmed during the 1940s. Driven to perfection, Upton focused intently on the military as his life's calling. Nothing else mattered. "He was the epitome of a professional soldier." Antisocial to an extreme, he rarely smiled and exhibited no appreciable sense of humor. He distrusted the volunteer army and put his faith in the professional. Upton eventually served in all three branches of the military and participated in most of the larger and more important engagements of the war. He showed incredible, almost reckless bravery in leading his men in battle. Sheer luck probably kept him from being wounded or killed on more than one occasion. He spoke his mind with the conviction of a much older man, inherently assured of his position. Upton stood up to his superiors and never shied away from verbal confrontation with the politicians back home in New York State. Over time, he became increasingly irritated with the civilian handling of the war.[5]

Upton initially had little time for the volunteer soldier. Yet his compassion for his men became apparent as they sought shelter when they were exposed, and he offered comfort and encouragement when they were sick or wounded. From his first post in Washington, he told his sister of his hard work, but he refused to complain when he realized how "hard the poor privates had to

Emory Upton as a young colonel.
Author's collection.

work." He deeply sympathized with the "soldier who is walking his two weary hours while" he himself slept. He told his sister that he liked army life, adding, "I would not leave war and return home to work for $500 per month. Excitement is what we want."

Jonathon Burrell reported that Upton's first action as a new commander occurred in a hospital: "Off with his coat and [he] commenced shaking up the straw in the beds of the patients" to provide them a minimum of comfort and relief. William Remmel told his parents that Upton's first action was to "move the invalids of our Regiment to a brick church not far off and have them at least comfortably sheltered if not medically treated." Henry Walker said that Upton "commenced his duties with the hospital and quartermaster department. I like him very much." Despite his doubts concerning the effectiveness of the volunteer soldier, Upton cared for his men. He saw the volunteer army as his path to higher command and responsibility and therefore made accommodations in his view of the world. He recognized that he could not lead a ghost command and that he needed bodies on the line to turn the regiment into an effective fighting unit.[6]

Upon his return from leave, Upton immediately went to work tackling a multitude of issues. Building on Colonel Clark's primitive schedule, Upton issued his own, which accounted for practically every minute of the soldier's day. He set reveille at 6:30 A.M., followed by breakfast at 7:00 and then surgeon's call at 8:00. He set company drill from 9:00 to noon, with an hour and a half for lunch followed by battalion drill from 1:30 until 3:45. At that time, the officer of the day set the guard mount and guards were posted. A full dress parade and retreat were performed at 4:30. Supper came at 5:00, tattoo at 7:30, and taps at 8:30 P.M. Upton modified the schedule on December 24, 1862, and on March 12, 1863, to include target practice in the afternoon.[7]

Upton's orders initiated drilling in the "school of the soldier," which dealt with everything from instruction on how to fall into a formation to commands such as "right face" and "fall out" to using arms in formations. He tapped Egbert Olcott to train the regiment's officers and Elias Mather to work with the noncommissioned officers. Both groups were then to pass their knowledge on to the privates in the ranks. Before training the common soldiers, the new "teachers" were to be given a proficiency test. Upton also cracked down heavily on unsoldierly conduct in the ranks. He expressly forbade spitting, raising hands, and gazing about while in formation. If a soldier wanted the attention of his leader, he was to fall out of rank "one pace" and raise his hand. These general rules of conduct applied to everyday formations and especially to dress parades. Spitting in ranks and general inattention were "strictly prohibited" and subject to report. Despite Upton's new regulations, Lt. Adam Clarke Rice found duties "quite light"; he enumerated them as drilling two to three times a week.[8]

Upton's strict upbringing and West Point education heavily influenced his relations with his new command. Dress parades and inspections became his specialties. The formal dress parades were nothing more than inspections on a larger, less personal scale. The reviews featured "columns of infantry in close order and covering a field as large as you could see." Normally, the reviews were held at the request of brigade, corps, and army commanders and sometimes by the commander in chief himself.

Upton issued clear directives concerning inspections and guard duty, the latter being one of the more onerous tasks of the soldier. Although guard duty lasted twenty-four hours at a time, the individual received the following day off as compensation. The private soldier spent the day before guard duty in preparation for the guard mount, which always took place at reveille. The first sergeant ensured the appearance of his men, who were required to wear their "best uniform, white gloves," and have their "boots polished." A supernumerary replaced any man failing inspection for the guard mount. In addition, the replaced man received extra duty. Army regulations demanded close inspections for guard duty, and Upton, always interested in the finer points, insisted on "particular attention to the uniform of the reliefs between reveille and retreat."[9]

The majority of the men in the regiment accepted the new regime. Delavan Bates, John Kidder's second lieutenant, thought that Upton "was worth four like Franchot." As an aside, he described Kidder as "a real nice clever man." He reserved his highest praise for Major Olcott—"as fine a fellow as you ever saw."

Upton's prior service impressed Sam Kelley: "Today, Col Franchot bid us adieu and introduced us to our new Col. by name of Upton, a West Point graduate and has seen *real service*. I for one shall have more confidence if we are called into battle than I would under Col. Franchot." Isaac Best, who later worked closely with Upton at brigade headquarters, spared nothing in his admiration of Upton. Best approved of the new commander's temperance and described him as "just," "strict," "efficient," "cool," "fearless and decisive," "religious," and "clean and without profanity." William Remmel thought that Upton would make the 121st a "very efficient regiment if he only has a chance." John Lovejoy delighted in the fact that Upton "was not long in bringing order out of confusion."[10]

Upton earned the "good feelings of all the boys," according to Jonathon Burrell. He thought that the new commander would make a good officer but took note of his strict disciplinarian way. Upton's insistence on instituting examinations for the officers frightened Burrell. Tongue in cheek, he expressed fear that he would fail and have to resign and flee to Canada: he told his sister Hatt that he would stop to see her on his way north but cautioned that she should not invite any friends to the party "as I shall not want a public reception." Fred Ford simply declared that Upton "was all I represented him to be, brave and gentlemanly. He seems to consider that, although we are slaves through necessity, we were once freemen by right. You may believe any good of him. The people may be assured that their sons will be dealt justly with so long as Upton commands." Years later, Isaac Best confessed that Upton had asked him to take an exam for an officer's commission but he had declined because he did not think it right for him to take the place of another who earned the post through "active service in the ranks."[11]

The Medical Situation

The poor physical condition of the regiment was apparent to all. As Jonathon Burrell told his brother, "If you could only be here at night after the men are all in bed and hear the coughing through the camp. It sounds rash. It is a hard place for a sick man and in most cases they get rather shabby attendance." At the same time, many men were using sickness as an excuse to avoid duty. If they were unable to persuade the regimental surgeon that they were unfit, many soldiers appealed to their officers for medical excuses and releases. Upton reprimanded his commissioned and noncommissioned officers for "excusing privates from duty." He reinforced the surgeon's authority in this area and reminded his officers that he had not delegated such authority or the responsibility to others, thereby stopping the practice. Between the time of Upton's appointment as commander of the 121st and the day he actually took command, he assumed responsibility for visiting army hospitals, talking to surgeons, and studying the medical system. He made every effort to learn the causes and cures of military diseases and to work toward their prevention and application.[12]

Under Upton's command, "the want of neatness," Chaplain Adams remarked, "is noticed and punished." Personal inspections, designed to improve discipline and morale, carried a much more subtle objective—personal hygiene and sanitation. Edward Wales put it simply: "It being Saturday we had orders to wash our clothes and ourselfs."[13]

Throughout the war, the 121st experienced the same tumult in its medical corps as it did in its commanders. William Bassett had no sooner taken the field as head surgeon than he resigned because of poor health, on September 30, 1862, soon after Franchot quit. Dr. Edward S. Walker replaced Bassett on October 24 but resigned eight months later, on July 1, 1863. John O. Slocum, a nephew of General Slocum, followed Walker as regimental surgeon. Four assistant surgeons, Irving W. Hotaling, Stephen B. Valentine, Daniel Holt, and James Kimball, all rotated through the regiment. Hotaling resigned a year into his assignment, on August 24, 1863. Holt lasted until his lungs began to fail and left the 121st on October 17, 1864, before the battle of Cedar Creek. Surgeon Slocum and Assistant Surgeon Kimball were the only two medical men who stayed until the end of the war, at which point they were ministering to one-third of the original number of men who had left Herkimer in 1862.

As much as he tried, Colonel Clark had not been able to slow the downward spiral of sickness and desertion that began under Franchot. Clark had used the regiment's first death on October 1 as an example of the terrible effects of the lack of shelter and equipment and of the unsanitary conditions prevalent throughout the camp. Helon Pearson, a native of Roseboom and a private in Company G, had died in a hospital tent from either exposure or typhoid fever, depending on the report. His comrades buried him the next day in a grave "forty rods from camp, under a large oak tree," near Bakersville, Maryland. He received a proper military burial with three drummers, a fifer, and about 300 mourners from the regiment. Chaplain Sage said a prayer, and a volley of muskets saluted the fallen soldier. Adj. Charles Dean blamed Pearson's death on Franchot and the lack of tents, the resultant exposure to the elements, and the heavy marching for no purpose. John Lovejoy, also a member of Company G and a fellow Roseboom resident, believed that homesickness, directly related to letters received from home, had killed Pearson: "It is the worst disease a soldier can have." Sgt. John Hartwell participated in the funeral procession and empathized with the deceased as he thought of his own family back in Herkimer. Hartwell also unemotionally assessed the cost of returning a body to Herkimer by express—"$28. Not very costly. The total expense of a man coming after a body will be not much less than $100."[14]

Captain Kidder reported many illnesses in Company I and in noting Pearson's passing, he theorized that the larger men did "not endure as well as the smaller boys." He listed all the men in his company and their relative sizes as evidence of his thesis, stating flatly, "Some of my littler boys from Worcester are as tough as knots and make good soldiers." Marshall Dye told his friend Martha that he "was getting tough as a snake; all I have to do when it comes night is to roll myself in any blanket and drop down on the ground and sleep soundly till morning. I am happy to say that I never was more healthy in my life." Samuel French bragged that he slept on the ground without any cover and had not had a sore throat or cold since he left Camp Schuyler. Yet many men were not so lucky: even Clark fell ill during his short stint as commanding officer, and Egbert Olcott briefly filled in for him.[15]

The toll from disease mounted. Emmet Mather wrote home that his brother Elias suffered from a fever but it "turned" (that is, broke). Andrew Mather, the boys' father, accompanied his friend Adam Elliott to Fredericksburg to pick up the body of William Elliott, age eighteen, who succumbed to the measles three days after Christmas in 1862. William Herdman from Cherry Valley fell ill with typhoid fever but recovered. When he buried eighteen-year-old Peter Crounse, a private in Company G who lost his battle against the same disease, Herdman wondered why Crounse died and he did not. "He was one of our strongest and most healthy boys," he wrote of his friend. "When I see so many strong men die, I often wonder at my recovery now that I realize how many chances were against me." Frank Carran saw the stacked guns after the march, which numbered "about 560." "Quite a contrast," he observed, "between the regiment when at Camp Schuyler and now after two months campaign in Maryland." Another strong boy, Clarke Rice, expressed optimism that he would "be favored with unimpaired health" during his time in the service, a gift he never received. He died at age twenty-three in Georgetown Hospital of "bilious remittent fever," a year after the 121st had arrived in Maryland.[16]

Older members of the regiment, such as Stephen P. Wolverton of Little Falls in Company H and forty-four-year-old Samuel Cooke, the regiment's quartermaster sergeant, did not fare well at all. Wolverton had enlisted at age thirty-nine, one of the first to answer Lincoln's call. Because of his age and life experience, he immediately moved up to the rank of sergeant. During the Crampton's Gap campaign, he had only three days' worth of hardtack, but he shared it "with an Irishman who seemed the hungriest man in the command." Near Sugar Loaf Mountain, his squad became so exhausted that he placed the whole group on sick leave. The following day, the officers in his company became ill, and the command devolved on Wolverton for a time. He tried to deal with the heat, the march, the command, fatigue, and sunstroke, but ultimately, these factors caused him to pass out for several hours. Doctors evacuated him to the rear and bled him, but they failed to close his wound properly, and en route to Frederick City, Wolverton nearly bled to death. Thereafter, "the two causes combined produced nervous prostration of incurable character." Following the battle of South Mountain, Wolverton was shuttled between shelters, finally receiving his discharge in Philadelphia on November 17, 1862. His time with the regiment spanned barely two months, and he never saw battle, yet his brief exposure to the life of a soldier made him an invalid for life. As Dr. Holt pointed out, Wolverton should never have served in the first place. The other old-timer, Cooke, was a justice of the peace in Oneonta, and as a delegate from the Nineteenth New York District to the 1860 Republican National Convention in Chicago, he had voted for Lincoln when favorite son William Seward could not muster a majority. Cooke managed to hang on to his military duties until December 1862, when disability forced him out.[17]

Within the first week of November 1862, Holt personally sent 80 men to the hospital at Harpers Ferry and 100 to Hagerstown, Maryland. Like Charles Dean, Holt blamed the attrition on the regiment's "rawness," the time of the year with its changing weather patterns, and "above all the hardships which they have undergone." In October, the regiment had lost its first officer, 2nd Lt. George W. Davis. A twenty-nine-year-old native of Little Falls and a member of Capt. Henry Galpin's Company A, Davis died on October 10, struck down by typhoid after only two months in the field. The Reverend Henry Sage ministered to him by providing him with a comfortable place in an old house to keep him away from the noise of camp while some of the regiment served on picket duty. Sage feared the worst: "Poor fellow, he takes it so hard to be so sick away down here." Davis's father traveled from Herkimer County to be with him at the end and then accompanied his body home for burial.

Before the regiment left Camp Schuyler, Davis had spoken with the *Herkimer County Journal* and expressed his confidence in the army's mission and the correctness of his decision to enlist. "No alloy was mingled with the purity of his patriotism: no selfish design influenced his action," according to the *Journal*. Another second lieutenant, Angus Cameron, a twenty-five-year-old member of Capt. Clinton Moon's Company C, became the second officer to succumb to illness; he, too, came from Herkimer County. Diagnosed with a "fever" and then a "lingering wasting illness," he was expected to recover, but he died a month after Davis, on November 10. His family took his body back to Fairfield so he could be buried among his "school day friends." He, like William Remmel, had excelled as a Fairfield Seminary student and later as a teacher.[18] Henry Walker buried his friend Cpl. John I. Burlingham from Hartwick on October 26. Burlingham had joined Company E on August 3, a mere three months earlier. The deaths weighed heavily on the young recruits: Walker remarked that he "was sad to lay a comrade in the grave away from his home."

The deaths from disease continued well into the new year. Charles Staring, writing from camp at White Oak Swamp in January, told his brother the tale of three men in Company H who shared a tent on a fiercely cold Saturday night.

On Sunday morning, two of them woke to reveille and "tried to wake up the third," to no avail. "He was as dead as a log," Staring declared.[19]

After Antietam, Dr. Holt reported that "every house, for miles around," had become a hospital. Every available doctor was pressed into service, particularly those whose regiments had not participated in the battle, including Holt, who "extracted balls, dressed wounds, and amputated [limbs]" of both Northern and Southern troops. Exhausted, Holt promptly fell asleep. The scene repeated itself throughout the war. Meanwhile, diarrhea and dysentery became rampant. "We have to get rid of them [soldiers with those conditions] as soon as possible by sending them to hospitals," Holt insisted. Many should never have taken to the field.[20]

After the battle of Antietam, the members of the 121st were detailed to burial units or assigned to picking up stragglers and to picket duty, and the doctors were immediately ordered to care for the recently wounded. In addition to his normal regimental duties, which he handled alone because the other surgeons were working in the field hospital, Holt cared for the wounded on the field. During the war's initial months, regimental officers were solely responsible for medical care. Each regiment cared for its own wounded until they could be shipped back to a general hospital in Washington, Philadelphia, Annapolis, or Baltimore. The plan, long on theory, broke down in practice. Some regiments took higher casualties than others, causing regimental doctors in high-casualty units to be overworked while those assigned to reserve regiments were able to spend time in leisure activities. The workload proved onerous for some and unbalanced for all.

In July 1862, just before the 121st took to the field, Dr. Jonathon W. Letterman became the army's medical director. His sweeping reforms were adopted throughout the army and ultimately proved more effective in dealing with the dead and wounded. Letterman removed all ambulances from the Quartermaster Corps and placed them in the Medical Corps. The ambulance train consisted of one to three wagons per regiment—or, in the case of cavalry and artillery, per squadron or battery. Letterman allotted one medical wagon and two or three supply wagons per brigade.

The network depended on a field hospital and ambulance system, independent of the Quartermaster Corps, for all divisions consisting of at least three brigades. The medical officers not detailed to field hospitals "accompanied their regiments and established temporary depots as near as practicable to the line of battle." After a battle, the wounded went from the division or corps field hospitals back to base or a general hospital for the more severely wounded. Regimental doctors remained responsible for their own men—but only the sick and slightly wounded. The army tested the system at Antietam and broadened it at Fredericksburg at year's end. The 121st took the field just as Letterman's changes were being implemented. Chaplain Adams thought the idea of corps and division hospitals was an "excellent arrangement" as he made his rounds comforting the sick and the wounded and writing letters back home for them.[21]

When the brigade encamped in northern Virginia, Adams visited the division hospital at Potomac Creek Bridge regularly. Men not sent to the general hospital in Washington were kept there, 4 or 5 miles from the 121st's camp. When the regiment moved into battle, Adams became the equivalent of an additional medical aide. He remained with the surgeons behind the line of battle. During an engagement, he positioned himself in the field hospital, set close to the line of battle. When retreating lines caused disruption in the rear, the entire hospital moved back to "a knoll, or a road-bank," or to any available shelter. During the first few months, the daily routine for the doctors became overwhelming. After rising, washing, and eating breakfast, surgeon's call began. It would last two to three hours, during which time the medical men would see 150 to 200 men. Most surgeons followed that with a visit to the barn "hospital" near Bakersville. After the rounds of that facility, the doctors fanned out to visit the sick in their quarters—for those lucky enough to have quarters. Medicines, diet, and the general sanitation of the camp that Clark insisted on came under the medical men's scrutiny. Above all, reports were maintained and filed up the chain of command.[22]

The rapid influx of new troops overwhelmed the army's logistical services, but the system gradually responded to the increased population toward the end of 1862. Dr. Holt blamed the system's problems on all the "drunken or incompetent Quartermasters." They needed watching "above all others," he affirmed. He believed that they should not be paid; rather, they should pay the army for occupying their positions. "It seems almost of necessity that they are dishonest," he intoned. Edward Wales disagreed with Holt about the quartermasters and exulted in drawing three days' rations and a new pair of pants as proof, even as the good doctor complained about the supply lines.

Although the amount of sickness tapered off after the first few months, the 121st never fully recovered from its unhealthy start. And as diseases subsided, battle casualties took their place as a primary concern. As an aside, it is interesting to note that there is no discussion of venereal disease in the official records and regimental books of the 121st; neither doctors nor chaplains mentioned it.[23]

In November, Upton learned from his quartermaster that many men being held at Hagerstown could be released for duty. Upton requested the return of 87 men from Hagerstown, 25 from Harpers Ferry, 34 from Bakersville, and 9 from Washington. All were carried on the rolls as "absent-sick" from the 121st, and Upton asked Lieutenant Colonel Clark to round them up. Clark asked Rice to accompany him. The two traveled to all parts east to gather the convalescing men of the 121st. The extremely light duty gave Rice the opportunity to visit the Smithsonian, the House of Representatives, and "the National monuments" in Washington. His impressions of Harpers Ferry were harsh; he described it as "melancholy" and the "saddest place I ever saw." He found the armory in ruins, the town abandoned, the people "sullen and sorrowful, and the streets deep in mud." As he saw it, Harpers Ferry was the site of John Brown's martyrdom: its bedraggled and depressed condition was proof of divine retribution against the community for having hanged Brown three years earlier.[24]

Thomas H. Hyzer of Company K, from New Lisbon, New York, one of the men in the "convalescent camp" at Harpers Ferry, loathed his station in life, particularly the hard life of a soldier. On the march after Antietam, he had contracted a severe case of diarrhea, which he treated with "staunch weed." "It does not check it," he complained to his wife, admitting that he visited the doctors for some traditional medicine, which he took and hoped would cure him. Six weeks later, his wife begged Upton to release her husband from the army. Upton had politely and gently refused her unusual request on the grounds that it would set a dangerous precedent for the army. He told her that Hyzer fell out of the ranks near Berlin, Maryland, and was probably in the camp at Harpers Ferry. He assured Mrs. Hyzer, however, that her husband would have the best care possible while with the regiment. He finished by saying: "I shall always have the welfare of my men at heart, and as long as your husband is with me; so long you shall know he is not suffering." Hyzer stayed with the regiment throughout the war but deserted on April 29, 1865, well after Lee surrendered.[25]

Upton's attention to the details began to pay off, and the 121st's military proficiency and efficiency soon became known outside the regiment. In fact, Upton's strict routine "became so noticeable to the older regiments that they began to call [the 121st] Upton's Regulars." The West Pointer made a difference from the beginning. Jonathon Burrell, who repeatedly referred to the new commander as a "cadet," declared unequivocally: "Our colonel is called the best colonel in the division" even though his strict ways were no more severe "than any West Point cadet." Douglas Campbell remembered that "in discipline he was stern" and that "at first some of the boys thought his drills and discipline" were too strict. However, when "people began flocking from distant encampments to witness our dress parades" and after the regiment proved itself under Upton in battle, "these very men thanked the Colonel." The men responded immediately to the commander's new regimen. Fred Ford predicted that if Upton "only wears as well as he takes, in six months we shall be one of the finest regiments in the service. The secret of success in an officer is to give no unnecessary orders, to have necessary ones obeyed. He has the secret."[26]

Upton remained concerned about the welfare of his men as winter approached. He petitioned the ladies of Herkimer and Otsego counties to knit mittens for the boys of the 121st. He even specified that the gloves should be as "uniform as possible and with one finger each"—presumably, the index or trigger finger. Fred Ford reported that Upton removed all the sick to a brick church, with the comment that "his men should not lie in uncomfortable outhouses." According to Ford, Upton provided tents for the guards whereas before they had been "compelled to lay unsheltered when on guard duty," and he also supplied purchased or stolen straw on which the men could lie.[27]

Upton initiated one of the most important drills of all: target practice. Untested in battle, members of the 121st thought that target practice made more sense than the foolishness of marching in columns and polishing accoutrements. Fair and warm days were the usual favorites for on-line firing. Typically, the entire unit was drawn up as on a line of battle. Ten or more targets, each about the size of a man, were placed side by side 160 rods from the regiment (distances from 30 rods to half a mile were also used). By the spring of 1863, the regiment had experienced a "good deal of practice" suited "for real service." Norman Herdman confidently predicted that the 121st's weapons would "do execution at a mile."[28]

The Valentine Affair

Dr. Stephen B. Valentine, the first assistant surgeon, had been with the regiment through Franchot's and Clark's commands. Of the approximately ninety commissioned officers who went through the ranks of the 121st, including surgeons and chaplains, only Valentine would suffer the ignominy of being drummed out of the service.

Stephen Bargy Valentine was one of those few tragic souls of the 121st who would be dogged by bad judgment and bad luck throughout life. The Valentine family had lived in the town of Schuyler since before the Revolution. The doctor's father, also named Stephen, married twice, the second time to Nancy Bargy. Stephen and Nancy had four children, sons Sidney, Stephen, and William and daughter Marriette. They eked out a meager existence on farmland just north of the hamlet of East Schuyler in Herkimer County. Medical authorities declared Sidney insane in 1860 when he was twenty-six, and he spent the rest of his life in the Herkimer County Poor House. William died in 1862 at the age of twenty-two.

The younger Stephen Valentine was a patriot. He offered his services to the authorities in Albany immediately after war broke out in April 1861. The state approved his application to serve as a surgeon's "mate" in May, provided that a colonel of a completed regiment could appoint him. Nothing happened. In July, ignoring bureaucrats at lower levels, Valentine petitioned Secretary of War Simon Cameron, asking to be appointed an assistant surgeon. He attached a letter of recommendation signed by the prominent citizens of Herkimer County, including Eliphalet Remington and his sons, along with a certificate from Surgeon General Vanderpoel's office in Albany with its endorsement from the state's medical board. When Valentine received a positive response from

Cameron, he sent along further testimony of his health and physical qualifications. As a result, he was ordered to report to New York City for another round of examinations, to which he was opposed. Despite his objections, however, he took the new exams, but he failed them and was rejected by the army in August. He remained undeterred. By December, he had obtained a position as a contract surgeon with the 2nd Regiment, New York State Militia.[29]

Finally, with Lincoln's call for 300,000 more volunteers in July 1862, Valentine enlisted at Mohawk on July 23 at age thirty. He coasted along under Franchot, but as the regiment stumbled through Maryland during September 1862, Valentine came to the attention of his superiors. When Dr. Bassett resigned at the end of that month, Colonel Clark promoted Edwin J. Walker to replace him, but he also turned to Stephen Valentine as the next senior officer in the medical department. Clark recommended to brigade headquarters that Valentine be appointed to fill Bassett's vacancy and that Holt be promoted to take Valentine's spot. His recommendation was not accepted, though, and instead, Walker replaced Bassett. Holt, who reported to Valentine, hinted to his wife of the "storm brewing in the medical department of this regiment, which when it breaks will cause somebody to leave for home." Holt knew that Valentine was an alcoholic, and he refused to "have a drunken tyrant lord it over me as Valentine does." Beyond that, Holt deplored Valentine's medical ignorance and his low medical stature both on the field and back home. He predicted, "Just watch and see— he will be the man to leave—not me."[30]

Valentine did not escape Upton's notice. The ragged and weak physical condition of the regiment appalled the new commander, and the lengthy sick list proved Valentine's incompetence. Upton complained directly to Dr. Bradley, medical director of the Sixth Corps, calling Valentine a "surgeon of very little experience, no energy, and no disposition to do his duty." He charged that under Valentine's care, the sick were "neglected and uncared for," medical prescriptions were irregularly administered, and basic sanitation was neglected. Further, when the 121st crossed the Potomac into Virginia, Valentine "failed to provide himself with medicines, and it was only after constant and repeated urging that he procured them." Ultimately, Upton brought Valentine before a medical board "to determine his proficiency and fitness."[31]

Holt cheered Upton on. He blamed Valentine for the regiment's sorry state of health and readiness. "If he is not soon dismissed dishonorably from the service, I am mistaken," he bitterly predicted. He hinted at darker misdeeds and suggested that if he were the regiment's commanding officer, he "would look well into such transactions" and if necessary "prefer charges against an officer so offending."[32]

Holt was referring to an incident that would end Valentine's military career. For a payment of $150, the surgeon had signed the medical discharge papers of Pvt. Crosby John Graves of Company C. Upton wasted no time in bringing the matter to the attention of the army's adjutant general, Brig. Gen. Lorenzo Thomas. Upton demanded "prompt punishment" and Valentine's immediate discharge. He called "this last act" of Valentine's "dishonorable to himself and prejudicial to the interests of the government." Valentine was summoned to appear before the Medical Examination Board in Washington on December 18, 1862. Less than a month later, the army dismissed him from the "service of the U. S. . . . for incompetence." Holt was "greatly relieved," and he proceeded "immediately to put the machine in running order again." But before that, he held a day of rejoicing, inviting to a party in his tent all who had been "grossly swindled" by Valentine.[33]

Fred Ford of Company C was the regular correspondent for the *Herkimer County Journal*. His pen dripping with sarcasm, he wrote in his weekly report to the citizens of Herkimer that the regiment presented "its numerous friends back home with a 'valentine'—the most costly of the season, to *us* at least." The paper printed the pertinent excerpt from the special order outlining Valentine's incompetence, and Ford added that Valentine was "so long afflicted by this disease [incompetence] that it had become chronic and incurable, and toward the last, compounded '*cum digitatus longis et lapso lingue*' [with his long fingers—that is, stealing—and a slip of the tongue—meaning that someone finally turned him in]."[34]

Stephen Valentine left the service and moved back to Herkimer County, where, although disgraced, he resumed his medical practice. In June 1863, Elias Mather, on leave at home because of wounds suffered at Salem Church, received a medical certificate from Valentine stating that his condition prevented his return to active duty. As it turned out, Valentine barely survived the war himself. He died on April 15, 1865, at the age of thirty-three, just fifteen days after his mother died and four months before his father passed away. He is buried in the village of Ilion, German Flats, Herkimer County, next to his brother Sidney, who survived the rest of the family and spent half a century in the poorhouse, dying in 1904 at age seventy.[35]

Desertion and Discipline

Upton addressed the mounting problems of desertion and discipline immediately. He attacked desertion head on. Acting on a tip from Otsego County's sheriff, Andrew Mather, he brought charges against Lt. George St. John of the 144th New York. Upton claimed that St. John knowingly enlisted a deserter from the 121st's Company E, Edward Turp, in the 144th; Turp returned to the unit only to desert again at Gettysburg on July 3, 1863. As Clark had done before him, Upton sent to the respective county papers a complete list of deserters, indicating that "their names have been stricken from the rolls" of the regiment. He wanted to inform the citizens at home who the "cowards and deserters" were. Included in the list were five noncommissioned officers—three sergeants and two corporals.

The next month, Upton required that noncommissioned officers accompany all work details going outside the camp for fuel, water, rations, or any other reason. All details were to report to the officer of the guard when passing through the lines. He reduced in rank any officer returning with fewer men than he escorted out. He also appointed noncommissioned officers as babysitters to the sick, accompanying them on their way to medical quarters. He placed guards on all latrines to ensure that anyone using them would return to duty, not head away from camp. Finally, he issued passes to the officers' servants. The quartermaster sergeant, commissary sergeant, hospital steward, and sutler were the only persons allowed passes at all times. Upton also instructed the officer of the guard to note the return times of all enlisted men with passes, and he ordered all commanding officers (who were permitted to come and go at will) to "keep a black list" of all offenders.[36]

The letters and diaries of the men of the 121st as well as their hometown newspapers were replete with stories of desertion and its punishments. The local papers printed the names of deserters, and those they left behind had no time for them. Although the majority of desertions in the Union army occurred within the first few months in the field, they never stopped throughout the war. Men deserted before the 121st took the field in August 1862 and also in April 1865, just before and immediately after Lee's surrender. The 121st experienced desertion rates as high as or higher than the entire Army of the Potomac and the Union army in general.

Desertion was a complicated and pervasive issue. Most desertions were prompted by an immediate event, such as receiving a letter from a distraught relative or getting a paycheck (which provided the means to take off); in other cases, deserters left simply because they were cowards or were unable to adapt to the rigors of the field. Many had joined the army on a lark or for the money, and a good number of those who ultimately deserted had joined under the impression that the war would be over quickly and that they would not have to face the enemy and death. At first, the army did not address the desertion issue with force. It attempted to ameliorate the situation with light punishments, including humiliation. After all, the Lincoln administration needed every able-bodied man possible, and it eschewed drastic measures such as long incarcerations or the firing squad.

Two very distinctive waves of desertions hit the 121st New York Volunteers. The first occurred during the initial four months of duty in the field, September through December 1862, and was attributable to the slaughter at Antietam, the exposures at Belle Plain, and the incessant marching required of green troops who were away from home for the first time. The second period occurred immediately after that and can be directly attributed to the Union disaster at Fredericksburg on December 13, 1862; Gen. Ambrose Burnside's Mud March; and the conditions of winter camp from January through April 1863, including the lack of pay for more than four months. In each case—directly after the bloodbath at Antietam and then the loss at Fredericksburg—desertions in the army as a whole escalated enormously.

Thereafter, the numbers dropped, for several reasons. By 1863, the army had begun trying and executing deserters. And by that time, the men who remained under arms were by and large in it for the long haul; conversely, those most inclined to take "French leave" had already done so. Further, since bounty payments were another direct cause of desertion, the government had quickly realized that prudent stewardship of federal dollars called for offering a new enlistee only a partial payment up front and the balance of his recruitment bonus at the end of a successful enlistment. Similarly, paydays were scheduled just once a month (at the end of the month), the reasoning being that even though paying soldiers might improve their morale, would-be deserters would be less inclined to take off if their pockets were empty. Had the government or individual regiments kept line or bar charts of desertions, they could have plotted a direct correlation between payday and desertion day. As Jonathon Burrell put it, "There has been a good many desertions and I think there will be a good many more after payday."[37]

The first wave of desertions hit the 121st as Franchot's green troops took to the field. Well before the regiment mustered in, Henry Abbott enlisted in Company C in Little Falls on July 29, only to desert seven days later, on August 5, at Camp Schuyler. Pvt. John Lamb from Winfield and a member of Company C joined the 121st on July 24 and deserted on August 20. The company clerk remarked that the government "spent ten dollars in trying to catch him"; he did not say if the government received its money's worth. In September, after just a few weeks in the field, Marshall Dye reported that two boys from his company, John C. Richmond of German Flats and William L. Taylor of Little Falls, "either 'skedaddled' or have been taken prisoners." "They went to [Bakersville] last Thursday morning and have not been heard from since."[38]

After only two months in the field, Dr. Holt recorded that "over fifty [men had taken] French leave without waiting to say 'goodbye' to the colonel, or even call upon their surgeon to ascertain whether he thought it would be *healthy* to leave this cold weather without purse or scrip." Back in Otsego County, Sheriff Mather was authorized by Secretary of War Edwin Stanton to arrest deserters and turn them over to provost marshals. In effect, Stanton made Mather "a police officer under the general government." During his two-year term, Mather estimated that he arrested twenty-five to thirty men for desertion. He was sympathetic to most of them because many had enlisted under the impression they would never be sent into combat, since the war was soon to end.[39]

Nothing could keep the soldiers from dreaming of home. In their letters to those they had left behind, many men remembered scenes of hearth and family that may never have actually occurred. William Remmel's letters are replete with wishes to return home and have family and friends close by—and he was always careful to add "if I am spared." Jonathon Burrell, a steadfast soldier who was eventually killed, wistfully acknowledged the strong impulse to return home. In November, gripped by melancholy, he wrote longingly of home to his sister in Little Falls: "It must be look[ing] rather dreamy up there with so much snow and the wind whistling around the corner of the old house. Me thinks I can hear it now as it turns and squeaks down through the stovepipe and through the old kitchen door. Oh Hatt, I wish I was there just to step down cellar and help myself to some of your fine apples." As he continued, he became morose: "When I read your and F's [his brother's] letters this afternoon, I was all alone in my tent and as I read the letters, I could not keep the tears back. Brother and sister never fear you will ever be remembered by Brother Jonathon."[40]

On September 12, 1862, just days after the regiment had left Washington, Erastus Green of Company K, from the town of Otego, deserted. Sheriff Mather arrested him the following year and turned him over to the military authorities. Green was tried by a court-martial and sentenced to confinement and hard labor on public works; he would return to the 121st on July 27, 1863. His company commander, John Kidder, had wanted him and another deserter, George Bull, executed, and the *Otsego Republican* had expressed pleasure in Green's capture, though predicting it would "give the Copperheads another opportunity to howl against the Sherriff. They can put in another 'count' of 'arbitrary arrest' in their complaint to Governor Seymour." George Bull had deserted during the Mud March. When he showed up in Laurens, one of Kidder's corporals who was on leave recognized him and arrested him on the spot. By the summer of 1863, after Bull and Green had been charged with desertion, the mood of the army placed them in danger of losing their lives. Capt. Cleaveland Campbell, Company C, who presided over the court-martial of the two men, hinted to Kidder that both might be executed. In the end, Bull never received his sentence. He finished out his term of service with the regiment in 1865 along with Green.[41]

In December 1862, Mather "went down to Milford and arrested Cyrus H. Clinton and George Hyde, deserters." Both men had enlisted on the same day in Hartwick, both had served in Company E, and both were discharged before the end of the war. Clinton was thirty-six and Hyde eighteen at the time of their arrest. Clinton deserted again just eighteen days after Mather arrested him, and Hyde received his formal discharge from the army on February 1, 1864.[42]

Infractions and their punishments varied widely. The latter included forfeiture of pay, reduction in rank, incarceration, and extra duty, all employed to keep the men disciplined and obedient. One private, smarting from perceived ill treatment by his orderly sergeant, told the man to go to hell and as punishment was tied up by the thumbs for thirty minutes. The ultimate punishment for desertion—death by hanging or the firing squad—was not used on a wide scale until the latter half of 1863—midway through the war.

Upton pressed desertion charges against Elias Gage, a private in Company B who had deserted at Mohawk, New York, on August 31 as the regiment was leaving the state. He also pursued Delos Eddy from Company K, who deserted a year later, and Charles Mather (no relation to Sheriff Mather), a nineteen-year-old in Company K who eventually served until war's end, in order "to bring them speedily to trial to procure their punishment." One deserter, Francis S. Whitmore, from New York City and a private in Company H of the 84th New York Infantry, was assigned to Company K of the 121st as punishment and an opportunity for restitution. Under the Bounty Act of 1861, Whitmore was due $100 when he took off. The government stopped payment to him and recouped the costs of his arrest from his monthly pay of $30.

When he was apprehended, Whitmore had refused to cooperate with the arresting officials. He bellowed loudly that he would never put on the uniform of a soldier again. Sgt. Erastus Weaver sent him to a guardhouse, took his clothes away, and waited until "there was ice on the guard house floor, and the bleak, wintry winds were whistling mournfully outside." Weaver then gave Whitmore another opportunity to consider his situation, and after delivering a few more well-chosen words, Whitmore decided he would, after all, again don the blue uniform of the 121st. This event marked his first step on the road to becoming a model soldier.

Martin C. Ostrander, Company E, deserted near Stafford Court House, Virginia, on December 4, 1862. After his arrest, he returned to the 121st in February 1863. A court-martial found him guilty and sentenced him to Dry Tortugas Prison for one year of hard labor. The court ordered Ostrander to forfeit all pay and allowances due him in addition to "two dollars per month of his monthly pay while in confinement." He returned to his unit, was wounded at Spotsylvania, and mustered out with the rest of the regiment in 1865.[43]

Furlough could play a crucial role in the potential deserter's thinking. Not infrequently, friends, parents, spouses, and betrothed ones advised furloughed soldiers "not to return to the Army," and "there were many who harbored, fed and kept them in hiding." Chaplains Sage and Adams and Captain Kidder all blamed "friends at home" who encouraged deserters and then "tried to prevent their arrest and return." To thwart this practice, Mather wrote to the returnees' commanding officers to explain any mitigating circumstances, such as sickness in the family, and to ask the officers to go easy on the boys. He maintained that "disloyal friends of theirs had more to do with their not returning to the army than anything deserving of punishment." Jonathon Burrell told his sister that if any of the 121st showed up in Herkimer County "without proper papers," they should be "arrested and confined" until the authorities could deal with them.[44]

Captain Kidder took the desertions personally, especially among the men he had recruited from Laurens. He noted that desertions by recruits from Herkimer County were more prevalent than those by men from Otsego County, and he labeled them "disgraceful." He questioned the men's patriotism—"shame on such Americans," he exclaimed. Kidder remarked on the native-born American's lukewarm patriotism, contrasting it with the immigrant's passion for his adopted country (he himself was an immigrant). He wished that there were more efficient methods to catch "the scoundrels" and suggested that some would have to be shot as examples to others. He cursed those who deserted immediately after being paid. Disregarding Sheriff Mather's efforts, Kidder lamented the fact that no one in authority arrested the deserter who went home, much less returned him to his unit. Like Upton, Kidder and others sent the names of deserters to local papers for publication. He also enlisted his wife's assistance in arresting Sam Snediker from his company, who he knew was headed home to Laurens. The *Herkimer Democrat* echoed Kidder's embarrassment by printing the sentiments of an anonymous member of the 121st who had written to the paper. Concerned with the enormity of the desertion problem, he asserted that it would be better "to lose every drop of blood on the battlefield, than to bring such disgrace upon ones-self and his connections."[45]

Although he never deserted, William Remmel ran into trouble almost immediately, for he was often absent without leave and belligerent to the point of being insubordinate. He told his company commander, Captain Kidder, that he "did not care for extra duty," and he frequently left camp without permission. Kidder punished him with incarceration for six days along with fatigue duty (policing the camp and cleaning the camp streets) every morning from 9 A.M. to noon. In the afternoons, instead of battalion drill, Kidder ordered Remmel to walk around with his rifle on his shoulder for half the time and move at a double-quick pace (that is, run) for the other half. Remmel told his parents, "The boys in our company do not like their captain very well and think that he had better go home." After he served his punishment, however, he became a model soldier. Cpl. Adam Van Nort, a boy from Otsego in Company E, was reduced to the ranks for "incompetence and insubordination," and according to Sergeant Wales, an unidentified man in the regiment was "docked one month's pay for disobedience of order and kept under guard for five days."[46]

At times, Upton's discipline proved too severe for the offense. In a moment of egregious micromanagement, for example, he told Captain Kidder to hang a young private, Edward Pattengill, by the thumbs for possessing two shares of a government tent instead of the authorized one. Kidder ignored Upton's drastic response to the situation. The issue revolved around the fact that George Teel had sold his tent half to Pattengill (although he had no right to do so) and

Pattengill had refused to give it up when an officer asked him for it. Rather than tie Pattengill up by the thumbs, Kidder tried to reason with him, but when the soldier eventually refused to surrender his extra share in the tent, he arrested him. Bates watched the whole affair from a distance and thought that Kidder did the right thing by his men. He considered Upton's approach "arbitrary." According to Kidder, the men in Company I agreed with his approach as well, and his stature as a leader improved with this incident. But the folks back home in Laurens reportedly feared Kidder's strict disciplinarian methods. His tough treatment of the men drew Bates's criticism. And as much as Bates approved of Upton's strict ways, he did not shy away from criticizing his regimental commander as well.[47]

Writing years after the war, Bates remembered one officer handing in his resignation because Upton "insisted that he should draw the lines a little closer with his command." Upton also continued Clark's policy of clamping down on fraternization between officers and enlisted men. When all complied with the new regimen, the machine ran well. When an occasional violation occurred, no matter "how trifling the offense, a severe punishment was meted out to the unfortunate victim." Bates hinted that when other officers adopted Upton's harsh methods, "in some succeeding battle a so-called accidental shot would wound or perchance kill the officer against whom the memories were treasured up."[48]

Although desertions continued to plague the 121st throughout the war, incidents of French leave became less prevalent over time. After a second wave in the first few months of 1863, desertions eventually tapered off, and they did not materially increase in the remainder of the war for a variety of reasons. But they did stay constant. New factors such as draftees, substitutes, and bounty jumpers kept the rates of desertion level. But of course, not all soldiers were disposed to run. Even though letters from home incited some men to leave their posts and return home, patriotism was still an important part of the equation, and there is abundant evidence that patriotic pressures from the home front, which appealed to a soldier's pride, kept men on the front lines. Jonathon Burrell pledged, as many of the men of the 121st did, to remain at his post no matter how rough the situation became. Burrell stated quite clearly to his brother and sister that he would never dishonor the family's reputation or do "anything that would bring a stain on myself or on my friends."[49]

Chasing Lee

Between Antietam and Fredericksburg, from September 17 to December 14, 1862, the 121st, with the Sixth Corps of the Army of the Potomac, chased Robert E. Lee's army back into Virginia—a move "not generally liked by the soldiers who have fought there," William Remmel reported. At first, progress was snail-like, and the troops found the inaction worse than the unseen battle or the forced marches under Franchot. They complained of McClellan's slowness and the lack of movement. Thomas Hyzer, though, remained confident that McClellan "was determined to rush it right through. I think it may be settled in the course of two or three months." Remmel thought that the 121st would not see any action until the following spring. Talk in the ranks predicted that Richmond, "that hot hole of secession," would be taken during the "Indian Summer"—a desire more ambitious than Horace Greeley's. Some in the regiment were pleased that "Democrats and Conservatives" were enlisting and experiencing the perils of war in person. Fred Ford, writing in the context of the Emancipation Proclamation, did not care if the war ended slavery or not as long as Richmond fell—whatever the shortest course to peace demanded. Passionately and elegantly, he wrote: "You see that while the thing grinds *your pockets* it is wearing on our flesh and blood."[50]

Most of the days consisted of marching, interspersed with drilling, setting camp, breaking camp, and marching again. Henry Galpin found the weather "splendid and traveling delightful." "Nothing can surpass the beauty of the autumnal foliage that meets our eye on every side," he enthused. Southerners viewed the soil of Virginia as sacred, and "[if] thus sacred, will not everyone demand that it be henceforth consecrated to freedom?" Adelbert Reed remarked on the "handsomest stands of woods of oak, walnut and cherry." Seeing the thick, dark pines and the "darkies" watching the troops march by was all a new experience for the young man. He noted that some of the blacks he encountered were "nearly white. It is seldom that you see a white man." Meanwhile, William Remmel said it was with trepidation that he left the "loyal" state of Maryland, where there were a "good number of loyalists," for the "secessionist" state of Virginia, where "in the heart of rebellion . . . hardly one in a hundred" professed loyalty to the Union. Back home in Cooperstown, Sheriff Mather wondered and worried about sons Elias and Emmet—he had not heard from them for some time, but he knew that they had missed the heavy action at Antietam.[51]

The 121st left Bakersville, Maryland, on October 31, and by Sunday, November 2, it reached the Potomac at Berlin, a few miles south of Harpers Ferry. There, it crossed the Potomac on pontoons, since the Confederates had burned the bridge, and during the entire month of November, the army moved back and forth over the gently rolling hills of northern Virginia. The army line extended so far back into Maryland that it took one week for the entire column to traverse the pontoons and reach the Virginia side. On Thursday and Friday, November 6 and 7, the 121st stopped briefly at White Plains, Virginia, and then moved on Sunday, November 9, to Thoroughfare Gap. The army began maneuvering for a clear and decisive blow at Lee's army. Samuel French, in Company F, recorded the grueling routine in his diary. He arose every morning (usually at a different time each day), cooked breakfast, struck his tent, packed his knapsack, loaded his haversack with a day's rations, filled his canteen, shouldered his weapon, put on his cartridge and cap boxes, marched "12 or 15 miles per day," pitched his tent, and cooked supper in the evening. Frank Carran remarked that the latest march ranked as the "severest one we have as yet experienced" mainly because of the bad roads. Hope sprang eternal, though. He predicted that by the end of the year, Richmond, "this hot hole of treason and rebellion may be in the hands of its lawful owner, the famous Uncle Sam."[52]

Food has been a concern of armies since the beginning of time and warfare. As the 121st pushed through the rain and the mud in November 1862, Samuel French wondered if the downpour would ever stop and Edward Wales questioned if the troops would ever be fed. Foraging, rather than relying on army rations and the logistical supply system, provided a viable alternative for the men in the field. William Remmel and Adelbert Reed found it strange to be taking straw to sleep on and livestock and corn to eat in order to make up for what the army did not provide. Taking someone else's property was alien to many of the troops, but it rapidly became a common practice. "Confiscating is carried on quite extensively here when an old Secesh is found," French reported. "The boys go and take cattle, sheep, hogs, and poultry, and kill and eat." Wales agreed: "Had pork and beans for dinner which was beautiful." John Ingraham asked his parents to send him new boots, with a "hunk of old Herkimer Cheese and cookie or two in the boot leg," and he implored his brother to send some butter and more of the old Herkimer County cheese. Remmel correctly predicted that the men would soon grow tired of the daily army fare of hardtack, salt pork, and coffee.

Remmel, among others in his regiment, expressed concern about the poverty of the enemy and the lack of necessities available to him. He recognized the dire conditions suffered by the lower classes of whites and the relative ease with which the upper classes moved to safety in Richmond, "although their sentiment is contrary to ours." He deplored the ravenous soldiers coming off a long march or immediately after making a new camp rampaging through occupied and empty houses in search of food. Another soldier remarked how "this wicked rebellion" cursed the people who brought it on. "All seem depressed with sadness and gloom," he recorded. "No steps seem to be taken to cultivate a few vegetables." He observed that the owner of a ruined plantation "has given up in despair and can be seen wandering, crying, 'I am a ruined man' as all advocates of treason will exclaim."[53]

5

Desertion, Disarray, and Despair: Winter 1862–1863

McClellan seems to stir us about for exercise, just as an owner would his horse but when night comes, it's the same old horse in the same old stall and the horse is getting to be only a spavined back.

> Fred Ford, Company C, November 6, 1862

Politics has ruled this war so far.

> Jonathon Burrell, Company A, November 11, 1862

Our men is a running a way and a dying off so fast that we have not got more than four hundred men left.

> John Ballard, Company G, February 2, 1863

New York Politics and the Emancipation Proclamation

Focusing on the victory at Antietam, the Lincoln administration promulgated a preliminary emancipation proclamation in September 1862. Its issuance provoked a maelstrom of controversy in the North that equaled or surpassed the reaction in the seceded states it affected. In the Empire State, where politics during peacetime was a blood sport, the proclamation exacerbated a witch's brew of partisan political warfare. Politicians waged the fall campaign of 1862 during an armed national insurrection in an atmosphere of mistrust and deception.[1]

Over the first eighteen months of the conflict, the political wars in New York State had subsided to the point of being nonexistent. Both Democrats and Republicans were quietly attempting to loyally get behind the Lincoln administration. As long as the administration kept the restoration of the Union as the goal of the war, the former Know-Nothings, Whigs, Free-Soilers, and others who coalesced into the new parties remained supportive of the war effort. Between July and September 1862, however, all that changed. After Antietam, General McClellan provoked the president with his unwillingness to pursue the rebel army. And in New York State, with the hint of emancipation in the air, the gubernatorial election season began to take shape.

The parties convened in September as the 121st joined the Army of the Potomac. Governor Morgan declined to run again, and the Democrats, meeting in Albany, made Horatio Seymour their thunderous choice. Seymour, a Democrat from Pompey Hill in Onondaga County, had served as the mayor of Utica from 1842 to 1843 and as governor from 1853 to 1854. Until lawmakers changed the state constitution in 1877, a governor had a two-year term and could opt to serve an unlimited number of terms. Morgan had served two consecutive terms from 1859. The Constitutional Union Party's convention, a sideshow in Troy, attempted to win the support of the old Whigs for the Democratic Party. Denounced as a sham and a "humbug," the party never amounted to much, but its existence added to the political stew that boiled throughout the state.

The Republicans nominated Brig. Gen. James S. Wadsworth, a former Free-Soiler. He had been military governor of Washington, D.C., in 1861, and was an abolitionist whose credentials made him palatable to the party's radical wing. Reflecting the continued confusion, the Republican convention then picked a war Democrat, Lyman Tremain, as Wadsworth's running mate. Wadsworth, a successful and intelligent New York businessman, believed that the South had erred in its defense of slavery and that the North could justify the war if it could bring the "peculiar institution" to an end. When war broke out, Wadsworth procured supplies and the necessary transportation, particularly steamboats, and moved the materials to awaiting troops in Annapolis. Later, he accepted an appointment as a major on Gen. Irvin McDowell's staff. Serving in that capacity at the first battle of Bull Run, Wadsworth distinguished himself for "coolness, high courage, and great capacity."[2]

New York Democrats, meanwhile, walked a perilous line. Labeled peace democrats, they advocated reuniting the country at any cost as long as the Constitution could be saved. Oversimplified descriptors of the different factions did injustice to the two political parties. Members of both factions believed that the "Radicals"—or abolitionists—were really responsible for the secessionist movement, but those labels stuck with the Republicans. Once war began, Northern Democrats distanced themselves from their Southern brethren. They were loyal and supportive of the war—but only to preserve the Union, whatever that meant. To some, it meant bringing the Southerners back into the fold; to others, it meant letting the wayward brothers and sisters go their separate ways.

Democrats insisted on the preservation of the Union and the Constitution above all else and held that the federal government possessed no right to interfere with the Southerners' right to hold slaves. Although some in the Republican Party held these same views, the Democrats were labeled traitors, conservatives, and, ultimately, peace democrats and "Copperheads."

Several converging and unfortunate events conspired in the late fall of 1862 to doom the Republicans' chances in New York and give the gubernatorial victory to Horatio Seymour. He took office in January 1863 against a complex backdrop: the drafted Emancipation Proclamation, Lincoln's suspension of habeas corpus, the issuance of the final proclamation, the general rancor and discontent among the citizenry after the losses at Fredericksburg, and the perceived attack on the Constitution and the personal liberties of citizens everywhere by the Lincoln administration. Lincoln further angered so-called conservatives (those in either party who were opposed to the "radical" notion of emancipation) when he fired Democrat George McClellan as commander of the Army of the Potomac and replaced him with the man who was the loser at Fredericksburg—Maj. Gen. Ambrose E. Burnside.

Wadsworth gave only one stump speech, and Seymour only gave two, but Seymour's views were well-known from previous public utterances. In the fall of 1861, he had delivered a speech in Utica in which he voiced his strong support of the Union and the Constitution and rejected abolition and immediate emancipation. The latter, he argued, would not stop the war; in fact, it would only be the beginning of a "lasting, destructive, terrible domestic conflict." None in the North would agree that "four millions of free Negroes should live in their midst," and further, he asked, by what right did the North demand that the South "should be subjected to the evils, the insecurity, and the loss of constitutional rights, involved in immediate abolition?"

With an obvious and clear reference to the Lincoln administration, Seymour warned against leaders who trampled on personal freedoms and overstepped their constitutional powers, for they would suffer the consequences of the despots of old. He asserted that Lincoln held the view that "a whole nation with a battered constitution was preferable to an intact Constitution for a remnant of the Union." Seymour's argument did not cover the issue of traitors in open rebellion against the constitutional government who were not required to suffer equally for their actions. In his inaugural address on January 7, 1863, he again condemned emancipation, calling it "a proposal for the butchery of women and children, for scenes of lust and rapine, and of arson and murder, which would invoke the interference of civilized Europe." Seymour promised that "the democrats had no desire to embarrass Lincoln—they only wanted to bring Washington to a realization that the war's purpose was solely the suppression of the rebellion. It was not fought to change the social status of the states."[3]

Seymour and Lincoln were polar opposites. The well-mannered and cultured

Seymour was a contrast to the prairie lawyer who became president. Schooled in the art of debate (as Lincoln was), Seymour possessed a canny political sense. He tended to surround himself with yes-men who played to his sensitivity and quick temper. Lincoln, by contrast, embraced his detractors and rivals. One contemporary described Seymour as "a gentleman of commanding talents, high culture of bland and winning manners, admired in social and domestic life." In the end, his party prevailed with a plurality of 10,000 votes. The Radicals were crushed. George William Curtis, political writer for *Harper's Weekly*, attributed Wadsworth's defeat to the "mad desperation of reaction." He blamed the "military disasters, financial embarrassments, and the emancipation proclamation." In Curtis's opinion, "All of the reverses, our despondence, our despairs bring us to the inevitable issue, shall not the blacks strike for their freedom?" The election of Democrats not only to the governor's office but also to half of the seats in the state assembly especially troubled the Lincoln administration, as it "created the anomalous situation of partially turning over the state that furnished the greatest number of troops and supplied the principal financial backing to the Union to active opponents of the administration."[4]

Seymour's election followed a bitter campaign fueled by New York City newspapers in which "personal vilification largely supplanted argument." The *Freeman's Journal* could not contain its glee. It exulted in Seymour's victory and Otsego County's thirty-six-vote plurality, calling it "a great democratic triumph in New York." In the Herkimer town of Litchfield, politics and General McClellan's departure split the Carran family. Frank Carran's cousin, J. A. Goodier, argued that McClellan's dismissal would help the war effort: the move "takes very well around here," he reported in reference to Herkimer County, "we hope it is for the best." But Frank and the boys in the ranks thought the general's departure spelled disaster. Beyond that, Frank's dislike for Seymour angered his cousin Harrison (William H. H. Goodier). Frank's mother, Philenda, would have no part of it; in her heart, she knew Seymour was a "secesh." Brother William summed up in a few words the meaning of the election—"I suppose Seymour is elected Governor," he said, "but I tell you old Litchfield didn't go for him nor this county either. I suppose you will be at home in about 90 days after he takes the chair [office] for he says the war will be over then."[5]

With New Jersey and New York now solidly in the Democratic camp, Lincoln courted Seymour for obvious reasons. As the leader of the largest Union state, from which much manpower and financial strength emanated, Seymour was in a position to be either a large headache or an enormous help to the government in Washington. Lincoln wooed the new governor with a short, direct letter in March in which he asked Seymour for his help despite any personal or political differences the two might share; if there were any, he suggested, they should exist in the realm of *means* and not *purpose*. And when their differences involved *means*, Lincoln told Seymour, "they should be as small as possible." The president conceded that New York's cooperation in the war's prosecution "was indispensable. This alone is a sufficient reason why I should wish to be at a good understanding with you." Seymour, however, was none too receptive to the president's overtures. Citing the overwhelming burdens of office, he waited three weeks to reply to Lincoln's missive. He finally sent a cold, perfunctory answer that sidestepped the main issues. He reiterated his love of the Constitution and the "preservation of the Union" and said he was prepared to "make every sacrifice" for either. However, even though Seymour continued to oppose the administration's policies, he did not hinder the recruitment of new troops, and he supplied as many as were asked of the state by the federal government.[6]

The election of an anti-Lincoln administration in Albany, the impact of the Emancipation Proclamation, and Burnside's replacement of McClellan affected the troops in the field. The autumn of 1862—the first in the field for the men of the 121st—was marked by a mix of politics and military drama that drew reactions from the men. They were not allowed to return home to vote, and absentee ballots were not yet in use. Their feelings, however, were split as evenly as the vote back home. Company A, determined to stage a straw vote among the men notwithstanding the fact that a number of them were too young to vote, cast 45 votes for Wadsworth and 18 for Seymour. Lt. Frank Bolles reported that his Company F voted 41 for Seymour and 28 for Wadsworth and that all the 29 men he had enlisted from Unadilla were Democrats.

Some soldiers expressed their anti-Seymour sentiments and deep dismay over the election's results. Jonathon Burrell reacted bitterly to Seymour's win—"the thing can hardly be swallowed." Upton told him that Seymour's election would shorten the war and that it would end in compromise, but he did not indicate whether he supported a compromised ending. For his part, Burrell wanted to see "about 100,000 old hard shell democrats brought down here and be obliged to face the music," with Governor Seymour "in the front rank."

Frank Carran agreed with him, bemoaning the election's results and expressing concern over the direction shown by the voters of New York. "Do they intend to send us down here to fight the battles of the country and the world and then betray us at the ballot box?" he asked, adding, "*For shame.*" In a scathing series of letters to the *Herkimer Journal*, the 121st's official correspondent, Fred Ford, angrily scolded those at home: "The army believed that you of the North would of course support the war and Administration." He reported that the "sneaks" in the ranks were thrilled at the election results and the prospect of a speedy return home. But for his part, he despaired of the proslavery, antiwar Congress that the Democrats provided. He criticized Americans who abandoned their patriotism in favor of party loyalty. Ford blamed the whole mess on Lincoln's perceived tentative execution of the war and his relentless search for a strong military leader. Sadly, he concluded that "a commonwealth which knows how to play at war only and not to fight in dead earnest had better die, that something better may spring out of its decay."[7]

The recruits of the 121st embodied nineteenth-century views of slavery and blacks. They perceived the interconnections and interplay in the recent election, the lack of support for the war in the North, and the Emancipation Proclamation. They were careful in their distinctions between the idealized concept of emancipation and the equality of blacks and whites. They also splintered over their feelings for McClellan, Seymour, and the emergence of the Copperheads.

The men recruited from Herkimer County were generally more accepting of the notion of freedom for blacks than those recruited from Otsego, for several reasons. At the time of the war, freed blacks were living in both counties, but they were much more prominent in Herkimer. Progressive schools with progressive agendas, such as Fairfield Academy in Herkimer County, taught a broad, classical liberal arts education. Herkimer's manufacturing base and the east-west corridor of commerce through the Mohawk Valley allowed its residents a more cosmopolitan view of the world. For example, during the month of December 1863, nearly a year after the Emancipation Proclamation, when the managers of the skating rink at Excelsior Park in Utica, New York, made the rink off-limits to blacks, the *Utica Herald* quickly approved of the ban. But at the *Herkimer County Journal*, editor J. R. Stebbins, a Fairfield Academy graduate who was appalled and "ashamed" of the *Herald,* issued a stern rebuttal. He called the decision a "mistake" and said that the new policy ran counter "to the good sense" and "wishes of the great masses of those who [used the facility]." When Lincoln's preliminary proclamation first rang out over the land after Antietam, the academy's students celebrated with a rally and a ringing endorsement of the announcement. No such incident occurred in Otsego.[8]

Herkimer County residents Ford, Galpin, Rice, and Holt were particularly opposed to slavery and outspoken in favor of Lincoln's move. Fred Ford thought that the proclamation would destroy the Confederacy and noted that "from the tone of the Southern papers and politicians, they think that it will be the most stunning blow of the war." He incorrectly predicted that a slave insurrection was inevitable and that the Confederate army, preoccupied with the Union forces, would not be in a position to put it down. He feared that McClellan's plan would foment a black-and-white war; if so, he warned, "the whites may have a fair chance to hammer down their black beasts of burden." Clarke Rice called the war the "great moral struggle of the century." He wished that the North was as united in purpose as he perceived the South to be. He recognized slavery's deep roots in American history and expressed his belief that it was in its death throes, while maintaining a condescending but hopeful attitude toward the slave. "They certainly possess many superior traits," he wrote, "and under the sunshine of a liberal civilization, will yet attain to the higher circle of the family of man." Rice and his fellow soldiers reserved their hatred for the Copperheads, whom they called "our deadliest foes, more to be dreaded than the minions of the South."[9]

Henry Galpin believed that the Emancipation Proclamation would have shortened the war had it been issued earlier. But he differed with his regimental comrades in his belief that "the only man at present who can control and satisfactorily lead the grand Union Army" to victory and the nation to reunion was George McClellan, not Abraham Lincoln or Ambrose Burnside. The country's only viable future, he maintained, consisted of a full and restored Union without the stain of secession and slavery. Galpin berated those back home for their "lack of soul and principle" in prosecuting the war. By comparison, he said, they could not measure up to the "fixed determination, the indomitable will that characterizes the Southern people." He excoriated those who wanted to return to the old Union, for that would imply the continued existence of "the black cancer of slavery spreading and gnawing at our vitals." The men of the 121st joined the service because of a passion to save a better Union. Galpin equated the slaveowner's loss of property—slaves—for the common good of the country with the Union man's sacrifice of blood and treasure to put down the rebellion, also for the common good. Or, he asked rhetorically, "is the two-legged property more sacred in the eyes of those faint and feeble-hearted Unionists at the North than the blood of our noble men, or more to be regarded than the vitality of our glorious old Union?"[10]

Dr. Holt captured the conflict between freedom for an enslaved human being and Negrophobia. He saw the war and the emancipation of millions of people in moral terms. In the first few weeks of the conflict, he shared his love of the Maryland countryside with his wife, telling her that it reminded him of the Mohawk Valley. He wrote that he would not mind settling there "were it not for the baneful curse of slavery." In his mind, no free man could adopt "any of the rules which govern the peculiar institution." He criticized the Lincoln administration for not using blacks to fight the war; he could not understand why the government "distrusted" the black man and did not use him to win his own freedom. He firmly believed that the war's only natural result had to be emancipation.

At the same time, Holt admitted that as great as his "love for a black skin" was, he had not met one black with whom he would be "willing to be on a *perfect* equality." Education formed the basis of inequality, he believed: "It is engrafted in me, I cannot help it." Yet when the regiment encamped in the Shenandoah Valley, Holt encountered poor whites who followed the army and found them "far less attractive than the poorest Negro." He described them as "snuff-dripping, tobacco-chewing and smoking creatures, filled with domestic whiskey," far inferior to the black slave, in his eyes. In the end, he preached, "We

Daniel Holt, assistant surgeon. Proudly posing with his Sixth Corps badge, Holt was a garrulous observer and commentator on every aspect of the war. Poor health caused him to resign just before the battle of Cedar Creek. His health continued to deteriorate, and he died two years later after reestablishing his medical practice in Herkimer County. From Isaac O. Best, *History of the 121st.*

cannot roll the sin of slavery under our tongue as a sweet morsel and claim the divine favor. It is impious to call upon God for a blessing while we dare have such cruelty in our hearts."[11]

The meaning and understanding of the new war effort cut across not only intellectual and educational lines but also class lines. Herkimer resident John Hartwell, a house carpenter and builder with no formal education, held a perceptive insight into world affairs and had an agile vocabulary to express those views. An older, married man with a family, he understood that the "chivalry" of the South protected the evils of slavery and that the war's root cause could only be slavery. He blamed the Democrats and Copperheads for their deadly collusion with the rebel armies to cause harm to the soldier in the field.[12]

Chaplain Adams saw Lincoln's issuance of the Emancipation Proclamation as "a military necessity" to "weaken the enemy." The proclamation withdrew "aid and comfort to the Southern States," and Lincoln had a moral obligation to issue it. But he worried that many officers would make good on their threat to resign because Lincoln had changed the purpose of the war from the salvation of the country to the abolition of slavery. Phillip Van Horne, a corporal in Company E from Springfield, wrote to his father on George Washington's birthday with a full understanding of the day's meaning. He saw the elimination of slavery as the only means by which the country could continue to exist as the forefathers intended. Eloquently, he depicted the land that was destined to be "sacred to freedom" instead "trembling and writhing with slavery's accursed fangs tearing at its vitals." Like others in the ranks, he complained that those who remained at home really did not appreciate the war's severity or the importance of its successful conclusion. In Company K, 1st Lt. Lansing B. Paine felt that the rebellion could be quashed only with force, and he expressed his willingness to fight "a spell longer."[13]

When Lincoln changed the war's objectives, the boys from Otsego County were not in an accepting mood. Their home county's isolation and the residents' insular way of thinking and living precluded the unconditional embrace of the proclamation and its impact on the war's meaning. There were few blacks living in the county in 1861, and most of the young farmboys had never even seen a freedman or slave. Their letters and diaries reveal that they were far less open to progressive worldviews and ideas. Their writings are replete with derogatory references to blacks, more so than that of the least educated Herkimer County soldier.

James Hall, a private in John Kidder's Company I, typified the young, naïve, and uneducated farmboy suddenly introduced to women—both black and white. He asserted that the women in Laurens were better-looking than the women he saw in Maryland. When one woman ventured through camp, he wrote home: "You can bet there was a gazing at her." He longed for the girls of Laurens to come to camp. The black women of the South were a disappointment to him—he wrote scathingly of the "dark, cullard wimmin." In his opinion, they did not look "as well as the boys thought they would. They look black and nasty." His friends carried *cartes de visite* (small paper photographs the size of calling cards) of the girls back home, which they used to compare to the women coming into camp or those they encountered "away from camp."

Ten Eyck Howland of Cherry Valley, first sergeant in Company G, summed up the conflict inherent in the change of direction for the war when he declared that he "was sick of fighting for the niggers. When we were fighting for the Union, I was satisfied, but now it is fighting for the black niggers." He went on to say that the United States no longer merited his continuing citizenship: he would rather leave the country and live anywhere else in the world. His thoughts were echoed by Charles B. West, a private in Company F from Edmeston who complained that it "was hard times to enjoy life in these war times and it's hard to fight under such a damn nigger administration." When Delavan Bates became eligible for a colonelcy in a colored regiment, as it was called, his letters were laced with racial epithets. As the 121st stepped off at the beginning of Grant's overland campaign, Francis Morse, Upton's adjutant, observed a procession of blacks bearing a coffin to the cemetery. Morse bumped into Chaplain Adams as he strode to perform his ministerial duties, "looking very solemn." Morse asked Adams if "it was early in the season to go *black burying*; [Adams] deigned no reply, but looked shocked at my irreverence."[14]

The Emancipation Proclamation enraged Cooperstown's anti-Lincoln *Freeman's Journal*, whose editors realized that it meant unconditional surrender and no peace talks. They cited the section of the proclamation that spoke directly to the slaves and wondered how a group of people who could not read would benefit from what they called a "joke" and a "miserable humbug." They viewed the proclamation as a victory for the Republican Radicals who had lobbied for the measure since the war began. In the *Journal's* estimation, the proclamation would only prolong the war. Now, victory consisted of complete domination of the Southern people, and if the new strategy failed, they asked rhetorically, "whose fault is it? On whom rests the responsibility and the shame?" They answered their own question: "On the weak and incompetent ABRAHAM LINCOLN!"[15]

Philenda Carran forcefully reiterated that the blacks would soon be fighting for themselves rather than the armies now in the field fighting for them. From her home in Herkimer County, she expressed the wish that Lincoln had "sustained Fremont and Hunter when they issued their Proclamations of freedom, [for] it would have been better for the country." On the formation of the new black regiments in the West and the South, she concluded: "I hope the day is not far distant when the word slave will be done with in this enlightened land."[16]

Burnside Takes Command

In November, Ambrose Burnside replaced George McClellan as the commander of the Army of the Potomac. Lincoln replaced McClellan because he had failed to vigorously follow Lee after Antietam. The president worried that the effect of the weak victory at Antietam, the issuance of the preliminary Emancipation Proclamation, and McClellan's political ambitions posed a major threat to the war effort. The general's inability to estimate his own army's strength and the enemy's strength, coupled with his fear of failure, crippled him as an effective leader. His slow and deliberate movements at critical times infuriated Lincoln, who wanted Lee crushed as soon as possible. When McClellan missed his chance on the Peninsula and after Antietam, Lincoln decided to make the change.

The men of the 121st watched as the veteran regiments bemoaned the loss of McClellan as commander of the Army of the Potomac. In their eyes, he had welded them into an effective fighting machine with high morale. McClellan's firing added another ingredient to the flammable atmosphere within the ranks of the 121st regiment, already fanned by the proclamation and Seymour's election. Jonathon Burrell reported that some officers in the older regiments had offered their resignations in protest of McClellan's firing: "It is wonderful how much that man is thought of by the old regiments," he wrote. He repeated camp rumors that Burnside was firing officers rather than accepting their resignations. If the North had embraced the Emancipation Proclamation, Lincoln would not have fired McClellan, Burrell argued. He reasoned, if you were anti-proclamation, you were pro-McClellan. And in retaliation, Lincoln fired the Democrat McClellan. Burrell envisioned a prolonged war because of the negative reception emancipation received in the North; because of the New York elections; and, yes, he grudgingly admitted, because of McClellan's military failures. He predicted a long war if McClellan was the standard-bearer on the Democratic ticket in 1864.

Surprised by the depth of admiration the old regiments held for McClellan, Burrell still favored the change—"better than the election of Seymour." Had the soldiers voted, he asserted, Seymour would never have been elected. "Politics has ruled this war so far," he complained, and now the country wanted a compromise to end the war. "And if a compromised peace came, we would be at war again in a few years." Burrell believed Lincoln's removal of McClellan in the midst of the war imperiled the Union. If the country were as true to McClellan as he had been to his soldiers, the war would be over quickly, he argued. He told his siblings that "there has been considerable commotion in the army since the news became public that Burnside had been appointed to the place of Little Mac," but he hoped for the best. Reluctantly, he accepted Burnside as his new commander. "I think you will see the fur fly," he predicted.[17]

Clinton Beckwith observed that "it was a strange sight to see these battle-tried veterans swarm to the roadside and yell and cheer and run after McClellan." He himself confessed to dueling loyalties. Although he supported Lincoln, he disagreed with the change's timing. He linked McClellan's supporters with the antiemancipation crowd who saw the proclamation as the fruition of a long-planned plot by abolitionists who "declared had they known they were coming down there to fight for the nigger they would have staid at home." When both Burnside and McClellan reviewed the troops near Stafford Court House, a member of the 121st described the enlisted men's noisy enthusiasm for both officers to the *Herkimer Democrat*. Frank Carran reported that the soldiers were "carried away with excitement." The older soldiers showed no "confidence in any other general."

"Napoleon Bonaparte McClellan" did not impress Fred Ford. He accused the general of humiliating the Army of the Potomac. "McClellan seems to stir us about for exercise, just as an owner would his horse but when night comes," he wrote in a picturesque metaphor, "it's the same old horse in the same old stall and the horse is getting to be only a spavined back." Ford spoke with disillusioned soldiers who talked of desertion and with officers who threatened resignation—"all talked of nothing but getting home." His own formula for victory called for the "right kind of a leader and the right kind of fighting principles [which] would, before the New Year, change the Army of the Potomac to the army in Richmond."[18]

In one of the more important moves before his removal, McClellan established a board of officers "to examine into the capacity, qualifications, propriety of conduct, and efficiency" of volunteer officers "as may be ordered before it." Placed on the board were Col. Alfred T. A. Torbert, 1st New Jersey; Col. Henry B. Brown, 3rd New Jersey; Capt. Henry Seymour Hall, 27th New York; and Col. Emory Upton, 121st New York. The board remained in existence for at least the following eighteen months, giving Upton a structure by which to rid his command of incompetent officers.[19]

Burnside Forges a Plan—and the 121st Suffers at Belle Plain

Lincoln turned to Burnside to solve his third problem—Union losses. Accordingly, Burnside determined to seize Fredericksburg and then move on to capture a defenseless Richmond. Only surprise and speed could place him between Lee and Richmond: an attack would be on Burnside's terms. The plan appeared solid and, on initial review, possible. In order to bring victory to the Union and his president, Burnside immediately embarked on an ill-advised reorganization of the Army of the Potomac into three grand divisions. The Left Grand Division consisted of the Sixth Corps, now commanded by Maj. Gen. William P. Smith, and Maj. Gen. John F. Reynolds's First Corps; the division was led by Maj. Gen. William B. Franklin, the former commander of the Sixth Corps. Maj. Gen. Joseph Hooker led the Center Grand Division, comprising the Third Corps and the Fifth Corps. Maj. Gen. Edwin Sumner commanded the Right Grand Division, consisting of the Second Corps and Ninth Corps. McClellan's original plan, approved by the president, had called for the army to engage Lee at Warrenton, Virginia. Burnside decided instead to move on Fredericksburg and rely on supply and water lines to Washington via Aquia Creek.

Although the plan was ill fated from the beginning, Maj. Gen. Henry W. Halleck and Lincoln reluctantly agreed to it. Fred Ford doubted that the men in the 121st or in his brigade would accept Burnside or his plan. "I think that the old troops will not fight as well *for the first time,"* he wrote. "McClellan seems to be the idol of the army," although the entire force itched to move on to Richmond. Fredericksburg represented a minor impediment as they reached for the grand prize. "When we do start, the General will have to ride with gag bit to keep us out of Richmond."[20]

Burnside's plan, simple and direct, required the cooperation of both Lee and the weather. The pontoon bridges that Burnside needed to cross the Rappahannock River were delayed. Perceiving the town of Fredericksburg to be lightly defended, Generals Edwin Sumner and Winfield Scott Hancock pushed Burnside to ford the river with their commands. While Burnside delayed and awaited his pontoons, the Confederates began reassembling to challenge the new Union commander. Longstreet's corps arrived from Culpeper, in northern Virginia, between November 21 and November 25. Jackson returned from the Shenandoah Valley, and Lee ordered him to take up positions along the Rappahannock, just south and west of Fredericksburg, by December 1. The weather became a large factor two weeks before the battle. Heavy rains in the third week of November made the fords impassable, denying the federal troops' initiative to strike early. With the arrival of December, the rain turned to snow, and after a 6-mile march to Belle Plain, located northeast of Fredericksburg on an inlet off the Potomac, the Sixth Corps slowed and finally ground to a halt.

On December 5, rain produced shoe-deep mud, and toward evening, the rain turned to snow. Snow and freezing water covered the ground. The plain was the worst possible location for winter quarters, for its flat, vacant ground offered no shelter from the strong northern and westerly winds. Men and animals "were wet to the skin." And with no shelter, the regiment's collective physical condition became alarming. The men were on open ground, windswept and barren of firewood. Emory Upton realized the danger to his men. They had passed a lush pine forest that would have been an ideal bivouac area. If he could move his men to the shelter of the forest, he reasoned, they would be secure. Accordingly, he petitioned the acting brigade commander, Col. Henry Lutz Cake, who denied his request.

Cake commanded the 96th Pennsylvania, a brigade companion to the 121st and a regiment that would suffer with it at Salem Church, Rappahannock Station, the Wilderness, and Spotsylvania. As a politician-soldier, Cake had become the colonel of the 25th Pennsylvania, a ninety-day regiment, in the early stage of the war. He was thirty-three years old at the outbreak of the conflict, with ambitions for high office, and he saw his military service aiding that cause. In Pottsville, Pennsylvania, Cake owned a newspaper and dabbled in the emerging anthracite coal industry. His fellow officers uniformly reviled him. They deplored his disregard for military protocol and his "unorthodox management of the regiment," which skirted "military regulations and procedures." Before leaving Pennsylvania, Cake ran for a seat in the state senate. He personified the politician–volunteer soldier that Upton loathed. His lack of empathy and his weaknesses were readily apparent at Belle Plain. John Ingraham said of Cake, "He will get scooped out yet. He made two or three blunders the other day."[21]

The hard marching first through rain and then through snow ("large, soft, fleecy flake"), coupled with the slippery footing, left the men of the 121st wet, steaming with perspiration, and encamped in the open. Conditions worsened when the wind came up and darkness fell. Unable to find shelter in this hostile, windswept plain, the men huddled together to keep warm and dry as best they could. They marched onto a low flat near the river and were "ordered to go into camp and make [themselves] comfortable for the night." Sergeant Wales, Company G, wrote that "this was the hardest time I ever see or expect to see." Although the men of the 121st used "thin shelter tents over their heads . . . and one blanket for a covering," the lack of effective shelter and the exposure to the elements crippled the regiment. Beckwith found the situation unbearable: "I believe . . . the camping on the flats at Belle Plain Landing was the cause of the breaking down of a great many men. The misery of it is beyond description."[22]

Belle Plain ruined the health of numerous men. The "fearful night" seared the memory of Capt. Douglas Campbell. Many survived only through individual efforts at providing shelter and warmth by scrounging for fagots, wet and green twigs and branches, and anything flammable, and "the ice froze thick enough to bear a horse." Campbell was forty-eight years old. Within months, he would receive a discharge, diagnosed with "synovia" of the right knee. He contracted malaria at Belle Plain and finally mustered out April 27, 1863.[23]

John Lovejoy remembered the "terrible march through a cold drenching rain." He described the "open plain without shelter" and the water-filled "hollows" in the ground that soldiers tried to sleep in to avoid the fierce winds; they then froze to the ground. Old rails and wet firewood, some found 2 miles away, were added to any fires that were already started. The cold and the fear of freezing to death during the night made sleep impossible. Upton gave up his bed to a sick junior officer and tried to sleep on the ground. The next morning, coats and blankets were "frozen stiff as a rail," and many of the boys "looked like the last rose of summer." After two nights under these conditions, Upton finally received permission to move the regiment to higher, wooded ground—"dense cedar and a high ridge"—protected from the wind. He told his sister in a letter that day, "I like the regiment very much. The men know that they will be taken care of, and they are quite contented." John Ingraham agreed: "He [Upton] said he would not kill his men in that way. He is a man every inch of him."[24]

The extreme weather caused the tragic deaths of two Cooperstown men, father and son. Nineteen-year-old Robert Campbell "Cammy" Wood had joined Company E as a corporal in August with other young men from Otsego. He was the only son of Jerome and Martha Wood and a student at Cooperstown Seminary. An unassuming boy, Wood possessed a "gentle and modest nature" and was "one of the last" one would consider a soldier. He enlisted against the wishes of his parents, who worried that his youth and "frail constitution" would betray him. An active correspondent, Cammy described the horrors of the Antietam battlefield, which sickened him. In December, at Belle Plain, less than four months into the field, he fell ill with typhoid. His father, an employee of the *Otsego Republican,* rushed to his side in a hospital in Washington "through the kind offices of Judge Turner," Cooperstown's "own" sitting assistant judge advocate. Jerome Wood reached his son before he died on New Year's Day 1863.

James Cronkite brought the news from Washington to the regiment and Company E that Campbell had died. From a box of food and clothing intended for young Campbell, Cronkite retrieved a pair of boots for the dead soldier to wear home, but Jerome Wood arranged for the transportation of his son's body.

He "watched faithfully over [his son] until he closed his eyes in death, and brought his remains to Fort Plain," north of Cooperstown. Once he arrived back in the Empire State, Jerome fell ill with typhoid and died in his brother's home two weeks after his son had passed away. His wife buried both her husband and son in Lakewood Cemetery in Cooperstown. The troops in the field read of Jerome's death in the *Otsego Republican*. "Poor Mrs. Wood," lamented Henry Walker, "how heavily afflicted . . . I trust that God will give her grace to bear up under this double affliction as he did for the first."[25]

The raw experiences at Belle Plain were indirectly responsible for other deaths. Almost certainly, Pvt. Stephen T. Austin, a Frankfort native in Company D, succumbed to exposure on the cold, open plain. During that ordeal, he had described how the men banded together, fixed their bayonets, and plunged them into the freezing ground. They affixed their tent canvases to the inverted muskets and crawled into the makeshift shelters to lie in the mud and snow all night long. In the morning, he found himself literally frozen to the mud. Austin reported that he caught a cold and "felt like an old man for a good while." The New Year found him in Finley Hospital in Washington. Nearly a year to the day after the 121st's arrival in the nation's capital, Austin succumbed to typhoid fever on September 2, 1863—in Washington.[26]

Miraculously, many survived the few days at Belle Plain and eventually recovered enough to engage in simple duties such as repairing roads and unloading boats. Beckwith made it through a cold and damp night and the next morning was down at the river on the landing where Union supply boats unloaded provisions on waiting mule trains. With "diplomacy" and cash, he secured a supply of "substantial food" and hard liquor to wash it down. He obtained the latter from the Depot Commissary. Beckwith wrote that he gave the functionary who provided him the goods a "Captain's receipt for the articles furnished, which I regret very much to say the Captain has never seen." The salubrious effect of the spirits and the provisions on his company mates caused some "to clean up the forest." A member of Company B reported to the doctor the next morning that he was crazy and that he "never knew one of his father's family to be crazy before." Beckwith reported that the ailing soldier received a dose of quinine and whiskey "to prevent a recurrence of the attack."

Captain Kidder, it seems, enjoyed the same "medicine." George Teel, his tent mate, reported that "on Saturday night the ground froze six inches deep and we lay in our tents and suffered everything but death. On Sunday morning Captain Kidder got tight as a brick; he is a fine specimen of an officer." Teel became a victim of the extreme exposure during the army's stay at Belle Plain and the hard marching to and from Fredericksburg. He lay on the ground in the regimental hospital for a week and got very "poor care," during which time he counted eight victims of typhoid. Before he transferred to Ward P at Harewood Hospital in Washington, two more men died, and "one was dead over one hour before the nurses knew anything of it." William Remmel commented on the prevalent sickness that the regiment could not shake and observed that "many of our brave boys are fast going to their long homes." Fred Ford blamed inactivity for whatever health problems the 121st suffered and offered his advice: "If the leaders wish to save the army, as well as the unity of the states, they will let us take Richmond this winter." On December 10, 1862, the regiment, with three days of rations and sixty rounds of cartridges for each man, left Belle Plain and began the march on a corduroy road toward Fredericksburg. The day before, Egbert Olcott had predicted "that the 121st would be in a fight in less than six days."[27]

The March to Fredericksburg

For the first two weeks of December, as the 121st made its way to Fredericksburg, Burnside delayed until his pontoons and most of his army was in position. The battle of Fredericksburg would be fought in a river valley with high hills on either side. At the point of the river where Fredericksburg itself was situated, the river ran north and south instead of following its overall east-west orientation. On the southwestern side of the river, Fredericksburg sat in the valley with Stafford Heights across the river as the eastern wall and Spotsylvania Heights toward the west. The latter ran behind the town from a point just across the river from Falmouth to a few miles south of Fredericksburg. Marye's Heights was a spur off the more impressive Spotsylvania Heights. South of the town were river flatlands that reminded Corporal Beckwith of home: "The flats on each side of the river are much alike, and about the width as those at Ilion and Frankfurt."

At the point of the 121st's attack, the river widened to 400 feet. The open plain, with its exposed position and the city of Fredericksburg below a fortified hill, presented a huge military challenge. Burnside's plan consisted of throwing as many well-armed troops as possible at the rebels. One recent authority on battle tactics has called it "a tactical nightmare" and "ill defined": "It called for attacking across a river, in part through a town, uphill to steep ground on which Confederates posted artillery and could fire down onto the attackers." This was the first battle plan of the war "that would have cut right through a town. It would have been an illogical plan even if carried out with great skill." Below Fredericksburg on the southwestern side of the river were two parallel, significant creeks that played a part in the battle, Hazel Run and Deep Run. On Stafford Heights, on the eastern bank, the Union army assembled during the weeks preceding the battle.[28]

Burnside's reorganized army on Stafford Heights faced west toward the Rappahannock and Fredericksburg across the river. The Right Grand Division, with the Second Corps and Ninth Corps, were northernmost and directly opposite the city. The Center Grand Division, composed of the Fifth Corps and the Third Corps, occupied the line farther south, held a reserve position behind Sumner, and extended somewhat south of the city toward the lower pontoon crossing. It connected with the Left Grand Division, composed of the First Corps and Sixth Corps—the farthest south in the alignment—near the lower crossing point.

Burnside's strategy called for the Right Grand Division to attack the town of Fredericksburg. Elements of its two corps, the Second and Ninth, were to secure the upper and middle pontoon crossings, respectively. Burnside ordered the Left Grand Division to attack Jackson on Lee's right, west and south of the town. The troops south of town (which included the 121st)—positioned above George Meade's and John Gibbon's divisions—were there to cover any retreat by the troops attacking the town farther up and down the river. The pontoons at Franklin's Crossing were vital should the attack to the north by the two grand divisions on Marye's Heights fail and should Meade's and Gibbon's attacks to the south fail. The 121st, with its brigade and division, acted as a blocking device or safety valve—an insurance policy giving pause to Stonewall Jackson and John Bell Hood on the ridge above.

By December 10, troops in both armies were in readiness—unfortunately for Burnside—on both sides of the river. At daybreak on December 11, with the Left Grand Division, Sixth Corps, 1st Division, 2nd Brigade, the men of the 121st struck their tents, crossed the bridges, and moved into the open field below the city. "It was a splendid sight to see 75,000 men in motion," enthused Edward Wales in Company G. When the order came to strike the tents, "the largest body of men or horses you ever thought of seeing" began to move as one down to the river, where artillery played "smartly on the Rebs," Adelbert Reed wrote. Isaac Best remembered the bridges and the water covered with playing cards as the troops crossed. "It was evident to all that a bloody battle was to be fought and few men wanted to go to certain death with gambling devices in their pockets."[29]

Artillery covered the advance as the 121st crossed the river. "The picture presented by the bursting of those deadly missiles . . . in connection with the light of the burning city of Fredericksburg, presented a scene that was grand to behold, but awful to contemplate," Reuben Holmes of Company B declared. The 121st would cross the Rappahannock four times: twice on December 11, once again on December 12, and finally in retreat on December 15. After the men had taken some supper and bedded down for the night on December 11 in the flats south of the city, Upton appeared with orders to return back across the river. Officers roused the regiment, telling the men to remain quiet and "fall in with everything on." The regiment "marched on a dog trot back across the river." No one understood the quick retreat. Cassius Delavan commented: "The reason for our coming back I do not know."

The troops on the left flank, ahead of the right wing, became choice targets for rebel sharpshooters in and above Fredericksburg, who laid a heavy fire on the pontoon builders across the river, opposite the city. Union batteries could not cross the river in support of the advancing infantry. As the 121st spent December 11 on the east side of the river, Union artillery on Stafford Heights pounded the town in an attempt to dislodge the sharpshooters but with little success, since the "heavy guns of the reserve artillery could not make the same impression on masonry walls that the field batteries had produced on thicket and hut." The next morning, December 12, the 121st recrossed the river a mile and a half downstream at the lower bridges at Franklin's Crossing. Burnside remained unsure what to do, and the 121st was one of the units to suffer from his lack of planning.[30]

Approximately a mile behind Fredericksburg, Lee took advantage of Burnside's delay by entrenching on the heights behind the town. He occupied a strategic position on the high ground, with the river on his left and right. Lee brought his forces to bear when he became convinced that Burnside planned to commit troops to a frontal assault on his position on the higher ground. Longstreet's corps of five divisions sat on the Confederate left (north), and Jackson's corps of four divisions was farther south on the right. Below Jackson, James Ewell Brown "Jeb" Stuart's cavalry protected Lee's right flank.

The 121st, with Franklin's Left Grand Division, crossed the river the final time and positioned itself with Col. Henry L. Cake's brigade in a small valley or gully through which Deep Run formed a U. It nearly touched the Bowling Green Road, also known as the Old Richmond Road. Ahead of them, Brig. Gen. David A. Russell's brigade took advanced positions, and behind them, Alfred T. A. Torbert brought up the rear. Their brigade consisted of the 5th Maine, the 16th New York, the 27th New York, and the 96th Pennsylvania. The brigade lay in the Old Richmond Road, clinging to the cover provided by the banks of Deep Run throughout the night of December 12.

The Battle Is Joined

The next morning, December 13, the 121st prepared breakfast prior to resuming picket duty. The fog that morning blanketed the lowlands as it had the day before. Nineteen-year-old Levi Doxtater in Company B went off to fill his and his companion's canteens in the cold creek. Urged by his older brother, Jerome, to "hurry up," Levi replied that it was unnecessary to hurry because he was going to get killed anyway. Before the men were able to brew coffee, the orders changed, and the 121st moved forward under cover of the Deep Run gully in order to replace the advanced skirmish lines established by the 15th New Jersey. Scrambling out of their makeshift camp, they followed the creek for "a considerable distance" until they reached an open field. Under the fog, the Union troops to the 121st's left prepared to assault Jackson's corps.[31]

Burnside ordered the Left Grand Division to attack Jackson's men on the heights first. Rebel artillery zeroed in on the advancing federal troops under Generals Meade and Gibbon. The 121st and the rest of the brigade, a little to the north and right of the main attacking force of Meade's and Gibbon's men, were on the receiving end of the fire. Federal 12-pound Napoleons were called in to respond, and in order to make way for the caissons and guns, the 121st moved out of the road. "The battery swung into position in front [of them] on the highest part of the rising ground immediately before [them]," where they were unlimbered and began returning fire. "To this the enemy replied with equal vigor." Clinging to the ditch at roadside, the 121st watched the interchange of batteries firing at each other and performed nothing more glamorous than intermittent skirmishing and some picket duty throughout the remainder of the long day.

Beckwith told of each shell's distinct sound—notes and tones "and none of them could be called musical. Some fiendishly seemed to say 'I've got you, I've got you.'" No sooner had the barrage begun than Edward Spicer, an eighteen-year-old private in Company B, became the 121st's first battle casualty. He had enlisted with Dennis Dewey from Plainfield, in the valley of Unadilla Forks. Spicer, one of the tallest boys in the regiment, earned the position in the first file as head of the company. As the men hugged the ground, Company B's commanding officer, Captain Holcomb, called Dewey over, saying that Spicer had been killed. A fragment from a shell that fell behind the prone men of the regiment had struck him in the back of the head, killing him instantly. Spicer never knew what hit him. Dewey gathered his friend's personal belongings to send them home to his family.

On the same day, in a hospital in Hagerstown, Maryland, Edward's brother Oscar, also a private in the same company, died from diphtheria. The brothers were from Plainfield, Otsego County. They had joined the army on the same day, August 1, 1862, and were mustered in together in Company B. During a lull in the rebel artillery barrage and within a half hour of Edward Spicer's death, the men of the regiment buried him. Wrapping him in his blanket, they laid him in a shallow grave and gave him a Christian burial under a cedar tree in a quiet nearby grove. The chaplain said a few words, but the Confederate artillery found the burial party in range of their guns and cut short the ceremony. Much later, before the regiment retreated back across the river, Spicer's comrades found time to carve his name in the tree and then into a wood plank that became his head marker. As Dewey later remembered, "The prayer ended when it was scarcely begun" but "there was more love and loyalty in that pine board than goes with many a costly shaft of marble or granite."

In Company E, Fernando Hubbell, from Middlefield, was hit in the right arm with a bullet that also grazed Elijah H. Hawley, a third sergeant in a hole next to him. Hawley jumped to Hubbell's aid, tied a handkerchief around his arm, and rushed him to the rear, dodging bullets all the way. Hubbell lost his arm to a surgeon in the rear. Hawley meanwhile returned to his cover and "waited patiently" for the sharpshooter taking aim at him, and when the man raised his head again, Hawley fired with deadly accuracy. Charles Compton's canteen took a direct hit. Another member of Company E became enraged when a rebel sharpshooter grazed his neck with a shot. "He jumped up and fired and the same time said, 'take that you son of a bitch.' I think he hit his man," Hawley deadpanned.[32]

Longstreet recognized that the first assault would be on Jackson's corps, not his. He took comfort in his impregnable position on the high ground above the river. As the fog lifted around 10 A.M., the elements took "a hand in the drama about to be enacted, the warmth of the sun brushed the mist away and revealed the mighty panorama below [the Confederate lines]." Franklin's 65,000 men were there. Longstreet recorded that "the flags of the Federals fluttered gaily, the polished arms shone brightly in the sunlight, and the beautiful uniforms of the buoyant troops gave to the scene the air of a holiday occasion rather than the spectacle of a great army about to be thrown into the tumult of battle." Longstreet could see "almost every soldier Franklin had, and a splendid array it was."[33]

In the clear air, the men of the 121st could make out, in the distance, small white puffs of smoke coming from a rail fence, followed by the sounds of whizzing bullets. They had heard the distant sounds of battle at Crampton's Gap and Antietam, but they had never experienced a direct assaulting fire. The battle of Fredericksburg began in earnest and turned deadly immediately. To the north, the Center Grand Division and the Right Grand Division began assaulting Marye's Heights. The 121st waited on the right of the Left Grand Division. Jackson's troops, in the woods at the crest of the hill in a commanding position, began shelling both of the Left Grand Division's flanks, and most of the men of the 121st expected an attack at any moment. Directly opposing them was Maj. Gen. John B. Hood.

As small bits of dirt kicked up on all sides, Corporal Beckwith found his tin plate in his haversack and began to dig a hole for shelter. Ingraham Smith remembered the bullets coming over the troops' heads "like hail. We hugged the ground close for a spell. Mostly they had some sharp shooters that picked at us once in a while and towards night they hollered at us to stop firing 'you damned rascals.'" On Beckwith's right were Levi Doxtater and twenty-seven-year-old Cpl. Asabel Davis. A Confederate marksman shot Doxtater through the head. He died instantly without uttering a sound. Davis was also killed outright. Doxtater's brother, Jerome, standing next to him, received a minor flesh wound. Jerome buried his brother next to Edward Spicer along the Bowling Green Road and marked the spot with a board. (Four Doxtater sons and their father served in the Union army at the same time.) In Company G, eighteen-year-old Jabez Willson of Roseboom, Otsego County, also died violently, shot in the neck. Three others were shot accidentally either by themselves or by their comrades. Beckwith was slightly wounded in the arm.[34]

Upton "leisurely" rode the line, exposing himself to the enemy's fire but showing "no concern or fear." At his encouragement, the regiment returned fire. Beckwith and Benny West kept firing at the puffs of smoke from the edge of the timber on the crest above them. Beckwith remembered that a man from the brigade, within earshot of his position, "breathing through the blood that was fast choking him to death, made an awful sound." Each man began to wonder how long the shelling and firing would last, if he would have to charge across the open field, if others were in a similarly bad situation, and if any of them would survive. Beckwith, West, Charley Carmody, and Joey Warmoth were all in their teens (Beckwith had just turned seventeen), yet here they were "doing men's work, and doing it well."

The high-profile action occurred to their right. Wave after wave of Union troops in the Center Grand Division and the Right Grand Division assaulted Marye's Heights as the 121st remained pinned down south of the town. Confederate troops on the hills behind Fredericksburg, in the sunken lane, and on Marye's Heights poured deadly fire into each succeeding line of federal troops attempting to take the entrenched positions. Burnside threw thirteen separate assaults at the heights where the Confederates were four deep and firing directly into the approaching Union lines. Behind the Confederate infantrymen, a line of artillery added punishing fire on the advancing troops. No bluecoat got within 25 yards of the wall at the top.

For the remainder of the day, December 13, the men of the 121st hugged the ground, protecting themselves from the Confederate fire on the ridgeline above. Advance or retreat meant certain death. The men remained inactive, awaiting further orders. A small detail of twenty men managed to slip over an open plain between their position and the river to reach the pontoons, cross the water, and retrieve rations from the baggage trains. The men quickly became easy targets for the rebels, but they managed the maneuver without incident or injury. Had the Union artillery not arrived and drawn the attention and fire from the Confederate batteries on the heights, the 121st probably would not have incurred any casualties that day. That night, the men of the 121st slept on their weapons.[35]

Burnside finally gave up after dark. Over the next two days, December 14 and 15, he continued to agonize over what action to take next. Most bets in the regiment were on another day of fighting; Burnside tried but the battle was over. At midnight, the officers were told to get their "men up as quick as possible and with as little noise as possible." At 1:00 on Sunday morning, December 15, the 121st began to retreat across the river. At dawn, the Confederates probed the Union lines and found an empty field. Burnside had decided to withdraw, and he skillfully pulled his entire command with its "grand divisions" back across the Rappahannock. But his troops had suffered more than 12,600 casualties, many of the dead lying on the hillside below the Sunken Road and above Fredericksburg. With the withdrawal of the pontoon boats and bridges, Burnside conceded defeat. That day, under a flag of truce, both sides recovered and buried their dead.

John Kidder knew he had been in the thick of the fight, but he had no way of knowing at the time the extent of the fighting and of the losses. A week later, Sheriff Mather recorded in his diary: "Received a letter from Emmet and Elias, they were well." Frank Carran's younger brother, Tommy, articulated from afar his youthful enthusiasm for a battle experienced by his brother. He wished that he could be there with his brother, "fighting for his country." He asked Frank how it felt to cross the Rappahannock into Fredericksburg. "Didn't you feel as though you were in danger or did you march right through after them old raskels and send them a messenger or a chunk of cold lead after them?"[36]

Chaplain Sage was proud of the regiment and its young West Point commander. The regiment had experienced real fire for the first time, and the "boys behaved splendidly," with no cowardice. Sage confessed that he was incapable of effusive praise; he allowed that the men and officers were "made of the right stuff" and that Emory Upton was "one of the noblest, truest and bravest Colonels who grace the service of the United States." His "temperate" behavior in all things drew chaplains and Isaac Best to Upton. Sage feared, as did others of the regiment, that their unit would lose Upton to a higher rank. Sage observed "to the friends of the 121st Reg't. . . . he is young yet, but richly deserves a star."[37]

After the battle, Upton returned to his "by the book" military training. Although his men had made him proud in their first ordeal under fire, he did not relent as a disciplinarian. Immediately after the battle, as the army licked its wounds, Upton reprimanded and punished two corporals and four privates for an unnamed offense before the battle, probably malingering. He threatened them with the death penalty, but he attributed their crime to "want of experience" and "inflicted" a far less severe penalty with the hope that they had learned their lessons. Cpl. Michael Hartford and Cpl. William Thornton from Company B were reduced to the ranks and, along with the four privates from Company D, were given extra guard duty for thirty days.[38]

No one, from President Lincoln down to the lowest private, thought that the Army of the Potomac did well that day. Burnside nearly lost his force with his insistence on repeated piecemeal assaults against a heavily armed and entrenched enemy across an open field. The 121st escaped the horror of the battle, given its role as a covering force. The older regiments praised the men of the 121st "for their coolness under fire." (Many of the old-timers had bet that the 121st would not last longer than two hours on picket duty.) For his part, Emory Upton minced no words. "We have subsided into perfect quietude since the recent battle of Fredericksburg," he told his sister. "I can hardly bear to think of it. We have been defeated so often when it was not the fault of the brave soldiers, that I am losing patience." Upton warmed to his topic: "There is imbecility somewhere, but it does not do to breathe it. Our defeats emanated from Washington." If it were not for certain generals, "the courage of our troops would surmount the obstacles the rebels oppose to our march."

Upton longed to describe just one victory or to witness that one general who would rise up to "lead us to great deeds. No army ever entered the field like this—brave; one victory would make it enthusiastic; two formidable; three irresistible." He lamented the lack of "great generalship displayed on our side. It is astonishing and depressing [to] one's spirits to know and feel this." He thought of his men with only thin tents and blankets for protection from the elements— "How they keep warm is a mystery—they say they do not suffer." At first, Sam Kelley thought that the federal army succeeded, but after a few days' reflection, he characterized Fredericksburg as a "regular *back down*, the plans our generals had in view were like . . . perpetual motion, they could not get them to work."[39]

6

Burnside, Mud, and Hooker

Yesterday, each one of the regiment had a red cross put on the crown of his cap.

John Hartwell, Company C, April 15, 1863

The Mud March

After the debacle at Fredericksburg and a week before Christmas, the 121st found itself east of the town in the vicinity of Belle Plain at White Oak Church, among giant, age-old oak trees. There, the regiment prepared for winter quarters. The church resembled a great, dilapidated barn. Boards along the walls as high as a man's reach had been scavenged for use elsewhere as building supplies or firewood. Troops and horses were housed in the former slaves' quarters. The regiment encamped 4 miles from Fredericksburg, planning to stay in relatively comfortable, semipermanent, log-reinforced shelters until spring. Emory Upton determined that it would be best to quarter his troops at the edge of the woods in order to drill in the open fields beyond.

Immediately after the battle of Fredericksburg, Lt. Francis W. Morse prepared to join the regiment. A native of Cherry Valley, he was the son of one-term congressman Oliver Andrew Morse and the grandson of Judge James O. Morse, founder of the Alpha Delta Phi fraternity. His neighbors were the Campbells and the Olcotts. Governor Morgan gave him his commission in Albany on December 15, 1862, with orders to report to the 121st's headquarters. With no prior military experience, a short time at West Point served him well in his relations with his new regimental commander. (He never explained in his memoirs why he left West Point, nor did he even acknowledge that he had attended the academy.) Like the Campbells and the Olcotts, he enjoyed the privilege of being a member of one of the first families of the small village. His grandfather was the cousin of Samuel F. B. Morse, telegraph inventor and painter of upstate dignitaries, many from Cooperstown.[1]

The day after receiving his commission, December 16, he returned home, put his affairs in order, said his good-byes, and prepared to set out later in the week for Washington via New York City, arriving there on Sunday, December 23. The next morning, he applied to the provost marshal's office for a one-day pass to the front, which he received from a "very pompous little lieutenant." Unfortunately, that evening, a porter mishandled his baggage and switched it with that of a minister. By the next morning, Morse's bags were located, but by then, his pass had expired. Morse groveled before the same lieutenant the following day for an extension, which he received with the gratuitous suggestion that it would be wise to travel to the front that same day. He complied, and on Wednesday morning, he sailed down the Potomac in a "rotten transport."[2]

Disembarking at Aquia Creek, Morse discovered that his recently retrieved baggage was not on board and had mistakenly been sent to Baltimore. With no time to deal with the lost luggage, he barely caught the train to Falmouth. On boarding the train, he settled himself on a bale of hay for the two-and-a-half-hour ride covering 15 miles. Leaving the train, Morse asked directions to the 121st, and as darkness fell, he embarked on a 4-mile walk to White Oak Church. A staff member of Brig. Gen. John Newton's 3rd Division, of the Sixth Corps, offered him shelter for the night—Christmas Eve—which he welcomed. On Christmas morning, he shared his first meal in the field with Newton's staff; they also provided him a horse and an orderly, and within an hour, he reported to Emory Upton. Upton received him with "military courtesy" and assigned him as a second officer to the company of his choice. His new home in Company G was comfortable, but his situation "was dubious." "No clothes, cold weather, miserable tent, and little to eat. The romance of a soldier's life vanished," he wrote years later.

His first assignment for the next two days dealt with picket relief on the Rappahannock and gave him his first view of rebel soldiers. In the afternoon of December 27, Upton summoned Morse to his tent and asked him to act as adjutant for the evening's dress parade. Though he did so with trepidation, Morse performed his duties so well that when the parade ended, Upton told him that he would recommend to Governor Morgan that Morse be appointed to the vacant adjutancy. All this happened to the eighteen-year-old within a mere fifteen days of his enlistment and just one week in the army! Morse's elation evaporated, however, as he returned to his tent to discover orders from Secretary of War Stanton dismissing him from the service for being in Washington without a pass. The pompous lieutenant had done him in.

Upton moved immediately to set the record straight. Armed with a letter to the Adjutant General, Brig. Gen. Lorenzo Thomas, and endorsed by

Generals Joseph Bartlett, William Brooks, John Sedgwick, and William Franklin, Morse appealed to Levi C. Turner to intercede with Stanton on his behalf, and before long, Stanton relented and reinstated him. Politics and cronyism thus allowed Morse the liberty to choose his own regiment already in the field and to benefit from Levi Turner's help in clearing up the "misunderstanding." Clearly, having friends in high places in Albany and Washington did not hurt certain members of the 121st.

The time for the army to go into winter quarters arrived, but Burnside, smarting from the ignominious defeat at Fredericksburg and wishing to redeem himself, had other ideas. He would attack Lee again when he least expected it—during the winter and within the month. Both armies spent Christmas Day in as traditional an observance as possible under the conditions. Across the Rappahannock, the Confederate troops were celebrating with "men cheering, bands playing and guns firing." Some of the men of the 121st spent the day on picket duty but were rewarded with a "good dinner" when they returned to camp.

The day after Christmas, Burnside issued orders to attack Fredericksburg again. Lincoln vetoed his plans because he lacked adequate information about them, which made him uncomfortable. Burnside, however, persisted. In January, the weather began in a benign manner, being generally cold and clear. The roads remained passable when frozen, but during thaws, mud became "king" due to sporadic downpours. Meanwhile, the 121st settled in comfortably for the winter. Officers moved into cabinlike shelters, with walls of logs and tent material for roofs and dirt banked against the walls on the outside to fend off the cold winds. Some built makeshift fireplaces and found wood to burn. The weather "was not cold enough to wear an overcoat much of the time," and Upton required drills every day.[3]

Although the fighting had temporarily ceased, disease continued to take its toll. Alonzo "Lonnie" Coon, of Company B, died in the camp of the 149th Pennsylvania from "hardship, exposure, and homesickness." Lonnie, a sickly boy, had never "slept outside the parental roof until he went to be a soldier." From all indications, he exhibited signs of clinical depression. According to his comrades, a trip to the hospital proved useless because the doctors were unable to find any physical ailment behind his complaints. Chaplain Sage on several occasions carried his gun for him and tried to cheer him. He observed Lonnie on the march, with "lagging step and pleading look, the very picture of homesickness and despondency, to which he fell victim." He would stagger into camp, "drop down at the first fire he came to, put his elbows on his knees, pull his cap over his eyes, and crouch over the fire until roused by some comrade from his lethargy." One day, he simply did not show up. He fell out on the march to the Rappahannock and wandered about "in a state of mental derangement," unable to find his regiment. He strayed into the 149th Pennsylvania's camp.

The next day, a man from the 149th went to the 121st and reported that one of their men had drifted into his camp and lain down by the fire; they discovered him the next morning lying unconscious on the ground. They put him on a makeshift bed and called for a doctor, but he died a few hours later. Led by Chaplain Sage, the men of Coon's company walked 2 miles to the 149th camp, and "there under a solitary pine, on a beautiful knoll . . . gave him a Christian burial." Later, his father came to claim his body. When his comrades disinterred his body, "he looked as fresh as when he was buried," although the blanket used to bury him had left an imprint of its texture on his skin. Sage wondered if the loneliness and disease were taking a larger toll on the men than battle: "I have come to dread disease far more than bullets of the enemy," he said. The *Cherry Valley Gazette,* reporting the death of Oliver Ottman of Company G from Roseboom, plainly and simply blamed "dumb generals and politicians."[4]

The Confederate army remained in Fredericksburg, and Burnside remained determined to drive it out. Accordingly, he devised a simple plan that called for Hooker and Franklin to march west along the Rappahannock's north bank, cross the river, and attack Lee above Fredericksburg. A week earlier, John Kidder had gotten wind of a plan to reinforce the roads with logs—to "corduroy" them for easier movement of troops, livestock, and equipment. Kidder took charge of a large detail that included men from both his own company and a New Jersey company. He guessed that Burnside intended to move across the river. On January 15, all units were placed on alert, with the men ordered to draw nine days of rations and sixty rounds of cartridges and be ready to march the next morning. Four days later, on January 19, Burnside issued his orders early in the morning, and the troops broke camp.[5]

When Francis Morse arrived at Falmouth on returning from his successful sojourn in Washington, he found his regiment and the entire army gone. "I looked where the army was, and, like the Irishman's flea, it was not there. I saw the end of an immense army train disappearing on a distant hill, and was told that the whole army moved at day-break on that day, and it was, of course, at that late hour in the afternoon, many miles away."

As the Army of the Potomac began its latest move, the rains came. Morse started out on foot, and for the next four hours, through downpours, more mud, and extreme discomfort, he cursed the pompous lieutenant in Washington—the source of all his troubles. At first, the rains were a nuisance. They quickly became an annoyance, and eventually, the muddy goo became a life-threatening hazard. Morse found the Sixth Corps, and thanks to a kindly quartermaster, he climbed under a stalled wagon, pulled his cape over his head, and went to sleep in the mud. Soon, pontoons, caissons, ammunition wagons, mules, horses, and men became mired in the mud. The men of the 121st "could distinctly see the rebs on the opposite bank of the river" huddled around their fires as they watched and mocked the Grand Army.

Jonathon R. Sage, chaplain. Detested by his men, Sage resigned during the war and became a weatherman in Iowa after the war. From Isaac O. Best, *History of the 121st.*

The next morning, after enduring a night of torrential rain without shelter, the men of the 121st tried to cook breakfast but were stopped from doing so by their officers, which angered most of them. They had awakened lying in 1 to 2 inches of water, and they crossed the Aquia Creek Railroad about 3 miles below Falmouth on empty stomachs. The rains came in torrents, and the mud, 6 to 24 inches deep, became thick enough for a soldier to sink in up to his knees. They followed the pike that paralleled the river, encamped, and pitched their tents in the rain. "That night was a sleepless night to many a weary soldier," Carran reported, "for the storm which had been raging for the 24 hours previous had not yet ceased nor could there be seen the slightest evidence of its cessation." Henry Galpin characterized the mud that they encountered the next morning as "a foe more to be dreaded than the grey backs." After three days without shelter and in the rain and the mud, Burnside reversed himself and ordered everyone back to camp.[6]

Morse caught up with the 121st at Banks' Ford on the river. He found Upton, who, with his fellow commanding officers, pronounced the cause hopeless: it would be impossible to cross the river during the torrential downpour. They ordered a general pullback. The 121st, part of the rearguard action tasked to deter any attack from the rebel army, ensured that horses, mules, and equipment returned to camp in serviceable condition. Briefly, Upton placed two companies, A and F, on the river as pickets as the regiment began retreating. When the entire army began to move back to its former position, the men of the two companies halted, stacked arms, unslung knapsacks, and were ordered to "play horse," dragging the pontoons out of the mud. The boats were still on wagons, and the men of the 121st, along with sixteen mules, pulled the boats onto higher and supposedly drier ground. The pontoons were now as useful as if they were back in the Washington Naval Yard "or had never been built." Carran saw four and six teams hitched to one wagon and still no movement. Fifty to a hundred men with ropes in addition to mule and horse teams worked to free man and beast from the mud. The artillery found it impossible to move. In one incident, Carran saw nine teams try to move one artillery wagon. Eventually, supply wagons, ammunition wagons, and whole wagon trains were pulled along until they reached the corduroy roads Kidder and his detail had built for the original march.

Fatigue mounted, and tempers flared. Adelbert Reed tried to explain the mud: "The old soldiers say they never saw its equal, not even on the Peninsula." Commissary liquor, mud, and still more rain combined to turn the entire affair into a slapstick comedy, which the men of the 121st began to enjoy. They all realized the preposterous spectacle the Army of the Potomac made stuck in the mud. James Cronkite wrote that "the distribution of a barrel of 'commissary' to each regiment" rescued the army trains and artillery from the mud. William Remmel, bowing to his strict Germanic upbringing, confessed to his father two months later that he indeed had "taken liquor" because he determined it was "beneficial" as the army "returned from the Rappahannock after marching through mud knee deep all day. This is the only time I ever drank in the army." Daniel Holt agreed about the benefits of the liquor: "If no worse use is ever made of liquor than this, surely the cause of temperance has no reason to complain."[7]

The army returned to where it had begun a few days earlier. The soldiers had mixed reactions: most were glad to be back in a warmer and drier atmosphere, but others were incensed at what they just experienced. "We are stuck in the mud and it is growing worse instead of better all the time," Jonathon Burrell grumbled. He told his brother that "the capper was when we was on our last march to the river and return that was the hardest time that I ever saw . . . I thought I had seen mud at home but I am now satisfied that I never did." Ever the optimist, he added, "But I believe if we had had good weather we would have cleaned the Rebs off them hills about Fredericksburg . . . the whole army seemed determined to fight to the last and I know that the 121st would have fought good." Echoing Beckwith's earlier Darwinian theory of the survival of the fittest, he admitted they were down to 600 fighting men—but all of the "puny ones and sneaks were all gone."

On a large old door taken from one of the homes in Fredericksburg or the surrounding countryside, an energetic rebel painted an inscription large enough to be read across the river by the mud-encrusted federals; it read: "Burnside Stuck in the Mud." The sign proved to be the ultimate insult to all the men in Burnside's army who were trying to execute an ill-conceived campaign. Carran proclaimed that the Sixth Corps saved the day: "You may say that Brook's Division pulled Burnside out of the mud."[8]

Everyone described the march as a nightmare. Just before beginning the march, some of the soldiers, including Frank Carran, had received a box of food and other creature comforts from home. Carran, like most of the boys, was not about to waste free food, especially if it came from home. He estimated that the latest box weighed about 70 pounds, and rather than leave its contents behind, the men stuffed every available knapsack and haversack with the bounty. When the strategy proved too cumbersome, they decided to eat as much of the food as possible. The pies were the most sought after—and they eventually did the most damage. Carran got "as sick as I have been since I joined the army" with a severe case of diarrhea. As he explained, they could not carry all the pies, "and being naturally stingy, we ate them down and the consequences, were what I stated above."

Henry Galpin summed up Burnside's folly: "This moving an army in the mud, you know nothing of it at the north, only those who have made the attempt can form any correct idea."[9] But Galpin did not blame Burnside for the Mud March. Instead, his forgiving nature blamed his commander's failure on the elements. Burnside's subordinates, however, were in open rebellion, which placed his very career in jeopardy. Lieutenant Burrell felt that if the politicians in Washington did not do *something* and do it immediately, "we are goners. We might as well lay down our arms and tell them [the Confederates] to make the terms." He had no answer to the government's dilemma and what it would take to win a battle "that is of any account." He concluded that cutting off all communication with Washington and the politicians there and letting Burnside or McClellan finish the job in the field would bring victory. If they did not win soon, "We are down. And what will become of the Country, God only knows."

John Ingraham tried to remain optimistic, but the latest debacle depressed him. "I must heartily say that I am heartily discouraged and it is enough to make anyone discouraged and the soldiers are all discouraged. They use men here; oh it is wicked to mention it," he told his parents. Henry Galpin expressed equally apprehensive emotions: "The clouds that envelop our country look thick and heavy and I am fearful," he wrote, "that our good old ship of state will not be able to stand the storm that threatens her with destruction." General Franklin concluded that Burnside "was fast losing his mind." Franklin "looked on the rain which stopped [the Mud March]" as "providential interference on our behalf." Finally, on January 26, Lincoln replaced Burnside with Joe

Hooker as commander of the Army of the Potomac. Hooker had lobbied Lincoln for the job; Burnside had crawled and whimpered his way to Washington to complain to the president of his problems with his rebellious subordinates and to reiterate his lack of interest in keeping his position. As Lincoln gave Hooker the command, he admonished him: "Beware of rashness, but with energy, and sleepless vigilance, go forward, and give us victories."[10]

The Army in Disarray

The debacle at Fredericksburg in December and the Mud March in January threw the Army of the Potomac into disarray. The government in Washington could not explain the army's ineptness, and the specter of disaster haunted the troops, down to the individual soldier. The shocking carnage at Fredericksburg as reported by the newspapers demoralized the country. Those who witnessed the outcome of the battle could not understand how the defeat of a well-trained force by an army half its size could have happened. The stature of the great Army of the Potomac was significantly diminished.

Some in the ranks expressed confusion as to what had actually happened at Fredericksburg. Even though he participated in the battle, Fred Ford did not know what went on overall. "Rumors are flying about amongst our troops of our being defeated in the late battles and having to skedaddle," he reported. "There certainly was some severe fighting going on, within our hearing . . . but as to being defeated, I believe nothing of it at present." Chaplain Sage remained optimistic. "I am for the war up to the hilt. We can bring the insurgents to terms," he told an audience back home. He portrayed the battle as "an expensive little trip" but did not regard it "as nearly so disastrous as many." William Remmel, an observant reporter, described the battle as "an awful affair." His pessimistic but realistic assessment admitted defeat. "Notwithstanding the boldness and good fighting we gained nothing and lost much. I trust that the next movement will be carried on with a different leader or different management," he wrote. He deplored the sacrifice "of life . . . for nothing" and the impact it would have on public opinion in the North. Delavan Bates, in Capt. John Kidder's Company I, presented an equally practical assessment to his father: "The repulse at Fredericksburg seems to have thrown such a chill over the anticipations of our leaders so that they do not know what to do next."[11]

Lieutenant Burrell expressed surprise and pleasure in his continued physical health, but he admitted that his spirits were dampened by the defeat. Attempting to put the best light on the battle, he wrote home that it was not as "disastrous as at first represented to tell the thing just as it is." If the regiment had stayed on the other side of the Rappahannock another day, the results would have been much worse, he said—an assessment shared by Pvt. Merton Tanner, of Company E. Tanner wrote his mother that the men were "sick of the war and are longing for a settlement." Laurin Ingalsbe, a private in Company E, spoke for many in the ranks when he wrote his wife that, whether Democrat or Republican, politicians were all the same: the war would be settled only if the politicians came down to the front and listened to the soldiers' complaints. "Although you suffer from the effects of this war, I think your sufferings are not a comparison to that of the poor soldiers," he said. Ingalsbe succumbed to typhoid a month later.[12]

Although the diminished sickness rate minimized "that miserable feeling of down-heartedness," Fred Ford and Henry Walker vented their frustrations during the inactive, cold, and rainy days that followed. Ford admitted that "the good spirits and confidence of the men and indeed of the army . . . have been steadily ebbing ever since the fight and butchery at Fredericksburg." Although morale in the army was very low, it did not match the despair expressed by the army's "friends [up] North." How, he asked, could soldiers "be full of courage" when the writers back home were "totally devoid of back bone?" He blamed upstate New Yorkers' support of Seymour for the 121st's recent setbacks—"spending Indian summer at Harper's Ferry by political generalship, wearied by long marches . . . plunged recklessly against that stone-wall" at Fredericksburg, and finally "settled into the Stafford County mud." Ford's morale reached its low point when he complained bitterly that half of the deserters from the 121st were good soldiers and that they "had the good wishes of the whole regiment, almost without exception. Men here attach no disgrace to desertion." He allowed that his feelings were shared by the "common soldier of the army."[13]

Henry Walker blamed the almighty dollar and those who were being pinched by the war—those back home who had hoped to profit from the war. He viewed them as soft and willing to settle the fight "in any way." His view of the end of the war did not include a cessation of all hostilities and a return to the status quo but a plea to look to the future and the potential that a truly free country could bring. "I sometimes think that half the norths have not got hearts as large as a pin head," he griped. He did not believe that the folks back home really wanted to preserve the Union, and by returning to the prewar conditions, he said they could "share with the south the common miseries which a dishonorable peace would bring."[14]

The carping at command level began almost immediately with Burnside's defeat at the hands of a smaller force. Burnside's generals attacked his proficiency and questioned his effectiveness. Reportedly, Union troops booed him after the battle. The commander of the Left Grand Division, Maj. Gen. William B. Franklin, under whom the 121st served during the battle, had regarded Burnside highly until Fredericksburg, when he "lost all confidence in his ability." He said that Hooker and Sumner felt the same. Joe Hooker, commander of the Center Grand Division, voiced his opinions to anyone who would listen. And for his part, Burnside felt he was ill suited for his position at the head of the army. Reluctantly, Lincoln had gone along with his advisers, Secretary of War Stanton in particular, in nominating Burnside for the job in the first place. And the president had only halfheartedly endorsed Burnside's plan to move south against Fredericksburg and then on to Richmond, thereby scrapping McClellan's original strategy of fighting it out with Lee in the Warrenton area.[15]

In New York, the threat of a statewide and national draft circulated for months, and the threat came closer to reality with each new need for fresh recruits. The new men would not be well received by the two- and three-year veteran volunteers. Jonathon Burrell predicted that the "drafted men will stand a poor show[ing] here among the rest of the army for I think they would not have many favors shown them." He warned his sister to tell her friend "Gordon" that if he received his draft notice, he should hire a substitute "as it would be sure death to a person of his disposition, especially if he was forced into it."[16]

Desertions Continue

The 121st had barely acclimated to the rough life of march and countermarch, death and disease during its first four months in the field when it experienced another period of desertions, low morale, and dissension. The mud, a failed second attempt to mount a military operation, and bitter cold conspired to wreak havoc on morale throughout the entire army. By mid-January, morale and the problems besetting the entire war effort bottomed out. At that time, no fewer than 19 enlisted men and noncommissioned officers deserted from the 121st Regiment within one twenty-four-hour period. Jonathon Burrell stated bluntly: "Our Company is getting pretty small." He counted only 60 muskets for Company A and rations for only 660 men for the entire regiment. Rhetorically, he asked: "Where have they all gone?" He answered: the hospitals, discharges, and "a good many in their graves."

Cherry Valley native John H. Ballard of Company C wrote his brother that his friend from Burlington, Alvy Nichols in Company F, ran away, along with a "great many more out of our regiment." As Ballard put it: "Our men is a running a way and a dying off so fast that we have not got more than four hundred men left." Although he overstated his estimate, he claimed that the regiment was "decreasing prity fast." He thought that the early battle casualties were small in comparison to the number of men who were "left sick and died and runned a way." Henry Galpin complained to his sister Abby that during the night before he wrote her, "three men deserted [from his Company A]; the first that have left the company in that manner since we came out; two deserted from Company H, two from Co. B and 7 from Co. D." "These bounty men," as he called them, were less reliable than the men in his old 44th New York. Any man stealing from the government, he said, ought to be hunted down, arrested, and some ultimately "punished by having a bullet put through [them]." He called those individuals "animals" and "scapegoats." And those back home were just as complicit, in his eyes, when they wrote of the hardships they were enduring and inadvertently encouraged the soldiers to desert so they could return home to help out. "I think more of a rebel," he wrote, "than of that class of persons, for in my opinion they are no worse than the rankest Tory."[17]

By mid-February, 90 men were listed as deserters in the *Herkimer Journal,* and the *Freeman's Journal* reported 90 from the 121st and 60 from the 152nd in mid-March. Company E had the most, 18 men, and Company A the fewest, the 3 Galpin reported. Reuben Holmes, from the all-Herkimer Company B, sarcastically told the editor of the *Herkimer County Journal* that the 121st became "renowned" not for its battlefield prowess but for its desertion and resignation record. The provost marshal in Herkimer County maintained his vigilance for all deserters, especially those who foolishly were still wearing their uniforms. He arrested Benjamin Gifford of Company H at his father's home in German Flats and sent him to jail. Gifford and another soldier had gone into Confederate lines, where they purchased phony parole papers as evidence of their "capture" and release. They walked all the way home from the Rappahannock River camp, except for the last 20 miles when they caught a ride in a wagon. Sheriff Mather arrested a large group of deserters in March and sent them to the military authorities in Albany and Utica.[18]

The administration in Washington recognized the "evil disposed and disloyal persons" who were enticing soldiers to desert and thereby "giving aid and comfort to the enemy." In an attempt to stem desertions, Lincoln proclaimed an amnesty for all soldiers who were absent without leave. The amnesty covered all costs except for the forfeiture of pay and allowances that were incurred during the perpetrator's absence. Lincoln remained firm, however, toward those who chose not to return to their units: they were "cruelly exposing the gallant and faithful soldiers remaining in the ranks to increased hardships and danger" and would still be treated as deserters "and punished as the law provides."

In response to this proclamation, eleven men eventually returned to the 121st: two each to Companies E, F, and I; one man to Company G; and four to Company H. Upton reinstated all without punishment except the forfeiture of pay and allowances, in accordance with the spirit and letter of the amnesty. Benjamin Gifford, one of those from Company H, eventually returned to the 121st under the Lincoln amnesty in 1863 and received an honorable discharge from the regiment two years later. Henry Lewis from Company I, despite John Kidder's offer of a $5 reward to anyone in Laurens who could find him, escaped capture and also returned under the amnesty program. He was later wounded at Spotsylvania and finished the war in a reserve corps.[19]

Pursuing his parallel strategies to deal with the dissension and desertions, Upton employed punitive measures but also appealed to the folks in Herkimer and Otsego counties to help him and his officers maintain a semblance of order and encourage their soldier boys to return to duty. During the severe winter of 1862–1863, he called once again on the residents of Cooperstown to provide simple comforts, particularly blankets, coverlets, sheets, pillows, and ticking, for the troops whether their relations were in the regiment or not. Campbell Wood's father, James, asked readers of the local papers to deliver the goods to Cockett and Marvin's general store for transfer to the front. The ladies of Herkimer and Otsego counties also answered the call, albeit feebly at first. Sometime in March, the regiment received a quantity of mittens that were a large disappointment. Surgeon Holt berated his wife and called them "an insult." The mittens became the laughingstock of the regiment, and the men made "all manner of sport of them," which in a perverse way raised morale through its communal rejection of the shoddy products from the good ladies back home. Rising to his full literary powers, Holt fulminated: "It looks as if they were made out of the seats of worn out satinet breeches, and two year old babies sewed them together." A month later, another batch arrived that the regiment received enthusiastically. "They were all [that] our fancy painted them," Holt said. He called them *"good, first rate, a great improvement of the last lot sent."*[20]

Chaplain Sage sent hometown newspapers lengthy treatises on the evils of enticing young soldiers to abandon their posts and return to the hearthside. Although he encouraged the home folks to write to the soldiers in order to keep up morale, he cautioned them to offer "good Christian counsel, and words of cheer and encouragement." He warned them to avoid discussing politics and the course of the war—the soldiers got enough of that in "such treacherous sheets as the *World* and the *Herald* and their satellites." He asked them to keep their troubles and "theories" at home. In a morsel of "Sage" advice, he told them: "All things don't go just right in Washington, in Congress, at Albany; they never did go *just* right." He urged his readers to "spike the guns of the miserable copperhead traitors in our rear; we will attend to their butternut friends in our front." He concluded with a story about a fellow who went into convulsions after receiving a single discouraging letter and later died.[21]

Henry Galpin agreed with Sage's main point: "Too many gloomy, desponding letters come to the army from home. This is wrong." He blamed the "stay at home bodies . . . for all or nearly all of the desertions" and appealed to the hometown crowd to help the army arrest and return those who deserted. "You at the North can make desertion such a black, damning spot upon a man's character that even a man without character would stand in fear." Meanwhile, Colonel Clark threatened the troops "that if this talk of going home, etc., was not stopped," they would be "left to the tender mercies of a field battery." John Hartwell reported that Clark's "pep" talk "put us in position in less time than it took him to tell it."

New York City newspapers, the *Herald* and the *World,* were singled out by the articulate, educated boys from Herkimer. When Hooker demanded that the army's subscriptions to both papers be terminated, Clarke Rice exulted: "Bright signs begin to appear . . . Hail, O, spirit of war! Strike death to treason wherever you find it; hush every voice that whispers dissensions." Henry Walker avoided the two papers and expressed no desire to ever read them. In his opinion, the papers did a "great deal of mischief in the army." The hometown papers, though, especially the *Otsego Republican,* were very active in their attempts to discourage desertions. In one particularly florid piece, the *Republican* warned: "Go Back Deserters! Hasten; the time draws nigh . . . when a price will be set upon your heads, and your breasts will be pierced by your comrades' bullets, or perchance, in some by-way town the hemp cord will twist about your necks."[22]

Upton used Hooker's ambitious plans to improve the Army of the Potomac to weed out the weak and incompetent officers in the 121st. He also turned to the legal means at his disposal and began to deal with serious issues through judicial proceedings.

Court-Martial of Private Johnson, Company D

Inevitably, someone concocted a fantasy scenario that provided cover to men who were entertaining the notion of deserting. In Capt. John D. Fish's Company D, where desertions were particularly rampant, Pvt. Henry Johnson, from Frankfort, Herkimer County, somehow determined that the federal government had erred in mustering him into the army. He spread the belief that his company and his regiment had never actually mustered into the service of the United States and that both units were being illegally retained. Whether Johnson really believed the fabrication he served up is unknown. However, he acted on it by urging his comrades to stack arms (that is, lay down their weapons), refuse to drill, and disregard all legal orders by their superiors. He followed his own counsel and affirmed that he would be first to stack arms and disregard orders. And that stirred Upton to action beyond writing letters to the newspapers back home.

Upton could not contain his temper and ordered a court-martial for Johnson on January 31. A fellow New Yorker, Gen. Joe Bartlett, commander of the 2nd Brigade, 1st Division, presided. Two counts were leveled at Johnson—"Mutinous and Seditious conduct and Exciting Mutiny" and "Neglecting and Refusing to impart to his Commanding Officer knowledge of an intended mutiny." The latter charge specified that Johnson knew of mutinous activity among his mates and refused, even when questioned, to report it to his superiors—"All this at the Camp of the 121st N. Y. V."

The court-martial convened on February 5, 1863. Johnson shrewdly pleaded not guilty to the first charge and guilty to the second. "After mature deliberation," Bartlett found Johnson guilty on both charges. The court ordered that Johnson was to forfeit all pay and allowances due him and that he was to be confined for one year of hard labor at Dry Tortugas Prison. In addition, Bartlett fined Johnson $10 per month from his monthly pay for the year he would spend in the guardhouse. After serving his term, Bartlett ruled, Johnson would be allowed to return to his regiment but with half his head shaved, and "when discharged," he was "to lose all bounties or emoluments usually received by soldiers." The punishment as a whole exceeded Brig. Gen. William "Bully" Brooks's tolerance level, and on March 20, he reduced Johnson's sentence by overturning the one year of hard labor provision and the humiliating half-shaved head requirement.

The real issue centered on the government's sporadic pay scheme. Johnson, described by his comrades as a "mischief breeding cuss," circulated the rumor that if the government failed to pay them in any four-month period, their contract with the government would become null and void. The men had received one month's pay at Camp Schuyler in August 1862 and nothing more until mid-February 1863, when they received nearly three months' pay.

Once the men were paid and Upton took action to curb Johnson and others, the troops settled down into a winter quarters routine and the desertions slowed, but the grumbling and potential for desertion remained. Many continued to blame the Lincoln government for their lot—"it was a blanked nigger war anyway, and they were not going to fight for the Negro or 'nigger' as they called him." Johnson eventually mustered out with the regiment in June 1865, honorably discharged and unscathed by the war and his brief episode as a guardhouse lawyer.[23]

Charged, arraigned, and tried for desertion on February 19 were Sgts. Langford Burton, Francis N. Piper, and Aaron S. Miller and Cpls. George H. Gilbert and N. P. Tanner of Company D, from Schuyler and Frankfort. They took off during Burnside's Mud March and remained absent until they turned themselves in to authorities at White Oak Swamp around 4:00 in the afternoon on February 19, long after the regiment had left on the march. All pleaded not guilty. The court disagreed and sentenced the five men to a reduction to the ranks and forfeiture of $10 pay then owed them. They received eighteen months of hard labor at the Rip Raps—a man-made island at the mouth of Hampton Roads built in 1817 as a part of a harbor defense system. They were to pay the government $10 per month during their incarceration and were to be returned to their regiment upon completing their sentences. Brooks concurred with the findings and ordered the sentences carried out.[24]

The five ended their enlistments on honorable terms. Burton returned to the 121st and was commissioned a second lieutenant on October 29, 1864. A month later, Piper received a commission and a transfer to Company B. Both were honorably discharged with the regiment in June 1865. Piper remained active with the 121st's Regimental Association into the 1920s. Tanner and Miller were reinstated, were wounded at Spotsylvania, and died of their wounds.

Gilbert returned to Company D and served out the remainder of his enlistment as a first sergeant.

With too much time on their hands, many men were distracted by thoughts of home and leaving the field, playing too much cards, drinking easily available liquor, and sometimes arguing. Dean Pierce, in Company D, characterized February 1863 as the worst time he had spent anywhere. Between the mud, the knee-deep snow, the occasional rain, the miserable picket duty exposed to the weather, and the extreme boredom in camp, he was led to extracurricular activities. When he got his pay of $47.25 on Valentine's Day, he blew it on an all-day whiskey bender but proudly boasted that he did not get sick.[25]

Fred Ford, the regiment's voice in the *Herkimer County Journal,* never shrank from an open debate. The lack of activity on the front during a particularly wretched winter quarters prompted bickering and harsh words among friends. Ever since the recruiters of the 152nd New York, from Herkimer and Otsego counties, admitted that the 121st got the cream of the two counties' manpower material, the 121st had maintained a feeling of superiority over its "sister" regiment. The 121st had been thrown into the fray almost immediately, whereas the 152nd found itself in the nation's capital performing comparatively light guard duty. Additionally, the 34th New York, another regiment from the two counties, comprised two-year men who volunteered during the first phase of the war without the benefit of liberal bounties as war broke out. The frictions that resulted between units were never far from the surface, and they boiled over when Ford referred to the 152nd's light duty "in a big mud puddle of the suburbs of Washington" and the fact that the "121st has been ordered into active service and the 152nd is grubbing away in the sand hills at Washington."

Both the 152nd and the 34th retaliated by saying that the men of the 34th had signed up out of patriotism and not because of the "golden inducements . . . of two, three or five hundred dollar bounties." Ford in turn wondered if "one who hires out to butcher his fellow for 'eleven dollars per month and no reward,' is infinitely meaner than he whom a larger sum induces to do the same thing." The argument came to a draw when yet another regiment, the 97th, stepped in and mediated the settlement by pointing out that they were all in the situation together and should not be picking at each other; they were old classmates and close friends, and they needed to focus on the larger picture and direct their anger elsewhere.[26]

Hooker Reorganizes and Reforms the Army

"Fighting Joe" Hooker replaced the ineffectual Burnside. He hated his nickname, but the sobriquet would follow him through his career. As to his last name being used as a synonym for the camp followers, or prostitutes, traveling with the Army of the Potomac, no evidence exists to confirm or deny the connection.

Hooker finished in the middle of his West Point class, without distinction. Although he was a New England Yankee from Hadley, Massachusetts, and not a blue-blooded Brahmin, Hooker had a distinctive manner. When Clarke Rice saw him up close during a review, he described him as "one of the finest looking men" he had ever seen. "He is a very tall man, well proportioned, with high massive square head, bright black locks and healthy red cheeks. He has all the military airs, as much so as McClellan, and at the same time, appears more intelligent and active," he wrote.[27]

After West Point, Hooker established his reputation during the Mexican War, where he fought bravely and commanded with heart. When political generals would not fight, Hooker would. After the war, he went west to make his fortune but instead gained a reputation as a gambler and a drinker. One historian described Hooker and his California days in a few spare words: "The dashing army officer had descended almost to the level of a beachcomber." During his time in Mexico and California, Hooker managed to alienate two of his future commanders—Winfield Scott, the hero of the Mexican War, and Henry W. Halleck, now Lincoln's general in chief of the Union army. He fell out with Halleck over a business deal in California, accusing him of misconduct in a land deal gone bad. When Fort Sumter fell, Hooker offered his services to the government, and Winfield Scott, who had not forgotten their relationship in Mexico, tried to block him. Hooker went to Lincoln after the disaster at Bull Run and convinced the president that he could lead men.[28]

By the time of his appointment to command the Army of the Potomac, Hooker had distinguished himself on the battlefield once again—and also advanced his reputation for speaking before thinking. After Fredericksburg, word reached Lincoln that Hooker thought the nation and the army needed a dictator. Burnside thought Hooker should be relieved of command for criticizing his leadership. Instead, Lincoln replaced Burnside with his nemesis, with the warning that he, Hooker, was to worry about prosecuting the war while Lincoln would "risk the dictatorship." Despite having enemies in Burnside, Halleck, and Scott, Hooker could count on the president and an additional unlikely candidate, Edwin Stanton, who did not dismiss him out of hand.

Hooker's first move was a complete reorganization of the Army of the Potomac. He abandoned Burnside's grand divisions and consolidated the army into seven corps. He kept John F. Reynolds as commander of the First Corps. He gave the Second Corps to Darius Couch and the Fifth Corps to George Meade. New Yorker Dan Sickles received command of the Third Corps and Oliver O. Howard the Eleventh Corps. Henry Slocum, Richard Franchot's old friend from upstate New York, took over the Twelfth Corps. "Uncle John" Sedgwick received command of the Sixth Corps, home of the 121st. Commanding the 121st's division would be Bully Brooks. Hooker also cast his eye on the cavalry and consolidated those troops into a single corps as the Confederates had done eighteen months previously. Hooker appointed George Stoneman commander of the new cavalry corps. None of the eight new commanders had led a corps before. He left the artillery unchanged, assigned to the divisions.

Hooker also attacked the plague of desertions. He asked each command for the names of all men missing from the ranks without permission. He cut off mailed packages from home that contained civilian clothing. He offered a cash bounty to Northern law officers, such as Sheriff Mather, for turning in deserters. He tightened the circle of pickets and provost guards around the Rappahannock camps. And he enhanced Lincoln's amnesty proclamation by asking that it be extended to those deserters who were already in custody or "awaiting sentence."

The Enrollment Act of March 3, 1863, established mandatory military service for Northern men between eighteen and forty-five years of age. Its passage soon diminished desertions, for two primary reasons: it made the deserter eligible for the draft if he showed up at home, and it made enlistment appealing because it allowed a measure of freedom for the recruit. Norman Herdman chided his brother Sperry back home in Otsego County: "Perhaps you may have an urgent invitation to come down here to help us finish up this little rebellious job. How would that set on your stomach? Hard to digest, I reckon. Let old Abe send along his conscripts soon and as many as he pleases; there will be a place and business for all without doubt."[29]

Hooker's institution of a consistent and reliable system of furloughs helped raise morale and inhibit desertions. He allowed two men per every hundred (two per company) to go on furlough at a time. When two returned, two more were allowed to leave. Unfortunately, going home meant that an enlisted man from upstate New York would need $30 for a round-trip. Furlough meant being at home, in Washington, or anywhere but in camp or in the field on picket duty. Most furloughs were between ten and thirty days long, including travel time, and a ten-day leave meant four days of travel and only six days at home for upstate New Yorkers. Most thought that the time spent with loved ones more than justified the expense.[30]

Introducing the corps badge became the most long-lasting, albeit largely symbolic, strategy that Hooker and his chief of staff, Maj. Gen. Daniel Butterfield, devised. Maj. Gen. Phil Kearny had used a diamond-shaped piece of red felt, attached to each soldier's uniform, as a means to prevent straggling and to identify men of his command on the Peninsula. Expanding on that concept, Butterfield came up with a whole range of colors and shapes to identify Hooker's new corps. The Sixth Corps received the Greek cross, for example. Since each corps consisted of three divisions, each division wore the same symbol but in different colors: red for the 1st Division, white for the 2nd, and blue for the 3rd. Thus, the 121st adopted the red cross as its badge of honor. Dr. Holt had his picture taken with his new badge on his chest; Sam Kelley did as well. John Hartwell noted the new symbol in his diary: "Yesterday, each one of the regiment had a red cross put on the crown of his cap."[31]

Other changes Hooker implemented included establishing a regular payday, thereby addressing a source of extreme irritation in the ranks. The regiment had not been paid since Camp Schuyler, and many men depended on receiving the pay to send it home to families who were left nearly destitute when the head of the household had left for war. Jonathon Burrell held out eternal hope for the paymaster. It did not take a brilliant tactician to realize the correlation between no pay and low morale. Chaplain Adams, always concerned with the welfare of the men under his care, recognized that "to be shut out of pay for six months" caused officers and enlisted men to "growl terribly." "The boys grumble a good deal on account of the hard marches and the short rations . . . much grumbling. We have got some in our company that can do it [grumble] as well as the best of them." The troops felt that the government, justified or not, planned to lose 10,000 to 15,000 men in battle and could "thus save paying so many." Pay was distributed to the various units unevenly. At the end of January, for instance, the paymaster visited the rest of the brigade but not the 121st. The *Freeman's Journal* warned of the "worst consequences" if troops were not soon paid and reported "trouble" in several unidentified regiments. But in February, the paymaster paid the troops retroactively through January 1.[32]

Hooker also strongly encouraged inspector generals to ferret out and punish incompetence and fraud. And most important, he gave the troops real food. Soft bread and fresh vegetables were hailed by the enlisted men as godsends. Members of Company A reported having fresh shad for breakfast, along with "plenty of potatoes, good bread and butter and tea." Even though some thought eating pies was "not fashionable down here," Ten Eyck Howland took pleasure in the delicate dessert. "I dove in some of the pies head first clear up to my shoulders. It seems good to get something fit to eat down here." Adelbert Reed reported that one of the Wood boys, George, baked bread for the entire brigade. "We get soft bread four times a week, onions and potatoes twice or three times, beans twice, pork and fresh meat twice," he proclaimed, "so we are having the best of times away down in Dixie." Fred Ford, in his continuing campaign against Governor Seymour, mentioned the food situation even as he blasted the *New York World* and the *New York Herald* for their support of Seymour: "Those two papers are probably glad to learn that under the auspices of that 'Pet of the Abolitionists,' General Hooker, the army is daily and surely increasing in efficiency. One order of his, giving fresh bread and plenty of vegetables to the troops has made him popular." Ford rejoiced along with his comrades about the little things that Hooker seemed to understand were essential to the morale of his men. "Soft bread and vegetables are plenty. All these little things do far more than you can guess," he explained.[33]

Hooker turned the Army of the Potomac's morale around in two months. As the troops went into winter quarters, a new wave of optimism and hope spread through the camps. An abysmal January was followed by a flurry of activity in February. In March, as spring approached, the mood reflected the eternal optimism promised by the new season. Officers' wives visited, and parties were not uncommon in the upgraded huts and shelters. And though the men still focused their thoughts on the home front, they realized that the path home ran through the ordeal of fighting and defeating the enemy. Even the parade reviews became a source of pride and a boost to morale. In April, President Lincoln visited the Army of the Potomac, and Isaac Darling reported on the day's "grand spectacle—some 60,000 men, all armed with burnished bayonets gleaming in the sun." He thought the president looked "very much worn out." But the beautiful morning brought out the best in everyone. "The boys are all in fine spirits and doing well," he observed. Private Beckwith believed that Hooker's new command had produced a "better feeling among the men" and that the troops were slowly accepting the reality of his appointment.[34]

They inevitably compared him to his predecessors. "I did not like Hooker's appointment in the place of Burnside at all but I like his orders so far very much," Henry Walker admitted, adding that "there seems to be a great deal of vigor and a just conception of affairs in them. I like Hooker better and better and think that is generally the case with the soldiers and I hope that we shall not be disappointed in him." Clarke Rice compared him to all of the classical and historical figures he could remember from his studies at Fairfield Academy. He recounted Hooker's propensity to visit his troops unannounced and sometimes unrecognized in order to see the "workings of the smallest wheels in the stupendous machinery of the army." As Rice told his brother Charley: "I assure you that he fills a higher place in the hearts of the soldiers than ever McClellan did." Hooker now commanded an entirely different army—enthusiastic but tempered by eighteen months of hard fighting and tough times. In its hardened condition, it looked to the next engagement—"another effort to crush the enemy was soon to be undertaken."[35]

During the months in winter camp, Upton spent as many of the good-weather days as he could on drilling the men and the officers of the 121st in the ways of warfare. Drills on all levels and target practice continued. "Our officers are becoming pretty well acquainted with tactics, and the men learn very fast," William Remmel wrote. Norman Herdman described target practice. It might involve the entire regiment in line of battle "firing at ten targets placed side by side about the size of a man." Practice would start with firing at a distance of 30 rods and end with firing at targets a half mile away. Herdman was convinced they could hit anything a mile away. And by the way, he told his brother Sperry, while they were out shooting, the "balloons" went up every day to check on the rebel positions on the other side of the river. The balloons were not a new sight to Norman; he reminded Sperry that they had gone together to Fort Plain "once upon a time to see one."[36]

Upton and the Crisis of Leadership

Capitalizing on Hooker's propitious reforms, Upton began improving his command's leadership. He remained concerned about the quality of his officers and refused to play the political game of "who do you know" with politically connected subordinates. He also wanted to set guidelines and standards against which all officers would be judged. His attempt to purge his ranks of the unqualified officers did not meet with total success. Some of the targeted men caved in and resigned immediately. But other moves he tried backfired on him almost completely. Upton waged the battle on two fronts: one with the governor's office and the other within the regiment's ranks. He began with Albany.

When Sgt. Andrew Davidson's friends in Cooperstown lobbied for his advancement, Upton wrote to Governor Seymour with his very real concerns. Audaciously, he told the governor that he set standards in choosing officers for the regiment. He predicted that Davidson would someday earn a commission because he was "a good soldier," but he refused to recommend him. Upton insisted that candidates for officers' slots take a rigorous examination. He only desired to "bring the regiment to the highest state of efficiency." And the only method he understood resided in the careful selection of leaders. His criteria were simple. All candidates had to "be neat in their personal appearance, military in their deportment, prompt in obeying orders."

"Those who are incompetent," said Upton, "shall occupy positions which others can and shall fill." Upton alluded to pressure from "influential men both in Herkimer and Otsego Counties to promote their friends." He refused to allow pressure from home to influence him "for the reason that most men outside the Army have no idea of the qualifications of a good soldier." At the same time, he would not automatically eliminate a candidate merely because his upstate friends interceded for him, and he would allow the potential officer to take his examination. He took this stance even though he admitted there were "about ten vacancies in the Regiment." Upton promised the governor that when he found men "with the requisite energy, firmness and intelligence," he would forward their names to him. Moving to the very edge of protocol and propriety, he boldly assumed that the governor would agree with him and leave him alone, with the promise that he would field a regiment that would be "not only an honor to the State, but to the Country."[37]

The conflict with Seymour's administration proved to be a turning point for the young Emory Upton—a lesson in the ways and means of the "real" military. The incident also honed Upton's skepticism of the politicians in charge. Throughout the war, he experienced one situation after another that bolstered his desire for a complete overhaul of the nation's military policy. The incident with Seymour marked the starting point of his lifelong quest to reform the army. After this episode, he made clear distinctions between the volunteer soldier, the professional from West Point, and interfering politicians.

Hooker's changes immediately impacted the officers and men in the Army of the Potomac. With Upton firmly in command of the 121st, changes in the army were mirrored in the regiment's leadership. Lieutenant Colonel Clark, unable to impress either Olcott or Upton, left the unit. Burrell thought that no one in the officer corps of the 121st could withstand Upton's rigid examinations, and old-timers in other regiments doubted that anyone could pass the requirements of the "West Point Cadet." During the same period, most of the regiment's original officers resigned. Lieutenants Cameron and Davis died. And Stephen Valentine held the dubious distinction of being the only officer dismissed from the regiment.

The rest of the officers who resigned simply went home. Adj. Thomas Arnold, after his promotion to captain, replaced John Ramsey, Company H, when the latter resigned. In all, twelve lieutenants and five captains had resigned since the regiment took the field. Burrell reported that "one captain and two lieutenants" were asked to resign in November and that Upton threatened to ask for more resignations. Sackett Olin, who had recruited Company K, became ill as soon as the regiment took to the field. He suffered with several different symptoms from mid-September 1862, when doctors treated him in the regimental hospital, through his discharge on December 31, 1862, at White Oak Church. His medical chart noted piles, diarrhea, and heart disease. The diagnoses proved beneficial when Olin applied for a government pension after the war.[38]

Although all the resigning officers were honorably discharged, families and friends generally did not welcome resignation, and some equated it with desertion. The hometown reaction confirmed Upton's judgment in deciding to weed out the weak. Irving Holcomb's resignation provoked strong reactions. The men in his company were relieved when he left, but the people in Litchfield viewed his resignation as an outrage. Holcomb had recruited many of the men in Company B from Litchfield and the surrounding villages, and he resigned his commission and received his discharge on January 20, right after many Herkimer men deserted. Philenda Carran, Frank's widowed mother, attacked Holcomb and made her feelings known to anyone who would listen. "Now what do you think of Irv Holcomb?" she asked Frank. She found him no better than a deserter. When Holcomb returned home, Philenda reported that he took care "about being seen by the people here . . . I do not envy him his position, he is censured very much. It is nothing uncommon to hear the expression he ought to be shot and I heard that one man who has a son in Co. B told him he had a good mind to shoot him."

Mrs. Carran guessed that the soldiers in the company were happy that he had returned home, "for I imagine he was not very kind to his men." She knew that he "had not come home with any more honor than did Del Harris whom he made so much fun of last summer when he was attending war meetings." Holcomb told people in the community that his superiors "would not let him be as kind to the men of his company as he wished to be." In a brutal conclusion to her letter, Philenda told her son: "If I had been in Holcomb's company he would not have come home without some one or more bullet holes through his coat if not through his body. He never ought to have been permitted to have left alive." Holcomb's resignation came as a surprise to others; in fact, Jonathon Burrell said Holcomb was the last person he thought would resign, adding, "Not very welcome at home, I hear."[39]

Although his vitriol could not match Philendra Carran's, Fred Ford fumed that the editor of the *Herkimer County Journal* refused to print his list of resignations. "Justice to these men and to other men would demand their names," he insisted. "We have . . . few of our original officers left . . . and shall soon have still fewer. Enlisted men have no way of escaping, except through desertion; officers none, unless by resignations. If there had been fewer of the latter, there would have been less of the former. At home the two should be on a level." After Congress passed the Conscription Act, John Kidder expressed the hope that all the resigning officers would be drafted and would have to come back as privates.[40]

John Hartwell served under Lt. Charles Bradt of Company C and owed his sergeant's stripes to him. When Bradt resigned in April, Hartwell reported that the boys of the 121st were sad to see him go. He had earned their respect for his attention to the men and for instilling in them an esprit de corps through drill and discipline. "It is seldom a man who enlists as a private," Hartwell observed, "attains the rank of first Lieutenant in less than eight months which he did." A few months earlier, however, Upton had arrested Bradt for leaving his guard post and retiring to his own tent. Upton took Bradt's sword and confined him to quarters for a week. He ultimately forced Bradt out.[41]

That winter, just before the onset of the good-weather campaign, the regiment's ten officer vacancies hampered its efficiency. As Dr. Holt complained as early as November 1862, only months into the field, "*Resignations* are frequent. Some companies are commanded by non-commissioned officers; some by Second Lieutenants." Holt noted many who had died during the first two months, including Cameron and Davis. In January, Jonathon Burrell confirmed Holt's concerns: "We now have but twenty line officers—ten short of our complement. Captain Moon has resigned. Lieut. Staring of Co. D received his papers tonight and I think . . . three or four more . . . will resign before long." Cautiously but with missteps, Upton began to replace them with officers from outside the unit and from within. In his attempt to instill a higher state of discipline, he threw open the competition for promotions "to every deserving efficient and meritorious soldier."

Between January and April 1863, the regimental books were filled with the reassignments, promotions, and demotions of several men back and forth between the enlisted and commissioned ranks. In an attempt to replenish the ranks, during a dress parade in February Upton extended a general invitation to all privates wishing a commission to "hand in their names" for immediate consideration. By mid-March, he made five changes relative to promotions and resignations. The promotion of Sam Miller as a newly minted second lieutenant in Company C came as a surprise to many, and Henry Walker thought that "friends at home procured" Miller's commission for him. By the beginning of May, just before the battle of Salem Church, Upton had made twelve more changes and assignments. He dipped into the ranks of the noncommissioned officers and sent their appointments on to Albany. Others, such as Mather, Olcott, Sternberg, and Cronkite—all second lieutenants—were promoted to first lieutenant.

Upton temporarily placed Miller in command of Irving Holcomb's Company B until Lt. Marcus Casler transferred from Company H. Miller and Casler were well liked. Frank Carran thought that Miller made a better soldier than a civilian and would rather have had him in charge than Holcomb: "He behaves like a man." Upton's other decisions did not set as well with the regiment. He brought in Robert P. Wilson from General Bartlett's staff as a major; Cleaveland John Campbell of Cherry Valley, the brother of Douglas Campbell, as a captain; and his own brother, Henry Upton, from an Illinois regiment as a second lieutenant. The young regimental commander made a huge misstep with his brother's and Wilson's appointments. Both proved controversial.[42]

Jonathon Burrell, like Chaplain Sage, believed the rumors that Upton might be promoted and that the 121st would lose him. That prospect reopened the regimental guessing game of who would move up the food chain from below. The betting on Upton's replacement favored Olcott and Clark. Burrell felt that Olcott "would come the nearest but Lieut. Col Clark stands in his way. I don't think the Major has an enemy in the whole regiment. Not so with a good many of the others." For the immediate future, however, Upton remained in command and Olcott remained third in command. When Clark finally resigned the number two spot effective March 23, 1863, Upton immediately promoted Egbert Olcott in his place, stirring new rumors. Who would be Major Olcott's replacement and essentially third in command of the regiment? There were but a few eligible captains ready to move into the slot, including John Kidder, John Fish, Emmet Mather, and Henry Galpin. Here, Emory Upton made his first tactical error in management and administration. He went outside the 121st for a major, choosing Robert P. Wilson.[43]

Wilson, variously called "the Spook" or "Snoop" by the men of the 121st for unknown reasons, had entered the army as a private in the 16th New York—Isaac O. Best's regiment in April 1861 at war's outbreak. He rose quickly in the ranks, to lieutenant on July 4 and adjutant on September 24. The army assigned him to General Bartlett's staff as a captain and acting assistant adjutant general in March 1863, and then Upton handpicked him as major of the 121st on April 10 as the army prepared to move once again against Lee. Wilson read about his appointment in the newspaper. He understood his status as an outsider and knew that he preempted Henry Galpin's chances of becoming the next major. He reported to the regiment but quickly refused the appointment, returning to Bartlett's staff. He realized that his presence provoked controversy and stepped aside to avoid an internal battle. He appeared to be an honorable man. Isaac Best, who was also on Bartlett's staff, found Wilson engaging and friendly. An ardent supporter of temperance and always on the lookout for big drinkers, Best said of Wilson that he occasionally imbibed but was never drunk in his presence. He also cited Wilson's business-like approach to leadership as one of the reasons that the 2nd Brigade functioned smoothly and efficiently.[44]

When Wilson's brief appointment did not work out, an uproar ensued. Henry Galpin, the most eligible candidate for promotion, threatened to resign, but Upton refused to allow it. Galpin countered with the threat of going over Upton's head to Washington. Wounded in the Peninsula campaign, Galpin had prior service with Ellsworth's Avengers. Promoted to sergeant on the field for gallantry when the president's call for 300,000 men was issued, he quickly recruited a company that assumed the honor post of the regiment as Company A. Captain Fish, Company D, also threatened to resign. Before yielding to the unrest that Wilson's appointment caused among his officers, Upton told them that they must live with his decision or get out of the service and that Wilson would have "added another brave and good officer" to the regiment. Despite the hard feelings on both sides, Wilson helped Upton with his abrupt return to Bartlett's staff.

Upton compounded his troubles by sending Capt. Emmet Mather's name to Albany for promotion to major just before the Chancellorsville campaign. Mather had begun his army experience on the wrong foot. As the regiment made its way to the front, he took two bottles of liquor away from some enlisted men during a stop in Baltimore. When he smashed them on the sidewalk, one of the men threatened Mather, saying that "his time will soon come and when we get in a battle he will remember it." Now, the appointment of Mather, an insider, as a major in the 121st caused more controversy than Wilson's appointment had. The officer corps and the men in the ranks held no regard for Mather. And he was chosen over Galpin, Kidder, and Fish, despite the fact that he ranked below all of them. The men of the 121st regarded Wilson, the un-known outsider, as an interloper. They viewed Mather, the "too well known" insider, as the usurper. He had just been promoted to captain in January.[45]

Mather had actually been Upton's first choice. When Albany rejected that nomination, Upton turned to Wilson, whom Albany immediately accepted. Then, when Wilson turned down the promotion, Mather became Upton's de-fault choice. Although Galpin respected Upton, he told him on more than one occasion that he wanted a promotion with the regiment and that he would leave if that did not happen. In response, Upton told Galpin that he needed him in his officer corps but that he would never recommend him for promotion be-cause he fraternized with the men under his command. Ultimately, even though Galpin "had friends at Albany working for him" to deflect any competitor, he did not get the post.

Inside and outside the army, Galpin had earned the reputation of being too easy on his men. After the 121st left for the field, an unnamed politician in Little Falls told Galpin's brother that Henry would not make a good officer because he "was too mild, not stern enough"; he would be "too easy with the men" and "would not have control and the respect of them to obey [orders]." The brother responded naively that Henry would win the respect of the men with love, not fear. John Kidder, who was pro-Galpin and anti-Mather but who pressed for his own promotion, felt that Galpin could "lead twenty men into battle where Mather could not lead one." According to Kidder, the decision to promote Mather over him "displeased" the entire regiment, "men and officers" alike; moreover, he said, "Mather's company perfectly hate him"—not a man "speaks well of him." The men disliked Mather because he was an "over bearing and tyrannical" martinet, and although he may have been a good officer, the "men had no confidence in him." Kidder also thought Mather possessed an ego larger than life: "I think he is larger in his own estimation," he wrote, "than General Hooker." Kidder scathingly told his wife that Mather was not liked because "he is such a fop . . . all dress that seems to be his style." (Paradoxically, Kidder had remarked on two other occasions that "[Mather] is a good officer and will do his duty" and that "Mather can fill the office well as he is a good officer also.")

Kidder's pro-Galpin stance was surprising, since the regiment universally re-garded Kidder as a tough disciplinarian. Indeed, his wife heard stories back in Laurens of his uncompromising manners in drill and discipline. Yet when Upton (and Clark before him) tried to keep the officers from fraternizing with the en-listed men, Kidder regarded the policy as "a mistaken notion" while adding, "but we must obey orders." Kidder disdained the policy because his two enlisted brothers and an enlisted brother-in-law served alongside him in the regiment.

Dr. Holt offered his own uninformed minority opinion. He thought that Mather "was a first rate man and officer possessing the confidence of the en-tire regiment." Delavan Bates recognized Mather's ambitions. He knew that

Mather longed to someday command a regiment, perhaps a colored regiment: "He didn't believe either in the 'jolly good fellow' business or in singing 'We won't go home till morning' songs." But Mather could be foolhardy and naïve. As Henry Upton, Emory's brother, convalesced from wounds suffered at Salem Church, Mather called for the establishment of a commission to determine if Henry had stayed away longer than authorized. Nothing came of his actions, however, and Henry Upton left the service two months later.[46]

Mather succumbed easily to flattery, and he became an "Upton man." In a letter to his brother, he confessed that "the Colonel seems to take quite an interest in me." Before the battle of Fredericksburg, Upton had put Mather in charge of Company G even though he was a junior lieutenant and outranked by two twenty-year-olds from Mohawk, James D. Clyde and Charles T. Ferguson. At that point, the two men could either resign or go before an examining board to seek promotion. Both chose to resign in November, just two months after enlisting.

Mather dealt particularly harshly with Company B's first lieutenant, Henry Keith. He predicted that Keith would not last through his three-year commitment and told his own brother, "He is actually stupid." He also predicted that Irving Holcomb, Keith's commanding officer, "will shield him a good deal, but it is doubtful . . . if he saves him." According to Mather, Upton threatened him and all the captains that he would transfer them to another command if they continued fraternizing with the enlisted men. He impressed on Mather that enlisted men were required to salute an officer before speaking with him and to remove their caps indoors; further, officers were "never [to] laugh at one of their [the enlisted men's] jokes." Mather told his brother that if a vacancy occurred in the company, "I shall try to get it." Sgt. Lansing B. Paine (who would become a lieutenant) understood Mather's ambitious streak; a year later, when Mather applied for and received a commission to head up one of the new U.S. colored troops, Paine remarked: "Did you ever see a fellow go ahead as he does in everything?"[47]

Bringing in new recruits from other regiments was acceptable, but the men in the regiment did not take kindly to the presence of an officer from another unit. And if an inside candidate rose in the ranks, he had to be popular. Captains Cronkite, Gorton, and Casler were all promoted by Upton from the ranks of the men who had left Camp Schuyler together. For the near future, however, the fate of the 121st New York Volunteers remained in the hands of Upton, Olcott, and Mather, and the men of the regiment had no choice but to accept the situation without complaint. The turmoil in the officers' ranks did not escape the notice of the enlisted men. John Ingraham rated the officers, placing Galpin as number one, followed by Fish, Kidder, and finally Mather—and yet "they jumped him [Mather] over the whole of them."

One soldier, probably from Galpin's Company A, aired his views publicly but anonymously, by expressing his displeasure with Mather's appointment over Galpin to the *Herkimer County Journal*. He attributed Mather's promotion to politics and "the influence of families and home organizations, Church and Free Mason Societies" with the "weight even among the Captains in the selection of officers in this time of rebellion. It is discouraging sometimes." The process of selecting officers from the ranks of the privates disturbed him, especially when capable noncommissioned officers were overlooked. He hinted that outside influences in promotions demoralized the regiment.[48]

Another anonymous rambling, a scathing letter posted from Mohawk, appeared in the *Herkimer County Journal* on April 23. The writer took Upton to task for not promoting men from the original corps of Herkimer County or Otsego County volunteers. In what could have been a direct condemnation of a few of the 121st's officers, the writer asked: "Is the 121st Regiment to be the recipient of every ruined profligate, who may have a friend in the field?" Did every vacancy have to be filled by "an outsider who is a 'boon companion'" or by a "youth from West Point who has left that institution on account of sore eyes" or by "my friend's son who is rather wild and wants a good position? Or my *particular* friend, who has spent a fortune in riotous living and dissipation and wants to keep up appearances?—Where are those who have nobly earned those positions?" The recent appointments dissipated the good feelings of the previous few months. The writer accused Upton of being a "cat's paw," carrying out the wishes of the powerful to the extreme detriment of the regiment. In fact, Upton bore the brunt of the writer's wrath: "The regiment has been grossly insulted by the introduction of officers who are strangers to the Regiment," particularly since the regiment already possessed the necessary talents. The writer accused Upton of reneging on his promise to fill the vacancies from within and concluded with a call on Governor Seymour not to "be a party to anything so unjust."[49]

Upton did not escape criticism from his own men. At the beginning of July, the regiment welcomed a new surgeon, John O. Slocum. An 1847 graduate from Castleton Medical College, Slocum had served with the 122nd New York Volunteers from the Syracuse area, where he had enlisted on August 14, 1862, at age forty-two. He received his commission as regimental surgeon for the 121st on June 23, 1863—over Dr. Holt. At first, the two doctors got along well. After a two-hour discussion, Holt pronounced Slocum a "good fellow, and if inclined to be half decent, we shall get along well enough." His appointment still offended Dr. Holt, though Holt directed his anger toward Upton, not Slocum.

But favoritism had reared its ugly head. Holt was displeased that he had been passed over again not only by a man who was, in his opinion, much less qualified but also as the result of a political favor. He blamed Upton completely. He was convinced that because Upton owed "his promotion from Lieutenant in the regular service, to colonel of volunteers, to the influence of General

Slocum," he had given Slocum's brother a place in his regiment—over Holt—in order "to reciprocate the favor." Holt's knowledge that both he and Slocum were assistant surgeons, albeit in different regiments, and that Slocum was nonetheless promoted over him made him furious. He also felt slighted by the lack of respect he received from his commanders and from Albany. "I have been a pack horse long enough," he told his wife, "and I ought to get a little more compensation for the service I bestow." He threatened to resign over the issue in a letter to the New York State surgeon general, John Van Pelt Quackenbush, in Albany. Quackenbush reassured him that he was needed and appreciated and promised him a promotion. "We shall see," Holt told his wife. But within a month, he and Slocum agreed to work together, and Holt dropped the issue. Slocum, however, never forgot the furor that Holt had kicked up. The two worked together in an uneasy truce.[50]

Slocum and Holt were two entirely different personalities. Holt did not drink, and from all the evidence, he abstained from all vices—except acerbic criticism of his enemies and his excessive sensitivity to perceived slights. He had a prim and proper demeanor and an easily upset equilibrium. Slocum, by contrast, was a drinker and card player (he preferred whist). He kept his finances under tight control, recording every penny he loaned out and all outstanding debts. Despite their differences, both doctors attempted to make the best of the hard lot of marching and dealing with all the suffering experienced by the entire army. They eagerly pursued the luxuries denied to the enlisted men, as both sought that extra edge over the troops. Each one expected a high degree of respect as an officer and doctor. But Slocum never really warmed to Holt. In an enigmatic entry in his diary in February 1864, he wrote: "Dr. Holt told me about Taylor's talk with Olcott. No peace for me while he remains ____ Doctor." But after Slocum signed Holt's release papers in October 1864 and he himself returned to the regiment from a division assignment, he told his diary: "All seemed glad that I have returned, and I am not sorry Dr. Holt has gone."[51]

Meanwhile, Andrew Davidson offered a vote of confidence for his leaders, singling out Upton, Olcott, and Wilson (who was back at brigade headquarters)—"all sterling, energetic, brave and kind officers. In this respect the 121st cannot be surpassed." And despite Upton's missteps, the men displayed overwhelming confidence in and unabashed affection toward their commander. Adelbert Reed proudly boasted, "You don't know what a good name this 121st Regiment has got—it is pronounced the best looking regiment in the whole corps, the best drilled in the brigade. Our Colonel thinks the world of it. He says we beat the regulars who have been in the service for 3–4 years and he is not afraid to lead us anywhere and we will follow him wherever he goes." John Bain, a sergeant in Company G, indiscriminately liked all his superiors. He called Upton "one of the best officers in the Army of the Potomac." "He is kind to the boys," he observed, "and so long as they do what is right he will use them well, but when they do wrong he is certain to punish [them]." He attributed the regiment's high state of readiness and discipline to Upton, Olcott, and the line officers who remained.[52]

Upton's concern for the officer class and for strict discipline exempted no one who defied authority from serious charges and courts-martial. He placed Lt. Jonathon Burrell, for example, under arrest on a charge of conduct prejudicial to good order and military discipline. Upton's motives were admirable. The lack of military professionalism and the obvious need to instill respect for officers caused him genuine concern. Burrell never disclosed the reason for his arrest, but the court-martial records reveal a Marx Brothers performance by all the actors. Burrell claimed ignorance of the incident and innocence of the charges. The latter were initially preferred by Douglas Campbell, commander of Company E. According to Burrell, Captain Campbell was also "fishing for the office of Major," and the case offered him a way of showing his military prowess.

The facts of the case involved Burrell's refusal to assist Campbell in "finding some spades" that men of Company A had stored in their tents. Further, Burrell was said to have encouraged the enlisted men to defy Campbell and make "unseemly noises and hissings without rebuking them or aiding [Campbell]" and then refusing to identify the men "who so grossly insulted him." Cross-examination revealed that the noises were "in imitation of breaking of wind made by the mouth." Burrell introduced a statement of his own, pleading his innocence.

Capt. John Fish, Company D commander; Lt. Frank Bowles of Company F; J. G. Barnes, Captain Galpin's cook; and Sgt. M. H. Harrington were called as witnesses. They added nothing to the knowledge of the court in the case. Trivial testimony revolved around the number of spades, their ownership, whether Campbell wore his accoutrements as officer of the day, and who made the offensive noises and what they sounded like. The court, consisting of Colonel Cake of the 96th Pennsylvania, Campbell, and Lt. Frank Lemont of the 5th Maine, decided against Burrell, finding him guilty. The brigade commander, Bully Brooks, reprimanded Burrell, adding that "the sentence is made thus lenient by the Court in consideration of his manifest inexperience of the service."

Burrell made light of the incident, feigning enjoyment during the period of arrest while waiting for his trial with nothing to do. He basked in the envy of his fellow officers. "I like my leisure as well as any of them," he wrote facetiously, "but I hate to be obliged to have it." According to Burrell, Capt. Douglas Campbell lost the most from the whole affair. His popularity plummeted among the officers and men of the regiment, "especially Co. A and as for that matter, I might extend it to the whole Brigade." Burrell was annoyed that Campbell acted as his accuser, "one of the Board of Officers that constituted the court and also the principle witness against [him]." But in the end, none of that mattered, as he "came out all right." The inconsequential trial played out during the suffering at Belle Plain on the march to Fredericksburg. And ultimately, Burrell was correct in his assessment of Douglas Campbell's desire to become a major. When he was passed over for the promotion, the super recruiter who had enlisted two companies of men from Otsego County quit and returned home to Cherry Valley. James Cronkite, a rising star who had joined John Kidder's Company I as a sergeant, replaced Campbell just before the battle of Salem Church.[53]

Throughout the war, the 121st found itself chronically short of enlisted men and officers, due to death, resignation, promotion out of the unit, and discharge. Although it experienced two large infusions of new recruits, it never regained its original strength of 1,000 able-bodied men. False hopes of increasing the numbers were raised on a regular basis. The army became a mighty rumor mill that promised new recruits were on the way. Those in the field saw an influx of fresh men as a way to "settle this cruel war" early because when the rebels heard of the new enlistments, surely they would give up. Upton expressed genuine concern that he might lose his command because it had fallen below the official regimental level, and he reportedly used the entire drum corps in his head count to bring his regiment to 500 men and thereby keep it from being swallowed up in a consolidation with another regiment.

These various incidents and experiences became the curriculum in the education of the young Emory Upton. Although he proclaimed that he loved his men and would do anything for them, he quickly became disillusioned with the volunteer army. And he began questioning the politician-soldier, the politician back home who retained the power to place politically connected individuals in regiments and positions of power.[54]

7

Chancellorsville and Salem Church

There is very little sickness in the regiment at present, the only thing that troubles us is that we are *spoiling for a fight*. When the day of battle comes, the 121st will be heard from.

Andrew Davidson, Company E, April 22, 1863

Our boys was all cut to pieces . . . there is not half the Regiment left, the most wounded that I ever saw and the Old Sergeant says that it's the hardest fight we . . . had.

Dean Pierce, Company D, May 3, 1863

I came out lucky this time. It was the hardest battle that ever was fought with the rebel army.

Dolphus Sayles, Company D, May 6, 1863

Crossing the Rappahannock Again

With the spring thaw, the grass began to green up, the apple trees budded, and the peach trees pushed out blossoms; the Virginia roads became dry and hard for man and beast. Robert E. Lee sat with his army west of Fredericksburg, and Joseph Hooker meant to engage him there. The 121st's first winter quarters were cold, wet, and uncomfortable. The cruel April weather's harsh, strong winds alternated between bouts of snow and rain followed by mud. The bitter winds dried up the mud but also drove many from their huts when their fireplaces belched a reverse draft. On April 27, the wind diminished and the day broke "clear, bright and warm." At month's end, the weather cleared. Briefly, the men enjoyed a game of pitching quoits. On the parade ground, many soldiers of the 121st played baseball. The officers challenged their peers in the 16th New York to a game the following Saturday, a game that would never be played. The warm spring breezes carried rumors through the ranks that the army would soon move, and attendance at prayer meetings jumped dramatically. During a "hard shower," more than eighty men, two ministers. and two representatives from the Christian Commission held a service on Friday, April 24. The Reverend Adams of the 5th Maine held another service on Sunday.[1]

Robert Turner reported that Hooker "ain't a going to move not till he knows where they are and how many there are in number." Hooker intended to send a diversionary feint below Fredericksburg "in the vicinity of Franklin's crossing and make honest demonstrations on the Telegraph and Bowling Green roads, where the main Rebel bodies behind their defenses are posted," he informed his commander in chief. He would personally lead the main body of the army north and west, outflanking Lee and coming in behind him. He placed the diversionary force under the command of Uncle John Sedgwick; it included Sedgwick's own Sixth Corps together with the first Corps and third Corps. Hooker ordered Sedgwick to demonstrate against Lee in order to convince the general that the main attack would be below Fredericksburg. His movement masked Hooker's maneuver to the north above the town at Falmouth on the Rappahannock.[2]

On April 26, 1863, the Army of the Potomac could look across the river and see the rebel tents and conclude that a large contingent faced them. The next day, the federal army broke camp. On April 28, Sedgwick moved his troops behind Falmouth Heights, where they rested while pontoons were carried to the river by hand under cover of darkness. Just before daylight on April 29, Bully Brooks's 1st Division crossed in boats, and "the 121st moved off with the rest." Martin McMahon on Sedgwick's staff remembered that the rebels, hearing the movement of heavy equipment over the pontoons, called out to the federals in the dark, "Hallo there Yank, what's going on over there? What are you doing?" To which the federal pickets answered, "Johnnie, we're coming over after you." General Brooks reportedly told a group of men that he could take Richmond with the 121st New York: "He says he will march them down near the city and encamp and that they will steal the city before morning." The 121st continued as an element of the 2nd Brigade, still commanded by Brig. Gen. Joe Bartlett. The rest of the brigade was comprised of the 5th Maine, the 96th Pennsylvania, the 23rd New Jersey, and the 16th New York. On the night of April 30, the troops slept on the ground in the trenches before the rebel lines. Henry Seymour Hall of the 27th New York spent the night on the picket line with Emory Upton, "listening and watching for the enemy's movements."[3]

The battles of Chancellorsville, second Fredericksburg, Salem Church, and Banks' Ford were all individual segments of a larger action known as the Chancellorsville campaign, waged between April 27 and May 6. The 121st played a part in the initial probe across the Rappahannock as the 1st Division once again crossed the river opposite Deep Run, where the 121st had crossed in December. The remainder of the Sixth Corps joined the division and the other two corps as they settled in below the town, on April 28 and 29.[4]

The orders were to move quietly into the boats, with no commands given above a whisper. The crossing proved uneventful. With soldiers from engineer brigades, sixty men per boat silently slipped into the covering fog and darkness to cross the Rappahannock. They were to negotiate no more than 80 or 100 yards across the watery expanse, but to the men in the boats, the distance loomed large and time seemed to stand still. The advancing troops met no opposition—nothing but an "ominous silence on the other bank"—until, through the clammy fog, the men heard a single word, "Fire." The opposite bank along a 200-yard front erupted in small-arms fire—too high to hit the men in the attacking boats. The bluecoats crossing the river maintained their silence until an exultant yell came out of the fog telling those who followed that their comrades had achieved a successful landing. A scattering of rebel pickets were quickly driven from their rifle pits. Farther south, where General Reynolds's First Corps crossed, the troops encountered heavy fire, delaying their movement until late in the day on April 29. That day, the Union army employed balloons to ascertain the Confederate lines and movement. On the ground as the 121st attempted to cross the river, a story circulated among the men that a rebel woman in a house in town near the lines would expose herself and when the Union troops "showed themselves above the rifle pits, [they] would be fired on by [Lee's] sharpshooters." On the orders of an officer, the next time she showed her face, Union infantrymen shot and killed her.[5]

Capture of Marye's Heights

The diversionary force below the city could hear the sound of muskets and cannon up and beyond Marye's Heights on the Orange Plank Road toward Chancellorsville. Lee was not fooled. He perceived Hooker's intent, and his bold move to divide his army to meet both perils became legend. He detached a small force of 9,000 men under Jubal Anderson Early to keep Sedgwick occupied near Fredericksburg while he sent his main force against Hooker at Chancellorsville. As Hooker pulled into a defensive position, he reeled from Stonewall Jackson's brilliant rout of the federal Eleventh Corps under O. O. Howard. Hooker left Sedgwick and his Sixth Corps alone below the city, where Sedgwick followed his instructions to demonstrate against Early and not engage him fully in battle. Meanwhile, conflicting orders from Hooker, received at 5:00 in the afternoon on Friday, May 1, directed Sedgwick to move against the Confederates in the town on the heights. Just as he began his attack, the orders were countermanded.

The next night, Saturday, May 2, Hooker, realizing his perilous position, or-

dered Sedgwick to come to his aid in Chancellorsville. Further, Sedgwick's orders were to "attack and destroy any force on the road, and be in the vicinity"
of Hooker's forces by daylight. Now, the orders were for full battle, and the only
road to Chancellorsville led through Fredericksburg. Oddly, Hooker told Sedgwick to cross the river at Fredericksburg to attack the city, although Sedgwick
had crossed on the south side below the city earlier. Sedgwick thought these
new instructions were too time-consuming. He therefore ignored them and instead decided to move his command straight up the Bowling Green Road toward the town. Years later, with Sedgwick dead, Hooker pointed to Sedgwick's
refusal to follow his orders as the main reason the federals lost the battle of
Chancellorsville.

On Sunday morning, May 3, the men of the 121st roused from a fitful sleep
at 1:00 and headed toward the town of Fredericksburg. As the morning broke
on a clear spring Sabbath day, the regiment received artillery fire, which it responded to with its outlying pickets. Pickets exchanged fire for about an hour
and a half until a concealed battery began throwing grape and canister at the
advancing federals. The barrage wounded and killed many in the brigade. Adj.
George W. Bicknell of the 5th Maine, who later became that regiment's historian, was seriously wounded and removed from the field. A few members of
the 121st were wounded as well. Sedgwick, leaving the 121st in a reserve position, assaulted Fredericksburg, traversing the same bloody ground toward
Marye's Heights that the Union troops had faced the previous December. On
the heights, a strong but small contingent of Brig. Gen. William Barksdale's Mississippi veterans and southern artillerists opposed the advancing bluecoats.

Heavy artillery from two batteries positioned on either side of a road leading to the crest repulsed the first federal attempt. Infantry power from the
heights also produced an effective, raking field of fire. Sedgwick devised a plan
involving two storming, converging columns and an old-fashioned line of battle
that met at the tollgate halfway up the ridge to Marye's Heights. Early's men
were driven from their positions by the 6th Maine and the 5th Wisconsin, supported by siege guns from the other side of the river. The assault was not without loss, and Sedgwick reported "most destructive fire" while capturing prisoners and guns. By 11:00 A.M., the federal troops were in the town and atop
the ridge. The second battle of Fredericksburg ended with the stars and stripes
floating over the city. "National pride, thrilled the breast of every soldier, when
we saw them wave triumphantly over the heights," Clarke Rice told his brother.[6]

The 121st remained below the town and missed out on the action on the hill
behind Fredericksburg. With some skirmishing and artillery duels, it once again
found itself on the Bowling Green Pike. One hundred and fifty yards away, a
line of rebel rifle pits occupied by sharpshooters took aim at a nearby Union artillery battery. Upton, immediately perceiving the situation, called on a squad
of men, who quickly trained their Enfields on the puffs of smoke from the

enemy pits. Within a short time, they snuffed out the threat, and around eleven in the morning, the men noticed that the firing in town and on Marye's Heights stopped, followed by cheers from below the city. From the south of town, the 121st could see the unit and Union flags of the rest of Sedgwick's command on the heights. Brooks's division was the freshest on the field. He was ordered "to march his division upon the heights and follow the panic stricken rebels." The 121st took to the Bowling Green Pike and headed toward Fredericksburg, passing the graves of Doxtater, Spicer, Davis, and Willson, to join the victorious troops on the hill where the federals had routed the Mississippi troops. The regiment halted briefly "to restore a long breath" when they were "again put in motion."[7]

They passed through the devastated city, where "evidences of the fierce nature of the struggle just ended were present." The 121st stopped momentarily in the town and then passed over the same ground Sedgwick's men had just traversed. There, the "deadliness of the enemy's fire accumulated and behind a ruined brick building," Clinton Beckwith saw "a ghastly row of desperately wounded men." As the 121st crossed Marye's Heights, the "dead were in every position, just as they had fallen." Martin McMahon remembered years later that "the morning dew was yet fresh upon the grass upon that pretty slope which led from the city limits to this crest of death."

Sedgwick pressed on toward Chancellorsville, realizing that Hooker's original plans for a pincer movement against Lee had now turned the hunter into the hunted. Having pushed Early off Marye's Heights and to the south, Sedgwick found himself beyond his support lines as he headed west to meet Hooker. And as Sedgwick proceeded, Early seized the opportunity to slip troops around him. Complicating the situation, Brig. Gen. Cadmus M. Wilcox, a North Carolinian, posted his command on the early morning of May 3 at Banks' Ford on the south bank of the river. Wilcox had graduated from West Point in the class of 1846 with such illustrious classmates as Stonewall Jackson, George McClellan, and George Pickett. He served with John Sedgwick in the Mexican War, and he was Emory Upton's instructor at the Point.[8]

Wilcox's assignment was to prevent a federal force crossing at the ford to reinforce Hooker or Sedgwick. While visiting his rebel pickets, he noticed that the federal pickets were wearing their haversacks, which led him to believe that no force threatened the river at that point. He therefore turned his attention south to the Orange Plank Road, with the thought of reinforcing Lee at Chancellorsville. His pickets on that side of the field spotted federals advancing up the road no more than 1,000 yards away. Pulling together a few scattered artillery pieces, Wilcox opened on them, and they scattered. Wilcox then rode to the vicinity of the Marye House just north of Fredericksburg, where he spotted Sedgwick's corps moving west. He returned to his troops and realized that his men were the only obstacle between Sedgwick's corps and the rear of the main Confederate force at Chancellorsville.[9]

"With the enemy in full view on the crest of the first range of hills in [the] rear of Fredericksburg, and with three times [his own command]," Wilcox "felt it a duty to delay the enemy as much as possible in his advance." After a few batteries threw shells into Sedgwick's advancing men, Wilcox thought that they were reluctant to move quickly. In effect, the rebel batteries were behind the woods near Salem Church and could not clearly see the advancing federals to fire on them effectively. The barrage did hit a few men, including one who "was literally torn to pieces." Wilcox took advantage of the moment and posted his men perpendicular to the Orange Plank Road at the "red church." In the road, he placed two rifled pieces, which temporarily halted the advancing skirmishers of the bluecoats. Skirmishers exchanged fire as the federals brought up a battery to respond.

As Wilcox wrote later, the "line of battle was formed, crossing the road at right angles." He placed the 11th and 14th Alabama on the left of the road (north) and the 10th and 8th Alabama on the right of the road (south). Between the two wings and in the road were four pieces of artillery. Two companies were placed in the church and the school. The federals stopped at the tollgate house on the road about 1,000 yards away from Wilcox and began returning artillery fire, attempting to reach the Confederate lines of infantry. The artillery barrage ended around 5:00 P.M. when the advanced federal skirmishers engaged in a heavy exchange with their rebel counterparts for some fifteen or twenty minutes. Open fields between the opposing forces gave way to a small ridge, behind which lay the Confederates. A small, thick copse of woods occupied either side of the road. Behind the woods and in a road with ditches on both sides, the Confederates lay in wait. James Cronkite described the landscape years later: "This road, having a trench on either side, was a fair specimen of many Virginia turnpikes. The dirt from these made a good rifle pit." Salem Church sat south of the road in a clearing that was filled with rebel snipers. Dennis Dewey remembered, "It was a beautiful Sunday afternoon." The scene was set.[10]

The Attack at Salem Church

The Sixth Corps walked toward the waiting rebels. Joe Bartlett's 2nd Brigade of Bully Brooks's division marched down the Plank Road; Bartlett would complain that the tiring, hot, and debilitating march damaged his command. Bully Brooks disparagingly referred to the 121st and the rest of the volunteers under him as "two hundred dollar sons of bitches" as he sent them into battle, a comment that still rankled Daniel Holt months later. Bartlett halted

(top left) Lt. Thomas Arnold, who left a position as Herkimer County supervisor, sold his business and left a wife and small daughter to join the 121st. He was falsely accused of accounting improprieties by the Herkimer County Board in the spring of 1863. He fought the charges, but then succumbed to wounds received at Salem Church. Author's collection. (top right) Major Andrew E. Mather. Kidder called him a "martinet" and he was despised by his men. He left the regiment in 1864 to become a Lieutenant Colonel in the 20th U.S. Colored Troops. Courtesy of the New York State Historical Association. Research Library, Special Collections, Civil War Collection. Hereafter, NYSHA. (above) Sixth Corps before Salem Church. Civil War author Earl J. Hess has re-attributed and re-identified this photograph based on recent research. Originally thought to depict troops in the trenches before Petersburg in 1864–65, Hess maintains that it is "one of the best group photographs of Civil War Soldiers ever taken." He believes that it depicts "Bully" Brooks' 1st Division, 6th Army Corps south of Fredericksburg during the Battle of Chancellorsville before they began their march westward toward Salem Church. The men shown in this photograph could be members of the 2nd Brigade and possibly members of the 121st. Courtesy of the Library of Congress.

the federal skirmish line at the woods, where "it became evident that . . . farther advance was to be contested with all the forces of the enemy." But Brooks countermanded Bartlett and ordered him to set his troops in line, prepared to engage the enemy.

The 5th Maine held the far left, next to the 96th Pennsylvania; the 121st was on its right, and the 23rd New Jersey was on the far right, with its right wing on the Plank Road. Directly behind the Jersey regiment, Bartlett placed the 16th New York in support. Across the road were two other New Jersey and Pennsylvania regiments. Meanwhile, behind the dense woods and in the church, Wilcox's Alabamians awaited the oncoming federals. After the Union troops made a short march forward, the Confederate batteries opened on the advancing federals. The "popping sound of musketry" indicated the forward movement of the federal skirmish line, consisting of New Jersey troops with white knapsacks and the first signs of Confederate resistance. The 121st and the forward line of battle followed to the edge of the woods, where they encountered a wooden fence. Upton's orders were to push through the woods "and engage the enemy, who were supposed to be hastily withdrawing."[11]

The rebel skirmishers soon yielded to the advancing blue lines, which disappeared into the woods "thick with harsh, unyielding undergrowth, with little timber." As the attacking troops walked forward, they moved into the fire zone. Confederate musket fire became more intense, and halfway into the woods, Upton ordered the regiment to fix bayonets. The federals managed to reach the far edge of the woods, "where the rebs were lying flat on their bellies waiting to give us a volley as soon we stuck our heads out." A hundred yards away, the Confederates held their fire as an eerie silence fell over the field. The approaching federals crossed another 20 yards, and still the rebels held their fire. Wilcox's men watched the federals who had halted momentarily 80 yards away. And then, "giving three cheers, they [the federals] came with a rush, driving our skirmishers before them," Wilcox reported. The Union line had walked right up to the rebel line.

The Confederates' withering first volley missed the target. They fired from behind the protection of the ditch in the road, and as a result, their fire went well over the approaching bluecoats' heads. Had the fire been an inch or two lower, James Cronkite remembered, it "would have almost annihilated our command at the outset." With the second volley, adjusted for maximum effectiveness, Wilcox's men "delivered a close and terrible fire upon them, killing and wounding many and causing many of them to waver and give way." Clinton Beckwith recalled that, suddenly, "a line of men rose up and delivered their fire almost in our faces." Benton "Bennie" West, running alongside Beckwith, fell almost immediately. Bounding up against Beckwith, he died without a sound. Bennie had served as a nurse under Dr. Holt's supervision. That morning, he had been given a rifle—"all the nurses had to carry guns and go into action and we lost 5 out of 8," John Ingraham wrote. "I happened to be one of the 3 that came out all sound." William Remmel recorded that he thought "nothing but the rear guard were here but we soon found different, for we were mowed down like grass before the scythe."[12]

The 121st halted and returned fire. Lieutenant Casler ordered his company to kneel when he saw that the rebels were firing high. The 121st and its flank support pressed forward as the rebels left the ditch closest to the federals and fell back to their rear—another ditch on the other side of the road and on higher ground offered a clear firing lane into the advancing federals. The Confederates left their dead and wounded were they fell. The 9th Alabama occupied the church and a schoolhouse nearby in the churchyard. They poured fire into the advancing federals, who bunched together around the buildings in order to avoid being hit. Eventually, the federals prevailed, and the two buildings were captured with all of their occupants. "We were driving the Rebs toward Hooker looking for nothing but success," enthused an optimistic Adelbert Reed, "thousands of prisoners were being taken and we were close upon there heels. We had made one of the most desperate charges ever known."[13]

In the fighting, Upton's horse, "Manassas," was hit by a rebel ball, and he reared up. When the wounded horse became unwieldy and dashed toward the enemy lines, Upton threw himself from the saddle to avoid being captured. Members of the 121st, seeing the empty saddle, feared the worst. At the same time, Adj. Francis W. Morse's horse received a ball through the neck that wounded him but did not disable him. A second shot struck Morse's saddle, and a third finally struck the animal in the head, killing him. Morse landed on his rear end on the ground, unhurt. On the other side of the churchyard and at the road perpendicular to the Plank Road, the 121st ran into the entrenched Alabama troops, but "the fire was received without creating the slightest confusion." The 121st pushed the 10th Alabama back, exposing the flank of the 8th Alabama next to it. The entire brigade, led by the 121st, had penetrated the rebel line. Recognizing the danger his troops faced, the 8th Alabama's commanding officer, Hilary Herbert, ordered his men to fire directly into the flank of the hard-charging 121st New York Infantry—with devastating effect.

Herbert later recalled that "if Upton had had another line coming up fifty or a hundred paces in the rear, I think we must have yielded, and if we had done so it would have been a very serious blow, because our lines were greatly extended and there were no troops near by to succor us." The 96th Pennsylvania and the 23rd New Jersey came up on either side of the 121st for support, and Egbert Olcott tried in vain to get the Jersey regiment to countercharge. The regiments became disorganized and disoriented, and it became "impossible to remain longer." Upton attempted to rally his regiment, "almost crying as he spoke, implored them in the name of their country, to stand by the old flag, and make an attempt to avenge their fallen comrades." Cleaveland Campbell remembered Upton was everywhere at once. Upton stood at his elbow and his voice could be heard over the musket fire: "Don't flinch men—stand by me—I'm not afraid of the *Devil*." And Pvt. Dennis Dewey remembered that "he called out to us, '121st, help is coming.'" The 16th and the 121st New York held their positions as long as possible, but the 5th Maine and the 96th Pennsylvania gave ground. Clarke Rice told his parents that the papers credited the 96th with leading the brigade in the charge, but he clarified the record: "I assure you that it did lead it in the retreat. It never was known to fight well but once, and that was at Crampton's Gap." Upton and Olcott, seemingly oblivious to the enemy's fire, encouraged the men to remain calm and cool "and all with a fearlessness that seemed to defy both injury and death."[14]

As Morse stated (and many others later verified), "No mortal could stay and live where we were, and the line moved back and retreated in confusion." Dennis Dewey recalled that "this was the hottest place the 121st ever saw." Hilary Herbert knew that the troops attacking his Confederates "were unused to battle by the way they hung on." An anonymous writer told the *Herkimer Democrat,* "Our boys were falling like hail on all sides but we held our ground about twenty minutes." Dewey used all forty rounds in his cartridge box, and when his musket became too hot to handle, he took a dead man's gun and cartridges. Spook Wilson rode up from Bartlett's headquarters screaming, "Damn you, don't you know enough to fall back?" Stragglers stumbled out of the woods and were shot as they sought cover. As the Alabama troops pursued them, Wilson pressed the men to retreat to the tollhouse where the rest of Brooks's command had gathered.

Wilson warned the regiment's remnants that they would be captured if they remained in the open field halfway between the woods they had just left and the support that never came to their aid in the rear. Morse picked up the colors and started to run to the rear. He fell over his spurs and saber three times but managed to escape capture. He claimed that he met Colonel Bartlett in the field, gave him the colors, and immediately fell to the ground, wounded in the ankle. Using his saber as a crutch, he hobbled to friendly lines. Wilcox's Alabamians pressed the "confused mass of the discomfited enemy" down the Plank Road. If Wilcox had had a good battery to "play upon this retreating mass, the carnage would have been terrific."[15]

Wilcox's and Brig. Gen. Paul Semmes's commands were the only ones that followed the retreating federals: "Night and want of ammunition prevented a farther pursuit." The Union remnants eventually rallied in the rear with "20 or 30 from the Ninety-sixth Pennsylvania Volunteers" and a few men from the New Jersey brigade. They gathered first around the flag and then farther to the rear, out of harm's way. Veterans of earlier campaigns told Adelbert Reed that they "never came into so hot a fight where the bullets flew so much like hail and the parties stood so determined neither willing to give up." Reed was puzzled that he had survived the fight, which he estimated lasted no longer than ten minutes. He never heard the moans and shrieks of the wounded because of the rattling musketry and the earth-shaking cannonading. He cursed the 96th Pennsylvania for breaking ranks and fleeing, leaving the 121st's left flank exposed to Herbert's 8th Alabama and his efficient raking fire. He also blamed the 16th New York on the right for retreating, leaving the right flank exposed.

Nearly 200 men from the 121st were killed or wounded, and Wilcox's losses were comparable. In the battle's aftermath, "everything was in chaos. Fragments of fifty regiments were drifting around in wild confusion," Clarke Rice wrote. The fields were littered with the dead and the wounded "and stragglers running, they knew not whither." Upton proclaimed that he "never saw one that equaled it," yet he remained businesslike. Joe Bartlett's distress came through loudly in his official report. That document also revealed his affection for his brigade: "It was the first time they were ever repulsed; it was the first time they were ever ordered to hold a position which they were unable to do; it was the first time they retired in the face of the enemy, and their losses attest their regret more feelingly than I can express it."[16]

The Cost

The fighting ended within twenty minutes, exacting a horrible toll. The point-blank fire decimated the regiment: the wounds of the survivors and the dead bore witness to its intensity. Emmet and Elias Mather were wounded—Emmet in the shoulder and Elias in his right arm below the elbow. Kidder shared brandy with them and "nine others." Kidder's brother Edward, a private in Company F, received a minor wound in his left arm, which was saved. DeWitt Wells of Company E was hit in the groin, and Capt. Andrew Davidson was shot seriously through both legs. Sedgwick ordered the wounded removed to Fredericksburg, putting them in harm's way due to the proximity of Barksdale's Mississippians. Davidson, bleeding profusely and unable to use his legs, urged Wells to take care of himself, but Wells stayed with Davidson until ambulances could carry both men across the river to safety.

Sam Kelley, slightly wounded in the right arm above the elbow, was removed with others to Potomac Creek Hospital, 5 miles distant from Fredericksburg. He told his mother: "Well, Ma, the 121st regiment has seen what it is to fight. Our regiment is badly cut to pieces." Many of the wounded were hit in the forearm or in the head, since they were trying to load their muskets while hugging the ground "as close as possible." "If we would raise our heads we would feel the wind of a bullet going by us from some sharpshooter," John Ingraham reported. Lester Murdock in Company E "saw a gun aimed at his head and jumped behind a small tree; received a bullet through his clothes, cutting his suspenders and raising a contusion across his back as large as a broomstick." He joined only fourteen others to answer roll call later that evening. Twenty-five-year-old Robert Caldwell of Laurens was not among them: he died soon after being shot in the head. His comrades buried him on the field. Isaac Miner, a sergeant in Company H, fell while helping a wounded comrade off the field.[17]

Dr. Holt found Emory Upton's brother Henry, who had taken a ball through the shoulder and upper portion of his right lung. It fractured his clavicle and passed through his scapula, leaving his left arm paralyzed. Henry was carried off the field, and surgeons stanched his hemorrhaging. He survived and returned to duty on November 5, 1863, just before Rappahannock Station, but exertion and military duties kept his wound from healing. He was medically discharged the following year.[18]

Dr. Holt also found Capt. Thomas Arnold of Company H lying next to Upton, mortally wounded. A thirty-year-old lawyer, Arnold had left a viable practice in Fairfield when he enlisted. He lived in the village of Herkimer with his wife of four years and a new baby girl; he held the office of excise commissioner of Herkimer County. When he enlisted, he sold his house and settled his debts, and with fellow lawyer and recruiter Clinton Moon, he raised a company for the 121st. Colonel Franchot, impressed with his intelligence and work ethic, asked Arnold to become his adjutant, with the rank of captain.

As the army was suffering at Belle Plain, the clerk of the Herkimer County Board of Supervisors had announced that he intended to prosecute Arnold for not filing his annual report as excise commissioner. Furious and unable to leave the field to defend himself, Arnold resorted to writing long letters of explanation. He enlisted his father to aid in his defense. "Herkimer County prosecute me!!" he railed. "And in my absence too when I could buy not for love or gold, a permit to visit my wife and child, much less my native place. Why? I came down here to fight, and shed the last drop of blood for her firesides and free homes. He, who knows me, knows I did not come for money." In a chilling prescient comment, Arnold continued, "If I prove not true, may some higher power lay me cold on the first battlefield, which is not far off." When he was wounded at Salem Church, his father and wife rushed to his side as friends and family prayed for his recovery, but he died in the Potomac Creek Hospital on May 18. After his body was embalmed, it was returned to Herkimer County, accompanied by his widow and father. Eventually, the charges brought by the Herkimer board were dropped.[19]

Fred Ford had just been promoted to second lieutenant of Company G on April 15. In the fighting in May, he took a minié ball through his groin or thigh, which cut a main artery. "Bleeding profusely," he asked John Kidder of Company I to help him stay out of the line of fire and the heat of the sun. Kidder carried him back behind Salem Church, where he left him as his life bled away. At first, the *Herkimer County Journal* reported that its correspondent had been seriously wounded and that there was little chance he would survive. The paper hoped that sympathetic rebels had captured and cared for him. His father, Albert, left Herkimer for the battlefield to find him. When he did, his worst fears were confirmed. He notified the paper that "Fred, alas! Is Dead." Confederate troops had buried him after stripping him of everything but his shirt. When Ford's body was exhumed, Clarke Rice remarked, "Though he had been exposed for two days, yet he looked remarkably natural." Albert Ford authorized disinterment and returned home with his son's body. There, the Reverend Dolphus I. Skinner of Utica performed the burial service as family and friends laid Ford to rest in Eaton Bush Cemetery. Skinner preached a spellbinding sermon to an overflowing crowd of mourners, including those who drove their wagons and carriages to the open church windows to listen to him. It was reminiscent of Lt. Angus Cameron's funeral six months before, at which, despite hard rain, "the crowd was nearly as great." Rice took Ford's death hard. Both Ford and Arnold were mourned in the *Herkimer County Journal* as two sons of the county who fell on the same battlefield: "And thus from the same neighborhood are taken two officers, brilliant, virtuous and beloved by large circles of friends and relatives."[20]

Two days before the battle of Salem Church, Capt. Nelson O. Wendell had a premonition of death. He gave Dr. Holt $250 and all his earthly belongings with the request that Holt safeguard them. He kept $5—"a sum sufficient for a few days' requirements, and a sum sufficiently large enough to fall into the hands of the enemy." According to one account, Wendell was shot in the head while leading his Company F. Another claimed that he went down, wounded in the arm and then in the chest, while leading his men forward. Emory Upton reported that he saw him in the path of his own horse, Manassas, after Upton had fallen from the saddle. The horse struck Wendell as the two crossed paths after the horse had charged into two privates. Upton tried to warn him, but the horse's shoulder struck Wendell in the back, "throwing him several feet. He got up and was almost immediately shot through the head, producing instant death."

Adelbert Reed claimed to be the last to see Wendell alive and insisted that he was not killed instantly; rather, he said he saw him propped up against a tree with his head in his hands. "As one of our men passed him they spoke to him but he made no reply. Whether he was dead or wounded is not known." James Cronkite did not see Wendell fall but learned from others that "he was shot through the head as the battle was drawing to a close, and was doubtless instantly killed. His death shed a gloom over the whole regiment." Wendell's nephew, Fernando Wright, wrote his aunt, Wendell's wife, that he had been shot in the temple, the ball tearing through his head and coming out the opposite side. Wright saw his body four days later "and could still recognize him." He told his aunt that Wendell was buried in a pit with 200 to 300 others; he added that he had tried to cut off a lock of "Uncle Nelly's" hair, but the rebels would not let him near the body. Wright, hit in the neck, lost the use of his left arm.

Dr. Holt also saw Wendell in death, ignominiously dumped naked into a watery pit. "His greenbacks would have served a poor purpose towards clothing him for the tomb," Holt reported, "and as I looked upon all that remained of so pure and worthy a man as he, I thought how well it was in life he had provided against such a contingency as I now saw in his death." The *Otsego Republican* remembered Wendell, a survivor of Bull Run and the Peninsula campaign, as a "man of fine education, an honest and upright citizen . . . peace to his ashes." James Jewell, a member of his company, also saw Wendell fall and later described the entire battle experience: "We got whaled outlandishly, it is a wonder how many of us escaped." In addition to Wendell, Company F lost twenty-three men out of fifty-five.[21]

During the battle as the rebels fired a third volley into the regiment, Ulysses F. Doubleday, lieutenant in Company H, died instantly, shot between the eyes with a ball to the forehead that exited the "back side of his head." Waving his sword wildly, he died urging his company forward: "Go on boys, you are driving them." Sgt. Rosselle Firman had the presence of mind to gather Doubleday's hat, sword, and belt as the 121st retreated. He lost the cap but retained the sword, which he promised to return to his family. Battlefield conditions prevented recovery of Doubleday's body. His family believed that fire consumed him when it engulfed the field near the church.[22]

The dead were the lucky ones that evening. "As darkness came over the scene a lurid flame, kindled by the fire of our batteries, was consuming the dry leaves and underbrush, in the wood in which our helpless wounded lay," James Cronkite related years later. Henry Crittenden of Company C, the brother-in-law of John Hartwell, perished in the fire. Crittenden had feared crossing the river and that he "would not live to return." Hartwell did not see him fall, but others reported that Henry was shot in the forehead and in the mouth, firing two rounds as he went down. Hartwell believed that Crittenden died in the flames because he and others were "near the fire" when it started. He also thought Henry had killed a large Confederate on the third shot at him when the rebel "threw his arms wildly in the air and fell over backwards." Hartwell would forward Crittenden's personal belongings home.[23]

Delavan Bates, second lieutenant with Company I, moved with his company as it hit the schoolhouse and the regiment struck the church. He was surprised at the regiment's resiliency with no appreciable shelter. Standing next to him, Phillip Potter was busily loading and firing when he took a ball in his arm. Potter coolly turned to Bates with a smile and said: "Lieutenant, I am shot. What shall I do?" Bates ordered him to the rear, and he would remember him as an example of the spirit of most of the regiment that day in May.

During the retreat, Bates and Kidder came out of the woods together and were rallying the men to fight when Kidder lost sight of Bates. Lieutenant Butts saw Bates limping at one point, and Kidder feared the worst. As it turned out, a rebel private had captured Bates and demanded his sword, but Bates refused to turn it over to anyone other than an officer. The private walked Bates along the road to Chancellorsville, where he dutifully surrendered his sword to a major. His captors allowed him to keep his slouch hat and rubber overcoat, and two days later at Guinea Station, he and nearly 4,000 Union prisoners were loaded on trains for Libby Prison. Libby turned out to be fairly well run, much to Bates's surprise, and while there, he learned how to play chess, enjoyed card games and checkers, and read the latest papers and even a few books. From the windows, he could see the James River, Tredegar Iron Works, and Belle Island, where enlisted prisoners were kept. He managed to keep clean and had plenty of provisions. And his luck continued. On his sixteenth day at the prison, "the exchange roll was called and the last name on the list was 'Delavan Bates, 2nd Lieutenant, 121st N. Y. Vols.'" By June 11, Bates had returned to camp at White Oak Church, reunited with his regiment.[24]

Company I bore the brunt of the attack. Five men in Kidder's company were shot through the head—an indication of the point-blank ferocity of the barrage that the first wave experienced. Aaron Stephens of Company F took a bullet through his knapsack, probably while in retreat mode, but the ball passed through the sack and "entered the back of his head," killing him instantly. Adelbert Reed retrieved a ring from Stephens's pocket and sent it to his mother. Washington Babcock, an eighteen-year-old in Casler's company, took a minié ball in the stomach above his hip, and the bullet exited his spine. Alfred Casler helped him to a nearby house for shelter. There, he passed the night comfortably but refused to talk because it pained him. "He died the next morning," Casler wrote.

Cherry Valley counted its blessings after the battle. "Considering how many of the 121st were residents of our town," one local noted, "it is almost miraculous how many escaped unharmed." But the town of New Lisbon suffered the most. Of the eighteen men from that town recruited by Emmet Mather, nine in Company K died instantly. Pvt. James Bowe was shot in the forehead and killed outright. Elliot Barnes of Oneonta left a wife and several children. His widow had already lost a son at the battle of Fair Oaks earlier in the war. Another son, discharged for poor health, served with the 44th New York. The *Oneonta Herald* called the awful retribution of this "cruel war" a humbling experience "before our Maker," one that should "cause us to relinquish our sins, and call upon the God of battles for his help in this hour of our National distress and affliction." Company K had twenty-seven men wounded, some of them mortally, and three went missing. Three others from New Lisbon were killed in subsequent battles. Years later, Dennis Dewey recalled: "Oh! The heart aches in Otsego and Herkimer counties after that dread battle."[25]

Lt. Lansing B. Paine, one of seventeen from New Lisbon who survived, was angry. "I feel like avenging their deaths and no man must talk to me of Southern Brethren, men who have murdered my schoolmates and companions." Paine noted that all the file closers of Company E were wounded except himself and Sgt. Philip Woodcock—"I feel rather gloomy," he complained. Of the nine missing from Middlefield Center, just one answered roll call. Only the men of Company D escaped the Salem Church nightmare. They had been a part of the assault on the heights at Fredericksburg and were left behind "below the city as rear skirmishers." They ran to catch up to the action but arrived too late. Captain Galpin praised his men: they fought "nobly, they advanced steadily, received and returned volley and volley with great coolness and bravery," though he admitted afterward, "I do not feel like writing, but felt that I must give an account as soon as I could."[26]

From the town of Otego, one of the southernmost towns in Otsego, Jacob Gould enlisted as a private in Company K at age forty-two. The 1860 census had listed his age as thirty-five and his wife Sally's age as thirty. They had five children. Orrin, the oldest boy, enlisted two weeks after his father, at age eighteen. He outranked his father, mustering in as a corporal in the same company. Orrin died on the battlefield. Father Jacob, mortally wounded, lingered until he died three weeks later. At age thirty-two, N. H. Bill Harrington, better known to his friends as UHB (it stood for "UnHappy Bill"), joined the regiment from Little Falls in July 1862 as one of the oldest privates in Company A. He died on the field. According to one of his friends, Harrington "was under a cloud from the very beginning, for the presentiment was with him continually that he would be killed in battle."[27]

A minié ball fractured Frank Carran's leg. The rebels held him for a time, and when he returned to the army, he improved in Potomac Creek Hospital. But assigned to a small wooden bunk with "only one tick," filled with wheat straw, he soon developed a bedsore. By June 1, his mother had arrived, and she tried to make him as comfortable as possible. He joked that one leg would probably be an inch and a half shorter than the other. Despite his mother's presence and ministrations of the ladies from the Philadelphia Sanitary Commission, his condition worsened, and on June 5, he died. Thomas McGowan, a member of Company H who hailed from Little Falls, had a ball pass through his liver, lodging in his left hip. With others, he boarded the steamer *John A. Warner* at Aquia Creek to recuperate at Finley General Hospital in Washington. With the ball lodged in his bone, it caused little bleeding. His dressings were changed regularly, and he received opium to sleep at night. By the end of May, he began to improve, but the doctors could not break his addiction to chewing tobacco.

Major Henry Galpin, who vied
with Mather and John Fish for the
major's slot when Upton and
Olcott were promoted. Well liked
by his men, he was faulted by his
superiors for his familiarity with
the enlisted men. He served
during the first year of the war
as an enlisted man in Ellsworth's
Avengers and resigned after being
wounded at Cedar Creek.
Author's collection.

Then, on June 1, he took a turn for the worse, and he died two days later, still
using tobacco. McGowan's autopsy showed a gangrenous and ruptured liver
caused by pyemia, or an infection of the blood producing puslike abscesses.[28]

Banks' Ford and Dr. Holt's Adventure

On the morning after the battle of Salem Church, Monday, May 4, the
Union army was holed up in two inverted U formations, with both open ends
touching on the Rappahannock approximately 3 miles away from each other.
Hooker had 75,000 men in a strong defensive position, and his only escape route
was over the river at U.S. Ford. Sedgwick, pinned against the river in a similar
configuration, relied on Scott's Ford and Banks' Ford as his escape hatch. Jubal
Early, who had moved off the field of battle to the south after the Sixth Corps
passed through Fredericksburg, returned up Telegraph Road and became a part
of the right wing of the Confederate army covering Sedgwick on three sides.
Lee split his army and left A. P. Hill at Chancellorsville with 25,000 men facing

Hooker. That morning, he personally moved with his remaining troops down the Orange Plank Road toward Fredericksburg and joined Early to form a large U around Sedgwick. While Hooker remained in a defensive position with no attacks coming from the rebels, the fight resumed on Sedgwick's front.

The federal troops thus awoke that morning with Confederate troops on three sides and the river at their backs. Several times during the night, a sleepless Sedgwick had petitioned a bewildered Hooker for help. Hooker finally responded around 8 A.M., essentially telling Sedgwick to fend for himself. Remnants of the 121st formed up behind a battery of 3-inch guns and waited. All during the day, the 121st could hear firing off to its left toward Fredericksburg, where Early engaged Gen. Albion Howe's division of Vermonters. The rebels continued directing a steady rain of artillery toward the bluecoat lines. "A little way off a dead man lay who had been struck with a cannon shot and the back of his head had been carried away," Clinton Beckwith remembered, "and the fact that his features remained life like and natural caused comment, and we all went back and looked at him, and he was not buried until afternoon, so heedless were those whose duty it was to give him burial."[29]

Lee had wanted to attack Sedgwick early that morning, but the delay in bringing the troops up from Chancellorsville and preparing them for a coordinated attack foiled his plans. The delay kept Hooker from coming to the aid of Sedgwick because Hooker perceived no threat and therefore thought no action was required on his part. The delay and the decision by Lee to attack on his right flank spared the 121st from further serious action because of its position near the center, which remained relatively untouched by the Confederates. Sedgwick, however, found himself in an increasingly dangerous position. Surprisingly, his corps was able to fend off the waves of assaults until darkness spared all of his command. And as Emory Upton remarked, "Thank God, they will have to light candles, soon." The left of the line, away from the 121st's position, sustained the majority of the losses.[30]

That night, in an incident that can only be described as worthy of a Gilbert and Sullivan opera, Dr. Holt, leading a team of medical assistants in the dark, stumbled into General Wilcox's lines. Under orders, Holt was moving his base of operations even as he tried to save the life of a New Jersey man who had been shot in the armpit and was bleeding profusely from a severed artery. He closed up his field hospital with the admonition to his attendants to stay together and avoid straggling at all costs; if they were to go "to the devil, we would all go together." As Sedgwick's men headed toward Banks' Ford and the river, Holt, hearing voices in the dark ahead of him, stopped a captain leading his company and asked what brigade was before him. The response was "Kershaw's." Holt found the answer curious, but since "Brigadiers were as plentiful as blackberries in the army, I did not know but our own side had many such names in it, but of *that* fact, I knew nothing."

After giving that piece of information, the officer in the dark responded with his own question: "To what regiment do *you* belong?" Holt's men were piling into his heels in the dark, so he tried to stop them with the command "*Halt, Halt, Halt,*" and then he answered the voice in the dark: "The 121st." Meanwhile, all along the line, Holt's men repeated his call to "Halt" until the doctor realized that his commands had brought "the entire rebel army" to a standstill. Once this piece of physical comedy ran its course, the dialogue continued when the rebel commander asked, "The 121st what?" to which Holt replied, "121st New York." The voice in the dark then asked Holt's rank. Next, a rebel officer rode up in a rage demanding to know who gave the order for his men to halt. When Holt revealed that he did so in order not to run over the rebel army, the Confederate officer replied, "Federal Army be damned! And you too!!" He then placed Holt and his contingent of hospital wards under arrest.

Holt treated the entire incident as a lark. In turning over all his property to the rebels, he remarked that he "never had a transfer of property more complete and thorough . . . it was charming." The rebel army had established a hospital in the church, and there, his captors escorted Holt into a small room with his entourage. Three or four guards charged with watching them immediately began to barter with the prisoners for pocket knives, watches, canteens, and any other items not already confiscated.

The following morning began the real work as Holt and his team started ministering to the wounded. In the church/hospital, a number of men from the 121st lay dead or dying. "All over and around the building the best blood of Herkimer and Otsego was dripping away upon the rebel soil of the Old Dominion." Holt and his men took short rest breaks and food when they could over the few days as they tended to the wounded. Had General Wilcox not "kindly supplied me with food from his own table, and made me a guest rather than a prisoner," Holt reported, he probably would not have survived. On one of the days after the battle, Holt left his captors looking for the body of Bennie West, who had wielded a musket that Sunday morning. An overzealous "young gray back" accosted Holt and then threatened to shoot him. Once the doctor talked his way out of the predicament, he returned to his own regiment. Holt also witnessed the burial of many of the 121st's dead in one large mass grave, among them Fred Ford, Captain Wendell, and Bennie West. Isaac Darling, a prisoner of a few days, had received permission to go on the battlefield, where he found the bodies of Fred Ford and Nelson Wendell and other friends from Herkimer.[31]

Holt also made the acquaintance of Confederate surgeon George Rogers Clark Todd, Mary Lincoln's brother, who described his sister as a "poor weak-minded woman." Todd spoke with an impediment, and at first, he did not impress Holt. But Holt eventually warmed to his congenial manner. Todd immersed himself in the medical issues at Chancellorsville and earned an excellent reputation as a surgeon. He told Holt that he had amputated the arm of Charles Nichols, from Company I, at the shoulder. The man's survival was remarkable and a testimony to Todd's medical prowess, since that particular amputation killed nearly 100 percent of its victims.[32]

General Lee visited Holt during his captivity, and the two discussed the merits of medical care on both sides. In addition, Lee sent the medical director of the Confederate army to Holt's aid, as amputations by this time "had become imperative." Holt and Lee discovered that they were both Masons, to which Holt attributed his short captivity. He realized he could have been "an inmate of Libby [Prison]" if Lee or other Confederate officers had not treated him as well as they did. The rebels had taken his horse, saddle, and several personal items, which he finally retrieved as the army moved north toward Pennsylvania. Supposedly, Holt had asked Lee for the return of the items personally, and they had been returned within four days to the Union army; the provost marshal general, for unknown reasons, retained them all until the army began moving. Holt also wrote a personal note to Lee a few months later, thanking him for his kindness (although he wondered how it would appear for him to be corresponding with the enemy). "How could I but feel a sense of unalloyed kindness toward such a man whose word is law and who as easily might have caused my death?" he asked.[33]

When the fighting ceased, the rebels praised the bravery exhibited by the 121st, but "[they called] the Eleventh Corps base cowards." James Jewell reported that the rebels "never saw a new regiment fight better than the 121st." Unanimously, the men of the 121st characterized the leadership of Emory Upton and Egbert Olcott as inspirational, and they praised their valor and courage. Upton and Olcott returned the feelings. Marcus Casler told the *Herkimer County Journal* that after Upton lost his horse, "he took the ground and fought like a perfect demon. He don't know what fear is." General Bartlett pronounced that the men of the 121st finally "won for themselves the proud title of soldiers," and Upton declared the regiment fit for future battle despite its enormous casualty list.

The men in the ranks, though they admired their commander's courage, thought the whole affair a waste. Some blamed the disaster on the "generals." Delavan Bates blamed Hooker and ridiculed his moniker, "Fighting Joe": if he had fought, Sedgwick and the 121st would not have suffered as they did. Dr. Holt remarked: "The 121st exists in *fact*—the *name* glorious and abiding will remain, but how poorly compensated by such renown." In a letter home, Lansing Paine left the distinct impression that the 121st had fallen into an ambush. Dr. Holt's thoughts were similar, and Francis Morse characterized the whole affair as pointless. Clarke Rice blamed Sedgwick and the Lincoln administration but made excuses for Hooker. Isaac Best—the reformer, the temperance zealot, the converted teetotaler—had the "real story" on the highest of authorities—

the bugler on Hooker's staff—that a drunken Hooker had failed the Union troops at Chancellorsville.[34]

That night, May 4–5, the Sixth Corps, under cover of darkness, moved quietly over the river, ending the battle of Banks' Ford. The 121st crossed the river last, as daylight began to illuminate the scene. "You can imagine our anxiety as the morning hours began to approach," Clarke Rice told his brother Daniel. "That was the most horrid night I ever experienced." The only sounds breaking the stillness were the "lonely screech of the owl and the doleful screech of the katydid." The retreat demoralized the regiment. "To think after we had fought so hard and lost so many men, to think that we had to fall back on the other side was grinding on a fellow," lamented John Ingraham. Running the last 4 miles across Banks' Ford with the rebels on their heels, the men of the 121st at last found shelter on the other side of the Rappahannock. Many were so exhausted that they "dropped down in the road" and were captured. Dean Pierce told his diary: "They closed hard uptight on us, they had reinforcements come and they let into us awful. They shelled us all night and this morning but we have got accrost the river out of their reach now." Also in Company D, Malcolm Graham told his sister Sarah that although the regiment suffered greatly, his company counted only two wounded, despite the fact that the regiment found itself outnumbered three to one and Dr. Holt and the drum corps had been captured. The retreat tested the most heroic: "I tell you what; there was some scratching when we withdrew, for the rebels had us nearly surrounded." Further upriver, Hooker quietly slipped back over the Rappahannock at U.S. Ford the next day, much to Lee's anger. Lee reported that with the "blessing of Heaven," he drove Sedgwick "over the river. We have reoccupied Fredericksburg, and no enemy remains south of the Rappahannock in its vicinity."[35]

Thirty years after the war, Dewitt Clinton Beckwith, who had been a corporal at the time but was now a colonel, walked through the halls of Congress with a close friend. In a committee meeting room, the two came upon former Confederate colonel Hilary Abner Herbert, who had "enthusiastically" rejoined the Union. He was a captain in the Greenville Guards from Greenville, Alabama, where he practiced law. Wounded at the battle of the Wilderness, he would serve seven terms in Congress after the war as the Democratic chair of the Committee on Naval Affairs. His highest public service in the government came as a member of Grover Cleveland's cabinet, where he served as secretary of the navy from 1893 to 1897.

Beckwith's friend, Buell, asked Herbert if he remembered that Sunday afternoon on the heights behind Fredericksburg near the Salem Church. Herbert's response mixed recognition and respect: "Were you one of Upton's men?" he asked Beckwith. Herbert had been twenty-nine years old when he was pressed into service after Col. Young L. Royston, commanding the 8th Alabama, went down with a serious wound. Herbert told Beckwith that the Alabama troops were sure none of the New York troops opposing them had gotten away except Upton himself. "He rode through our line and back, and though we emptied a hundred rifles at him he escaped unhurt. We killed his horse and his men. We covered the ground with them after we drove you back." Beckwith interrupted him with a correction: "We were ordered back." Herbert recalled burying the dead New Yorkers in an icehouse, adding, "We took those dead Yanks and put them in the pit as close together as we could." Two months later, on his way to Gettysburg, Herbert had passed the same icehouse and discovered it was on fire. The image was seared into his memory. Herbert joked about his futile attempt to kill Yankees. If one "put them in an icehouse for a grave . . . they would come to and set themselves on fire to keep warm." It was Herbert's awkward expression of his admiration for Beckwith and the spirit of the troops who opposed him that day. But his story also spoke to the brutal nature of the first real battle experienced by the 121st New York and its young commander.[36]

Upton's Challenge: New Leadership and Fresh Recruits

As the 121st limped back across the river into its former campgrounds on May 5, the men reflected on the past ten days. The battle's full impact struck them when they filed quietly into the regiment's silent streets. Empty tents, some missing one or two occupants, and some tents gone altogether, met their stares—"scarcely one third of the tents up that there was just 12 days ago," Adelbert Reed glumly wrote his mother. "Oh mother," he continued, "there are too many vacancies. It makes ones heart ache to go over the ground and see the tents left. Is it possible that so many are gone?" James McCurry of the 16th New York merely wrote in his diary: "A fine day and all with sober faces."[37]

The *Cherry Valley Gazette*, lacking real information, printed a headline on May 9 that read: GLORIOUS NEWS FROM HOOKER'S ARMY. But no "glorious news" greeted the survivors. Several could not really comprehend what they had experienced and struggled for the right words to express their sentiments. Reed's parents read his latest letter to them at a public meeting in Edmeston, which was not to the young man's liking. In his next letter, he said he wished he "could explain the fight" to his mother in a way "fit for the public." He summed it up best in saying, "How I wish I could write and tell you all about the thing, but it is impossible." A few of the regiment marked the anniversary of the battle on May 3, 1864, noting that although one year had passed since the awful engagement above Fredericksburg, its effects still preyed on their memories. Writing thirty years later, Clinton Beckwith remembered the month following the battle with a different perspective: "It had now gotten into June, Salem Church had got to seem an ugly dream and except for some acute reasons its pangs were scarcely felt."[38]

William Remmel blamed the Union loss on Hooker and the "disgraceful con-duct" of the Eleventh Corps, which ran in the face of Stonewall Jackson's bril-liant attack at Chancellorsville on May 3. He understood the battle's effect on the public in general. He noted that although Robert E. Lee suffered large losses, the general "was jubilant over what they term achievements or series of suc-cesses and Lee informs his clique in Richmond that the loss of the Yankees must be double his own." Remmel blamed Hooker for striving to put a good face on a disaster: "It shows a disposition in both commanders to smooth his own loss and make the enemy's as large as possible." Delavan Bates, in the officer corps, reinforced Remmel's observations. He concluded that no leader in the Army of the Potomac equaled Robert E. Lee. Salem Church and Chancellorsville were unmitigated disasters inflicted by an army half the size of the Union army—a Union army hunkered down behind breastworks. When the bluecoats were able to come out from behind their comfortable and defensive positions, they still lost. Lee, he stated, "has proved himself the first general of the day. The South has unlimited confidence in his abilities, have entrusted him with the whole military power of the Confederate States and no one questions any of his acts."[39]

The survivors looked to their leaders and the surgeons for any news of their missing and wounded comrades. The care of the wounded became a priority for the authorities. Many of the seriously wounded were sent to hospitals in and around Washington and as far away as Philadelphia, Annapolis, New York, and Boston. Via the steamer *John A. Warner,* Arthur Proctor and Wilbur Champ-ney, both of Company B, sailed to hospitals in Washington. Proctor had been hit in the knee, and Champney had received arm and leg wounds. Henry Walker was shot in the left shoulder either on May 2 or May 3—he could not remem-ber which. If only the ball could be extracted, he expected to be back in action "within two or three weeks." He was moved to the Potomac Creek Station to recuperate and received a commission on May 3. The Mather boys were allowed to return home to be treated by Dr. Horace Lathrop of Coopers-town.[40]

At Salem Church, the 121st experienced war firsthand. Daniel Holt strug-gled to describe the battle and its effect on his comrades. Before understand-ing could begin, he said, one needed "to hear the incessant discharge of mus-ketry, see men leaping high in the air and falling dead upon the ground—others without a groan or a sigh yielding up their life from loss of blood—see the wounded covered with dirt and blackened by powder—hear their groans—witness their agonies, see the eye grow dim in death." His words proved inad-equate. As he became inured to the gore around him, the feelings of excite-ment, rage, revenge, and retaliation became paramount. His conviction about the war's higher calling and moral objectives kept him in the service and pre-vented him from returning to his comfortable home in Herkimer County.

Inevitably, duty called, and he continued to labor among those who needed his skills. Even though the medical team was short staffed, Holt welcomed the resignation of Surgeon Irving W. Houghtaling, who left the regiment abruptly in August. Holt condemned Houghtaling for deserting during the battle of Salem Church—a sight witnessed by several men of the regiment. "Never has he been where duty called when an action was pending, but was always in the rear far out of danger with sneaks, dead beats, bummers and cowards."[41]

Political channels were never far out of reach to resolve problems in the field. And the wounded were never far from Captain Kidder's mind. He railed against the system established by the surgeons and doctors that required the walking wounded to march and keep up with their regiments. After Salem Church, his anger boiled over, and he once again opted for a political solution. His customer and friend William Craig Fields had built a prosperous woolen and cotton industry in the village of Laurens. Fields, a lifelong member and founder of the Republican Party in Otsego County, staunchly supported Lincoln. He earned his reputation through service in several public offices in Otsego County— justice of the peace, county clerk, and county supervisor. (Otsego County voters would send him to Congress after the war, where he served one term during the heated days of Reconstruction, 1867–1869.) When Kidder's frustration boiled over, he asked his wife to "speak to Fields about how my wounded men are used and have him write to Levi Turner."[42]

Emory Upton now dealt with other serious problems. Just as he satisfied himself with his choices for command positions in the regiment, the awful toll of Salem Church put him back to rebuilding his broken command. Lee's situation was no different. He too was plagued by inadequate manpower in the ranks and in leadership positions. Replenishing his losses also challenged Lee as he began to make noises across the Rappahannock again. Upton, appalled by the losses suffered by the 121st, expressed his irritation at his supervisors' failure to recognize his military leadership. He confided to his brother his continuing frustration more than six months after the battle. Although extremely proud of his men and their performance in moments of extreme duress, he understood the toll those few minutes of intense fighting had taken. "The conduct of the regiment challenged the admiration of the enemy," he complained, "but it was not mentioned by our commanders, where others with a loss little more than half as large were mentioned in the highest terms." Upton also fretted about Henry's resignation and his return to upstate New York. "Henry's course surprised" him. He assumed that if he and Henry generated any enemies in the regiment, they would misconstrue this action as favoritism by the commander when, in fact, Henry's wound precluded him from continuing to serve.[43]

Three weeks after the battle, the 16th, 18th, 27th, 31st, and 32nd New York regiments completed their terms of service, and the troops began returning home. Nearly one-third of the Army of the Potomac—some 23,000 men—left, their terms legally over. The 16th and the 27th were especially singled out for commendation by the commanding general, Bartlett, for their two years of service. The men from all five regiments whose terms were not expiring were sent to Henry Seymour Hall, who was then inspector general for General Bartlett at 2nd Brigade headquarters; Hall organized them into the 16th New York Consolidated Battalion. Upton, alerted to the possibility that men from four retiring regiments might be available, stepped in and made an "urgent request" for Hall's service along with the eighty men under his command in the new battalion.

Upton petitioned Martin McMahon at Sixth Corps headquarters for all the three-year men he could deliver—Upton counted "about 275—still below its maximum organization." Bully Brooks, the division commander, blessed the deal, and the 121st received the new men into the ranks. And, as might be expected, the transfer of the new men "created considerable trouble." Men from the 16th New York with three-year commitments had been offered their regiment of choice—a Massachusetts artillery battery, a Regular Army battery, or the 121st. But according to Gen. Newton M. Curtis, the 16th's commander, the government ignored their requests and summarily transferred them to the 121st. Curtis claimed that a majority of the transfers had selected the 121st, noting that "all were indignant at this treatment, but, with the exception of four, all forgave the deception and entered upon duty" with the 121st. The four malcontents enlisted elsewhere or deserted.[44]

Two new recruits from the 16th New York were Isaac O. Best and James Henry McCurry. Best was born in 1841 on the New York–Canadian border in Oswegatchie, St. Lawrence County, into a family of four with English parents. Prior to 1860, his family moved to Ogdensburg, where he attended Ogdensburg Academy. He enrolled in Hamilton College in Clinton, New York, in the autumn of 1861. On being assigned to Company A in the 16th New York, Best joined many of his old friends from Ogdensburg. He served only a year for the remainder of the 16th's legal existence and saw action at Fredericksburg in December 1862 and Chancellorsville the following May; he also took part in the Mud March of January 1863. When the 16th mustered out in May 1863, Best, although officially assigned to the 121st, became a secretary on the adjutant general's staff in Sixth Corps headquarters.

James Henry McCurry came from Company F of the 16th and joined the same company in the 121st. With his original regiment, he had assaulted the heights of Fredericksburg and helped gather the dead and wounded as his unit passed through the town toward Salem Church. He lost his brother Wellesley, also in Company F, 16th New York, at Salem Church. He was detailed as a butcher, and for the next year and a half, he assiduously recorded slaughtering five to six head of cattle daily for the regiment.[45]

The 121st Regiment picked up nearly 200 men from the 32nd. The malcontents that Curtis glossed over were in John Kidder's words "mutinous," and 20 of them refused to perform picket duty and were marched out under guard to their posts to ensure that they would perform up to minimal standards and not run away. To Kidder's surprise, most of the men, once they accepted the fact that they would have to fill out the remainder of their enlistments, chose his company. Upton, who proposed the idea of giving the new members of the regiment their choice of company, did not let them all fill Kidder's ranks but spread them around. As a result, Company I became as large as John Fish's Company D. The point of contention revolved around the men's impression that they enlisted for the life of the regiment. Stanton, however, insisted that after a certain date, all enlistments were for three years or the duration of the war. The War Department won that argument. Emory Upton rounded the malcontents up, "explained to them their position, the position of the War Department, and his determination to enforce a rigid compliance of orders, and at the same time appealed to their pride and patriotism, and succeeded in winning [them over]."

In the officer corps, the appointment of Hall along with Lt. Lewis C. Bartlett into Company G and Capt. Albert Tyler into Company H—all from the 27th New York—infuriated the other officers. They could accept bringing in new men from other areas of New York, but it offended them to have new officers from outside Otsego and Herkimer while the regiment's own were overlooked. Bartlett, who was Gen. Joe Bartlett's brother, started military life with the 27th as a quartermaster sergeant. They—Hall, Bartlett, and Tyler—appear to have been part of a scheme Upton engineered to obtain more men for his regiment. All three officers, although officially assigned to the 121st, were detailed to General Bartlett's staff and never served with the regiment. Bartlett's appointment eventually boiled up at war's end, upsetting the surviving and senior officers of the regiment. Upton did promote Frank Gorton, James Cronkite, and Marcus Casler from the regiment to the rank of captain and Henry Walker to second lieutenant, moves that were palatable to all concerned. Cronkite rose the fastest, from a noncommissioned sergeant to captain of a company in less than a year.[46]

But those who were passed over continued to be discontented—it did not matter to them if a new promotion came from within or from without. William Ackerman, age thirty, and Thomas Adams, age twenty-three, were both natives of Edmeston, and both were sergeants in Company F. Upton promoted Adams to second lieutenant in April and first lieutenant a month later, and the commander's decision infuriated Ackerman. Adelbert Reed thought that Upton did the right thing because the men in the regiment thought highly of Adams and viewed him as a brave soldier, whereas "not one boy in the company" liked Ackerman. Upton's judgment prevailed, as Adams became a captain a year later. He was discharged in September 1864 with wounds suffered at Spotsylvania Court House. That same month, commanding officer Olcott reduced Ackerman to the ranks as a private.[47]

8

After Gettysburg: Becoming Abolitionists, June to October 1863

The heat was deathly, dust filled our throats; but still the march was kept up all night with no time to rest, no time to eat, no time for anything but suffering.

Francis Morse, adjutant, Memoirs

I don't know as they have got a place picked out yet but it is getting about the time of year for a Bull Run fight.

George Collins, Company C, June 19, 1863

Today marched 35 miles and we are here in Pennsylvania at a place called Gettysburg and there is a continual roar of cannon.

Dean A. Pierce, Company D, July 2, 1863

On to Gettysburg

Falmouth, Virginia, is approximately 125 miles from Gettysburg, Pennsylvania. Before the war, most men in the 121st had never heard of either town. Now, they were soon to leave Falmouth and travel by foot over those miles in little more than two weeks—and back again in another two weeks. After Salem Church, the 121st had around 250 men fit and present for duty, one-quarter of the number who had left Camp Schuyler. Before the march north, the regiment replenished its ranks to bring its total strength to approximately 500. The companies looked like squads. Sam Kelley deeply felt the absence of missing colleagues but held out the hope some would return; he knew, of course, that many would never be back. He took consolation in recalling that "they fought like men and died the most honorable of deaths."[1]

On the other side of the Rappahannock, Lee's men were exhausted, ill equipped, and malnourished. Yet they appeared to be in better condition relative to the Army of the Potomac after Chancellorsville. They bene-fited from the accepted wisdom that Lee had won and Hooker had lost that battle. But Lee had lost Stonewall Jackson. And his "offensive-defensive" strategy placed him in opposition to Jefferson Davis. Davis preferred that Lee stay near Richmond to defend the capital. James Longstreet suggested that the Army of Northern Virginia remove itself to the western theater to mitigate Grant's threat to Vicksburg by striking at Rosecrans in Tennessee. Meanwhile, the members of the 121st were "patiently awaiting the news of the capture of Vicksburg." One wrote, "I sometimes think we should attack here for fear they might profit by withdrawing some of Lee's force away to reinforce General Johnson." Lee rejected the idea and proceeded to plan a second invasion of the North. He concluded that Vicksburg could not be saved and that he could not spare his men from the eastern theater for fear of being unable to defend Rich-mond. Lee heard the same Copperhead voices that the men in the ranks of the 121st were hearing. He feared that another Northern offensive would strengthen the peace process and end the war on the North's terms. Again, he would use the Shenandoah Valley as his screen to move his army north toward Maryland and Pennsylvania.[2]

Since Chancellorsville, the Army of the Potomac had been encamped across from Fredericksburg outside Falmouth, Virginia—north of the Rappahannock. By mid-May, the trees were fully leaved and the fields had greened up to a bright spring sheen. Despite the regiment having had its first real experience of death at Chancellorsville, the 121st's camp took on a carefree attitude as the men whiled away the time by playing cards, gambling ("George Ackerman lost all his money playing cards"), reading novels, writing letters home, bothering those trying to catch up on their sleep, and generally relaxing as much as the condi-tions permitted. Some men even began improving their tents and shelters in the optimistic hope that the army would stay put. Several wives came into camp to visit their husbands. "A live Yankee woman in camp," George Teel proclaimed, "oh what a night; you had better believe there was some looking." The bands ("George Wood is in the band . . . and he is enjoying himself") performed on quiet evenings. Sam Kelley joined with others in impromptu glee clubs sere-nading the officers. Occasionally, Daniel Holt enjoyed being the sole audience for those who stopped by his tent and treated him to a song.

Teel returned to his company, but he would have been dropped from the rolls if his commanding officer, John Kidder, had not intervened on his behalf. In Ot-sego County, Teel's wife learned that the army considered him a deserter, and she blamed Kidder for her husband's predicament. Teel sent several letters home to clear his name and to reclaim Kidder's reputation. And Henry Walker finally received his commission—"a very respectable looking piece of sheep skin with a red seal and signed by Governor Seymour," though he wished that "it had a more respectable name attached to it."[3]

Copperhead activity, particularly in Indiana and Ohio, dampened the regiment's mood. Indeed, Lee intended to secure the sympathy of the peacemakers in the North with his invasion. On May 5, 1863, authorities arrested former congressman Clement Vallandigham, for treasonous and seditious activities, at his home in Dayton, Ohio. His friends had tried to warn him of his imminent arrest, and then they tried to rescue him. Vallandigham was jailed in Cincinnati, but his friends remained in Dayton, where they cut telegraph lines and burned the offices of the local newspaper, the *Journal*. Andrew Davidson, an articulate member of Company E and the future editor of the *Otsego Republican,* was well-known for his loathing of the Copperheads. He described them as *"low, cowardly, sneaking traitors,"* who were "held in contempt by all *true* men at home, as well as the soldier in the field; and sooner I would point my rifle at the cowardly copperheads' breast, than at the braver [rebel soldiers]." Davidson ridiculed the Copperheads' use of copper cents on their lapels, insisting that their words and actions were enough for reasonable men to understand who they were and the cause for which they stood.[4]

Many letters from the front expressed identical sentiments. Although the men abhorred camp boredom and the terror of battle, they believed that only continued force would bring the rebel armies to heel. They were glad that Lee had decided to take the battle north. A rebel invasion would show those who "blew" hard on the war without experiencing the battlefield horrors what the man in the field faced. Sam Kelley and Adelbert Reed articulated the growing animosity in the ranks toward the peacemakers and Copperheads who advocated accommodation. Kelley urged the people of the North to stop talking and "prepare themselves to join us." He invited the Northern posers to come "help put down this wicked rebellion." If they did, the South would soon sue for peace. Reed predicted that Lee's invasion "is going to wake up the north" and open the eyes of draft dodgers to the real dangers of the war. "Tell them the show is free, tis one of the greatest shows on earth," he directed his parents in a letter. He attacked one of his friends still in New York who had avoided the draft. "We think as much of him as we do a deserter," he asserted. "He is a *coward*. He has got a pretty poor estimation from the boys of this regiment." John Ingraham reserved his anger for Copperheads and draft dodgers. He called Lee's move "a bold dash into Maryland, I think, and Pennsylvania." "I wish they would get to New York," he sneered.[5]

Washington received word of movement by the Confederate forces around Fredericksburg. Stanton and Lincoln believed it, but Hooker remained dubious. His scouts and intelligence told him that a large body of rebels remained encamped directly across the Rappahannock from him. In reality, Lee had left a small force at Fredericksburg when the bulk of his army began heading northward as May turned into June. Scouts, balloons, direct observations, and informants indicated that Lee intended to stay put. On June 5, Hooker, still uncertain of Lee's movements, sent Sedgwick and his Sixth Corps, including the 121st, across the river to determine the whereabouts of the rebel army and perhaps decipher the rebels' next move. Supported by Union artillery on the north bank of the river, the Sixth Corps once again crossed the Rappahannock. After the artillery softened up the Confederate troops, the Sixth Corps lowered its pontoon boats into the water and crossed the river. The invaders drew light resistance from Confederate pickets. Once on the opposite riverbank, the 121st set about improving the rifle pits along a "regular line" on nearly the same ground it had occupied in April at Franklin's Crossing. The line extended from the crossing, parallel along the Richmond Road for a distance, and then back to the river.

The men sat there for eight days, occasionally trading fire with rebel pickets. No one in the 121st knew why they were there or what to expect next. Either they were participating in another Hooker strategy to outwit Lee or they were part of a new, large offensive. As it turned out, neither scenario came to pass. But in the meantime, William Remmel reported that everyone was "puzzled by this move; some think that General Hooker is making a feint to keep the rebels in Va. and prevent Lee from reinforcing the western Generals." Others speculated that a synchronized assault on the other side of the river would coincide with an attack by Grant "and make the expected victory in the West a more decisive one." Remmel confessed that he really did not understand the grand strategy but noted that the men of the 121st hoped a third battle in Fredericksburg would not be fought. They vowed they would fight "any where else than at this place for we have never had success and always met with heavy slaughter," he wrote. Clarke Rice guessed that the action would occur to the south again, on the Peninsula and then on to Richmond.

Sam Kelley felt that the rebels would not fight but that if they did, the Sixth Corps would make short work of them. "Everything seems to hang in uncertainty now," Henry Walker reflected. Hooker, for his part, remained ignorant of Lee's plans. Lee had taken off north, leaving behind a large enough contingent to convince Hooker that he remained in the area. On June 9, at Brandy Station, Jeb Stuart's cavalry force, until then billed as superb and invincible, fended off a surprise attack by a Union force led by Brig. Gen. Alfred Pleasonton. The clash persuaded Hooker that the Confederate army was on the move, and he realized that he had to stay between the enemy and Washington. Lee crossed the Rappahannock headed north, but no one in the Union army knew his ultimate destination. He intended to use his old familiar route, under the cover of the Shenandoah Valley, into Maryland and ultimately Pennsylvania. At last, Hooker began to mobilize the Army of the Potomac. He shipped all the sick and wounded and all unnecessary baggage to Washington. He no longer believed he faced the rebels in Fredericksburg and vicinity.[6]

With a blinding thunderstorm covering its withdrawal, the 121st abandoned its "useless works" at midnight on June 13 and went back across the river. The regiment was the last to move. On the other side of the river, the rest of the army had a head start on the Sixth Corps. The rain continued unabated, pelting the moving mass of men in the dark. "Who will ever forget the start," John Lovejoy asked. "Sprawling and slipping over corduroy roads amid peals of thunder, flashes of lightning and the laugh and cheer of comrades who happened to be a little surer footed than those who fell." They slogged on through the darkness. The next day, Sunday, June 14, as the weather cleared and became oppressive, the column rested near the Potomac Creek Bridge. Some were beginning to suffer from fatigue and sunstroke. The roads quickly dried out to a thin dust. On June 15, the Sixth Corps passed the Chantilly and Bull Run battlefields, where recent heavy rains uncovered the gruesome signs of earlier struggles. The shallow graves revealed their grisly contents. Bones and skulls had resurfaced to mingle with the detritus of war, which included mutilated trees, mangled equipment, and earlier earthworks.

The 121st was involved in an unorthodox artillery movement that delayed four of its companies in joining the entourage north. Yankee artillery mounted a 100-pound gun at Fredericksburg on June 12 on a hill opposite the city. The commander who initially placed the gun explained to John Kidder that he meant it merely as a decoy. The plan worked almost too well. The men in charge of the gun delayed the decision to take it down, and around 5:00 P.M. on June 13, the rebels found the gun's range with rounds from a Whitworth battery that came within 20 rods of the watching Yankees. One round sang over John Ingraham's head, and he watched it bound away. He sauntered over to pick it up, only to promptly drop the hot metal. Lt. Ralph H. Cummings of Battery A of the 1st Connecticut Volunteer Artillery thought that before moving the gun, it would be interesting to fire the 100-pounder just once. The shell went toward the rebel lines and obliterated the rebel battery, but it also blew the big gun off its carriage. "The gun kicked out of the trees," George Collins exclaimed, "and stood right up on end." Kidder took a detail of forty men from the 121st to retrieve the gun and load it on the carriage. They worked all night in a pouring rain to accomplish the task and were able to join the 121st at Dumfries on Monday, June 15. By that date, it was apparent that the armies would soon collide somewhere in Maryland or Pennsylvania. Lee headed through Maryland for Pennsylvania, with at least a two-week lead on Hooker. At midmonth, Lincoln put out a call for 100,000 militia, primarily from Maryland, Pennsylvania, West Virginia, and Ohio, to repel the invasion.[7]

By June 16 and 17, the Sixth Corps and the 121st, along with the Second Corps and the Twelfth Corps, were well on the road north, having passed through Stafford Court House, Dumfries, and Fairfax Station on the Orange and Alexandria Railroad. The remainder of the army—the First, Third, Fifth, and Eleventh corps—was farther west. June 16 brought another day of stifling heat and choking dust on the roads. Some of the regiments of the Sixth Corps were called out at 3:00 in the morning. The roads were clogged with wagons, stragglers, and abandoned equipment, making the march more difficult than it needed to be.

On the night of June 17, the 121st stopped at Centreville. The hard marching over existing roads and the corduroy roads that the forward units had prepared became unrelenting, day and night and in every kind of weather. When it rained, the mud sucked at the men's boots; on clear, bright days, the dry roads covered them with dust. Even the older soldiers, veterans of the Peninsula, were impressed at the hard time the troops experienced in making their way north. Night marches, although much cooler, were increasingly difficult. In the darkness, "the boys would often stumble down and become all over besmirched with mud." Adelbert Reed told his parents, "The roads were filled with the sick, tired and weary." His feet were blistered. To lighten his load, he threw away his knapsack and everything else but his blanket, tent half, and accoutrements.

The army moved in "quick time," a paced march in step, until those who could not keep up fell out of the ranks. "The long line splashed through the dust, which rose in clouds," an anonymous soldier wrote, "and where it touched the skin it burned like particles of molten brass." He described the "hard yellow glare of the burning sunbeams" that "seemed to eat into one's brain," adding that "the temptation was strong to lie down in the cool recesses of some one of the copses of timber through which we passed, and abandon all else to bodily comfort." The roadway became littered with military detritus, including canteens, which he described as "those tin receptacles of luke warm water [that] are the last thing a soldier throws away." He told of thousands of "weary feet" treading "over the hot, strangling dust, through cool vistas of forest, by scattered farm houses, whose occupants had left their labor and leaned on the fences, looking with curious wistful faces at the long column rolling up to the front." The horses pulling artillery pieces were equally stressed, and soon, brigades began to resemble regiments and regiments, companies, as men fell out by the roadside.[8]

On June 19, Hooker revealed his ignorance of Lee's movements when he alerted General Halleck that "Lee's delay in my front has caused me to doubt his intention of throwing over any considerable force on Maryland shore." His information indicated that Lee intended to attack east toward Washington from the Shenandoah Valley. He told Halleck that the Sixth Corps had arrived at Germantown that day. Twenty-four hours later, he reported that he had laid a bridge at Edward's Ferry that evening in order to cross into Maryland. With tongue in cheek, George Collins told his cousin: "I don't know as they have got a place picked out yet but it is getting about the time of year for a Bull Run fight."[9]

While the main body of the Army of the Potomac remained west of the regiment, the 121st settled into camp for a week. William Remmel told his parents that the army knew Lee's location in Maryland and that he intended to invade Pennsylvania. "The hellish traitors must be dispersed and we will do it" if properly led by the Union generals. He told a brother, "Affairs for the present look dark, indeed." Cynically, George Teel remarked that the "Army of the Potomac is making one of their splendid retreats." George Collins agreed: "I suppose General Hooker does not call this a retreat, only a change of base; but I think if the Rebs should cut up this same caper we should call it a retreat." Most of the news came from the Washington papers—news confirmed by captured rebels who spoke of the cavalry fight at Brandy Station and Lee's general movement north.[10]

By Thursday, June 25, after a week of inaction, the pace picked up with renewed urgency. The rest of the army remained north and west of the Sixth Corps. At 3:00 A.M. on June 26, the 121st moved out. Over now muddy roads, the corps moved out of Centreville and Germantown and reached Dranesville, Virginia, where the regiment halted for the night. The Sixth Corps replaced the First Corps, which had moved on farther west and north the day before, crossing the Potomac at Edward's Ferry and stopping in Barnesville, Maryland.

The next day, the Sixth Corps crossed the Potomac at Edward's Ferry, only going as far north as the area of Poolesville and Hyattstown, Maryland, a distance of 10 miles. The ford became a bottleneck as men, cattle, wagons, guns, and equipment waited their turn to cross into Maryland. Sam Kelley, still recovering from a slow-healing wound received at Salem Church and now much bothered by it, doctored himself. He applied a mixture of silver nitrate to clean it out, a procedure that pained him "beyond description." Distraught, he wrote his mother, "I do not know where we are going nor do I care." Dolphus Sayles wrote his father that he expected "to have another large battle at Antietam."[11]

The march proved different things to different men. Pvt. Sedate Foote made it all worthwhile when he became the supplier of cherries and other fruit to his comrades in Company I. In Company B, "although orders were stringent against foraging," Clinton Beckwith recalled that he "took chances and secured an abundant supply for our mess." Along with his tent mates, Beckwith managed to slaughter a heifer with their muskets just as Gen. David Russell and his staff passed their position. When one of the raider's minié balls, intended to bring down the cow, nearly hit Russell in the head, the general ordered Beckwith and his comrades to report to him. The men scattered, and Beckwith chose to run and hide in the woods until the next morning. The guilty parties eventually caught up to the regiment the next day, exhausted and without their beef. For another man, the serious and sober Adelbert Reed, the march represented an epiphany of sorts. He admitted to his parents that as a civilian, he had complained about small things, but now, army discipline had taught him not to grumble and to move without question. The Mud March in January marked the last time he knew the army's destination. In the past, he had worried about the army's ultimate objective. Now, like Sam Kelley, he really did not care where the regiment headed—he would fall in with the rest, an obedient soldier.[12]

Upstate Democratic newspapers derided Lee's threat and the Lincoln administration's response to it. According to the *Herkimer Democrat*, "the scare in Pennsylvania" amounted to no more than 10,000 "mounted men" and probably only 5,000, with a force equaling no more than 20,000 men altogether; the paper called the situation a "disgraceful panic" in light of "such figures." The *Albany Statesman* fulminated: "The War Office deserves to be horse-whipped for the fuss and timidity which it has created among our old women of both sexes." The *Democrat* also reported on the dry and dusty conditions faced by Hooker's army. Antiwar and antiadministration reporters were blatant in their stories describing the Army of the Potomac's tribulations with weather conditions, stragglers, sunstroke, and other "untold miseries" as it plodded north to meet the threat.[13]

By June 27, Lincoln had tired of Hooker's dilatory ways, and he fired him. Hooker's relief from command "affected the men visibly," James Cronkite recalled, "as they had great confidence in 'Fighting Joe'; but they were still willing to meet the enemy bravely under their new leader." John Lovejoy remembered that "this could hardly be believed. All had confidence [in Hooker]" and "why to change went from lip to lip. Astonishment was written on every face." The men freely expressed their indignation. "Hooker was well known to the Army," many felt. And why would anyone want to replace a known quantity? Clarke Rice articulated his frustration about having to defend the Northern homeland now that Lee had stolen the march on Hooker. He remained loyal to Hooker and expressed sorrow at his firing. He thought the general ranked as one of the best leaders of the Army of the Potomac who had been appointed to date by the president. He blamed Halleck for the debacle. Isaac Best, writing with hindsight some sixty years later, thought that Hooker's removal made sense; after all, in Best's opinion, Hooker was a drunkard.[14]

General Meade assumed command immediately, and in his acceptance dispatch on the morning of June 28, he confirmed Hooker's ignorance of the situation by admitting he did not know the condition of his own troops or the "position of the enemy." He surmised that the threat lay north and west of Washington and that the Susquehanna River might be the battleground. That day, fresh intelligence told Meade that Richard S. Ewell's men were positioned on the Susquehanna at Columbia and Harrisburg, Longstreet occupied Chambersburg, and Hill had placed his men between Chambersburg and Cashtown. Armed with that information, Meade pushed his new command north, and the army doubled its marching output, halting between Emmitsburg and Manchester, Maryland. The men of the Sixth Corps held the rear as they marched 20 miles that day into the heart of Maryland. Meade's 1st Division, with the 121st, broke camp at Edward's Ferry at 4:00 that morning and marched to Hyattstown,

18 miles up the road. "The inhabitants seem to be pleased to see the army came to defend them," John Hartwell recorded in his diary. "Flags were occasionally displayed and of the right stamp." The Pennsylvania citizens pleasantly surprised Hartwell as they greeted the soldiers with a warm welcome, which included food and water at every turn. The army followed the same routine the next day, Monday, June 29. They broke camp at 4:00 A.M., and via Monrovia, New Market, Ridgeville, and Mount Airy, Maryland, the 121st tramped another 22 miles, finally encamping near New Windsor, Maryland. June 30 found the 1st Division of the Sixth Corps and the 121st another 23 miles up the road through Westminster—finally encamping 2 miles from Manchester, Maryland.[15]

The regiment marched all through the night of June 30, until the Sixth Corps halted southeast of Gettysburg in Manchester, Maryland. As the men of the 121st passed the milestones by the roadside, they counted off the miles: the army in Manchester still faced 35 tough miles to reach Gettysburg. And no one really knew that Gettysburg was the final destination. The 121st pulled up the rear of the brigade, which, in turn, brought up the rear of the division and the Sixth Corps. Along with Pleasonton's cavalry, the Sixth Corps represented the most easterly unit in the Army of the Potomac. When the rest of the army stopped to rest, the Army of the Potomac rested on the Pipe Creek Line that ran from Middleburg to Manchester, Maryland. The Sixth Corps held the far right. Meade's headquarters were in Taneytown, nearly the center of the line: the general knew that the battle would take place along the Pipe Creek Line. But the next day, June 30, he learned from Brig. Gen. John Buford at Gettysburg that the Confederates were massing there. Meade dispatched Gen. John Reynolds, in charge of the First, Third, and Eleventh corps, to Buford's aid. The Sixth Corps remained in place, prepared for anything, including a presumed attack by the rebels on Baltimore.[16]

The next day, July 1, as Reynolds found Buford "warmly engaged," Meade alerted Sedgwick that the Sixth Corps would probably need to stay put for the time being. Orders came down to the various units; the 121st rested. Instantly, cooking utensils and coffee-making gear were unpacked and put to use. Local residents came into camp offering food and beverages to the footsore troops. The men spent the entire day relaxing while the action to their north and west escalated. Unknown to the men of the Sixth Corps and the 121st, Confederate troops were engaged with the First Corps in heavy skirmishes west of Gettysburg. They lingered at Manchester throughout the day, July 1.

That night, no sooner were the pork and hardtack set out for an evening meal than the order came to march in the direction of Gettysburg. Meade needed the Sixth Corps to reinforce the Union lines. Word came that a great battle had begun, that the First Corps had been badly cut up, and that General Reynolds had been killed. Meade abandoned his headquarters at Taneytown around 10:00 P.M. and headed north to Gettysburg, where he arrived around 1:00 in the morning of July 2. According to James Cronkite, General Sedgwick was resting under the shade of a tree by the road when a staff officer rode up and "informed him that the 6th Corps was wanted at Gettysburg with out delay." The Twelfth and part of the Third corps reached Gettysburg around 7:00 P.M. Within the next hour, the troops of the Sixth Corps in Manchester dropped all preparations for their evening meal and coffee and formed on the road. The Sixth Corps moved on, the 1st Division taking the lead. Striking out for Gettysburg, the regiment marched for forty-five minutes. Commanders gave the troops fifteen minutes to rest in each hour. Horatio Wright said that the 1st Division "pushed on to Gettysburg, without halting," except "for a few moments each hour" to enable the men to catch their breath and one half-hour break to make coffee and rest.[17]

That evening, July 1, Brig. Gen. Joe Bartlett temporarily turned over command of his brigade to Emory Upton. At once, Upton began the march from Manchester toward Taneytown as instructed, around 10:00 P.M. Meade's orders to Sedgwick were to get to his headquarters in Taneytown as soon as possible and then head north via the Taneytown Road to Gettysburg. By now, the troops were calling themselves "Sedgwick's foot cavalry." As the corps approached Westminster, a countermanding order arrived from Meade encouraging Sedgwick to take a more expeditious route. Sedgwick then moved his entire corps off the Taneytown Road toward the Baltimore Pike, a move that caused additional grief among the men by inflicting a much longer march on them. The change probably added 3 miles to the trek.[18]

As the corps marched along the smoother Baltimore Pike, the pace picked up. At intervals, the men paused but only briefly. The brigade band played national airs to keep the footsore men moving forward. When the band stopped, Upton ordered "the regimental musicians to strike up one of their best marches to regulate the steps of the weary men and cheer them onward." Years later, a private in a Wisconsin regiment remembered the march to Gettysburg as the only time he heard music played en route. The 121st marched "all night long without halt, worn out, eyes aching from want of sleep, faint from want of nourishment," wrote Frank Morse—"but without a murmur, or complaint. The heat was deathly, dust filled our throats" as they marched through the night with "no time to rest, no time to eat, no time for anything but suffering." Twice during the night, Morse fell off his horse "while asleep." They completed the last two days of the march without food or sleep. Doctors had ordered Sam Kelley not to carry a gun because of his wound. And since he could not go into battle unarmed, he was forced to remain behind when the regiment moved forward toward Gettysburg. He slept alone in the woods and remained in the rear until the battle ended. Frank Morse later asserted that the road to Gettysburg and the battle itself marked the war's turning point.[19]

As the rays of sunlight signaled a new day on July 2, the exhausted men of the Sixth Corps were allowed to file off the Baltimore Pike to boil coffee.

Before many of them could unpack their gear, however, Sedgwick ordered the corps back on the road. They trooped on through the oppressive heat and thick dust. Some began falling to the side of the road. As they approached the sleepy Pennsylvania village of Littlestown around 2:00 P.M., the men of the 121st could hear the cannonading and sounds of battle to the north. The citizens of the village offered what food and drink they could, and when they ran out, they offered their good wishes as the bluecoats hurried forward. The wounded were streaming past the advancing corps in the opposite direction, giving the men a grim foretelling of what awaited them on the road ahead. Within hours, they were in place south of Gettysburg.

General Bartlett's 2nd Brigade of the 1st Division under command of Emory Upton arrived on the battlefield about 3:30 in the afternoon on July 2, "having marched since the preceding evening 32 miles." Other divisions either preceded or followed them in rapid succession. The 3rd Division, the first to arrive, went to the immediate help of the Fifth Corps. Sedgwick scattered the remainder of his command at points along the line on the Union's left that were being sorely tested by Longstreet. Upton's brigade formed two lines on Cemetery Ridge just north of Little Round Top in support of Maj. Gen. George Sykes on the Union line's far left flank. As it moved into position after a rest of three hours, Bartlett returned to command of the brigade and Upton returned to the 121st.

The regiment found itself overlooking the Devil's Den, the Peach Orchard, the Wheatfield, and General Sickles's Third Corps below. Its fraternal comrade, the 5th Maine, was to its left. By 6:00, Upton had positioned the 121st with the rest of the brigade, and during the next twenty-four hours, it sat on the ridge. Sedgwick ordered the 121st to "reinforce that part of our line which was engaged near Round Top Mountain," Upton explained in his report after the battle. During this maneuver, Bartlett relieved Upton of command and returned to the head of the brigade. The 121st "took position in line of battle to support a battery to the right of the summit of Round top, the right of the regiment resting on the road leading out to the Emmitsburg pike." According to Upton, the regiment arrived, exhausted from its long march, "just in time to reenforce our left, which was hard pressed by Longstreet, and slowly giving way. Ten minutes later, and the battle had been lost." John Ingraham bragged that "when the rebs saw the 6th Corps coming up, they fell back. They didn't want to meet us."[20]

The 3rd Division of the corps and two Pennsylvania regiments were thrown into the action just as Longstreet withdrew, resulting in few casualties. Sedgwick and Bartlett held the 121st in reserve. There, once the immediate threat of Longstreet's assault passed, "what we had endured during the past two days soon had full effect on us," Francis Morse remembered. Overcome by exhaustion, "we dropped where we stood, and the men instantly fell in a deep dead

sleep." Morse himself "rolled off my horse, and resting my head upon the body of Captain Casler was soon forgetful of battles." During the night, the men of the 121st tried to sleep on their weapons, but around 3:00 A.M., pickets on both sides began firing, awaking and alerting the entire Sixth Corps. Sleep eluded them after that. Both Morse and James Cronkite remembered "hearing the agonizing cries of the wounded whom we were unable to succor." All around them were "the dead of both armies, and several hundred yards [in their front] were the frowning lines and batteries of Longstreet."[21]

The next morning, July 3, broke hot and oppressive. The day began with cannonading off to the north on the extreme right flank of the Union army. Lee tested the "eye" of the fishhook at Culp's Hill. Federal troops stretched out south along Cemetery Ridge below the village of Gettysburg. On the left flank, Upton wondered what the next few hours would bring. The 121st could be called to attack down the rocky hillside in front of them, hold where they were and repel a rebel assault, or just remain vigilant. He recalled later that "a feeling of enthusiasm possessed" him at that time. He confessed to his brother that he never envisioned himself as a speaker, but "for the first time in my life, words and actions came to me spontaneously." He appealed to the patriotism and pride of the men in his regiment, affirmed that he would lead them, and "asked them to follow." Their enthusiastic reaction replaced the anxiety as they followed his speech with "a cheer that would have raised the hair of a confronting rebel." That moment instilled in the young commander a new sense of courage, both professionally and personally. "From that instant I had as much confidence in them as in myself," he declared.[22]

Near the crest of Little Round Top and the end of the Union line, they waited and watched. They were in an enviable position. "No place could have been fitter for artillery, for the inside lines of maneuvering, for reinforcing, for the cover of walls, and of natural defenses," Francis Morse recalled. But the men of the 121st did not participate in the most notable battle on American soil and in American history. Instead, they became eyewitnesses to a spectacular military maneuver rivaling the charge of the Light Brigade in the Crimean War. What they saw taxed their abilities to retell effectively. Delavan Bates vividly described the unfolding drama: "The whole day long was a living panorama of events that I would almost give the balance of my life to see once more." Below the 121st in the Devil's Den, sharpshooters on both sides were trying to kill each other with precision. Writing years later, Bates said of Col. Hiram Berdan's sharpshooters and their handiwork, "For about two hours we had a free entertainment equal to Buffalo Bill's best endeavors in the Wild West Show." At noon, through field glasses, Emory Upton watched his first love—the artillery—massed on Seminary Ridge by the enemy. He told those near him that he could see the Confederate infantry forming behind the 150 guns pointed toward the Union lines. "There will be hot work this afternoon," he predicted, according

to Delavan Bates. Further, he prepared the men to protect themselves as "best they could" from the barrage and the infantry assault he felt sure would come when the guns fell silent. Before the opening shots, the men took advantage of the lull to cook, eat, and sleep. Under some large shade trees, Upton, Morse, and Major Mather were at rest, lying on a poncho. Just as Morse turned to Mather to tell him he thought that either side would launch an attack soon, a Whitworth round sailed over their heads. As they moved off the poncho to determine the origin of the fire, a shell grazed it in the general area where the three had been discussing next moves.[23]

At 1:00 in the afternoon, Confederate artillery opened on the center of the Union line in earnest. "Forty minutes, fifty minutes were counted on watches that ran too slowly," Francis Morse recalled. Two hours later, the guns ceased. As an unnatural quiet settled over the shallow valley, the tension mounted in the wet heat. Across the open space on Seminary Ridge, the combined forces of Generals Pettigrew, Pickett, and Trimble began their legendary journey into Confederate memory as the 121st watched from their safe vantage point on Little Round Top. "There they come," someone yelled out as the advancing Confederates left the cover of the tree line on the ridge and headed for the Emmitsburg Road and ultimately the copse of trees on Cemetery Ridge. Nervously, all eyes were on the "Johnnies" as they moved toward the road and past the farmhouses and barns in the open fields. As the rebel force crossed the road, Brig. Gen. George Stannard's Vermonters—short-timers with a few days left on their nine-month enlistments—were holding the left flank of the Second Corps, facing west as the attack passed them.

With a "rapid pivot to the right," the Vermonters realized, they would be "facing northward and squarely on the Confederate's flank just as they were attacking" the Union center. The 121st heard "the yells of the Johnnies . . . drowned out by the cheers of the Vermonters as they swept down upon them and gobbled them up." Further up the line, the noise subsided as soon as it began, and from its vantage point, the 121st watched the Confederate survivors' slow retreat. "It was a splendid sight to see our men advance," Marcus Casler noted, and to see "our batteries pouring their iron hail and shell among the rebel ranks, leaving great gaps, and blowing up their caissons, killing their horses and putting all to rout. It was indeed a perfect thunder." Emory Upton called Lee's assault "imposing and sublime. For ten minutes I watched the contest, when it seemed that the weight of a hair would have turned the scales." As the men of the 121st were held in reserve, their adversaries from Salem Church—Wilcox's and Herbert's Alabamians—were being held in support on the Confederate side. They were called at the last moment and too late to come to the aid of General Pickett. Meade held the Sixth Corps in support. Parts of it were dispatched from one end of the line to the other, including the center, but as Sedgwick said in his official report, "they were at no time seriously engaged."[24]

After Gettysburg—The Race to the Potomac

The next morning, the Fourth of July of 1863, dawned with dark and heavy skies that would pour rain all day. As the gloomy morning broke over the village of Gettysburg, the horrors of the battlefield lying below the 121st were revealed. Upton led his regiment on a reconnaissance into the infamous Peach Orchard, where dead horses from rebel batteries lay mingled with the stinking, putrefying corpses of both Union and Confederate soldiers who lay where they fell. The harsh sun of the previous day had hastened the blackening and bloating of the bodies of men and animals alike. The pouring rain made the scene surreal—a "horrid sight for even those who were most familiar with battle scenes." In a strange way, it appeared as if nature were attempting to wash away man's folly. Francis Morse noted the "hundreds of dead bodies of our late enemies, scarcely buried. Dismounted cannons, broken down ambulances and straggling rebels plainly showed the line of retreat." When the forward troops discovered that the Confederate army had not yet moved off the field in retreat, they stopped in their positions and spent the remainder of the day burying the dead and treating the wounded. Lee pulled back his left flank on the northern part of the battlefield but maintained his right across from the Round Tops.[25]

The importance of the recent battle did not escape the men of the 121st. Daniel Holt told his wife that the recent battle would forever be known "as one of the hardest fought, most destructive of human life and most decided in its results of any on record." He did not know what it would be called, but since it was "fought near Gettysburg, Pa., I presume it will be known as the Battle of Gettysburg." John Kidder credited George Meade for the miraculous "forced march" on July 2. When Hooker had replaced McClellan, the McClellan contingent in the army bemoaned his loss. But Kidder knew if Little Mac had been in charge during the 32-mile march, "Lee would have been in Baltimore before he [McClellan] got out of Virginia." Marcus Casler remarked in a letter to the *Herkimer County Journal* that July 3 would be a day long remembered: "It saved the nation and killed rebellion. Lee's army is demoralized." Emory Upton echoed Casler's words. In a letter to his sister written on July 4, he proclaimed that "yesterday was a glorious day for the country and the Army of the Potomac," adding that the "contest seems the decisive battle of the war. Our men are in good spirits over the success."[26]

The rain continued on July 5 as Lee began his long march back across the Potomac into Virginia, with the Union army in pursuit. Meade decided, after a counsel of war and with fresh reports from his signal corps, to use the Sixth Corps to discover Lee's intentions. Because the Sixth had arrived last on the field and played little or no part in the combat at Gettysburg, it was assigned the task of finding the Confederate lines. At first, scouts probed the lines but found no indication of whether Lee's army had left the field or had merely regrouped for

another attack. Sometime between 3:00 and 5:00 A.M., Sedgwick's troops, with Horatio Wright's 1st Division and the 121st, began probing the movements of the retreating rebel army as it cautiously moved out on the Emmitsburg Road toward Seminary Ridge. Dutifully, the 121st moved into the valley, between their position on Cemetery Ridge and Seminary Ridge. They discovered that the Confederate army had left the field. Wright's division occupied the ridge just evacuated, and his artillery opened on targets to his right, which, in his words, "soon disappeared without replying, moving off to the rear in retreat. This marked the last firing at Gettysburg on either side."[27]

There, according to John Lovejoy, were "sights such as never was seen before." Following the battle and the attendant flight of its participants back into Virginia, medical care became of utmost importance. Many of the wounded in both armies had been left in barns and farmhouses along the way, from Gettysburg to Fairfield "and even to the South Mountain Pass." Occasionally, a tent shielded the wounded. Lovejoy, on sick leave, had not participated in the battle, but after the war, he wrote a brief account of the conflict up to the battle of Rappahannock Station. He gathered information from those who were present, including reports of seeing a barn that was burned to the ground by artillery fire and the "charred remains" of the wounded: now, dead Confederates "were plainly visible as they lay under the ashes of hay and straw." According to Lovejoy, "men lay dead everywhere. Horses in groups of a dozen or more in a place lay swollen and filling the air with a stench almost unbearable." Marcus Casler and Clarke Rice were both moved by sights they directly witnessed and never wished to see again. Casler expressed grief for the "wounded men, imploring death to relieve them from their sufferings—praying for the care of nurses and physicians and surgeons whom the rebel generals, in their inhumanity, neglected to leave them, wounded in every part of their body." Confederate surgeons remained behind tending their wounded as best they could but complaining bitterly that they were unable to relieve the suffering "in a proper manner for the want of medicines and surgical appliances." The Union army, where practical, supplied them. The rebels took the walking wounded with them, and the less injured were piled into wagons. Only the most hopeless were left behind. The Confederate surgeons on the ground estimated their wounded at 15,000. Francis Morse's cruel assessment argued that the Confederates were barbarians and had filled the Pennsylvania barns with their wounded, leaving them "to our tender mercies." In Morse's opinion, Confederate actions proved that the Union treated its wounded better "than the barbarous way the high minded sons of the south did to theirs." Rice described the devastation of the retreating army, leaving nothing of value in its wake: "None of the rules of civilized warfare were respected." He accused the rebels of pillaging "the quiet homes of unoffending families . . . laying their sacrilegious hands upon their most cherished house hold goods."[28]

Meade could not afford to delay to pick up debris from the field, let alone the wounded from both sides, whom he left in Gettysburg. He managed to bury some of the dead of each army, but he left many bodies for the citizens of the town to deal with. Dr. Jonathon Letterman, head of Medical Services of the Army of the Potomac, shifted the responsibility for first care of the wounded from the regimental to the division and corps levels. In accordance with the reorganization, casualties received temporary aid at the division level. Dr. Holt, detailed to a division hospital with fifteen other surgeons, attended the wounded. Sick and wounded soldiers were then sent on to the general hospitals in Washington, Philadelphia, and Baltimore, "where greater comfort and better nursing" were offered. Holt's responsibilities included finding locations for the establishment of field hospitals, supervision and direction of ambulance trains, and "care of [the trains'] occupants." Despite the workload, he found prestige in being detailed up the chain of command: he called it a "matter of distinction." Although he disliked leaving the men of the regiment, he noted that "none but the most competent" doctors were sent to division and corps hospitals. However, the distinction could never outweigh the "dirty" and "disagreeable" job of "dressing sloughing, stinking gun shot wounds."[29]

Just as Clarke Rice expressed his displeasure with the 96th Pennsylvania after the battle of Salem Church, Francis Morse became vocal about the 119th Pennsylvania after Gettysburg. As the Confederate army retreated, the Union army picked at its rear guard. Meade decided on a full pursuit of the enemy as it headed away from Gettysburg on the Cashtown and Fairfield roads. The Sixth Corps took the Fairfield Road. Around 8:00 A.M., the corps found itself 2 miles from Fairfield, where the rebels were occupying the road through the pass. Throughout the day, July 5, the sides traded fire. In the late afternoon, Sedgwick and Wright kept up a "brisk artillery fire" on the retreating rebels, followed by an infantry assault. Wright's 1st Division overtook the rebel rear guard about 2 miles from Fairfield at 5:00 that afternoon. Wanting to know more about the enemy and its condition, Sedgwick sent his inspector general, Lt. Col. J. Ford Kent, "with a squadron of cavalry to our [the 121st's] regiment, with orders for us to accompany Kent out on the Fairfield road on a reconnaissance," Frank Morse remembered. The Union intended to set up a skirmish line and harass the retreating Confederate rear guard. The resistance proved stronger than anticipated. As the 121st held the line, Morse, "being the only officer mounted" on the left of the line attacked by the enemy with some success, became alarmed by their advances. He found Upton and informed him of the situation. Upton told Morse to report the problem to Sedgwick, which he did. He found Sedgwick sitting in the rear on a stump, surrounded by his staff. When Morse finished relating his story to the general, Sedgwick quietly asked him how he "knew anything about it" as the 121st "was not in the party." Morse replied that he knew all "about it" because the 121st had been in the thick of the fight. When

Sedgwick turned to Kent and informed him that he had ordered out the "119th Pennsylvania . . . not the 121st New York, Kent's confusion was great," superseded only by Morse's "indignation." He expressed his extreme unhappiness with Kent for confusing the two regiments. As Morse so aptly stated: "To think my precious life had been exposed by mistake all that morning, when some Pennsylvania adjutant might as well have been in the same place." Summing up his unrelenting animosity for the Pennsylvania troops, Morse wrote, "From the way the natives of the Key Stone State had treated us the life of one of them had but little value in our eyes." By the time he returned to the 121st, around 3:00 in the afternoon, the firing had ceased, "the enemy had retired in confusion, and our object was gained."[30]

No sooner had the regiment been relieved after its skirmish near Fairfield than it reversed course, packed up, and moved to Emmitsburg. Sedgwick's Sixth Corps chased the rebels to the mountain gap outside Fairfield. The general reported to Meade that the formidable gap could too easily be defended by a very few enemy troops. As a result, Sedgwick decided to take the Emmitsburg Pike and march his command over South Mountain. By July 6, Meade admitted that he did not have "reliable information" as to where Lee and his army were. He told Halleck that he believed "the enemy is retreating, very much crippled, and hampered by his trains."

Soon, the 121st found itself at the base of the Catoctin range of mountains—specifically, South Mountain. Even today, the mountain is thickly covered with heavy vegetation, and the regiment was forced to move over the mountain through summer's thickest foliage, in an absolute deluge and at night—"the darkness so dense that it could almost be felt." Even before the move upward, the men and animals were exhausted. John Ingraham reported that the horses were so worn-out that they "dropped down" and "trembled like a leaf." As the 121st went over and around South Mountain, with a deep ravine on one side and a steep mountain incline on the other, the march to Gettysburg began to pale in comparison. Artillery, cavalry, and infantry troops were all attempting to march straight up the 4-mile incline with room for only two men abreast. John Kidder wrote his wife: "I never suffered so much in my life as I did that night." Delavan Bates never forgot the night and the immense suffering endured by the troops. Several of the men characterized the night as "dark as pitch." Clarke Rice, never without a classical allusion at the ready, remarked that it "was as dark as the shades of Erebus could make it."[31]

By midnight, Upton and a handful of men had reached the summit. "Some officers had no men," according to Clarke Rice, who counted only six men in his own company. Perhaps just twenty-five men from the 121st made the climb; Sam Kelley estimated only 150 from the entire brigade got up the mountain. The mountainside ascended so steeply that when the men halted, their knees touched the ground in front of them. The rain intensified, and the wind picked

up as the ground became saturated. Bates and Kidder shared two pieces of hardtack between them and the only two men from Company I nearby. Cpl. Mason Jenks of Company I tried to maintain discipline with his usual "Damn it boys, this is the military. Stop your grumbling and keep in ranks." And the rain fell unceasingly. Men easily fell out of ranks and into a deep sleep, some lying in 2 inches of water. Clinton Beckwith gave up halfway up the mountain and fell asleep in a brush heap on the side of the road. In the dark and the rain, those who pressed on faced the real possibility of pitching into the ravine below. Finally, Kidder and Bates gave up, too, and fell to sleep on their rubber blankets on the side of the road. Bates wished never to see another march like that one.[32]

The next morning, the stragglers, including Beckwith, caught up with the regiment and the brigade on the summit. Beckwith passed General Sedgwick sitting on his horse in the rain, encouraging the men to move along and rejoin their commands. Sam Kelley awoke to find only two or three other officers and a few enlisted men nearby from the 121st. Rations had been distributed the day the regiment left Gettysburg, and they were now running low. If Silas Pierce had not shared rations with him, Kelley feared that he would have perished right there on the side of the mountain. When the army finally marched into Middletown, rations were replenished with fresh beef and bread. By that point, most of the men had worn out their shoes and remained barefoot—except for Clinton Beckwith, who convinced a local citizen to part with his shoes for a useless federal voucher in payment. Over the next few days, the Union army played a game of cat and mouse with the retreating gray backs. From Emmitsburg, over South Mountain, the Sixth Corps marched to Middletown by way of Hamburg and then to Boonsborough. Both armies continued south toward Hagerstown, Maryland, and Williamsport on the Potomac. On July 11, the rebels retired farther toward Funkstown, Maryland.

On that day, the two forces collided at Funkstown, with Lee playing a delaying game and Meade remaining tentative. Lee desired to build a line of defensive trenches before Williamsport, where he intended to recross the Potomac back into Virginia. The Sixth Corps and Buford's cavalry pressed him. Once Lee began to construct and improve his trenches, Meade's army faced him along a 9-mile line. Sedgwick positioned the Sixth Corps just below Funkstown. In the only action experienced by the 121st, on Sunday, July 12, Joe Bartlett tasked Captain Cronkite with taking out a line of Confederate skirmishers who were situated in the first of two rebel lines, barely 800 yards in their front. Wright ordered Bartlett to take the "crest occupied by the enemy's skirmishers." With segments of the 5th Maine and Companies E and H of the 121st, Cronkite led a party to dislodge the skirmishers with Bartlett's instructions: "Captain, the sun is now an hour high, and you must occupy that ledge before it goes down." Cronkite led his detachment in a "partially successful" attack, driving off the rebels. But he soon realized that the Confederate skirmish lines were closer to their own main line of battle than to the Union lines. Pushing forward to any degree would have been foolhardy. At a minimum, nine privates were wounded, two mortally. Cronkite counted three enemy killed.[33]

This action marked the last engagement of the Gettysburg campaign for the regiment. Meade dug in around Hagerstown—positioning the Eleventh Corps on his right and the Fifth Corps on his left—and Lee had dug trenches along a 10-mile front from north to south, which he manned with pickets on July 13. Occasional sharp skirmishing erupted, but nothing more serious occurred. The next day, Joe Bartlett received intelligence that "the enemy was not in sight." He advanced his skirmishers and "a small scouting party" to determine Lee's intentions. He met no resistance and concluded that the rebels had crossed the Potomac. He then moved on with the rest of the army to Williamsport. Lee returned to Virginia unaccompanied by the Union army. "[When] we got to the river," William Remmel wrote, "we saw that all our efforts had been in vain." Hance Morgan captured the essence of the operation: "We find we were just soon enough to be two hours too late to catch them." From there, the Union army followed Lee into Virginia through Boonsborough, Middletown, Burkittsville, and then Berlin, Maryland. The 121st decamped at 7:00 A.M. on July 19, crossed the Potomac at Berlin, and camped at Lovettsville.

By July 20, the regiment found itself on the Aldie and Snickersville Pike. By month's end, the army settled in or near Warrenton, and the men of the 121st camped in New Baltimore, Virginia. They passed familiar fields near Antietam and Crampton's Gap, which stirred memories of the previous year when they were new to war and resembled a healthy brigade instead of a sickly regiment of nearly 400 weary men. Upton remained in command, with Maj. Emmet Mather being second in command. Egbert Olcott missed the entire Gettysburg campaign on sick leave, and only fourteen line officers were present for duty. Charley Dean thought that Meade should have fought the rebs at Williamsport. John Kidder disagreed with him, arguing that Lee's strongly entrenched position deterred Meade. The concept of attacking reinforced lines in trenches became a discredited idea, and it began to take hold with some of the men, if not the generals.[34]

The New York Draft Riots and Governor Seymour

While the troops of the Army of the Potomac were preoccupied with chasing after the Army of Northern Virginia, a serious development occurred in New York City that would prove to have an indirect impact on the 121st. The Enrollment Act passed by Congress in the spring was implemented by summer. The troops in the field received the news of the draft with mixed reactions. Many were torn between hoping the man back home would have to serve and hoping he possessed the wits to escape the long arm of the draft agents and the enticements of the recruiters. John Hartwell expressed sorrow that "people are so foolish as to resist the draft as it will certainly take effect even if the army of the Potomac has to enforce the law." To replenish battle losses, as well as losses from desertion, death, disease, and resignations, individual units in the field sent recruiters back home. Such recruiters gave the regiment a chance to burnish its image for hometown folks.

Albert Bailey predicted a hard time for the recruiters and an even harder time for the potential recruits. He did not blame them for "not wanting to come for they will see hard times" like those experienced by the original members of the 121st. In August, the 121st detailed "six officers and six privates in New York after conscripts." New York draft officials, alarmed at the desertion of bounty jumpers, attempted to close off the northern border into Canada, "which was becoming the refuge of half the men deserting in the state" in 1863. Others believed that the time had arrived for the shirkers to do their duty in service to their country. Charles Rice, Clarke Rice's brother who never served, believed that the volunteer possessed a purer heart than the "hirelings and conscripts" generated by the draft. According to Charles, his brother Clarke and only more like him would save the country. George Teel agreed: "The draft does not trouble us; we had rather be volunteers than conscripts." The Lincoln administration obviously viewed the situation differently.[35]

As the war dragged on, it became painfully obvious to the federal government that more men were needed. The country grew restless after Gettysburg. The war entered its third year in April, volunteers were drying up, and those whose original enlistments expired were going home. The Conscription Act of March 1863, the pro-Southern sympathy of New York City, and the federal government's insistence on forcefully enforcing the new and fatally flawed law would be a toxic brew for Governor Seymour that eventually brought about his political downfall. The legislation called for all men between the ages of twenty and forty-five to serve in the military. The match that ignited the volatile mix was the provision in the law stating that anyone could escape the draft by paying an acceptable substitute $300. The unintended consequence of that provision was that the man of wealth could escape military service and the poor man could not.

The passage of the bill in March, on the heels of the Emancipation Proclamation, resonated deeply with the urban poor, particularly New York City's large Irish population. They saw service in a war for the Union as a way of losing their jobs to freed blacks—a threat to their well-being. White workers in the North equated the $300 substitution price with the cost of a slave at $1,000—an unreasonable and unfavorable comparison. Governor Seymour, already on record in his opposition to the Emancipation Proclamation as unconstitutional, attacked the Enrollment Act with the same arguments. Although he paid lip service to the law, he challenged its constitutionality in court. His comments did nothing to calm the political waters, which were already roiled by social and economic factors produced by the war. Riots soon broke out in New York City, and between July 13 and 16, 120 people were killed and nearly $2 million in property damage was caused by looting and arson. Irish American laborers attacked police, abolitionists, and blacks, beating many to death. Rioters torched the Colored Orphan Asylum and sacked Brooks Brothers clothiers as troops rushed from the Gettysburg battlefield to quell the crowds.[36]

In his feeble attempt to calm the waters, Seymour traveled to the city and addressed the mob with his famous salutation, "My Friends," followed by a promise to telegraph the president and ask him to suspend the draft—words that marked the beginning of his political end. Seymour's comments were picked up by his opponents, who gleefully perpetuated the "My Friends" comment to the governor's detriment.

The men of the 121st held no respect for Horatio Seymour. John Lovejoy and his comrades were not amused by the governor's words. Can you imagine, Lovejoy asked, "the governor of the Empire State calling such men his 'friends' and pledging to use his power and influence to aid them in resisting a constitutional law of our land?" Marcus Casler agreed and called for Seymour and his friends, including New York mayor Fernando Wood, to go the way of Vallandigham "or perchance [to] a more ignominious [end]." Casler ingeniously lumped the Union victories at Vicksburg, Gettysburg, and Port Hudson with New York City, believing that "there was a pre-concerted plan of action between Lee and Davis and their friends and sympathizers in the North and in New York City." He charged that Wood's and Seymour's words were "giving aid and comfort to those in arms against this Government." John Ingraham wanted to go to New York and fight the Copperheads. He viewed the Seymour speech and the draft riots as a "disgrace to us and to New York" and its soldiers. He was outraged that New York City "acted so shamefully."

John Kidder, not acknowledging Seymour as "his" governor, chided his wife in August: "I see by the papers that your governor wants men raised by volunteering. I suppose that would suit every copperhead to have Republicans and loyal democrats volunteer so that the copperheads could control the state and get up a fire in our rear." Kidder perceived a deep and dark conspiracy between Seymour and Lee and expressed approval of Lincoln's determination to pursue the draft. He believed that Seymour delayed the draft in New York to allow Lee time to recruit for his own army. Once the Union troops were ready to fight, Lee would have trained and placed his men in the field, prepared for battle against a new group of federals. Kidder wished that the Copperheads would join the army—especially his company, where he would show them the errors of their ways. If they were disposed to run, he would have his file closers bayonet them, and if one tried to sneak away, he would personally shoot him. He dismissed Seymour as a Copperhead and "a scoundrel" who deserved to be shot.[37]

New York State was hardest hit by the draft because of its size. By 1863, 20 percent of the Union's population lived in New York State. Further, the state supplied more men for the army, "accounted for more bounty money, and was the center of operations for more bounty jumpers and bounty brokers than the other union states combined." The state shared a long and wide-open border with Canada, the goal of many bounty jumpers. Seymour's words on that fateful day in the city were perceived as part of a pattern of obstruction, noncompliance, and refusal to cooperate with the Union war effort, which eventually led to his defeat at the polls the following autumn. Most men of the 121st, appalled by Seymour's behavior, condemned him in the most unflattering and intemperate terms.

But back home, the results of the draft produced very little in the way of new recruits, and most of the men in the regiment viewed it as a failure, despite their initial high hopes for its success. The $300 loophole prevented the draft from becoming effective. Herkimer and Otsego counties led the entire state in the percentage of commutations—draftees who were able to buy their way out of military service. The percentages in the two counties were nearly identical—88 percent and 87 percent, respectively. Yet neither county was particularly wealthy. The high commutation rate belied the widespread belief that the conflict was a rich man's war but a poor man's fight. The evidence suggests that no correlation between wealth and commutation existed. In the 121st, shouts of joy and laughter accompanied the reading of the names of those who had been drafted in the local paper sent from home. The "Middlefield boys were much 'tickled'" when they heard a Copperhead's name read aloud. The men in the field wanted more men—whether draftees or substitutes—so that the war would end sooner and they all could go home.[38]

In Otsego, the town leaders were stymied in their attempts to meet the need for fresh men at the front. The state legislature that summer passed a measure that prohibited the various local governments from offering bounties for enlistments but allowed the payment of substitutes. The state wanted to stop the competition for men to fill local quotas. But the new law failed to correct the flawed system, leading to corruption and evasion. Instead of offering a bounty per se, the town of Otsego passed an ordinance allowing the payment of direct cash aid to drafted men who were heads of household, in order to provide some assistance to the families they left behind. The ordinance recognized the class inequality of the draft, as it began to scrape the bottom of the local population for soldiers.

The town showed a remarkably human and progressive face in its consideration of the less privileged. The *Freeman's Journal* suggested that the town pay "one or two hundred dollars" to married draftees to help them pay for substitutes. A second idea proposed by the *Journal* called for the establishment of an "insurance association" that would pool private donations to pay for substitutes for needy draftees. At the end of the year, the town fathers defied Albany by passing a town ordinance authorizing a bounty of $600 to any man volunteering for service—directly in violation of state law. Throughout the remainder of the year and well into 1864, the towns and villages under duress to provide new men to the war effort struggled with creative ways to meet the need. By September 1864, the amount offered to induce new volunteers in Otsego had ballooned to $1,025.[39]

Conscription proved to be an unpopular and ineffective means to provide the manpower needed to sustain the war effort. The men in the 121st referred to the "Three Hundred Dollar Clause" as a "rat hole" for drafted men to crawl through. The men who had signed on as volunteers were offended by those receiving large payoffs to fight for their country. Men were needed, not money, to save the Union, and, as Henry Walker opined, the money being offered to induce men to fight made "enlisting unfashionable and those who would be influenced by the money will be influenced by fashion too." Walker worried that the autumn would not produce any material results in ending the struggle and that the fight would have to continue over another spring, when many older recruits would return home, their terms of service completed. Such a turn of events would embolden the enemy as well as the "unprincipled and the rebel wretches of the north."

John Kidder, who had left a struggling carriage- and wagon-making business in Laurens, welcomed the Conscription Act but expressed his displeasure with the $300 commutation fee. His partner, Elisha Fisher, who, with Kidder's wife, Harriet, managed what remained of the insolvent company, asked Kidder for $300 to stay out of the army, which presented Kidder with a dilemma. If he sent his partner $300, Fisher would stay in Laurens and keep the firm afloat. If he refused to do so, he might lose Fisher to the draft. Kidder ultimately declined, despite the possibility he would lose the man holding the company together. On the surface, his response appeared puzzling, for his early letters home had articulated his fear of losing his business and eventually becoming impoverished. Fisher's presentation of the "pay to stay" option forced Kidder's patriotism to trump his concern for his business's continued prosperity.[40]

By July 15, the riots had played themselves out. Two regiments from the 1st Division of the Sixth Corps were reassigned from Gettysburg to help New York City bring calm to the streets. Clarke Rice was horrified that the government would send troops against its own people: the idea of taking out of the field men who were fighting a rebellious people in order to coerce other "loyal" citizens to join the fight defied all logic. "We have fallen upon sad times indeed," he moaned. "I think those riotous manifestations will help the rebellion very much." He told his brother Charley that he had changed his position concerning the draft and its resisters. He expressed surprise that the "spirit of resistance prevailed so freely, and that it received so much countenance from the chief officials of the State."

When other states peacefully conducted the draft, Seymour's critics pronounced him mortally wounded politically. Three days later, Lincoln turned to one of his Cooperstown friends, Democrat John A. Dix, to replace Maj. Gen. John Wool as commander of the Department of the East—"a transfer of authority which put Dix directly in control of draft resumption." All through August, Seymour defied Dix in every way possible. Once the veterans of the Army of the Potomac restored order, he relented but still maintained his verbal attacks on the Lincoln administration. The president simply let him rant.[41]

Execution of Deserters

Desertions continued during and after the Gettysburg campaign, although now, a more stringent line of discipline became the norm. Even the 121st continued to be plagued by deserters. As the regiment got into position near Little Round Top at Gettysburg, Stephen Bolt, a farmer from Morris, began limping to the rear. John Kidder drew his revolver and strongly encouraged Bolt to return to the front line. "I shall not be troubled with cowards," he declared, allowing that he would have shot Bolt without a second thought. Four men fell out on the march. Only two of them had returned by the time the regiment fell into the line of battle. Two others shot their fingers off to get out of the battle but were arrested and ordered back into the line. By the time the Sixth Corps approached the Taneytown Road below Little Round Top, new orders authorized commanders to shoot stragglers on the spot. Kidder probably deserved the reputation as the strictest disciplinarian on the march or, for that matter, in the regiment. His sergeant, George Teel, liked him and told his wife that all the men did, too. At times, though, Kidder would go over the line in disciplining the men, and Teel believed that Kidder would lose his influence. He confided to his wife that Kidder had struck one of his men three times with his sword and that when the march concluded for the day in a temporary camp, he had ordered the man tied up by his "hands for two hours without breakfast"; Teel added, "After a long march this can send a bad feeling through the regiment." Kidder admitted to his wife that some men in the regiment "desired [his] fall by rebel bullets."[42]

No stragglers from the 121st were shot by their officers, and the 121st executed no one for desertion. Its sister organization, the 5th Maine, executed two deserters. Except for Company I of the 121st, which remained behind for guard duty, the entire regiment witnessed the execution of thirty-three-year-old English laborer Thomas Jewett of Rockland, Maine, on August 14, 1863. A member of Company D, 5th Maine, Jewett had left his post once before while serving in the English army. The second time, he left his unit "in the presence of the enemy" as the troops struggled at Salem Church on May 3, 1863. Authorities in Washington arrested Jewett and returned him to his regiment on July 17, where a court-martial tried him.

The proceedings began at 1st Division headquarters on July 30, 1863. Three members of the 121st were on the court: Capt. John D. Fish from Kidder's Company I; Capt. Marcus R. Casler, Company B; and Capt. Cleaveland J. Campbell, Company C, sitting as the judge. Four witnesses testified against Jewett, who pleaded not guilty to the single charge. His company commander, 1st Lt. Daniel Clark, and the company's second lieutenant, Frank Patterson, testified that Jewett was not present at the Salem Church battle on May 3. Neither, however, could recall any previous infractions, and both attested to his good character. 1st Sgt. Alonzo Haley, originally of Company D, although he admitted that he "never knew him to display cowardice," presented damaging testimony that Jewett indeed moved up to a fence line with the 5th Maine but when the firing started "made pretty good time going back from the fence. I think he started on a double quick." He did not seem tired to Haley.

The 5th Maine's regimental surgeon, Francis G. Warren, testified last for the prosecution. Warren had treated Jewett for diarrhea in April, but on the day of the battle, he excused only two men for medical reasons, neither of whom was Jewett. He swore he never excused him from duty anytime after the regiment crossed the Rappahannock. Jewett spoke in his own defense, saying that he fought against rebel skirmishers on the army's left flank and then fell back to stay alive. With the bridges out and in order to save himself, he threw his weapon and accoutrements into the river and swam across. Once on the other side, Jewett met up with two men from the 96th Pennsylvania—John Live and Luke Delainy—who persuaded him to desert. The two Pennsylvanians told him that a Pennsylvania regiment "was going home and they could get away with it." He defended himself by saying that he feared he would be "court-martialled for throwing away my things if I went back to the regiment and I was therefore induced to go with them."

On August 7, the court, "two thirds concurring," sentenced Jewett to death "with musketry" by a firing squad on August 14. Upon sentencing, Jewett asked for Chaplain Adams of his regiment to prepare him for his death. Adams saw him several times a day in the last week of Jewett's life, and the two prayed and talked. "His whole inquiry is," Adams wrote to his wife, "how he can be saved from the second death. It is affecting to hear him pray, so earnest in his supplications, the big tears furrowing his cheeks." On the day of his execution, scheduled between noon and 4:00 P.M., he shook hands with his friends as he was handcuffed. Surrounded by guards, he walked to an awaiting wagon. He sat on his coffin on the wagon and rode 2.5 miles to the site of his execution.

Adams accompanied him on a separate horse until they were half a mile from the awaiting 1st Division of the Sixth Corps. At that point, Adams dismounted and climbed aboard the wagon with Jewett, and they rode together into a three-sided square formed by the entire division. Two bands played funeral dirges as guards drove Jewett around the inside of the square, composed of two lines of men. Adams, Albert Bailey, and John Ingraham of the 121st described Jewett as "calm." He appeared to be going "on to a church instead of a coffin," Bailey wrote. When the wagon arrived at the open end of the square, it halted, and the convicted man got "off his coffin, jumped out of the back end of the wagon pretty spry." His guards unloaded the coffin from the wagon, led Jewett to it, and ordered him to sit on it. Chaplain Adams sat on the coffin with him, and the two prayed for a short time. While the executioners stood 2 rods away, Adams said a last prayer as the execution squad blindfolded Jewett. The provost marshal read the sentence, and then Adams stepped away. No word commands were used. When the provost dropped the point of his sword, the squad fired. In strikingly similar terms, Bailey and Ingraham described the execution: "The poor fellow never saw what hurt him as there were six balls passed through his breast and one through his head. It threw him right over his coffin. His head struck the ground before his feet." Ironically, the execution squad consisted of ten volunteers from the 96th Pennsylvania, and watching the squad do its work was a "sorrowful sight." Chaplain Adams reported that Jewett never asked for a reprieve, noting, "All his thoughts have been centered on . . . the good of his soul." Dr. Holt said his end could not be compared to death in battle "when all is excitement and you are looking for it."[43]

Members of the regiment turned the execution into an opportunity to criticize Governor Seymour. Andrew Davidson, responding to another execution witnessed by the 121st, sarcastically called on the governor to seal the New York–Canadian border with a picket line of militia to prevent further desertions. Capt. Marcus Casler, a member of the Jewett court, witnessed the execution and remarked that it took place "in less time than I could tell it, amid the most *awful* silence." With the recent draft riots in New York on everyone's mind, Casler pushed the bounds of propriety when he wrote, "How everyone in his heart wished it might have been Gov. Seymour . . . instead." He believed that Jewett's courage must have allowed him to endure such a suspenseful and horrible death. Apparently referring to Governor Seymour and all manner of Copperheads, Casler blamed Jewett's actions on those "cowardly wretches who have been instigating and enticing men to desert, by speaking and writing it in all their actions ever since the war commenced, and using even greater endeavors as the rebellion nears its final overthrow."[44]

Daniel Holt personalized the traumatic experience. He prayed that he would "never witness such a scene with one of my own sons, nor hear of disgrace attaching to their names by any soldierly conduct; and I believe I never shall. I feel that in them I may safely trust their own as well as my own reputation." Yet in

October, the division witnessed the execution of another deserter, Joseph Connelly from Company H of the 4th New Jersey. Rumors spread that two more men from the 119th Pennsylvania would be executed soon, along with one from the 121st—a rumor that proved unfounded. John Ingraham remarked: "When I am shot, I want to be shot by the Johnnies."[45]

A Change of Heart

Despite occasional raids conducted by both sides and the tedium between them, the remainder of the summer and the autumn of 1863 were extraordinarily pleasant, although some days reached 100 degrees. On those days, the air was as saturated and heavy as the wool uniforms the men wore, and sweat dripped onto the paper as men wrote letters home. The men returned to familiar diversions. The idyllic countryside bolstered men's psyches, and the boredom of camp soon replaced the terror of the battlefield. To some, it made up for the marching and trials of the previous weeks. "All is told us by drum and fife," Delavan Bates observed. The army provided "music for everything"— music for rising, music for retiring in the evening, for breakfast, dinner, when to clean the streets, when to drill, stop drilling, and "when to go to church . . . and when to come back." Although he complained, Bates enjoyed the brigade and regimental bands, which "made the afternoon pass very pleasantly." The 121st's band made him particularly proud. He boasted that others considered it the "best in the brigade." Returning to the regiment at the end of August, John Lovejoy expressed his relief at seeing old friends but admitted that the "regiment don't look much as it did when I last saw it." He had toured the federal hospitals since January. Now, he bunked with Howard Sherman of Westfield. After the two put up a tent, Lovejoy slept "first rate" for the first time in a year and "had more to eat . . . than I have before in a week." He discovered that he lagged in his drills and training. A few days later, he served on picket duty, "something new" to him. He learned that the night held "no fun . . . when we know the rebels are prowling around us on every side."[46]

Many of the farmboys from Otsego County were concerned with the coming hop harvest and the size of the crop being taken to market. They had left home a year ago just as the hop season began. Now, they pictured their loved ones, often only the women they had left behind, laboring under the hot sun in the hop yard. The *Freeman's Journal* ran a weekly column entitled "Hops Intelligence" that provided hops farmers with market news for their product. A friend of Sam Kelley, Matilda Sykes, complained of the boredom of picking hops with a ratio of twenty girls to one boy—"it is dull times," she wrote. Kelley might have thought about hops, but he also found time to flirt long distance with Calista Bailey of Cooperstown. He confessed to his mother that he harbored a fondness for her and had asked her for her picture. Within a month, he changed his mind. He now claimed that he did not love Calista but that he asked for her picture as a favor for another man in the company. By December, the relationship had cooled to the point that the two were returning each other's photographs and requesting one another to destroy earlier letters. Kelley also kept up a determined mail relationship with Alice Miller, with whom he traded photographs. Alice came from the rural crossroads of Davenport Center and was a student at the Delaware Literary Institute, in Franklin, Delaware County. Kelley had met her during a brief working stint in a rake and grain cradle factory before moving to Cooperstown. Her father was a wealthy landowner. Throughout the autumn, they carried on an increasingly friendly conversation by mail.[47]

Yet even though the men were in good spirits and morale continued to be high, something basic had changed after the horror of Gettysburg. The men of the 121st, who earlier expressed concern and sympathy for the rebels and the families they left behind, discovered their feelings were turning to bitterness, hatred, and revenge. The men from upstate New York suffered enormously, but more so, many of them were disappointed with Meade and his inability to crush Lee and end the war. After enduring the excruciating experiences of Salem Church and the Gettysburg campaign, the men of the Sixth Corps and particularly the 121st found themselves roundly condemning the Southern people and their "acts of treason and treachery." They cited the devastation that Lee's army wrought in Pennsylvania as the reason for their rage. They poured their anger out through their letters home after Gettysburg. All of a sudden, the war took on a very different tone for them.

In a very public letter published in the *Herkimer County Journal*, Marcus Casler articulated the policy of all-out war. "I tell you that this time through Virginia," he wrote, "we will show them no leniency. Their sheep and swine, and whatever would give them aid, should we move in another direction are seized and consumed, or put in such a shape that they will be of no use to any person." In a statement predating the total war of 1864 waged by Grant, Sherman, and Sheridan, Casler declared that once the federal army ravaged the rebel land, "Let them *all* beg for mercy, together, and if they should still be obstinate, let them all starve together." He quoted Marshall Ney's remarks to Napoleon during the Spanish campaign: "It is not an army we fight, it is a people." He viewed the populace as "obstinate," "self-willed," and immune to "soundness of reasoning." He compared both sides with their hardened positions to hungry wolves: "We are now snapping and snarling and showing our teeth at each other, 'one afraid and the other dare not,' aspect on both sides, satisfied with picking what few 'sheep' stray from either fold."[48]

The men of the 121st insisted that the Confederates had scavenged all they could get their hands on when they traveled north and then taken all that remained on their way back south. Houses of loyal citizens were ransacked and burned, livestock were killed or commandeered for the benefit of the Confederate army, and unconfirmed rumors abounded of rebel soldiers having their way with Northern women. John Hartwell visited one house where all the furniture was stacked in the center of one room in a large pile, topped off by a chamber pot filled with "a solution usually kept in it to save night traveling." Hartwell decried the stories of rape and assured his wife that Yankee troops were incapable of such acts. He justified the Union troops' actions as not stealing but merely "getting our pay for what the Rebs got from us." Hartwell naively believed unsubstantiated stories and rumors about the abuse of Yankee prisoners in Confederate hands. Three members of the 121st who were captured after Salem Church and marched to Richmond's Belle Island told stories of fellow prisoners who were bayoneted by their captors when they were unable to keep up on the march. "Is that not a mild way to treat prisoners?" he asked in a letter to the *Herkimer County Journal*. "But that is all we can expect of traitors. May God with our armies annihilate them," he continued. "No punishment is too severe for them. No harm too great to befall them, and God in his wisdom *will* punish them for their misdeeds."[49]

The bounty of the land impressed John Ingraham. He excused the soldiers who were taking all they could get their hands on. Echoing Hartwell's words, he wrote: "We are taking our pay, for what the rebs done in Maryland and Pennsylvania." George Teel told his wife that the "inhabitants about here look upon us with dread for we take things where we can find them. We confiscate everything we want, if we can find it." Clarke Rice, moved by the devastation of the once-beautiful valleys ravaged by war, painted a word picture of hopelessness and justified retribution to a haughty, proud state that "hauled down the flag of our fathers, and raised her unrighteous arm against the Government of the land." He told his sister of those who became ardent abolitionists and who found their voice of rage against the enemy. The malaise and the condition of the rebel citizens were attributable to their immoral behavior as rebels.

God had inflicted his divine retribution: "There is no use concealing it," Daniel Holt told his wife; they "are anything but a happy people now, and this unhappiness [is] all their own folly and wickedness." He described the fruits of foraging and the slaughter of livestock as the "indubitable evidence of a sanguinary conflict with the living property of an outraged Confederacy." William Remmel described the land: "The country through which the army passed is almost desolated. Grain to a great extent is destroyed. Fields [are] all cut up with roads, fences nearly all destroyed for cooking and other purposes." He saw farms without cows and no healthy horses. Adelbert Reed declared that the Virginia soil was "stained with the blood of many a brave and daring soldier of the Old Empire State," and he offered no mercy to those who killed his comrades. Delavan Bates's men disappointed him. Even though Virginia was "suffering tenfold than she ever did before," he reported that his soldiers "steal and plunder everything they can lay their hands upon" and burned down a nearby barn. "I don't like this way of doing business," he declared, "private property should be respected the world over. The rebs did . . . [this] . . . in Pennsylvania but that does not justify us who have plenty of victuals of our own."[50]

John Kidder retained a modicum of sympathy for the poor whites and the slaves he encountered. He told a group of contrabands that wandered into camp that they were free. Initially unbelieving, they accepted Kidder's truthfulness, and in the end, they refused to work for free anymore. Kidder realized that they were intelligent but had been kept in ignorance by their masters. Two young men, aged twenty-four and twenty-six, both married, told him that they would spread the word of their freedom to others. The younger one had lost his wife the year before when owners sold her away farther south. They told Kidder that their masters had said the North fought in order to steal the slaves and then sell them to Cuba. Kidder saw the devastation of the land that stripped all the families of Virginia of their livelihood and sources of subsistence. He saw resignation and capitulation in the white population after Gettysburg. Where once there existed bravado in loud proclamations that they would "wade in blood up to their knees before they would submit to Lincoln's government," they now begrudgingly accepted their impoverished circumstances. Supply and demand pushed the prices of common staples such as butter, bread, and sugar beyond the reach of the dirt farmers as well as the "FFVs," or the "First Families of Virginia." Salt became scarce, and homegrown milk and vegetables were all they could muster in a meager diet.

The Union troops bragged about their bounty. Marcus Casler boasted of a sumptuous meal of "quails, stewed apples, quail soup and hard tack." The quail were shot with revolvers and prepared over an open fire. Sweet blackberries and wild cherries, along with an abundance of all manner of other fruits, were available for breakfast. The army enjoyed an adequate supply of beef. Thousands of cattle were "liberated" from Lee as he led his 46-mile-long wagon train from Gettysburg back into Virginia. The Union troops sold their coffee rations to the poor of Virginia for $1.50 to $2 a pound, sugar for $1 a pound. Vinegar sold for $4 a gallon, and flour was dear—$27 per barrel. "No wonder they wish this war may end soon," Casler remarked, for although the First Families were accustomed to such goods, "they have been deprived of all the luxuries a southern man so much appreciates." And he knew of their plight through letters the men of the army recovered on the march or after Gettysburg on the battlefield. "Their families are poorly supplied with the necessities of life," he wrote. Their women are "praying that this war might end, saying they know not how to live through the coming winter. Food is scarce."[51]

Henry Walker, although still in the hospital, celebrated his promotion with the purchase of a $20 sword. He described it to his sister: a "good blade and steel scabbard, silver plated which will keep it from rusting, and save scouring as long as the plating lasts." While the rebel army and the "secesh" population were suffering, the Union troops were living well. The 121st boasted of fresh soft bread, potatoes, fresh vegetables two to three times a week, and pickled cabbage once a week. They ravaged the cornfields that produced edible corn as officers looked the other way. When six men were arrested picking corn in a Virginia field, John Fish asked Dean Pierce if he would ever do it again. When Pierce answered, "No sir," Fish replied, "Remember that your captain likes corn." Clarke Rice looked forward to the quiet time and reveled in all the "perks" afforded an officer, including better quarters, an enlisted cook assigned to him, pack mules on the march carrying his equipment, and all the necessities of life from the commissary. "Sutlers bring in many of the luxuries, so we are enabled to live very well, indeed."[52]

John Ingraham, John Lovejoy, and two other boys from Roseboom and Cherry Valley, Peter Simmons and Ten Eyck Howland, walked the mile and a half to visit the 152nd New York, the other Herkimer-Otsego County regiment and renew acquaintances whenever they could. Lovejoy enjoyed seeing the men but missed his brother Jonathon, who had mustered out that September for disability. His cousin Henry served in the 152nd's band. In October, Lovejoy read in the *Cherry Valley Gazette* that his brother Jonathon had died. He had not received a letter from home for a few weeks and wished that the "sad intelligence" could have come from a family member rather than the newspaper.[53]

The 152nd did not participate in any significant action, and after a year guarding the highways and byways around Washington, it remained untested. As a result, the men of the 121st were unmerciful in their criticism of their "brother" regiment. John Kidder, always tough in talk and action, thought that the 152nd would be a better regiment if it were led by a man such as Upton. Expressing the feelings of many of the men of the 121st, Delavan Bates, who had experienced firsthand the horrors of war, said that "the boys [of the 152nd] find it different business from laying around in the city." According to Ingraham, they could not make coffee properly, they cursed the war, they did not know how to cook, and they did not have anything with which to cook. "They have never done any fighting or marching," he wrote, "they ain't seen nothing compared to us."[54]

Casler criticized the hypocrisy of Southern slaveholders. Although the so-called First Families continually railed against miscegenation and the fear of the black race diluting the white masters, Casler remarked that he had not found a "real, genuine negro" in all of Virginia. "They are the offspring of white men and slave mothers, which is manifest by their lemon color, blue eyes, almost straight hair and a certain degree of *inborn independence* of a *higher-duty-to-perform* manner than is noticeable in the full blooded African." Casler also denounced the white masters who openly sent their illegitimate offspring to the North for schooling "on account of their beauty and talent." Of course, slavery remained the root cause of this "wicked war." Initially, the war's intent was to restore the Union; now, Casler wrote, "Let us . . . strike at the root of the evil which produced it, and wipe slavery from the category of crimes for which the inhabitants of this once God favored land are guilty." He called the Confederacy nothing more than a "political abortion whose cornerstone is human slavery." Clarke Rice decided that the more "he saw the negro race, the better is my opinion of him." But they were not, he said, his equals. He admitted that they possessed "many superior traits." Condescendingly, he held out hope that "under the sunshine of liberal civilization, [they] will yet attain to a higher circle in the family of man." John Kidder expressed astonishment that summer: "Since we returned to Virginia after the Battle of Gettysburg, the soldiers have all got to be abolitionists—those who used to blow about black Republicans are the most radical abolitionists."[55]

The newly embraced abolitionism among the soldiers of the 121st varied, presenting a more complicated picture than Kidder portrayed. A few celebrated the black man's freedom. Others viewed emancipation as a justified loss of property for the white owners—a just revenge for the class of men who would dare rebel against the central government and tear the Constitution apart. Kidder's words were partially true when it came to those from Otsego County. In countless diaries and letters, the men from Otsego referred to slaves and blacks in the most pejorative terms. Herkimer County men rarely did.

The Southern people were not the only targets of the frustration building in the army. During the pleasant autumn months of 1863, the men of the 121st turned on their own back at home, and as before, in many letters, both public and private, they lashed out at the stay-at-homes, the Copperheads, the draft dodgers, the $300 men, the perceived lack of support by their fellow Northerners, and those who refused to support the cause. "When I think how the men of the North are acting it makes my blood boil," Adelbert Reed wrote. With melodrama, Daniel Holt wished for "the voice of Gabriel and the power of the Infinite" to raise "the North to a full and perfect consciousness of its condition. I would ring in the ears the thunders of Sinai and tell them to arouse from their lethargy and strike for freedom. Never . . . was a nation so profoundly slumbering over its own destruction." A great many men of the 121st wanted to see the North send more men to end the war conclusively and with what they continually referred to as an honorable peace. In Roseboom, draftees were announced to the troops in the field, and John Lovejoy expressed pessimism that they would be hard-pressed to come up with the $300 commutation fee. Meanwhile, Delavan Bates just wanted "the fun of drilling some of them."[56]

9

To Rappahannock Station

Our brigade got into a scrap with some wild Yankees and got cut all to pieces.

Thomas Benton Reed, 9th Louisiana Regiment, November 7, 1863

Heavy firing at Rappahannock Station this afternoon. Galent success on our side.

James Henry McCurry, Company F, November 7, 1863

Many ludicrous things about which I will tell you when you return.

Andrew Emmet Mather, to his brother, November 11, 1863

The relatively uneventful summer and early autumn of 1863 in the east gave Emory Upton an opportunity to reflect on the war, his role in it, and the grand strategy he would employ if he were in charge of the entire effort: ideas that germinated in this period blossomed into full bloom after the war in his theories of armies and warfare. Both armies were quietly regrouping after Gettysburg—a necessary move in Upton's opinion. The lull in fighting allowed each side to reinforce its army to "far outnumber the enemy." When the next struggle came, the war in the east would tip the balance toward an ultimate Union victory. But in the meantime, the supply lines in the west supporting General Rosecrans were too long to be effective. Rosecrans needed to accumulate six months of provisions and store them at Tullahoma, Tennessee, where additional men would have to secure them so they could supply his troops. "Nashville would be too far in his rear for his depot." Upton predicted that Rosecrans would move as far south as Atlanta.

Upton thought that Grant should detach 25,000 of his men and send them to Maj. Gen. Nathaniel P. Banks, commanding the Nineteenth

Corps, Department of the Gulf in New Orleans, so that he could keep the Mississippi clear. By impressing all the watercraft available, Upton would have Grant make a feint at Mobile while Banks attacked Port Royal, South Carolina, eventually coming down on the rear of Charleston. To Upton, Charleston represented a critical target as the center for Confederate blockade-runners. Once Charleston was "bagged," Upton would have Banks's army move north and west to Augusta, cutting the Confederacy in half and foreshadowing Sherman's march to the sea a year later but in the opposite direction. Upton thought that Lee would counter by taking badly needed men from Gen. Braxton Bragg and Gen. Joe Johnston and try to drive the Army of the Potomac back to Washington. Such a move would not harm the Confederates, as they suffered from the same long supply lines the Union army experienced. Upton predicted that the rebellion would be "crushed," and he felt that the draft should remain in place as a great idea; it was, as he put it, "manly."

He retained his youthful impatience with his own commanders. During the summer and fall, he read Plutarch's *Lives,* which taught him that "success begets confidence and resolution, which is a battle half won. No soldier in the world can equal the American, if properly commanded." Upton saw the American soldier as combining the determination of his British counterpart and the enthusiasm of the Frenchman. He criticized the leaders of the Union army for not paying close attention to the men in their command and to the psychological importance of a well-placed word or symbolic action. He felt deeply that commanders should urge their men on in the heat of the fight, appealing to their patriotism, and, even more important, that they should say "thank you" to their men after a hard fight—approaches that were critically lacking in the current army. Upton noted from his own experience how a few well-chosen words had served him at Blackburn's Ford in July 1861, where, despite his reluctance at public speaking, he appealed to pride and country to carry the day. He also lamented the losses at Salem Church and expressed admiration for his men— an admiration that went unreciprocated by Union commanders, but was expressed by the enemy.[1]

September 1863 marked the 121st's one-year anniversary in the field. By that time, the regiment bore little resemblance to the youthful, naïve group that had left Mohawk for the front. Some of the men observed the anniversary by writing letters home attesting to their "hardening" from the fighting and marching. Adelbert Reed remembered the long, painful marches but now reveled in the notion that the troops could do in "one day what we did in two or three days then and do it as easy as we are giving it to the Johnnies." On one march, Henry Walker, marveling at how good the roads were, reported that "the evening [was] pleasant and the men were very merry. There are several pretty good singers in the Company and they sang every common song they knew," including "Yankee Doodle" and even "Dixie." The boys from upstate New York had witnessed

the horror of Antietam, participated in the debacle at Fredericksburg, been decimated at Salem Church, and suffered through a 500-mile round-trip march
through Gettysburg. Since the 121st joined the battle, Lincoln and his administration had changed the meaning of the war, and positions on both sides had
hardened and remained unbending. The regiment slowly reinforced itself with
new conscripts, yet the total number of troops remained well below the 1,000
who had assembled among waving flags and handkerchiefs at Camp Schuyler
the year before.[2]

Upton and Olcott—Raiders

Those who had survived the marches to and from Gettysburg began
to enjoy the fruits of the Virginia countryside during the relatively quiet months
of August, September, and October 1863. Behind the regiment were the night-
mares of Fredericksburg and Salem Church and the intense summer marching that took them to Gettysburg, where they could merely view the battle raging below and before them. In mid-September, the 121st found itself on the
march again as the rear guard at the tail end of the corps as it moved on through
Warrenton. The regiment encamped on the Fayetteville Road near the picturesque village of New Baltimore, 6 miles from Warrenton, within instant communication with Washington "and paymasters regular in their visits." John Ingraham thought that Warrenton was a "nice town" but strongly "secesh, [with]
a good many niggers and mulattos." But the war had ravaged it. Harpers Ferry
bustled with military activity: the civilians had deserted the town. Its picturesque setting and pretty white houses were subjected to the constant changes
in the front lines of combat. Many of the houses had been torn apart to provide firewood to keep exposed troops warm in the winter. Frank Morse made
the acquaintance of two lovely ladies from the First Families of Virginia, both
of whom lost their heart to "some officer" as the corps moved through Warrenton. He complained that the regiment passed through town so rapidly it did
not allow the young men "time to say goodbye." The female attention given
to the young men prompted Morse to conclude, "If this is war may there never
be peace."[3]

Horse racing became popular in the 2nd Division, and Henry Walker witnessed the first heat in a $400 race between two officers' horses. He told a Coo-
perstown friend that the brigade hosted "one or two horse races . . . and it is
quite the rage now in the Army of the Potomac."

Captain Galpin and Lieutenants Paine and Hiram Van Scoy were sent to New
York to escort new recruits back to the regiment, with the expectation that they
would return with at least 300 more men. Meanwhile, during August, September, and October, the 121st "camped on fine land" with abundantly growing
fruit, including lots of blackberries. Frank Morse could ask for no more: "We

are perfectly contented," he cooed. Delavan Bates remembered the beauty of the land and his surroundings, of which the regiment and the army took advantage to refresh themselves after the previous three months of hell. Emory Upton returned to his regiment immediately after Gettysburg, and between July 1, 1863, and the following spring when Grant began his Overland campaign, the 121st was, at different times, under the command of Upton, Olcott, and Mather. Upton wrote to his sister that he liked the temporary feel of higher command: "The command of a brigade is a half-way step between Colonel and Brigadier General and I shall try to take the full step in the next battle."[4]

A new threat, especially to the 121st, soon became apparent. Bands of guerrillas, particularly those led by Col. John Singleton Mosby, conducted raids in the area, taking supplies, ammunition, occasional prisoners, wagons, and horses—anything they could use or, more important, anything they could deny the Union army. Upton decided that Mosby and his men posed no threat to the Union lines. "If he becomes impertinent he may get chastised," he said, "but I do not think there will be much trouble." Two days later, Upton reversed himself and decided to "try his hand" at apprehending Mosby and his mob with the 121st New York State Volunteers—or, as he described it, to "carry Jefferson Davis' Conscript Act into effect." Upton and Olcott split up the regiment and decided to hunt down Mosby's guerrillas. Francis Morse went with Olcott. Upton's group included John Kidder and Delavan Bates. The two groups moved through White Plains to Middleburg and Salem—all towns known to harbor Mosby's men—to search for guerrillas and in general harass the local citizens.

Between August 8 and 11, Upton targeted Middleburg and Olcott headed for Salem. Rumors abounded that Mosby's men were looting and killing indiscriminately. Although their mission comprised a serious military objective, the men of the 121st treated the days they spent chasing Mosby as a lark. Flagrant rumors, repeated independently by no less than four members of the 121st, told of one of Emory Upton's aides being hanged by guerrillas after Upton sympathetically responded to a lone woman who requested a guard for herself and her property. John Kidder not only reported the incident but also argued that it gave Upton the excuse to go after Mosby. Upton sympathized with the area's citizens and their requests for guards, and he continued to grant their requests. But he warned the residents that the government would confiscate their property if they threatened their protectors. Daniel Holt knew of the rumored story, but he never mentioned anyone being hanged. Ingraham told his parents, "The report is they hung him but I don't think so."[5]

There were 300 men in each party sent to hunt down the guerrillas, and the first detachment achieved its objective when it found Mosby's home "on the mountain side between Thoroughfare Gap and the new Baltimore Pike." At Salem, Virginia, a small rural town of 600 people, Olcott's men surrounded the

(above left) An early protégé of John Kidder, Delavan Bates went on to command the 30th U.S. Colored Troops and was wounded at the Battle of the Crater at Petersburg, where he also won a Medal of Honor. After the war he moved west and became a community leader and mayor of Aurora, Kansas. Courtesy of the New York State Historical Association Research Library, Special Collections, Civil War Collection. (above right) Lt. Henry Walker, a Cooperstown native and temperance man. Courtesy of the New York State Historical Association Research Library, Special Collections, Civil War Collection. (right) Captured with Kelley and Olcott at the Wilderness, Lt. Lansing Paine was later exchanged and survived the war. His little village of Garrattsville lost several men at Salem Church, nearly wiping out his entire company. After the war he returned to Otsego County and became a clerk in a lumberyard. Courtesy of the New York State Historical Association Research Library, Special Collections, Civil War Collection.

village with a line of pickets. Methodically, the regiment swept the town house by house, looking for guerrillas and for "all of the forage" they could take. Olcott, according to Adelbert Reed, did not want the men "grumbling for the want of rations." He cautioned against outright pillaging and told the men to take only what they could eat and use—two directives that were loosely interpreted. But he ordered them to take every horse they could find and to "arrest every male citizen between the ages of 18 and 45." He particularly admonished them against abusing any females, a directive the men took seriously. He also ordered them to shoot "every man that attempted to run through [the army's lines]" and to shoot "any citizen" attempting "to molest [them] in any way" but to make no effort "to take guerrillas alive." They arrested all the white men in town, including the preacher, and liberated a few blacks. And just as abruptly, Olcott's detachment left Salem with only the men as captives.

The next day, they stopped at the estate of John A. Washington and liberated his horses for the U.S. Army. When the regiment reunited, some 38 miles later, they released the white men, who were faced with a long walk back to Salem. "The negroes would not return" but stayed with the army. One of them, named Peter, decided to remain with the regiment and offered to be a guide on the next expedition. He said he would show them "Mosby's cave" in the mountains, where he kept "his stolen property and prisoners." According to Reed, the detachment took twenty-five of Mosby's men and sixty-four horses. In the meantime, Upton's contingent marched to Middleburg, where it arrived at 2:00 in the morning and, after an hour's sleep, "completely invested" the town "by daylight." The citizens "came on their doorsteps and displayed the *white flag*, in the shape of the *tails of their under garments*, as they fluttered in the breeze." Mosby had left the day before with forty-one men. James Cronkite held forty-three horses, which most of the men rode. They arrived back in camp with "turkeys, chickens, and ducks strung across their necks." Knapsacks were filled with apples, potatoes, onions, preserves, and butter, and canteens were filled with milk instead of water. "We milked all the cows we could find," Remmel told his brother Caleb. The rest of the brigade was so impressed with the "new" horsemen that they encouraged the 121st to consider becoming a cavalry regiment because it was "not afraid of the devil."[6]

In White Plains, citizens directed the venom of two years of war at the blue-coated detachment as it marched into town. White Plains, a hotbed of guerrilla activity and partisan resistance, witnessed the retreat of the irregulars before the advancing federal army. The men from the 121st attempted to extract information from the noncombatants who remained behind. The townspeople greeted the regiment with a cautious cordiality tempered by a deep-seated enmity for the Union. "Were it not for that notorious robber and murderer Mosby," Remmel remarked, "the people would not be molested." The few men left behind were, according to Clarke Rice, ready to return to the Union. The same could not be said for the women. Their unbridled hatred for all things Yankee manifested itself immediately. "Indeed," Rice wrote, "they are perfect fanatics in their devotion to their unholy cause," giving great succor to the rebel soldier. They were, in contrast to the Northern women, unbending in their devotion to the "cause." Where Northern women encouraged their men to return home, the Southern women urged their "brothers and their sons to fight till the last Yankee bites the dust—until their flag shall wave triumphantly over the ruins of the Union. Their zeal, so mad, knows no limitation."[7]

Mosby's Attack on Headquarters

The raids against Mosby's guerrillas accomplished little of lasting value. They proved to be nothing more than a trial of men and animals over rough terrain for three days. At the end of the month, with Upton off sick in Washington, Olcott led another expedition to Thoroughfare Gap but turned up nothing but "citizens." The tough duty did nothing to diminish the respect the men reserved for Upton and Olcott and their strict ways. They continued to praise both of them. Calling Olcott a "man we could trust leading us," they singled him out for his leadership during the rough expedition. He sustained the men's spirits. "We would follow him through fire if he would ask us to," Reed wrote. Of Upton, James H. Cox of Company C wrote that he "won the esteem of his men. In fact, all of our officers, with a few unimportant exceptions, command the respect and admiration of all good and well meaning men." Upton returned the compliments, telling his men that they proved themselves "second to none in battle," and he persisted in his goal to make them "second to none in discipline." Yet Mosby continued to prey on targets of opportunity, and the Union army responded weakly.

A month later, General Bartlett, undeterred by the occasional annoyances of Mosby's rangers, continued to allow himself indulgences about which the enlisted men could only fanaticize. At New Baltimore, Bartlett established his headquarters away from his troops in a beautiful grove near the "home of a Southern lady with several accomplished daughters." The good-looking Bartlett was one of the army's most eligible bachelors, and some expressed concerns about his intentions and behavior, given the proximity of the attractive woman; many wondered, as well, about the prudence of being closer to a woman of questionable loyalty than to his own troops. But Bartlett was unaffected by these concerns. Besides, Gen. John Singleton Mosby roamed in the area with his troops, and his presence constituted a real and present danger. "To the average man the presence of a lovely woman will overbalance many dangers," Delavan Bates later commented, "even when they can be plainly seen." Purportedly, the woman's husband and sons were guerrillas and were passing information on the Yankees' whereabouts and movements to the regular Confederate troops. "The inhabitants around here are all rank secesh," complained Henry Walker.[8]

Before retiring on the evening of September 4, Bartlett ordered pickets set up around the perimeter of his camp. He had established his headquarters 600 yards from the tents of the 121st, in a peach orchard surrounded by a high wooden fence. A dirt road ran from the New Baltimore Pike to the mansion and then on toward another house. The pickets of the 96th Pennsylvania were posted on this road. A hundred yards in the opposite direction, the brigade band encamped. Around 2:00 in the morning, guerrillas, presumably from Mosby's contingent, attacked the sleeping camp. An advance Confederate scout got the drop on a picket, and when asked for identification, he answered, "Cavalry men, friends, returning from a scout." When ordered to dismount and provide further identification, the "scout" leveled his revolver at the head of the picket, shot him in the face, jumped from his horse, and with other guerrillas promptly attacked the brigade band tents. Realizing their error and just as the entire camp began to respond to the attack, the guerrillas sought out General Bartlett's tent.

By now, Bartlett and the rest of his men were awake. Bartlett grabbed his pistol but not his trousers and proceeded to fight "his would-be captors in the uniform nature had provided." George Collins described the chaos as the men were routed out in the middle of the night and "got under arms after a good many funny moves have been gone through with." Most of the men of the brigade were half dressed, but all were armed with a "gun and a cartridge box"—things that "would not be tolerated on dress parade." Olcott got into the fray and, in the dark, almost killed Col. Clark S. Edwards, commanding officer of the 5th Maine. John Ingraham allowed that "it was quite exciting to wake up out of a dead sleep hearing musketry and Reb cavalry riding along." Delavan Bates grabbed his weapon and with the rest ran toward the action in minutes. When the guerrillas realized the futility of their raid, they departed as hurriedly as they had attacked. The next morning, scouts scoured the countryside for them, "but nothing but harmless citizens were found." Bates wrote that "a good many think these harmless citizens by day are guerrillas at night." Bartlett laughed off the attack, whose major casualties were the brigade band's bass drum, a canteen, and Bartlett's trunk—each of which took a single bullet. Another bullet had gone through Isaac Best's tent as he and a staff orderly chased after the intruders. "Brigade headquarters were not moved; the ladies of the house were as pleasant and sociable as ever," but after that, Bartlett ensured that a cohort of soldiers were stationed in the area just behind his tent.[9]

Bartlett's behavior did not escape the notice of the enlisted men. At first, there were general good feelings toward Bartlett, but some men became disillusioned as they perceived they were being "misused" by him. Henry Walker wrote home saying that "a good many think he is jealous of Colonel Upton and afraid he will get a Brigadier General's commission before he [Bartlett] does. Bartlett's appointment as Brigadier General has not been confirmed yet."[10]

Chasing Lee in Circles

George Meade remained in command of the Army of the Potomac, although rumors persisted that he would soon be replaced with yet another leader. "Better to hold on to a fair man, than to change for an untried one," wrote Dr. Holt. "This has been death of us in more senses than one." Meade continued to smart from the criticism he had received for allowing Lee to escape from Pennsylvania. He needed a victory to elevate his stature over his predecessors' record and to expunge the disappointment after Gettysburg.[11]

That summer and autumn, the nation's attention focused on the western theater. Lee's army was recuperating. The Confederate commander pulled his army below the Rapidan while Meade plotted to defeat him. Early that fall, Lee sent a part of James Longstreet's corps west to Georgia. Word of that deployment prompted Meade in mid-September to attempt a broad turning movement near Culpeper to attack Lee. Rumors spread among the troops that the Third Corps and the Fifth Corps were also going to join the western units under Rosecrans. The Sixth Corps was said to be destined for Texas or Charleston or assigned to serve in defense of the nation's capital—all news coming courtesy of Dr. Holt. But by September 24, Meade was forced to send his Eleventh and Twelfth corps to Chattanooga after the federal loss at Chickamauga.

Lee intended to press Meade and threaten Washington, which Meade had pledged to defend. The two played a game of cat and mouse, Lee looking for a weak point in the Union army and Meade retreating, realigning, marching, and delaying. The slow response and meager effort in attacking Lee's retreating and wounded army angered and disappointed some, but others chose to defend Meade. The strategy remained a mystery to the enlisted men. They knew that Lee's army was "demoralized, poorly fed, almost shoeless, discouraged and worn out," and they could not understand why their own army did not deliver the knockout punch.[12]

Meade pulled his still larger army back along the Orange and Alexandria Railroad in early October when Lee attempted to turn his right flank. As the army approached Bristoe Station, a major confrontation brewed. On October 9, Lee moved north to turn Meade's right flank in order to get behind the Union army and to either threaten Washington or hit Meade's supply source at Culpeper. On October 14, Meade moved the Sixth Corps out onto an open, level terrain. The sun played on the changing autumn leaves on that bright, brisk morning. Meade drew the Second, Fifth, and Sixth corps into a 3-mile line of battle accompanied by artillery in the rear and Buford's cavalry skirmishing ahead.

As the line moved forward, the flags fluttered gently in the breeze. Sunlight glinted off the steel muskets and bayonets. "The whole army moved together," Bates told his father, "columns of infantry, artillery, ambulances, pontoons, and wagon trains going side by side. It was a grand sight." George Collins wrote that he would "never see the likes again" of the spectacle before him. Isaac Best also witnessed the Grand Army maneuvers as they unfolded and called it "the most spectacular movement" he witnessed during the war. But as Collins reminded his reader, "It is better to see a show than to be a part of it oneself." The men were watching the opening moves of the battle of Bristoe Station, which proved disastrous to the Confederates and A. P. Hill, who impetuously attacked Meade without a strategic plan. The Confederate losses were three times the Union's in terms of men killed, wounded, and missing, a decided loss for Lee. Again, the men of the 121st did not participate; they merely bore witness to the proceedings.[13]

In November, the two armies jockeyed between Centerville and Culpeper Court House at least twice. Meade remained perplexed. "As yet, I have not been able to arrive at any satisfactory conclusion, though most earnestly anxious to bring matters to a termination," he told Halleck. Meade could not determine whether Lee had moved, but he admitted to Halleck that he had not moved his army either. Lee returned to familiar territory just below the Rappahannock and set his defenses at Rappahannock Station.

Clinton Beckwith saw the evidence of the broken Confederacy as he followed the fleeing rebels back into Virginia. The debris-strewn ground convinced his comrades that the Confederates had little with which to oppose the pursuing Union armies. The discarded militaria gave evidence of the "entire destruction" of the retreating armies. "So we got to believe almost any story of their demoralization," he wrote, "and it was with feeling of exultation that we thought we saw the end of the war as soon as we could strike them again." Clarke Rice remarked how the Union army missed the chance to crush Lee and his forces and end the war in Maryland. He did not blame Meade for the escape and wished that Hooker still led them. He cited the rebels' low morale, low ammunition, confusion, hunger, and exhaustion, all "pressing them to the ground." But he had learned in his year in the military that duty required him "to exercise a good deal of charity" toward the high command.[14]

Many of the boys discovered in the soft Virginia autumn that picketing could be a desirable pastime. Although the men of the 121st described their enemy to their family and friends in atrocious terms, their targets were in the abstract. When they were face-to-face on the picket line, they interacted with their foes in a warm and friendly way. The men of the 121st befriended their counterparts across the picket line, exchanging papers, tobacco, and news with the tacit agreement that neither side would fire on the other. The lines became so close, in fact, that one officer claimed if they had stood there "three days longer, we and the Rebs would be picketing the same line." A few members of the 121st played euchre with the rebel troops.

William Remmel enjoyed talking to his enemies, as they did to him. They admitted that they would like to meet Yankees on friendly terms and "have a nice soldier talk over the war." Remmel exchanged newspapers with the Johnnies and found their papers "interesting." John Ingraham was posted so close to the rebels that he could hear the 4th Georgia relieve its pickets across the river. As each rebel left his post, he doffed his hat, waving good-bye to the Yankees on the other side. From their positions, the 121st's pickets could see the rebel signal station south of the Rapidan, 40 rods from the federal lines. There was no "firing on either side although it is very easy musket range." When the men of the 121st were able to put a human face on their enemy, they were able to relate to him on an equal basis. The soldiers were not killing each other; they were carrying out officers' orders. Left to the enlisted man, the war would be over immediately.[15]

As summer melded into autumn, the men of the 121st were convinced that winter quarters were in their very near future. Many began fantasizing about a quiet, six-month hiatus in comfortable quarters somewhere along the Rappahannock. The 121st spent seven weeks in New Baltimore, Upton drilling and marching his charges relentlessly. At the end of September, he trotted out three companies of the 121st—A, G, and J—for a lesson in the skirmish line drill, "with a few illustrations in the shape of a sham fight."[16]

The 121st spent September and October going in circles as Meade kept his army between Lee and Washington—"it would take a Philadelphia Lawyer" to keep track of the regiment's movements, Daniel Holt joked. The circular marches wore down the army, and some soldiers were convinced that Meade and his generals had concocted a mysterious grand strategy. "I hope that all our running will amount to something," wrote Henry Walker. "I would rather march than fight if the same ends can be accomplished." But most agreed that the regiment was faring much better than it had a year before. Fifteen-mile marches through mud and at night were well tolerated by the toughened troops. Grumbling had died down, and straggling had became nonexistent. Discipline improved because Hooker had replaced McClellan, and Hooker "changed the army for good." The third week of September became, in John Hartwell's words, "the easiest time since leaving home, having nothing to do but a little camp duty and to make ourselves comfortable."[17]

On the "Grand March," the men recorded every little town they marched through, including some for a second and a third time. They passed through small towns to the west of Washington that reminded them of home. One of the men compared Warrenton's size to Cooperstown, and another thought that Middleburg resembled Newport in Herkimer County. In late October, the regiment passed the old Bull Run battlefield, with its human bones still exposed. A recent skirmish there had left some dead Confederates in a ditch.

On one march in September, the 121st passed the Eleventh Corps, moving in the opposite direction, and the two columns exchanged greetings. The men of the Sixth Corps needled the men of the Eleventh for skedaddling at Chancellorsville and Gettysburg. Their ranks were sadly depleted, "their colors tattered, and there seemed to be a sullen, gloomy feeling over them and a lack of interest in their surroundings," Beckwith remembered.[18]

At one of many stops in Warrenton, the 121st occupied the deserted camp of a New Jersey regiment. They discovered a jerry-rigged merry-go-round made of an old buggy wheel at the center, two 30-foot poles radiating out from the horizontal wheel, and two buckets at the poles' ends for joyriders. One foolhardy soul from the 121st tried to ride the contraption. As he attempted to get out from the middle of the whirling, hazardous ride, it sent him "head first against a stump."

When the 121st returned to New Baltimore in late October, where it halted momentarily, the regiment drew up in a line of battle, stacked arms, and waited. Presently, a flock of some "40 sheep came into view"—as Henry Walker said, "probably for mustering"—and there ensued "a grand rush" toward the unsuspecting animals. Although officers tried to stop the rush and resultant massacre, "in less than ten minutes," Teel wrote, "the sheep were dead." He himself got an old ram and ate the hindquarters, which were "rather strong."[19]

In September 1863, Adam Clarke Rice completed his first year in the army with the 121st. He had escaped the perils of combat and survived the long and arduous marches. He had enlisted as a private and was promoted to sergeant in Company C. He swiftly moved through the ranks to first lieutenant a month before Salem Church, serving successively in Companies D and F. When Capt. Nelson Wendell died at Salem Church, Rice took over command of the company, a position in which he took "more pride and interest." His family variously described him as "ambitious, poetical, impetuous, and whole-souled." His ambition knew no bounds. After he became a first lieutenant and transferred to Company F just after Salem Church on May 14, 1863, he boasted to his brother that he commanded the best-disciplined company in the regiment; he also said that he kept his eye on the next step. He knew that Upton forwarded his name to Governor Seymour for a captaincy, but it concerned him that he might not be promoted until the regiment's new recruits brought the 121st up to strength. He stayed focused on the future—once the war was over, he would go to college and then practice law. "I shall try to aim high in life," he told his brother, "but I shall not be awfully disappointed if I do not hit the mark." He admitted that he loved public speaking and thought that the opening western lands would be his destiny. He predicted that the West could "offer better inducements to a young man than the east."

While the regiment was camped at White Plains, Rice complained of an earache. A secessionist family treated him for what may have been a precursor to the disease that would soon take his life. Rice's family knew nothing of his illness until they received word from administrators at Seminary Hospital in Georgetown the day before he died. His cousin W. Ward Rice wrote his parents that Clarke suddenly took ill in Warrenton and that doctors had sent him to Washington immediately. He had read of Clarke's death in the *Washington Chronicle*; the paper used only initials but gave his regiment as the 121st U.S. Infantry. Ward hoped that the surgeons had made a mistake. They had not. Clarke's brother Eleazer reached his bedside on Sunday, and the next day, Eleazer telegraphed his parents that he was returning with his brother's body to Little Falls. Within twenty-four hours, Clarke had succumbed to typhoid, among strangers—in the company of hospital personnel but no family members.

Dr. Holt told the family that he initially diagnosed Clarke's illness as nonthreatening after ministering to him for four or five days. Holt anticipated an army move, and that was what prompted him to order Clarke to Washington, not because he felt Clarke would receive better treatment there. It was Holt's opinion that the ride Clarke took by ambulance wagon to New Baltimore and thence to Washington killed him. By the time Eleazer arrived, morticians had prepared Rice's body for a burial with full military honors. After the embalming was completed, Eleazer started off for Little Falls with the body, arriving on Thursday. There, he was met by the family along with a delegation of students and faculty from Fairfield Academy. Rice's body went home for the last time, where his family could greet mourners. The next day, Friday, September 25, "was a dark, cold day, and the rain poured in torrents almost, as we lowered him into the damp ground," his brother Charley wrote. Adam Clarke Rice was buried within a week of his death.[20]

Emory Upton wrote a letter of sympathy, now lost. According to the family, Upton praised Rice as "one of the best officers in the line," who won the admiration of his "superiors and men by strict adherence to duty, as well as many kind and unselfish acts." His brother Charley affirmed Clarke's honesty in all his actions: "A person could not help to admire, respect and love him." John Kidder described him as a "noble officer, and we feel his loss very much," he wrote his wife.

Unfortunately, the men in Rice's company felt differently. The hot, dry summer months had been a factor in increased tensions among the men, and drills held in the heat only exacerbated the situation. In his diary, Dean Pierce wrote on the evening of August 3 that "our boys had a general row last night with the officer of the guard, Lieut. Rice." The following day, he wrote of officers tying up men by the thumbs and wrists "for nothing, only talking after taps last night after they had been told to go to sleep." Rice's subordinate, Adelbert Reed, had no time for Rice. At the time, two lieutenants served in Company F: 2nd Lt. Silas Pierce and 1st Lt. Adam Clarke Rice. Pierce came from Otsego County. The captain and commanding officer, Seymour Hall, had been assigned to Joe Bartlett's staff at brigade headquarters. Reed wrote his parents that Rice was "not liked at all. He hates other people as though they were snakes." To ensure that his parents understood whom he was referring to, Reed told them that one of the officers was "the son of the County House keeper [Pierce] and the other is *a Herkimer chap* [Rice]."

Reed's unrelenting contempt spilled out on the page: "He is too mean to live. We cannot do anything to please him and have given up trying and do anything we can to displease him in hope we can get him put out of the regiment. The boys would give one month's pay to see him leave." Seven weeks later, Rice was dead and Reed changed his tone. He was reluctant to speak ill of the dead: "We have lost our First Lieutenant, he died in the hospital. His loss is much regretted by the men and officers of this regiment for he was a bold and ambitious fellow. We have a pretty good Second Lieutenant; our Captain is on Bartlett's staff." Reed also noted that his friend Lt. Thomas Adams received a presentation watch from the men of Company B. "How I wish we had an officer we felt like that towards," he wrote awkwardly.[21]

New York Politics

Back in the Empire State, Governor Seymour managed to keep the political pot boiling while alienating the men in the field. In the winter of 1863, the Republicans in the state assembly sent the governor a bill that would allow citizens to vote with an absentee ballot. Before legislators wrote the bill to allow proxy voting, Seymour threatened to veto the idea on the basis that it would lead to fraud. The Republicans intended to embarrass him, and Seymour signaled that he would accept a constitutional amendment allowing absentee voting. He knew that the amendment would take another two years to go into effect, and by then, either the war would be over or Lincoln and the abhorrent Republican administration would be out of office. The bill eventually reached Seymour's desk in April 1863, and he vetoed it on the basis that it was unconstitutional. He thus placed himself in the position of being *against* the troops in the field, which "damaged the Democrats at the next election for the assembly in the autumn of 1863." With the additional baggage of his "Friends" speech, Seymour was a wounded executive, and the Republicans circled for the kill.

Only the legislature stood for reelection in 1863, an "off year." It was a rehearsal for the following year's presidential elections. As the fall elections began, the anti-Seymour papers reminded their readers of his actions during the draft riots in the city and his veto of the absentee voting bill. New York Republicans took the unusual step of changing their party's name to the "Union" Party. Political meetings and conventions were labeled "Union" gatherings, the party organs called themselves "Union" presses, and the candidates were "Union" nominees. In September, the Central Party formally changed its name to the Union Central Committee. Although the Democrats continued to call their opponents Republicans, the name Union gradually replaced Republican over the course of the year. The Democrats used only native New Yorkers as their party spokesmen. The Union-Republicans imported national figures from Northern states to campaign for their candidates—many of them loyal Lincoln men. In October, the election results began to roll in from Ohio and Pennsylvania, showing a decidedly Republican slant. In the first week of November, nearly 18,000 soldiers were granted leave to return home to middle and central New York—a move immediately denounced by the Democrats. Seymour and the Democrats were defeated by the thousands of veteran soldiers when the fall elections were held. After Salem Church in May and June, the men of thirty-eight New York regiments had completed their two-year enlistments; they returned home—and voted. The Union-Republicans carried the state by 30,000 votes. Voters rejected Seymour and rewarded the Lincoln men.[22]

Even though they were unable to vote in that election, the soldiers of the 121st were cheered by Seymour's "defeat." To most in the regiment, Seymour and the Democratic Party were synonymous with the Copperheads. Lansing Paine reported that "the boys are all very strong Union and very glad the Copperheads were defeated in New York." Those who wanted to restore the Union to its prewar configuration has been asleep for the last five years, Silas Pierce remarked. He wrote his father that protection of the Union and the Constitution had cost too much in blood and treasure over the past two years to turn back. "Could every man at the North, who thinks of voting the Copperhead ticket, have stood where the 121st stood," they would "have hung their heads in shame, like men who had been caught stealing." Richard Turner in Company B wrote to his friend Thomas Carran of his pleasure at the turn of events back home:

> Well Thomas, I am glad that the old Empire State has gone union throughout the state with a great majority. I am glad to hear that the soldiers of New York State can have the privileges of voting for the next president. It makes the soldiers feel as they had got some friends at home when we hear that the state has given a great majority for the soldiers to vote. I am proud to think that I am one of the empire state soldiers that can have the privilege of voting next November.[23]

The legislature took no action to allow the soldiers to vote, but the soldiers interpreted the election as a victory for their right to cast a vote from the front.

Turner, not an educated man, realized that the election outcome meant that he might be allowed to vote in the future. An anonymous private wrote: "York State has proclaimed that her soldiers shall have the right of suffrage while absent, battling for one of the best governments that ever existed." Adelbert Reed was pleased to hear the "glorious news from the old Empire State" and to know that the state would "go Union." So were John Kidder and Andrew Davidson. Davidson saw the election as a "retrieval" of "what was lost last fall" with the election of Seymour and the Democrats. Legislative victories by Democrats would only "encourage Jeff Davis and Company," he wrote. Davidson pronounced Seymour "politically dead" and vowed that the soldiers would never forget his veto of the bill allowing absentee ballots. Kidder told his wife that the election made it very clear: "The soldiers know [who] their friends are."[24]

Henry Walker believed that the soldiers' vote would have shown "how few Modern Democrats there are in the army." Walker, who proudly wrote "New York Volunteers" after his name and had just turned twenty-three, grew concerned about the *next* election as talk of McClellan's potential candidacy circulated in the army. "But McClellan is dead," he stated, "dead past all political resurrection. Lincoln is very popular among the soldiers," and he would be the candidate the next November. "The Union victories all through the North from the east to the far west are very encouraging to those in the field and will [also] have a good effect in Dixie." Dr. Holt echoed young Walker's feelings. The vote represented a voice "louder and more fearful" to the Confederacy "than all the cannon of the universe pouring death and destruction into [them]," he exulted. With the vote, it appeared to Holt as if "the whole North [blazed] with patriotic fire. The Army is in a perfect frenzy of delight over the joyful news." John Fish called it a "noble victory over the northern traitors—Three times three for the old Empire State. She is redeemed."[25]

Delavan Bates remained unconvinced; he held a nuanced position. Although he found no common cause with the Copperheads, he was still a Peace Democrat and adamantly believed that the war represented a fight for Union and Constitution. Contrary to Copperhead canon, Bates felt that the war demonstrated to the rebels that the Constitution and the Union were paramount, and he would welcome his wayward peers back into the Union, where everyone could return to the status quo. He whispered about a McClellan testimonial that supposedly received widespread acceptance by the majority of the regiment and about the rumor that "officials" in Washington had "suppressed" it—both dubious tales. Naively, Bates told his father that "politics are but little discussed in the army."[26]

An anonymous soldier told the *Otsego Republican* that the *Freeman's Journal* was the "meanest and most traitorous paper" in camp and ought to be barred from being sent to the troops. A week before the election, its pages were "black with lies and treason about the war and the Army of the Potomac." The writer hoped that the election would "make old Seymour tremble in his boots." One can only imagine the glee enjoyed by the editors at the *Republican* in publishing the letter.[27]

The Battle of Rappahannock Station

On November 6, Meade told Halleck that he intended to cross the Rappahannock at Kelly's Ford and at Rappahannock Station. The Army of the Potomac sat astride the Warrenton Railroad approximately 17 miles from Rappahannock Station—at Auburn and Catlett's Station. Cavalry skirmishes in the area revealed that rebel transportation trains and skirmishers were posted at Kelly's Ford. Gen. Wesley Merritt in Buford's cavalry command wanted to press the few rebel skirmishers on the north side of the river but instead received instructions to watch their movements and not attack unless he was struck first. Meade determined that the alignment of both armies made this an ideal time to launch an attack on Lee. He reconfigured his command, designating two columns. He gave command of the "left column," consisting of the First, Second, and Third corps, to Maj. Gen. William H. French. John Sedgwick received command of the "right column," consisting of the Fifth Corps, under Maj. Gen. George Sykes, and his own Sixth Corps, under Horatio Wright.[28]

On the night of November 6, Meade issued orders to leave the next morning. General Bartlett took command of a brigade in the Fifth Corps, and Meade assigned Emory Upton to lead the 2nd Brigade. At headquarters, Francis Morse volunteered to deliver the order and the good news to Upton personally, knowing that he would be asked to be Upton's aide. Upton turned command of the 121st over to Major Mather, leaving Morse to perform new duties "which were more pleasant than those of an infantry adjutant." That night, Egbert Olcott began a fifteen-day leave of absence after his horse rolled over on his leg, injuring his knee in a freak accident. The next morning, November 7, 350 men and 17 officers of the 121st New York left Warrenton and marched briskly toward Rappahannock Station, "little dreaming," wrote John Fish to his brother, "that before night we should assist in one of the most brilliant things done in the war." As they marched along the Orange and Alexandria rail line, the buoyant mood and conversations were punctuated with jokes and comments on the recent elections in New York, which made Fish and the others "feel jovial." Andrew Mather incorrectly predicted that when they left Warrenton, they would not be in a fight "for several days at least."[29]

Eight days of rations, consisting of hardtack and pork, were issued to everyone. Upton complained that it was too much food for too long a time. While on the march, soldiers of the 121st, like the rest of the army, carried their rations in their knapsacks and haversacks. On the road, these "lunch boxes" were constantly jostled, thrown, and used as pillows. As a result, most food carried in them crumbled beyond recognition. Food that remained whole became dirty, lost, or, in the rainy seasons, wet and invariably inedible. In camp, the men were allowed to keep their eight days' rations, and according to Upton, soldiers with much time on their hands were prone to nibbling away at the source of food. Inexplicably, the men were issued the same amount of rations whether in camp or on the march, a concept that made no sense to Upton. The day before the Rappahannock Station campaign, he correctly pointed out to his superiors that the men needed more calories on the march than in camp. His words went unheeded. The rations were issued, and the next morning, they struck off on the road to the Rappahannock.[30]

Rappahannock Station no longer exists. In its place is the small town of Remington, Virginia. The battle occurred north of the Rappahannock River on fairly level ground. The Orange and Alexandria Railroad and the road to Warrenton, running parallel to each other, crossed the river at that point. Combat had destroyed the railroad bridge earlier in the war. On the north bank, Lee established a *tete-de-pont,* or bridgehead, of well-established and connected rifle pits; the pits were occasionally interrupted by "forts" placed on any elevated terrain available, "which covered all approaches from the front." The rifle pits ran parallel to the river, providing a position of "unusual strength." Behind the lines, Confederates threw a pontoon bridge across the river, which Lee envisioned using as a safety valve to move across and then up or down the south bank of the river in the unlikely event that his troops were overrun.

With broad, wide, and level plains on both sides gently sloped to the river and behind their lines, Confederates placed artillery batteries on the low ridge and hills. In the area where the men of the 121st arrived, a gentle upward slope halfway between their position and the Confederates on the river provided cover from the rebel lines. Lee expected Meade to leave a small force at the station and use his main force to cross the Rappahannock a few miles below, striking at Kelly's Ford. Should this occur, Lee could efficiently cross the river on pontoons and deliver a flanking blow to the Army of the Potomac at the ford. Lee chose Maj. Gen. Robert F. Hoke's and Maj. Gen. Harry T. Hays's two brigades and four artillery pieces to guard the bridgehead at Rappahannock Station. Both brigades were veteran units. Hoke's 1st Louisiana Brigade, consisting of the 5th, 8th, and 9th Louisiana and the 6th, 7th, and 54th North Carolina regiments under Hays, were in the trenches and rifle pits with orders to hold the position if Sedgwick attacked.[31]

Between 10:00 A.M. and noon, the rebels noticed Union troops moving toward them, with a large column breaking off and headed to their right. As Lee expected, Meade divided his troops. Maj. Gen. William French, in charge of the "left column," began crossing the Rappahannock at Kelly's Ford, 5 miles downstream. Meade intended the move at Kelly's Ford to be a feint designed to convince Lee that it represented the main attack. Lee moved to meet French at the ford, hoping to rapidly dispatch the threat and then return to defeat Sedgwick at Rappahannock Station. French, however, drove the Confederate defenders at the ford back across the river. At noon, Sedgwick positioned the two corps straddling the railroad, north of the river: the Fifth Corps on the left, the Sixth on the right.

All through the afternoon of November 7, Sedgwick used the six batteries of 20-pound Parrot rifles from his two corps to pound away at the entrenched Louisiana and North Carolina regiments at the bridgehead. His strategically positioned artillery fire tore into their rifle pits. Nine rebel regiments were entrenched on the north side of the river, but they had placed artillery batteries on both sides of the river and responded with solid shot and shell. Because Sedgwick's artillery maintained a steady fire throughout the afternoon and did not appear to be preparing an infantry assault, Lee remained convinced that French's demonstration downstream at Kelly's Ford posed the greatest threat. With the approaching darkness, Lee became increasingly confident that Sedgwick would not attack until the next morning.

The division waited throughout the afternoon in the dense woods overlooking the river, 1.5 miles from the rebel works. Facing them on the crest of a long hill a half mile away were Lee's Louisiana Tigers, deployed as skirmishers. Upton's brigade consisted of the 121st, the 5th Maine, and the 95th and 96th Pennsylvania. They were accompanied by Col. Peter Ellmaker's 3rd Brigade, made up of the 6th Maine, the 5th Wisconsin, and the 49th and 119th Pennsylvania. Both brigades were part of Brig. Gen. David A. Russell's 1st Division, Sixth Corps. Nearly 20,000 federals in the Fifth and Sixth corps were facing 2,000 Confederates. The key to the battle proved to be the skirmish line. Skirmishers who had been out front in a kind of no-man's-land since 2:00 that afternoon traded shots with their Confederate counterparts.

As dusk descended on the battlefield, Sedgwick asked Russell if he could take the Confederate works on the river with his division. Without hesitating, Russell quietly told Sedgwick that he could do it. Russell devised, in essence, a "sneak attack," under the pretense of merely relieving the weary skirmishers who had remained in place the better part of the afternoon. Russell and Upton instructed all the troops involved to appear to be relieving the skirmishers on duty but, once they were all together, to push forward and attack the Confederate fort on the railroad. Within minutes, the 6th Maine and the 5th Wisconsin, with the 49th and 119th Pennsylvania as support—all from Ellmaker's 3rd Brigade—were headed toward the middle of the field. Upton picked Companies B and D of the 121st as a part of this "fake" skirmish line and Captain Fish as commander of the line. Marcus Casler led Company B, and Lt. Daniel Jackson led Company D. Six companies of the 6th Maine were deployed to Fish's left. The rebels were on a gentle, upwardly sloping crest 800 yards from the river. According to Upton, "the enemy saw the whole operation, but supposing it simply a relief, paid but little attention to the matter. The first or old line of skirmishers were notified of the intention, the second line came up to where the first lay, when both rushed upon the enemy's redoubts, and were almost inside before the enemy recovered from his astonishment."[32]

Upton instructed Fish as follows: "When the line advances upon your right, *you* will advance—you will drive the enemy off that crest, you will use your judgment and act as if you had a separate command: but remember one thing—I want my brigade line to get there as soon as any of them." Fish, on horseback—a symbol of his responsibility—acknowledged his orders and went back to his men. Momentarily, the line on the right rose, and Fish ordered his men to step off. He gave his men an order not to fire unless fired upon. The silence was deafening on both sides. The Tigers watched and waited, and no one fired a shot. To Clinton Beckwith, with Company B in the skirmishers, it felt like "an age" before they fired. Morse said that every "moment seemed [like] hours." Morse waited on a little knoll with Upton, General Torbert, and Brig. Gen. Henry D. Terry and the staffs. Upton told Morse to return to the brigade when Fish and his men made contact with the enemy.

Fish noticed a second line approaching to his left and rear. He apparently had not understood Russell's objective because he asked a lead officer if they came to relieve him. "No," the officer replied, they were there to reinforce the line and together were to charge the rebel works. Fish wanted to be sure that even though his men were running low on ammunition, his command arrived first to grab the glory. With no further word from Upton on where to go and what to do, he decided on his own that "if the works were taken I wished our Brigade to have some of the honor." According to Delavan Bates, Fish shouted to his men: "They are going to charge! By God boys, we will go in with them. Forward, the skirmish line!" He ordered the men to fix bayonets as the two lines merged in the gathering dark. The men in the new detachment, informally joined in the heat of battle and without specific orders, charged toward the river. Accompanied by derisive yells from the rebel lines, they disappeared in the smoke and darkness as the steady firing continued. Standing on the railroad embankment, Isaac Best watched the drama unfold below. As night fell, he followed the assault from the muzzle flashes of Union muskets firing into the rebel breastworks.[33]

The skirmishers had reached a point within 80 paces of the rebel line when the "dance" began. Two rounds "ripped" through Fish's horse's mane as the wind blew it up. Andrew Mather expressed pride in his horse, who behaved "splendidly as well under fire as in parade." The Union skirmishers returned fire, and Fish ordered his men forward on the "double-quick march." The Tigers "turned their backs and ran for dear life." Fish's command followed them over the crest and watched them dive into the rifle pits along the riverside. Beckwith and comrades ran after them and almost caught one. The 121st and the rest of the assaulting skirmish line found shelter in the wide-open space in a shallow ditch between two roads. Fish's horse became unmanageable, and he let him go as both sides traded serious volleys. The assault on the Tigers appeared successful.[34]

The objectives were the redoubts and a fort that rested on a gently rising knoll near the river, with a bridge over the Rappahannock behind the two fortifications. The intense fire did not deter the attacking column, and halfway up, Fish was hit with an unknown missile, which threw him on his back. At first, he thought he had been shot, but when he regained his composure, he recovered and caught up with his advancing comrades. As an anonymous private in Company D later related, "Leaping into the entrenchments, the first object that met my gaze was [Captain Fish]. There he stood, dressed in full uniform—a prominent mark for the rebel hordes that were standing three feet deep in the ditch at his feet. To see him there, almost single handed, confronting that long line of rebels, was enough to remind one of Leonidas and the 300 Spartans."

Indeed, Fish remarked later that he gave no thought to his dress until the next day: had he known that he would have been so exposed, he would have worn just a shirt. As Fish jumped the breastwork, a rebel took aim at him. Fish aimed his revolver and fired, killing the Confederate with a ball between the eyes. When the men of the 121st jumped into a ditch, they discovered it filled with rebels. Fish yelled at the top of his lungs for the Confederates to surrender, a command echoed by some of his men. "Four guns, one color, and two hundred prisoners were captured on the spot." Fish and his men now faced a serious problem. To their left, the 6th Maine and the 5th Wisconsin had secured the fort and breastworks, but the Mainers were being badly mauled. And to Fish's right, the rebels were still in force, and now they were making a desperate effort to recapture the works. As the Union force received fire, the men huddled in the fort for safety and protection. The rebels were not going to stop and were preparing to attack the fort.[35]

Capt. A. M. Tyler on General Wright's staff alerted Upton to be prepared to support the initial attack. With Fish and the 3rd Brigade's 5th Wisconsin and 6th Maine clinging desperately to their newly won terrain, Upton and the rest of his brigade watched the proceedings from the shelter of the woods on the hill, approximately 1,000 yards from the river and the rifle pits and 300 yards from the slight ridge held by the forward contingent. Many of the men stacked arms and made coffee while the action to their left near the river continued hot and furious. General Russell, watching the action from the rear, moved forward to find Upton. "Upon arriving . . . Russell pointed out a rifle pit from which the enemy maintained an enfilading fire," John Hartwell remarked. Russell ordered Upton to take two of his regiments and "dislodge the enemy" on the right, who poured an enfilading fire into the "skirmishing" attackers.

Upton went with his two favorites to carry the works. He chose the 121st and the 5th Maine, leaving the 95th and 96th Pennsylvania in reserve. He never spoke publicly against the Pennsylvania regiments. The 121st and the 5th Maine formed a strong bond, and most were contemptuous of the two Pennsylvania units. A. S. Daggett, of the 5th Maine, remembered years later: "There soon rode out in front of the Brigade one whose very presence on such occasions would electrify even the most obtuse. It was Upton. In clear and distinct tone rang out the command, 'Forward!' It was enough."[36]

Upton and Morse rode out before the charge, and Upton told Morse that "in less than a minute all this artillery will open on us." At that, the rebel shells found their distance—one shell struck in front of them and bounded over their heads into the band behind them. When Upton moved on to initiate the charge, Morse hung back, and as he wrote an order on the side of his saddle, another round hit nearby, causing him to think he had been shot. Turning around, he discovered that the man standing next to him awaiting his order for delivery "was torn to pieces, his shoulder severed from his body."

To save time, Upton directed the regiments to load while marching, and as they did, they stepped up to the "double-quick." They advanced under a heavy Confederate artillery fire. As John Gray remarked, the shells were bursting overhead, and on all sides, there "was no comfortable place." Upton's detachment moved toward the enemy positions and rested under cover of a slight ridge within 150 yards of the rifle pits. There, as they paused, he ordered knapsacks unslung and bayonets fixed. Knapsacks were put in a pile and given a guard. Many began to gather sticks to light fires and cook coffee, expecting to stay a while. Some spread blankets for the evening. John Hartwell took the opportunity to steal "out from the ranks" to check out the job that lay before them. "Things looked rather dark I confess. I saw where we had got to pass over a wide plain all the while exposed to their cannonade." He calculated his chances of surviving the charge over open ground. "But as the boys say, I resolved to let 'em rip and I would take shot if I could not dodge it."

In the gathering dark, the regiments moved another 70 yards on the double-quick. When they were within 30 yards of the rebels, Upton ordered his command to hold its fire and to charge the lines, which were on a "summit of a gently rising knoll." He later wrote his sister that the Confederate banners "could be plainly seen outstanding against the sky; while their saucy heads appearing everywhere above the parapets forewarned us how deadly might be our task." As the Union soldiers approached the enemy lines, the rebels fired the initial volley—a signal to the advancing federals to storm the ridge before a second volley could be prepared and delivered. Fortunately for the attacking Union soldiers, they were protected by a shallow ditch. The defenders fired high, missing their intended targets. Mather credited the darkness with saving lives because the rebel batteries could not see well enough to be effective on the advancing Union lines.[37]

According to Upton, "a few words to the 121st New York sufficed to rouse their determination to the highest pitch." He encouraged the 5th Maine by reminding them that Maine had distinguished itself on every battlefield and that they must not disappoint now. Then, with orders not to fire a shot, the two regiments advanced at quick step within 30 yards of the rebel lines. "It seemed to our men a forlorn hope," A. S. Daggett wrote years later. Without a shot, Upton and his men were over the ridge of the hill, and the enemy capitulated in the gathering darkness. Upton's only shouted command consisted of "Charge bayonets, double-quick march!" Although the rebels fought stubbornly, the fight at that point in the line ended within five minutes. "To execute my orders we had only to remain where we were, but a more brilliant success was in store," Upton wrote.[38]

The Louisiana Brigade of Stonewall Jackson's old division, not yet directly engaged, backed and filled to form farther to Upton's right, the men remaining "sanguine and defiant" in their rifle pits. Upton could see their colors in the gathering night, inscribed with "Cedar Run," "Manassas Second," "Winchester," "Harpers Ferry," "Sharpsburg," "Fredericksburg," "Chancellorsville," and "Gettysburg." Without waiting for Russell for further instructions, Upton sent Capt. Seymour Hall to tell Russell that he had accomplished his mission and had reformed his lines parallel to the rifle pits that were still crawling with rebel soldiers. He intended to attack again.

With Colonel Edwards of the 5th Maine, Upton marched parts of the 5th Maine and the 121st New York alongside the rebel lines. When nearly opposite the entrenched rebels, Upton addressed his men in a loud voice. According to witnesses, he told his command, "Our friends at home and your country expect every man to do his duty on this occasion. Some of us have got to die, but remember you are going to heaven. When I give the command to charge move forward. If they fire upon you, I will move six lines of battle over you and bayonet every one of them." Others said that Upton merely remarked: "Don't fire a shot—if they fire at you lie down—there are three lines of battle behind you and storm the works." Still others remembered that he said: "Boys, or rather Old 121st, I am with you again. We are going to make a charge, and some of you may fall, but you will all go to heaven. And I am going with you over the works." They all agreed that he guaranteed a heavenly reward. Upton modestly claimed that he told the men not to fire and "stated in a loud tone that four lines of battle were supporting [them]."

Whatever his words, his men attacked and within minutes routed the remaining rebels in the trenches. Captain Wilson, with a wounded right arm, reportedly shouted, "Forward every lover of his country." Major Mather cried, "Remember Salem Chapel." The column, once in place, did a left face and fell on the enemy. "We went in with a yell that would almost deafen a man," George Teel wrote. Peter Mickel in Company K reported they charged "with a yell that sent terror to the hearts of the foe." Upton stated: "The work was carried at the point of the bayonet, and without firing a shot. The enemy fought stubbornly over their colors, but being overpowered soon surrendered."[39]

The attacking troops overran Col. Archibald C. Godwin's 6th, 54th, and 57th North Carolina regiments with fierce face-to-face, hand-to-hand combat. As Upton secured the rifle pits, the enemy attempted to escape using the pontoon bridge laid across the river. Upton directed Major Mather to take a portion of the 5th Maine and the 121st and seize the bridge to block any retreat. Mather's ad hoc command stopped a majority of rebels trying to cross on the pontoon bridge and detailed a detachment upriver to capture those attempting to swim to the other side.

One of Mather's men went after Lt. Col. Hamilton C. Jones Jr., commanding the 57th North Carolina Regiment. In the melee and confusion, he tried to swim away. According to Mather, Jones cried out in the freezing water: "Oh, God, how cold it is." A sergeant of Company H yelled back that he would make it hot for Jones if he did not surrender to him. Jones refused to surrender to an enlisted man, and when he could no longer stand the cold water, his enlisted captor realized he had bagged a lieutenant colonel. He took Jones to Mather, who told his brother in a letter a few days later, "I wish you could have seen him." Col. William Monaghan and Maj. William H. Manning of the 6th Louisiana, Lt. Col. Thomas Terry of the 7th Louisiana, Capt. James Garrity of the 6th, and 6-and-a-half-foot-tall, 300-pound Col. William Raine Peck of the 9th swam the river. In the darkness and confusion, the men in the Louisiana Brigade of Stonewall Jackson's old division laid down their arms and surrendered. Rebel troops on the south side of the river watched helplessly as their friends were taken prisoner.[40]

Capt. William Johnson Seymour of New Orleans was one of the swimmers. He served on Brig. Gen. Harry T. Hays's staff as an assistant adjutant general. A rabid Yankee hater, his memoirs were replete with references to drunken enemies. That night, he swam the icy Rappahannock in the company of higher-ranking officers fleeing for their lives. He later wrote of the Union attack and being hemmed in on the left and attacked on the center, with nothing but the "deep unfordable river" in the rear. Under those circumstances, the only "alternative left to our regiments" was to surrender. One wonders what reaction members of the New York regiments on the battlefield would have had if they had known Seymour was a distant relative of their own governor![41]

Those who did not surrender while swimming the river probably drowned. The rebels who did give up were marched to the rear under guard. As John Gray moved forward, he came upon a squad of half a dozen rebels. Gray said he "ordered every damned one of them to surrender or I would run them through." One scared rebel speedily surrendered and offered to give up all of his gear. A "splendid repeating rifle"—probably a Spencer—and some cartridges were taken. Also seized was a sword carried by a Confederate lieutenant who had taken it from a federal the past summer at the battle of Winchester, together with a scabbard that came from an officer at Gettysburg. "So of course it is a very nice prize [for me]," Gray wrote.[42]

Everyone in the regiment, except for Isaac Best at brigade headquarters, took part in the action. Staff officer Robert Wilson suffered a severe wrist wound but remained throughout the battle, capturing a flag; Seymour Hall and Francis Morse entered the rifle pits with the rest of the men. Surgeons Slocum and Holt were with the troops up to the walls of the fort. As Dr. Holt so eloquently explained: "Not finding it on my card of instructions to storm a fort without gun or any other article of offensive warfare, I concluded to remain outside while others reaped more glory, perhaps by going in." Adelbert Reed wrote his sister that "not a man flinched. On we went in one solid long line of battle—on steady and firmly holding aloft in the enemy's faces the good old flag." Young drummer boy Henry Wood described the scene years later almost as if he were describing a child's set of toy soldiers lined up for a bloodless battle. He wrote of the forts, the rifle pits, the flying colors, the shells bursting overhead, the drums beating, and "soldiers marching like on parade," their ranks being torn by artillery and then re-forming in the gaps. The shell that Francis Morse had described struck the ground in front of the drum corps, kicking up gravel that drew blood on Wood's face. Another shell burst overhead, and a fragment went through his drum, destroying his ability to play, but, he said, "I kept my place."[43]

Colonel Jones told his captors that he knew Upton commanded a reserve of hundreds waiting to pour over the beleaguered rebels. Andrew Mather maintained that the North Carolinians remembered the 121st New York from Salem Church and were chagrined that they were overwhelmed by such a small force. Jones admitted that they were fooled by a very smart Yankee officer. The sight of a marching body of men off to his side confirmed his suspicions. In the confusion of the assault and the gathering gloom, he did not know that they were actually captured Confederate soldiers moving to the Union rear. The captured soldiers asked how many Union corps were engaged. When told that only two regiments carried out the assault, the rebel "mortification" was "extreme."

The captured Confederates surprised John Fish. He thought that "the Rebs were a sort of puny, sallow looking sort of men—but I never saw so many *very* large men together in my life as we took prisoners that night—Some were really giants." Two days later, the *Richmond Enquirer* called for the dismissal of Hoke and Hays, who were in command of the rifle pits. Two days after that, the paper struck a more sympathetic note, saying that all the troops behaved splendidly and that there were just too many Yankees. Several Confederates were convinced that they were assaulted by "overwhelming numbers" and were "compelled to yield." Upton remained modest about his accomplishment. He told his sister a week later that only a few words to his men were sufficient "to rouse their determination to the highest pitch." He confirmed that he gave orders to unsling knapsacks, fix bayonets, remain quiet, hold fire—and then charge when they were within 30 yards of the rifle pits. "The work was carried at the point of the bayonet."[44]

The Importance of the Victory

The results were surprising to all concerned, from the lowest privates to Generals Meade and Lee. The South was horrified. "The success at the Rappahannock had a most electrifying effect throughout the army," Upton reported, and the men in his brigade were ecstatic. They captured 7 colors, 103 officers, 1,300 enlisted men, and 1,200 stands of weapons. They suffered 63 killed and wounded. The officers of the 121st and the 5th Maine embraced. "Oh if you could only have felt the same feeling that we all felt at that charge," Adelbert Reed told his parents. "How my heart swelled and beat for joy."

The 121st suffered only 4 killed and 23 wounded. Those killed were Pvt. William Watson and Pvt. Wilbur Eastwood, Company D; Pvt. Asbell Lamont, Company I; and Cpl. Deloss H. Platt, Company D. Lamont, who had enlisted from Worcester with Delavan Bates, took a round in the head as he ran alongside Bates and William Remmel and was killed instantly. Kidder lamented the loss "of such a good fighter," one of the thirteen who rallied with him at Salem Church. The attacking 121st found no time to care for his corpse until the next day, when they gave him a burial "under the sheltering branches of a friendly tree." Those casualties who survived took direct shots to the body; most suffered wounds to the left arm. George Herdman, who had been captured at Salem Church and had returned to the regiment a few weeks earlier, was hit in the right leg and died three weeks later. He was buried in the Military Asylum Cemetery in Washington. By comparison with the 121st, the 6th Maine suffered heavily, with 17 officers killed and wounded out of 22 and two-thirds of its enlisted men.

Frank Foote, the 121st's acting adjutant at the battle, reported that the 121st alone captured 4 rebel flags, 3 colonels, 2 majors, 17 captains, 27 lieutenants, and 651 men—2 for every 121st man engaged in the battle. In addition, he declared that the brigade took 1,250 small arms. Several officers and men of the 121st bragged of taking weapons, particularly swords, as war souvenirs, destined to hang over hearths at home. Delavan Bates took 4 swords and kept 1 rusty weapon that he seized from a North Carolina rebel. The insignia "US" on the basket hilt had been altered to "CS," and the item became a prized souvenir of the battle. Captain Kidder took 4 swords. Francis Morse accepted the surrender of 6 Confederate officers and attached their swords to his belt all at one time. Henry Walker celebrated his birthday that day with a rusty sword he took from an officer, and he promised to send it home. John Gray prized his newly acquired Spencer rifle—a souvenir not only of Rappahannock Station but also of Gettysburg.

One member of the 122nd New York, observing his tent mate swapping his well-worn Enfield for a bright new Springfield rifle, decided to do the same. As he jumped down into the pit to make the swap, he found himself lying on top of three dead rebels. "I did not hold them down long or stop to trade guns," he recalled later. On the other side of the river, the 121st managed to get into several Louisiana troops' tents and opened all of their trunks, taking Confederate uniforms as war booty. One week after the battle, the 121st "raked the bed of the river" behind the rebel positions and "fished out 60 dead bodies, 2 heavy field pieces and large quantities of guns, swords, and small arms."[45]

Lee never imagined that his stronghold on the Rappahannock would falter. Two rebel colonels reputedly told General Sedgwick that their bridgehead could withstand an Army of the Potomac corps but not four undersized regiments. Never before had a line of skirmishers led a successful attack on an enemy's entrenched position. Darkness, the suddenness of the attack, Confederate underestimates of the forces facing them, the battle experience of the Union troops, and "poorly planned and built" fortifications all contributed to the Union success in the battle. The many hours of discipline were evident as well. The men accepted the orders given them and executed them as their training dictated. They attacked an entrenched enemy and overran it with little bloodshed, which came as a shock to all who participated. The reactions among the enlisted men were wonder and disbelief. Many thought an attack in broad daylight would not have left "many of the 121st . . . to tell the story." Clinton Beckwith could not understand "why those johnnies did not kill every one [of them]." Delavan Bates saw the victory as vengeance for Salem Church. "All say that for the numbers engaged it was one of the most brilliant feats of the war."[46]

As a result of the battle, four men of the 121st were cited for their daring and bravery. Pvt. Philip Smith, Company E, and Pvt. Silas Waterman, Company I, had sprung from the ranks in front of their own advancing lines and wrestled the flags from their bearers. Capt. Seymour H. Hall, Company F, received the Medal of Honor for distinguished gallantry first at Gaines Mill on June 27, 1862, and then at Rappahannock Station. Smith was a transfer after Salem Church from the 16th New York. Waterman, an original member of the regiment from Worcester, was killed the following spring at Spotsylvania. Barney Trainor captured a bare color pole from which the rebel color-bearer had ripped the flag. According to some sources, the pieces were retrieved and sewn back together.[47]

Emory Upton shared the spotlight with the other commanders. He gave all credit to General Russell, whom he applauded in a private letter as "one of the best and bravest officers in our service." To Russell belonged "the credit of this brilliant success," due mainly to his selection of the "time and mode of attack." Upton feared that a daylight attack would have been a disaster, probably at a high loss of life—1,500 men. In the end, neither side lost many in killed and wounded, and Union troops were successful in capturing large quantities of arms and men. General Russell returned the favor in his official report, saying that Upton led the 5th Maine and the 121st "to the assault upon the rifle pits with unexampled coolness, steadiness, and bravery." The enlisted men were equally impressed with their commander. Adelbert Reed hoped that Upton would be made a general in the near future, adding, "[he] deserves it" and soon "if he keeps on. He is one brave fellow." Upton was jubilant. He called Rappahannock Station "one of the prettiest fights of the war." It had been his "pleasure to participate as Brigade Commander."[48]

General Meade needed the victory badly. One Maine newspaper charged that if Meade had not been forced to grant leaves to soldiers from New York and Pennsylvania to go home and vote, he would be in Richmond that month. To stress the importance of the battle, Meade invited representatives from the two brigades to bring him the captured flags. Fifty men from each regiment involved in the heaviest fighting formed into companies—one for each rebel flag taken. The captured flags were flown at the head of the column of companies, surmounted by the Union flag. With banners flying and bands playing, soldiers lining the road cheered the column all the way to Meade's headquarters.

Upton proudly led the delegation. Clinton Beckwith and Sam Kelley from the 121st accompanied him. Meade generously praised Upton and General Russell for their fine work and leadership. He made a short speech as the ad hoc command presented seven flags and one bare pole to him. All were captured by the 5th Maine and the 121st New York, except for one taken by a member of the 6th Maine. Officially, Meade reported the seizure of 1,600 prisoners, 4 guns, 2,000 small arms, 1 bridge train, and 8 battle flags. Early newspaper accounts credited the army with capturing 7 pieces from one battery, some bearing the inscription "US Watertown Arsenal." Meade assured all of his admiration for them and that he had related their daring to the president. He also expressed his pleasure with the army's success at Rappahannock Station. Lincoln told Sedgwick only "Well done" but in an aside wondered if the 400 Confederates captured at Kelly's Ford were included in the number of captures—1,400—that Sedgwick had reported earlier.[49]

Meade sent the flags on to the War Department in Washington in the care of General Russell. He ordered the words *Rappahannock Station* inscribed on the 121st's battle flag. He thanked all the troops for their service, a band played a few tunes, and Meade invited the officers—"all the Generals of note in the army were there"—to his tent for several glasses of champagne. "After a few moments of congratulations and social intercourse, the deputation took leave and returned to camp."[50]

Mine Run

After Rappahannock station, many of the 121st were convinced that another major battle would occur before they moved into winter quarters. Emory Upton believed that the troops in his command, "far from wishing it deferred," were "anxious for it." At Payne's Farm, the 121st drew up into line of battle with the Sixth Corps to support General French's troops. The Union army hoped to follow up the victory at Rappahannock Station with another rout of the rebels. But as both sides stumbled into each other, neither had the stomach for a fight. General French, arriving late and never becoming a player in the intended assault on Lee, angered Meade. His incompetence caused unnecessary pain and suffering among his men. John Kidder thought that French ought to be dismissed or shot. Firing—heavier than at Gettysburg, according to Kidder—actually began with heavy skirmishing and nothing more.[51]

Up north, the president of the United States belatedly decided to attend a ceremony at Gettysburg to dedicate the new military cemetery being created as a final resting place for the Union soldiers who died there. On November 19, Lincoln made a few brief remarks following a two-hour speech by the scholar of the day and featured speaker for the commemoration, Edward Everett. When both finished and the festivities ended, Lincoln shook hands with the crowd for an hour. New York governor Horatio Seymour, his nemesis, attended the festivities. Seymour reviewed the New York troops attending the ceremony and praised their patriotism and courage but never embraced the war and its goals. Newspapers played Seymour's statements to their advantage; a Republican paper claimed that the New York governor's experience at the dedication "stimulated Seymour's patriotism." Many of the men of the 121st would have agreed.[52]

Lincoln proclaimed the Thursday after his trip to Gettysburg as a day of national thanksgiving. The press picked up the concept, and the men of the 121st promptly recognized the day in their letters and diaries. Many took note of the day with a moment of prayer or reverent remembrance. Further adding to the optimism of the season, on November 27, Upton read a telegram to all the troops detailing Hooker's, Sherman's, and Grant's victories in the west at Lookout Mountain and Missionary Ridge, further invigorating the men. Henry Walker suggested that perhaps "Lee would soon share the same fate as [Confederate general Braxton] Bragg." He hoped to be with his family at this first Thanksgiving and took pleasure in knowing that the news of Grant's victories "added to the occasion."[53]

On November 30 and December 1, 1863, Lee and Meade once more probed each other's lines for weaknesses. Meade still smarted from his "press" after Gettysburg but was emboldened by the successful action at Rappahannock Station. Both incidents whetted his appetite to find a way to fall on Lee and crush him before the winter hiatus. During those two days, Meade tried to flank Lee's army entrenched at Mine Run, a godforsaken land once rich in iron ore. The verdant forests had fired the smelting process with their fuel. Once the land was played out and even tobacco could not be grown there, nature reclaimed it with a vengeance. In one observer's words, the area "became so thickly overgrown . . . that a dog could scarce force his way through." At 2:00 in the morning on a frigid Sunday, November 29, the Union troops entered the dense wood to their right in sight of Lee's formidable position. What they found before them chilled them as much as the weather. The two armies were separated by a 5-foot-deep, 12- to 15-foot-wide run of water. Cut saplings in the form of abatis were protruding from the opposite bank, their sharpened points awaiting a Yankee assault. On the ridges, strategically placed Confederate batteries were trained, through the dismal rain, on the large Yankee force before them. The Union army, ordered not to start fires that would alert the enemy to their presence, ate only hardtack. A harsh north wind tore at them in their exposed positions.[54]

That night, Upton and Seymour Hall collected dead leaves to use as pillows and mattresses and lay down wrapped in buffalo robes, where they "remained until daylight, chilled to the marrow" by the intense cold. At daylight, the "full strength of the enemy's position and fortifications" was menacingly revealed. Upton and other generals perceived one weak spot on the right of the line where an attack might have a better chance of success. When Upton ordered fixed bayonets in preparation for a frontal assault, the men recalled the recent success on the Rappahannock but also realized that a frontal assault would doom many of them. Rallying his troops, Upton challenged Gen. Alfred Torbert, saying that his men would beat Torbert's into the enemy's pits. The rivalry extended to the Fifth Corps and the Sixth Corps as well, to the point that the two units "sent committees inviting each other to a reunion in the enemy's works, each one promising to be there first to receive the others."

Preparations for a major assault were in place. Warren and his Second Corps were to attack first, then Sedgwick. The 121st occupied the first line, the dubious position of honor. The 5th Maine and the 95th Pennsylvania formed the second line, and the 96th Pennsylvania held the third. To their right were Jersey and Vermont brigades. "By daylight," according to Francis Morse, "we were just as willing and ready to be killed by iron and lead as by cold." Seymour Hall saw men "coolly and deliberately prepare for death." They took off their knapsacks, placing them in an orderly fashion on the ground. They left a last message with a friend or in their knapsacks. And in a move not witnessed before, many "put some mark on their clothing by which they could be identified."[55]

But the final order for Sedgwick's command to charge never came. Based on information provided by the commanding general of the Fifth Corps, Gen. Gouverneur Warren, the engineer of Gettysburg fame, it was decided that an attack as proposed would be disastrous. Warren wanted to call off the attack.

Meade, unconvinced, rode out to Warren's position to see for himself. By the time he understood the situation, the rebels had fortified their position to the point that an attack would have been suicide. Meade, however, continued to vacillate. At first, he decided not to make a decision on the Sabbath but rather to wait until Monday. He finally reconsidered and countermanded the order to attack Lee's heavily fortified positions.

When he finally made his decision not to attack, the men had waited for three days in weather "as cold as any we ever had in New York in the same month." Although he earned the enmity of Northern news editors for his decision, Meade won the admiration of his men for avoiding a sure disaster. The men on the front line felt they had been granted a reprieve from a death sentence. They were convinced that an attack on Lee would have resulted in their never returning to home and hearth. "Bully for him," wrote George Teel; "he is the man to lead us to victory." Richard Turner in Company B told his friends back home that there "never was a happier lot of men in the world," and John Hartwell wrote his wife that if they had attacked, Meade would have been without an army and she "would have been without a husband." Only the bitter cold and the constant strain, "more on the mind than the body," threatened them now. Meade decided to give it up for the season and go into winter quarters.[56]

In their continuing battle with other regiments, when the 121st returned to its original position to the line occupied by the 96th Pennsylvania, Clinton Beckwith discovered that the knapsack and blanket he had left behind in preparation for the attack had disappeared. He did not miss those two items, probably taken by someone in the 96th, as much as he lamented the loss of a family Bible and "papers." The loss of the latter caused him unnecessary trouble after the war when he attempted to prove to the Pension Office that Dewitt Clinton Beckwith and Clinton Beckwith were one and the same person.[57]

Immediately after Mine Run, Dr. Holt, with Dr. Daniel W. Bland of the 96th Pennsylvania, commandeered a house to use as a hospital. The outbuildings, formerly slave quarters, were occupied by the enlisted men to get out of the cold. The property owner, a tanner, fled, leaving behind his daughters—"Fair specimens of Southern Chivalry—snuff dipping, dilapidated, lantern jawed bipeds of neuter gender"—to greet Dr. Holt and his fellow surgeons. When informed that the federal army had taken their house as a hospital, the "ladies" expressed the hope that it would burn down with "every damned Yankee in it!" Dr. Bland assured them that when they were finished with it, he would personally grant their wishes—but without the Yankees in the house. Within six hours, the medical men had finished their tasks, after which they torched the house, all the outbuildings, and the tannery, destroying thousands of dollars of leather and finished inventory—and, in the process, shelter for several slave families. Sadly, the few possessions of the slaves went up in flames also. Holt portrayed the incident as one of liberation that was welcomed by the slaves even though they were now homeless, left with only the clothes on their backs on one of the harshest nights of the winter. He depicted them as welcoming their freedom and grateful that federals had burned out the master. By denying the enemy a few dwellings, the officers and men of the 121st became liberators. The freed slaves boarded baggage wagons headed for Alexandria, where the government provided for them.[58]

John Hartwell watched the tannery, house, and slave quarters burn. A homeless child cried, moving him to tears. "The heavens brightly lit up by the burning houses, colored families with their little effects shivering in the cold and fear a little distance from their burning huts." He wondered if it was right to torch the property. "I could not say yes," he wrote. "But such cases are common and such the bitter fruits of this terrible rebellion." God wreaked retribution on a wayward people for their transgressions against the Constitution and the Union. The incident did not escape the attention of Lee and Early, both of whom condemned the Yankee barbarity. Henry Hall did not know who ordered the burning or why but wrote in his diary on December 1, "So ended the Mine Run campaign. Mr. Johnson had his house and tannery burned because of his brutal treatment of our wounded." Hall believed that simple statement answered the Confederates' charges of barbarity.[59]

IO

Winter Quarters, December 15, 1863, to May 4, 1864

I believe this regiment puts on more style than any other in the United States. Even a private here in this Regiment thinks himself better than a commissioned officer in most any other Regiment. I saw in the *Journal* they call us up north what they call us here—Upton's Regulars, and we are not ashamed to own it.

John Ingraham, Company D, February 14, 1864

Colonel Upton is an excellent drill master and the way he makes the men charge on imaginary rifle pits and batteries is not so slow after all. But after our charge is over we fail to find any more colors and it looks like boys playing storming snow forts that we used to build when we went to school.

John Hartwell, Company C, November 16, 1863

Life in Winter Quarters

Between December 15, 1863, and May 1864, the 121st took up winter quarters at Welford's Ford on the Hazel River. General Sedgwick commandeered the Welford mansion opposite the ford as his headquarters. It belonged to John Minor Botts, a strong Unionist who had been ill used by the Richmond government—particularly Jeb Stuart, who briefly imprisoned him. Within two weeks, Botts's woods, crops, and wooden fences were stripped by the occupying forces. The 121st occupied a miserable location on the south side of the Hazel River, a small waterway between the Rappahannock and Rapidan rivers, flowing into the former. Lee remained nearby on the Rapidan.

The men prevailed upon Upton to move to the other side of the river near a substantial house with commodious sheds and barns. A wood of clean pine trees and pleasant grounds stood near the house. They connived with the surgeons to declare their present camp unhealthy and with the chaplains to lobby for more appropriate surroundings for their devotions. Eventually, Upton relented. He persuaded General Wright who in turn convinced General Sedgwick that the idea merited his consideration, and within days, pontoons were laid and the 121st New York moved to the other side of the river "completely isolated from the [rest of] the army." According to others, they convinced Wright that their move would offer protection against any guerrilla raids on the army. In any case, the result was that the men now had quarters far more pleasant than those of the year before. The location placed them between the forks of the Rapidan and the Rappahannock, with the Blue Ridge Mountains to the west. Within this triangle they passed the winter, 3 miles from their supply nexus to Washington at Brandy Station.[1]

Boasting that they were quartered in the best accommodations of any regiment in the entire Army of the Potomac, the men of the 121st quickly made themselves comfortable. In a lesson learned the previous winter, they used a nearby stand of timber for fuel, leaving the pine trees for shelter. The camp soon sported wooden sidewalks and streets 30 feet wide and 200 feet long. The regiment separated into five "divisions" of two companies per street. The design and decoration of the log huts were limited only by the occupants' imaginations. The logs were 8 to 10 inches thick, split in two, "notched and built up cob house style about six feet high with . . . shelter tents for [a] roof." The cracks were filled with Virginia mud. Evergreens graced the hospital entrance. A sutler's tent, a post office, and stables completed the village.

James McCurry built himself a shanty, furnishing it with a floor, a table, and some stools. Lansing Paine's elaborate quarters had a door with a wooden latch; the beds were made of poles and evergreen boughs, and there was a fireplace at the far end. Boards from a "Virginia residence" were used for the floor. The walls were insulated with mud, flour plaster, and newspapers. "You see we understand soldiering better this winter than we did last," Paine wrote. The camps of a year ago bore no resemblance to the new ones. The previous winter took the "patience of Job to endure," John Ingraham told his friend Mary Green. "About a year ago I came very near giving up in despair," he confessed. "We were getting defeated on all sides. Our army was demoralized but not so at the present. Our army is in good spirits and ready to take Richmond or some other good place."[2]

The quarters for the officers were grander, especially Colonel Olcott's. He designed and constructed a "gothic structure" for his quarters, and it was outfitted with the best of everything. As the local papers said, "It excels anything in the army." Olcott's quarters were "made of straight poles hewn on one side and laid up like a log cabin. It was not only commodious but elegant and nicely furnished inside." Olcott commandeered carpenters in the regiment to work on his billet—men who were willing to ply their trade instead of policing the streets and latrines of the camp all winter.

Delavan Bates was in Olcott's quarters once, "which was enough to leave a picture on my mind," he wrote later. "The floor was neatly carpeted; a comfortable cot, an easy chair, a couple of camp chairs and a center table, upon which was a full set of Christopher North's *Noctes Ambrosiana* elegantly bound. How I wished that some day I could be a major and live in such style as that." Bates envied Olcott's library: he "always had a supply of choice literature in his tent." Upton's headquarters were in a "large substantial house" with attendant barns and sheds, which officers had commandeered from a Mrs. Major. The brigade took the land, and the staff occupied the great house. Upton's quarters "were considered to be the most aristocratic, stylish, and comfortable in the army of the Potomac." Morse remembered, "For the first few evenings we did nothing but congratulate ourselves upon our elegant quarters, and in the day time took care that the men were made comfortable." Morse could not have been happier. He was "vastly delighted" by "the idea of beds and four substantial walls."[3]

Once settled, the officers on Upton's staff threw a party for Sedgwick and his staff as guests of honor, with enough champagne "to float the pontoons of the 50th engineers." Midway through the festivities, a loud crash resembling the sound of many bottles of champagne falling down stairs caused partygoers to avert their attention, with "that ludicrous kind of politeness of looking unconscious" that anything had happened. Upton turned white, and Seymour Hall's eyeballs "started from their sockets" at the idea that bottles of champagne had just died on the stairs. When the head cook produced champagne and an explanation that two windows had tumbled down the stairs, all breathed a sigh of relief and continued drinking. As the dinner party broke up, the adjutant general assured Morse that he "could have a leave any time" he asked for it. By mid-January, Morse was in Cherry Valley.[4]

The 2nd Brigade staff continued in party mode. The men decided that a celebration honoring General Bartlett two days before Christmas would be an excellent idea. They invited 150 officers from the brigade and General Sedgwick's staff, took up a collection, and bought Bartlett a watch and a Sixth Corps badge. The staff arranged for the food and decided early on that the guests should have plenty to drink—"enough whisky to kill them all." Morse determined that he and his friends would brew the "most villainous compound that man ever drank and survived." The concoction consisted of 30 gallons of commissary whiskey "with enough sugar to make it very sweet and smooth, six bottles of brandy, six bottles of gin," finishing up with claret wine and lemons. As the guests began to drink, Morse and the others stood back to watch the effects, much like "men blasting rocks wait behind a tree for the explosion." Morse warned his "host," Mrs. Major, that the fun would commence soon and that the Yankee officers might be as effective during the party as they were on the field of battle. Bartlett and Sedgwick arrived, and everyone drank to everyone's health—except Morse and his coconspirators. Sedgwick sipped the concoction and "suspected the properties of our soothing little lotion, but said nothing." Chaplain Adams made the presentation, Bartlett responded, and all began to feel the effects of the "punch." When things got out of hand, Mrs. Major cursed Morse and his "crazy Yankees." Eventually, the party broke up, and Morse retreated to his quarters.

In February, General Bartlett reciprocated with plans for a full-fledged ball. All eligible officers were invited, and the ladies in camp were to be their dates. To facilitate the ladies' presence, the staff commandeered unused ambulances to transport them from their quarters. When a crotchety surgeon at division headquarters balked at the notion, Morse petitioned General Sedgwick directly. Sedgwick told him to take as many ambulances as he needed as soon as he needed them, but in a wink and a nod to the earlier party, he warned Morse to stay away from "any punch that tasted weak." The ball began at 9:00 P.M. at Fifth Corps headquarters. Eventually, the corps hosted "several hundred ladies and gentlemen dressed in the height of civil or military fashion." The dance went on into the early hours of the morning, to be interrupted at 1:00 A.M. for supper, after which more energetic dancing resumed. "Spurs, sabers and sashes caught in dresses and coat tails; and the whole room was a scene of chaotic confusion." An hour after supper, Morse returned home in his ambulance and reached his quarters "at peep of day, and went to sleep, thinking of ladies and Sedgwick punches."[5]

While the enlisted men dreamed of home and sleighing across the snowy, open fields of upstate New York, the officers who were not partying were free to leave at any time; Dr. Holt, for example, went home for ten days at Christmas. It took weeks, however, for an enlisted man to obtain leave. Those who reenlisted had to weigh spending another three years in the ranks versus enjoying a thirty-day furlough. In March, Upton, Olcott, and Captain Cronkite took off for Washington, leaving the regiment in the hands of Henry Galpin. On March 9, Galpin held a battalion drill, and, as Dolphus Sayles told his diary, "he made some big mistakes."[6]

Visitors from home found their way to the banks of the river and the 121st's encampment, where they were warmly welcomed in gentrified shelters by the less fortunate soldiers who had not been able to secure leave. One "guest" was the maligned, recently resigned Irving Holcomb. Richard Turner barely acknowledged his existence, saying only that "Irving looks natural" and that the situation forced the two to shake hands. The visit of Lt. Erastus Weaver's wife brought stares and vulgar remarks. But Dr. Holt, who had known her in New York, considered her a perfect lady, and upon his return to camp, he reminisced about the old days back in Herkimer County when they used to travel together. George Teel wished his wife would visit him, but he did not want her subjected to the same abuse. "The anxiety of soldiers to see a live Yankee woman is great," he told her.

If Francis Morse is to be believed, women overran the camp that winter. With his wild imagination, he counted 2,500 women in camp, making it resemble a peacetime garrison. The band gave several performances, which offered opportunities for galas and balls. As Morse "moved among the girls generally," Seymour Hall fell in love with a woman who did not reciprocate his affection. Daniel Jackson's wife traveled from New Lisbon to keep "him out of mischief." William Remmel saw the new situation as a "pleasant and highly delightful winter vacation," and George Eaton remarked, "It is quite a novelty to see a lady down here, so the boys think." The dress parades, parties, and women were a welcome relief after the deadly marches and battles the men had endured. As John Ingraham recounted: "We were reviewed today by generals Russell and Sedgwick and also by 15 to 20 ladies, which made it a great deal pleasanter of course."[7]

In winter camp, the mail came regularly from Washington. Sutlers provided amenities not available on the march. Engineers built an amusement hall using pine poles, where the men displayed their acting and singing talents in regular "show nights." The bands and informal glee clubs provided music. When the 121st Regiment first went into the field, Upton, Colonel Clark, and Major Olcott had urged the men to form a glee club. They wanted some "good singing for the Sabbath and also some glees for other occasions." In those first perilous days in the field, most of the men and officers viewed music as a luxury. Members of the 121st joined with their counterparts in the 5th Maine to form a "theatrical troop." The troop folded when the 5th's term of service expired.[8]

The men fashioned countless ways to pass the time and yet remain vigilant. "The officers and the men devoted themselves to unlimited festivity, balls, horse-races, cock fights, greased pigs and poles, and other games such as only soldiers can devise," wrote one general. Games of chess, checkers, and cards (particularly poker) were universally played, sometimes in Egbert Olcott's grand quarters. On occasion, Cleaveland Campbell joined the game. John Slocum's weakness was whist, and the doctor strictly accounted for his losses and gains. Eventually, he too took leave to return to upstate New York but only in January when Holt returned. The 121st spent the days of good weather in drill and, when not on the drill field, enjoying outdoor activities including baseball and football. The grind of picket duty proved less burdensome than it had earlier. By Christmas, John Kidder had embraced the soldier's life and all the camp amenities that had been unavailable the year before.[9]

Letters, newspapers, boxes, and photographs were highly prized. Receiving a box from home when the army settled into camp was the highlight of the week. Soldiers asked their loved ones to pack as much into a box as possible, with food and clothing being the most requested items. The boys from upstate New York knew to ask for warm woolens, socks, and boots, and those from Herkimer craved their cheeses. George Teel begged for all the photographs his wife could send. The pictures helped pass "many a lonely hour. Lots of men have six to twelve pictures," he wrote; "they draw the mind from many camp vices."

Gradually, the sick and wounded from Fredericksburg, Salem Church, the Gettysburg campaign, and Rappahannock Station returned to the regiment. Ingraham Smith had probably toured the inside of every Union hospital then in operation. After Fredericksburg, he was transferred to Armory Square Hospital, then to Finley in Washington, then to Satterlee in Philadelphia, then back to Finley, and finally to Camp Convalescent in Alexandria. He rejoined the regiment in its new quarters after being dropped off at Brandy Station and walking the last few miles to the Hazel River. Compared to the hospitals, he found the regimental accommodations superb and the food superior, and he declared his joy to be among his comrades once again. The food especially proved a "good introduction into camp life again." By December, neither the Army of the Potomac nor the Army of Northern Virginia entertained any notion of fighting until spring.[10]

For the weary soldier, the railroad was the preferred path to Washington. The gateway, Brandy Station, lay just a few miles up the tracks from the 121st. As the army's depot, it bustled with activity, offering soldiers an array of goods approaching the commerce of a small city. Tradesmen in makeshift shanties hawked "Oysters!" "Fresh fish!" "Condensed milk!" "Beer!" and numerous other temptations to separate the soldier from his pay. Army supply trains moved in and out with forage and commissary stores, express boxes from home, and clothing. Newspapers were readily available at 5 cents each, and many soldiers got the news of an impending move from them rather than their officers.

In camp, relations with other units were both strengthened and strained. The 95th Pennsylvania and the 121st differed greatly. The 95th, a proud "city" regiment from Philadelphia, had little in common with the country boys from upstate New York. Named after their first commander, Col. John M. Gosline, the 95th adopted the Zouave French regimental traditions and were known as Gosline's Zouaves. They wore the flamboyant sack jackets and knee-high boots with pleated trousers tucked into their tops. They joined the brigade in May 1863 and performed admirably every time Upton asked. They led the brigade across the Rappahannock before Salem Church and were in the forefront of the Overland campaign. Olcott and Fish occasionally visited their camp. In a statement more revealing about Olcott, Delavan Bates remembered that "Olcott did not have very congenial companions at the headquarters of the 121st." Meanwhile, with two men from the 5th Maine, Sam Kelley joined a glee club and took up singing, which reminded him of his cold Cooperstown winters. With friends from the 5th Maine, the singers moved from tent to tent serenading comrades in both camps. The 95th Pennsylvania reciprocated with a serenade at regimental headquarters.[11]

Generally, then, the men of the 121st related well to their peers in the 95th, despite their differences. But the 96th Pennsylvania presented another kind of challenge. The men of the 121st had not forgotten that Colonel Cake, commander of the 96th, had put them through their winter nightmare at Belle Plain the year before. The 96th came from Pottsville, a small coal-mining town at the center of triangle equidistant from Scranton, Harrisburg, and Allentown-Bethlehem, and consisted of coal-mining Germans from Schuylkill County. Dr. Holt was brutal in his assessment. "From the first," he wrote, "our boys could not endure the Sauerkraut illiterate lunk heads, and they appeared to equally despise us." Holt called them "braggadocios and abusive," "Neanderthals," and "cowards." After several run-ins, he said, "they ceased to annoy us and kept where they belonged—at the farthest verge of the brigade." But Bates remembered the "coal heavers" as "fair fighters," suffering in proportion to the 121st. He praised their valor at Crampton's Gap and acknowledged their suffering at Spotsylvania.[12]

John Kidder despised both Pennsylvania regiments equally. The 95th and 96th had as many or more casualties than the 121st when the final battle statistics were tallied. At Payne's Farm, according to Kidder, the 95th and 96th Pennsylvania were placed in the front battle line of the 2nd Division to keep them from running, and the 121st and the 5th Maine were placed behind them to put the bayonets to them should they try. "They are cowardly regiments," Kidder hissed. Both units proved themselves in battle, but some never viewed them as serious soldiers. When reenlistments were sweetened with a thirty-day furlough, the 95th re-signed nearly every man. They were "a lot of jolly good fellows, and many were the pleasant gatherings at their headquarters when the troops were in camp," Bates remembered. He praised the 95th's officers as "brave, courteous, genteel and jolly good fellows socially"—and fighters.[13]

In camp, the pain of the long marches was forgotten, the horrors of the battlefield sublimated, and the sick rolls dropped dramatically, leaving the large new hospital unused. Unlike the previous winter, only two men died that year, both on the same day and both from Company E. On January 4, 1864, thirty-year-old Isaac Whipple of Springfield and twenty-four-year-old Allen Matteson of Exeter died. Henry Walker thought Matteson died of "dirt," probably meaning unsanitary conditions. John Kidder added that Matteson never took care of himself and that "no one knew he was sick until two days before he died." Chaplain Adams of the 5th Maine presided over the ceremony as the two were laid to rest together. Walker recorded the scene: "It was a sad and dreary sight to see them borne out of camp just at dark—the ground covered with snow and still storming—the solemn dirge and muffled drums and escort marching with reversed arms."[14]

That winter, a few of the boys in Company D went to visit the grave of

(above left) Capt. John Kidder. He left a languishing carriage-making business in Laurens, Otsego County, to raise a company. A tough taskmaster, he was wounded at Spotsylvania. He survived the war and became a major player in the regimental association. From Isaac O. Best, *History of the 121st.* (above right) Capt. John Fish. After distinguishing himself at Rappahannock Station, he led an unsuccessful recruiting party back home in the spring of 1864. He was killed at Spotsylvania as he carried ammunition to gunners at the Salient. His body was never recovered. Courtesy of the United States Army Historical Military Institute, Carlisle, Pa. (left) Maj. James Cronkite, who began as an enlisted man and eventually led the regiment. He barely survived the war. Immediately after the battle of Sailor's Creek, he was accidentally wounded when a loaded gun discharged a round into his left leg, which was amputated. Author's collection.

Deloss Platt, who was killed at Rappahannock Station. "Everything was right," John Ingraham reported. "The ground had settled some on the grave but not to amount to anything." Meanwhile, death did not confine itself to the battlefield and camp. Thirty-two-year-old Chauncey Colton of Company I, from Morris, received news of the deaths of his two small children from diphtheria. His wife contracted it from the children and nearly died as well. Colton was killed four months later in the Wilderness and was buried in an unmarked grave.[15]

Those in Confederate hands could not enjoy the leisure experienced by their comrades on the Rapidan. Just before Christmas, Joe Heath told the *Little Falls Journal and Courier* that several members of the regiment had died in rebel prisons. He reported that Robert Bradshaw of Company E, Benjamin Covell and George Eaton of Company A, Norman Zollar of Company C, Isaac Dawson of Company D, Stephen Crocker of Company G, and Horace Field and twenty-nine-year-old William Turner had died at Andersonville, Florence (South Carolina), or other Southern prisons. He also reported that Milo B. Tanner, Company D, and Libemus Lettis, Company G, both captured at Spotsylvania, had taken "the oath of allegiance to the Southern Confederacy." Heath added, "A disgrace upon them forever."[16]

Only one foray into the field to support George Custer's cavalry pulled the 121st out of its comfortable quarters. A raid into Albemarle County lasted four days (February 28 to March 2). Custer was to move on Charlottesville in concert with the notorious Judson Kilpatrick–Ulrich Dahlgren raid on Richmond. Part of the Sixth Corps crossed Robinson River to the tiny hamlet of Madison, to support Custer if necessary. The 121st was part of the support effort, and for most of the time in the field, it alternately rained, snowed, and blew bitter cold—and the regiment was without tents. "It was quite a time for us," Norman Herdman told his brother, "and you may bet it was a hard time." Many men fell out on the return march, some arriving back in camp the next day. Herdman, although he "stood the march as well as most," complained of a cold, a severe headache, and backaches on his return.[17]

Sam Kelley fell in love during camp that winter. He had started corresponding with Alice Miller of Franklin, New York, the previous year, beginning a long-range relationship that consumed the winter months. Alice expressed genuine interest in Sam. Her letters survived the war, even though she asked Kelley to destroy them after he read and responded to them—proof of his more than casual interest in her. Alice, a bright student, showed a keen interest in politics, unusual for a young woman of the mid-nineteenth century. The autumn elections in the western states energized her as each state's results rolled toward New York. Too young to vote, she called herself a Republican and hoped for a "union" victory. She admitted that she corresponded with a member of the 144th New York, who usually wrote "very lively letters" to her but of late expressed apprehension over the war's course. Writing as she sat before a cozy fireplace on a rainy day, she told Sam that she empathized with the soldier in the field exposed to the elements. "I am certainly not indifferent in their behalf."

In December, when Calista Bailey of Cooperstown wrote Kelley that she wanted to call off their long-standing relationship, Alice inserted herself more aggressively into Kelley's life. In February, when she had not heard from him for some time, she inquired whether he no longer wished to write to her. She reminded him that they had been corresponding for a year. She told Sam that she liked to be *"free* and *easy,"* a progressive comment for a woman of the period that revealed much about her and her views. She also preferred to be addressed as "Dear Alice" rather than "Friend Alice" or "Miss Alice," and she pressed him to divulge more of himself. In one cloying letter, she acknowledged receipt of his latest that morning, and in her eight-page response, she teasingly told him that she had been reprimanded at school for walking in the rain under an umbrella with a gentleman. As part of her reprimand, she received the school's rule book, which she promptly burned. "I have walked with a gentleman forty times or more," she wrote defiantly. She told Kelley that she sat for her picture but was not sure she liked it. "I guess that I am a pretty hard subject," she teased. "I don't see why I should be for I have dark eyes and hair, and I thought that was all that was necessary." Further, she said she was going to a party that night but wished he could be there so that they could sit and talk.

Later that month, she sent him her picture, which Kelley told her he liked. She confessed that she thought of him often. Although his words flattered her, she did not care for flattery. She talked of soldiers in the Army of the Potomac getting married, and chiding him, she wondered aloud if she was "corresponding with somebody about to be married." It is unknown if Sam answered her. He wrote his family in March telling them about Alice and declaring his liking for "gay" women, but he said he made no "arrangements to marry." Alice wrote at least three long letters in early spring before the Overland campaign, which were preserved but are largely illegible.[18]

Sam Kelley's life changed dramatically during winter quarters. He visited a fortune-teller in mid-February and learned that he would, indeed, marry the girl he loved, a fate he never realized. He became a sergeant in March and at the end of the month, Capt. Frank Gorton, Company G, alerted him that he had been put forth as an officer candidate. As Gorton predicted but sooner than expected, Kelley went before Emory Upton the next day and passed the rigorous test for officer promotion. Upton made every effort to trap Sam, but he missed only one question and would have corrected that if Upton had allowed him to do so. He toyed with the idea of joining the new colored regiments but decided to stay with the 121st because he would be "paid faster." Kelley became an officer with a date of rank retroactive to January 1, 1864. A week before pushing off on the Overland campaign, Dolphus Sayles noted in his diary: "Sergeant Kelley put on the shoulder straps." During that winter, Kelley had tried to keep up with his splintered family. Soon after he had joined the army, his father, Almond, left his family and enlisted in the 51st New York. Almond was nearby during the battle of Fredericksburg and the Mud March. Soon after, the 51st transferred to the Department of the West, and with the Ninth Corps, it arrived in Vicksburg in June 1863. It rejoined the Army of the Potomac in the spring of 1864, and father and son were briefly reunited. Almond survived the war and mustered out in Minnesota.[19]

In April, Sam learned that his two employers in Cooperstown had died within a month of each other. Harvey Marvin succumbed to consumption, and three weeks later, his partner, James Cockett, blew out his brains with a shotgun, leaving a wife, one child, and a sizable fortune. The account came to Sam from his minister and the rector of Episcopal Christ Church, Stephen H. Synott. The minister congratulated Sam on his promotion but warned him that when the war ended, he would return home to many changes. Synott signed off with the hope that the coming spring campaign would "give the rebels their death blow," but based on past experience, he held out little hope for success.[20]

John Hartwell professed his love for his wife and longed for the day they would be reunited, if he lived. Married in 1854, they had one child, and Hartwell had enlisted over his wife's objections. His candid expressions of love were rare. He told her of a dream in which he surprised her and stayed "all night" with her. "What I should have done in so long a time as that I cannot tell but might have come off the loser, so if you ever see me, look out—as a soldier is to never be trusted is the army saying." At Christmas, he wrote her that he longed to be one of her students. He hoped that the first lesson "would be to stay home and love the school Marm." He knew he would be a good pupil.

Despite the odds, Hartwell attempted to see his wife. Like others, he tried to arrange a meeting with her either in Washington or in New York. That winter, she traveled to Washington, but he failed to obtain a pass—a keen disappointment to both of them. That he was unable to meet his wife, who had traveled a great distance to see him, made Hartwell miserable. On the day the regiment went on alert to support Custer, one of the rainiest days they had seen, Hartwell told his diary: "Thus passed the first 24 hours after my cruel disappointment and it has indeed been a gloomy day to me." Reenlistment offered one way of returning home for a month. Hartwell discussed that possibility with his wife, but he rejected it because it meant time added to his original enlistment, further delaying his permanent return home. He questioned his original decision to join up. He had never anticipated the anxiety he would feel in being separated from her. His guilt increased when his wife became seriously ill and he could not help her. He had to rely on the kindness of neighbors to nurse her back to health. He missed her more with each passing day and told her so in his letters. "I never realized how much my happiness depended on you," he wrote.[21]

Adelbert Reed, in a playful letter to his father, told him that he stood a good chance of getting a wife "down here. What do you say to a southern daughter in law? Ha, ha." One fellow, a transfer from the 32nd New York, thought that the idea of a Southern bride made sense. Unfortunately, he also had a wife and child back home. His comrades roundly jeered him, even though his Southern woman was "said to be fine girl." The humor and lightheartedness with which the men discussed such matters merely covered their fears about the coming campaign and all it might entail.[22]

Francis Morse heard that seventy rebels crossed the federal lines at the beginning of December and gave themselves up because they were tired of eating a steady diet of corn—not easy-to-digest ground corn but corn right off the cob. During a lull, the rebels shot sheep between the lines, and both sides warily came out together and dressed and divided the meat. The rebels told the Yankees that they craved meat after all the corn. That Christmas, Lansing Paine and James Cronkite dined on goose.[23]

In a poignant moment, members of the 121st discovered a woman in a comfortable and gracious home who had never seen the flag of the United States until she saw the 121st's. According to Henry Walker, she found the stars and stripes "pretty" but allowed that she "did not like them as much as the bars." Walker and his comrades were shocked: "Just think of it," he wrote, "that any human being should have lived in these United States to reach middle age and never see or know the flag of their country."[24]

Court-Martial of Trainor, Smith, and Walrath

Six days after the fighting at Rappahannock Station, Barney Trainor, Philip Smith, and John H. Walrath, all privates from Company E, pushed foraging too far. Smith and Trainor had just won laurels at Rappahannock Station for their bravery in wresting the colors from rebel hands. But on November 13, they decided to ransack two farmhouses on the river at Frances Ford—one of which was owned by J. W. Lyon. Lyon was visiting his next-door neighbor's house about 300 yards away when he noticed Union soldiers approaching. The soldiers were led by Private Walrath, who was wearing a sword and a hat with cords—impersonating an officer. In threatening tones, Walrath asked Lyon and his neighbor if others had searched the property for weapons. When Lyon's neighbor replied that no one had searched his property since Lee moved into Pennsylvania, Walrath, along with Smith, Trainor, and others, decided to do so themselves. "They searched the house, and took some tobacco out of a bureau. They searched the chamber, and one of the men searched the lady's trunk."

When they were satisfied, the men proceeded to Lyon's house on the hill. Lyon took out after them, but the hapless homeowner could not stop them. By the time Lyon arrived, Walrath and his men had begun their work. Under the pretense of looking for weapons, the soldiers ransacked bureau drawers, trunks, and closets, scattering the contents throughout the house—all while the Lyon family looked on. They even searched Lyon's daughter's room on the second floor. When the soldiers turned their attention to the family's farmyard and live-stock, chaos ensued. They began killing sheep and chickens and threatened Mrs. Lyon's horse. When she tried to protect the animal, Walrath became angry and moved as if to draw his sword, threatening her and the horse. Lyon tried to as-suage Walrath, telling him that he should pay no attention to what a woman had to say, to which Walrath retorted, "I like to be respected." Trainor, mean-while, grabbed Lyon's daughter's four-year-old colt from the stable as she pleaded with him not to take it.

As the men began shooting the farm's livestock, they drew the attention of Maj. O. O. Robinson of the 3rd Regiment Pennsylvania Cavalry. Robinson was checking his picket lines when he heard the shouting and shooting from the other side of the river. Lyon's son met Robinson at the river's edge and explained what was happening. At first, Robinson thought that rebel guerrillas were the source of the commotion when he observed Walrath and his party crossing the river. Robinson detained the group, but still believing the men he sought were rebels, he let them go. Walrath had told Robinson that he and his band were at-tacked by guerrillas. When Robinson got to the farmhouse and learned the true story, he sent a squad of men to find as many of those he had just released and bring them back. Walrath, Smith, and Trainor were rounded up with incrimi-nating evidence in their possession, including a pillowcase of clothing and Lyon's horses. Walrath still carried the officer's sword and wore the hat with the officer's cord. The contents of the pillowcase were odd—a pair of drawers, stockings, a pair of pantaloons, and a pair of scissors.

Capt. John Fish presided at their court-martial. Other members of the court included Col. Clark Edwards, commander of the 5th Maine, and Capt. James Cronkite, Lt. Frank Foote, and Lt. Charles Butts of the 121st. Others were from the 95th and 96th Pennsylvania. The three defendants were charged with two counts: violation of the 41st Article of War, "Straggling beyond the cavalry picket lines without proper authority," and violation of the 54th Article of War, "Pillaging without proper authority." All three pleaded not guilty, and all three were convicted on both charges. Walrath received the stiffest sentence. He was to forfeit $8 per month for six months and to walk a circle 20 feet in diameter in front of the guardhouse, carrying a log of wood weighing 20 pounds, from 9:00 A.M. to noon and from 1:00 to 4:00 P.M. for thirty consecutive days. He was also to wear a sign around his neck that read *Marauder* in 3-inch-high letters. The other men received the same sentence but with the forfeiture of only $5 per pay period for their indiscretions.[25]

Barney Trainor was released from the army on March 16, 1864, when his term of service expired—but not for disciplinary reasons. Trainor had enlisted in the 31st New York for two years on April 24, 1861, in New York City; he mustered on May 24 and deserted on July 31. Authorities arrested him a year later, on May 12, 1863, and assigned him to the 121st as his penalty, to serve out an additional nine months and twelve days—until around mid-February 1864. The thirty-day punishment resulting from the "marauding" sentence delayed his official release date. Philip Smith returned to the 121st and fell at the Wilderness on May 5, 1864—shot in the left hand and left hip. He received his pay while recuperating in the hospital, which was lightened by $5 to fulfill his sentence. He left the army one year later when his term of service expired, not because of misbehavior or wounds.[26]

The ringleader, Walrath, went on to bigger and better things. Dr. Daniel Holt encouraged his penchant for stealing horses. Walrath appealed to Holt's darker and lazier side, and Holt was always on the hunt for a horse, any horse so that he would not have to walk. Walrath filled the bill on two occasions, while the doctor looked the other way. During the heat of the Overland campaign in the spring of 1864, Holt boasted that his man Walrath was "stealing all the horses and mules he can get his hand upon. Another good one is added to my stock." Only later did he express doubts: "My man Walrath is off after horses. He had my blankets and rations. I think this does not pay." But in August, Holt reverted to his old tricks, buying a gray colt from the man for $50. Walrath survived the war and mustered out with the rest at war's end.[27]

Upton Charges Olcott

Winter quarters, with its boredom, inactivity, and general tedium, caused many men to seek creative ways to spend their time. Gambling and drinking were ready and easy solutions. Chaplain John Adams, recently of the 5th Maine but at the end of 1864 the chaplain of the 121st New York, naively wrote his wife that he forwarded his monthly report to Washington "rejoicing in the statement made regarding the officers of the One Hundred and Twenty-First Regiment,—'Not one of them uses whiskey.'"[28]

Adams turned a blind eye to the officer corps and its drinking. As William Remmel told his parents how proud he was of his brother Caleb in the 152nd New York for refusing to take a drink, he conceded that it "was very fashionable to step up to take a glass of rum [these days]." The men of the 121st were no strangers to the "evils of drink," and the officers failed as examples to the enlisted men. In the Shenandoah Valley in August 1864, John Slocum shared two bottles of rum, one bottle of whiskey, and six ales with Capt. Horatio Duroe and Capt. James Cronkite. The idle moments led to gambling, swearing, and drinking—a catalog of vices kept by George Teel. Of the three, drinking topped the list. He especially singled out the officers of the regiment, with the exception of his in-law James Cronkite. He assured his wife that he harbored "no inclinations" toward the many vices offered in camp because the mere thought of his wife and family kept him pure.

Francis Morse understood the tedium of camp life: "While there are cards, whisky and wines in an army they will be the ruling pleasures." Morse disliked cards, and his stomach could not take commissary whiskey, which left him "at wit's end for amusement during the long evenings." Delavan Bates remembered fondly the whiskey issued to every man as a reward for their hard work during the Mud March the previous January. He recalled few officers at the division and corps levels who abused the bottle, although one officer on the staff usually "could mix a cocktail if the occasion demanded, and the necessary ingredients were always easily obtained." As for the 121st, he could remember but two names "out of the thirty-five original officers . . . who loved the flowing bowl." Those were probably John Fish and Egbert Olcott, who were joined occasionally by John Kidder. During one payday episode, Fish became so "beastly drunk . . . he could not do business." In that episode, Olcott took Fish's sword away from him, effectively placing him under arrest.[29]

Tedium led to drinking, and drinking led to trouble. In the autumn of 1862, the first Thanksgiving holiday in the field was canceled. Instead, the troops were drilled all day. In Upton's absence, Major Olcott was commanding the regiment, and as Edward Wales told his diary, "the major got drunk as a brute and drilled us longer and harder than usual." During battalion drill, an enlisted man described Olcott as "pretty tight." That evening, in counterpoint, the chaplain read a few lines from the hymnal. "This was the manner the 121st New York Regiment spent their Thanksgiving Day." Daniel Holt, ever in a love-hate relationship with his commanding officers, thought Olcott a "first rate officer even though he does imbibe." A few months later, Holt wrote of liberally flowing alcohol—it filled every available container. Even Colonel Franchot partook of intoxicating beverages. Everyone "down to the officer's servants will stand ready to see that none of it is wasted."

The enlisted men were no exception, and the regiment's bad boy, Clinton Beckwith, age seventeen, could find whiskey readily. Word reached him and his comrades that a sutler in a nearby camp had liquor, and Beckwith easily obtained "several or more bottles of army whiskey." They proceeded to down the powerful liquor, causing time to pass "rapidly and, all unconscious to us we reached a frame of mind which despised distance"; as a result, one of the inebriates declared that he would just remain right there. As one member of the group recalled, "It was only by the combined exertions of the others that we enticed him back to camp upon our backs." John Hartwell deplored the use of alcohol but broke down as the 121st took to winter quarters. He asked his wife to send him a bottle of wine but to "label it elderberry juice for colds."

Temperate members of the regiment such as Isaac Best and Henry Walker were always concerned about their comrades and heavy drinking. Walker worried about fellow Cooperstown officer Francis W. Foote. He hoped that Foote found Dr. Adams's sermons comforting. He liked Foote, finding him "very intelligent—sociable and good hearted, and a good soldier," with a seeming respect for religion. He pointed out, though, that "if he would not get tight and have a spree once in a while he would be a very fine fellow." Right after Rappahannock Station in winter quarters, whiskey caused an uproar in Sam Kelley's company, which resulted in a fight and the arrest of two enlisted men. The incidents of drunken officers going unpunished contrasted sharply with those involving enlisted men, for the latter received severe penalties for the same offenses. The inequities became the root of simmering discontent in the ranks of the 121st.[30]

Just before Christmas 1864, the officers of the 121st began their celebration. On December 23, recently promoted Brig. Gen. Joseph Bartlett visited the brigade bearing presents in the form of one barrel of ale for each regiment, to celebrate the Savior's birthday and his own new rank. The officers supplemented their rations with other hard liquors from the enlisted men's commissary, and by Christmas Day, a majority of the officers were sleeping it off. Sgt. Lester Baum sent a "prayer" to the *Herkimer Journal,* hoping that "that which intoxicates and makes men appear so silly" would not be given to any man—officer or enlisted. He finished his prayer with "And would that our superiors might set us an example that would shield us from all punishment."[31]

Egbert Olcott could not refrain from the bottle on Christmas Day. In a hedonistic display worthy of a Roman emperor, he cleared the regiment's empty hospital and decorated it with festive greens and chandeliers made of bayonets. At the head table, there was a large bow with Olcott's name in the center—all in keeping with the season. He invited John Kidder; surgeon Slocum; Captains Fish, Cleaveland Campbell, and Gorton; and Lieutenants Upton, Walker, and Lewis Campbell, Cleaveland's brother from the 152nd New York. The lavish meal they enjoyed featured goose, turkey, and chickens, supplemented with potatoes, onions, apples, cranberry sauce, and numerous other items, including five different cakes for dessert. Although the drinking continued unabated, nothing untoward happened that day.

Olcott partied into the next day. Joining him were the officer of the day, Campbell, and the sutler, Sam Miller, formerly a lieutenant with the 121st. The trio began drinking in a spirit of celebration, but things soon turned ugly. Olcott chose to take on Cherry Valley's first family, the Campbells. He bullied Miller into holding Cleaveland Campbell down while he poured liquor down his throat. As Campbell fought, Olcott taunted him: "Will you take it, Captain? Drink it! Drink it!" Numerous enlisted men witnessed the incident, and the crowd soon became disruptive and unruly. In a lull, Campbell slipped away to his tent, which only pushed Olcott further. He ordered Sgt. William Remmel to go to Campbell's quarters and arrest him for having his sword and belt off. He told Remmel to get ten men to round up Campbell; if that were not enough, Olcott bellowed that Remmel should get his whole company out, and if *that* did not work, he authorized him to call out the entire regiment. In a boozy haze, Olcott promised to make Remmel an orderly sergeant if he succeeded in bringing Campbell back for more abuse.

Remmel refused, and Olcott turned to the corporal of the guard, William Cady, in Company A. Olcott gave him the same speech but with no promise of promotion. With Pvts. Milton Snell, Benjamin Covell, and Boyton G. Priest— all also from Company A—Cady pulled Campbell from his bed and delivered him to Olcott.

The following month, January 1864, all of these men as well as Campbell, Lt. Col. Andrew Mather of the 20th U.S. Colored Troops, Kidder, and Captain Douw were called as witnesses in Olcott's court-martial. Upton preferred the charges. The trial ended in a severe reprimand for Olcott and "threats of dismissal if further indulged in"—and nothing else.

George Teel and John Hartwell mentioned the incident in passing, but only Dr. Holt spoke of it directly. Holt insisted that Mather preferred charges, but the official transcript of the trial clearly indicates that Upton was the charging officer. He also elaborated greatly on Olcott's charges in addition to drunkenness— "gambling and obscene behavior"—charges not supported by the transcripts. Holt admired Olcott's courage and his military discipline, but he did not respect him. He used Olcott's troubles as an opportunity to reproach the man and his character, describing him as "anything but a temperate, virtuous man. Wine and women are his Gods, and to indulge his appetite in the matter, he has taken to the card table to supply an empty purse." Holt believed that Olcott coerced everyone in the regiment, including the officers, to make loans to him to "keep his bottle full, and gratify his lust while on leave of absence." He blamed Mather for setting the officer corps "and many of the privates" against Olcott, which is why Holt insisted that Mather brought the charges against Olcott.

Teel recorded that the officers enjoyed a "great supper and broke up in a drunk, which lasted until last night [December 26]." They offered James Cronkite whiskey, but he declined. According to Teel, Bates and Kidder refused to be involved in the "big drunk." Cronkite expressed disgust "with the way the officers do business," and Hartwell told his diary, "Officers all drunk as fools tonight. Oh Misery." He told his wife that there were "a great amount of drunkards for several days," and he expected the situation to last at least another week. He wrote that "scenes too ridiculous for pens to record are enacted every night by our officers; they act worse than the men if possible." Hartwell voiced the concerns of his comrades who shared his strict, fundamentalist upbringing when he criticized those who could not control their actions and who became irresponsible in the amoral setting of the army. "Their only aim," he wrote, "seems to be to drink, gamble, quarrel, desert, mingle their blood with the African race, force southern defenseless women to submit to indignation too disgraceful to tell." John Kidder shaded the truth about the events of the day, telling his wife that "Christmas passed off merrily with us. The men and the officers enjoying themselves well." Albert Jennings in Company H echoed his words with the additional information that the men were issued a ration of beer, "but there was not enough to affect the brain, nor was the quality the most tempting."[32]

Cleaveland John Campbell could authentically be described as a blueblood. The Campbell and Olcott families were of different social strata in their hierarchical, small Cherry Valley village. The Campbells, led by father William, were not above using their family influence for status or rank in the military. William Campbell, the well-known justice, traced his ancestry to the Argyle clan of Campbells in Scotland. An erudite and articulate barrister, he wrote history as a hobby and had three sons in the service. As his obituary indicated, he "possessed genial social qualities of a high order."

Cleaveland's friends characterized him as a solid citizen with a strong intellect nurtured by a liberal education, "the best that wealth could give." After college, he toured Europe, where he learned German. He returned home as the war loomed. One of the first to volunteer, he joined the newly forming Ellsworth's Avengers, the 44th New York, in September 1861. His father pulled many political levers to get a better situation for him. Cleaveland's status as a mere private offended his father: his son deserved better. William petitioned a fellow New Yorker, Gen. Innis Newton Palmer of Buffalo, to place Cleaveland in a more important and demanding position somewhere in the army. In William's opinion, Cleaveland's proficiency in German made him an excellent candidate to lead the newly forming German troops. And clearly, his lowly rank of private did not befit his upbringing and social status. "That is not the place for him," William pronounced. His talents and organizational skills were being wasted as an enlisted man.

William Campbell offered to write to Secretary Seward, whom he "knew well," and his mere "acquaintance," the secretary of war. Then he might petition "our good old Chieftain, General Scott." Campbell approached none of them but offered to do so if Palmer endorsed his idea. Within two weeks, Cleaveland received a promotion to second lieutenant in the 1st New York Cavalry. Less than a year later, in October 1862, he joined his brother in the 152nd as a staff adjutant for a brief, six-month stay. Campbell had learned of the formation of the 152nd from his father in August, just as the 121st left Camp Schuyler for the front. William offered to put in a good word with the recruiters of the 152nd on Cleaveland's behalf, and he urged his son to line up "proper testimonials for your qualifications." Lewis Campbell, Cleaveland's brother, was booted out of the 121st for some unknown reason and wanted to recruit a company for the new 152nd. Father Campbell felt unbridled pride in his two other sons: Cleaveland's rapid rise through the ranks and Douglas's recruiting efforts in getting up a "crack company of a hundred men." "He makes a fine looking officer," his father bragged of Douglas, "I think he will make a good one too." Cleaveland joined the 121st on April 22, 1863, as a captain of Company C, where he soon became a good friend of Capt. John Fish. That relationship would strengthen as the war progressed.[33]

In an anecdotal but revealing story, Cleaveland Campbell eagerly volunteered soon after joining the army for a task he believed would require a monumental deed of bravery. Instead, he received a shovel to clean out the regiment's sinks. At that moment, he determined never to volunteer for special duty again. On another occasion, he became a candidate for a judge advocate's position when he answered the interviewing officer's only question: "What is the first duty of a staff officer?" Seeing the questioner's ample sideboard burdened with alcohol, Campbell answered, "To know how to mix a cocktail," and he received the appointment.[34]

Like Campbell, Olcott was a native of Cherry Valley and had served previously with the military, but his origins were much more common. His father, Horatio Olcott, began work at eighteen as a cashier for William Campbell, owner of the National Central Bank of Cherry Valley. In 1844, the elder Olcott sold his thirty-nine shares of stock in the bank to the Campbell family for $1,350. Right after Fort Sumter and Lincoln's call for 75,000 men, George Tuckerman of Cherry Valley raised a company and became its captain. Egbert Olcott and Cleaveland Campbell became its lieutenants. But New York reached its quota before the regiment could be filled, and the company did not muster into federal service. So, instead of going to war with the boys from Cherry Valley, both men began their military careers with the 44th New York. Olcott's brother Delos became a captain in the 127th New York, and a cousin of the same name received a lieutenant's commission in the Regular Army. Egbert and Cleaveland joined the 44th on the same day, where they were assigned as privates to Company C. Olcott transferred from the 44th with a promotion to the 25th New York (known as Kerrigan's Rangers) on November 21, 1861. Egbert Olcott, the son of a cashier, vied for position with Cleaveland Campbell, the son of a judge and the bank's owner. They were not peers.

When Olcott joined the regiment, he received ample press coverage. When he became a lieutenant colonel, the *Cherry Valley Gazette* called him "one of the best and most popular officers in the army," adding, "and the appointment is justly deserved." When he died after the war, the *Freeman's Journal* and the *Otsego Republican* ran his obituary; none appeared in the *Gazette*. However, when Campbell died from wounds suffered in the infamous mine explosion at Petersburg while leading the 23rd U.S. Colored Troops, the *Gazette* favored him with an entire column and a half of effusive language extolling his many virtues, and the *Otsego Republican* devoted a prominent half column to his obituary. The *Gazette*, mourning his loss, wrote with Victorian excess: "His last few days, spent amid the beauties of his Uncle's estate at Castleton on the Hudson, were calm, repentant, gentle." The *Gazette* barely noticed Olcott's return from the war with a one-line announcement: "Col. E. Olcott, of the 121st Regiment, arrived home last week."

Whereas Campbell actually lived in a privileged and material world, Olcott merely attempted to either affect or achieve it. As Delavan Bates pointed out, Campbell "was one of those men we read about: an intellect of high grade, an education the best that wealth could give, in pedigree coming from one of the noblest families in Otsego County, he far surpassed in many respects any other officer we had in the regiment, not excepting our gallant Emory Upton." Bates remembered that Campbell came from a "high-toned, wealthy parentage, and had a liberal education." He correctly compared Olcott to Upton when he remembered, "Outside of the art of war he was probably in all respects the equal of Col. Upton." But whereas Upton was temperate, rigid, God-fearing, and a strict disciplinarian, Olcott had learned the ways of a man of the world. His lineage did not compare to the Campbells', but as a social animal with natural instincts, he could belly up to the bar with the best of them. In that respect, Olcott "was far better adapted to meet the demands of society, and especially at the festive gatherings which sometimes are indulged in by congenial spirits," Bates remembered. Olcott's sartorial tendencies were well documented. "His taste in dress was as refined as that of any lady," Bates wrote, "and not a wrinkle could ever be seen upon his elegant uniform." When Olcott finally snapped at Christmas in 1863, he took his drunken rage out on his rival, Campbell.[35]

In mid-February, both men's fathers visited camp, Judge Campbell on February 13 and Horatio Olcott four days later. In Cleaveland's absence, Henry Hall, Cleaveland's good friend, greeted the elder Campbell, entertaining him royally at brigade headquarters. Hall showed him around and introduced him to Generals Sedgwick, Pleasonton, and Todd (Mary Lincoln's brother). Cleaveland Campbell soon took the examination to become an officer for one of the new colored regiments, and when he received an appointment to lead a regiment, that removed him from Olcott's sphere of influence. Both of their fathers became principals in the Cherry Valley National Central Bank at war's end. Horatio became the bank's president—after years of being the cashier—and Judge William Campbell was made a member of the board of directors. In Cherry Valley, Campbell still trumped Olcott.[36]

Captains Fish and Kidder Head Home to Recruit

At the end of January, Lincoln called for 500,000 more men for the coming spring offensive. The 121st continued to be well below its authorized strength. On February 1, Dr. Slocum irreverently noted in his diary: "A new recruit arrived to day—the first *one*." During the winter, the 121st lost several of its more effective officers and a few enlisted men to promotions into the new colored regiments. The Union, in a political and practical military move, enlisted freed African Americans into the ranks of the Union army. The government got over its fear of arming blacks by allowing only white men to lead them. The examining board required a rigorous examination for anyone seeking such positions, and many officers saw the chance to lead the new troops as a way of furthering their own fortunes. Two sergeants from the 121st, W. Ward Rice and Nathaniel Gano, were promoted to first lieutenant, with Gano going to Company H of the 25th U.S. Colored Troops and Rice to the 32nd USCT.[37]

Capt. Delavan Bates eventually got his wish to live as handsomely as Colonel Olcott when he received command of the 30th USCT as a colonel. He had taken the examination on a lark. He went to Washington on leave and visited the Capitol, the Smithsonian, the Patent Office, and other sites in the city. One day, "just for fun," Bates went before the examination board and so impressed them that they offered him a lieutenant colonelcy in a colored troop. Now all he needed was for more blacks to enlist so that he could be mustered as a commanding officer. The opportunity came more quickly than he anticipated, and on March 17, 1864, he turned over his official duties in the 121st to Lt. Frank Foote and left to be a full colonel, not a lieutenant colonel. He later confessed to Kidder that he forged his name on the leave slip that got him to Washington, which he "knew would be all right as you would have done the same had you been here." He professed undying loyalty to the 121st and expressed his sorrow at leaving for an unknown future.[38]

Cleaveland Campbell received his assignment as a colonel of the 23rd USCT. He so impressed his examiners that they offered him a seat on the board. John Devendorf Gray received a promotion right after Gettysburg to second lieutenant and mustered into the 23rd USCT as a captain a week later. Sgt. Andrew Davidson also became a captain in the 30th, handpicked by Delavan Bates as the regiment's adjutant. The two became fast friends—a friendship that lasted well after the war. As Bates fondly remembered, he and Davidson shared the same military education: "eighteen months' service under Colonel Emory Upton." Maj. Andrew Mather received command of the 20th USCT as a full colonel—a move that unleashed another round of backbiting and jockeying to fill his vacant position. Capt. Henry Hall became the commander of the 43rd USCT with the same rank. In the end, more than 200,000 freed black men served in the U.S. Colored Troops. They were led in these few instances by some of the most capable men produced by the 121st under the close tutelage of Emory Upton.[39]

Bates and Campbell approached their individual commands based on their backgrounds and their feelings for the men serving under them. Bates was very much a man of the nineteenth century when it came to describing his new enlistees, employing less than polite terms. Campbell, by contrast, came from a progressive family environment that bordered on abolitionist. The Campbell family was more cosmopolitan and worldly when it came to the issues of emancipation, equality of the races, and the abhorrence of slavery, and members spoke out on these topics often. Douglas Campbell wrote his older brother Cleaveland after the disaster at the Crater at Petersburg, where "in a hopeless task," the 23rd Colored Regiment took the brunt of the action. He regretted the outcome not only because it was a personal setback for his brother but also because the fight seemed to prove to the Copperheads that "black men will not fight, but with good officers, and fair chance as white men get, I see not why they should not." Bates grudgingly accepted his charges when they proved themselves in battle with valor and courage, and he eventually came to accept them as valued fighters. He also moved from calling them "niggers" to "American citizens of African descent."[40]

George Teel and William Remmel were both promoted to sergeant. Teel took his promotion as a sign of accomplishment and a reward for a job well done at Rappahannock Station. Upton told the men of the 121st that they were "as good a fighting regiment as is in the regular army." He praised their work on the rifle pits and the redoubts along the river. He told his men that they honored themselves, their country, and their friends in making the 121st "second to no regiment in the army." Henry Walker, though less ambitious than some, still desired promotion. During winter quarters, he acted as the regiment's adjutant, reporting to Lieutenant Colonel Olcott. Now he wished that Upton would get his star, for surely he would take Morse with him as his adjutant at brigade headquarters, and Walker could replace Morse. He coveted a horse and "a good one" as a perk. Yet it bothered him that he received preferential treatment over 2nd Lt. Frank Foote and Andrew Mather because he thought that they were better officers.[41]

Sam Kelley, with his promotion and his selection as one of the few to present the rebel flags to General Meade after Rappahannock Station, did not receive orders for a recruiting mission—even though John Kidder had asked him to join the group going to Otsego and Herkimer counties. Kidder recruited in Otsego and Fish in Herkimer. Each took one sergeant, one corporal, and two privates along. Replacing Kelley, Sgt. Edward Wales accompanied Kidder. Kelley remained philosophical about his rejection. Prophetically, he wrote home: "I am not disappointed for I do not seem to be always one of the fortunate."[42]

When the fighting ended at Rappahannock Station, Emory Upton rode up to Capt. John Fish in the dark and heartily congratulated him on a job well done. Upton expressed his relief to see Fish alive and complimented him by saying, "You have done yourself honor. I am proud of you." The compliments took Fish aback because Upton had twice passed him over for promotion, leaving

Fish to assume that his commander thought very little of him. Twice Fish tendered his resignation, and twice Upton rejected it. Now, Upton saw Fish through different eyes, and Fish felt sure that he would be promoted the next time around. "We are good friends now," he wrote. Indeed, they were friendly enough so that Fish went up to brigade headquarters after the battle at Rappahannock Station, dropping in on Upton unannounced and without an appointment. According to Fish, Upton welcomed him warmly and seemed glad to see him. Upton told Fish that he had mentioned him in his official report and that General Howe had asked the name of the brave officer who led the advance skirmish line. His name also made the rounds at "Meade's headquarters the day before, where I was spoken of in General Meade's presence with approbation— so I am paid," he wrote. "If I should happen to be mentioned in General Orders I should be doubly paid."[43]

Now in Upton's good graces, Fish joined John Kidder to find new recruits for the 121st back home. Upton and Olcott had recommended the two men to General Sedgwick, who forwarded the recommendation through army headquarters to Washington "with the strongest endorsement possible." Taking no chances, Kidder pulled all his political connections to get home to do recruiting. He wrote his friend William Fields requesting that he write to Levi Turner to ask the War Department for the assignment to return home to recruit. Kidder knew many in Otsego County, so the assignment fit him perfectly. He knew he could sign up all the willing and able-bodied men he could find and persuade them to join the 121st.

Kidder told Fields that a "committee from Herkimer sent a very strong recommendation to Col. Olcott to have an officer sent to that county to recruit." He went so far as to have dinner with Upton. There, over "a good fat turkey," Upton assured him that he had put in a good word for him. Kidder knew that once a young recruit saw the wonders of army life, he would sign up without hesitation. In an absurd stretch of the imagination, he told his wife he once thought that women "had much to do in keeping men in a quiet, civilized state but I think that when men are away from the society of females as they are here . . . they are much more civil and quiet. We never have any quarrels or disturbances. All is peace and harmony among soldiers." Whether he wrote those lines with a straight face or whether his wife believed the fiction is unknown.[44]

All through January, the two awaited orders. That month, the War Department rejected their request, with the explanation that no more men would be sent home on recruiting efforts without the approval of Governor Seymour. Olcott and Upton reacted by writing to Seymour immediately. In the meantime, members of the regiment watched representatives from the 152nd New York go home for new enlistees—an insult from a regiment that had not suffered nearly as much as the 121st and that was, in the eyes of most, in no need of new men. George Teel heard of a man from Otsego who enlisted in the 152nd and could not understand why anyone would want to join such an inferior regiment. By mid-February, word finally came allowing Fish and Kidder, with their detail of men, to head to Washington to begin their recruiting efforts. Joining them as they traveled into one of the coldest winters in upstate New York in many years were four sergeants, Erastus Weaver of Oneonta, Augustus Gage and Henry Timmerman of Little Falls, and Edward Wales of Cherry Valley. Cpl. Samuel G. Button of Winfield, Cpl. Charles I. Metcalf of Otsego, and Cpl. James Taft of West Exeter were part of the recruiting party as well, with Pvt. P. T. Van Horne of Springfield Center and Pvt. Rufus L. Robinson of Frankfort rounding out the detail.[45]

Fish took charge of the group. Gage, Timmerman, Button, and Robinson joined him in Herkimer County. Kidder took Wales, Weaver, Metcalf, Van Horne, and Taft with him to canvass Otsego County. Fish commissioned broadsides and advertisements in the local papers to stimulate recruitment. In a commanding broadside with a majestic eagle spreading his wings over symbols of American power, he asked for 300 men to fill the regiment "to the maximum standard." He urged them, "Rally on the colors, men! We know they're old and tattered, and the staff is marred and shattered, but Rally, Rally on the Flag, brave Boys." The broadside promised the federal government would pay $400 for veterans and $300 for new recruits, augmented by state money of $150 for veterans and $75 for new men. Fish also promised recruits the highest possible town and county bounties available. In another, less picturesque broadside, he emphasized the unit's well-deserved history of service in putting down the rebellion, asking for "sympathy and assistance" in filling up the depleted ranks savaged by disease and battle. He claimed that he came to ask potential recruits to "send us into the next and final campaign, with full numbers and increased efficiency." Fish promised new recruits strict military discipline in a regiment with some of the best officers in the field, men who were "faithful, energetic, brave, and who have at heart the comfort, reputation and well being of their men." After nearly seven weeks in upstate New York, Fish and Kidder and their contingent returned to camp empty-handed.[46]

Fish may have believed his recruiting pitch about the officers of the 121st, but others did not buy into his argument. The atmosphere in which Fish and Kidder and their band of recruiters found themselves had changed dramatically since they had joined in the autumn of 1862. Despite generous offers of larger bounties, the recruiting detail failed for a variety of reasons. The news reports and the letters home told of the hardships of the life of a recruit. Potential candidates refused to sign up for infantry duty knowing that the coming spring campaign threatened to be meaner than the preceding two years of heavy fighting. The recruits of 1864 were keenly aware of the reality of war. In addition, newer and more regiments increased competition for Fish and his recruiting contingent. The cavalry enjoyed a reputation for higher survival, and the new heavy artillery units proved to have an even higher survival rate, with their guard duty in the national capital and its environs. The latter would turn out to be a bad bet for the recruit seeking a safer slot, for the incoming commander, Ulysses Grant, saw the underutilized heavy artillery units around Washington and ordered them to the front in Virginia to bolster his upcoming Overland campaign. Fish and Kidder also found themselves competing with existing units in the field that were offering incumbents thirty-day furloughs to re-sign with their original regiments. And finally, the fever pitch of patriotism that had characterized the early days of 1861 had waned.

Kidder and Fish discovered similar difficulties existed in both counties when they caught up with each other in Herkimer and grabbed the train for Albany. From there, they traveled to New York City and on to Washington, where they caught up with Upton, who welcomed them back. Back in camp, they were warmly greeted by their fellow officers.[47]

The enlisted men were not impressed. Adelbert Reed could not understand the lack of recruits. He concluded that potential enlistees either were cowards or knew of the trials and hard times of the 121st, which caused them to turn away from the soldier's life. In either case, Reed did not want such men anyway, as he took great pride in the regiment's strong battle record.[48]

Muddying the waters of the recruiting detail to New York was the problem of the major—or rather, the absence of the major. Upton, still a full colonel, commanded the brigade without the benefit of having a brigadier general's single star. Olcott commanded the 121st as a lieutenant colonel. Now, with Andrew Mather's brand-new commission as a colonel and his assignment to the U.S. Colored Troops, the vacancy left in his wake set off a scramble among those eager to fill his old slot. The two most eligible candidates were the old rivals Henry Galpin and John Fish, and the 121st's officer corps quickly split over the two. Kidder favored Galpin, although he confided that he thought that Fish would make a good major. Cleaveland Campbell was a Fish man. Rumors abounded. Upton favored Fish—according to the latest gossip. With Upton's newfound respect for Fish, that rumor gained credibility. Others were convinced that if one got the position, the other would resign.[49]

The battle for major of the 121st echoed in the halls at Albany. While recruiting in New York, Fish traveled to the state capital to evaluate firsthand his chances for promotion. He dropped in on the Adjutant General's Office and there viewed the recommendations that had come in for Galpin, his chief competitor. He described Galpin's references as a "cloud of witnesses, to the fact that he is a pretty good fellow and don't drink." He also gained access to Emory Upton's and Egbert Olcott's strong letters in *his* favor. Initially, Upton had urged Adj. Gen. John T. Sprague in Albany to leave the position vacant for a while to enable Upton "to make the best selection possible." He asked Sprague to defer "all action" on the vacancy until he could get to Albany in early February.[50]

TO THE CITIZENS OF
HERKIMER & OTSEGO
COUNTIES!

The 121st Reg't, N. Y. V.,
YOUR Representative Regiment
ASKS YOU FOR MEN!

TO FILL UP ITS RANKS. We claim that we are entitled, by our past history, to your sympathy and assistance. Recruited in the first instance almost exclusively from the two Counties, we have never disgraced the flag presented to us, or the friends who sent us. The casualties of disease and battle have reduced our numbers, and we have come to ask you to send us into the next, and *final* campaign, with full numbers and increased efficiency, and we promise you in return, that you shall have no occasion to regret that we represent you.

To the *Patriotic men* of the different towns, who are interested in filling *local quotas,* we say that it is for your interest to fill them *quickly.* The sooner your men are in camp, the sooner will they become acclimated, disciplined and efficient soldiers, ready for the purpose for which you raise them---*service in the field.* And to the men who enlist for you, we can say that we offer them places on equal terms with us, in a Regiment which, in drill, discipline, patriotism and good fellowship among its members, is not rivaled in the service; commanded by officers who are faithful, energetic, brave, and who have at heart the comfort, reputation and well-being of their men.

In the County of Otsego, Capt. John S. Kidder, of Laurens, Sergeants Edward Wales and E. C. Weaver, Privates C. J. Metcalf, P. J Van Horne and James A Taft, are sent to co-operate with you, while myself, with Sergeants A. M. Gage and H. A. Timmerman, Corporal S. G. Button and Private R. L. Robinson, are ready to work with you in Herkimer, for the mutual benefit of ourselves and the country. Respectfully your Ob't Serv't,

JOHN D. FISH, Capt.,
Commanding Recruiting Detail.
Head Quarters at Herkimer, Herkimer Co., N. Y.

121st recruiting poster. John Fish and John Kidder commissioned this broadside when they visited Herkimer and Otsego Counties in the late winter and early spring of 1864 looking for new recruits to fill up the regiment. Their trip produced no new replacements. Author's collection.

Olcott's support of his candidacy pleased and encouraged Fish, especially since Olcott's nemesis, Cleaveland Campbell, also supported him. Campbell had surreptitiously furnished Fish with a letter signed by a group of officers and enlisted men critical of him and his candidacy. Fish acknowledged that "the paper you sent me is certainly a strong one," but he doubted it would hurt him. But the knowledge of *who* signed the letter galled him: Daniel Holt's name appeared with others. Fish told Campbell that Holt "must be 'queer' else I have always been so very unfortunate as to misunderstand him."

Newly minted first lieutenant Daniel Jackson of New Lisbon backed Galpin, a move that was "inexplicable" to Fish. Just a few days earlier, Fish had received a letter of support from Jackson, who was "hoping to see" him "come back major." In addition, Campbell told Fish that both James Cronkite and Sgt. William Tucker favored his candidacy, but Fish doubted him. "I cannot possibly understand what should make the officers so bitter against me," he wrote Campbell. "You say they are afraid of me. Well bless their souls, I won't hurt them. I am not at all dangerous, and although I have teeth, I won't bite." He confirmed the same "severe feelings against" him from other sources. He said that he never intended to treat the officers of the 121st "unkindly or in an ungracious manner" and that he held the highest regard for many and wished to make amends if he had offended them.

There were others whose opinions he wanted to hear, but he would not "run after" them. Fish felt sure that these letters were all part of a larger plot to rid the regiment of Olcott and Campbell himself. He based his insight on a conversation in Albany with an unidentified person in the Adjutant General's Office. The individual asked after Campbell and Olcott and wondered aloud if Fish thought that they "were likely to remain with the 121st"—and that, he said, "caused me to smell a very large 'mice' instantly." Fish realized during his conversation that he was speaking with a Mather and Galpin supporter, with whom Galpin had recently been in touch. Fish's source refused to show him "the papers—pro and con—in our matter, but I saw them, I did." He sensed he could not win, and he refused to ask "the copperheads" in Albany "to plead for [him]." If Upton's and Olcott's recommendations were not good enough for a promotion, Fish remained "content to serve as a Captain until I wear my legs [down] to six inches in length" by marching and standing in formation. He signed off his letter to Campbell by asking to be remembered to his friends, especially Colonel Olcott, but to keep the news in his letter quiet.[51]

Mitigating the failure of the recruiting detail—and despite the backstage theatrics—neither Fish nor Galpin returned empty-handed. Galpin accepted a commission as the new major of the 121st as it prepared for the upcoming spring offensive. And Fish remained a captain but got the consolation prize—an appointment on Emory Upton's staff, which entailed more prestige and fewer hazards. John Hartwell wrote of Captain Galpin in his diary, "He is worthy of it. Success to him." As one of his first duties, Galpin carried the regiment's flag to Washington for repairs and to have the names of three battles—Salem Church, Gettysburg, and Rappahannock Station—embroidered on it.[52]

Emory Upton suffered his own setbacks in his advance up the ranks. He now commanded a brigade as a colonel, but he wanted the accompanying star signifying his stature as a brigadier general. Even though he complained bitterly about political interference in officer appointments, he soon learned to play the political game. He wrote his sister in the spring of 1864 that he never "fully despaired of receiving promotion." He much preferred receiving it on merit alone, not as a political favor.

However, his actions belied his assertion. He tried but failed to curry favor with those in high places to achieve his goals. In 1863 and early 1864, he attempted various strategies to get his star. In 1863, he received glowing recommendations from several brigadier and major generals, to no avail. The next year, he tried the direct political approach. "My own affairs I consider almost hopeless," he complained to his sister. "I cannot as yet secure the influence of Senator Harris and [former] Governor [Edwin] Morgan." He wrote directly to Morgan, his benefactor when he replaced Franchot as commander of the 121st. He even tried the loyal states' governors—an approach that was for naught. General Meade warned him "that without their influence," he would "never be promoted." Upton remained confident that his good deeds would eventually vindicate him, but he hedged his bets by soliciting and receiving the endorsements of powerful high-ranking officers. "Had there been but one friend in Washington, my services would have been rewarded."

Upton took on the president. "Mr. Lincoln has secured my papers and although General Sedgwick wrote that my claims were superior to those of any other in this corps, yet he has appointed two colonels over me. How could he do such an act of injustice?" Lincoln's attitude perplexed him. Why would Lincoln ignore his peers and superiors and, even more important, those he might lead? he wondered. Upton received endorsements and recommendations from officers and men in the division's 1st Brigade, all with the thought that he would be assigned to command them. A New Jersey brigade flattered him when they picked him over all the colonels from the Garden State.[53]

Preparing for the Spring Campaign

In preparation for the spring initiative, a campaign that no one envisioned would last eleven grueling months, the Lincoln administration turned to yet another commander in whom the president himself placed every hope for stamping out the rebellion. Ulysses S. Grant, fresh from his successes in the west, took command of all Union armies except the Army of the Potomac, which George Gordon Meade continued to command. Grant decided to place his headquarters within Meade's army, as he continued to wage war on the Confederacy at all points. His ascendancy to command initiated the third and last phase—unrelenting war and unconditional surrender. Because of Grant's record of successes in the west, his new command was imbued with confidence. At the end of April, the general reviewed the Union troops, moving among the men accompanied by his staff. He visited with the 1st Division, 2nd Brigade, and the now-famous 121st New York Infantry. He inspected Pvt. Adelbert Reed's musket, asking him where he got it and then pronouncing it "a very good looking one." Reed wrote of his pride and confidence that the government had found a leader who would take them to Richmond. John Hartwell summed up Grant's review: "The hero of Vicksburg is a fine looking man. He took no pains to show off."[54]

The faces and names of the line officers changed dramatically before the spring offensive. Emory Upton was in command of the 2nd Brigade and Egbert Olcott the regiment. With captains detailed to brigade or division duty, a few of the regiment's companies were commanded by first lieutenants. Four companies were reduced to just one officer; Company A continued with all three. The staff consisted of only two surgeons, Slocum and Holt; Olcott in command; Galpin second in command; and Morse on detail to Colonel Upton at brigade headquarters. Theodore Sternberg continued as quartermaster.

The regiment looked to its cadre of noncommissioned officers for leadership. The regiment that left Camp Schuyler in September 1862 no longer looked like a brigade. No one could know that within the next eleven months and after the heavy battles that lay ahead, the regiment would end up looking like a company. Daniel Holt predicted that the army would soon "enter upon the hardest and bloodiest campaign," ending a moral struggle between good and evil. He guessed that the Confederacy had completely exhausted its resources and continued the fight on "pluck" alone. "But," he suggested, "this very commodity will keep them alive and kicking long after they should have been entombed." He "shuddered at the thought of the carnage" that he knew would follow when the two armies met again. He prepared himself for the worst and asked his wife to pray for the best.[55]

Upton earned his reputation and that of the 121st in part through drills at the regimental and battalion levels. On good weather days, the troops were put through their paces until, throughout the division, the 121st became known as Upton's Regulars. The dress parades were detailed down to the white gloves, which prompted John Lovejoy to remark, "It don't make a bad show to look at the boys of the 121st N.Y." There were drills at every level of command, including real-life exercises. Toward the end of April, Upton drilled the brigade in single lines and charged the command against "imaginary rifle pits and forts at a double quick over ditches, stones and brush," completing the charge twice over a half-mile range in a four-hour period. He left no areas of instruction uncovered, even including the natural instinct to duck. Clinton Beckwith told of several occasions when Upton lectured men for ducking when they heard an incoming round whistling about their heads. He told them that their actions, though natural, "were foolish." "The shot that strikes you," he said, "you never will hear, and remember a shell makes more noise than it does harm. When you hear the hiss of a bullet or the rush of a shell its power to do you harm has departed." Beckwith argued that with his unusual attention to detail in all matters military, Upton instilled confidence in his men to the point that they would willingly follow him anywhere. The men of the 121st learned the art of warfare, and under Upton's tutelage, they quickly became an effective fighting team. Upton covered all the "arts and business" of warfare—self-protection while doing as much damage to the enemy as possible, concealment, how and when to take cover, "as well as advance on the enemy, was carefully demonstrated by practice."[56]

As the troops of the Sixth Corps drilled in preparation for the spring offensive, Upton and his brigade came to the attention of Oliver Wendell Holmes. An aide-de-camp to Gen. Horatio Wright commanding the 1st Division of the Sixth Corps, Holmes was a Harvard graduate, a Boston Brahmin, and a future Supreme Court justice. He was an avid people-watcher and social commentator. In one of his last diary entries before the spring campaign, he recorded his observations of many of the brigadiers and senior officers. "Upton's Brigade appeared well, in connection with his handsome camp," he wrote. "The 121st N.Y. afterwards went through the manual very nicely—some fancy dodges."[57]

Earlier in winter camp, in the dead of the season, John Ingraham wrote his brother of his pride as a member of the 121st New York. The unique, nine-button New York jacket worn by the regiment impacted the regiment's morale materially. By the time the 121st went into winter camp, the jackets had become threadbare. Egbert Olcott and Emory Upton believed that the garments were important to the regimental esprit de corps, and thus they petitioned Governor Seymour for 200 replacements that winter. Upton gave Olcott's request a warm and politically savvy endorsement. He asked Seymour to consider the request sympathetically because it would reflect favorably on the "state and the regiment." He wrote: "The men are proud of their uniform and would regret to have it changed." But the jackets were not forthcoming. As Ingraham correctly perceived, they were not making them anymore. Although he stated that he preferred the New York jacket over a dress coat any day, he told his brother that he still believed that the 121st "puts on more style than any other in the United States." "Even a private here in this Regiment thinks himself better than a commissioned officer in most any other Regiment. I saw in the *Journal* they call us up north what they call us here—Upton's Regulars, and we are not ashamed to own it. Our Regiment is quite noted." Alluding to the fact that Upton invariably joined Sedgwick and others when they reviewed the troops so that he could see the 121st, Ingraham wrote, "He hasn't forgotten his old regiment [even] if he is commander of the Brigade. We owe it all to him. He was the making of the Regiment."[58]

In early April, Grant ordered all the women and other visitors in camp to leave without delay. The first contingent left on April 11 and 12. Francis Morse and his cohort Captain Daniels traveled down to Brandy Station to see the first group off during day one of the two-day process. The remainder of the 2,500 visitors left the next day. Morse and Daniels sat on a bale of hay "till the most affecting scenes were over, and then attended to our own little business in that line." Dr. Holt saw his patients off to Washington and to safer environs the day before the 121st broke winter camp in preparation for the spring offensive. He accompanied them down to the trains at Brandy Station. He and they "had a rough time of it generally." Sam Kelley wrote letters home, sent his newly won commission to his mother, sent his pictures to his father, drew his pay, and railed against the cowards at home who were no better than "wooden men" because at least wooden men would fill the awful vacancies in the ranks and "stand until they were knocked over." He bunked with Jonathon Burrell, whom he liked very much. "I think he is a good man," he wrote to his mother. "He seems to like me [also]." When he had mustered in, Burrell told him he would try his hardest to ensure that Kelley would stay in his company—"I guess he has been successful."[59]

Like the rest of the army, Kelley prepared himself mentally and spiritually for the coming struggle. Rumors of every stripe rippled through the camps as most men realized that the spring offensive might well become the definitive campaign. Many found religion. The passionately religious bemoaned the absence of a regimental chaplain. Kelley and others exerted the energy to travel to the 5th Maine's camp to hear a rousing sermon by a guest minister from New York. The powerful sermon caused "the tears to trickle down the cheeks of the hardest hearts." The religious zealots in the regiment—Ingraham Smith in Company G from Middlefield, Henry Walker, John Lovejoy, and most recently William Remmel—were witnesses to the revival happening throughout the Army of the Potomac. On Saturday night, April 30, several of the boys attended a prayer meeting with standing room only. Those who could not get in prayed outside the wooden shanty used for such gatherings. Remmel publicly expressed his salvation to the crowd, much to Smith's surprise. Smith expressed delight at those seeking the Lord, a feeling he had not anticipated when he joined the 121st. The coming campaign motivated a majority of the religious cases. Long letters home extolling God's mercy and tenderness were the declarations of fearful men preparing for what many believed might be their last battle. Smith wrote his mother, "We feel that many of us will be in eternity perhaps before another Sabbath for we expect to move every day now." He closed his letter with a solemn request: "I ask your prayers for your unworthy son that if he falls he may fall in the arms of Jesus."[60]

But John Lovejoy epitomized the extremely religious soldier motivated by a sincere love of Jesus Christ as his savior. John filled every letter home to his cousin Cynthia with his desire to purify his soul and put his trust in the Lord. He melded his religious fervor with the Northern cause. In nearly all his letters, he referred to the "unholy rebellion." While others ranted about this cruel war, Lovejoy viewed the struggle as a moral imperative—not to end slavery but to stop the killing and the madness. His brother's death in January 1864 marked his moment of revelation. He told Cynthia Jonathon's last words: "Tell my brother to meet me in Heaven" were "the first words that ever sent the arrow of conviction stinging through my conscience." He claimed that he abandoned his former life and turned to God.

Before the Wilderness campaign, scores of soldiers were taking part in a religious revival. At first, there were only twelve in Lovejoy's prayer "association." By April 8, 1864, that number had grown to sixty, albeit with some backsliders. Prayer meetings were held on Sunday, Tuesday, Thursday, and Saturday evenings, even though there was no chaplain to direct them. Bible classes were held on Wednesday and Friday evenings. Lovejoy shrugged off the ridicule and scorn he received from his comrades for praying aloud in his tent. "I mind it not," he wrote, "for I know if I do my duty the Lord will bless me."[61]

On May 1, 1864, Captain Holt, Captain Kidder, Major Galpin, and hospital steward Newton Phelps visited the men of the 152nd New York as they made their final preparations. The 152nd had recently left its guard duties around Washington. The men were new to the routine of "hurry up and wait." The unit's quarters were not as pleasant as the 121st's were, and its men were not reluctant to leave them. John Kidder visited his brother George for the last time. He believed that because of his officer status, he would not survive the coming battles but that George might. The two wished each other well and parted. As it happened, George fell in the Wilderness and John escaped, wounded, at Spotsylvania.[62]

Olcott Takes Command

When Gen. George Gordon Meade told Emory Upton that he would never become a general officer without political influence, Upton responded with an arrogant and optimistic answer. Throughout his life and military career, Emory Upton exhibited both those traits, arrogance and optimism, and they served him well. He never doubted that he would be promoted; if not, his friends would have ample proof that he deserved promotion but that his supervisors unfairly judged him. A month after his conversation with Meade,

Upton proved himself worthy as he won his star on the battlefield in an audacious move against all odds.

Egbert Olcott succeeded Upton as commander of the 121st—following the man who recently had brought court-martial charges against him. Although Olcott did not have Upton's self-control, he in fact resembled him more than Upton would probably have admitted. Olcott was, after all, a volunteer. He learned at the foot of the professional soldier. He possessed the necessary qualifications to replace Upton in spite of his intemperate alter ego. According to Delavan Bates, "when Upton assumed command, he and [Colonel] Clark did not work well together, so much so that Col. Clark resigned, but Major Olcott was an apt pupil, and with Upton's assistance, soon became competent to handle a regiment or a brigade as well as the best." His prior service with the 44th New York and the 25th New York gave him a wealth of experience in addition to being an understudy to one of the most competent commanders in the Union army. At only twenty-two years of age, he joined the 121st as the regiment's major. Like Upton, he insisted on attention to details.

Also like Upton, he demanded "strict compliance with military etiquette." He made his commanding officers responsible for acquainting the men with the rules of "saluting, removing hats when entering officer's quarters and all that pertains to this branch of discipline." He reminded noncommissioned officers that they were to perform their duties as pristinely as possible as examples to the enlisted men, with "patience, obedience, fortitude and courage." If not, they would be reduced to the ranks. On one occasion, Olcott reduced Cpl. Albert S. Tanner, Company I, to the rank of private for not saluting the brigade commander. Even after Lee surrendered, Olcott was unrelenting in matters of military order, decorum, or readiness. As late as May 1865, he ordered his commanding officers to inspect their units' weapons and equipment "each day before retreat." He employed corporal punishment, which sometimes exceeded the infractions. In April 1864, he reduced Cpl. Nathan F. Jones, Company D, to the rank of private after guards found him walking around the camp and visiting the sutler's tent after being excused from battalion drill for a "severe headache." Jones complained to the doctor that unbearable headaches would not allow him to "bear the light without great panic." Jones perished a month later at Spotsylvania.

As Grant crafted his plans for the spring offensive against Lee, the 121st prepared to follow both Upton and Olcott into the war's fiercest fighting. But up north, hometown papers in Otsego and Herkimer counties were calling the regiment Upton's Regulars, a sobriquet that went unchallenged even though Olcott finished the war as the regiment's commander. The men in the regiment adopted it as a badge of honor. Their reverence and devotion to Upton only increased with time. Olcott never received the same level of adulation. The men loved and respected Upton; they respected and feared Olcott.[63]

II

Grant's Overland Campaign, May to June 1864

I've known instances of men going into battle, they would make the remark they knew they were going to be killed. Something forewarned them and sure enough they were killed. That proper time had arrived.

John Ingraham, Company D, April 26, 1864

We feel that many of us will be in eternity perhaps before another Sabbath for we expect to move every day now.

Ingraham Smith, Company G, May 1, 1864

Do not come to the front to claim your loved one's body—they are being properly buried and marked.

Cherry Valley Gazette, June 1, 1864

The Wilderness

The word to move out came down at midnight, May 3. Leaving the relative luxury of the past few months, the 121st joined the brigade and the Sixth Corps on the south side of the Hazel in the small hours of the morning. At 3:00 A.M. on Wednesday, May 4, the men of the 121st awoke to a new day and the beginning of a long journey from which many of them would not return. More than 400 men stepped off smartly, with their new regimental colors inscribed with the names of Salem Church and Rappahannock Station.

The regiment had 21 officers and 456 privates present for duty. Another 5 officers and 92 men were on detachment to other units. Dolphus Sayles predicted that his father would "hear of a big battle before long." Daniel Holt reflected sadly on the "thought that scores of those now moving out in military pride and perfect health will in a short time

Sixth Corps Fighting in the Wilderness, a sketch by Alfred A. Waud. Courtesy of the Library of Congress.

become food for worms." Two months earlier, Norman Herdman had predicted that Grant would not attack Lee directly but would "skillfully maneuver on his flanks." A victory here with Grant's army would "decide the matter." John Slocum echoed his words and the thoughts of many: "In my opinion the next ten days decides the spring campaign." He remembered that May 3 marked the anniversary of the battle at Salem Church.

The rivers, recently swollen with spring rains, had receded, making the roads manageable. The country placed its confidence and hope in Ulysses Grant to reach Richmond. William Remmel prayed that the Army of the Potomac would be successful under his and Meade's leadership. Remmel visualized an opportunity to finally "crush the rebels . . . trying to enslave four millions of human beings to save their own necks from labor and to lead the lives of Lords and Masters." A member of the 121st told the *Little Falls Journal and Courier* he expected to "spend the month of October" in Richmond, with Grant at the army's head and Upton leading the brigade. If Grant should get as close as McClellan did, the soldier wrote, he would not turn back: "We expect to see the bloodiest battle this spring that was ever fought on this continent; we mean to be victorious in our achievements."[1]

After the men ate a meager breakfast, the army began its journey from its comfortable winter quarters, going south over the Rapidan. "[For] once in the history of the war, we start punctually at the moment designated," Dr. Holt noted. The Army of the Potomac consisted of the Second, Fifth, and Sixth corps. Ambrose Burnside's Ninth Corps, guarding the long supply trains, reported directly to Grant, who later incorporated the unit into the Army of the Potomac. The First and Third corps disbanded, and their remnants were placed with the other corps.[2]

The Sixth Corps crossed the Rapidan at Germanna Ford following the Fifth; the rest of the army used Ely's and Culpeper Mine fords. The 121st struck out across the river. According to John Slocum, the men were "as full of play as though they had done nothing." Ahead, Lee and his army awaited them. Lee had spent the winter in Orange County, below the Rapidan. Between Lee and the Army of the Potomac were the abandoned embattlements at Mine Run, entrenchments that ran parallel to the Germanna Plank Road and a few miles west of it. Lee's signalmen saw the federal army's movement from the signal station on top of Clark's Mountain. Meade's signalmen were on Pony and Stony mountains watching Lee's signalmen. With a combination of intelligence gathered from his men on Clark's Mountain and indications as early as May 2 that the Union army had moved, Lee quickly discerned his enemy's direction and strength.[3]

Both armies were familiar with the landscape. If one were to overlay a modern map of the eastern part of the state of Virginia over its 1864 version, the routes taken by the armies once they got through the Wilderness and Spotsylvania would roughly parallel modern-day U.S. Interstate 95 from Fredericksburg to Richmond. Many times before, different Union army commanders had tried and failed to reach the Confederate capital. But now, with a new commander, the army came out of its winter quarters with high hopes of being in Richmond by summer's end. At the same time, the troops were apprehensive about how this man from the west, Grant, would deal with Robert E. Lee and the Army of Northern Virginia and how he would manage the Army of the Potomac. Skepticism was rampant given the history of the army and its commanders over the previous three years.

Although Richmond continued to be a long-term goal, Grant intended to find Lee and destroy him. He believed that his predecessors were wrong to focus on Richmond while Lee's army lived on. Based on his record at Vicksburg, army rumors said Grant would draw sixty days' rations, cut off all communications with Washington and "the rest of mankind," and annihilate Lee's army.[4]

The two forces collided in the Wilderness, just west of Chancellorsville, Salem Church, and Fredericksburg. Grant did not want to engage Lee in the wild and impenetrable forest. His troops quickly moved through the thick woods to reach Spotsylvania before they could be discovered. He intended to move on a straight line southeast, interposing himself between Richmond and Lee. The head of his column would eventually be the left flank, the tail his right flank when the men turned west and confronted Lee. For his part, Lee initially wanted to avoid an engagement but later favored the idea of cutting this strung-out "snake" in half.

The Wilderness was not an ideal location in which to engage an enemy. Heavy foliage limited vision to a few yards. Tangled thickets of deciduous trees and regenerating oaks covered the ground. The pine trees provided a steady supply of needles—"pine straw"—and pinecones, both highly flammable when dry. The oaks resembled "scrub oaks," ugly plants that thrive in the sandy soil and rarely grow taller than 6 or 8 feet. Their stunted trunks and branches are sharp, twisted, and gnarled. In the gloom, their silhouettes are foreboding and more suited to a cemetery; their branches snag and tear at passersby.

Equally unwelcoming, the terrain was not level for 50 feet in any direction—with ravines lying left and right of the dirt roads that ran through the primeval forest. Low areas in the midst of the pines were often soft, muddy, or filled with water. With the exception of the Orange Plank Road, Brock Road, and the Orange Court House Turnpike, the roads narrowly accommodated a troop column marching four abreast. Vegetation grew up to the edge of the roadway. Artillery, useless except in a few clearings such as the Tapp farm, could only be employed on the length and breadth of the roads; its effectiveness was negated by the thick brush. The highways slashed through the woods, and only because of continuous human use did the roads resist the forest's unrelenting march to reclaim them. The Orange Turnpike ran north and parallel to the Orange Plank Road in a generally east-west direction. Only 3 miles from each other, they came to a T with the Germanna Plank Road. Off the Orange Plank Road, Brock Road ran south toward Spotsylvania Court House. Parker's Store and the Tapp farm along the Orange Plank Road were cleared areas. Along the Orange Turnpike, to the north, the Lacy House and the Wilderness Tavern were situated in or near a clearing where that road intersected Germanna Plank Road.

The thick woods presented military planners from both sides with minimal visibility and little maneuverability. Holt called the area the "raggedest hole" he had ever seen. "No wonder we cannot find or see a reb until we get right upon them. Swampy, hilly bushes thick as dog's hair, grape vines, rotten logs, and fallen trees, make up this pretty picture . . . a perfect quagmire." Grant put it bluntly: "The roads were narrow and bad. All the conditions were favorable to a defensive position." He wanted to strike when and if the "enemy could be drawn from his entrenchments," if the Union army did not entrench itself. Lee wanted to pin him in the woods. Unfortunately for Grant, he had to slow down to await his lumbering wagon trains. He could not afford to outrun his valued supplies.[5]

Nothing occurred on May 4. The regiment, with Emory Upton leading the 2nd Brigade of the 1st Division, crossed the Hazel River on pontoons and forded the Rapidan. Sedgwick camped a few miles north of Germanna Plank Ford that night after making little discernible progress. On May 5, he encamped north of the Wilderness Tavern near Meade's headquarters. Grant had stayed behind the day before, but he joined Meade at the tavern on May 5. The 121st found itself about 6 miles from the site of the prior winter's Mine Run campaign. The rest of the army was strung out along the Germanna Ford road from north to south—Warren in the middle and Hancock on the left along the road into Chancellorsville. Grant held Burnside's Ninth Corps in reserve to the north.

The morning of May 5 dawned bright and clear. Grant determined to press into open areas past the Wilderness. As he moved south, word came that a Confederate force of unknown strength approached from the west along the Orange Turnpike. When Grant sent Warren to investigate, the dance began. The armies collided along the two turnpike and Plank Road corridors—the northerly Orange Turnpike first. The 121st fell in line as the Sixth Corps moved down the Germanna road that day. Ahead, the Fifth Corps engaged Ewell's men. By noon, the firing had intensified. Moving in a column of fours (four men across), the division's regiments maintained a large space between them so that, if necessary, they could rapidly deploy off the road into a line of battle in the thick woods.

Lee sent Ewell down the turnpike against the middle of the Union line and Gouvernor K. Warren's Fifth Corps. Three miles south, on the Plank Road, Gen. A. P. Hill's men engaged Hancock's corps along the Brock Road in an entirely separate engagement. Meade ordered the Sixth Corps onto the Wilderness Road, a minor and less developed road, in order to hook up with Warren's right flank. The orders came down at 11:00 A.M., and the relief corps was "to touch to the left and regulate the advance by the right." Upton moved his men through "the dense pine and nearly impenetrable thickets which met us on every hand." Warren's right flank, the far right end of the Fifth Corps, posted just south of the Orange Turnpike, and Sedgwick's left rested on the turnpike. Sedgwick's right flank rested on thin air, hooked to no other unit, surrounded by dense woods.[6]

As Upton's 2nd Brigade moved to connect with Warren's right, the 95th Pennsylvania held the brigade's far left in position to make the connection. Upton sent his adjutant, Francis Morse, to tell the 95th's commanding officer, Lt. Col. Edward Carroll, to move forward. Two minutes after he left Morse, Carroll stumbled into a group of the enemy and was killed instantly. There were no battle lines, although Upton reported that his left advanced 200 yards ahead of Warren's troops and he felt it important to hold his position there. As the 121st and the 2nd Brigade of the 1st Division came up to strengthen Warren, the lines momentarily stabilized. The 3rd Brigade came up on Upton's right. The left of the Sixth Corps successfully hooked up with Warren's right and closed a dangerous gap between the two corps. The armies joined in a death struggle in the dark forest where regiments and companies disintegrated, re-formed, and fought again. Their commanders lost contact with the troops in the dense woods, leaving pockets of armed men killing each other without supervision or direction.

Delavan Bates wrote thirty years later: "Imagine a body of strong, able-bodied men, three times the entire population of Cooperstown—men, women, and children—armed with guns and bayonets and moving steadily through a dense forest until they meet another of equal numbers, well armed and waiting to receive them with bloody hands and desperate courage." Eventually, the smoke from the overheated muskets hung low in the air. The hot weapons kindled the pine straw, dead leaves, and other debris on the forest floor. The fires that erupted cremated the dead—many of whom were burned beyond recognition. The living, including wounded men, also "perished in the flames, as corpses were found partly consumed." Upton erroneously thought that the Confederates had started the fires.

Nothing more transpired that day, and the regiment immediately began digging entrenchments and throwing up log defenses. That night, the men tried to sleep on their weapons. The cries of the wounded and dying left on the field foretold the fighting and suffering to come in the days ahead and kept the living awake through the night. As John Hartwell tried to sleep, the anguished cries of the wounded—"Oh my god, must I die here?" or "Come and help me off"— foiled his efforts. Isaac Best lay down next to a soldier and only the next morning discovered that he shared his bed with a "crisped corpse." Clinton Beckwith remembered the cries as "something terrible to hear. Some prayed, some cursed, some cried and some asked to be killed and put out of their misery." Rebel soldiers fired on a rescue party in the morning, which beat a hasty retreat but not before the charred corpses of soldiers on both sides were discovered. Under cover of white handkerchiefs, a second attempt to recover the living "succeeded in bringing in some of the wounded."[7]

During the night of May 5–6, Lt. Gen. John B. Gordon and his brigade moved into position opposite Sedgwick. Gordon confronted a situation he later described as astounding and "inconceivable": he had stumbled on the very end of the Union army. Scouts confirmed that there were no skirmishers, pickets, or any other Union forces farther to Sedgwick's right. Gordon himself surveyed the scene on the morning of May 6 as the men of the Union right wing ate breakfast in the woods, sat in their rifle pits, drank coffee, and talked. Gordon's discovery "amazed" and filled him with "confident anticipations of unprecedented victory." Some 400 yards from Sedgwick's unprotected flank, an open field and wood line offered an opportunity to form for an attack on the federal lines.

Gordon asked for permission to attack at daybreak that morning, Friday, May 6. With heavy skirmishing all along the front, Upton's brigade also prepared to make a daylight attack on the Confederate positions. Headquarters later countermanded the order, but the men remained on alert. As indiscriminate firing continued during the day, the 121st busied itself digging and reinforcing rifle pits. "Continually the rain of iron was sweeping over us, men slept on their muskets, and staff officers, with their horses saddled, were constantly on watch," Morse remembered. Much to Gordon's frustration, Ewell and Early mulled over his proposed plan during most of the day. Finally, Robert E. Lee, overriding his two generals, decided that the charge made sense. As dusk began to gather, Gordon realized that the whole day had been wasted.[8]

Late in the day, Adjutant Morse became aware of an "unusual peal of musketry" in the direction of Sedgwick's headquarters and the extreme right of the Union army. It "deepened with a steady choking roll," he wrote. Around 7:00 P.M., Emory Upton got word from Lt. Col. James N. Duffy, the division's inspector general, to hurry two regiments to the extreme right—"that flank of the corps having been turned."

When the word came to assist on the line, half the men were digging trenches and the other half were stacking rifles and preparing dinner. The regiment had drawn fresh beef for rations, and some were making a hasty dinner. Now, the urgent need to come to the aid of their comrades became apparent. They grabbed their equipment, scurrying to follow Duffy. Their beef dinners went untouched. Upton picked the 121st and the 95th Pennsylvania to reinforce the faltering line, and before Olcott "could get his men in hand, they dashed off with this crazy, foolish officer," Francis Morse wrote. Duffy tried to find Olcott, and when he could not, he commandeered the 121st and the 95th Pennsylvania and rode off in great confusion. The responsibility for holding the Union right fell to these two veteran regiments. Racing to the rescue, they received fire from their left and soon became entangled in the undergrowth. As they came into contact with the enemy, they lost all sense of direction.

Clinton Beckwith remembered that the rebels seemed to come from all directions. In the dark, the lines intermingled, with both sides firing in confusion. The rebels fired into the 121st, and the men fired back. For a time, Beckwith found himself behind the Confederate lines, and after an order to surrender, he threw down his weapon and fell on his face, expecting to be hit with a round at any moment. When nothing happened, he jumped up, retrieved his musket, and found his regiment in the dark. In the meantime, Upton finally located his horse and started after them, leaving the remainder of the brigade in the hands of a subordinate. As he approached the front lines, retreating federals began to break on several points into a disorganized run to the rear. Upton valiantly rallied half of them, holding the right with fragments of several different commands 300 yards to the rear. Ultimately, the command and control of the two regiments broke down completely.[9]

In the melee and the gathering gloom, Olcott attempted to reunite his regiment. In his first real test as a commander, he decided to ride to the front "to ascertain the position of affairs." Sam Kelley and Lansing Paine joined him as all three attempted to rally the men to meet the growing rebel threat. A Confederate sharpshooter spotted Olcott, coolly pulled the trigger, and with one shot brought him down with a bullet to his forehead. Miraculously, the round fractured his skull but did not kill him. As he fell from his horse and attempted to gather his wits and escape with Kelley and Paine, all three men were captured by the advancing rebels. Twenty others were taken with them, including Sixth Corps brigade commanders Gen. Truman Seymour and Gen. Alexander Shaler. "They had completely flanked us," Kelley wrote. "And in trying to form our line to the right, I was taken prisoner by the enemy who were directly in our rear." Kelley got permission to stay with Olcott, which he did "until the morning of the 7th." Kelley carried Olcott "about a mile and a half through the woods to a hospital and slept by his side during the night."

Phillip Goodman found Olcott's riderless horse, and as he led him to safety, he bumped into the returning Clinton Beckwith. The *New York Tribune* picked up Olcott's story detailing his wounding and capture and tried, without success, to discern Olcott's fate. The *Cherry Valley Gazette* picked up the *Tribune*'s story for its readers on June 15, indicating that more than a month later, his whereabouts and condition were still unknown. The *Tribune* profusely detailed Olcott's military career and his rapid ascent to regimental command. In a closing statement that raised the eyebrows of most of his men, the paper declared that Olcott personified a soldier of the highest order. With unabashed puffery, the paper said it could not understand why no reports of the missing included his name, "for no officer in his regiment was more loved by his soldiers or honored by its officers."[10]

Others from the 121st were nearly taken in the confusion. George Teel barely escaped capture "with everything but [his] gun, one boot," and his kepi. John Hartwell and Lt. Hiram Van Scoy of Company F, the only commissioned officer in the immediate area, rescued the regimental colors and literally rallied around them. John Slocum remarked that he had never worked so hard: "cut, cut all day." He knew that the federals were "getting the worst" of it. That night, he got lost in the woods and stayed there all night. The next day, he recounted loading 51 ambulances and 60 army wagons with wounded. Major Galpin and others caught up with the men who had the colors as they continued the fight well into the darkness. Galpin now commanded the regiment.[11]

The 121st and the Sixth Corps barely stemmed the rebel tide. At nightfall, the battle subsided. Darkness allowed commanders to reunite their disorganized and scattered commands. As sporadic fighting continued, Gordon's plan partially succeeded: the fading light halted his effort. Around 10:00 P.M., Upton fell back near the Wilderness Tavern to fortifications between the turnpike and Orange Plank Road. James McCurry told his diary: "The Ball opened at day light—hard fighting all day—we are falling back toward Fredericksburg." The brigade and the 121st were only a few yards away from the enemy lines but were able to disengage without loss. Near the Wilderness Tavern, the 121st quickly threw up earthworks to fend off another assault. Gordon felt that the attack would have completely routed the army, much as Jackson's attack had done a year before on nearly the same field—if only Ewell or Early had allowed him to attack earlier. It infuriated him that both superiors questioned his soldiering. Had they not, he might have turned the Union's right flank and rolled into Grant's headquarters at the Wilderness Tavern.[12]

The battle of the Wilderness culminated in a draw as both sides pulled back in the smoky forest. Rather than retreat as predecessors had, Grant continued to move south the next day—a move that surprised and pleased the men in the ranks. George Teel wrote that when the fighting subsided, the 121st threw up rifle pits "under heavy fire. Our lines were attacked on several points, the rebs were repulsed with heavy losses, we changed position that night." The next day, May 8, was much the same: "We charged the rebels and drove them two miles, with heavy losses on both sides." The 2nd Brigade suffered severely, with 111 casualties. The 121st took 73, most of them captured or missing.[13]

Dennis Dewey was taken prisoner after being wounded in his right leg. After the war, he wrote, "The enemy chopped off my good right leg, and I came very near to death's door." As the armies raced to the open fields around Spotsylvania, Sam Kelley, Lansing Paine, Egbert Olcott, and others were marched to Orange Court House, where the officers were allowed to sleep on the floor inside, the enlisted men outside. The next day, May 9, they were placed into a "nasty cattle car" and sent south to Gordonsville. There, the prisoners were placed in a floorless, "dirty shed" for safekeeping and were then moved by rail to Lynchburg—the officers in passenger cars, the enlisted in cattle cars. After several officers were caught trying to escape, all were placed in cattle cars en route to Danville.[14]

After a long and exhausting train ride through the rest of Virginia, through North Carolina, to Columbia, South Carolina, and to Augusta, Georgia, the prisoners found themselves at the end of the month on the fairgrounds of Macon, Georgia, a southernmost post for captured Union officers. The enlisted men were sent farther south to Andersonville, and many did not return to the regiment until Lee surrendered. Dewey went to Richmond and claimed that he had been imprisoned at Libby, a prison usually reserved for officers. Enlisted prisoners sent to Richmond were kept on Belle Isle. When Sam Kelley was captured, his captors escorted him into a room where they searched him, relieving him of $10. With 100 others, he joined 1,000 prisoners from the Army of the Potomac and Sherman's western troops penned in a small area. The new arrivals were greeted with cries of "Fresh fish," "Keep your hands out of his pockets," "Don't put that louse on him," and "Hold on to your haversack." Once the pleasantries were dispensed with, the earlier occupants, with a "grand rush," swamped the newcomers for the latest news from the front. Kelley, with meager rations and no blankets for cover, slept on a rubber blanket in the open air. Lansing Paine sold his watch for $100 in Confederate money. At month's end, cold and lonely, he could only think of home, his family, and any "joy if I am ever permitted" when they were reunited again.[15]

Meanwhile, as the troops on both sides prepared to move south again, the 121st learned of a casualty that occurred on the other side of the field late in the morning of May 6. The news brought to a conclusion a story that reached back to the 1862 New York gubernatorial election. The old lion—Maj. Gen. James Samuel Wadsworth, Governor Seymour's opponent who went on to serve admirably in the Union army—lay mortally wounded. When the fifty-seven-year-old Wadsworth ran for governor as a Republican, he maintained his status in the army after his friends and supporters importuned him to take on the campaign, and many men in the 121st voted for him. On May 6, he commanded a division of Warren's Fifth Corps, and in leading a charge to repel yet another rebel assault, he was shot in the head, the bullet lodging in his brain. Taken to a Confederate field hospital, he died in his sleep on a dirty floor two days later. The Confederates buried him on the battlefield. His body was eventually recovered and reburied in his hometown of Geneseo, New York.

On another part of the field, in Burnside's Ninth Corps were brand-new U.S. Colored Troops and their new commanders. In Brig. Gen. Edward Ferraro's 4th Division were two brigades with seven new colored regiments. Within the 1st Brigade, the newly minted colonel Delavan Bates commanded the 30th USCT, and his comrade Lt. Col. Hiram Seymour Hall commanded the 43rd USCT. In the 2nd Brigade, Cleaveland Campbell commanded the 23rd USCT. All three commanders were alumni of the 121st and the school of Upton. Their men were minimally involved in the Wilderness, playing a supporting role. Many doubted their ability to fight, and they were detailed to do little more than guard supply trains and ambulances. They had trained for only a few weeks when they were ordered to report to Burnside's corps.

The Salient (Muleshoe) at Spotsylvania

In the evening of May 7, the army moved south, with Upton's 2nd Brigade leading the 1st Division. Twelve hours later, Field's division in Anderson's (formerly Longstreet's) corps in Lee's army led the Confederates toward Spotsylvania. The crossroads at Spotsylvania were the gateway to Richmond, and the army that held the intersection controlled the road. Grant did not want Lee to get to Richmond and move on Maj. Gen. Ben Butler on the Peninsula. Above all, he intended to interpose himself between Richmond and Lee's army. Warren's Fifth Corps and Hancock's Second Corps moved south on Brock Road. Simultaneously, the Sixth Corps took the Chancellorsville-Fredericksburg

Upton at the Salient, a sketch by Alfred A. Waud. Courtesy of the Library of Congress.

road south, turning onto the Piney Branch Road past the Piney Branch Church. With many missing comrades rejoining the 121st, the regiment stopped for a hurried breakfast before moving off with the rest of the corps. The fate of the 121st's commander, Egbert Olcott, remained unknown. Breakfast rumors had him dead; others told that he survived his head wound but fell into rebel hands. Whether Olcott was dead or alive, Maj. Henry Galpin acted in his stead.

The morning dawned hot and oppressive. As it swung south on the Piney Branch Road, the 121st found itself on part of the old Chancellorsville battle-field. One of the men discovered a human skull, presumably from the previous year's horrendous battle, and as the regiment moved down the road in forma-tion, the men amused themselves by kicking the skull as they marched. Some speculated whether they handled a Yankee or a rebel skull, and some wondered if the original owner would mind if they continued to amuse themselves with it. Eventually, they grew tired of the game, and one of the men "threw it in the leaves by the roadside." The skull and the horseplay reminded Beckwith of the small symbols of the "horrors of war, and how easily men became hard-ened" by the rigors of the task before them. John Hartwell's comments were to the point: "We passed over Hooker's battlefield of breastworks and bones.

Human skeletons were seen at any point especially skulls. I saw three in the road."[16]

As they marched toward Spotsylvania, the men of the 121st could hear the firing in the deep forests off toward their destination. Shortly after noon on May 8, the regiment converged on the rear of the Sixth Corps as it followed the Brock Road. Evidence of recent fighting abounded. The wounded occupied every available shelter. The woods were on fire, and many of the veterans who had recently reenlisted in Joe Bartlett's brigade of seven veteran regiments were among the dead and dying who were being consumed by the flames. "It was a horrible sight, enough to make the most hardened soldier shudder." The regiment fell into line of battle that evening around 6:30. On the next day, May 9, the brigade moved to the left of the Spotsylvania Road. From then until the afternoon of May 10, as they received incoming artillery fire and sustained several casualties, the 121st watched and waited.[17]

The federals lost the race to Spotsylvania. Longstreet's corps, now being led by Maj. Gen. Richard Anderson, reached the site first and entrenched east and west of the Brock Road. Both sides poured onto the battlefield for two days, May 8 and 9, reinforcing the initial troops. Both sides also entrenched, but the Confederates built a large salient out from their lines in the shape of a horseshoe, or, as the Confederates named it, a muleshoe. The salient's outer line was simple but effective. The nose of the muleshoe pointed due north. On its eastern and western sides, small trees were cut down and placed lengthwise on the ground forming a wall, or breastworks. Behind the trees, the Confederates dug trenches some 3 feet deep, throwing the dirt from the excavations on top of the logs in front. Behind the main line were a series of trenches and complex, interconnecting earthen works. This trench warfare, the precursor of World War I combat, allowed a man to stand upright in the bottom of the trench and fire through openings in the log wall. The sides of a defensive position such as the muleshoe were vulnerable if not heavily supported with artillery. With a straight battle line, an assault could only come on one's front. In the case of a salient, a frontal assault on one of the sides, if strong enough, would crumple the pocket, turn the inside of the formation into a killing zone, and rout the defenders. Artillery would be a key component in keeping such a fragile "bulge" from collapsing. Lee relied on both infantry and artillery to keep his line intact.

During May 9 and 10, Grant probed first one and then the other Confederate flank, to no avail. On the morning of May 9, Francis Morse decided to grab a "few leisure minutes," and he "sat down to eat something." Within moments, Maj. Charles A. Whittier of Sedgwick's staff rode up with the news that Sedgwick had been shot in the face. As Whittier went for an ambulance, he reported Sedgwick's dire situation. Morse had just left Sedgwick and Gen. Martin T. McMahon, his chief of staff. Sedgwick, jovial, avuncular, and well liked by his men, had joked that morning with McMahon as the Union troops about 100 yards ahead of them finished work on their rifle pits. Sedgwick chided them for ducking and weaving and wondered aloud what they would do when the real firing commenced. After all, Sedgwick said, "they couldn't hit an elephant at this distance." With that, he was hit with "a dull, heavy stroke," wrote McMahon. Sedgwick fell on McMahon, knocking them both to the ground. Word came to the men that a Confederate sharpshooter had shot John Sedgwick— ironically and fatefully, just after Sedgwick gave an Upton-like lecture on ducking to his men. The command of the Sixth Corps became of immediate concern. Sedgwick had always favored Horatio Wright to replace him, and Meade quickly agreed with that choice. That afternoon, the men of the Sixth were summoned to heroic duty under their new corps commander, Wright.[18]

Most of the men were distraught when they heard of Sedgwick's death. A compassionate leader who showed concern for the men he led, Sedgwick had been a favorite of his troops. By contrast, crusty John Kidder, a compassionate husband and father, showed little sympathy when men in command were killed in the line of duty. He seemed to believe that the ill fate visited on an unfortunate recipient redounded somehow to his own fault or a character flaw. When Confederate riflemen at Gettysburg had cut down John Reynolds, one of the most respected men in the army, Kidder harshly remarked that any general who led his men "as Reynolds did and have not more judgment had better be out of the service. I think that the service is much better off without them. Poor fellow, he lost his life by it." Sedgwick's death upset him. He felt that he "threw his life away. He had no business out on the skirmish line," he wrote his wife.[19]

Several officers might be given credit for the idea of using a massed attacking column rather than a traditional single-line attack on the salient. It is unclear who conceived the notion to bunch up several regiments in a columnar assault on the heavily entrenched Confederate lines. Wright, Russell, Upton, and Randall McKenzie all played a role in the preparation. In the end, it appears that a committee boiled several ideas into a consensus. On the night of May 9, McMahon met at army headquarters with Wright, Grant, Meade, and several other high-ranking officers. Shortly after everyone assembled, Meade told Wright that he had ordered a general attack along the entire line the next day at 4:00 P.M. According to McMahon, Meade hatched the plan to attack in columns consisting of twelve to fifteen handpicked regiments from his corps. Meade closed the deal when he pledged that Brig. Gen. Gershom Mott's division from Burnside's corps and a part of the Fifth Corps would support the special column's advance. Wright rode off to his headquarters, where he promptly put General Russell of Rappahannock Station fame to work on the details of the attack. Russell in turn chose Emory Upton to lead the assaulting column.

The morning of Tuesday, May 10, broke warm and humid. At daylight, the firing commenced, to continue nonstop for six hours. The log-constructed

Gen. Horatio Wright, who took command of the Sixth Corps after Gen. John Sedgwick was killed during the Overland campaign. Courtesy of the Library of Congress

breastworks on both sides shot splinters of wood in every direction as rebel fire tried to hit the federals behind them. A few balls made it through the thick logs. The 121st's regimental battle flag, with its latest victory at Rappahannock Station proudly emblazoned on it, took a direct hit by Confederate fire. Another missile hit Judson Chapin's musket, bending it in half toward John Tucker, who was near him. Other than it being frightening, neither man was hurt. For the remainder of the day, most of the men remained pinned down by the constant fire. Dr. Holt dealt with the wounded, who soon began to overwhelm his small aid station in the rear. Three times, he moved back out of range of the screaming shells. Around 3:00 P.M., word filtered down to the troops that a frontal assault on the rebel muleshoe was planned.[20]

That morning, Upton had gone to Russell's headquarters, where Wright and Martin McMahon presented him with the list of twelve handpicked regiments. As Upton carefully studied the list, Wright told him, "You will assault the enemy's entrenchments in four lines—Captain McKenzie will show you the point of attack—Mott's division will support you." McMahon then spoke: "Upton, what do you think of that for a command?" When Upton raised his head from the paper, "his face lit up with satisfaction." Upton replied, "I golly [sic], Mac, that is a splendid command; they are the best men in this army." McMahon said, "Upton, you are to lead those men upon the enemy's works this afternoon, and if you do not carry them you are not expected to come back; but if you do carry them, I am authorized to say to you that you will get your stars." Upton responded confidently and enthusiastically: "Mac, I will carry those works; if I don't, I won't come back." McMahon then laid out the rest of the plan, promising support on both flanks. It was Upton's job to punch a hole in the Confederate lines, and Mott would be right behind him exploiting the opening by rolling up the enemy's flank at a right angle.[21]

As Upton rode off to assemble his command, he stated, "Mac, I'll carry those works; they cannot repulse those regiments." Earlier that day, artillery wizard Randall Mackenzie, of the U.S. Corps of Engineers, had surveyed the ground over which Upton's attack would occur. That afternoon, Upton consulted with Mackenzie, who showed him the point of attack, the nature of the ground the regiments were to traverse, and the earthworks that the rebels constructed. Near the Scott House, "about half a mile to the left of the Spotsylvania road," Upton concentrated on his new command. His troops were to charge through an open field parallel with and on either side of a primitive wood road leading 200 yards from the Union tree line to the heavily fortified rebel entrenchments. They were to assemble in the cover of the woods on either side of the road and eventually strike the western face of the salient. After both Russell and Upton examined the terrain before them, Upton brought all the regimental commanders to the point of departure and reviewed the "work before them." The topographical realities of an attack over open fields with twelve regiments, requiring them to squeeze into a small breach in the reinforced defenses, dictated the columnar assault. A two- and three-line attack would have been impossible.

Of the chosen regiments, the 121st New York, the 5th Maine, and the 96th Pennsylvania were in the first line of the column. The 49th Pennsylvania, the 6th Maine, and the 5th Wisconsin manned the second line. The 43rd New York, the 77th New York, and the 119th Pennsylvania occupied the third line, and the fourth line consisted of the 2nd, 5th, and 6th Vermont. Seven of the regiments were from Russell's brigade and five from Upton's. The road divided the advancing column, with four regiments on the right and eight on the left. Each of the four lines of three regiments received a different assignment. On the right and in the first row, the 121st and the 96th Pennsylvania were instructed to immediately turn to their right when the walls were breached and charge the battery. On the left, the 5th Maine's instructions were to "change front to the left and open an enfilading fire" on the enemy in their front. The second line prepared to "halt at the works, and open fire to the front if necessary." The third line, held in reserve, was to lie down behind the second line. The fourth line would remain at the line of departure at wood's edge. All men were ordered to load their weapons and fix bayonets; only the first line capped its muskets.

Upton returned to his headquarters and roused the napping Francis Morse with the words "Wake up adjutant, and mount your horse." Morse did not have to ask any questions, as he saw the assembled regiments moving past him without knapsacks.[22]

The instructions were dismally clear: Upton ordered that no one was to stop to care for a wounded comrade. As the troops moved into the assembly area in preparation to launch the attack, Upton rode the line with Major Galpin and Adjutant Morse as the three reviewed sketches of the field and rehearsed their roles in the attack on the muleshoe. Upton stationed himself to the right of his old regiment at the head of the attacking column in order to command the entire detachment. When they moved off, the "officers were instructed to repeat the command 'forward' constantly from the commencement of the charge till the works were carried." With an attack traversing 200 yards of open field, it did not require a genius in military strategy to understand the danger and the risk confronting the regiment. Dorr Devendorf knew he would not survive the charge. He and his tent mate, Clinton Beckwith, pledged that the survivor would gather the other's belongings and respectfully ship them home. Devendorf confided in Beckwith that he "dreaded the first volley, they have so good a shot at us."[23]

At 6:00 P.M., the artillery barrage ended, signaling Upton to move out. He had no time to confer with Mott and coordinate the attack. After he formed the lines into columns, he shook hands with Russell and his staff and with his own staff, wishing everyone well. Then Upton mounted his horse and rode to the center of the entire detachment. The light began to fade as the men all stepped off. In a "clear full" voice, Upton gave the commands: "Attention!" "Forward double-quick!" "March!" As Morse remembered, "The clear voice of Upton rang out: 'Attention! Forward!'" The order to move out rippled up the ranks to the first line. The heavy, humid air grew hazy from the skirmishers' firing. Beckwith felt his "gorge rise" and his "stomach and intestines shrink together in a knot, and a thousand things rushed through" his mind. As they moved past the 65th New York skirmishers, Beckwith "realized the terrible peril I was to encounter." Premonitions, based now on solid recent experiences, prevailed everywhere. Beckwith looked into the faces around him, and "they told a tale of expected death. Pulling my cap down over my eyes," he wrote later, "I stepped out, the extreme man on the left of our regiment."[24]

When the officers commanded "Forward," the lines of blue-uniformed men began to move slowly at first. But as the adrenalin and nerves began to kick in, the impulse to run and to scream at the top of their lungs overtook them— despite orders to the contrary. Once the skirmish lines were cleared, the race began. "Away we went," John Lovejoy wrote, "with cheers that made the wood ring above the musketry." According to John Kidder, Upton trotted his horse right "up to the enemy's works" just in advance of his own lines. There wasn't another horseman on the field.[25]

On the parapets ahead, small white puffs of smoke appeared, followed at once by the sight of men in the blue ranks falling at random. "The rebs poured the balls into us like hail," Lovejoy said. "Many fell before we reached the works." Some of the attackers fired at the protected enemy, thereby losing any advantage of firing for effect once they reached the entrenched rebels. Lovejoy, positioned on the right of Company G, came out of the charge unscathed with six other men. One shot came so close to his head that it blistered his ear and "the force of the air" knocked him down, probably saving his life. Once the "terrible front and flank fire" was endured, the parapets were breached, and there, intense hand-to-hand combat ensued. All the men in the first line to make it over the wall were killed with shots through the head. The rebels sat in their rifle pits with their bayonets fixed and held upright, hoping to impale the attacking hordes. Lt. James Johnston mounted the parapet just as a rebel thrust a bayonet into his thigh. He focused on the offending rebel with his sword, and when the Confederate asked for mercy, Johnston granted it, sending him to the rear as a prisoner. Other Union men, seeing the fate of those ahead of them, held their muskets at arm's length and fired downward; some used their bayoneted guns as spears and threw them into the mass of Confederates below. One of the leading officers mounted the parapet, "shouted 'come on men!' and pitched forward and disappeared, shot."

The men from the 121st followed on, using their weapons as spears and clubs. Several received bayonet wounds. Thomas Hassett and George Pierson were both wounded as they attacked the first line of breastworks. Pierson helped Hassett off the field. Upton boldly "jumped his horse over both pits and went down past the battery with us." The men pushed on to the left and right as they executed the battle plan perfectly. The Confederate battery to the right managed to fire one load of canister when Upton ordered his men to charge it, but the fired-up regiment easily took the battery. The troops pressed on, capturing the second line behind the battery "until there was nothing in our front, except some tents near the roadside, and no firing upon us of any magnitude," Beckwith remembered.[26]

They had breached the salient. Devendorf survived the charge, and he and Beckwith and others looked around for debris to spike, or disable, the guns if they should have to leave them behind. That done, the men moved on over the last line of entrenchments. By that point, the rebels had regrouped, and they began counterattacking, supporting their beleaguered comrades on the front line. Upton immediately recognized the danger as he halted his horse and saw the rebels closing in on the left flank. The cruel irony did not escape Upton. Mott's division and Burnside's Ninth Corps were supposed to rescue the federal troops. The Confederate lines were "broken and an opening had been made" for Mott's division to support the left, but as Upton mournfully wrote in his report later, "it did not arrive." Instead, the rebels began pouring back into the salient, and the bluecoats began taking serious casualties.

Inside the muleshoe, Upton's command slammed into Brig. Gen. George P. Dole's Georgian brigade of Maj. Gen. Robert Rodes's division and pushed it nearly 100 yards to the rear. Gordon's leading brigade—Johnston's North Carolinians—re-formed and made a direct assault on the federals. John Gordon's brigade also leaped into the breach. The wounded from both sides were in the no-man's-land between the two lines and were now receiving fire from both sides. Henry Wood, a drummer, was pressed into service as a stretcher-bearer to help bring the wounded off the field. He described a "perfect rain of shot and shell for three hours." The young Wood had a slight build, and with too little food in the previous few days coupled with the intense stress, he permanently injured his back and legs. He wondered how he survived. Many enemy soldiers were shot in the back by their own men as they surrendered to the federals. The survivors were moved to the rear by their captors. The lost momentum irritated Upton, who could do nothing but give the order to fall back to the first line of pits for cover—a command he gave as "deliberately as though we were on the parade grounds drilling." The battle plans were discarded in favor of the strategy of "every man for himself" and doing anything to hold the ground already taken.[27]

Dr. Holt, several yards to the rear, ministered to the wounded, who walked off or were carried off the field. He expressed surprise that he had not been killed himself. As he cared for one wounded man, a second round found the man as Holt held him in his arms, killing him instantly. Meanwhile, Upton moved back outside the perimeter, intent on bringing up the Vermonters who had been held in reserve. But instead, he found them, along with the 65th New York skirmishers, heavily engaged in the battle on their own. He asked for volunteers to rush a second battery and then, getting no response, asked, "Is there none of my old regiment here?" A few of the 121st were there, but those who could continue were out of ammunition. Upton, still under the impression that his order for the last line of three regiments to be held in reserve was observed, rode back and found the fourth line already committed. Years later, he wrote, "You know what confusion arises in every assault. The orders communicated before the charge were in the main carried out, but the twelve regiments had become so mixed up that there was not a single unit under my control." As darkness fell, under unrelenting fire from the rebel lines, Upton found that his hold on the ground already taken was untenable. He conferred with Russell at woods' edge, and Russell concurred in his assessment of the situation and ordered a pullback. Upton wrote the orders to withdraw and sent them along the line with Capt. Frank Gorton of the 121st. Thereafter, "under cover of darkness, the works were evacuated, the regiments returning to their former camps." The Union attack along the entire front had failed. Conflicting orders to Upton to "pile more men" in and to retreat probably caused the deaths of several men inside the rebel works.[28]

On his way back to the jumping-off point for the aborted charge, Beckwith came upon a wounded man and carried him to safety on his back. When he reached the trenches that the 121st had dug behind the line of woods, he found them occupied by the 95th Pennsylvania. He searched in vain among the dead and the dying for his tent mate Devendorf, backtracking the ground over which he had recently charged and retreated. When he realized the futility of his search, Beckwith "sat down in the woods" and focused on his "desolation and misery" and "cried like a little child." Devendorf had been killed, Henry Galpin was wounded, and Capt. Thomas Adams in Beckwith's company and a good friend of Adelbert Reed was wounded in the shoulder. Adams was discharged in October.

Captain Butts and Lt. Silas Pierce were dead. Butts had been wounded in the initial charge across the open field "while leading his men in an assault on the rifle pits of the enemy." As his comrades helped him to the rear, he was hit again and killed instantly. In the face of withering enemy fire, the men left his body on the field, with the hope of retrieving him after the battle. That was never accomplished. His grieving family and friends wrote after the battle that it was "impossible to obtain his body at that time and it is extremely doubtful whether we shall ever be able to." After South Mountain and Antietam, Butts had finally received his coveted commission. He rose through the ranks quickly and made captain in April 1864, just three weeks before the army left the winter camps. He had quickly adapted to army life from student life and began to enjoy it. Rather than succumbing to the temptations around him, he felt that he had been strengthened and now lived "closer to Jesus here, than at college." But the risks were never far from his mind as the army engaged in one fight after another. At Salem Church, he momentarily took over Captain Wendell's company when Wendell fell mortally wounded. Butts wrote home a week before he died, as the Sixth Corps left winter camp. He told his family that "only God" knew his fate but added that with "all his faults," he maintained a belief in the protection of the almighty—"God be with you all," he signed off, "Good bye, Charlie."[29]

Francis Foote, a first lieutenant in Company I, was struck with a minié ball through his thigh, which "bro't me down," he wrote his mother. He was wounded while attempting to turn the captured guns on the enemy within the first few minutes of the attack. He lay on the field until he was taken by rebels to a rebel hospital. The Confederate surgeons discovered that his bone had shattered, and they amputated his leg. By the end of the week, he had arrived in Libby Prison, where he tried to get as comfortable as possible. A few of the missing troops straggled in later. Captain Cronkite was wounded with five other officers. He and Lt. Edward Johnson were wounded simultaneously as they mounted the parapet. Johnson died later that day. Captain Kidder, by virtue of seniority, took charge of the regiment—a position normally held by a lieutenant colonel or a full colonel. And the wounded remained where they fell. "The woods were full of these unfortunate creatures, and sounded all night with their cries and groans."

In the light of the new day, the enormity of the army's losses became horribly obvious. Up and down the depleted lines, the thinned ranks told a story of loss that was only hinted at Salem Church one year earlier. "We were filled with sorrow for our lost comrades, and deep forebodings for the future," Beckwith remembered. "A splendid regiment had been nearly destroyed, without adequate results." The cold rain, Sedgwick's death, and the attack's failure cast a pall over the regiment. The bungled attack put Beckwith in mind of Tennyson's famous lines from the "Charge of the Light Brigade": "Not tho' the soldiers knew some one had blundered: / Theirs not to make reply, theirs not to reason why, theirs but to do or die."[30]

The regiment suffered dearly. According to the assistant adjutant, Joe Heath, the regiment had started out with 446 men and 15 officers "and came out today with 4 officers and not [a] hundred men." With the heat of the battle still on him, he reported, "I have just taken the census, and find we have just 94 men today, May 13th." There were 7 men left in Company A, which started the day with 56. Company G reported 11 men able for duty. Sgt. Eli Oakes, twice wounded, was in charge of the company. Hometown papers erroneously reported that Sam Kelley and Frank Foote had been killed in action but at the same time held out hope that they had survived. John Slocum, exhausted by his exertions, ministered to the wounded: he counted 218 ambulances sent out by May 13. Company E suffered outsized casualties. The unit had charged with 27 men and 2 officers. Joseph Birch, who had joined the regiment from the 32nd New York, noted that after the charge, "there were only two of us—not enough to make a stack of guns so we ran our bayonets in the ground." Four more returned to the company the next day, bringing the total to six. Heath was optimistic that Richmond would be taken soon, and the news of Sherman's "doings" in Georgia encouraged him. "This has been the greatest battle ever fought on this continent."[31]

Cpl. Dolphus Sayles was gone, counted among the missing and presumed dead. He had written to his father a year earlier, longing to return home to help him in the farm fields. He wished the cruel war would soon end: "Then the poor soldier can come home once more." His last diary entry, dated Monday, May 9, and the previous day's as well—the last two of his life—dissolved in the unrelenting rain. There were no entries for May 10, 11, and 12. The entry for May 13 began, "Found this diary near rebel." William Clark of the 14th New

Jersey retrieved the diary, and for years, it remained that of an unidentified sergeant from the 121st in Company D.[32]

Pvt. Jared Fuller of Company G, from Middlefield and an only son, was killed in the attack. He was absent without leave earlier in the war and was reduced in the ranks from corporal to private because he went home to visit his dying sister. She died eight days after he returned to the regiment from her bedside. Thirty-seven-year-old George Drake, a recent draftee from Otsego County, was another casualty. He had befriended Norman Herdman, with whom he bunked. Although Drake received far more dollars to fight for the Union than Herdman had, the latter grudgingly allowed that Drake went into "soldiering just as at everything else, with great vigor." But Herdman wondered if Drake would have "it" once he tasted battle. Drake was killed inside the salient on May 10.[33]

The mood continued to be dark. Commanders praised the 121st for its bravery and its tenacious and flawless execution of the battle plan despite the lack of success. Blame for its failure clearly lay with others—Mott, Burnside, Grant, Russell, and Wright. Upton did the job assigned to him. He called the attack a "complete success." His command traversed "two lines of formidable entrenchments, and made a break at least half a mile long," he wrote. "Had fresh troops, in good order, been at hand, the enemy must have been badly beaten." Mott's nearly impossible task called for his troops to traverse the Confederate open ground, a virtual killing field, in order to come to Upton's aid. Upton never understood what happened to Mott. Several observers blamed Mott's failure on the "demon rum." Once again, Isaac Best had it on good authority that Mott was drunk. The Vermonters who were in the last line were duly impressed with Upton. They had not been led by him before, but now, they told John Kidder that "there never was such a splendid man and officer as General Upton."[34]

Before the engagement, General McMahon and others had promised Upton his star if he could successfully lead twelve handpicked regiments against the Confederate entrenchments at the muleshoe. But that evening, McMahon found a despondent Upton brooding over the day's events. McMahon told him how impressed he was with Upton's loyalty and fondness for his old regiment as well as his new brigade command. According to McMahon, he himself facilitated the presentation of Upton's first star. He scouted up a pair of brigadier general's shoulder straps with single stars, and the next morning, with stars and paperwork in hand, he approached Upton. After reminding Upton that if he lived he was to earn his stars, McMahon produced the straps and handed them to the incredulous young commander, who at first thought he was joking. McMahon delighted in Upton's joy. Upton told him that the men in his command would be glad to hear that their work was not in vain.

Whatever role McMahon played in making Emory Upton a brigadier general, it was probably not as grand as he described it. General Grant had received presidential authority to "promote officers on the field for special acts of gallantry," and he conferred the rank of brigadier general on Upton "on the spot." Grant understood that Upton and his regiments had carried the works but that "a lack in others of the spirit and dash possessed by him lost it." Grant also remembered that Upton was wounded in the assault.

The reasons for the promotion were "gratifying" to Upton, especially since he did not exert political influence to get it. He knew that War Department records would mention his performance for "gallant and distinguished services"—a record that would "help him for life." He was elated that everyone, even his enemies, acknowledged the fact that he "fairly earned it [the promotion]." It was only the beginning; he "had not yet ceased to aspire." To his sister, he wrote, "I shall not be content until I get a division, and time will bring that about." Despite the fact that he had tried to earn his stars through political influence, he actually won them the old-fashioned way—through his own performance on the field of battle.[35]

The Bloody Angle

Once again, Grant tried to assault the muleshoe, this time with a larger force. He believed that Upton's columnar attack on the western face was a prototype for success. By using 20,000 troops during the second attempt, he felt he could break Lee's back. Grant determined that a larger force could successfully hit the salient on its apex and 250 yards on either side of it—a decision that would forever name the area "the bloody angle." On the morning of May 11, Grant sent his famous telegram to Lincoln promising to fight it out on this line if it took all summer. Conflicting stories concerning Lee's mind-set that day portrayed him as either expecting another flanking movement from Grant or anticipating that Grant would abandon Spotsylvania and move on toward Fredericksburg. His scouts reported that the federal troops in front of them were gone. Under the assumption that Grant had moved on, Lee removed the artillery that had been so essential in supporting the infantry's defense two days before. Meanwhile, during the night of May 11–12, Grant decided that Hancock's entire Second Corps could do the job with Burnside on his left, Wright's Sixth Corps to his right, and Warren's Fifth Corps on the far right flank. The Sixth Corps moved all over the field through the night.

By 8:00 the next morning, the corps and the 121st had halted in a pine grove as the 152nd New York passed nearby. Briefly, the regiments stopped and swapped information from the other side of the field. In a driving rain that had shown no sign of abating since the previous afternoon, the men of the 121st struggled to cook pork and boil coffee. Men, equipment, animals, and weapons were drenched. Word reached them that a Union attack on the salient had begun at 4:00 that morning. After a long night of positioning his men rather than retreating as Lee thought, Hancock had his command drive in the Confederate pickets near the Landrum House, and then he attacked the salient once again with a larger force. The rain fell without letting up all day, and the lowering skies seemed to be an omen of the slaughter going on in the trenches below.

At first, Hancock's early morning attack with Brig. Gen. Francis Barlow and Maj. Gen. David Birney's divisions succeeded in capturing Gen. Edward Johnson's entire division as its men were just rousing themselves from sleep. Three thousand rebels, including thirty stands of colors, two generals, and twenty of the guns that remained from the assault on May 10, were taken. The 121st cheered the news. The federal strategy was simple and straightforward: based on Upton's partial success two days earlier, Grant massed a large body of men and hurled them at an entrenched enemy behind reinforced fortifications. Unfortunately, no one had learned the hard lesson of Upton's attack two days before—that a large body of men would soon become unmanageable because of the tight spaces in which they found themselves once they hit the rebel entrenchments. As Norton Galloway of the 95th Pennsylvania wrote later, "The great difficulty was in the narrow limits of the Angle, around which we were fighting, which precluded the possibility of getting more than a limited number into action at once. At one time our ranks were crowded in some parts four deep by reinforcements." Tragically, the Union soldiers abruptly stopped their advance to gather souvenirs and prisoners. Lee took advantage of their momentary loss of focus and the lull in the fighting. The Confederates recovered and regrouped, and suddenly, the slaughter became worse than that of the May 10 attack or any previous action experienced by either side. In the words of one witness, the battle was the "fiercest, most stubbornly contested and most deadly of any fought during the entire campaign."[36]

By 6:00 A.M., the Confederates had regained nearly all the lost ground. Grant reacted by pouring in more men. The Sixth Corps and the 121st led the resurgence just as the Second Corps was repulsed. During the night, Upton had moved to the army's left. When Hancock's attack faltered, the Sixth Corps went to support him. Complying with his orders, Upton retraced his steps. He set his men in motion north toward the Brown House as he attempted to position his forces on the army's right wing. For the next hour, Upton moved his troops in a circuitous march to the hottest part of the battle. He marched his brigade within 400 yards of the Brown House, at which point it turned to the right. It emerged from the rear in the vicinity of the Landrum House. Upton's brigade occupied the rear of the Sixth Corps near the Shelton House, opposite the western face of the salient where he had launched his attack two days before.

Lieutenant Colonel Duffy met Upton as he came out of the woods with his troops: "We are going to lose the day," he told Upton. "The battery you captured on the 10th is now firing to the right, and instead of attacking them, the corps is moving off to the left." With no one in command of the melee in front of the salient, Upton moved his troops into a swale for relief from the incessant fire coming from behind the rebel works. There, he found the different commands intermingled and confused. He engaged in a useless argument with Col. Joseph Parsons of the 10th Massachusetts and Col. Oliver Edwards commanding the 37th Massachusetts as to where troops should and should not be placed.[37]

In frustration, Upton, once his brigade had settled into position, ordered the 95th Pennsylvania to move over the first crest in an attempt to get inside the Angle and to the second line of pits that his command had captured two days earlier. But a delay caused the attack to falter momentarily. Upton told the 95th that when they broke through, they were to lie down and fire from the prone position. Galloway wondered if it could hold on until the rest of the brigade got there. The 121st, the 5th Maine, the 96th Pennsylvania, and eventually the entire 1st Division were thrown in to hold the Union position. The troops huddled together in natural swales, some of which ran dangerously perpendicular to the salient; others that were parallel provided a modicum of protection. The heavy rains turned the ground into ankle-deep mud. The firing became increasingly intense. As each federal line received reinforcements, it seemed to the attackers that the rebels put in another line. In truth, it just appeared that way: from midmorning on, the Confederates fought largely with the same force. Galloway remembered that the rebels crawled forward under cover of the dense smoke and rain "until, reaching a certain point, and raising their usual yell, they charged gallantly up to the very muzzles of our pieces and reoccupied the Angle."[38]

On his horse, Upton seemed to be everywhere at once. "Hat in hand, he bravely cheered his men, and begged them to 'hold this point.'" Upton continued to rally his men up and down the line. As one of the few remaining officers on horseback, he became an increasingly tempting target for Confederate riflemen. Delavan Bates believed that Upton led a charmed life and was immune to the hail of fire around him. According to Bates, Upton remarked: "Boys, if we can hold this line, a record will be ours that never will be forgotten." As it turned out, he was never hit, and his command won the dubious distinction of holding the line at all costs. As the fighting intensified, Upton ordered Morse "to ride back and get a section of" First Lieutenant Gillis's 5th Artillery Battery C, under the command of Lt. Richard Metcalf, and take it forward. Metcalf complied with the request, "remarking that he never expected" to see his men, horses, and equipment again. The battery "came up on the run, unlimbered, and the pieces were run up as close to the rebel works as they could . . . and opened into the crowded trenches with canister." The rebels tried to capture the artillery pieces. They never took the cannon, but they managed to kill the entire battery and all the horses.[39]

John Fish, no longer a line officer with the 121st but a member of Upton's staff, remained safely out of harm's way. The regiment's line officers had been decimated two days before, but staff officers, because they were removed from the action, experienced a higher survival rate. Fish felt it was his duty to help with the task that unfolded before him. He offered to help move canister from the caissons to the guns. Just as he cried out, "Give it to them boys, I'll bring you the canister," a sharpshooter killed him. As his colleague Delavan Bates remarked, "Bravery on the battlefield is . . . always commendable, but his death was a greater loss to the army than all the benefit derived from the work he was doing." Upton tried to shut down the sharpshooters. He ordered Sgt. Thomas Smith of Company K to choose four men to silence the Confederate team. Smith chose Erastus Fritts, William Gardner, James Phillips, and Oliver Young from his company. Within minutes, two of them were dead, and a third died that night, his jaw shot off. Smith and Young survived. After Rappahannock Station, Emory Upton had greeted Fish with the comment that he was glad he survived the assault. Fish believed that luck kept him from harm. He believed in the randomness of a death in battle, but if it were to happen to him, he said, "God help my poor wife and little ones. I would not care so much but for them."

In the afternoon of May 12, Capt. Frank L. Lemont of the 5th Maine fell on the crest of the entrenchment, killed as he engaged the Confederates in front of him. He weighed in at 200 pounds, and when his comrades found him to attend to him, he was "simply a mass of riddled flesh." There probably was not a "square inch of surface" left in his body without a bullet hole. All day long, he had lain there as a target for Confederate minié balls. Lemont was one of seven captains in the 5th Maine who survived the May 10 assault, and Isaac Best remembered him as a "splendid man."[40]

Francis Morse doubted he himself would survive the day. "It seemed impossible that troops could stand so severe a fire." He called two orderlies to his side to give them a written order, and both of their horses were shot from under them. Morse delivered the messages himself. All day long, both sides took withering fire; the ranks were repeatedly decimated, only to be refilled by another mob in a continuous killing cycle. Morse recalled the "heaps of dead . . . impeding our operations." Upton instructed his men to fire at the head logs on the rebel breastworks, which "splintered like brush-brooms." The Sixth Corps and Upton's brigade may have destroyed the large, 22-inch-diameter oak tree near the salient and the target of many minié balls, although many federal troops claimed responsibility for the tree's demise. It fell in midafternoon into the Confederate lines inside the muleshoe.

The torrential rain found the men in mud up to their knees, and as Norton Galloway remembered, "by our constant movement the fallen were almost buried at our feet." That afternoon, George Teel killed two rebels. So, too, did Henry Henicker, a twenty-eight-year-old corporal from Laurens, despite a bayonet wound to his hand. John Kidder claimed to have shot four during the attack. Under the breastworks, the men of the 121st would rest their loaded muskets on the top log, raise the butts, and fire into the crowd of rebels on the other side. Occasionally, one would jump on the parapet, fire a few shots into the huddled masses below, and then fall dead on the breastworks. As the skies opened, artillery batteries on both sides kept up a withering, point-blank fire into the men engaged in hand-to-hand combat. Smoke hung low in the driving rain, adding to the hellish scene being played out with each savage attack and counterattack. Artillery and infantry ammunition boxes were brought forward, and when they were expended, they were filled with dirt and used as protection in their front.[41]

Well into the evening hours, musket balls and lethal sheets of artillery fire from both sides cut through the rain. Neither side gave ground, and for "eighteen hours raged the most sanguinary conflict of the war." During the afternoon, a group of eighty rebels had advanced toward the 121st under a flag of truce. As brigade commanders ordered the regiment to cease fire and allow the men to surrender, the Confederates directly behind the "surrendering" cadre opened fire on them, killing many of their comrades who were attempting to give themselves up. The battle raged at its hottest from 9:30 A.M. until 5:30 P.M., when Upton's brigade was relieved. At dark, Upton's men, exhausted and filthy, withdrew and regrouped at the Union rifle pits. Beckwith refused to go with them. He waited until after dark, lying on the ground under the incessant fire. When he did get to the rear, he stumbled into what remained of the regiment, and "little was said." The survivors were covered in gunpowder, mud, and blood, and they were soaked to the skin. They quietly cooked a meal of pork and crackers and then fell asleep wrapped in their rubber blankets—despite the occasional shelling that went on through the night.[42]

The dead and wounded were intermingled everywhere, not neatly laid out in single rows as they had been at Antietam but piled six deep in some places. The heavy, close-in firing reduced many bodies to jelly. When their comrades tried to move them, the bodies merely slipped away—disintegrating in the hands of the rescuers. They were "perfectly powdered, and bones cut up as fine as dust." The dead horses that were riddled by bullets "were so cut up that there was not a bone of them left as large as a finger." Some of the wounded wriggled beneath bodies three and four deep. During the fighting, piles of the dead became breastworks themselves, providing protection for the living soldiers firing behind them. At one spot, Isaac Best counted five rebel bodies piled on top of each other, with the limbs of the lower ones still "quivering in the death struggle." Clinton Beckwith, the youth who had defied his father to join the army at age fifteen, became a man that day. He remembered: "It was a day never to be forgotten in its fierce fighting, bull dog tenacity and horrible slaughter. This was the worst day's experience I ever had, and thoroughly disgusted me with war."

Theodore Briggs in Company K wrote his wife from a hospital bed at the U.S. General Hospital in Baltimore. He had survived with a gunshot wound on his left thigh—and if he had not turned his body, it would have exited his right thigh, a sure death warrant. As he put it, "If the ball had not changed course, I never should have left that battlefield." Daniel Holt simply stated: "An *awful* day this. Strange it is *how* we live at all. The atmosphere is perfectly pestilential from decaying bodies of men and horses. One thing is certain of this campaign thus far, and that is that *more blood* has been shed, more lives lost, and more human suffering undergone, than ever before in a season."[43]

The next morning, May 13, work details were ordered to the scene of the carnage to find and bury bodies and care for any wounded—despite occasional and intense harassment from rebel sharpshooters. Beckwith "counted sixty-three dead men in one little space on our side. The dead were already past identification by their features." For a brief moment, the sun penetrated the gloom, and it "seemed to add a new horror to the scene." His comrades gave up the search for John Fish's body when they concluded that he had been sucked into the mud under the feet of the men and the wheels of the battery. Fish had enjoyed his mention in Upton's official report after Rappahannock Station. Sadly, he would never read Upton's words of praise for him after the Bloody Angle: Upton remembered Fish as a "brave, zealous, patriotic officer" who "distinguished himself in every battle in which he had been engaged." Many of the fallen were merely dumped into the rifle pits dug the day before and were covered over with the earth originally intended to protect the occupants. Norton Galloway reported that "hundreds of Confederates, dead or dying, lay piled over one another in those pits." On the recovery detail, Thomas Smith "saw a terrible sight" that made his "blood run cold." In a pit full of dead rebels, a wounded survivor opened his eyes and stared directly at him. He discovered another rebel pinned to the ground by a fallen pine tree, cut down by a torrent of minié balls.

The demoralization within the ranks of the 121st was nearly universal. Initially, only 118 men from the Otsego-Herkimer regiment could be accounted for. The survivors talked in small groups, wondering about the fate of many of their comrades. Some wandered back into camp throughout the next several hours. Others were never heard from again: they merely disappeared into the mud and the maelstrom. The survivors were convinced that they would not live to see the end of the war. They correctly perceived that the nature of the conflict had changed and that a grim future awaited them. Many voiced concern that Grant might eventually be responsible for their deaths, and in truth, more frontal assaults against impregnable defenses *were* in the plans for this new commander from the west. Others marveled at their survival when their comrades were dead, wounded, or captured. Death was all around them, and the stench of battle was in their nostrils. "Our fellows, myself included," Beckwith wrote, "were a sad, sober crowd those days."[44]

A minié ball broke Adelbert Reed's shoulder blade. His good friend Lt. John Adams, promoted to captain on the battlefield, was unable to enjoy his new stature. Reed was with him when Adams was wounded in both arms; the left arm was amputated. Reed was evacuated to Fredericksburg with the rest of the wounded. "You would laugh to see the fellows here with only one leg or arm hopping and dancing around," he wrote his parents. Many were happy to be alive despite their wounds. By May 24, Reed was safely tucked away as a resident of Lincoln Hospital in Washington, a stay that put him out of harm's way for the duration and gave him a front-row seat to the war's end and Lincoln's assassination.[45]

Around noon on May 12, John Kidder had been wounded in the face, the bullet entering his left cheek and exiting near his ear. He carried himself off the field and walked 2 miles to the rear, attempting to find medical care. He was ordered to Fredericksburg. Recent rains had turned the roads to mush, making his ambulance ride from the field hospital to Fredericksburg a nightmare. Eventually, he climbed out of the ambulance and fell asleep on the side of the road. When he awoke an hour and a half later, his cheek had ballooned so large that his left eye was swollen shut. Transferred to a hospital in Annapolis, he was assured that his wound was not life-threatening or permanently disfiguring, even as his perforated left eardrum continued to produce pus. He would be "perfectly deaf" in that ear for the remainder of his life. Sadly, his brother George was mortally wounded at the Wilderness. Through his grieving and healing, Kidder maintained his composure. He told his wife that she could not "imagine his feelings" when he heard of his brother's death.[46]

The two armies had spent an unprecedented eighteen hours in a hammering rain trying to kill each other. James McCurry simply noted, "Hard fighting commenced at day light and it lasted all day and it is desperate. Fight at dark." John Kidder had to eat his words. After Gettysburg, he had written a tutorial on warfare to his friend William Fields. He told Fields that skirmishing differed from an all-out assault. Whereas skirmishers took occasional shots at each other, assaults usually lasted no more than twenty minutes, he said. "I do not believe that any one Regiment ever fought for more than one or two hours at one time. Most charges are either successful or are repulsed in 15 or 20 minutes and a majority are in less time than that."[47]

So many were wounded. William Remmel went to Fredericksburg before being transferred to Emory Hospital in Washington. Before the regiment reached the rebel rifle pits on May 10, he received an arm wound and on his right hand a smashed finger, which he feared he would lose. He soon won a thirty-day leave to return home to recuperate. James Cronkite, Maj. Henry Galpin, Lt. Daniel Jackson, Capt. Frank Gorton, Lt. William H. Tucker, Lt. James W. Johnston, and 2nd Lt. Edward P. Johnson were all on Delavan Bates's mind when he wrote after the war that "the fighting from the 9th to the 12th of May cleaned out most all the commissioned officers in the 121st regiment." After the battle, Bates told his father that he "missed a bloody time by joining the colored troops . . . We may have our turn before it is through yet, but can't fare worse than the 121st did, whatever comes. The 121st N. Y. Vols is entirely used up, having only 4 officers unhurt." He repeated the rumor that only seventy men were left for duty. Many of the wounds were bayonet cuts, a rarity in the war, "but at Spotsylvania there were plenty of bayonet wounds," Upton remembered. Simeon Mann, a transfer from the 18th New York in Company G, was shot to death in the charge "but had a rebel impaled on his bayonet."[48]

"Upton's Run" or Myers Hill

Grant pressed on. May 13 was uneventful, with very little firing from either side and no combat. All day long, he attempted to find the Confederate army. Toward evening, he decided that Lee's weak spot was his right flank. Lee had abandoned the salient the night before, that piece of ground over which so many were killed. He contracted the nose, eliminating the bulge. His army was strung out from Anderson's cohort on the left resting across the Po River, past Laurel Hill, and skirting the southern part of the muleshoe where Ewell's men looked into the salient; his right flank under Hill rested at Spotsylvania Court House. Impulsively, Grant ordered a night march of Warren's and Wright's corps *around* the rest of the army, past Hancock in the center and to the left of Burnside.

That night was dark, windy, and foreboding, like the mood of the troops. The 121st, along with the Sixth Corps, followed Warren's Fifth Corps to Spotsylvania. Warren had to move his army around Wright's Sixth Corps. Upton sent Morse ahead to a crossroads to alert him when the last of Warren's men had cleared the Sixth Corps in order to begin his movement. Morse sat on the roadside, sick, worn-out, and feeling sorry for himself. The flickering light of the campfires revealed the tired and haggard faces of the passing men. Once the Fifth Corps had passed, Morse sent word to Upton, and within minutes, the Sixth Corps began passing, "slipping and sliding in the mud," toward Hill's right flank.[49]

May 14 found the 121st on the Union's far left. The regiment had just 185 men and 4 officers. Noncommissioned officers were acting in place of officers. Other units straggled in from 4 A.M. until late morning. The element of surprise was lost, but Wright's night march caused Lee to counter Grant's movements. The brigade crossed the Ny River and seized Myers Hill near the Fifth Corps. The 121st set up its picket lines in front of a large mansion on Myers Hill. With the 95th Pennsylvania in reserve, the 96th Pennsylvania, the 5th Maine, and the 121st New York continued the picket line from the Fifth Corps to the river. With the Ny behind them, the troops took down rail fences, piling them in front of themselves for cover from enemy fire. Behind the rail fences, the men made fires and cooked breakfast. Directly in front of them was 600 yards of open field, with a wood line covering the rebel positions. From the left came word that the rebels were planning to attack the 121st. Within minutes, the rebels emerged at woods' edge with a strong skirmish line. Upton moved Lt. Col. William Lessig and his 96th Pennsylvania together with two 2nd New Jersey companies into the open toward the edge of the woods near the house to deny the Confederates any advantage.

To determine the rebels' strength and position, Lessig sent a scout toward the woods, but he came reeling back with four Georgia regiments on his heels. The Confederates were in full strength—four lines of battle, each more threatening than the one ahead of it. They were supported by an artillery battery. Upton ordered the 95th Pennsylvania and the 10th New Jersey forward just as the rebels emerged in full force to the left of the house, enfilading the left flank. Compounding Upton's dilemma, the Confederates opened up on both of his flanks with artillery and a contingent of dismounted cavalry. With that, the federal lines broke. As Daniel Holt eloquently recorded the action in his diary: "An advance is made of about thirty or forty rods, when we came flying back in all sorts of a hurry. Every man for himself. Here we had another run for sweet life." Joe Heath remarked that the regiment had just settled itself into place to relax a few minutes "with thoughts of the scenes just past upon our minds and the anticipation of many more before us when Generals Wright and Meade came up and ordered an advance of our skirmish line." He estimated the ratio of attacking Confederates to Yankees as eleven to one.

The rebels immediately occupied the makeshift breastworks of fence rails that the 121st had made and began lobbing shells at the retreating troops. Several federals found the river too cold and were fished out by their comrades. Henry Wood nearly drowned. His drum kept him afloat until his feet found the river bottom. After additional maneuvering and recognizing the enemy's strength, Upton appreciated the situation's untenable nature. He ordered his command to leave the field in haste, to cross the river, preferably using the bridge, and to regroup on the other side. After dark, the Confederates abandoned the Myers Hill fortifications, and Upton's men reoccupied them for the next two days. Frank Morse described the brigade as "very much shattered." In the lexicon of the 121st, the skirmish at Myers Hill forever remained known as Upton's Run or Upton's Height.[50]

To the North Anna and Cold Harbor

Troops from the 2nd Brigade, 1st Division occupied Myers Hill for a few days before they moved south toward the North Anna River with the rest of the army. Both armies moved out of Spotsylvania in the evening and night of May 21–22. That day "represented a low point in the campaign for both [leaders]." Each was more concerned with "what the other might do, and each missed chances to strike telling blows."[51]

In a successful action at Jericho Mills, Warren's Fifth Corps attacked entrenched Confederate positions south of the river. The artillery saved the day, finally giving Union troops something to celebrate for the first time since the beginning of the campaign. Grant read the day's events as a sign of Lee's willingness to move south and accept Warren's victory. On May 24, Wright's Sixth Corps, with the 121st, joined Warren across the river and headed south with the rest of Grant's army—right into Lee's trap. Lee had deployed the Army of Northern Virginia's left flank between the Little River to Ox Ford on the North Anna and the right flank southeast in an inverted V. In order to get from one side of the field to the other, Union troops had to cross the North Anna twice. In effect, Grant's army was split in two and trapped between Lee and the river. With an effective stalemate in place, Grant withdrew and moved the next day over the swollen North Anna on makeshift bridges. Wright and Warren slipped undetected back across the river. Grant continued east and south to cross the Pamunkey River and head toward Hanovertown and Richmond.

On May 31, Grant ordered Phil Sheridan south with instructions to take and hold the crossroads at Cold Harbor, a high piece of ground with roads radiating from its center, only 5 miles from Richmond. Perceiving Grant's intentions, Lee moved south to counter him. There, Fitzhugh Lee's horsemen met Sheridan and his troops. The rebels gave battle when Anderson reinforced them, but Sheridan forced them from the field.

Grant ordered Wright to move from the army's right flank to Cold Harbor to support Sheridan. At 1:00 in the morning of June 1, the 121st, with the rest of the brigade, marched off for Cold Harbor. The men were tired and unhappy with the latest maneuver. "They had torn up railroad near the North Anna River on May 26, marched without sleep all that night and the next day, continued to Crump's Creek on May 28, pushed out to Hanover Court House on May 29, marched twelve hours on May 30 to Totopotomy Creek, and skirmished all day on the 31st." After a mean, hot, 15-mile night march, the 121st arrived with the corps on the army's far left and southernmost flank the next day. By 5:00 that afternoon, the 121st was in line of battle with the 95th and 96th Pennsylvania regiments and the 5th Maine. That evening, Wright and Maj. Gen. William "Baldy" Smith's Eighteenth Corps prepared to make an assault across open ground against heavily defended enemy lines.[52]

The 2nd Connecticut Heavy Artillery, an 1,800-man contingent from Litch-field, Connecticut, led by Col. Elisha S. Kellogg, joined Upton's brigade in May. When Grant assumed command of the armies, he decided that the capital, defended by 25,000 troops, required fewer heavy artillery components and the Army of the Potomac needed more infantry units. "The boys say it is a good regiment," James Cronkite told John Kidder, echoing Clinton Beckwith, who remembered the 2nd Connecticut as a "magnificent organization of fine looking men, many of them veterans . . . Their bright clothes, clean and soldierly appearance was very attractive to us, and their imposing battle array made their arrival doubly welcome." In three front lines, the Connecticut Yankees spearheaded the ill-conceived attack on the entrenched Confederate veterans. They were supported by the 95th and 96th Pennsylvania, with the 5th Maine and the 121st New York fourth in line acting as provost guard to intercept stragglers. Part of the 121st was ordered to the skirmish line, where the men did their job admirably, clearing out the Confederate skirmish line.[53]

As soon as "the heavies" began their charge, the enemy "works were bordered with a fringe of smoke," Beckwith recalled. Kellogg's enthusiastic troops began "to fall very fast," and the wounded made their way to the rear. Just in front of the rebel line was a hollow that Beckwith watched as it seemed to swallow up the advancing bluecoats. The withering fire destroyed all before it. He saw the men "fall in all shapes; some would pitch forward" as though they tripped. Others "would throw up their arms and fall backward" or "stagger about a few paces before they dropped." Kellogg stopped the command to bring it into line before the final assault. The men of the 121st, watching the horrifying scene, wondered why they had stopped. Kellogg led the charge on foot. He went down immediately, riddled with minié balls. The regiment lost its major and adjutant. Although the 2nd Connecticut captured 300 Confederates, it lost nearly 400 of its own on its maiden combat mission. The 121st recorded only one casualty—Richard Bennett, who was killed by "friendly fire." A federal shell took his leg off, and he bled to death the next day.[54]

On June 2, large-scale charges were ordered and countermanded as the troops traded sporadic fire. The 121st replaced the 96th Pennsylvania at the front. The rebels maintained a strong position north of the Chickahominy River. Both sides stayed in their rifle pits, and it was unsafe "for a man to elevate his head." According to James Cronkite, the "bullets fly promiscuously about and every hour some one is carried to the rear." Somehow, the men wrote letters. George Teel, "so accustomed to the din of battle" under flying bullets, rarely gave it a second thought. Four men in the 5th Maine were wounded by one bullet. Around 7 P.M. on June 2, the rebels rose up in a furious firefight to which the 2nd Brigade responded. Neither side gained an advantage. Upton had three horses shot out from under him, but he escaped any injury. The 121st was led by Maj. Henry Galpin, and as John Hartwell remarked, "He stayed by us too."[55]

Although on the front in a skirmish line, the 121st did not participate in the slaughter on June 3. The 2nd Brigade spent most of the day under heavy fire, "laying flat on the ground in front of the breastworks" on a slight decline toward the enemy's works. John Hartwell wrote that the men were "obliged to lay our heads downhill which made it very uncomfortable." The main attack came from the Second Corps, the Eighteenth Corps, and a part of the Sixth Corps. Convinced that Lee would soon capitulate, Grant launched a ferocious and ill-advised attack at 4:30 that morning. He lost 7,000 men in the space of twenty minutes that day, due to a decision he later regretted. Daniel Holt called June 3 "the worst day of the campaign." The fury of May could not compare to Cold Harbor's extreme barbarity. "Discord and disorder on every hand. The woods full of dead, dying and wounded men. Stench like that of putrid carcasses, flavors your food, while the water is thick with all manner of impurities. Never was there such a day's work or such a wholesale slaughter!"

Later, Lee and Grant agreed to a two-hour cease-fire to bury the decaying bodies on both sides. Holt went out from the lines to look over the battlefield— "A ghastly sight indeed: Do not like it. Stench awful!" Thousands of putrefying bodies between the lines caused great suffering "from the odor arising from them" and prompted the cease-fire. As the burial parties went about their solemn duty, "both armies stood on their respective works, and commenced shaking their blankets." Soon, both sides, only 200 yards apart, were engulfed by a dust cloud all along the line. John Adams joined the rescue operations to help the overworked surgeons. He loaded stretchers and carried men and officers to wagons because there were not enough ambulances. Cedar boughs, laid on the bottom of the wagons, proved insufficient to the "legless and armless sufferers over rough road at night," and many died en route to the hospital at Fredericksburg. At 6:00, a battery signaled the end of the truce, and "like magic the two corps disappeared behind their works, and renewed the scathing fire." Sporadic firing on the line characterized June 10. Opposing pickets began talking to each other again, as they had the previous summer and autumn. "We felt no wish to fire on them," John Hartwell remarked.[56]

No one was really sure who won the Overland campaign or even if it had ended with any certainty. George Teel believed that despite fighting all night, on May 12 at Spotsylvania Court House, "our men got the best of the day, took the rebel works, seventeen pieces of artillery and about 4000 prisoners." But he admitted it was "an awful slaughter." He himself was nearly captured on May 14, "but thanks to a good pair of legs," he escaped. By May 16, he was convinced that "on the whole we are gaining on the rebels." Delavan Bates, now commanding the 30th USCT guarding the army's supply trains, described the

National flag of the 121st after the Overland campaign, presented to the regiment before Grant's campaign. Ironically, the only two battles decipherable afterward were Salem Church and Rappahannock Station, two very meaningful battles to the members of the 121st. Courtesy New York State Military Museum and Veterans Research Center, Saratoga.

recent fight at Spotsylvania as "an awful one, both armies fight with desperation." "There have been two days of incessant fighting there without any definite result," he told his father.

Between June 3 and June 12, the 121st hunkered down behind entrenchments. John Slocum wrote in his diary, "hot, hot, hot," several days in a row, then "hotter." From June 12 onward, attacks were ordered and planned, but then either they were canceled or the enemy retired. For the next two weeks, the 2nd Brigade and the 121st New York marched and countermarched in the area around Petersburg. Daniel Holt was not impressed with the constant motion: "Tom fooling all day. Regiment changed position from left to right and from right to left—up and down the middle, equal to any French dancing master, about the same results: pushing itself after all its evolutions, in just about the same spot as when the farce commenced." By month's end, the 121st faced the fortifications of Petersburg. Grant overshot Richmond by a few miles, but he had decided to strangle Lee's army and the population of the Confederate capital by besieging Petersburg and its converging rail lines.

By May 22, after more than two weeks of fighting and marching, John Slocum wondered if he would survive "the hardships and privations" he experienced. In his opinion, the Overland campaign was a "failure." He and Holt kept track of their countless amputations. A few days later, he fell asleep on his horse and awoke only as he was falling off. Daniel Holt found time to tell his wife that if the Union army had succeeded, it escaped his notice. "If losing 60,000 men is a slight loss, I never want to see a heavy one. We as a regiment have almost ceased to exist," he said, and soon, no one would "be left to recite the wholesale slaughter which has taken place upon the scared soil of Virginia."[57]

The constant fighting, marching, and countermarching took their toll mentally and physically on all the men. Like John Slocum, Francis Morse fell off his horse in a state of exhaustion on June 10, and with Slocum's medical excuse in his pocket, he was recuperating in Cherry Valley by July. Daniel Holt noticed that he had developed a cough that he could not shake, and he turned to Slocum for medical attention. But there were men of stronger constitutions in the ranks as well, among them John Hartwell. Hartwell reported after a 30-mile tramp over a two-day period that "hundreds are unable to reach camp for lack of strength and perseverance but I came in and stacked arms although nearly discouraged. *Pride* only kept me in the ranks. This march will cost thousands of valuable lives."[58]

Grant's strategy was to join Benjamin Butler on the Peninsula and go into Richmond. In the west, William Sherman was to cut the heart out of the Confederacy in a swath 60 miles wide, beginning in Chattanooga, going through Atlanta, and then on to Savannah and ultimately to Columbia, South Carolina. Grant's plans did not include a siege of Petersburg. Lee, perceiving the danger to Richmond, entrenched his entire army from the capital to Petersburg. He ordered Jubal Early west, into the Shenandoah Valley and up toward Washington, once again threatening the Union capital—cat and mouse. With the rest of the Army of the Potomac, the 121st dug in before Petersburg for the duration. Upton estimated his brigade's losses at 329 killed, 713 wounded, and 263 missing, for a total of 1,405—losses that affected him deeply.[59]

Once again, the 121st was much changed. Earlier, its ranks had been decimated by disease and desertion. Now, the lists of the dead, wounded, and missing in the local papers replaced the lists of deserters that were once sent to the hometown editors. Before the terrible battles of the summer campaign, Henry Walker's shoulder wound at Salem Church caused him to resign his commission and return to Cooperstown. Henry Upton's wounds forced his resignation also. George Teel, Ingraham Smith, and Adelbert Reed were in Washington-area hospitals. On May 10, at the salient, Smith had been shot in the mouth, the minié ball exiting just below his left ear. Henry Galpin, Egbert Olcott's replacement, was also wounded and temporarily out of action. Francis Morse spent July and August at home in idyllic Cherry Valley, recuperating from physical exhaustion. Jonathon Burrell was ill in the division hospital. John Fish was dead, and John Kidder was wounded.

Olcott, Sam Kelley, and Lansing Paine were prisoners in Macon, Georgia. Frank Foote lost his leg to amputation and was in Libby Prison. Delavan Bates, Andrew Mather, and others were commanding regiments in the U.S. Colored Troops. The 121st suffered 174 casualties throughout the Overland campaign: 44 killed, 91 wounded, 31 missing, and 4 captured. At Cold Harbor, Kidder's company lost Richard Bennett, but beyond that, only three men were wounded. One was Sedate Foote. In twenty minutes at Salem Church a year earlier, the 121st had 75 killed, 39 wounded, 5 captured, and 5 missing, for a total of 124 casualties. But May 10 at the muleshoe was nearly as deadly. There, the regiment had 30 killed, 53 wounded, 8 captured, and 4 missing.[60]

The 121st no longer resembled the regiment that had left Camp Schuyler two years before. Now, there were barely 160 men present and fit for duty. Capt. John D. P. Douw was in charge of the regiment until Galpin returned. After he received a commission as a first lieutenant in Company I, Douw had been asked by Maj. Gen. Henry Slocum to join his staff at 1st Division, Sixth Corps, as an ordnance officer. He returned to the regiment after Fredericksburg in Company K. In March 1863, Upton recommended Douw and Sgt. Fred Ford to Governor Seymour for promotion to captain and second lieutenant, respectively. Now, however, Douw was in Upton's place as regimental commander, and Ford was gone, killed at Salem Church. Only Lt. Hiram Van Scoy from Butternuts and 2nd Lts. Sheldon J. Redway from Little Falls, Erastus Weaver, and James Cronkite were line officers fit for duty. Sgt. Joe Heath served as acting adjutant.[61]

The losses from frontal assaults disturbed Upton. After Cold Harbor, rumors abounded that the Army of the Potomac would "swing around on the James River and not assault" strongly held rebel positions. "Charging is about played out," James Cronkite told Kidder; "[it eats] up the men too fast. I hear this is Colonel Upton's mind at present." Upton had now seen "the hardest fighting of the war." He lashed out at the commanders and the "generalship displayed." The poorly planned assaults inflicted death on an unacceptable scale. The "murderous" slaughter lost brave men who were expected to perform the impossible and "obviate all difficulties." Upton confessed to his sister that as long as he saw "such incompetancy, there is no grade in the army to which I do not aspire." He knew that some of the current corps commanders were "not fit to be corporals." He complained bitterly that officers refused to ride the lines to see a given situation firsthand and yet unhesitatingly ordered men into battle with an ill-conceived plan.[62]

I2

To Washington and the Valley

We are so accustom[ed] to dig back to Harpers Ferry that we have changed the name of our corps to *Harpers Weekly.*

John Hartwell, Company C, August 30, 1864

Well ma, you know about how many boys there was that came in this Regiment from our town [Russia] and now there is but one left besides myself.

George Fahey, Company C, November 2, 1864

John Kidder was not a model patient. Inaction did not suit him, and his irritants closed in on him as he convalesced. He complained about Pennsylvania troops, heavy artillery units, sneaks, and cowards to anyone who would listen. He kept up a steady rant about all of the shirkers and malingerers who were in the hospital under false pretenses. He particularly took after a Lt. Julius Townsend from the 152nd New York, whom Kidder accused of malingering. When he heard that the heavy artillery units around Washington were being pressed into service on the front, he expressed his "most supreme contempt" for them. He called them "poor, miserable, cowardly scoundrels." Kidder told his wife he "would prefer old women with broom handles." He praised her for not believing every piece of gossip she heard, including stories of his death. "I am better than a dozen dead men," he bristled. He tried desperately to leave for home.

By June 6, while his comrades recovered from the Overland campaign at Cold Harbor and just a few weeks after being wounded, Kidder attempted to leave. He did not shrink from using his friends in high places. When an equally stubborn Dutch doctor, Bernard A. Vanderkief, turned down his first application for leave, Kidder asked James Cronkite to plead his case to Levi Turner. When that tactic failed,

Kidder wrote to Turner himself and got his assurance that he would help get Kidder a leave to return home. Then, Kidder caught Vanderkief in a lie. The good doctor told Kidder that he neither approved nor disapproved Kidder's leave application when he sent it up the chain of command. When Kidder discovered that the doctor had, in fact, disapproved his application and that of other officers as well, he gathered up all of the other officers' leave applications and sent them on to Turner with a cover letter "stating the facts." Kidder also asked his friend William Fields to intervene, to no avail. Fields reassured Kidder that no one had discriminated against him and that other officers were not receiving permission to travel home to recuperate. Surgeons finally released him from the hospital on July 21, 1864—"it seems like getting out of prison," he remarked—and he began his journey to the Elmira, New York, prison camp for Confederates and some light duty.[1]

Losses in the Wilderness and in Grant's Overland campaign affected those left behind in upstate New York as well as the men in the 121st. Death and disfigurement touched many of the small communities where everyone knew everyone else's relations or neighbors. The families and wives in rural Otsego County were on constant alert for news from the front. The lack of information only increased their anxiety. George Kidder's death devastated his widow. He had instructed the surgeon attending him just before he died to tell his wife that although he wanted to live for her and his son, "he had done his duty and lost his life in fighting for God, his country, his wife, and little son and that he had no regrets." If it were necessary, he was confident he would do it all over again. A month later, in a despairing moment, Ann Kidder penned a heartbreaking letter to her sister-in-law, Harriett Kidder. In language eloquent and elegant, she revealed an implacable sorrow that many others may have felt but were unable to articulate. Ann wrote the letter when the fate of Harriett's husband, John, remained in doubt. If John had been captured, hope endured. If not, he would return to the grieving family in death, and then "all hope is swept away." She wrote:

> Oh Hatt I find it very, very hard to be reconciled. George is in my mind day and night. I see him often in my dreams but awake to the sad reality that he has passed forever away from the earth. I shall never look upon that noble form again, never press those lips with the warm kiss of affection, never pen him another message, nor receive one written in his own right hand. No. All hope, all anticipations of the future are swept away by this terrible storm of destruction. War. Don't you think it hard to say "Oh Lord, Thy will be done"? I sincerely hope you may never realize my feeling tonight. I received his diary last Saturday night all stained with his own life current. Oh my God, what a thought. I think sometimes if this war goes on much longer, it will make me about crazy.[2]

Francis Morse's and Sam Kelley's circumstances confirmed the randomness of war. Kelley struggled with his captivity in a rank Confederate prison in Macon, Georgia, in the summer of 1864 while Francis Morse basked in the glow of family, friends, sparkling days and cool nights, and good food while tucked comfortably into his Cherry Valley home.

For the long, hot Southern months of June and July, Sam Kelley endured the separation, isolation, and humiliation of the officer's version of Andersonville. The camp on the fairgrounds in Macon, Camp Oglethorpe, was established in 1862 after the battle of Shiloh over the objections of the governor and the people of Macon. At first, the prison occupied an idyllic setting among hearty shade trees on 15 to 20 acres of gently rolling land. It possessed several buildings, with the best and largest used as a hospital; a strong well with excellent drinking water; and a stream so clean that the men could bathe regularly. But by the spring of 1864 when prisoners from the Virginia battlefields overwhelmed it, the prison took on a grim appearance and reputation. The stream and the spring still flowed, but they were tainted by the influx of captured Yankees.[3]

Capt. George C. Gibbs commanded the prison—"not a good soldier, he is laughed at by over a thousand officers," Kelley wrote. But Gibbs's former commanding officer thought he was "peculiarly suited for the position" of camp commandant. The Georgian Gibbs had served as a colonel of the 42nd North Carolina Regiment for two years and resigned because his troops refused to serve under an officer from another state. At the prison camp in Macon, he built an unbreachable fence with platforms strong enough to support cannon trained on the prisoners. On a hill on the northwest corner of the camp, Gibbs augmented his fence guns with two 12-pound cannon, giving him a full sweep of the camp.

Confederate authorities were concerned with the situation at Macon. They feared that "1500 educated officers, courageous and desperate, cannot . . . be safely guarded" by the makeshift militia and home guards in charge of the prison. They were particularly worried about the 170 officer prisoners who "had been there for months" without any official paperwork documenting their existence. If not for their letters, the presence of Sam Kelley, Lansing Paine, Egbert Olcott, and countless others at Macon would have remained unknown to the outside world. New prisoners coming in from Sherman's army as it moved toward Atlanta brought news from the outside. Escapes over fences and through hand-dug tunnels were routine. One attempt to escape in a sutler's wagon proved unsuccessful. And when the Confederates discovered the tunnels, they took bunks away from the inmates, forcing them to sleep on the ground. On the Fourth of July during morning muster, defiant prisoners displayed a small American flag accompanied by "three times three" cheers for the Union and the Constitution. Commandant Gibbs was not amused. He ordered his cannon loaded and aimed at the prisoners and issued an order banning all speeches, patriotic songs, and any Yankee symbols.[4]

On June 3, 1864, Sam saw Colonel Olcott, his wound nearly healed. Olcott told him that his watch and hat were stolen after they were separated upon reaching Macon. Two days later, one month after he was captured, Sam Kelley fell ill. At first, he told his mother that he hoped to be released early. He remained in good spirits and told her that his care proved better than he had hoped. He contracted diarrhea and probably dysentery. He soon complained of headaches and a severe cold. The camp's inadequate sanitation systems were strained to the point where they became nearly nonexistent. The food and the shelter were, in Lansing Paine's words, "very bad." He protected Kelley when he became too ill to stand for prisoner formations by hiding him under floorboards, thus keeping him "from ruin." Paine believed that the "moisture contributed to [Sam's] health deterioration." And the corn bread and sliced bacon they received were "not fit for a sick man to eat." During July, Sam's health fluctuated.

Rumors thrived among the prisoners. By mid-July, word of the battles raging around Atlanta reached them within days. Paine and Olcott were with Kelley when Olcott, having improved enough, was sent away with fifty other officers, "maybe to be exchanged, do not know," Kelley wrote in his journal. Possibly, they were on their way to Charleston to serve as human shields to prevent Union forces from reducing the city to rubble. Another rumor a few days later had the men sent to Charleston to be exchanged.[5]

Sherman pressed the Confederate army and the civilian population in Georgia. By midmonth, the Confederate authorities were acknowledging that Macon "was an unhealthy locality, to which *our* troops ought not to be exposed." By the end of July, Kelley and Paine, along with most of the prisoners at Macon, were being prepared for transfer to Charleston. Richmond changed the order when the Confederates determined that there were so many Yankee prisoners in Charleston that additional transfers would "complicate negotiations for exchange of those [already there]." In August, captives made additional attempts to escape by tunneling out or by dressing in Confederate uniforms. Two captains were sent to solitary confinement for digging a tunnel. "Ex-change rumors run high," Kelley wrote in his diary as his health continued to deteriorate.

The water that the prisoners drank and bathed with began to smell and taste bad. Kelley developed a rash on his hands and other parts of his body, including mouth sores and a sore throat—all while his intestines were being ravaged by chronic diarrhea. He tried to occupy himself with higher pursuits. He read everything he could get his hands on, especially Shakespeare. The officers in his squad scraped together $50 and bought books from their rebel overseers, who were happy to sell to them. On August 20, 1864, Sam Kelley described in his diary the arrival of slave women to clean the camp's fetid refuse sinks. The women were accompanied by a large, menacing black overseer armed with a whip. That night, Kelley confided in his diary: "I think now I have seen slavery." Three days later, he observed his second-year anniversary in the army.[6]

The conditions affected all of the prisoners in the confined spaces at Macon. They suffered with "chronic and scorbutic diarrhea, scurvy, ulceration of the bowels . . . from insufficient and bad food, confinement, and want of clothing." Many were confined to bed for "four to 12 months." Eating only coarse and "sour meal and a little bacon" caused many to "move their bowels one to three times" an hour. Those who were imprisoned for nearly a year were penniless. They owned little clothing and were "too feeble to sit erect while using a bedpan." One doctor wrote of those he left behind: "Many . . . are greatly emaciated, very pale, and have edema of the lower extremities." Kelley undoubtedly survived Macon because of his generally healthy condition.[7]

By September, the prisoners were finally transferred to Savannah— presumably out of harm's way from the oncoming federal army. Lansing Paine reported that they were getting better treatment in the new prison, but Sam's mother had not heard from him for a month and began to worry that he had died.[8]

Frank Morse, back home in Cherry Valley in the summer of 1864, immersed himself into the village's social scene as though he had never left it. He arrived during a perfect upstate New York summer with a town "full of strangers." The nights were cool and dry. The days, when they were not overcast, were bright and clear as a diamond. The green hills and mature trees kept the valley hollows cool and moist. Friends were everywhere, and being young, they amused themselves with dinners, picnics, and social gatherings—all "incessant and charming." Douglas Campbell, out of the army since the previous year, saw Morse and remarked: "Frank Morse is here in all his glory, seems much improved."

Campbell wished that his brother Cleaveland, wounded at the Crater in Petersburg, would return to Cherry Valley, for its "pure air is famous for invalids, we would cure you up in a hurry," he wrote. Still ailing, Egbert Olcott wrote from prison in Charleston of his unimproved condition. The bounty surrounding Morse and Campbell in the village contrasted sharply with "the war-stricken and beggarly towns and country of Virginia" that Morse had described. The natives of Cherry Valley, well fed and well clothed, continued to support the conflict. "There were no traces of war here," he wrote, "save in the patriotic enthusiasm of the people." Those who leaned "Copperish" kept their mouths shut. As Morse saw it, the ruin and desolation in Virginia proved that "the guilty were being punished, [and] how severely the devil was treating his own."[9]

Monocacy, Fort Stevens, and Washington

By mid-June 1864, the regiment and the 1st Division were on the bottomlands of the James River waiting for 104 pontoon boats to form bridges that would facilitate their passage to the other side. Gunboats, tugs, transports, and vessels of every description filled the river. Although the air remained hot and bug infested, conditions had improved from the ordeal in the Wilderness; the open land offered a view "where you could see such things once more," wrote John Ingraham. The inordinate length of the water traffic and its turbulence "made a man walk as though he was about three sheets in the wind" while crossing the bridges. Once across, the regiment found empty mansions, their residents having fled to Petersburg and Richmond. The abandoned houses with manicured lawns and gardens and "nice graveled walks" struck Ingraham as surreal. He and James McCurry could see Petersburg's empty streets just 300 yards away.[10]

On the night of June 12, the 121st pulled away from Cold Harbor. The men crossed the Chickahominy at Jones Bridge on pontoons, heading toward Bermuda Hundred on the James River. Beckwith remembered how glad they were to get away from Cold Harbor's stifling climate, the "odors of the new made graves and vapors from the swamps" that caused the men to feel ill. The 121st settled into heavily reinforced fortifications at Bermuda Hundred, built earlier by black troops under Ben Butler's direction. The "elaborately fortified" works impressed Beckwith. He noted the "covered ways and bomb proofs" for protection, "redoubts and forts with mantelets covering the embrasures and rapid fire guns in battery, the first we had seen of that kind." John Ingraham found the black soldiers a pleasant surprise. Some told him they intended to show no quarter to the rebels—"They say they don't take any prisoners. They fight bully," he wrote.[11]

As the federal army pressed in on Petersburg, Confederate general Jubal Early remained on the loose in the Shenandoah Valley. Immediately after Cold Harbor, Lee had sent him to drive Gen. David Hunter out of Lynchburg to create a diversion and threaten the North once again. Hunter proved no challenge for the veteran Early, and once he dispensed with him, Early turned northward and began threatening Maryland and Washington. Both armies had long recognized the strategic value of the Shenandoah Valley. Since Jackson's campaigns two years earlier, it had become an important logistical asset to the Confederate army—both as a source of provisions and as a natural, protected highway to the heart of Maryland and Pennsylvania in 1862 and 1863. Its southwest-northeast orientation acted as a cannon pointed at the Union's underbelly by providing cover to Lee's armies as they marched north. The Union efforts during the war's first three years failed to neutralize the danger. Grant determined to put an end to the threat it posed.

On his way to Washington, Early ran into Gen. Lew Wallace of Shiloh in-
famy (and, later, fame as the author of *Ben Hur*) at Monocacy, Maryland. Early
handily beat off Wallace's smaller force, but the battle bought Grant enough
time to move reinforcements to the Washington area from the siege lines
around Petersburg to meet Early's probing army.

Grant wasted little time in dispatching help. Between July 1 and 9, the 2nd
Brigade and the 121st remained in camp near the Jerusalem Road. The last two
weeks of June were spent doing picket duty, tearing up railroad track and ties,
and building more breastworks. The Fourth of July passed quietly for the regiment. The Wilderness campaign had begun sixty days earlier, and John Slocum
sarcastically wondered why he saw "nobody drunk." By the time Early approached the Monocacy, the Sixth Corps had boarded railcars and then the
steamer *Tappahannock* on the James River for a journey that began on July 10.
As the 1st Division moved out, the 121st abandoned its rifle pits and trenches,
which were immediately occupied by the 30th U.S. Colored Troops under Delavan Bates.

The 121st and the 96th Pennsylvania marched down to the docks, where, at
5:00 A.M. on Sunday, June 10, they boarded the transport for a forty-six-hour trip
up the Potomac. The 121st was assigned to the right side of the boat facing the
bow. The 96th, "a regiment above all others which we hate," was to go to the
left side. The 96th boarded first and immediately occupied the spot assigned
to the 121st. The 121st complained, but the men of the 96th maintained they
were there first and were going to stay. The New Yorkers responded by grab-
bing the Pennsylvanians' blankets out from under their reclining bodies. One
word led to another, which quickly led to blows; before long, a "pretty lively
rough and tumble fight was started." Colonel Lessig of the 96th entered the fray,
drawing his sword and ordering everyone to stand down; he threatened to cut
them all down "if he was not instantly obeyed." Thomas Yeoman, a young recruit in Company B, grabbed his musket and foolishly threatened Lessig with
the warning that if "he struck him" with his sword, "he would blow a hole
through him."

With that, one of the 121st's officers arrived and separated the antagonists.
Yeoman went before the officers of the regiment, who investigated and settled
the issue. He escaped punishment only because examining officers determined
that the 96th had started the fight. The only casualty, a Pennsylvanian, either
was pushed off or fell off the boat but was quickly rescued. Lessig then
promptly got into another row with one of his own captains, whom he arrested
and sent belowdecks for the remainder of the trip. "The boys are all down on
the Colonel of the 96th," John Ingraham reported. John Slocum attributed the
trouble to a keg of ale that the 96th had smuggled on board.[12]

The next day, they steamed around Fortress Monroe in Hampton Rhodes
harbor and up the Potomac past Washington's Mount Vernon, arriving at the

Sixth Street wharf in the capital on the morning of June 12. Daniel Holt wondered if George Washington would be reduced to tears if he saw these ships carrying troops to put down a rebellion against a government he had helped establish. The trip provided a welcome, two-day relief from marching in the hot sun over dust-filled and parched roads. Boating up and down the James and the Potomac, the troops enjoyed the "panorama spread out along the banks" of the two mighty rivers.

After they landed at the Sixth Street wharf, the troops hustled up Seventh Street without having a chance to eat anything. The 121st hurried through northwest Washington—once again on a hot, dusty march. Young ladies and old women met them with water and ginger beer as they cheered and waved handkerchiefs at the passing troops. "The citizens around here are the fightenedest lot . . . I ever saw," wrote John Lovejoy. Free blacks particularly cheered them on with cries of "God Bless Massa Lincoln and the 6th Corps" and words to the effect that they were all saved now with the arrival of the "Red Cross Soldiers." The white citizens were equally ecstatic to see the veterans because they were sure that the rebs were coming down the street at any moment. One man with a spyglass swore that he saw a Confederate take aim and fire directly at him. "Such fellows can relate their adventures to Marines but not to 'old soldiers,'" Lovejoy scoffed. The whole affair incensed John Slocum. "The town mad with excitement," he told his diary. "Thousands of citizens [are] here to see a battle. I have no words to express my indignation at the conduct of this war. We deserve a disgraceful failure and they want a brilliant action."[13]

Early reached the outer circle of forts around the capital determined to penetrate the ring at Fort Stevens. Until genuine reinforcements arrived, the lines were manned by government clerks, "invalid reserves, convalescents" from the myriad Washington hospitals, "citizens, marines, and any and everybody that could or would be able to fire a gun." President Lincoln decided to throw caution to the wind and traveled out to Fort Stevens to see the action for himself. When a shot missed him, hitting another man, several soldiers quickly hustled him away from the front lines. General Wright escorted him back down Seventh Street, where the passing troops of the Sixth Corps on their way to Fort Stevens recognized him with their cheers. As the 121st and their comrades approached the Fort, Brig. Gen. Daniel Bidwell's 2nd Brigade of Brig. Gen. George W. Getty's 2nd Division of the Sixth Corps chased Early away from Washington, and the 121st saw no action. The rebels were convinced that they were facing ill-trained militia who would not fight and would run at the first volley. They were shocked to discover the Sixth Corps opposing them. When they saw the red crosses on their hats, rebel prisoners were heard to ask, "Where did you all come from, are you everywhere?" That night, the 121st rested after a well-deserved meal.[14]

The next morning, the regiment surveyed the unburied dead, lying where they fell. The wounded were carried off and tended to; the dead became the first in a new national cemetery at Fort Stevens. Three hundred Union casualties were sustained fending off Early's attack. George Teel and the others were persuaded that the Sixth Corps saved Washington. He firmly believed that Lee meant "to draw forces away from Petersburg." He also assumed that the 121st would never return to the Army of the Potomac.[15]

William Remmel, just coming off a convalescent leave at home, was delayed in rejoining the 121st in Washington because of the raid. He spent two days in Philadelphia when Early attacked the rail lines between Baltimore and Philadelphia. He reported a "great excitement" in town as he cooled his heels waiting to reach the 121st.[16]

With Sheridan in the Valley

Leaving Washington on July 14, 1864, the men of the 121st began chasing Early through northern Virginia and then Maryland, where they passed many of the places they had marched through when they first joined the fight two years before. During the last two weeks in July, they crossed and recrossed the Potomac. Until the middle of October 1864, the 121st traipsed back and forth between Washington and Harpers Ferry and up and down the Shenandoah Valley. The military movements during those hot, dry months were as critical to the life of the 121st as most of its previous experiences. George Teel complained about the marches in all kinds of weather, day and night, and in "all kinds of hell." But the most notable march involved the entire Sixth Corps wading across the Potomac with pants off and all accoutrements strapped above their waists, attached to their suspenders, or carried on their backs—"some laughing, some swearing. The sight was a novel one to see."

John Ingraham experienced a period of depression, which led him to speak of his feelings and emotions. He wrote regularly to Mary Green in Brockett's Bridge, whom he married on his return to upstate New York, and confided his innermost fears. "I sometimes think I never will enjoy myself again, never will be anything or anybody," he wrote. "And here I am spending my most precious and younger days in Virginia." He wondered if, when he returned home, people would recognize him as a civilian and not merely an army private. A resident in a democratic society, he observed, "if he behaves himself, he is on a level with all men. Not so with a soldier. He is inferior to all." John Hartwell, by contrast, welcomed the new duty after the horrors of the Wilderness campaign and away from the trenches at Petersburg. "Our business is to defend" Washington and Maryland from "any invasion or raids," he told his wife. He predicted easier times, which were overdue: "The 6th [Corps] has been constantly on the run ever since I joined it."[17]

His relief proved to be short-lived. By July 20, Union forces stopped chasing

Early near Snicker's Gap. Rumors were rife that he was headed back to Petersburg and that Grant had ordered the Sixth Corps to return to foil him. Wright believed that he accomplished his mission and that Early no longer posed a threat to the capital. The Sixth Corps headed back to rejoin Grant, moving through the capital preparatory to heading south. The thought of going back to the siege lines at Petersburg struck Daniel Holt as appalling and prisonlike. He observed that returning was too "horrible to contemplate and sad to endure." Petersburg represented "blood, death, carnage": it was an "unhallowed spot."

His medical comrade, John Slocum, became depressed. "The future looks darker than ever," he told his diary, "disaster and defeat overtake us on every side. Blindness and mismanagement will beat us." Yet July 25 found the 121st in Washington, where the men were paid and fed; they rested and visited Forrest Hall, an establishment in Georgetown "for men absent from their commands without proper authority." Forrest Hall was a building at 31st and N streets where, early in the war, prisoners and deserters were processed, but it was now a gathering place for those in the Union army looking for a good time off. James McCurry cryptically noted, "Very warm today . . . all laying back taking comfort." Dr. Holt confirmed the ribald nature of the unexpected return trip to Washington. He told his diary that after the men were paid, he witnessed a "general rush to Washington by officers and men [alike]." "Many visitors from the city. Fast young men and women in abundance. Stragglers in plenty. They have been to Washington! That's what's the matter." The "authorities" looked the other way, and two days later, the Sixth Corps retraced its steps on paths recently trodden and headed again in a northwesterly direction through Rockville, Maryland.

Once again, heat and exhaustion took their toll on the New Yorkers. Hundreds dropped by the wayside in brutal marches comparable to the road to Gettysburg the year before. Daniel Holt, who had withstood the rigors of the march and horrendous battles for two years, developed a racking cough that refused to leave him. And he could not understand the pointless marching and countermarching "when rebels are in sight or hearing." He felt sure that the endless movements would further decimate the regiment. The summer heat and humidity claimed their victims. "Dreadful hot," wrote James McCurry; "some of the men have fell dead on the road." On July 30, the 121st stopped by a cool Virginia brook, and many men jumped in to take advantage of the healing waters. During the march, Upton once again showed his compassionate side as he "did all he could to favor his men on the road and we felt thankful for this," John Hartwell wrote.[18]

With Early loose in the valley, Grant became concerned that his overall strategy of complete victory on all fronts had slipped away from him. Early easily disposed of Hunter at Kernstown, and Grant committed Phil Sheridan to remove the Confederates from the valley. He removed Hunter and replaced him with Sheridan in August. He consolidated four different military districts into one and assigned the Sixth Corps under Horatio Wright to Sheridan's new command—the Army of the Shenandoah. It consisted of the Nineteenth Corps, the Eighth Corps (the Army of West Virginia), and the Sixth Corps. For the first time in the war, the 121st left the Army of the Potomac and was assigned to another army.

With a combined command of nearly 30,000 men, Sheridan and his new army faced Early's force of 20,000 roaming freely through the valley. Grant and Sheridan overestimated Early's strength, and Lee and Early underestimated Sheridan's. Grant's instructions to Sheridan were simple—keep Early out of Maryland and away from Washington, keep him pinned down and unable to rejoin Lee around Petersburg, and avoid a general engagement. Grant told Sheridan to "do all the damage to railroads and crops you can. Carry off stock of all descriptions, and Negroes, so as to prevent further planting. If war is to last another year, we want the Shenandoah Valley to remain a barren waste." And he confided to Henry Halleck: "I hope Sheridan will wipe out the stain the Valley of the Shenandoah has been to us heretofore before he gets through." Daniel Holt considered Sheridan "first rate, and so do all." "He is a stirring officer, wide awake and alive to all around," he wrote. But he feared that Congress and "every department clerk" in the bureaucracy would impede Sheridan's ability to act.[19]

As Grant promoted Sheridan, Egbert Olcott returned to his regiment on August 22. Earlier in the month, he had gone as a human shield to Charleston, South Carolina, where he was exchanged in one of the last prisoner exchanges of the war. Fifty Union officers held in Charleston were moved to the harbor and exchanged for fifty Confederate officers on August 3, 1864. The Confederates were part of the 600 officers (the "Immortal Six Hundred") confined by Northern forces in a stockade on Morris Island, South Carolina, directly under the fire of Confederate guns by order of U.S. secretary of war Edwin M. Stanton. Supposedly, Stanton acted on information that Union officers were being held in Charleston as human shields and was merely countering the Confederate strategy.

Holt acknowledged Sheridan's and Olcott's leadership. Even though he thought poorly of Olcott as an individual, he recognized his skills as a leader and welcomed his return. "A complete overthrow in regimental matters of discipline. Glad to see it. We were getting demoralized, I am afraid," Holt revealed in his diary. Within a few weeks, though, Olcott reduced the number of hospital attendants from ten to four, cutting Holt's effectiveness and incurring his anger. "Very well," he wrote, "it is strange that military men cannot let medical alone. We have the power and will have our own way yet. This game has been tried by Col. Olcott and failed. It will now."

Holt's praise for Olcott can be construed as a thinly veiled criticism of Henry Galpin, who had filled in for Olcott. The enlisted men did not welcome Olcott's return. The men of the 121st continued to maintain a high regard for Galpin, the "easier" commander. According to John Hartwell: "Olcott is more strict and domineering, keeping the men on drill and duties which are of no earthly use for the old troops and which Major Galpin avoided." Galpin enjoyed being a *"great favorite with the men,"* who would literally do "anything for them." The night before the battle of Opequon Creek, when Olcott returned to the regiment after a short leave (probably in Washington), "few seemed glad to see him." Between Opequon Creek and Cedar Creek, Olcott ordered all eleven members of Company C to carry a rail on their shoulders and to walk in a circle until he told them to stop. He accused the men of making disparaging remarks about him and "cheering derisively." Although they pleaded their innocence, he did not relieve them of their punishment until nightfall, three hours later. Olcott questioned each man individually and then allowed them to return to their quarters. Hartwell boasted that veterans did not complain, but he called the actions "unmerited and unjust punishment" by a "head strong, willful commander," and he promised that everyone would not forget the injustice. Dr. Holt scolded Olcott in his diary: "Colonel Olcott must look out how he orders a whole company to be thus punished." The men felt sure that Galpin's good deeds "to help the men along in hard times and his acts of kindness" to them would "always be remembered." The winnowing process to find a new commander relegated Galpin to number two, leaving Olcott firmly in charge.[20]

Olcott moved immediately to reinstate military matters and manners that had slipped under Galpin, as he returned to the Upton model of perfection and precision. But as much as he tried to emulate Upton, he failed. Upton enjoyed a loyalty from his men that Olcott could not inspire. His cold, businesslike demeanor did not endear him to the men of the 121st. His insistence on stricter military discipline upset the enlisted ranks further. In a remarkable move a month after his return and during a very active and dangerous military campaign in the valley, he issued a broad set of orders covering the pertinent and the irrelevant. To ensure that units received the full component of fighting men, he ordered all company commanders to punish soldiers who were absent without leave—a commonsense approach to the severe situation faced by the army. Any officers failing to do so would themselves face court-martial for disobedience. Falling out on the march without a surgeon's release would result in a court-martial for the officer for disobeying orders and for the enlisted man for straggling. Olcott also ordered the officers of the company to march alongside their men when on the road. He gave authority to all officers to arrest any man for making a "nuisance" on the road and for using "loud and obscene" language. He reminded all that he would demand "strict compliance with the military etiquette," represented by the proper saluting of officers and the removal of hats in officers' quarters. He urged officers and noncommissioned officers to re-member that they were looked up to by the enlisted men as examples of "pa-tience, obedience, fortitude, and courage." The penalty for ignoring his admo-nitions would be immediate but undefined "severe punishments."[21]

Many of the sick or wounded men who had been away from the regiment returned and "increased its strength and appearance materially." But the con-stant hard marching throughout the month of August threatened to weaken the men once again. Sunstroke began to take its toll on the brigade. When pos-sible, men would fall out on the roadside and soak their heads with any avail-able water to cool down their bodies. John Ingraham saw two young women carry water to a few soldiers on the roadside, bathing them. When they were not marching, the men of the 121st encountered the enemy in rearguard ac-tions, on the picket lines, on the skirmish lines, but never in a full-fledged battle—until September 19. Many of the original members of the regiment re-called the month as the second anniversary of their enlistment and the begin-ning of the one-year countdown until they could return to their loved ones.

They passed through Harpers Ferry and Charlestown several times. They understood the historical nature of both places. The men expressed disap-pointment with Harpers Ferry's physical appearance. John Hartwell hoped to see the ruins of the armory and the great iron bridge over the rivers. Instead, he discovered a "wreck of a once Romantic village." He was so amused by the repeated movements through Harpers Ferry that he told his wife they decided to rename the Sixth Corps "Harpers Weekly." But he quickly recognized that the heat and rapid marches were depleting the men—"killing us slowly but surely: our once large and good looking corps of men are sadly thinned, the men . . . look haggard and worn out." By his count, the regiment had covered 364 miles by September 1, since the beginning of the Overland campaign.

On August 22, the regiment found itself on a skirmish line near Charlestown, West Virginia—the village where John Brown was hanged. They were posi-tioned in a field of recently cut wheat. In this deceptively picturesque farm set-ting with its gently rolling hills, the rebels were posted behind the outbuildings, fence posts, and wheat stacks. As the Confederate troops began firing, Upton ordered the men to lie down. He rode the line with the admonition "I want you to show the army that no rebel line of battle can drive this regiment from its position." Wilbur Champney, a young recruit from Litchfield in Company B, had been severely wounded in both legs at Salem Church and just rejoined the regiment. His colleagues warned him to take cover as sharpshooters found the 121st's range and were directing well-placed shots at the regiment—one into a soldier's gun stock, another into a blanket. Champney determined to take an-other shot. As he aimed at the sharpshooter, a ball pierced his forehead, killing him instantly. Under cover of darkness, his comrades took his body to the rear and buried him. John Lovejoy managed to get off five shots. As he took aim a sixth time, he was hit in the left ankle—putting him out of action once again. Confederate troops overran Company I, which occupied the skirmish line on the far right. The company moved forward too quickly, exposing its right flank. The men fled to the rear to join the reserve. In the exchange of fire, Samuel Babcock, "a good soldier and a good boy" from Laurens, was shot in the head and died an hour afterward. The men from the company "brought him off and buried him in a grove near Charlestown."[22]

The faltering troop morale caused John Hartwell to weaken momentarily. He considered reenlisting as a commissioned officer, but that would keep him from his beloved wife for three more years. His friend Daniel Webster Green from Fairfield had joined the regiment with the rest as a sergeant, but after being reduced to the enlisted ranks, he received a discharge to become a clerk in the Adjutant General's office in Washington on March 31, 1864. The idea of securing a safe desk job invigorated Hartwell, but he realized that he would need political help from Herkimer County to leave the 121st. Green offered to lend a hand but told him he needed recommendations from "men of Great Influence." Hartwell understood that before he would even be considered, he needed the intercession of former Democrat congressman Frank Spinner from Mohawk, treasurer of the United States, or from the Remington family in Ilion. He felt qualified for many of the duties in the office. A desk job would get him out of the army honorably and put him out of harm's way, but in the end, the possibility proved to be nothing but wishful thinking. He concluded that he did "not expect to ever go there."[23]

That autumn, the 121st welcomed back a familiar face. Chaplain John Ripley Adams of the 5th Maine had mustered out with the regiment when it left the field on June 24, 1864. When Chaplain John Sage returned to upstate New York, the 121st did not have a chaplain, so Adams did double duty as spiritual adviser for both regiments over a period of thirteen months. Sage paled in comparison to Adams in the eyes of the men of the 121st. Adams had graduated from Yale and had been a successful preacher for more than forty years when the war began. His reputation throughout the entire corps placed him in demand for funeral sermons and Sunday services. His connections with the Sanitary and Christian Commission produced supplies on his word alone. He had taught and preached for several years in the Empire State, and his son served as a chaplain in the 1st New York Mounted Rifles. The men of the 121st were so taken with Adams's style and substance that they prevailed on Governor Seymour to ask for his services with the regiment. In addition, other chaplains petitioned Albany to appoint Adams, "an exemplary Christian," as the 121st's chaplain.

Adams acquiesced and mustered back into service as the regiment's chaplain on September 15. Dr. Holt commented: "He is a *good* man and a *smart* one at that. We feel fortunate in securing his services. The Fifth Maine is now nearer

(above left) The Reverend John Adams, chaplain. Beloved by the men of the 121st, he transferred to the regiment when his enlistment ended with the 5th Maine. He served out the war and died within a year from "nervous exhaustion." From Isaac O. Best, *History of the 121st.* (above right) John Slocum, surgeon. A respected doctor and brother of Maj. Gen. Henry Slocum, he became Dr. Holt's nemesis when he was given the top medical post in the regiment over Holt. The two coexisted until Slocum recommended a medical discharge for Holt. Author's collection.

our hearts than ever." Delavan Bates effusively lauded Adams, calling him a "noble, whole souled individual, working from a sense of duty, and . . . second only to Col. Upton in influence with the regiment." Fellow Mainer Joshua Chamberlain called Adams his "admirable friend." Overall, the men loved Adams. Often while on the road in the valley, the men of the regiment would be roused before daylight and ordered to strike their tents and prepare to move, only to have the order countermanded and tents pitched again. Once, the men of the 121st surprised Adams by restriking his tent, with the comment that they would move out the next day—"we never fix up our camp and tents without moving." They moved out the next day.[24]

Adams's strong, God-fearing, New England Congregationalist bearing made an immediate and tangible impact on the 121st Regiment. He continued his practice of holding nightly prayer meetings. His fervor and tireless energy led him to visit other regimental camps for weekly services, and he often preached twice on Sundays—he devoted the afternoon session to a sermon and the evening to a prayer meeting. In January 1865, Adams petitioned the Christian Commission for seat boards to furnish his chapel in winter quarters. Normally, he would not have asked for seats if the 121st was operating in hardwood country, but since the only available seating consisted of pine benches, he asked the commission to furnish him ready-made seats. Pine's tendency to exude tar pitch made seating very uncomfortable and extremely sticky. "I want an impression to be made," wrote Adams, "on the head and heart, and not on the clothes."[25]

Three weeks after Adams assumed his new duties, Colonel Olcott issued his general orders, two of which concerned Sunday worship and obscene language. It is uncertain whether Adams crafted them, but the timing coincidence is remarkable, particularly since they were the first and only orders issued in the regiment that dealt specifically with those topics. The first made attendance at divine service "every Sabbath" mandatory for all "officers and men unless excused" by the regimental commander; the second banned "all obscene talk" within the 121st. From then on, all officers and noncommissioned officers were "to arrest and report" all violators. Since all commissioned and noncommissioned officers were considered to be "above" using obscene language and were therefore held up as role models, no provisions were made for *their* arrest.[26]

Adams insisted that the 121st should always maintain a fervent religious awareness. And if that was the case, then these two general orders were coincidental. In any event, there is no evidence that they were ever enforced, and Adams never mentioned them to his wife in his voluminous correspondence. But on October 5, 1864, the 121st New York Volunteers officially went on record as opposed to obscene talk and in favor of divine service on the Sabbath. This is not to minimize the reverend's good intentions. He truly considered his men's well-being, and he reserved his most charitable words to rebuke them for their bad behavior. In December 1864, when the division ferried back to Petersburg after spending the autumn in the Shenandoah Valley, Adams participated in a "suppression of mirthfulness." Catching several men playing cards on a Sunday, he reminded them it was the Sabbath. Charitably, he wrote of them: "When the day was brought to their notice, they at once suspended their games. It is not strange that men sometimes forget the calendar."[27]

The loss of the 5th Maine brought other changes to Upton's brigade. The addition of the 2nd Connecticut Heavy Artillery entailed a large influx of new men. The 95th Pennsylvania expected to return home soon, and many of its men chose not to reenlist. As a result, the 96th Pennsylvania and the 95th were consolidated. The new brigade nearly doubled with the addition of the 65th New York Volunteers, Col. Joseph E. Hamblin commanding. Meanwhile, the 121st, low on manpower at just over 250 rifles, prepared once again to meet the enemy—the familiar adversaries of past engagements: "The Louisianans of Rappahannock Station were there, the Alabamians of Salem Church, the Virginians and Georgians of the Wilderness, and Dole's and Battle's men of Spotsylvania, and we did not fear them," Clinton Beckwith wrote years later.[28]

On September 1, Grant sent Sheridan a dubious note to the effect that a single source in Richmond indicated Early had begun to move back to Petersburg to reinforce Lee. As a result, Grant intended to attach the Sixth Corps to his command. Early's men were all veterans—John C. Breckinridge, a veteran of the western theater, Robert Rodes, who faced the 121st at Spotsylvania, and John B. Gordon, the Sixth Corps's familiar nemesis at the Wilderness. Sheridan rebutted Grant the next day with his own intelligence, suggesting that although Lee had ordered Early back, the latter had not moved yet. His sources told him that Early remained to his front. When Sheridan tested his theory by ordering General Torbert and his cavalry to demonstrate against the enemy's pickets on the Opequon, he discovered that none of Early's troops had left the valley. Further conflicting reports came that same day, September 3, from Maj. Gen. C. C. Augur, commanding the Twenty-second Army Corps, to William Halleck; he reported that Early had returned to Petersburg in a "desperate effort" to "retake the Weldon Road" and that he left only Breckinridge in the valley with 20,000 men. Augur repeated his intelligence to Sheridan the next day, saying that Early was at Gordonsville and on his way to Richmond and that he regarded the information "as reliable." The uncertainty kept the Union commands on alert and on the move. Lee underestimated Sheridan's strength and recalled Joseph Kershaw to Petersburg.[29]

Opequon and the Third Battle of Winchester

Everything changed on September 18 when the Sixth Corps received orders to "move upon the enemy." Every day in early September, Sheridan had expected to engage the rebels. When he learned of Kershaw's return to Petersburg, he acted. He attacked Early on September 19. As one of his men recalled years after the war, "Sheridan had a bad habit of early rising and the army was astir by two o'clock." Following Wilson's cavalry, the 121st with the rest of the Sixth Corps headed due west, leaving the sleepy village of Berryville, on the pike to Winchester. The men of the 121st roused from sleep at that early hour but did not break camp until 3:30 A.M. Despite the early start, the heavy action did not begin until noon that day. In a welcome change, the infantry walked alongside the road, leaving the entire roadbed to the artillery and supply trains. They crossed the Opequon at 9:00 A.M. Wilson's cavalry started the general engagement, pushing the enemy back 2 miles over rough ground through a narrow valley and out into the open. The Nineteenth Corps and the 2nd and 3rd divisions of the Sixth Corps pushed on under heavy fire and musketry. The 1st Division of the Sixth Corps and the 121st remained in reserve.

For a time, Union forces carried everything before them. During the advance, an opening occurred between the two corps, which Rodes immediately began to exploit. Sheridan later reported to Grant that he swung his left flank to cut Early off from Winchester. "This movement would have been entirely successful," he wrote, "if it had not been for a part of Rickett's division . . . and a portion of the 19th Corps, which came back in confusion. This mishap was soon remedied by the good conduct of Upton's Brigade." He admitted that he and Grant had underestimated Early's troop strength.[30]

As the opposing forces surged and retreated, gaps were filled and charges made. Upton rallied his men forward to close the lines and ensure that the 65th and 67th Consolidated New York passed to the 121st's rear. Quickly becoming a veteran infantry regiment, the 2nd Connecticut remained slightly to the rear in reserve. In the confusion, a line of troops in the 121st's front was seen advancing, but no one could determine whether they were friend or foe. They were so close that Upton ordered his command to fix bayonets. His troops were to fire only on his word. When he determined that they were indeed Confederate troops, Upton ordered his lines to open fire, followed by the command "Forward, charge!" As the 121st reached the rebel lines, they came upon many of the Confederate soldiers lying on the ground and assumed they were killed or wounded. To their surprise, they found many of them untouched. They had fallen down to escape the volley poured into them and immediately surrendered to the advancing Union lines.

Firing continued all day. Around 4:00 in the afternoon, the 121st moved into some heavy timber, where the men came under increasingly effective fire. Disregarding the fire, they charged the Confederates and chased them all the way into the village of Winchester. Horatio Wright wrote of the Nineteenth and Sixth corps soldiers that they were "in the best of spirits, and nothing could resist their determined advance." In the charge on the Confederate lines, the heavy, loaded knapsack on Clinton Beckwith's back swung around to cover his chest just as a piece of exploded shell slammed into it as he ran ahead with the color guard. Shrapnel ripped through the flimsy canvas and passed through his rations of pork, sugar, and hardtack and then struck his tin plate, knife, fork, and spoon. He fell to the ground, and as his comrades inquired into his health, he carefully checked his upper body for blood and a wound. Except for "numbness and a bad bruise, I was unhurt and I soon got over it," he wrote. "I was some lame, but managed to keep on the march, getting into our camp by the roadside shortly after the regiment."

Edwin Ford, seriously wounded in his left side, died October 8 after the doctors had predicted his recovery. A young nurse from Winchester, Sarah Beck, cared for him until he breathed his last in a pleasant sleep. He had joined Company C as a Fairfield Academy student. His father, William, a prosperous Fairfield dairyman, traveled to Winchester to claim his body and accompany it back to Herkimer County. Once again, Company I, John Kidder's old unit, experienced intense fire. Lt. Joe Heath, commissioned that summer, took a minié ball to the face. His wound was noticed by George Teel, who remarked to his wife that the line officers of his company were the unluckiest in the regiment, a majority of them having been killed, wounded, or taken prisoner.[31]

Emory Upton realized his dream of leading a division at Opequon Creek. His friend and mentor Gen. David Allen Russell, who had tutored him at Rappahannock Station and shared in the glory of the captured flags there, died after a Confederate shell burst nearby as he led his old brigade on the charge. "He was killed instantly," Chaplain Adams lamented, "with solid shot or shell that lacerated him terribly." Upton, who had earned his star that spring, assumed command of the division as a brigadier general. He turned the 2nd Brigade over to Col. Joseph Eldridge Hamblin of the 65th New York.[32]

But Upton's new command proved short-lived. Slightly wounded at Spotsylvania in the spring, he was hit again, this time more seriously. When Chaplain Adams found him, a shell had torn a hole in one leg "three inches in length and one in depth." Upton lay on the field unconcerned about his leg but "rejoicing over the victory." According to Adams, he expressed his willingness "to give a leg for such a brilliant victory." He then "took the colors in his own hand" and yelled, "'come on men; follow me.'" John Hartwell reported that Upton led the "last grand charge and fell from his horse into the arms of his soldiers who carefully carried him to the rear as soon as possible."

Command of the division passed to Col. Oliver Edwards of the 37th Massachusetts, and John DePeyster Douw, Colonel Franchot's nephew, led the 121st. The men of the 121st praised their opponents as "the best" in the Confederate army but despaired over Russell's death and Upton's wounding. They knew at the time that Upton's wound was not life-threatening and that he would recover. Upton told Delavan Bates while recuperating that his wounding was "purely accidental." What his comrades did not know was that this would be their last battle with their leader and teacher. Sheridan gave all the credit to Upton and his brigade for stemming the tide at Opequon Creek.[33]

Upton went home to Batavia to recuperate. Frank Morse had spent the summer recovering from his exhaustion in Cherry Valley, but he returned to the regiment in September when he heard the news of Opequon Creek. Upton had written Morse telling him of his wound and that he was authorized to have an aide while he convalesced. He asked Morse to join him "when and where" he pleased. Morse decided to cast his lot with Upton, and when the latter recovered sufficiently, the two met up in Batavia.

In November, Upton visited Morse in Cherry Valley and then went on to New York and ultimately Washington, where Morse caught up with him. In the capital, Upton received his new orders to report to James Wilson as a cavalry division commander at Nashville. Morse and Upton traveled together to Harpers Ferry at the end of November to say good-bye to old friends in the Sixth Corps. Upton's brief speech offered praise and advice to his old regiment, the 121st. At Winchester, Upton's wound reopened and aggravated his general health, delaying his trip west until December. Morse went on ahead, and the two reunited in January in Louisville, where Upton took command of Wilson's 4th Division. They finished their service together in the cavalry during the war's last four months. The two were no longer associated with the 121st New York Volunteers, 2nd Brigade, 1st Division, Sixth Corps. The men were distressed to see Upton leave. John Lovejoy remarked, "He was always so kind to us." For his part, Upton credited the 121st for his promotion to brigadier. Members of the 121st remembered Upton until the last survivor died.[34]

Meanwhile, Sheridan duly reported his victory at Opequon Creek to Grant, calling it a "stubborn and sanguinary engagement" that completely defeated the rebels, ultimately driving them into Winchester. He counted the enemy's losses: his forces had taken 2,500 prisoners, 5 artillery pieces, and 9 flags. Besides Upton, Brig. Gen. John Ballie McIntosh lost his right leg, and Brig. Gen. George Henry Chapman received a slight wound. The next day, September 20, Lincoln wrote Sheridan: "Have just heard of your great victory. God bless you all, officers and men. Strongly inclined to come up and see you." Stanton followed up with the good news that Grant had recommended Sheridan for promotion to brigadier general in the Regular Army and offered him command of the Middle Division. They celebrated in Washington with a 100-gun salute at midday in honor of the victory. Grant, too, responded to Sheridan with a 100-gun salute, but he tempered his euphoria with a practical caution: "If practicable, push your success and make all you can of it." Secretary of War Stanton expressed his impatience as well. The army's dispatches telling the story of Opequon merely whetted his curiosity. He asked Gen. John Stevenson at Harpers Ferry for the latest news. "Your good tidings of yesterday and this morning," he wrote, "makes us anxious for more."[35]

At nightfall, James McCurry of Company F summarized the events of September 19: "Started at 2 o'clock this morning, heavy fighting opened at daylight on the Opequon Creek and our men drove them through Winchester. Losses are very heavy. General Russell killed."[36]

Fisher's Hill

The Union army chased Early up the valley. Leaving Winchester on September 20, they found him entrenched south of Strasburg, ready to give battle. They were in the narrowest point of the valley, where the eastern and western ridges were only 5 miles apart. His left flank stretched thinly to the west, and Sheridan immediately exploited it with infantry and Wilson's cavalry. On September 21, the Sixth and Nineteenth corps were in line of battle, on the left and to the right, respectively. Sheridan reported his troops were "fatigued" after the battle at Opequon Creek, but he continued to press them. Throughout the day and night, they maneuvered for position. By the next morning, Wright and Sheridan were satisfied that everything was in place. The infantry entrenched, and the strategically placed artillery came forward. The simple plan anticipated that the Union's Army of West Virginia would turn the enemy's left flank, and the Sixth Corps would attack its center. Perfectly placed Union batteries delivered devastating support for the advancing troops on the right as the rebel left flank turned as planned. The synchronization of attacking forces on the center worked beautifully, resulting in a "complete success." The rebel force became disoriented, and as a result, a chaotic retreat left rebel flags and artillery in Union hands. When the swarming federals gained the objective, they discovered carefully arranged musket cartridges on the breastworks, intended for rapid fire. Many of the Confederate positions were impregnable, and "yet, our men," wrote Wright, "flushed with the victory of the Opequon, disregarding all obstacles . . . moved gallantly forward, carried the works, and pursued the enemy till after dark." In Wright's opinion, the battle and victory were classic.[37]

The men of the 121st believed that Early had been beaten, a view shared by most of the commanders on the ground and in Washington. Sheridan and Grant were convinced that Early's force would slink away, a whipped army, and Grant believed that Sheridan's work would end in the fall of Richmond. James W. Forsyth, the chief of staff for the Middle Division, reported that "Early's army is nothing but a routed mob." When John Stevenson wrote Stanton from Harpers Ferry with news of Sheridan's victory at Fisher's Hill, he offered the opinion that "this is, in all probability, the finale of General Early"; in another message, he said that Sheridan had annihilated Early's army as an "effective organization."[38]

The Battle of Cedar Creek

By the end of September, the men of the 121st had begun to think of themselves as battle-tested veterans. Dr. Holt's spirits were lifted by the recent victories. He minimized the brigade's and regiment's losses in its burn-and-run operations in the valley and proudly boasted that the 121st had earned a "name and character in the army of which any command might well be proud." After the battles of Opequon Creek and Fisher's Hill and in accordance with Grant's directive, the 121st took an active role in laying waste to the Shenandoah Valley. Everything available to the rebels—barns, grain stacks, mills, and factories—was burned to the ground. According to Holt, the 121st single-handedly burned "119 barns" and every haystack in its path. "One heavy, black cloud of smoke hangs over the valley like a pall of death," he wrote his wife. Provisions, however, were a different matter. Food could be taken when found. Despite Holt's dark description, at Harrisonburg, the regiment's bad boy, Corporal Beckwith, found plenty of good things to eat, including apple butter, honey, chickens, and lamb. He remembered the fertile valley with its timberlands of oak and other valuable woods. He found the land "well watered." The built environment represented "wealth and prosperity" that the troops systematically burned. Rabid secessionists, through and through, were another matter. The children, well schooled in Yankee hating, regarded the troops "as barbarians" and willingly gave the invaders "some striking illustrations of their opinions." No one sympathized with the rebel civilians, "no matter how brave and honest in their opinion," as they ultimately did "their utmost to destroy us."

Undeterred, Beckwith and Philip Goodwin, a private from German Flats who was a member of Company B and a "first-class forager," thought they would do some scouting on their own. Near the village of Bridgewater, they hit pay dirt and came away with a treasure of good provisions. They were gone only a few hours, but when they returned to camp, they discovered that the 121st had moved on. "Loaded down with our commissary supplies," Beckwith remembered, they soon caught up with the regiment. No one said anything to them that night, but the next morning, the newly minted first sergeant Horatio Duroe ordered the two to report to Captain Douw. There, they received a lecture on being absent without permission—especially for foraging. Beckwith lost his corporal's stripes for the second time in the war. He also received extra duty policing the camp, which he did "without a murmur." After Lee's surrender, Beckwith's rank of corporal was reinstated.[39]

John Ingraham, though he wanted an end to the guerrilla raids and the end of the war there in the Shenandoah Valley, could still not endure the burning and destruction. He openly expressed his empathy for poor families with small children who lost everything they owned except for the clothes on their backs. "All unmovable property of any account is burned to ashes," he wrote to his parents. Refugees clogged the roads north and south, most preferring to move north. Released slaves and poor whites climbed aboard army supply trains to get out of the line of fire. Whenever Sheridan stopped the army for the night, every man made a straight line for the closest civilian houses to forage for food.[40]

Aside from the victory at Fisher's Hill, the army was inactive in the month between Opequon Creek and Cedar Creek, which surprised many, even as Sheridan ravaged the valley as far south as Staunton. During the month, Olcott petitioned Albany for more men, and he began to tinker with the companies and their structure. He asked for a new Company B, a move that could not only increase the regiment's efficiency but also improve his chances to be mustered as a colonel. The still-viable Early, with Kershaw's command rejoining him, probed Sheridan's lines for weaknesses. By October 14, Sheridan's army had rested on Cedar Creek's north bank, near the hamlets of Belle Grove and Middletown. The weather turned pleasant, the troops were paid, absentee ballots for the presidential election were passed out to the enlisted men, and an atmosphere of hope permeated the army. Many were happy not to be in the trenches at Petersburg as they learned of the debacle of the Crater in July. They also followed the progress of Sherman's army as it marched through Georgia.[41]

Sheridan traveled to Washington to meet with Grant and plan the next move. Grant wanted him to move up the valley (southward) as far as Lynchburg as a base of operations against Charlottesville and Gordonsville. Eventually, he wanted Sheridan to rejoin him at Petersburg, burning and destroying en route. Sheridan refused to endorse the plan. He wanted to set up a defensive position in the valley and send the Sixth Corps back to Petersburg. Before he left for the capital and without Grant's concurrence, Sheridan sent the 121st and the Sixth Corps on their way to Washington. Daniel Holt could not control his outrage at yet another move. He could not understand the painful and endless marches back and forth, to and fro. He complained bitterly of the ineptness of the commanders and the leaders in Washington, and as his health continued to deteriorate, he began to fret about his own fate. The Sixth Corps managed to get only as far as Ashby's Gap when Sheridan decided that Early posed a larger threat than he had previously thought. With that, the 121st reversed course to rejoin the troops in the valley.[42]

On the banks of the confluence of Cedar Creek and the North Fork of the Shenandoah River, the Union army stretched from south to north. The left flank of Gen. George Crook's Eighth Corps rested 1,300 yards from the crotch where the creek flowed into the river. Gen. William H. Emory's Nineteenth Corps held the center of the Union line as it faced the creek. Wright's returning Sixth Corps, near Meadow Brook, and a large contingent of cavalry consisting of George Custer's and Wesley Merritt's commands were on the far right. Opposing them on the south bank of Cedar Creek, Jubal Early's regrouped Southern army sat waiting and watching. The Valley Turnpike from Strasburg to Middletown ran directly through the center of both armies. On the east bank of the North Fork of the Shenandoah River sat Massanutten Mountain. Around the mountain base and between it and the North Fork ran the Manassas Gap Railroad.

Early's work in the valley remained unfinished. On October 18, he decided on a daring plan of attack drawn up by the 121st's old nemesis, Gen. John B. Gordon, now the senior major general in the Confederate army. It called for Gordon to cross the Shenandoah twice, following a narrow path along the western base of Massanutten Mountain with three divisions. After crossing the river at Bowman's Ford below the Union's Eighth Corps, he would deploy and then attack at dawn the next morning. Above Gordon's position, Kershaw's South Carolinians would cross Cedar Creek, join Gordon on his left, and attack the camp of the Nineteenth Corps. Brig. Gen. Gabriel C. Wharton, by way of the Valley Pike, would cross the Cedar Creek Bridge and attack on the extreme left. Artillery support would come from Hupp's Hill in the general area where

Wharton's division began its attack. One clear objective was the Sixth Corps, which was positioned behind the other two corps just west of Middletown. Belle Grove Manor, Sheridan's headquarters, was another objective; Early was unaware that Sheridan had gone to Washington. The battle was to consist of four distinctive phases: the surprise Confederate attack, the federal response, a controversial lull that would reverberate well after the war, and the federal counterattack late in the day.[43]

October 18 was a soft, mellow autumn day in Virginia; the leaves down the valley were at their peak colors. The crystal-clear air and the diamond-bright sky gave a peaceful aura to what would be yet another battle site. On Massanutten Mountain the day before, Confederate scouts and General Gordon himself had looked down into the federal camps below with impunity. As one historian has said, "From there, they had a panoramic view of Sheridan's whole camp. In this pre-camouflage era every position, every gun became clearly visible from the Confederate aerie. Gordon said he could see the color of the piping on the soldiers' jackets and the sores on the horses' backs."

At 8:00 P.M. on October 18, Gordon slowly began to wind his way around the mountain. Traveling all night, he positioned his entire command in front of the Eighth Corps. A bright, nearly full moon illuminated the landscape below. At daybreak, a rolling fog in the valley of the Shenandoah obscured all movements. It also hid the Eighth Corps and the Nineteenth Corps from the view of the Sixth Corps. Most of the Union army slept. The valley was "peaceful and quiet," with "no sign of war" evident. Guard fires were scattered around the grounds, and at 5:00 A.M., the guard changed as sleepy new sentries took their posts. Early's men in Kershaw's brigade had forded the creek at 4:30 that morning and were so close to the federal lines that they could hear "the early risers talking to each other in their tents."[44]

Gordon led the charge, as planned the day before. At 5:00 A.M., he attacked the sleeping federal army's Eighth Corps. Private Beckwith's guard duty occurred at precisely the same time. Beckwith had spent the entire night before gambling the cool hours away with some fellows from the 77th New York until an officer of the day dispersed the crowd. Instead of going to bed, he played penny ante with a few boys of the 121st until his relief time at 5:00 A.M. Olcott had attended a party of either the 65th New York or the 2nd Connecticut Heavy Artillery, where "they were having a jolly time." He recalled a bright, moonlit night and noted that down on the creek, "a streak of fog was rising, which in the distance looked like a long, narrow streak of snow against the side of the mountains." Reluctantly, the sleep-deprived Beckwith reported to his post. "The snoring of the men in the tents" was the only noise breaking the silence. The man he relieved grumbled at his tardiness, and Beckwith went around posting his guards in the proper places. He warmed himself at the campfire, sipped coffee, lit his pipe, and fought sleep by stretching and walking around. The quiet struck him as odd. He noted that the fog obscured his view of the other two corps.[45]

The sound of firing on the left seeped into Beckwith's consciousness. A deadly silence and then a volley on the right of the line followed in rapid succession. At first, he thought that Mosby and his bushwhackers had attacked them. But Gordon and his corps smashed into the sleeping left flank of the federal army. All along the Union line, the alarm sounded. Slowly at first and then with great urgency, the bluecoats began to realize their peril. The men of the Sixth Corps, farthest from the point of attack, dressed and donned their battle gear. As the roar of battle grew louder and more ominous, the Sixth moved toward the Valley Turnpike. The opaque fog increased the apprehension of the men all along the line as the sounds of musketry and cannons increased. Soon, out of the fog came not a horde of screaming rebels but members of the Eighth and Nineteenth corps, "partially clothed and without arms." In vain, their officers had tried to stop the stampede to the rear. The men had been rudely awakened by the rebels and were only able to escape with the clothes on their backs and nothing else. Beckwith remembered that they "were simply insane with fear." The men of the 121st were shocked to see veterans running for their lives in nothing more than the clothes they slept in when Gordon's and Kershaw's men struck them. Instead of rallying them, the Sixth Corps officers rode out in front of the fog and herded the unruly masses to their rear.[46]

Once all the retreating forces had passed through the 121st and the Sixth Corps, the fog lifted only slightly, allowing visibility of at least 50 yards. With the passage of the routed troops, Olcott determined to make a stand on a small ridge against whatever came out of the fog. The 121st was accompanied by the 1st Rhode Island Light Artillery, Battery C. With John Hartwell in charge, Olcott ordered twenty men from Company C to post themselves 600 yards in front of the ridge as skirmishers. When the wave of Confederates came out of the vapor, the 121st discovered that they were their old nemeses: Gordon's veterans and Hays's and Stafford's Louisianans, whom they had met at Rappahannock Station. The 121st and the Rhode Island battery held on for at least thirty minutes as the fog lifted and they realized the peril they faced. They were being flanked on both sides, Lamb's men were being picked off, and Gordon's men had seized the moment and charged the poorly defended cannon. The 121st held off the attackers and was able to withdraw to Lamb's position, where the men pulled the guns by hand to the rear. Hartwell noted that the rapid firing caused the regiment "to lose men fearfully" in their exposed position. William Henry Harrison "Tip" Goodier, Frank Carran's cousin, alongside Beckwith, was wounded. Capt. Jonathon Burrell and Capt. John Douw were both mortally wounded.

The 121st retreated with the rest of the army, which now resembled a mob, but it never panicked or became confused or demoralized. Olcott, commanding the 2nd Brigade, ordered his men to "retire slowly, from crest to crest, holding the enemy in check if he advanced." As they fell back to more defensible positions, they left the dead and wounded on the field. The "roar of artillery was indeed terrible," and the air was "filled by bursting and whistling shells and bullets." The lines were re-formed about a mile from the first encounter with minimum cover and were able to hold off the attacking Confederates for the better part of the morning. A second orderly pullback put the entire Union force a mile north of Middletown. The troops formed in two lines in a wood to the right of the 3rd Division, and "the Brigade remained in this position two to three hours." A mile south of the Union line, the Confederates filled the works the Union forces had recently vacated. Five hours had passed since the first rebel troops crashed into the Union left flank. Horatio Wright continued in charge of the army in Sheridan's absence. He quietly and efficiently shored up his routed troops and managed to re-form their lines. On the other side of the line, the Confederates paused—a suspension that would be controversial well after the war.[47]

At 10:30 A.M., Phil Sheridan, hearing the sounds of battle on his return from Washington, arrived on horseback at the collapsing and regrouping Union lines after a galloping ride from Winchester. He heard the artillery but took no notice of a battle until he arrived at Mill Creek, a half mile from Winchester. There, he saw the long line of fugitives and "trains and men coming to the rear with appalling rapidity," he later wrote. "I tell you he was awful mad when he saw them," John Ingraham remarked. Henry Wood also saw Sheridan as he rode up on his horse, Rienzi. "That beautiful black charger was covered with dust and foam," he remembered. Sheridan's legendary ride, memorialized in poetry after the war, became the rallying point for the Union army. Taking charge, Sheridan immediately completed Wright's line and began moving units around like chess pieces. He rode along the line of the Sixth Corps to let the men know he had returned, and stopping in front of the brigade, he exhorted everyone to give the rebels hell. Clinton Beckwith saw him with Col. Randall Mackenzie of the 2nd Connecticut, now in charge of the brigade, and with Colonel Olcott, riding the lines and positioning units as needed. He placed cavalry on both flanks, put the Eighth Corps in reserve, and ordered the Nineteenth Corps to pivot to the southeast around the Sixth Corps. After a half hour of pushing the gray-coated skirmishers in, he attacked at 4:00 P.M.

The rebels fought valiantly for an hour. Olcott succeeded Mackenzie when he was wounded. Gordon's line on the left broke when Custer got in his rear. The panic and stampede now reversed itself. According to John Hartwell, the rebels turned and ran "for dear life like a flock of sheep and we in hot pursuit pouring into their broken lines a terrible fire." Clinton Beckwith feared the charge meant certain death, but as soon as the 121st rose in line, "the devils behind the walls broke and ran as fast as they could." When the fleeing troops reached the south side of Strasburg, heading south, they bunched up in a traffic jam at Spangler's Mill. As a result, the Yankees were able to recover most of the rolling stock lost earlier that day. By 10:00 P.M., the exhausted troops ate a much-delayed breakfast "and then lay down and slept as sweetly as if nothing had happened."[48]

The battle of Cedar Creek created further gaps in the ranks of the 121st. The official reports told of 10 killed, 42 wounded, and 5 men either captured or missing. Chaplain Adams wrote his wife: "We are short of officers . . . our major . . . was wounded last week . . . only one captain is with the regiment." William Tucker, a first lieutenant from Roseboom and an original member of Company G, fell while "constantly encouraging his men" at the head of Company A. He had joined the 121st as a corporal and rose to the officer ranks. He left a wife and two small children. Several days after the battle, Olcott authorized Chaplain Adams to lead a detail that eventually found Tucker's body in a trench with two others. He was buried in a grave with the others, near where he fell. On a dreary, rain-soaked Monday morning, Adams's solemn detail exhumed Tucker's body and reburied him. "It is sad to exhume the dead, and see what changes death makes in the once manly form," Adams told his wife. The detail "reformed the grave, raised and turfed it, and placed a head board [on it]." That evening, Adams held a prayer meeting on the hillside.[49]

A minié ball struck George Teel in the right ankle, "cutting off the cords and damaging the bone slightly." He avoided capture as he managed to get off the field under his own power and stumbled into an army wagon in a passing train that was 8 miles long. Much like John Kidder's experience after the Wilderness, Teel spent twenty-two hours in the wagon "without stretching." He got as far as Martinsburg, where the wounded were placed in hospitals, churches, and private homes. Teel found refuge with a good Union family, who treated him kindly before he was sent to Jarvis Hospital in Baltimore.[50]

Oncoming rebels scooped up John Douw, whose right leg was badly wounded. According to one witness, the rebels held him for nearly eight hours. Anticipating that they might take advantage of his weakened condition, Douw opened the seam in his vest and stashed nearly all of the $160 he was carrying into it. He left the rest in his pocket, thinking that if he were robbed, the intruders would take only what they could easily find. As he lay on the field, rebel scavengers pulled off his "fine high top boots." The boot on his left leg came off easily; the wounded leg, though, caused him to writhe in agony. A compassionate Confederate came along and placed the wounded leg in some straw to ease his pain. When men from his regiment finally found him, he was rushed to the rear. Completely lucid and fully believing he would recover, he asked Cronkite to write to his father and his uncle Richard Franchot. After a 15-mile ride into Winchester, Douw went into shock. His badly mangled leg was amputated. The minié ball had struck his right knee joint, moved upward shattering his thigh bone, and eventually stopped in his groin. He alternated between depression and hopefulness as he slipped in and out of consciousness. Although he had cast his vote in the elections prior to the battle, he became delirious after surgeons removed his leg and told those hovering over him that he "was anxious to have his vote prepared and forwarded."

Despite his entrée to the officer corps through his uncle, Douw had turned out to be a decent officer. He earned the respect of Captain Cronkite, Colonel Olcott, and Emory Upton. He was made in the same mold as the other three—strict, disciplined, and ambitious. Upton had lured him away from a position on General Slocum's staff before Salem Church with the promise of a captaincy, which Douw readily accepted. Olcott knew, as he did, that the staff position brought prestige, privileges, and close relations with general officers, and "it ensured him daily comforts" not available to the line officer. Olcott particularly liked Douw's stoicism, and although the men liked him, that familiarity with his troops did not doom his ability to command, as was "the misfortune of many volunteer officers."[51]

Prophetically, Jonathon Burrell had written to his brother two years earlier and mentioned that he had a story for him that could wait until the next time they were together; he thought that would be soon, but at other times, he predicted it would not be "till the close of the war if I should be so lucky as to see that day." He never did. Like John Douw, he never recovered after doctors removed his wounded leg. John Douw and Jonathon Burrell died of their wounds one week later on the same day, October 26. The regimental quartermaster, Theodore Sternberg, comforted and consoled both men in their final hours. He wrote letters to their next of kin. He "sat holding a hand of each." Sternberg remarked how peacefully they died, "as a babe going to sleep in its mother's arms." At one point he thought that Douw had died "when suddenly he opened his eyes and said, 'my, didn't the rebels skedaddle.'" John Kidder, still in Elmira recovering from his wounds suffered in the Wilderness, learned from a visitor from Herkimer "that Captain Burrell was brought home in a coffin."[52]

That night, October 19, with the rebel threat pushed back beyond the point where it began, Henry Galpin went to the top of a small incline to determine if more could be done to drive the enemy troops further. A Confederate sharpshooter drew a bead on him and shot him cleanly through both thighs. That he survived a double hit without enduring amputation, when Douw and Burrell succumbed to their wounds, is remarkable. Galpin eventually recovered but not until he had resigned his commission and returned to recuperate at his brother's home in Little Falls. Supposedly, when he went to Albany to resign, officials had placed two pieces of paper on the desk before him. One document accepted his resignation, the other was a commission as lieutenant colonel. Galpin told his brother on his return home that, deep down, he wanted the promotion and not the resignation.[53]

William Remmel disappeared. As the 121st pulled back on the ridge with Lamb's battery, "the enemy was so close upon us," Clinton Beckwith wrote, "that we were obliged to abandon the effort" to recover the wounded "and they fell into the hands of the enemy." One of the five missing or captured listed in the official returns, Remmel fell unseen. The next day, John Hartwell led a detail to look for the dead and the wounded—specifically, "for three of our boys still missing." He reported that hundreds of the dead remained unburied, many of whom had been "stripped stark naked" by the ladies of Middletown. He claimed that large numbers of the wounded were murdered after surrendering and that all were "robbed of everything even to a penny pocket comb." William Remmel was not found.

James McCurry was on the burying detail the next day. Everyone was up at sunrise, "all busily burying the dead." The 121st initially listed Remmel among the missing but eventually changed his status to "killed in action." For years, his family hoped he had spent the last few months of his life at Andersonville, for eyewitnesses reported seeing him there. Indeed, well into the twentieth century, his sister vainly tried to determine his fate. She held out hope to the end that he would be found alive and return to his family. By war's end, most presumed that he had died at Cedar Creek. A year earlier, Remmel had written his brother that he was as fit and tough as ever. He fully expected to complete his three-year term of enlistment "if some careless bullet does not waylay me."[54]

As they "were driven back by degrees" during the morning's devastating rout, Pvt. Lester Murdock of Company E remembered an orderly pullback. He wrote that many were wounded and left to the "mercy of the enemy." Murdock, in his zeal to escape, nearly walked into Lt. James Johnston's sword as it flew through the air and fell at his feet when Johnston was hit. Just as Murdock picked Johnston up with his arm over his shoulders, a bullet went through Murdock's tin coffee cup, which hung on his knapsack. With Herculean effort, Murdock managed to get Johnston out of harm's way. It took the two more than an hour to fall back half a mile to the rear.

Once Sheridan arrived and rallied the men forward over their hastily constructed breastworks, the 121st recovered its initial position. With little rest and as night began to cover the field, the survivors struck out to look for their missing comrades. Although no one found Remmel, Murdock and his comrades located Pvt. DeWitt Wells of Company E. Calling out in the darkness, they heard Wells's weak response from under a pile of hay. His new boots were gone. A compassionate rebel had gently cut them off when Wells begged him to be careful of his wounded leg. The rebel succeeded in removing the boots and left his worn-out brogans in their place. As his comrades brought Wells back for care, he was able to tell them where to find Albert E. Smith and Charlie Hogle, also from Company E. They found both of the men badly wounded. Hogle died two weeks later, on November 1, 1864. A former employee of the *Otsego*

Republican, Smith had been hit twice—once in the right thigh and then in the left foot. Doctors amputated the right leg. Smith lingered well into the next year, when he succumbed to chronic diarrhea at Patterson Park Hospital in Baltimore on February 12, 1865. He left a wife and one child.[55]

At Salem Church, Capt. Nelson Wendell had picked up the regimental colors when the color-bearer went down. When Wendell himself fell moments later, Cpl. William Hassett, the brother of Thomas Hassett, both of Company F, grabbed the flag. James Jencks, from Company K and twenty years old, picked up the colors when Hassett fell mortally wounded. Somehow, Jencks survived and carried the colors through some of the worst fighting experienced by the 121st. John Brandon, Company G, apprenticed as a color guard under Jencks. Jencks received a hip wound in the initial rebel assault at Cedar Creek, the shot first going through his haversack. The two lines were no more than 20 rods apart, and there was a rebel flag flying in the faces of the Union troops, the two flags "looking defiance at each other."

Once the Nineteenth Corps had passed through the Sixth Corps lines, the 121st and the rest of the line poured heavy fire at the approaching Confederates. Jencks went to the rear with the flag to have the surgeons attend to his leg. When the 121st regrouped that afternoon behind a stone wall, Jencks returned. Brandon told him to stay out of the fight with his wound. Jencks replied, "If the regiment goes I will go if I get killed." With that, the 121st charged over the protection of the stone wall and attacked the rebels behind a rail fence. They successfully drove them back. Jencks, kneeling in the front line with the flag staff before him, was hit by a shell, which tore away the lower part of his face. Brandon picked up the flag for the second time that day "and lived to bring it safely home." Although badly wounded, Jencks's immediate survival astounded Dr. Slocum. He died a few days later.[56]

John Kidder learned of the regiment's fight at Cedar Creek from his wife. Galpin's and Jencks's misfortunes particularly saddened him, and he expressed hope for their recovery. He longed to share the glory in which the regiment basked. Kidder reflected on Jencks's unselfish and courageous service throughout some of the toughest fighting the regiment endured. He also lamented George Teel's wounding. But he never mentioned William Remmel. Perhaps word of Remmel's fate did not reach him immediately after the battle. Another member of Kidder's company, Parley McIntyre, was shot through both legs, as Galpin had been. He survived but never fully recovered from his wounds.[57]

John B. Gordon, the architect of the Cedar Creek attack, blamed his commanding general, Jubal Early, for not finishing off the bluecoats. Gordon believed that Early considered further pursuit of the Union army unnecessary. Early countered that he could not energize his troops because they stopped en masse to plunder the Yankee camps they overran. Eyewitness accounts by members of the 121st New York corroborated Jubal Early's description of the Confederate plundering of the Union camps. One veteran of the battle wrote years later that the rebels "were gorging themselves on the luxuries found in our abandoned camps when Sheridan took the offensive." Besides the testimony of the cruel treatment John Douw received, John Ingraham wrote home a few days after the battle describing the dire situation the wounded encountered after the fight. Both Douw and Burrell were robbed. The rebel soldiers "took about 100 dollars in greenbacks and a gold watch" from Burrell "and even the rings off his fingers. Robbed him of everything he had but the clothes he had on. They took a large amount of money from Captain Douw. They robbed all of our boys that fell in their hands wounded. They took 53 dollars . . . from Mert[on] Tanner and his photographs. He begged of them to let him have them but they would not." Most of the survivors of the 121st were reluctant to tell William Remmel's sister the truth. He probably had been stripped and robbed either as he was dying or when he was dead—making his identification impossible if he had received a disfiguring wound.[58]

George Fahey in Company C wrote his mother that he and Herman Johnson were the only surviving members of the contingent from the town of Russia who had all enlisted as teenagers, two years earlier. Clinton Beckwith and John Hartwell both escaped injury. Rebels nearly grabbed Hartwell as the 121st and the Sixth Corps retreated sequentially from one line to another. He faced capture or death unless he ran for his life. Off to the side, as his comrades were pulling Lamb's cannon out of harm's way, Hartwell became separated when a squad of Confederates bore down on him. After they unloaded a volley into the rails where he hid, he ran the gauntlet "in a zig zag course" over an open field and escaped after a very close call.[59]

With anxiety for his men in the 121st, John Kidder waited out his rehabilitation at Elmira. He voted absentee and expressed pleasure that one of his boys, Sedate Foote, supported Lincoln. He also received word of Sheridan's ride and ultimate victory in the valley. He could only hope for the best. When he returned to the regiment in the new year, he realized how much it had changed through the losses it sustained.

The regimental assistant surgeon, Dr. Daniel Holt, was one of the more prominent losses of the Shenandoah campaign. He had survived the horrors of Colonel Franchot's early marches, imprisonment, and all the major battles of the Army of the Potomac. But the hot and dusty forced marches from Petersburg to Washington and the valley and back again proved too much for his aging body. As early as July 1, when the army lay at Weldon Railroad, his racking cough became unbearable. On the boat trip to Washington, he slept in the open in a bass drum. As a physician, he knew that his body had begun to warn him. In the valley, his lungs and bowels began to fail, and he had little energy to perform his increasingly arduous duties. His lungs "so violently seized him" that it literally laid him low—"perfectly prostrating" him. Fatigue began to wear his body down, and he admitted that he often toppled from his horse in a sleep-induced haze. He told his wife, "Often I have fallen more like a dead than a living man, and only because I am worn out." In one telling diary entry, he admitted that he lost track of an entire day. Unknowingly, he slept around the clock. Two days before his comrades experienced the early morning surprise at Cedar Creek, Holt bid farewell to his friends and left camp with the 96th Pennsylvania, which had completed its term of enlistment. He made his way to Baltimore and eventually Washington, where he settled his accounts with the surgeon general. By the time the rest of the 121st celebrated its successful rout of the Southern army in the valley, on October 21, Holt was at home. His last army diary entry read: "Adieu to hard tack, salt horse, and stone pillows."[60]

It took commanding officer Major Cronkite three months to replace Holt. Temporarily, the 121st lacked a regimental surgeon after John Slocum reported to the division hospital. Prior to that, the regiment's hospital steward was permanently detailed to the division hospital, leaving Pvt. John J. Ingraham, "knapsack orderly," in charge of dispensing dangerous drugs to anyone who asked. He told of one crazed soldier who came to him for morphine, which Ingraham quickly gave him. He joked that he would take up a medical practice when the war ended and he returned to Brockett's Bridge. By January 16, 1865, Albany responded to the situation by assigning Dr. James P. Kimball to the regiment.[61]

I3

Return to Petersburg, December 1864 to April 1865

We are short of officers . . . our major . . . was wounded last week . . . only one Captain is with the regiment.

Chaplain John R. Adams, October 28, 1864

This business is mighty uncertain. Now you are here and now you are not. Now you see it and now you don't. Now you are in this world and now you are in the next.

Delavan Bates, January 18, 1865

We captured General [George Washington] Custis Lee and two stands of colors and over 1000 prisoners. This the 121st did.

Maj. John S. Kidder, April 10, 1865

Lincoln's Reelection and the Defeat of Seymour

August 1864 marked the lowest point of the war for the Union. In sun-drenched heat and humidity, Grant was bogged down at Petersburg, and Sherman slowed before Atlanta. The ingenious idea of blowing the rebels up at Petersburg with the construction of a tunnel filled with explosives backfired on the federals on the last day of July. With the loss of life around Richmond and the Lincoln administration's inability to bring the war to an end without further bloodshed, the Copperheads gained renewed strength. Jubal Early ran unchecked in the Shenandoah Valley after threatening Washington. The elation in the South contrasted sharply with the Northern depression. George McClellan accepted the peace democrats' mantle. The Copperheads and Jefferson Davis counted on him to crush Lincoln in the coming election. In August, friends and advisers persuaded Lincoln that

McClellan would be the next president, and he began making preparations to leave office. He asked each cabinet member to support the Union until the new president, presumably McClellan, came into power.

Within a month, however, everything changed. News of Sherman's capture of Atlanta and Adm. David Farragut's victory at Mobile knocked the planks from under the peace democrats and George McClellan's desire to negotiate an armistice and silenced the peace wing of the Republican Party, which wanted to replace Lincoln as its candidate.

John Hartwell and Surgeon Slocum expressed the earlier feelings of many of the men in the field. Slocum, a Lincoln man all the way, prophesied in his diary on March 4, 1864: "A year from today, old Abe to be inaugurated." In August, as the troops were ground down by endless marching through Virginia's humidity, they awaited word to return to the Petersburg trenches. Slocum noted in late July that the men were "all marched out." He questioned his own resilience, unsure he could endure the "fatigue much longer." In August, he wrote that he "was almost ready to give up the ghost."[1]

The army's constant movement and the war's brutalities tested Hartwell's allegiance to his president. The previous March, he had decided firmly for Lincoln. In an informal poll of the 5th Maine while both the 5th and the 121st regiments were comfortably in winter camp, Hartwell reported that all but two men raised their hands in favor of Lincoln. The two were immediately branded deserters and Copperheads. The troops' admiration for the president stemmed from his firmness—"willing at all times to give credit to whom it is due, irrespective of party." But by August, Hartwell's doubts about Lincoln's reelection had returned, and he became undecided as to whom to vote for because, as he told his wife, "things do not go to suit me at all." By midmonth, the regiment counted only 100 able-bodied men. The decimated troops were so discouraged by the constant marching and fighting that they were ready to vote for anyone willing to "put an end to this awful butchery." Hartwell reported that if the voting were held that hot day in August, McClellan would surely win. He convinced himself that no candidate deserved his support or vote. Another Lincoln victory would produce a prolonged and bloody struggle.[2]

By September, with the mood on the upswing, George Teel stated what many thought: "The victories at Atlanta and Mobile Bay have greatly encouraged the army, and stock in the Lincoln Market has risen about fifty percent within a few days." The Union victories at Opequon Creek and Fisher's Hill ensured an end to the hostilities. He predicted that Lincoln would be reelected in October when the "star spangled banner in triumph [would] wave over the land of the free and the home of the brave." The victories in the valley restored hope in all Union and Lincoln men. Maj. Gen. John Ellis Wool, former commander of the Department of the East and now retired at eighty-four and living in Troy, New York, exulted in Sheridan's success, which he described as "electric among the people. A few more such blows will accomplish the object which McClellan and the traitorous leaders of the Chicago convention say they seek, but by a different process—the surrender of the free states to Jeff Davis and his Government."

John Ingraham considered lying about his age to cast a ballot for Lincoln but decided otherwise. His fears of a McClellan victory were allayed now that Atlanta had fallen. He guessed that two-thirds of the army would go for Lincoln. "That victory seemed to change the tide," he asserted. When the nominations were in, Daniel Holt told his wife that the boys of the 121st expected General McClellan's nomination, but no one in the regiment thought he would be elected. Although the upstate New Yorkers remained loyal to Lincoln, Holt noticed a dip in the president's popularity in camp in early September. He feared that a McClellan victory at the polls in November would signal amnesty for the South. In a phrase reminiscent of later wars, Holt said he wanted "peace as much as any man, but not a dishonorable one." Chaplain Adams shared Holt's observation. He recognized that the McClellan platform "was disastrous to the country" and expressed encouragement that Lincoln sentiment continued "strong in the army." Still, he feared violence and bloodshed at the polls on election day.[3]

The men of the 121st perceived that their right to cast a vote was as important as their choice of candidate. The *Little Falls Journal and Courier* predicted that the soldiers in the field would have no stomach for the McClellan-Copperhead platform and would vote for Lincoln. But they could only do so if their friends back home made sure that valid ballots were in their hands and they then returned them in an expeditious manner by election time. The paper urged its readers to be prompt and return their valid ballots back to the local Union party representative. The *Oneonta Herald,* a Republican organ, printed Peter Mickel's letter. Purportedly, Mickel, a corporal in Company K, had originally endorsed a hard-line Democratic position. But he had been wounded in the Wilderness, where he underwent a change of heart—"how different [he] sounds from the howling of some of the so-called Democrats at home," the *Herald* trumpeted. Mickel eloquently laid out the case for union and the need to continue the present course. Only voting for Lincoln would "save the country from disgrace," he wrote. In his opinion, "the soldiers are nearly all of one mind." A vote for McClellan meant a vote against the men in the field.

On October 17, everyone was paid and absentee ballots were passed out. McClellan and Lincoln representatives were in camp, urging voters to consider their candidates. Each party bore the responsibility for its own ballots. The nineteen-step voting process was difficult to follow, and a vote would be disqualified when a supporter omitted just one of the steps. The Republican ballots were sent down from Albany by the American Express Company; the Democratic ballots, however, were in the custody of Seymour's "fifty or sixty agents," which drew immediate criticism from civilians as well as the boys in the regiment.

Seymour's brazen attempts to influence the election appalled Michael Hartford, a private from German Flats. After the election, he asked his sister her opinion of Seymour now. "He ought to be hung," Hartford wrote. "If I thought he had been changing my vote, I'm damned if I wouldn't kill him if I lived to get home again. A neat game that was he tried to play on the Republicans. Casting dead soldiers' votes for the Cops [Copperheads]." If Hartford had his way, life imprisonment at Fort Lafayette would have been the perfect punishment for "the old grey headed traitor." In addition to the absentee ballot machinations, many New York troops were furloughed home on election eve. Governor Seymour had asked Stanton to allow leaves for the New Yorkers with the hope they would tilt the contest away from his opponent, Reuben E. Fenton, and Lincoln. Fenton, a seasoned congressman from Chautauqua County in western New York, had left the Democratic Party to become a Republican in 1856. Stanton assured Seymour that the soldiers would be allowed home at election time.

In his last letter home, William Remmel expressed his pride at finally being of voting age. He did not say how he voted, but he anxiously waited to hear from his father that his ballot had been received and deposited in a timely fashion at the polls. And if his father could not get to the polls, he asked that a neighbor deliver it for him.[4]

The regiment went for Lincoln, although the final vote tally was unknown. John Slocum never doubted Lincoln's reelection. He reported a great deal of excitement in camp on November 8, but he confidently told his diary that "all is well." Herkimer and Otsego counties went for Fenton. A partial tally from the 152nd New York gave 54 votes for McClellan and 30 for Lincoln. Seymour won 54,000 more votes than he had two years earlier, yet Fenton outpolled him by 7,000 votes, carrying 41 counties to Seymour's 19. The soldiers' votes tipped the scale. Both Hartwell and Kidder voted for Lincoln, who carried the state by only 6,000 votes.

Far from the action, Adelbert Reed recuperated from his wounds in Washington's Lincoln Hospital as he enjoyed the city around him. He described the president's house and grounds and the Capitol as "beautiful beyond description" and "magnificent." On October 23, as his regiment recovered from the battle of Cedar Creek, Reed watched a rally for Old Abe that included a large torchlight procession. He kept in touch with the hometown news and was happy to learn that "they are 'wide awake' in Otsego as well as any other place." He was dismayed, though, by the anti-Lincoln meetings in Washington and the Copperheads' attempts to bring down the administration and elect McClellan. He steadfastly supported Lincoln, "and we will have him," he declared. "I can see the old fellow as often as I wish," he bragged. When Lincoln won, Reed explained that the Copperheads were like the Confederate army. Both rationalized defeat by claiming that they really did not expect to win, "but we know they did." Still stuck in Elmira, John Kidder and his mates threw a "jubilee . . . over the election news."[5]

John Ingraham's precocious insights about the presidential election during the battle of Cedar Creek belied his years. He contended that the best time to think about such things was during a battle because losing Lincoln as the country's president, in his opinion, would be a far greater disaster than any battle in which he fought. He talked with a wounded South Carolinian who acknowledged that 1864 heralded the Confederacy's last year. But, the man added, if McClellan were elected, the Confederacy would be recognized—a sentiment with which Ingraham agreed. When the ladies of New Town, bearing refreshments, came to visit the rebel wounded in federal care, one woman hoped aloud that her son in the Confederate army "would never disgrace himself" by taking the oath of allegiance to the federal government if the Confederacy collapsed. A wounded rebel lying on the floor looked her in the eye and said, "Oh shit, the confederacy is gone up."[6]

Delavan Bates, now commanding the 30th USCT, also weighed in on the election. Still a McClellan man, he accepted the results and resigned himself to another four years of the Lincoln administration. He contrasted the motive behind army voting with the Northern citizens' motivation. In the army, "it was union or disunion." But the civilian population saw the election as a choice between "union and peace with slavery or an abolition war ending—no one knew when—without slavery." He attributed the raw recruits' votes for McClellan to the fact that their "home opinions [were] strongly impressed upon their minds."[7]

Return to Petersburg

Early's Army of the Shenandoah remained in the valley after the battle of Cedar Creek, confining federal control to the lower valley. Contrary to the reports of its demise and despite its debilitating losses, the 121st continued to survive. It went into camp at Kernstown, where picket duty and guarding telegraph linemen were added to the usual drills and dress parades. A few men found time in November to visit Luray's natural caves.[8]

The 121st began its journey to rejoin the Army of the Potomac and the siege of Petersburg on December 1, 1864. The men broke camp that day and marched to Stevenson's Station, where they boarded the railcars for Washington. The next day, they piled onto steamboats in the capital and set sail for City Point, due east of Petersburg. Some of the men from the brigade got roaring drunk on board, and in the boisterous confusion of the moment, a three-year man with only four months left on his enlistment fell overboard and drowned. By December 4, the men were on their way to the front, where they relieved the 3rd Division of the Fifth Corps and moved into its well-developed camp.

They were west of the Jerusalem Plank Road, where they had departed five months earlier. The Sixth Corps settled in south of town on a 4-mile front spread across four country roads: Johnson, Halifax, Vaughan, and Squirrel Level. The Weldon Railroad "sliced through" the lines. After a one-day reconnaissance foray on December 9, they hunkered down for the winter, which proved to be one long month after another. The recovering wounded and sick, as well as those who had been away on leave or on detached service with another unit, returned to the 121st and swelled its ranks to close to 275 men, up from 200— "making a pretty tidy looking battalion on dress parade."[9]

The winter quarters of 1864–1865 were characterized by the siege of Petersburg, a sharp contrast with the previous year, which had been spent in the relative lap of luxury. The armies faced each other over more than 35 miles of trenches, foreshadowing the trench warfare that would characterize World War I. No one anticipated an easy time. "We are going to have a regular Vicksburg affair," observed John Ingraham. Continual firing and deplorable living conditions on the Southern side made life miserable. The Union troops threw stones at their Southern counterparts to draw them from their cover to make targets for Northern sharpshooters. The lines were so close that the men could hear their enemies' conversations. Exposing one's self in the rifle pits at any time drew fire. Deep connecting trenches were dug to move men from one pit to the next unhurt.

The men in the 121st counted the months: only seven to go before mustering out. Furloughs were distributed to those fortunate enough to get them. Though rare, they were still sought after, but their issuance depended on the officers and their moods; it was hard to predict if a soldier's wish to go home for ten days would be granted. "An officer don't care whether they accommodate a private or not," Ingraham complained, "all they care for is to gratify their own tribe and themselves."[10]

The Search for Officers

The 121st desperately lacked officers. Old comrades were doing well in the colored regiments. Delavan Bates had been promoted to brevet brigadier general—quite a leap from his starting rank of second lieutenant in John Kidder's company. Another Company I member, James Cronkite, now led the regiment, and he anxiously wrote around trying to find as many able-bodied officers as he could. Two days before Christmas, he asked Sam Kelley on his sickbed in Annapolis when he would be able to return to duty. He told Kelley that Olcott had left the service and that he himself was now in charge. "Please write me if any of our officers are in the hospital at Annapolis and who, and how, they are and when they may be expected here." On Christmas Eve, Cronkite asked the U.S. adjutant general to return John Kidder from Elmira, where he was still on light duty.[11]

Cronkite's best catch was Assistant Surgeon James Peleg Kimball. Since Holt's resignation and Slocum's detail to the division hospital, the health of the regiment had been in the unskilled hands of a medical assistant, John Ingraham. Kimball was new to medicine and the army. He had just graduated from Albany Medical College and had been a student at Hamilton College with Charlie Butts when war broke out. An intelligent and ambitious youth, he pursued his college studies simultaneously with his medical education through the Medical Department of New York University. As the 121st suffered through the Overland campaign during the summer of 1864, Kimball was assigned to the medical cadets at Fort Schuyler's McDougall Hospital in Throg's Neck, New York. There, he learned firsthand how to deal with the wounded, the dying, and the dead. One night, as he left the morgue with lantern in hand, he heard a low moan from somewhere in the rows of "corpses." With a colleague, he was able to revive the moaning man and move him to the general hospital.

After Grant's campaign, Kimball was afraid "the war would be over before [he] should be ready to share in it." He transferred from New York University to the Albany Medical College when he learned that he could get his degree by December 1864. "So it came about that one December day," he wrote, "I became a doctor of medicine, and the next day a surgeon in the 121st New York Volunteers." From New York, he traveled to City Point, Virginia, and thence to the front lines at Petersburg. He found camp a dreary place on wet ground stripped of pitch pines. He began the new year and his army service with a hearty welcome at headquarters, including a "tip-top supper of baked potatoes, pan-cakes, and mackerel." Following supper, he took possession of his own horse.[12]

Absent for nearly nine months, John Kidder returned for duty with the regiment at the end of January 1865. He had recuperated at home and then as the commander of a detachment guarding Confederate soldiers at Elmira Prison. Before the days of strict military regulations, Kidder realized that Elmira offered a perfect market for jewelry carved by rebel prisoners from the bones of chickens and other animals. Kidder sent for his brother-in-law Charley Matteson, who had been discharged from the army in 1863 when he lost his arm. Charley became Kidder's middleman in selling "bone jewelry." Kidder was soon sending rings to extended family members for resale throughout New York State while he was guarding prisoners. But even that sideline quickly bored him, and he longed for home or his regiment.

Kidder returned to a diminished military unit of 250 to 275 men, which shocked him. Meanwhile, those at home faced a new draft at the beginning of the year. John Lovejoy hoped that the draftees "will not tremble bad enough to get ague." Privates, promoted to fill the decimated ranks of line officers long departed, now led the regiment. Of the original corps of the regiment's officers on September 1, 1862, only Olcott and Kidder remained. In Olcott's absences, Cronkite or Henry Galpin had led the regiment. Galpin, with his wounds, relinquished command to Capt. Daniel D. Jackson of Garrattsville. A new adjutant, Lt. George C. Weaver of Laurens, had joined the 121st as a private in 1862. Sgts. Horatio Duroe, Langford Burton, Charles H. Barr, Newbern A. Armstrong, Nathaniel Post, and Eli Oakes received commissions after Cedar Creek. An ecstatic Duroe asked his father for money to buy an officer's "sword and clothes," which would cost a "hundred dollars." "By the way," he told his father, "our cavalry won another great victory—600 men and eleven guns. Hurrah for little Phil."[13]

The officers knew the rules very well. Just before Salem Church, Emory Upton made every effort to count as many men as possible to avoid having his officers lose their ranks and, worse, having the regiment merged into a larger unit. Rumors always swirled that the 121st might be dissolved and the men transferred to another regiment. General Orders No. 15 from May 1861 called for a minimum of 830 men in a regiment before the commanding officer could advance (muster) in the federal service to the rank of full colonel, the second in command to lieutenant colonel, and the third in command to major. Kidder, senior captain and next in line for the major's slot, lost the post because of his recuperative leave. Instead, Cronkite got the promotion. Olcott (who briefly resigned effective December 13, 1864, and then reconsidered two weeks later) received a promotion to colonel; Cronkite rose to lieutenant colonel; and Kidder, when he returned, was made a major. However, the promotions were unofficial because of the low census of the 121st. Recruiting parties were sent home to Herkimer and Otsego counties, but they produced the same results as the previous year, failing to enlist any new troops. In August 1864, Henry Galpin received a twenty-day leave "to go North and to excite enlistments" for the 121st, to no avail. At the beginning of 1865, recruits, who were paid more than the men serving in the 121st, were sent south to fill up the old regiments. Chaplain Adams called them "miserable men," who "for the sake of bounty pledged themselves to go in lieu of others [and took] the first opportunity to desert."[14]

The officers in charge, particularly Olcott and Cronkite before Kidder's return, "used every means in their power to obtain recruits." At year's end, 1864, they sent young men from the regiment to New York City to recruit. Isaac Bassett from the little Herkimer town of Russia felt uncomfortable "in the extreme" on recruiting duty in the big city—specifically, Brooklyn. Even so, he counted twenty-five new enlistees one day. Every night, he boarded a boat with the recruits and escorted them to Riker's Island. He wrote, "It is a nice boat ride 10 miles from here and we have a nice steamboat and there is always a great many ladies and gentlemen going to and from the Island."

Cronkite visited the provost marshal of the Otsego-Herkimer area, the governor, and the secretary of war to speed recruits through before the war ended and it was too late for their commissions. Kidder went directly to Levi Turner, asking him to petition Secretary of War Stanton for more men, and Olcott petitioned the new governor, pleading for more recruits to fill up the regiment so every officer eligible for a commission could be mustered. He appealed to Governor Fenton to "fill its ranks that it may go into the next campaign with some hopes of retaining its organization and its name." The Sixth Corps commander, Gen. Frank Wheaton, admired Olcott and endorsed his request. He reminded Albany of Olcott's meritorious service and pointed out that he had recommended him for promotion to brevet major general several times before. When Kidder returned, he began campaigning for the lieutenant colonel's position. He persuaded Olcott to recommend him, with an endorsement by the officers in the regiment, and he called on old friend Delavan Bates for a recommendation also. Pulling the levers of power, he knew that he would "succeed at Albany." Olcott probably knew of Kidder's "back channel" efforts and even may have encouraged them.[15]

In a magnanimous gesture, Cronkite resigned his lieutenant colonel's rank after hostilities ceased but before the regiment mustered out, allowing Kidder to have the position. According to Kidder, Olcott asked Cronkite to withdraw in Kidder's favor, since Cronkite could not muster because of his wound. By the time Kidder petitioned Turner, the chain of command all the way up to General Meade had endorsed Olcott's request for 400 more men. Meanwhile, Olcott, Cronkite, and Kidder remained at their previous ranks until the arrival of new recruits. Although officials had granted the regiment's request for more men, the contingent from Riker's Island did not arrive until a month after Lee surrendered. The new men brought the regiment's strength up to approximately 800 troops present for duty and "accounted for," which allowed all three men to be mustered as commissioned after hostilities ended: Olcott as full colonel, Kidder as lieutenant colonel, and Cronkite as major. Once they had received their full ranks, the army assigned 300 to 400 men to the 65th New York (no one knew the real number). True to Adams's prediction, most of those men deserted just before the transfer, and some were transferred while "absent without leave"—in other words, they were never really transferred at all.

The Bartlett Affair

In the midst of the attempts to find new leadership and as the army battled the Confederates in their last throes, the 121st continued to clash with Albany and the meddling politicians. The controversy over Lewis C. Bartlett came to the new governor's attention a few days after he took office. And as had happened the previous year when Olcott's promotion from major to lieutenant colonel reopened the fight over the major's slot, problems erupted when the promotion of one man set off a scramble for his vacated spot. This time, Henry Galpin left the vacuum. Despite his differences with Upton, Galpin was a regimental favorite and a very popular officer throughout his service. He was wounded at Spotsylvania and then again at Cedar Creek. His wounds plagued him, and when he developed tuberculosis and the pain became unendurable, he resigned.

Bartlett enrolled as a first lieutenant on the march to Gettysburg at Fairfax Court House on June 19, 1863, and reported to Company G. Bartlett took his mediocre record from Company G to Company K and later Company D. His brother, Joe Bartlett, commanding the 1st Division, Sixth Corps, to which the 121st belonged, assigned Lewis to the 121st in order to detail him to his staff. When Joe Bartlett transferred to the Fifth Corps, Lewis stayed behind with the 121st. Galpin's resignation on December 21 brought Bartlett's name to Albany's attention, and the firestorm erupted.

With little notice, the lame-duck governor Seymour commissioned Lewis Bartlett a major, raising the ugly specter of favoritism trumping seniority. The act of commissioning Bartlett meant he was promoted over six captains "and nearly as many First Lieutenants," causing a furor among the officers of the 121st; the absent John Kidder, next in seniority, should have received the commission. As much as Cronkite needed officers, he feared that he would lose some of his best by resignation if Bartlett was promoted. Courageously, the twenty-two-year-old captain sent his objections to the new governor, Reuben Fenton, and to Bartlett's brother Joe. Fearing no retribution by speaking the truth, Cronkite told Joe Bartlett that Lewis showed no interest in the regiment, that the officers felt this keenly, and that Lewis's continual absence from the regiment on high-profile assignments damaged his chances for promotion. Cronkite said his conclusion that Lewis should not be promoted over the others was "just" and that it was one "firmly held by the officers and which gives tenacity to their purpose."[16]

When Seymour promoted Bartlett on his way out of office and before Fenton was sworn in, Cronkite became convinced that Lewis's appointment was tainted. To Cronkite and "every thinking person," these opaque dealings called for an "investigation and judgment of the new Executive." Cronkite called Bartlett's appointment "this unjust act." He relayed the officers' feelings and boldly accused Bartlett of "injustice and fraud." By allowing a "junior First lieutenant to be elevated to a position" over an officer who had served with the regiment since the beginning was "an outrage," Cronkite wrote. He asked Fenton to revoke Bartlett's commission. Fenton agreed, and Bartlett withdrew.[17]

The jockeying for position played out against Lincoln's call for another 300,000 men on December 19, 1864. Delavan Bates wondered if the North would raise "such large bounties" or "wait and let the draft fetch out the quota?"

He concluded that the army "was in perfect rapture over the call and think that old Abe is really in earnest now."[18]

The Siege of Petersburg and Hatcher's Run

The city of Petersburg is 30 miles south of Richmond and sits on the south bank of the Appomattox River. Five railroads radiated from the city. The main line, the Richmond and Petersburg Railroad, runs north to Richmond. From the east to the west, the other four wind out clockwise from the city on the south side: the Petersburg and City Point Road, the Norfolk and Petersburg, the Weldon and Petersburg, and the South Side Railroad, which ran to Lynchburg. When the 121st left the Petersburg trenches, the Union forces controlled only the Petersburg and City Point rail line on the city's northeast side. Through the summer, Union troops occupied positions east of the city. The Confederates erected elaborate protective defenses named after commanders, such as Forts Stedman, Mahone, Morton, and Fisher. Supporting batteries, strung out at intervals between them, were designated with roman numerals. Both sides slid in a clockwise direction from northeast to southwest as Grant moved by his left flank and Lee responded in a countermove to his right until a half ring nearly enclosed the city on its southern side; the northeastern end touched on the river, and the southwestern end was still open.

The movements came at great cost to both sides. Lee was determined not to let Grant cut the last link to the south via the South Side rail line on his extreme right. Across the river, the critical rail line to Richmond on the city's north side was still open to the Confederates for communication between the two cities. By August, Union forces had captured the Weldon Railroad. When the 121st returned, the federal forces had constructed their elaborate complex of forts and both sides had extended their lines far from Petersburg to the southwest. Grant's attempt to sever the last rail link south of the town was aborted when Confederate forces stopped him at Hatcher's Run in late October and early November. With that, he went into winter quarters. Grant had thought he could end the war that summer. Men in both armies, stretched psychologically and physically, settled in for a long winter siege.

For the men of the 121st, the days melded into weeks and weeks into months as they sat before Petersburg. With winter's arrival and the return to an uneasy hiatus in the fighting, John Slocum, among others, returned to cards, whiskey, and the women of easy virtue at City Point. John Hartwell railed against the licentiousness of the troops and harbored no sympathy for them when they contracted venereal diseases. On Christmas Eve, Slocum predicted that the boys were "preparing to get drunk for Christmas." A few began early and got into a fight, resulting in their being tied up by their thumbs. News of Sherman's arrival at Savannah; the fall of Wilmington, North Carolina; and

George Thomas's defeat of Hood were welcome Christmas presents. The holidays were happily observed, despite the fact that boxes from home had been rifled by those needier than the troops on the front lines. New boxes soon replaced them. Besides, there were ubiquitous sutlers plying their wares, and the Sanitary Commission provided socks and mittens. The latter were necessary as cold weather bore down on the hardiest veterans.

Just before Christmas, John Lovejoy had returned to his regiment after four months in the hospital. In the meantime, Col. Ranald S. Mackenzie, of the 2nd Connecticut Artillery, had replaced Upton, and his stature suffered in comparison to the former commander. Lovejoy called Mackenzie a "mean little upstart." During a brigade inspection, he appeared before the troops "about two-thirds drunk." He seemed to enjoy finding fault with the men's appearance, but Lovejoy thought that "the men presented a more soldierly appearance than he did."[19]

For the men of the 121st, tending the siege lines before Petersburg during the winter of 1864–1865 bore no resemblance to the duties of their first two winters in the field. Although the armies were officially in winter camp, the circumstances of the siege made the experience like no other. Most men found picket duty to be the most onerous, for the siege line remained a dangerous place. The days were replete with boredom, coupled with the threat of instant battle. At any time during the siege, the regiment could be alerted to trouble and awakened by small-arms fire and yelling. Dutifully, the men would fall in behind the breastworks only to be called off when the firing stopped as abruptly as it began. Chaplain Adams was philosophical about their circumstances. He accepted the situation, "even though we have to dress in a hurry, and stumble over various things before we find matches, candles, etc."

Bates articulated what many thought when he wrote that he continued to be among the living: "I may be next week, next month, next year, and perhaps I may be occupying six feet by two in Virginia soil at either of those periods. This business is mighty uncertain. Now you are here and now you are not. Now you see it and now you don't. Now you are in this world and now you are in the next." Meanwhile, Grant's ongoing search for an opening in the Confederate lines created constant movement for the regiment.[20]

Clinton Beckwith wrangled a ten-day furlough that he stretched into five weeks at the end of February and into March. His trip to Herkimer County became another wild odyssey, including a run-in with a bunch of drunken marines on a boat from Fortress Monroe, an argument with a vendor at the fort over the price of a bologna sandwich and a pie, and a visit to Ford's Theater in Washington on his way home. At home, he convinced a local doctor that he suffered from "severe cold from exposure, threatened with pneumonia," and should remain home a bit longer. He then convinced a gullible major at St. Mary's Hospital in Rochester that his excuse was legitimate. Beckwith told the major about the 121st, its great leader Upton and others, and its battlefield record. The major was so taken in by his story that he let Beckwith return late to his regiment. As he finally headed back to the front, Beckwith was further delayed when the train he was taking was involved in an accident.

Upon reaching Washington, he met a fellow member of the 121st, Luman Baldwin. The two got on a river transport, which, to their delight, carried rations and commissary liquor to the troops downriver. Sending Luman up top as a lookout, Beckwith opened one of the liquor boxes; he and Baldwin soon sampled the contents, filled their canteens, and stuffed two bottles in their clothes. They rearranged the remaining bottles in the box so "that it would not be noticed" and reseated the box lid. Once ashore, they stumbled along the road and around midnight found the regiment. They roused their comrades, who fed them and heard their tales as everyone imbibed the free-flowing "commissary." The next morning, Beckwith reported to Olcott, who "was in a bad humor." Olcott grilled him about his delay. Undeterred by the commander's bad mood, Beckwith regaled him with his long and convoluted tale. In the end, with a flourish and with impeccable timing, Beckwith gave Olcott a "little box of cigars," and Olcott accepted his apologies and ordered him to return to his company for duty. Beckwith undoubtedly returned to his comrades with a self-satisfied smile on his face.[21]

A similar instance with another member of Company G showed Olcott's softer side. Pvt. Ebenezer Shelden from Roseboom took leave to go home during the early spring of 1865 while the regiment sat in front of Petersburg. Typical of most soldiers on leave at home, Shelden wore his civilian clothes. And because of that, "some low, mean miserable Copperhead," thinking that he was a deserter, "was mean enough to arrest him," John Lovejoy complained to his cousin Cynthia. And, Lovejoy continued, "to cap it all his furlough was not dated." Returned to his regiment under guard, Sheldon was taken by his captors to Olcott. He showed Olcott his papers and told him his story, and Olcott released him from arrest with orders to report to his company. Cousin Cynthia wondered if Olcott was the son of a banker from Cherry Valley. Lovejoy assured her that he was, adding, "and a smart young man he is too."[22]

Sam Kelley Returns Home

While his comrades were marching through Virginia and the military and political situation in the lower South deteriorated after the fall of Atlanta, Sam Kelley's health worsened. Facilities in Savannah and Charleston were overwhelmed with prisoners from Andersonville and Macon. Prison commander Maj. Gen. Sam Jones in Charleston complained to Secretary of War James Seddon that 1,000 men per day were arriving at Savannah. There were not enough troops to guard them, and none were available from the field. When Savannah could no longer care for the Union prisoners, Kelley's captors transferred him to Charleston on September 13, 1864, where the Sisters of Charity of Our Lady of Mercy cared for him. The sisters had established an orphanage and a convent, and during the war, they "came among" soldiers on both sides "distributing gifts to the well and bestowing care and medicines on the sick." They probably ministered to Kelley either in the racetrack infield located in north Charleston or in the city jail. Occupants of the city jail remembered it as a stinking cesspool; in contrast, they referred to the racecourse as an "oasis." Mother Theresa gave Sam a Catholic *Baltimore Catechism* published in 1847 during his stay. He welcomed his new surroundings and luxuriated in clean sheets, a bed, and bath.

In August, he learned of McClellan's nomination and the government's agreement on an exchange of prisoners, giving him hope of an early release. He left Charleston by November 11 and arrived in Savannah, where he boarded a ship for Annapolis on November 30. Later, the sisters' orphanage and convent were destroyed by the Union bombardment. On December 4, Kelley entered Officer's Hospital in Annapolis, where John Kidder had spent time the previous summer.[23]

Sam had lost contact with his mother during his time in Charleston, and no one knew his current condition or his location. In late November, Chaplain Adams mourned the capture of Lansing Paine and Sam Kelley and spoke of both in the past tense. He remembered the many happy glee club sessions with the 5th Maine and Sam's beautiful voice and "sweet songs." Finally, word came from Sam's nurse, Abbie L. Howe, who assured his mother that he was sitting and walking, although he still suffered from a debilitating chronic diarrhea. A few weeks later, Sam gathered sufficient strength to write, expressing hope that he would be well enough to return to his family soon and bring a few mementos to each of them. He also asked about the fate of the $100 that was due to him at the time of his capture. But three days before Christmas, Nurse Howe sent his mother an alarming letter: "Your son is growing worse," she warned. "You had better come at once—and not delay—for anything."[24]

Mary Anne Kelley, with two younger children at home, could not rush to her son's side. Another letter, somewhat more reassuring, came after the first of the New Year from Nurse Howe. She reported that Sam's health had improved slightly but said that his prognosis continued to be uncertain, and she once again urged his mother to come to Annapolis. Mary Anne Kelley finally arrived in mid-January as Sam's health continued to fluctuate. With Sam's father still serving in the 23rd Infantry, Veteran Reserve Corps, Mary Anne had decided to leave her older daughter, Sylvina, at home with younger sister Jessie.

Throughout the month, she was torn between being at the bedside of her severely ill son and being at home with her two underage daughters. She decided to bring Sam home. Before heading for Annapolis, she instructed her daughters to prepare the lower bedroom with the fireplace for him, with heavy quilts and covers. She arrived at Sam's side on January 20, 1865. When the doctors gave her permission to move him and she readied him for the trip home, he worsened. On January 22, all thought he would die. Doctors considered him the most fragile case in the hospital. But just as mysteriously, he rallied to the point where the doctors pronounced him fit for travel. Finally, at month's end, his mother accompanied Sam on a train from Annapolis to Cobleskill, New York, a small village north of Schenevus. There, bundling him with blankets to protect him from the bitter New York winter, she put him on a horse-drawn wagon for the overland trip down to Schenevus.

By February, Sam Kelley was home in the bosom of his family. His old friend the Reverend Synott in Cooperstown sent him get-well wishes. But all the care and love of family and friends could not repair his body, broken by Confederate prisons. Attended by his mother and sisters, Sam Kelley, at the age of twenty-three, died of chronic diarrhea in his home on February 16, 1865, two months before war's end. In Cooperstown, where he had tended store for Cockett and Marvin's, the *Freeman's Journal* ran a short obituary that referenced "rebel slaughter pens" where he "endured all the privations, sufferings and insult." Calista Bailey mourned his death. She offered to copy an ambrotype that Sam had sent her for his mother. She mentioned his Sixth Corps badge, which she thought he carried with him when he was captured. She hinted at things she wanted to talk about with Mary Anne Kelley, but she demurred, saying that she could not put her feelings in writing.[25]

Earlier, as Sam Kelley had reached home, the 121st went into action on the Petersburg line. Facing the Sixth Corps were A. P. Hill's veterans. Surgeon Kimball's naive initial impression of the service was replaced in one month by the cold reality of trench warfare, although he remained in awe of his new "veteran" regiment. On February 5, Grant again tried to extend his lines farther southwest in order to cut supplies to the city via the South Side Railroad and the Boydton Plank Road. The Second and Fifth Corps with Gen. David N. Gregg's cavalry division led the action. Grant ordered the Fifth Corps out of the trenches to secure the Plank Road. John Gordon, recently returned from the Shenandoah Valley, moved to stop Warren's Fifth Corps. The contesting armies moved back and forth between the Vaughan Road and Dabney's Sawmill.[26]

When Lee sent reinforcements to Gordon, Grant responded with the Sixth Corps and the Ninth Corps on February 6. The 121st broke camp between 8:00 and 9:00 P.M., February 5. They marched out toward the rebel lines and halted around midnight. Under a bright moonlit sky with stars ablaze, the 121st formed a battle line and went to sleep. There they lay until midday on February 6. At 1:00 P.M. on Monday, the regiment began "one of those eternal flank movements." The regiment marched an hour until it camped on frozen ground, where it rested for two hours. About 3:00 P.M., the men marched into "an open field fifty rods in width, on one side of which were the rebels, in the woods, behind entrenchments." They had crossed Hatcher's Run and were rushing toward Dabney's Sawmill. Warren's Fifth Corps was in trouble, and the 121st found itself in the midst of the action once again. Just as the 121st wheeled into line of battle, the Fifth Corps broke, and for thirty minutes "there was a perfect stampede." Ingraham declared, "You can't imagine what a sight it is when there is a stampede." The Sixth Corps and the 121st, along with the 97th New York, eight days away from mustering out, regrouped 300 yards to the rear. That line held, and in the evening, after the firing ceased around 10:00 P.M., the 121st slept on the hail- and snow-swept cornfield.[27]

By 5:00 A.M. the next day, the men of the regiment awoke covered by an inch of frozen rain and snow. They breakfasted on hardtack, coffee, and pork, and a few hours later, after marching through freezing rain, they were back in their quarters. Throughout the day, the wounded were transported on stretchers through a cold, unrelenting rain. James Kimball commandeered a "large white house in a beautiful grove of pine trees, put the occupants, an old gentleman, a middle-aged lady, two girls and a boy, into one room, and of the rest made a hospital." He made the parlor his operating room. In place of a happy family, "streams of human blood" ran; the groans of the wounded replaced merriment. That night, he slept, exhausted, on his rubber blanket with his case of instruments as a pillow and a thin blanket over him. John Lovejoy fell ill again from exposure.

Maj. Gen. Frank Wheaton credited Col. James Hubbard of the 2nd Connecticut Heavy Artillery and Olcott and the 121st when stragglers from the 3rd Division of the Fifth Corps stampeded through the front lines, and the 2nd Connecticut and the 121st reestablished the line in the dimming light and mass confusion. Captain Kidder "suggested to Colonel Olcott a point for the formation of a line of battle," which, if placed immediately, would provide the maximum effect. Olcott took Kidder's advice. "They checked the panic, restored order in that part of the field, and the rebels did not gain as much as they expected." Olcott took the regimental colors that evening, "under fire and great confusion," and led his men to the front to reestablish the line. Wheaton lauded Olcott again—he recommended him for the "brevet of Colonel for distinguished gallantry while commanding a brigade at Cedar Creek." Olcott held command for a year, and Wheaton expressed his disappointment that Olcott could not be mustered because the "regiment was small." As a result of the battle, the 121st moved its base farther west around Forts Fisher, Welch, and Gregg, abandoned by the Second Corps, which moved 3 miles west to the Vaughan Road crossing of Hatcher's Run.[28]

By that time, the 121st New York bore little resemblance to its original appearance. Egbert Olcott remained in command of the regiment after his return. Upton now commanded a cavalry unit in the west. Fish was dead, and Galpin had resigned. Mather and Bates had transferred to the 20th U.S. Colored Troops and the 30th USCT, respectively. And Olcott's confidant, Capt. John Kidder, had returned to the regiment ready for duty. Both men had been with the regiment from the beginning, both had risen through the ranks, and both had survived the war to that point. Bates described Kidder as "brave, cautious, and always reliable" and said his advice was more highly valued than that offered by men who "tried to move in higher circles." In the last campaign as the Sixth Corps and Grant's army pursued Lee, Olcott "often consulted with him when the regiment was in places that demanded prompt and vigorous action."

With Cronkite as his major, Olcott benefited from having two strong, "Upton like" officers on whom he relied to provide strict discipline in camp and effective execution of orders in battle. Olcott, Cronkite, and Kidder were all survivors and had earned their reputations. Although the county newspapers referred to their unit as "Upton's Regulars" during the war, other regiments probably did not refer to them as such. Regardless, they were hardened veterans recognized throughout the Army of the Potomac as a solid fighting regiment. Once, in March 1865 during a routine inspection, Generals Wright and Meade and their party rode up and asked if the regiment was a Regular Army unit. The answer came back that it was Upton's old regiment, the 121st New York State Volunteers. Supposedly, Meade remarked that there "was not a better regiment in the whole army." Despite the rave reviews, however, Olcott, Kidder, and Cronkite looked to Meade and the secretary of war to fill up the regiment's numbers so that they could each be mustered at a higher rank.[29]

February turned into March. The regiment's bad boy, Clinton Beckwith, found himself in trouble again. He was part of a detachment that set out from camp, with a team of horses and mules, to cut down pine trees and bring them back to strengthen the breastworks around Fort Fisher on St. Patrick's Day. The route to the pine forest led them directly past the camp of the Irish Brigade, which was celebrating the most important day of the year. Many of the boys, including Beckwith, were immediately diverted by the games and libations offered by the generous Irishmen. John Ingraham opted out. A few men continued on with the mission but could not complete their work because they were shorthanded. When everyone got back to camp at dark, Major Cronkite met them. He arrested them all, and each had a log placed across his shoulders and was ordered to march around in a circle all night. Log punishment was one of Cronkite's favorites. Joe Heath, in his role as officer of the day, let the prisoners take a nap or two. Another comrade brought them hot coffee. Nothing came of the incident except that Cronkite became the object of threats of vengeance. Philip Woodcock told his diary: "The officers: all drunk tonight." He did not mention a sober and alert Cronkite.[30]

Cronkite's methods of drill and discipline mirrored those employed by Upton, Kidder, and Olcott. In Olcott's absence, Cronkite instituted new and harsh punishments for those failing guard mount inspection. Replacements were inspected by the officer of the day for cleanliness and the proper equipment, including proper weapons and ammunition. Anyone failing this inspection would be replaced by a "supernumerary," who would be relieved of all of his normal duties for ten days. The man failing inspection was reported to the commanding officer and given the supernumerary's ten days' duties. The offender was also required to march in front of regimental guard quarters all day with a 20-pound log on his shoulders.[31]

The Fall of Petersburg

The noose tightened around the Confederacy in February 1865. Sherman left Savannah early in the month. He feinted against Augusta and Charleston, where panicked authorities sent important documents and government papers to Columbia—considered the safest place, in the middle of the state. In February, rumors of a peace agreement were stoked. Richmond sent peace negotiators north, and the 121st learned that Confederate vice president Alexander Stephens had passed through the siege lines about three-quarters of a mile from their position on his way to Washington. The news caused "some excitement" throughout the army, but John Ingraham and his comrades were not impressed.[32]

Sherman moved over swamps and through bitter cold, reaching Columbia on February 16. When he left four days later, the city was in ruins, burned to the ground by his troops, retreating Confederates, and remaining civilians. At midmonth, the peace talks collapsed. On February 18, Charleston surrendered to one of Gen. Oliver O. Howard's officers, and Union troops occupied the city while Union ships tied up at the city's docks. As he attempted to break the siege at Petersburg, Grant ordered Sheridan to leave the valley and join Sherman.

By March 1, Sherman was in North Carolina, preparing for the final act in the four-year-old drama. In front of Petersburg, men from Lee's Virginia regiments went home to take care of family matters. Georgians particularly were incensed about the Virginians' going home. Upset with the news of Sherman's depredations in their state, they also went home to see for themselves and care for their families: "General Lee can't make us fight for Virginia when he allows the Yanks to run all over Georgia," they groused. Increasingly, deserters poured into the Union lines—in squads of 5 up to large groups of 40, including officers with all their accoutrements. John Lovejoy reported getting 800 rebels in one week. They told of the miserable conditions on their side and expressed their fatigue with the war and the rebel cause.[33]

As Georgians and Virginians walked home that winter, the 121st noticed other deserters coming into Union lines, particularly from North Carolina. One North Carolinian named South came through the lines and observed that if all the rebs knew how well they would be treated after deserting, "Old Lee would not long have an army." Many desertions occurred during the day in places where the two opposing lines were so close that a few rebels slipping into the Union defenses would be unremarkable. Union soldiers would give their great-coats to rebels during a truce, and the rebels, wearing blue coats, would saunter into the Union lines, surrendering unhurt and unfired upon. Southern desert-ers also enlisted rebel sympathizers so that when the deserters made their dash to the other side, the rebels left behind would fire over their heads. As a final in-sult, they yelled back to their officers that "the Yankees would give them their fill of fight before next fall."

The sense that the war had run its course pervaded both sides. A flippant ca-maraderie prevailed across the lines. It would have "made a deacon laugh to have heard our boys and the rebs talk to each other," Lovejoy remarked. Talk-ing back and forth was easy, but "I desire to let them alone," he declared; how-ever, he also admitted that he enjoyed the fun. The rebels, when ready to fire, would warn the bluecoats to lie down to avoid being hit. The other side re-turned the favor. Both sides kept up a constant chatter when not firing at each other. In one exchange, a Yankee asked a rebel if he had any butter and told him that if he did, he should rub it on his clothes and slide over to the Union side. Rebel deserters were relieved to be in Yankee custody and immediately asked for rations. Several claimed that for every one who went over Union lines, ten went home.

The Confederates' unawareness of their army's true conditions perplexed Chaplain Adams. "They are kept in ignorance on the one hand, and told un-truths on the other, to keep their courage up," he wrote. Rumors that the rebels were evacuating Petersburg reached the regiment by month's end. As the ces-sation of hostilities began to look like a real prospect, hope replaced despair on the siege lines. War's end by summer became a very real possibility: "Every day brings forth glad tidings," John Ingraham reported. On the morning of March 27, the 121st received word of the fall of Wilmington, North Carolina.[34]

As the wet roads of February gave way to a relatively dry March, Grant wor-ried that Lee would leave Petersburg and head south to hook up with Johnston in North Carolina. Not until the end of the month did the final act begin. On Saturday, March 25, the 121st awoke to cannonading on the army's far right. The 121st's old nemesis, John B. Gordon, had attacked Fort Stedman. Lee him-self approved the 4:00 A.M. sneak attack. At 7:00 A.M., the men of the 121st, with three brigades of the Sixth Corps, hurried far to their right across the Jerusalem Plank Road to repulse the early morning assault. They arrived too late. The Ninth Corps recovered its composure, and seven Pennsylvania regiments and the 20th Michigan reoccupied the fort and its adjacent Batteries X, XI, and XII. By noon, the 121st was back in camp.

The rebel attack on the Union right indicated to all but the freshest recruit that Lee's line was thin and vulnerable. Did it make sense to attack along the front of the Sixth Corps? Meade pushed Maj. Gen. Andrew A. Humphrey's Second Corps and Wright's Sixth Corps to drive in the rebel pickets. By 4:00 P.M., the 121st was on the move again, this time sliding to the left toward Fort Fisher, one of the largest along the siege line. It soon found itself embroiled in the battle of Jones's Farm. It settled near the end of the Union left flank and between Forts Conahey and Welch. What had begun as a test of picket lines by skirmishers and two Ohio regiments was now a fight that engaged six brigades. At 5:00 P.M., with Colonel Hamblin leading the 2nd Brigade, the men of the 121st jumped off, instructed not to yell or fire until they could see the enemy. And once again, John Ingraham complained, "our brigade as usual had to make a charge just before dark." Egbert Olcott, on a fifteen-day leave in New York City, had left James Cronkite in command of the 121st. The enthusiasm of the rushing brigade outdistanced its support and flank protection, exposing it to galling fire on its front and right.

The regiment moved within 300 yards of the Confederate lines when it hunkered down in captured rifle pits. When Confederates attempted to turn their exposed right flank, Cronkite ordered two companies on the right to change front and open fire. The maneuver worked, although several men were wounded and Cronkite lost his horse—shot out from under him. Beckwith later concluded that the Confederate lines were thin; otherwise, the 121st would not have held its position. In the final maneuver, newly minted lieutenant Horatio Duroe died, gunned down with a minié ball in his brain. He became the last casualty from the tiny village of New Lisbon. His men carried his body to friendly lines.[35]

At sundown, the brigade withdrew. The regiment returned to its camp with losses and nothing to show for its work. On Monday, March 27, both sides agreed to a general truce in the area immediately in front of the regiment so that the wounded could be removed and the dead buried. Union troops carried the bodies of the enemy dead to a predetermined no-man's-land, between the lines, where they were claimed by the Confederates. During the truce, the Union officers went out "toward the rebel officers, shook hands, and engaged in conversation. Thus they met," to Chaplain Adams's surprise, "as though there were no war." John Hartwell exchanged papers, coffee, and tobacco with the rebels. That night, the sporadic picket firing competed with the "piteous cries of the wounded for help and water." Hartwell informed his wife that "Lieutenant Duroe was killed and is now in this camp for burial." Clinton Beckwith remembered him as "the largest man in the regiment, and a brave and impetuous officer." They buried him the next day. John Lovejoy summed up the action as "a severe fight but a splendid victory." The 121st remained in position until April 2, 1865, when the final act began.[36]

With Wright's engagement at Jones's Farm on March 25 and Sheridan's victory at Five Forks southwest of the city on April 1, Grant ordered and rescinded a general assault along the entire line on a daily basis. He was now convinced that Lee's lines were so thin they were near the breaking point. The Richmond papers kept up a good front. The war was not lost, just moving into a new phase, they said. Each day, the men of the 121st regiment rolled out of their tents at 4:00 A.M., prepared to move. They predicted hard fighting and marching: no one believed Lee would surrender easily. Increased camp activity, the issuance of four days' rations, officers drawing shoes and equipment, and enlisted men turning in tents and camp equipment all foretold a final push. The rains abated, and the roads dried.

The area immediately in front of the Sixth Corps was the weakest link in the chain. On April 1, Meade ordered General Wright to attack the Confederate lines the next morning. Wright reviewed the ground and went over the details with his commanders, outlining the objectives for the assault that would finally break the ten-month-long siege at Petersburg. Wright set his divisions to attack en echelon, with Maj. Gen. George W. Getty's 2nd Division in the lead and the other two on either side of the V, or wedge. The 121st would be on the attacking line's far right, anchored on Church Road. The troops were to move as far as their own picket lines and there wait until 4:00 A.M., when a cannon from Fort Fisher would signal the attack. Pioneers, woodcutters whose job was to eliminate wooden obstacles, were assigned to the assaulting troops to remove Confederate abatis in front of their lines, and artillerymen were assigned to various commands to turn captured rebel pieces against the Southerners. The assaulting column's point of attack was where the rebel line was broken by a shallow, 60-foot-wide ravine and swamp.

At 10:00 P.M. on April 1, a robust barrage opened up "along the whole line, so that the enemy could not understand the objective point of attack," Chaplain Adams explained. More simply, Grant wished to avoid a frontal assault if the artillery could scare off Lee's men. Around 11:00 P.M., the 121st and the rest of the Sixth Corps filed out of their rifle pits and marched "and laid under arms for a long time waiting for the moon to go down as we thought we were to make a charge," John Hartwell wrote. Positioning the men within 200 yards of the rebel pickets was a daring and risky move that, uncovered, could have been disastrous. The assaulting troops carried only rifles and ammunition, leaving noise-producing equipment behind. The Confederates did not hear the muffled shuffling of thousands of Union troops as they moved into position. The skies darkened further as a cold rain soaked the advancing troops. Despite the strict injunction to maintain silence, someone along the picket line, rebel or Union, opened fire. Beckwith thought it was covering fire. When it stopped, he remembered the Union troops called "April Fool" out to the rebels.[37]

As they waited for the attack signal, Anson Ryder told Clinton Beckwith he would prefer to lie in the cold, damp, and dark rather than charge into a hail of fire. "Our minds filled with all kinds of fearful forebodings for none knew what a rising sun would bring to them," John Lovejoy wrote. Chaplain Adams recalled, "[I] felt sad . . . when I saw our men in line ready to march out for the morning charge. Such an effort is always attended with great loss." Several men, including John Kidder, wrote out messages for their loved ones and gave them to the chaplain in the event they would not return. Adams spoke earnestly with many who feared it would be their last conversation. Most men of the Sixth Corps knew that the work ahead would not be easy, despite the break in the line. The rebels had strongly fortified their line with ditches, abatis, and rifle pits. The private soldier's only consolation was the knowledge that Grant had decided to send the entire army against the rebels.[38]

Hamblin's brigade formed two lines. The 121st occupied the second line immediately behind the 2nd Connecticut and next to the 95th Pennsylvania. By 3:00 A.M., nearly 14,000 Union troops faced only 2,800 defenders. When it became apparent that the unusual darkness precluded a charge at 4:00 A.M., Wright delayed. When the signal came nearly an hour later, the men of the 121st, within 100 yards of the Confederate picket lines, stepped off smartly. They moved forward on the double-quick as the rebels opened on them. Of the division's three brigades, Hamblin's had to cover more open ground. The Northerners were subjected to musket balls, shot, shell, grape, canister, and "other deadly missiles."[39]

As they moved out, the advancing federals could see the origins and directions of the rebel fire in the dissipating gloom. John Brandon and John Lovejoy were running side by side. They simultaneously saw a shot leave a Confederate gun and head straight for them. Brandon moved to the right and Lovejoy to the left to evade the oncoming missile. The shell passed between them. Directly behind them, Danube native James Hendrix, a private in Company A, was sliced in two by the shot. Had neither man ducked, Lovejoy would have lost his right arm and Brandon his left—or worse. After a strenuous run over three streams, brush, and briars, the men of the 121st came upon the enemy's abatis and had no way forward until someone found a road that gained them access. The regiment captured 200 prisoners and two guns. Sgt. Redford Dustin of Company F turned one of the guns against the graycoats. Another 16th New York transfer, Dustin had spent two years with the 1st Massachusetts Artillery, which prepared him for his role on April 2. Anson Ryder had been hit in the leg below the thigh, suffering one of the most deadly types of wound. Dr. Slocum told him it would kill him if he did not have his leg amputated and that he might die from the operation itself. Ryder preferred to take his chances and die with his leg attached, so Slocum patched him up: Ryder survived the war "with the rebel bullet and the shattered bone of his leg grown and cemented together like old friends." General Wright recognized that the seemingly meaningless actions of March 25 when the Sixth Corps carried the picket lines were critical to the success of this attack.[40]

Isaac Best closely followed the action to gain a better view, reporting, "Fortunately, just then the sun rose, the fog lifted and the whole field was spread out before me." After breaking the Confederate positions, the troops halted to reform their lines and then moved quickly to the left toward Hatcher's Run in support of the Ninth Corps. They chased the rebels until they submitted or were killed. Best noticed sharp fighting on his right and later remembered, erroneously, that a colored brigade charged a Confederate entrenchment. When the rebels contested the advance, he said, "the colored boys leaped in upon them and applied the bayonet."

The element of surprise carried the day. Olcott split the command of the 121st in half, with Cronkite and Kidder leading each part. Kidder was convinced that he would not survive the fight. John Hartwell reported that the regiment "rushed on the enemy with such impetuosity that before [the rebels reacted,] we had possession of a portion of their works and four forts." All across Wright's command, the hand-to-hand combat over the entrenchments was "brief but vicious." Cronkite's men gained the Boydton Road and the South Side Railroad and managed to stop and twist off telegraph wire with their bayonets. Hamblin's remaining command turned north toward Petersburg. Once through the lines, the momentum of victory created havoc for the commanders, hampering their ability to control their men. As a major portion of the Sixth Corps turned southwest toward Hatcher's Run to engage the remaining rebel lines there, Hamblin's four regiments stood pat.

When Wright arrived at Hatcher's Run around 10:00 A.M., he learned that the Sixth Corps was not needed. He turned his command toward Petersburg. On the right of the Sixth Corps, the Ninth Corps remained under heavy fire as it moved toward Petersburg, and the 121st, with the rest of the 1st Division, was detached to support it. Now, only two forts, Gregg and Whitworth, stood between the Sixth Corps and Petersburg, but the 121st did not participate in the action to take them. Exhausted at nightfall after fighting and marching for more than eighteen hours, the corps dug in east of the Turnbull House to wait out the night, as Grant and Meade ordered another attack the next morning. The men of the 121st, nearer the Jerusalem Plank Road in support of the Ninth Corps, lay down in the mud and tried to sleep. Their brigade had suffered the fewest casualties in the 1st Division because they were pulled away from the main action. All across the front, both sides hung on to whatever territory they claimed as darkness fell. That night, the tired soldiers could watch Confederate supplies burn as Lee departed.[41]

Grant ordered an attack for 5:00 A.M. on April 3. At three places on the Union line during the night, skirmishers and sharpshooters probed the Confederate lines for signs of weakness or withdrawal. But by 4:30, it became obvious that Lee had abandoned the city, and the federal troops moved in from every direction. General Hamblin's troops entered the city from the south, putting out the fire blazing on Pocahontas Bridge.

Hamblin ordered Olcott to take the 121st, the 65th New York, and the 95th Pennsylvania into the city when he believed that Confederate deserters filled its streets. They were authorized to take prisoners. Eventually, there were so many prisoners and the federals were so enthusiastic in their pursuit that they paid little attention to guarding them or getting receipts for captured prisoners or property. John Lovejoy enjoyed the regiment's new mission, namely, picking up "skulking rebels" who were hiding after the rest of their army either surrendered or escaped the town. As the regiment entered the city, Olcott took fire from a citizen in a private home. He was not injured, and no one was arrested for the incident, but a number of men from the 121st asked to ransack the house. Olcott reportedly replied: "We would not have time to halt, and the fellow was a poor marksman anyway."

Egbert Olcott ordered Cronkite to take two companies to hoist the regiment's colors in town. The 121st was also given the responsibility of placing national colors on all the public buildings. The 121st's flag "was the second Union banner that waved over that deserted city, a regiment of the 9th Corps having entered farther to the right and a few yards in advance of us," Cronkite related. Chaplain Adams jubilantly bore witness to history: "I was soon riding through its streets," he wrote, "and witnessed the joyous salutations of the colored population, as they bowed and clapped their hands and shouted." The newly freed slaves praised the lord and master Lincoln. One old lady reportedly said that she prayed on this day for "the stars and stripes forever." John Hartwell took credit for being the first member of the 121st in the city. He claimed that he and six others volunteered to precede the skirmish line by moving into the city and raise an alarm in case of an imminent attack. Hartwell asserted that when none materialized and the city appeared empty, he proceeded to the northern edge of the city, where he intercepted twenty-one rebel stragglers attempting to escape across the Appomattox. "They all surrendered to me," he boasted in his diary. The first elements in town took possession of the courthouse and all public buildings, including the post office where the souvenirs of choice were Confederate stamps and money.[42]

In the afternoon, the entire division returned to its camp to reclaim the gear it had left behind in preparation for the final attack. The Sixth Corps received the honor and credit for finally breaking the siege of Petersburg. It broke through Lee's lines southwest of town, putting him in full flight with the remnants of a once-proud army. Richmond fell the same day. Jefferson Davis and his cabinet were now trying to save the Confederacy and escape to the south and west. He was determined to make it to Mexico; Lee merely tried to stave off surrender. The race was on to end the contest with minimal bloodshed as both armies headed west from Petersburg. For the next two days after the two cities fell, the Sixth Corps made 10 to 15 hard-marching miles in pursuit of Lee's army. By the evening of April 3, the 121st found itself 10 miles from Petersburg, marching up the south bank of the Appomattox River. It had begun its last journey at 9:00 that morning. For the next two days, it joined in the pursuit of Lee.[43]

Sailor's Creek

By April 5, Lee was at Amelia Court House, his path blocked by Sheridan on the Danville Railroad. The next and last battle in which the 121st would be involved took shape near a small tributary of the Appomattox River. With Sheridan were Maj. Gen. Charles Griffin's Fifth Corps, Humphrey's Second Corps, and Wright's Sixth Corps. The Sixth Corps began the day at 3:00 A.M. when it moved toward Jetersville Station on the Danville Railroad. Lee had hoped to find railcars at Amelia Court House and rations for his army. Neither were there when he arrived, and he could only keep moving. John Hartwell expressed relief when the regiment got there and rested at Burkeville, just below Jetersville. His diary entry for the day ended with the words "layed down for the night . . . awful marching." Clinton Beckwith remembered "little jollity about the campfires that evening" as the troops reflected on the work that lay ahead of them the next day. They were told to prepare for a daybreak attack, and the next morning, April 6, the 121st moved out at 6:00 A.M. They expected to hear musket firing at any moment. They traveled through ravines, woods, swamps, streams, and thickets until they got on the road from Jetersville. "Everything and everybody now seemed to be in a hurry," Beckwith observed. They were racing to catch Lee, and at the rate they were marching, they were sure to catch up with him soon. The road led to Sailor's Creek.[44]

The 3rd Division reached the creek first. An open field stretched gently down to the water, and the 3rd deployed to the right of the road, moving forward in a line of battle. Across the valley of the creek and a mile up the bank, the Confederates stopped and entrenched to make a stand. Immediately, the 121st occupied a position in the line of battle to the left of the 37th Massachusetts, which had deployed first and was moving smartly into attack mode, forcing the 121st to catch up to it. As the men of the 121st raced toward the creek, they plunged into a thigh-deep creek. Under heavy fire, they waded into the swollen stream, where the water was chest-high, and then gained the other side. There, they regrouped, taking little or no direct fire because of the steep opposite slope and the partially timbered land.

After a brief halt, the 121st charged the hill and within minutes overran the hastily constructed rebel breastworks, carrying them "at the point of the bayonet." The men of the 37th Massachusetts struggled on the right, where the less defined ground, the heavy firing, and their exposed position placed them in extreme peril. Once the 121st overwhelmed the rebel works, Olcott "half-wheeled" the regiment to the right, perpendicular to the line of attack and toward the road crossing the creek where the 37th was engaged. General Wright characterized the 1st and 3rd divisions' work as done "handsomely." A Confederate marine brigade from Richmond under Gen. George Washington Custis Lee, Robert E. Lee's son, became a source of concern. The brigade of "boys" manned fortifications around Richmond and had not experienced battle. It made a countercharge that caused General Wright to remark, "I was never more astonished." The marines were flanked on both sides by the 1st and 3rd divisions, the 2nd and Wright's artillery were in their front, and Sheridan's cavalry was in their rear. Wright, already looking on the rebels as his prisoners, ordered his artillery to cease fire "as a dictate of humanity."[45]

Although the men of the 121 "fought like heroes," the short and deadly battle further depleted the ranks of the regiment. Beckwith's Company B commander, Ten Eyck Howland, died in one of his men's arms, shot through the heart. The son of Asa Howland of South Valley, he was a professor of religion before he joined the regiment as a private in Company G from Westford at age nineteen. He became a close friend of John Lovejoy. He was engaged to Ellen Simmons, the sister of Peter Simmons of Roseboom, a corporal in Company G. Howland and Lovejoy spent many hours talking about the war and every subject imaginable. Howland told Lovejoy that he had bought a ring for his intended, and Lovejoy, knowing where Howland kept it, vowed to get it to her. Lovejoy thought him a "noble young man, none braver. Only by his distinguished bravery [did he rise] from a private soldier to a lieutenant. None will feel his loss more than John M. L., for we were intimate friends." Although wounded at Cedar Creek the previous autumn, he had returned to the regiment for the spring offensive. He worked his way through the ranks, becoming a first sergeant and then a first lieutenant that spring, just prior to the Wilderness. In January 1865, he became a captain in Company B. Not fully recovered from his wounds, he left his sickbed on March 23 to rejoin the regiment against Olcott's wishes and despite the offers of his friends to seek his discharge.[46]

John Tracy Morton, a first lieutenant in Company C, from Edmeston, took a direct shot in the head. After making it through the noncommissioned officers' ranks, he had been commissioned in February. Isaac Bassett, a twenty-three-year-old from Russia, New York, was killed as he wrested the colors away from a tattered rebel standard-bearer. The regiment captured two stands of colors that day along Sailor's Creek. The prize belonged to the 18th Georgia Infantry, presented to it by the ladies of Savannah—"the prettiest I ever saw," according to John Ingraham. The heavy silk flag with beadwork in the form of a large castle "to represent the capitol of Georgia" bore the inscription "Our Hearts and Our Homes." The men of the 121st secured the ground in front of

Ten Eyck Howland, from Cherry Valley, Otsego County. His father implored him not to return to the front after he recovered from his wounds at Cedar Creek, but he insisted on returning and was killed in the 121st's last battle of the war—Sailor's Creek. His father, Olcott, Kidder, and Cronkite got into a nasty shouting match in the *Cherry Valley Gazette* over Howland's personal effects. Courtesy of the New York State Historical Association Research Library, Special Collections, Civil War Collection.

them, and the rebels indicated that they were willing to surrender. Cpl. Edwin Lewis of Company I and Alfred Coonrod of Company G were killed trying to seize the Georgians' colors. Coonrod fell "at his post doing his duty," with a shot to his head. When Lewis began to move toward the 18th Georgia's symbol, he was shot through the head and killed instantly. The rebels picked up their weapons and began firing on the regiment—"their brave and generous captors."

The reaction "for this act of treachery and the cowardly murder" was swift and brutal. James Sherman and George Shay from Company G were both killed instantly in the exchange. Warren Dockum of Company H finally secured the colors. He had transferred from the 16th New York when it left the service after Salem Church. Another Company H private, Benjamin Gifford from German Flats, captured a second flag from an unknown regiment. Both Dockum and Gifford received the Medal of Honor for their courageous work. All told, the 1st Division took six battle flags for their efforts at Sailor's Creek.[47]

In addition to the flags, the 121st captured scores of prisoners, baggage trains, mules, ambulances, and ammunition. The biggest catch of the day was Gen. George Washington Custis Lee. The 121st's Harris Smith Hawthorne, from the town of Otsego and a member of Company F, and the 37th Massachusetts private David D. White, of Company E, both claimed credit for the capture, launching a controversy that lasted over the next three decades. Both sides defended their respective positions years afterward, but Hawthorne, not White, received the Medal of Honor. Controversy aside, the decisive battle caused Lee to reexamine his fast-dwindling options. General Wright succinctly described the outcome of the battle: "The position was won, the right of the rebel army was annihilated, and the prisoners secured were counted by thousands."

Three men from the 121st won Medals of Honor for their actions at Sailor's Creek—Dockum, Gifford, and Hawthorne, all of whom lived into the next century. All kept their medals; only Hawthorne's exploits remained controversial. Prior to the events of that day, Gifford had turned his life around. He had deserted during the dark days of Burnside's Mud March, on January 1, 1863. Arrested on his father's farm, he had returned to the 121st under the president's 1863 amnesty proclamation, escaping punishment.

Colonel Hamblin commended Egbert Olcott for his quick thinking in moving his troops to the threat on the right and recommended him again for a brevet brigadier general's star. He came very close to crediting Olcott for saving the day at Sailor's Creek. Hamblin also singled out Captains Kidder, Johnson, Jackson, and Van Scoy, as well as 1st Lt. Thomas Hassett and Adj. Francis E. Lowe, for distinguishing themselves. As Kidder said, "The men fought well, never done better."[48]

One of the most poignant moments in the war occurred shortly after the regiment gained the hill on which the rebels took a stand above Sailor's Creek. The men stacked arms in the open field, just outside the woods. After wading across the swollen stream and charging the rebel position, they were wet, tired, and hungry. Some took their wet pants off to dry over the quickly built fires. No sooner had they settled in than a mounted officer rode up looking for Colonel Olcott. When he was not found, Major Cronkite stepped up to inquire if he could help. He was informed that the regiment was to move immediately and follow the 65th New York. Luman Baldwin and Clinton Beckwith overheard the new instructions, and Beckwith decided that a quick meal and dry pants were more desirable—and anyway, he asked himself, didn't the regiment usually move a "little ways to form a new line?" He thought that a better strategy would be to catch up with the regiment in the morning. In the meantime, Cronkite rode his horse around to the front of the stacked muskets in preparation for ordering the troops to fall into formation for the move. As an instantaneous report from a musket boomed, Cronkite cried out in pain. A loaded musket had fallen, discharging a ball into his left leg. Doctors later amputated it at the knee, and he eventually recovered. John Kidder blamed a "recruit" from the 95th Pennsylvania.[49]

Ten Eyck Howland's death roiled Cherry Valley. Ten Eyck had joined the 121st in 1862 over the his father's protests. Later in the war, Asa Howland had tried to prevent his son's return to the 121st after he recuperated from wounds received at Cedar Creek. Upon his return to the field, Ten Eyck had told his comrades that his father was so upset that he "wished he would be shot." Now, the young soldier was dead. On May 14, 1865, John Kidder wrote a letter to the grieving father, accompanying Ten Eyck's personal effects and an inventory of items he had possessed in the service. Kidder informed Asa Howland that he had sold, under Olcott's direction, some of the items to pay off Ten Eyck's out-standing debts, adding that he now held receipts for them. Kidder sent the re-maining items by express from City Point. He closed his note to Howland with the words: "We, as officers and men, in this regiment feel to mourn and regret the loss of your son, who was a true, gallant and brave officer, and we are very sorry that his father's wish [that Ten Eyck would be shot] has been gratified."[50]

The *Gazette* published Kidder's letter and Asa Howland's angry rebuttal. Howland was outraged that Kidder would dispose of any of his son's personal effects, including his officer's sash, without notifying him. Had he known that his son owed money at his death, he said, he would have sold everything he owned "before a single article belonging to him should have passed into the hands of strangers." Howland told Kidder he had no right to act as his son's ex-ecutor. In a searing personal attack, Howland reminded Kidder that he, Kidder, had joined the army as a captain and remained a captain at war's end whereas his son had risen through the ranks from private to captain—a position he achieved on merit, not favor. He declared, "I can hardly see how the example of the noble heroes of the 121st, who made a man of *him*, has failed to have some influence upon even *you*." Howland denied that he had ever spoken ill of his son, and he stated that as evil as the rebels were, he knew of "[no] instance where they have insulted the friends of our noble soldiers after death." How-land expressed shock that such a comment would be made to a grieving father and warned Kidder never to set foot in Cherry Valley.[51]

Howland's letter, printed in the *Cherry Valley Gazette* on May 24, stirred the officers of the 121st to join together in Kidder's defense. A week later, a letter signed by every officer of the regiment, including the ailing Cronkite and Colonel Olcott, soundly rebuked Howland. It is unclear who wrote the letter; it may have been Cronkite or possibly Olcott. Francis Lowe, the 121st's adju-tant, sent the letter to the paper under the date of June 7, with the clear expec-tation that it would be published. The officers explained to Howland that stan-dard army procedure required them to clear all debts in a case such as this: Kidder, as a duly appointed member of the board of survey, was merely doing his job. As to Howland's reputed wish that Ten Eyck would be shot, the officers' letter explained that the remark had circulated throughout the regiment and everyone therefore assumed he "would have no special desire to retain memorials" of his son. The officers were weary of the peace initiatives and the perception that the people up north were never in support of the war: they protested "the unkind remarks of those in the rear." The officers chastised father Asa by saying that they did not doubt Ten Eyck's veracity and that if he said his father wished him dead, they believed him. And they declared that "even petulance is no excuse for such a remark to such a hero." The letter concluded with a vote of confidence for Kidder and a reproach to Howland. The men of the regiment reasoned that if a man chose to publicly chastise one of his kin, he should expect a public rebuttal. The following June, Asa Howland successfully applied for a pension of $20 per month based on his declaration that Ten Eyck had provided him with nearly all his wages except what he retained for clothing and "a little spending money." John Kidder probably never traveled to Cherry Valley on his return to Otsego County.[52]

John Lovejoy made it his responsibility to write to Ten Eyck Howland's cousin Mote and his sister Mary. The letters Mote had written to Ten Eyck, expressing her concern for his safety, particularly impressed him. "I do not shed tears easily," Lovejoy wrote to his cousin Cynthia, "but the affecting love" that Mote showed for Ten Eyck "was more than I could bear. She will mourn deeply for him. I for one will miss him greatly." Lovejoy expressed deep concern that he could not attend Howland's memorial service back home. He objected to the fact that Ellen Simmons had chosen to take the place of the "first mourner"—a social faux pas in Lovejoy's eyes because she was merely the betrothed and not Howland's wife. Lovejoy's mother and aunt attended the "funeral" in South Valley. Lovejoy called the rumors from home that the regiment's dead remained unburied after Sailor's Creek "a lie." He assured his own mother that none "of the dead [were] left on the ground 24 hours." He explained that Howland and the others were buried where they fell; those who died of their wounds in a hospital were buried on hospital grounds. He told her that Howland's "lifeless body lies in a pine grove beside Sayler's Creek." The knowledge that he owned a good photographic likeness of Howland mitigated Lovejoy's sadness: "I would not part with it at any cost," he told Cynthia.[53]

14

Lee Surrenders and the War Ends

Grave and dignified General Officers behaved like mad men [and their] cut-up antics . . . would have made a reputation for a circus clown.

Dewitt Clinton Beckwith, June 13, 1894

Lee has surrendered, and the War is over. The Army is crazy, and we are having Fourth of July on a grand scale.

James P. Kimball, April 10, 1865

Lyman Smith introduced us to those assembled, and made a very fine speech, emphasizing the fact that we were real heroes. We were not used to that and hardly knew what to say.

Henry Hilton Wood, 1934

Appomattox and Lee's Surrender

Rumors, all favorable to the Union cause, were now in high gear. Released slaves wandering the countryside reported the fleeing Confederates' condition to the Union troops. They attested to their worn-out appearance, their haggard demeanor, and their hunger. Some knew the rebels wanted to reach Lynchburg, where they would finally have provisions—if they got there before the pursuing federals stopped them. On April 7 and 8, the 121st pushed on at the rate of 10 miles a day through Farmville and Rice's Station toward Appomattox Court House. As they marched down Farmville's main street in the dark, a band far ahead struck up "The Battle Hymn of the Republic." Other bands joined in, and soon, the "whole line took up the song." And through the still night "rolled a wave of song such as it had never heard before and probably never will again," wrote Isaac Best.

Shortly after daylight on Sunday morning, April 9, they were on the move again. The regiment marched within 4 miles of Appomattox Court House and along the way discovered evidence of the enemy's condition—broken-down wagons, caissons, and "half consumed yellow corn." When a prisoner or deserter safely rested behind their lines, he inevitably asked for hardtack. Occasionally, the 121st troops would pass an exhausted Confederate on the roadside who despaired of all hope. As they took their position to the left of the Second Corps, which preceded them, they noticed that little firing came from any direction, and "an ominous stillness seemed to come over the army." They heard that Lee was a mile or two in front of them and that as soon as the artillery arrived, they would put an end to the rebellion.[1]

While they waited, the men of the 121st speculated about the current situation and what awaited them and their counterparts on the other side. Reports that the war had ended began like a slow trickle of water. Rumors spread from regiment to regiment, battalion to battalion, and brigade to brigade. The news seemed too good to be true after all those years. Soon, mounted officers and an ambulance were seen racing past the 121st's camp, heading toward the courthouse. The latest rumor told of Grant traveling from his headquarters to receive Lee's surrender. Following on its heels came the news that Lee had surrendered. When the generals all started for the front lines, the men knew something important had happened; as John Ingraham remarked, "We soon began to smell a rat."

At 4:30 in the afternoon of April 9, the news came that "old Bob surrendered." The reactions of the men and officers were unrestrained. Once the rumors were confirmed, "we gave ourselves up to unrestrained rejoicing, demonstrating our joy by tossing some of our comrades in blankets, playing leap-frog with others shouting and cheering," wrote Clinton Beckwith. When men began firing off muskets, officers stopped them. General Hamblin, the 2nd Brigade's commander, brought the news. He fit the description of a bearer of auspicious news: at six feet, he was the "tallest man in the brigade," and he was "mounted on a large black charger." A "striking figure in more ways than one," he made three mad dashes back and forth between the regiment and the McLean House. His first message to all who could hear was, "Boys, the fox is about to give up." Each trip brought the latest news. He lost his hat on one run and cut his face on low-hanging tree branches on another. His last report brought tears to hardened veterans: "Lee has surrendered! Lee has surrendered! Boys, your long marching and hard fighting is over."

John Kidder remembered the euphoria: "We were perfectly wild with joy. Such cheering you never heard. The men threw up their hats, drums beat and cannons roared for about one hour. I never saw such a sight before." Isaac Best added that "some were too affected to cheer and stood with tears running down their faces." Mules, dogs, and horses joined in the chorus—"It seemed as though all nature was glad." The men received the news with disbelief. After four years of suffering, it seemed incomprehensible. As Best described it, "[the] news meant not victory only, but peace and home." John Ingraham told his parents, "Such cheering and shouting you never heard or never will hear. Bands began to play, colors were unfurled to the breeze and our batteries wheeled right about and unlimbered and fired salutes. Sky was black with hats." And as John Hartwell remarked, the men knew that "our fighting is done. Everyone seemed to give himself up to all sorts of gymnastic manifestations of joy. Batteries on every hill around us roared forth the national salute of 39 guns." He called it the "most exciting day of the war" and noted that the excitement "did not subside until after dark." Even the mules brayed. Best's dog jumped on him and barked loudly in chorus with others in the neighborhood. "The rebels [were] as glad as the Yankees," John Lovejoy exclaimed. That night, the men dreamed of home.[2]

From March 30 when the regiment began its decisive push before Petersburg to Lee's surrender, John Kidder's mood went from resignation coupled with the premonition that he would die to exaltation at the nearly unbelievable news that there would be no more fighting. Before Petersburg, he wrote out an informal last will for his wife. He settled all his debts, sold his blankets and other equipment, told his wife of debts still owed him, and noted that the government still owed him pay from December 31. He implored his wife to raise his little girls to remember their father and "educate them well." The day after Lee surrendered, he expressed a sense of enormous relief. He echoed the feelings of his regimental comrades when he wrote, "Thank God I have come through safe and sound."[3]

Herkimer County and Otsego County citizens soon learned the news. Within hours of Lee's surrender, Sunday night, April 9, the streets of Herkimer were filled with jubilant people. A spontaneous parade marched from Mohawk and Ilion, led by the Mohawk Valley Band. Speeches, cannons, bells, and songs marked impromptu celebrations across the state. In Little Falls, businesses closed, and by 10:00 the next morning, April 10, villagers had gathered in front of the Benton House to hear, among others, recently returned Col. Henry Galpin address the assembled throng.[4]

Washington reverberated with the news that Richmond and Petersburg had fallen and Lee had surrendered. The trees were greening up, and flowers finally appeared as the city's streets sprang into full bloom. Adelbert Reed, still recuperating, felt well enough to go "into the city to participate in the Grand demonstration" celebrating the "restoration of the Old Flag on Fort Sumter." He wished his parents could see the spectacle on which "no pains or cost was spared to make it the most splendid affair of the times." The capital presented "one blaze of light" from bonfires, candles, rockets, fireworks, and any incendiary implement the celebrating citizens could procure. The streets teemed with "soldiers, ladies and citizens." Reed caught a glimpse of General Grant escorting Mary Lincoln from her carriage at the War Department: "How the crowd did cheer at the sight of him."[5]

New Recruits and Jockeying for Position

The war ended in Virginia, but it boiled on in the rest of the country. Joe Johnston continued to resist William Sherman in North Carolina. In the west, the armies continued to contest the outcome. The last battle occurred in Texas on the Rio Grande at Palmito Ranch on May 13, 1865. But immediately after Appomattox, the 121st began to march south with the Sixth Corps to join Sherman.

On the way back through Burkeville, the regiment received the long-promised recruits needed to fill up the rolls and allow the officers to muster at a higher rank. Cronkite, with egalitarian flourish and at Olcott's urging, resigned the lieutenant colonel's rank to allow his friend John Kidder to be commissioned and mustered at that rank. Cronkite could not be mustered as a lieutenant colonel because of his wounding at the last possible moment. Olcott nominated Kidder for the position, and Governor Fenton agreed without delay. Three weeks before the governor's approval, Kidder bought a new officer's coat and lieutenant colonel's straps for only $38, marked down from the winter's high of $60. In his new position, Kidder escorted 200 of the regiment's fresh recruits from City Point to Burkeville.

The men in Kidder's contingent, to be mustered in as new members of the 121st, were a wretched lot, but John Ingraham estimated that the regiment would reach its legal limit of 800 troops. Although the new men who were sent to the front helped Olcott and Kidder attain their higher ranks, their deplorable quality never improved. They "were a tough lot," but they brought the regiment to its Antietam strength. Most of them were from New York City, particularly Brooklyn. Company G got twenty-five new recruits; three were conscripts, the others were substitutes. No one believed they would fit in with the regiment. John Lovejoy predicted that they would "be hard cases to deal with." Once Lee was beaten and the new recruits were reassigned to the 65th New York, many of them deserted. As Chaplain Adams pointed out, "Miserable men, for the sake of bounty, have pledged themselves to go in lieu of others, and improved the first opportunity to desert."[6]

With combat over, a scramble for rank began anew. A special act of Congress made James Cronkite a lieutenant colonel in the federal service. Henry Galpin, who had mustered out earlier, became a lieutenant colonel as well. Kidder received the permanent rank of major, although he continued after the war to use the higher rank in his private and public life. Lewis Bartlett, Francis Morse, and Robert Wilson were also "re-mustered from the time of their commissions." On September 15, 1865, additional honors went to others of the 121st's officer corps. Cronkite received a brevet of lieutenant colonel, a rank and title to which he quickly warmed. Kidder, Johnston, Jackson, and Van Scoy were also brevetted as majors. Frank Lowe, Morris Foote, and Thomas Hassett were brevetted captains.[7]

Lincoln's Assassination

The news of Lincoln's death in the early hours of April 15, 1865, reached the regiment at Burkeville after initial reports the night before indicated that the president had been horribly wounded. Olcott awakened Chaplain Adams to tell him the news. "Why has our joy turned into sorrow?" he asked. The soldiers' reactions ran the gamut of emotions. There were calls for revenge, justice, and the continuation of the fight until the South paid for the dastardly deed. Hours earlier, when doubt concerning Lincoln's prognosis had surfaced, John Lovejoy expressed the hope that he would live "to pass sentence on his would be murderers." Upon receiving word of his death, "many threats were heard," wrote Henry Wood, "as they thought the rebels were responsible for this catastrophe." John Hartwell told of the universal mourning in the army at the "cowardly and inhuman" act of murder. Words could not express the emotions rolling through the ranks. "Everyone seems to feel as though his father had been assassinated and all they ask for was another 6th of April [Sailor's Creek] to avenge his death on the rebel army," he wrote.

Chaplain Adams, at Olcott's request, conducted a service during which, he explained, "I tried to meet the occasion." The brigade band played "dirges and plaintive airs," making the "occasion" complete. In a controlled understatement, Adams summed up the troops' prevalent sentiment: "There has been a deep feeling in the army respecting the assassination." Adams saw the assassination as "one of the fruits of secession." Wistfully, he speculated that if Lincoln "had not pardoned those who conspired against him in Baltimore, and made a few summary examples of palpable offenders, the late tragedy would not have taken place." He remarked on the timing of events, expressing relief that the assassination did not occur *before* Lee's surrender for fear of the reaction of the Union troops in the field against their foes. Comments circulated in the ranks that had events been reversed and had there been another battle, few prisoners would have been taken. Adams and John Kidder wanted justice. The news hit John Ingraham particularly hard. He and Beckwith wanted revenge. The 121st had seen Lincoln three weeks earlier when, smiling and waving to the troops, he visited the conquered city of Petersburg. Ingraham regretted that the president did not live "to see the end of this Cursed Rebellion when so near at hand."[8]

Adelbert Reed rose early that day. As he made doughnuts in the hospital kitchen, word of Lincoln's death reached him well before his colleagues in the field. The exuberance of the preceding week turned to despair. Reed left the hospital and wound his way down to the rotunda of the Capitol, where the president lay in state. Writing on April 20, he reported that lines began to form at 8:00 that morning, and a steady stream of people entered the east door of the Capitol, "passing by pairs through the west side down the massive marble steps in to the beautiful park at the head of the avenue." Reed had seen Lincoln a few days before "in the best of spirits flushed with the recent victories of our armies" as he envisioned the "prospect of a speedy re-union." Now, Reed viewed the slain president "in his splendid coffin sleeping that everlasting sleep. He looks quite natural," he told his parents, "with the exception of being some dark in the face as when most persons are when shot." The mood in the city matched Reed's own: "The bitterest revenge was sworn by all patriots," he glumly reported. The lights of celebration so in evidence the week before were now all extinguished, and the buildings were draped in black crepe. It made him sick to compare the two contrasting periods—one of celebration, the other of despair. He predicted that no one alive would ever forget the day and its proceedings—surely he never would. "It was one of the most grand but solemn scenes I ever beheld," he lamented, "so heart rending to lose so good and so noble a man as he and in so cowardly a way."[9]

Lincoln returned to Little Falls on April 26. Four years earlier, he had come through on the way to his inauguration. Now, he journeyed through upstate New York as a fallen martyr. Just a week earlier, the towns and villages of Otsego and Herkimer counties had jubilantly celebrated the end of four brutal years of war. Now, they mourned their murdered president. In Little Falls in 1861, the bells had tolled joyously. Now, in the wake of his death, they "tolled with a solemn cadence . . . a mournful dirge and muffled drum-beat were the only music." The somber crowd that gathered on April 26 silently watched the funeral train as it passed slowly through town. Col. James Bowen, a native of Little Falls and in charge of the president's remains, accepted a wildflower wreath from the ladies of the village, woven in the shape of a cross and shield. J. R. Stebbins, editor of the *Little Falls Journal and Courier*, one of twelve villagers who formed a committee to meet the train, received permission to go aboard to pay respects to the president. He described the interior of the presidential car and the surroundings for his readers. The five-minute stop equaled the length of the president's first visit to Little Falls. As the train slowly pulled away, the crowd dispersed.[10]

Mustering Out at Hall's Hill

Although the fighting had ended, the marching continued. For the rest of April, Sherman continued to deal with Johnston in North Carolina. The 121st marched back to Burkeville, a trek of some 45 miles, and then moved on to Danville, Virginia, on the North Carolina state line—"in sight of the hills of North Carolina." Cronkite, Adams, and Kimball were invited to dinner at the home of a secessionist planter who purportedly was the first in Danville to raise the Confederate flag. The three ravenous Yankees determined that they would "not waste an opportunity to 'eat him out' when invited." Surgeon Kimball had not sat down to a meal at a table since mid-January. They feasted on roast turkey, ham, fresh vegetables, rolls, fruit, and cake, all of which was capped off with wine and cigars as young ladies entertained them at the piano. An hour later, cannons, bands, and shouts told them that Johnston had surrendered to Sherman. Now, the war truly was over, and the 121st was no longer needed. Their host soon went down to Sixth Corps headquarters to take the oath of allegiance, undoubtedly to protect his five large plantations with their 200 slaves. Johnston's peace terms with Sherman reached Washington on April 21 as the Lincoln funeral train began its long, sad journey to Springfield, Illinois.[11]

By April 26, Johnston and Sherman, with Grant's help, had concluded an agreement, and the rebels in North Carolina laid down their arms. The 1st Division of the Sixth Corps, with the 121st, returned to Burkeville by rail. The men had marched nearly 125 miles in eight days, arriving within a mile and a half of Danville. Along the road, they met rebels returning to their homes who, according to John Lovejoy, were happy to see the Union soldiers "and confessed themselves conquered." They were particularly loud in their denunciation of Lincoln's assassination. They feared that with Lincoln gone, their best chance for reconciliation and reunion was lost. "They know their best and most lenient friend is gone," Lovejoy wrote. Some even wished Jeff Davis dead.[12]

The 121st left Danville at 8:00 A.M. on May 1, and by May 5, it had returned to Burkeville. Four days later, after a march of 72 miles, the regiment was in the village of Manchester, just outside Richmond. Delays in setting up camp gave members of the 121st an opportunity to visit the burned-out city and its infamous Libby Prison and Belle Isle. Pvt. Luman Baldwin of Company B remembered that the rebels bragged that when war broke out, grass would be growing in New York City within three years, implying that it would be empty of all residents. Instead, the Union had prevailed and "the grass is actually growing in the streets of Richmond that I have seen," he reported gleefully. Richmond's largely deserted streets enjoyed a surprising state of "harmony and quiet." "Only 7 weeks ago war in all its fury" had raged there. John Ingraham intended to see all of the sights in the former Confederate capital and more— especially Jeff Davis's mansion. Referring to erroneous news reports that Davis had been captured disguised as a woman, Ingraham asked his parents: "Old Jeff will have to hang, won't he? They ought to hang him with his petticoats" and his "big boots" complete with heels and spurs.[13]

When the fighting stopped, the men of the 121st remained committed to federal service for at least another four months. Family and friends back home and in the ranks speculated that the regiment would be kept in service until August 23. The 121st concerned itself with the rumor that the 152nd New York would be mustered out before it would. Lovejoy called that prospect "shameful" if true; after all, the 152nd had not participated in a single engagement during the war's last phase that spring. Other rumors accused Olcott of extending the regiment's time until August or October. To straighten out the *Little Falls Journal and Courier*, Joe Heath wrote that the 121st would be home by the Fourth of July. The confusion came over the new draftees who filled the regiment's ranks at war's end. Those men were assigned to other commands to complete their commitments. As another correspondent to the *Journal and Courier* pointed out, the "original 121st will carry home their colors [soon]."

No one in the regiment believed that they would remain in the service that much longer—most were guessing they would be home by July 4. As it turned out, they remained in uniform for another two months, through May and June. And in those two months, they lived in a limbo between the desire to return to civilian life and the sense of obligation in regard to fulfilling their military commitment. There were now large amounts of time when nothing happened. With no more fighting to be done, members of the 121st resorted to various diversions to occupy themselves. And for the first time since they had joined the army, many talked optimistically of the future. Earlier, they had not allowed themselves that luxury. During battle, no one thought of the long-term future; their focus was on immediate survival. Now, paradoxically, John Lovejoy suddenly became morose. He worried that something catastrophic would occur to deny his return to friends and loved ones. He knew that in less than six months, he would be a free man, yet he feared that he would not live to see home again.

Several of the men captured a year earlier at the Wilderness and Spotsylvania returned to the regiment, in time for the final march back to Washington. In the two months remaining, the men of the 121st traveled from the North Carolina state line to Hall's Hill, Virginia—a mile and a half west of Washington. Hall's Hill was the promised land, the gateway out of federal service and into civilian life. The men of the regiment could not go directly home, though. They still had to go through Albany to be released from state service.[14]

The federal troops regarded their former enemies as a novelty. Just days before, these "new" Americans were shooting at them and trying to kill them, but now they walked among them like new yet somehow alien friends. On the line from Danville to Burkeville, the rebels had disrupted the Richmond and Danville Railroad by tearing up the tracks and burning the bridge over the Staunton River. The 121st waited until engineers repaired the bridge. Once the work was finished, the road reverted to the owners, who employed many of the same people who had been working on it before Lee's surrender. John Ingraham and John Lovejoy noted the irony of traveling on a train with engineers,

conductors, and firemen operating a train for the United States while still wearing their Confederate uniforms. (They were allowed to wear their old uniforms
if they stripped the military buttons, insignia, and lace or shoulder straps for officers.) Just six weeks before, these same men were running trains for the rebels
in an effort to keep their cause alive. A flood of former Confederates lined up
to take the oath of office in order to get access to the commissary stores and
much-needed food. The mad dash for aid and passes north indulged in by
"ladies," "rebel solders," and "contraband" amused Ingraham. Everyone joined
in the pervasive glee. Lovejoy enjoyed the respect shown to the victors, especially the Sixth Corps, which was "esteemed wherever [it went]." Before the war,
John Ingraham had never seen a black person. Now he described their language
and customs to the folks at home as if writing from a foreign land.[15]

As the army made its way north through Virginia for the last time, John Kidder found occasion to visit with former Confederates. Most of the men just
counted the days until they could return home. Kidder also took the opportunity to visit James Cronkite in the City Point Hospital at the end of April. He
found him in good spirits and recovering rapidly, although Cronkite's doctor
wanted him to wait until his stump healed sufficiently before heading home. Kidder also caught up with some of the men who had been held prisoner in Elmira.
Two were merchants, and another was a member of the Virginia legislature—
they were, he said, "first class men of Petersburg." He had dinner with them, a
friendly occasion enjoyed as though four years of war had never occurred.[16]

For free spirits such as Clinton Beckwith, the war's end meant more time to
nurture his carefree disposition, a temperament that army service never dampened. Beckwith found the locals cautious once the fighting stopped. His gre-
garious ways allowed him to meet many of Lee's men, who confided in him
that they expected to rejoin their commander soon even as they accepted rations and federal hospitality. The day after the surrender, Beckwith tried to cross
the lines to visit with the Johnnies and see Lee's surrender site, but he was
turned away. Bedraggled citizens he met on the march, although pleased that
the war had ended, remained fearful of a bleak future for their ruined land.
They told Beckwith that Davis and Lee would come to the rescue and "extri-
cate them from their present condition." "I do not believe that any General was
ever more trusted and loved by his men than was Lee," he recalled. Like his
comrades, he knew that with a word from Lee, the rebels would have broken
through the Union lines at Appomattox. The locals refused to admit defeat and
insisted that they were never conquered but were "just worn out." When the
regiment encamped in Danville, Beckwith and others foraged in the nearby
homes and farms. While they loaded wagons from a large farm, they were surrounded by freed slaves and locals who found them objects of "great curiosity."
An old black woman told Dr. Kimball of her joy at seeing the Yankee soldiers.
She reckoned that she now "belonged" to herself.

In one case, the mistress of a well-stocked plantation that had been discovered by the boys of the 121st managed to save her property through careful negotiation with the forage detail. She served them a first-class meal in the mansion's dining room. She asked them all to offer grace, and when all declined, she offered it herself. Once the niceties were dispensed with, the table linens and fine dishes were offset by a "solemnity and chilliness . . . which took the zest of the food away." The men finished their meal quickly. Years later, Beckwith wondered what feelings were really going through "that proud and haughty woman, presiding at a table" with a troop of "despised soldiers," men who were often described by the Southern press as a "hireling army." "Outwardly she was calm and self possessed," he wrote, "but who can tell the thoughts which surged through her brain and the desire to have the power to annihilate us." As the men of the forage detail moved off with the wagons and teams, they ensured that some of the smoked meat went with them.[17]

The James River separated Richmond from Manchester. One day, Olcott asked Beckwith to join him on a trip into Richmond as his mounted orderly. For the occasion, John Kidder lent Beckwith his white mare, a "clumsy sort of a brute." As he and Olcott attempted to thread their animals between the wheels of a stalled wagon and the edge of a pontoon bridge, the horse threw Beckwith into the river. The panicked animal headed for the river's bank with Beckwith hanging on to her tail as she towed him through the water. Olcott roared with laughter at his orderly's predicament, and as he galloped back to camp, he instructed Beckwith to follow him at his leisure. On May 22, Kidder mustered out as a captain and mustered in as a lieutenant colonel, a jump of two steps, which he celebrated by attending the theater in Richmond. He also bought a new horse for $125 and demoted the old one—the one that had thrown Beckwith into the drink—to a packhorse carrying his belongings.[18]

In Manchester, the regiment continued to drill and remain alert. Olcott worked to ensure that the new recruits assimilated into the regiment and learned a modicum of military discipline. After ten days of drill and much to Kidder's surprise, "they marched like old troops." Every man performed in full gear. The 121st impressed General Halleck, who reviewed the troops on May 24. He extolled the regiment as "the best in the corps." To reinforce that praise, he rewarded the regiment by detailing 100 men from the 121st as security to General Wright's headquarters.[19]

Before departing for Washington, Kidder, Lansing Paine, and 1st Lt. Morris Cooper Foote revisited the battlefield at Sailor's Creek. There, they found the marked graves of some of their comrades. For those graves in danger of being lost, Kidder erected boards inscribed with the names of the dead. When his party crossed the creek, it ran into a group of mounted Confederates doing the same thing. Kidder engaged them in friendly conversation as the joined group rode over the field, reliving the battle "as friendly as brothers"; as he later told his wife, he no longer feared them. He encouraged them to take some of the guns still on the field for their own use and protection. They refused for fear of being arrested with arms in their possession. As Kidder left the field, he discovered a shallow, washed-out grave that revealed its contents to the horrified travelers: it was, he said, a "shocking sight to behold heads, arms, and legs bleaching in the sun."[20]

On the road to Washington from Richmond, the regiment traveled back over the raw wounds of old battlefields. As the men marched across the 100 miles between capitals, memories of dead colleagues, dusty hot marches, intense battles, and anguished times flooded back to the survivors. They averaged 14 miles a day as they trooped past Cold Harbor, Spotsylvania, Chancellorsville, the Wilderness, and Fredericksburg. As in the days of intense battles, they marched on hot days and dry, dusty roads. When the rains came, the roads became impassable for the wagons and carriages. Chaplain Adams took a side trip back to the salient at Spotsylvania. He recalled the mighty trees felled by minié balls that flew furiously that day in May one year earlier. "I will not describe the appearance of the field as our men found it when they entered the works," he wrote. "I do not wish to recall the sights, they are too shocking." Adams referred to the sights the regiment encountered as it crossed the Wilderness-Spotsylvania battlefield. There, gleaming white skulls grinned at the men as they stopped for a lunch of hardtack and coffee.[21]

They reached the Washington area on June 2. The finished Capitol building could be seen just across the river. Proceeding to Hall's Hill, the regiment was only 5 miles from Fort Lincoln, where it had begun the long march three years ago with 1,000 men. (Hall's Hill per se no longer exists: it is now known as High View Park. After the war, it became an enclave for freed slaves, and it has since been an African American community in Arlington, Virginia.) "We have at last reached the end of our marching and you can't imagine how glad we are," John Ingraham gushed. He joked that the last hundred miles produced "cheek bones that I use to hang my hat on." The troops settled into the boredom of camp life again—washing clothes, putting up tents, cleaning and polishing their weapons, cooking, and writing letters. On sick leave for most of the trip to Washington, Lovejoy recuperated. He drew strength from the knowledge that he would soon see his beloved Cynthia. For three years, he had told her of his respect for her in letter after letter. He finally summoned the courage to tell her that he loved her. Within days, rumors rebounded from Otsego County that the two were to be married when he returned home.[22]

Once near the familiar environs of Washington, John Hartwell revisited the idea of pursuing a commission. He rejected the notion immediately, with reasoning that went a long way in explaining his character and his lingering resentment for those who initially joined in 1862 and were commissioned only to resign a few months later. Hartwell told his wife that it "would sound well to have a Lieutenant for a handle to one's name." He had accomplished and seen more than those who first joined at Camp Schuyler but left the field without finishing the job. He knew he would carry more respect and appreciation as a sergeant for his commitment to duty. He summed up the political atmosphere that prevailed to the bitter end. He had earned his sergeant's stripes "while thousands had stars and eagles and bars light on their shoulders in profusion and apparently unsought but money and a few influential friends will overcome the most formidable barriers."[23]

Once Lee surrendered, regiments began leaving federal service daily. In June, the pace picked up to three a day. Within sight of the Capitol dome, the green fields of northern Virginia were covered in nothing but blue for miles as the troops settled in for the final bivouac. "And mightily the hills ring," wrote John Lovejoy, "with the shouts of the boys who are leaving the field for their home and friends." Many Pennsylvania regiments were given preference to leave first, due to Meade's influence. Only 320 New Yorkers were eventually discharged from the 121st. Of that number, 275 were original members of the regiment; the rest had joined during the last few months. Promotions, transfers, deaths, and desertions had reduced the regiment to a third of its starting strength.[24]

Return to New York

The 121st New York Volunteer Infantry Regiment formally mustered out of the U.S. Army on June 25, 1865, at Hall's Hill, Virginia—but not before the bureaucrats across the Potomac received all the necessary paperwork, filled out in multiples. The mustering-out process began on June 2 and continued until everyone had received his discharge papers, a process that took nearly the entire month of June. Company clerks were given blank muster rolls to complete. Olcott ordered John Lovejoy to take on the dreary job of filling out descriptive rolls and final pay rosters. Brigade headquarters threatened to withhold officers' pay if they could not complete the rolls within the next four days. As they began the tedious task of filling out every line, someone found a batch of peaches soaked in brandy, which, after being liberally shared by as many soldiers as possible, greatly delayed the completion of the red tape.[25]

On June 8, the 121st New York participated with little enthusiasm in a second grand review in Washington. The Sixth Corps had arrived late in the Washington area and missed the "official" review held for the rest of the army. All the elements of the Union army except the Sixth Corps had paraded before the dignitaries two weeks earlier for two long, brutally hot days, on May 23 and 24. The rest of the Army of the Potomac participated the first day; the rough-hewn western armies passed in review the next day.

The Sixth Corps reprised the ceremony on June 8 in equally intense heat. And all the important Union officials, including President Andrew Johnson, reprised their roles to watch the men of the Sixth Corps—who, barely a year before, had saved the city from Early's attack—march proudly past the reviewing stand. Most of the men were no longer mentally engaged. The heat, combined with the regiment's exhausted troopers, produced a memory no one wished to remember. They began the long day at 4 A.M. and hiked 5 miles to the capital over the Long Bridge on the Potomac. They marched down Pennsylvania Avenue and past the reviewing stand, saluting the new president and their hero, Ulysses S. Grant. The *New York Times* covered the second review and gave equal billing to each unit, specifically singling out the 121st and its performance at Rappahannock Station. Lt. Eli Oakes, a veteran from the war's first days, suffered a second heatstroke attack—the first had occurred on the long, hot march to Gettysburg. Egbert Olcott led the regiment, and the paper noted how he showed "vestiges of the terrible wounds and treatment which he received at the hands of the enemy in the battle of the Wilderness."[26]

Henry Wood carried his drum. Unlike his comrades, Henry would find his memory of the grand review enhanced over time. He proudly marched down Pennsylvania Avenue before the cheering crowds and the assembled dignitaries. "Our uniforms were faded and rent by bullets and our flags had been torn by shot and shell," he remembered sixty years later. In an assessment closer to reality, Isaac Best remembered the "experience more pleasant to look back upon than to participate in. I have never heard an enlisted man enthuse over the memory of that review." As the troops marched past the cheering crowds, many residents were reminded that the Sixth Corps had arrived to save the capital a year before. Maj. James Cronkite watched the parade from his balcony at Willard's Hotel, nursing his wounded leg.[27]

By June 12, Olcott told his men that they would go home to Albany as a unit and that they could retain their arms. On leaving Albany, every man could choose to either turn in his weapon and equipment or purchase it for $6. Lovejoy decided that since he had been issued a brand-new Springfield, it made sense to purchase it and the accoutrements. After all, he joked, "I shall be fully armed in case there should be a second war." John Ingraham blamed Governor Fenton for not using his influence "to get the York troops home." Meanwhile, talk of a grand reception for the 121st in either home county circulated through camp. The day before the regiment mustered out, 6 officers and 448 enlisted men were transferred to the 65th New York. One of the officers, Surgeon Kimball, had recently joined the regiment. Among the others were Hassett, who had received his captaincy shortly before; 1st Lt. Eli Oaks; and 2nd Lt. William Henry Harrison Goodier. Oaks never got his straps because he succumbed to the temptation of a furlough to Washington, where he got into "some difficulty." After his arrest, he returned under guard to the regiment. Goodier and 100 others formed Company I of the 65th New York Volunteers.[28]

By Saturday evening, June 24, Captain Van Scoy had turned in Company G's paperwork to the officer handling the mustering out at the 121st's headquarters, where the materials were reviewed. If they were in order, the regiment could leave the next day. They were not, however, correct. They were sent back, and Olcott promised he would personally deliver the corrected rolls by 9:00 the next morning to brigade headquarters. And so he did. The 121st officially mustered out of federal service at 4:00 on Sunday evening.

Between Sunday, June 25, and July 4, 1865, the regiment traveled from Hall's Hill to Little Falls, Herkimer County. In the evening of Monday, June 26, the men of the 121st loaded into baggage cars for the ride to Baltimore, retracing their steps of three years before. The men changed trains in Baltimore and rode to Philadelphia, arriving the next day at noon. Around 7 P.M. on June 27, they boarded the trains from Philadelphia for an overnight trip to New York City, where they arrived at dawn the next morning. There, they encamped in the armory at Grand and Center streets. The regiment spent the remainder of the day at the armory; a few of the men ventured out in the big city. The next day, June 29, the regiment left New York City via the Hudson River Railroad, arriving in Albany at 8:00 P.M. for a welcoming dinner. The official refreshment committee greeting the 121st in Albany fed 328 members of the regiment that evening. The men proudly marched down Broadway with the captured rebel colors taken at Rappahannock Station and Sailor's Creek. As Beckwith recalled, "We received a great ovation." Lovejoy told his cousin Cynthia: "I wish you could see the 121st. We have a stand of Rebel colors and our own flag." He reveled in the honor of bearing the flag home from Virginia. He ripped a star off of the American flag and enclosed it with his letter with the intent that it be "a Union badge hereafter." The committee and citizens of Albany "made ample provision" for the soldiers' "wants at the Stanwix Mansion, Blake's and Brayton's," after which they "marched to the Troy barracks." They were now back in the Empire State.[29]

Three original members of the 121st—Egbert Olcott, John Kidder, and James Cronkite—led their return. They were all secure in their new ranks. They were Otsego County men; members of the Herkimer County contingent had died, resigned, or been honorably discharged with wounds. The three had been severely wounded, and Olcott had spent time in a Confederate prison. Kidder and Cronkite managed to deal with their wounds, but Olcott never recovered completely. Thirty-eight officers were casualties; half of them, nineteen in all, were killed or died of disease in the three years in the field. Company K achieved the dubious distinction of being the most unlucky company in the regiment. It lost every officer assigned to it during the war. Thomas Hassett, its last captain, received his commission after Lee surrendered. A total of 737 men were listed as casualties during the regiment's three-year tour of duty. Altogether, nearly 1,800 men served in the regiment's ranks from the day it left Camp Schuyler until that day at Hall's Hill.

Charlie Dean, John Kidder's protégé, mustered out at Hall's Hill in absentia. Throughout 1863, he was alternately well and deathly sick. His parents wanted to visit him in camp, but he dissuaded them. If he had a hospital bed, his mother would at least have a place to sleep while she cared for him. Kidder consulted with Dr. Holt and Major Mather, who were successful in getting him into a hospital in Washington. He left the regiment in September, as it returned from Gettysburg. Initial reports listed him as "absent sick" in Douglas Hospital, Washington, as of September 16. His trail went cold at that point, but he showed up on the bimonthly returns for the regiment in March and April 1864 on detached service in Levi Turner's Office of the Adjutant General of the Army.

John Kidder urged Dean's father, Delos, to write to Levi Turner to get Charlie a furlough: "With his help, he could get one," he said. There is no evidence that Kidder played a role in Dean's appointment to Turner's office, but the ease with which Kidder communicated with Turner and his high regard for Charlie Dean indicate that Kidder probably secured Dean's position. In early June 1864, doctors diagnosed Dean with "dyspepsia and general debility" and recommended a thirty-day leave of absence. By mid-June, Turner wrote to Col. James H. Hardin in the War Department saying that Dean came to him from a hospital and that although he was "a fine young man," his "bleeding piles" made him physically unfit and "too feeble to be of any use." Turner labeled him "permanently disabled" and recommended that he "be discharged immediately." A month later, another doctor at Douglas General Hospital in Washington listed him as not fit for duty with his regiment but "physically fit for light duty as a clerk."[30]

By July 31, 1864, Charlie Dean found himself in yet another hospital, Judiciary Square Hospital in Washington, where he was admitted with the diagnosis of "Bilious Fever." He ultimately deserted from this hospital. Thus, in two years, he went from a promising young clerk under John Kidder's tutelage to a deserter. In late autumn 1864, Kidder stated that he believed Charlie had gone to live with relatives in Canada. Dean later admitted he had deserted during the war and received a partial pension for his brief service.[31]

While the 121st waited in Albany for its final pay, two potentially ugly incidents nearly ruined the joyous homecoming. Both occurrences were instigated by officials from the state's Adjutant General's Office, and both were examples of New York's attempts to maintain its states' rights prerogatives to the bitter end. The first episode began innocently enough. Since the regiment's return to New York State, the 121st's officers had loosened up on the enlisted men. The regiment officially moved into the Troy Barracks, but Olcott allowed individuals to rent out hotel or private quarters if they could afford them, with the stipulation that all men were required to report to the barracks once a day. The three Wood brothers "secured a place in a private home," and Henry Wood remembered that they "enjoyed going about the city and eating real food." Olcott also ordered the suspension of daily drills and dress parades. When the command in Albany wanted them reinstated and Olcott refused, tensions mounted. In addition, the Albany commanders wanted the regiment to surrender the seven captured Confederate flags it held in order to turn them over to the state's Adjutant General's Office. John Kidder, second in command, refused to obey the order. He argued that the flags did not belong to the 121st but to the U.S. War Department; unless he was ordered to do so by the president, the secretary of war, or General Grant, he refused to relinquish them. The Adjutant General's Office sent a small detachment to the camp of the 121st on Troy Road to take the flags away from the newly returned veterans. Kidder reacted by putting a portion of his men under arms. He met the detachment with the warning that it would have to fight the grizzled veterans of so many bloody battles if it wanted to take the flags. The headquarters detachment backed down, and the colors remained with the 121st.[32]

The second episode involved the Albany headquarters and the citizens of Little Falls. Herkimer County adopted a more aggressive approach than Otsego County in its attempts to give a royal welcome home to the 121st. At the end of May, the *Little Falls Journal and Courier* called on both counties to make a "public expression" of appreciation for the returning veterans. The *Courier* proposed that a committee of an equal number of citizens from each county meet to plan an "affectionate welcome." "Preparations cannot be made too soon," the paper warned. The good people of the Mohawk Valley ignored the suggestion to include Otsego County and moved ahead with their own preparations. Little Falls, ahead of both counties, secured the appearance of the 121st in a grand parade down Main Street. In early June, the *Freeman's Journal* tepidly suggested that the boys would soon be home after their hard-fought battles and would "deserve a cordial reception." No one knew when to expect them until Lansing Paine wrote to the editors of the *Otsego Republican* that the regiment would probably be mustered out on June 22 and start for New York on the following Monday. The *Republican* guessed that the troops would arrive around July 1, putting it directly in line with the opportunity to infuse the Fourth with additional meaning and heighten the symbolic importance of the day. The paper knew that Herkimer County planned a celebration at Little Falls and would undoubtedly include the returning regiment. But, the *Republican* reminded its readers, Otsego County had as many men in the 121st as did its northern neighbor, and it called for at least a portion of the regiment to be on hand. On July 1, far too late for any sort of celebration for its returning heroes, the *Republican* urged its readers to act. "Should steps be taken to secure this end," the paper argued, "they must be taken *at once.*" Otsego County lost the race to its northern neighbor.[33]

The year 1865 marked the eighty-ninth anniversary of the nation's independence. It would be the first Fourth of July celebrated without the clouds of war and as such carried a double meaning. Little Falls laid out an elaborate plan for an all-day celebration as a final tribute and salute from the citizens of Herkimer County for the regiment. Cooperstown, miffed at missing out on the occasion, expressed its disappointment at not being able to welcome home "the Otsego boys in the regiment on that day" in the pages of the *Freeman's Journal*. At the same time, the commander of the Albany Military District decided to throw a party with a long Fourth of July parade involving *all* the returning New York regiments, and he ordered the 121st to participate. Olcott and his men wanted nothing else to do with Albany after the flag affair and much preferred a homecoming welcome among families and friends in Little Falls. Representatives H. P. Alexander and H. M. Burch made the trip from Little Falls to Albany to ask the Adjutant General's Office if the regiment could be present at the Fourth of July celebration in the village. When they were rebuked, the matter was appealed to the War Department in Washington. Olcott telegraphed Secretary of War Stanton asking for help. Stanton immediately furloughed the entire regiment for forty-eight hours and countermanded the orders from Albany. The second incident made it abundantly clear that the troops were still under federal control. The 121st boarded a train for Little Falls and marched in its last parade on the Fourth of July in 1865.[34]

With the arm wrestling over where the 121st would celebrate Independence Day concluded, Clinton Beckwith and a few others were allowed to leave the regiment early, and they headed west. They stopped in Schenectady "and explored the town, and after a good deal of trouble, got to Utica" on July 3, "camping in the depot." Beckwith went home for twenty-four hours and then joined the rest of the regiment in Little Falls the next day. He found the regiment's men scattered about the village, camping wherever they found a comfortable spot.[35]

Everyone who attended the Little Falls welcome home party agreed it was unforgettable—a fete for the ages. The morning of the grand celebration broke cool and clear. The festivities began "with a heavy gun at daybreak and a national salute at sunrise." Organizers focused completely on the returning men. By 9:00 A.M., wagons, carriages, and people on all sorts of conveyances and on foot began "pouring into the village from every quarter." By 10:00, a flood of humanity bearing every conceivable form of food descended on the village park. They came with baskets and pails and arms full of food for their heroes. Mutton, boiled ham, beef, 50 cold chickens, 200 pies, 60 gallons of fresh milk, 2 hogsheads of biscuits and bread, 2 bushels of hard-boiled eggs, and 2 large washtubs of pickles—to cite just a few examples—provided enough food "to feed five times the number in the 121st regiment." Newspaper reports quoted officials who estimated that between 6,000 and 15,000 people turned out to welcome home the boys in blue.

Despite the short notice, decorations on public and private buildings sprang up everywhere. Homeowners festooned their porches with red, white, and blue bunting accompanied by large signs welcoming home the boys of the 121st. They carried variations on the same theme: "Welcome Brave 121st," "Brave Defenders, Home Again," and "Welcome, Gallant 121st." Along the parade route, Barch and Company's general store sported a heavy red, white, and blue banner over the words "Welcome Brave 121st—that's never known defeat." At the rail depot, a somber inscription read: "In Memoriam. The Gallant Dead of the 121st Regiment." Railroad officials trimmed out the freight depot with evergreens topped off with a sign reading, "Brave Defenders, Home Again."

The Honorable William I. Skinner, a delegate from the Twentieth Senatorial District to the 1864 Democratic Convention in Chicago, constructed an arch across Main Street, which consisted of flags and wreaths of evergreen. A greeting below the arch and on its supporting columns listed the regiment's twenty-five battles. The *Journal and Courier* offered the opinion that Skinner doubtless produced

> the neatest and most expensive decoration on the route of the procession. There were no prizes offered for the best design, but if they had, merchant A. S. Richmond would have won the honors hands down. His elaborate and comprehensive design included a black draped picture of the assassinated President with an arch containing the words: "For this day we have waited three years." He accompanied that sentiment with a depiction of the 6th Corps badge with the inscription "The 121st—pride of the glorious 6th Corps."

Fifteen minutes before 11:00, the train carrying the men of the 121st arrived in the depot. The crowd surged perilously close to the tracks and the incoming train. Approximately 250 men debarked to join the 100 or so who had arrived earlier. Waiting anxiously, Henry Galpin spied his old color-bearer, John Brandon, alighting from the train. Galpin ran and embraced his long-lost friend. True to military discipline, the able-bodied men fell into formation on the platform. The wounded rode in carriages. Horace L. Greene, local Republican leader and publisher of the *Mohawk Valley Register* in Fort Plain (his mother was a Herkimer), offered a few words of greeting to the arriving soldiers. He recounted the regiment's bloody encounters. He offered words of solace for the dead and a warm welcome to returning natives and those in the regiment who were from elsewhere. He particularly made mention of the captured battle flags that bore silent testimony to their valor and courage. In two short sentences, Egbert Olcott accepted the village's gratitude. Lt. George Snell supplied the *Journal and Courier* with a brief history of the regiment, which it printed for its readers.[36]

At 11:15, the parade began. The 121st took the place of honor, leading the entire entourage. The 300 survivors present for duty marched with their captured Confederate banners and their own tattered regimental colors through the town. They walked proudly behind the torn flag they had received three years earlier from the citizens of the two counties. The Brockett's Bridge Band, the Little Falls Citizens Band, and the Newville Brass Band provided the martial music for the handkerchief-waving citizens of Little Falls, who thronged the streets and stood on housetops to catch a glimpse of the returning heroes. Marching behind the regiment were veterans of the Revolution and the War of 1812, as well as veterans of other units involved in the recent fighting. The twelve to fifteen veterans of the War of 1812 "seemed to light up with the fire of youth, at the recurrence of scenes of military life with which they were once so familiar." The *Journal and Courier* called the Savannah Volunteer Guards' flag the most interesting war prize of the lot. The paper exhaustively described its white silk lining and its stars, mottos, and emblems. Its captor, Warren Dockum of Company H, proudly carried it in the parade. Fire companies followed the rest, their hose carts decorated in wreaths of evergreens and bouquets of flowers. Pictures of Grant, Sherman, Sheridan, Lincoln, and Washington were placed among the foliage on the hose carts.

By 12:15, the parade had reached its destination at the village park. The men were stacking arms when one of them caught sight of the small creek that ran through the park between two stone walls. Without a word, like lemmings, men and boys jumped the walls and washed their faces and hands in the creek as if they were still in the field, to the "laughter and rich enjoyment of the people." The impromptu mass cleanup gave a glimpse of camp life to the assembled and amused crowd. When the men finished washing, everyone sat down to devour the feast. The bountiful meal was served by young women in white dresses, blue scarves, and red bows—quite a sight for the men, most of whom had been away from women for three years.

After the noonday meal and before the speeches and other festivities began, the soldiers had time to mingle with their families and friends. The day's orations, including a reading of the Declaration of Independence, consumed the afternoon. The featured speaker, the Reverend B. I. Ives, spoke for two hours. The *Journal and Courier* devoted several column inches to his oration. The paper reported that the reverend used no notes, yet it captured nearly every word— a prodigious and dubious feat. Despite the oration's length, the paper generously reported that Ives held the crowd's attention. He began with the Israelites. He gave a nod to the Pilgrims, the English during the days of chivalry, Christopher Columbus, and George Washington. He censured a morally bankrupt South and offered no olive branch to its recently vanquished people. Ives made it clear that the Confederate attack on the *Star of the West* as it delivered provisions to the besieged Fort Sumter in the spring of 1861 plunged the nation into war. The South's loss was part of a divine plan. Ives believed the war saved the Union, "wiped out slavery," and made the United States preeminent in the world. On slavery, Ives exclaimed, "Thank God! It is now dead." The war restored the Union not "'as it was' but as it should be under the constitution," guaranteeing every American the same privileges in Massachusetts as in South Carolina. He predicted that soon, "school houses and churches" would replace slave pens and auction blocks in the South.[37]

The day ended with a high-wire act near the Benton House in the town center and fireworks at dark. The people generally behaved themselves, and the event was marked by fewer brawls and fewer drunks than previous Fourth of July celebrations. The local paper singled out the regiment for its gentlemanly conduct from the time it arrived until it left for Albany. Immediately after the fireworks display, the men of the 121st returned to the railroad for the trip back to the state capital to collect their final pay and muster out of state service.

The celebration cost nearly $800, and the regiment's old comrade, Henry Galpin, who had returned home earlier than the rest, provided $270 toward the total. The round-trip transportation for the regiment made up a large part of the celebration's cost. Clinton Beckwith remembered the day as "great and glorious." It was an unforgettable experience. "Nothing was too good for us," he wrote, "we owned the town. The girls gave each of us a bouquet." But Isaac Best felt "like an Ishmaelite in a strange country." He was not a citizen of either county and knew no one at the celebrations; he also conceded that he knew very few of the men in the regiment (although he would later write about many of them in the 121st's history). He did, however, express pride at being considered a member of the regiment.[38]

In the crowd that day was a young boy named H. L. Remmel, the brother of William and Caleb, who had served proudly with the regiment. "As I looked into those bronzed faces, and those broken columns," he remembered years later, "it told a story of the heroic fortitude with which these men met death in the midst of carnage, while battling to maintain the integrity and unity of our great country."[39]

The citizens of Cooperstown proceeded with their celebration, calling on Chief Justice Samuel Nelson as the parade's president and various dignitaries of the village as other officers of the day. Lumped together and placed at the end of the parade were "soldiers of 1812–15 and of 1861–1865; wounded and disabled soldiers in carriages, and military," respectively. The festivities paled in comparison to the celebrations in Little Falls.[40]

By defying the officials at Albany, the regiment missed the official presentation of regimental flags to Governor Fenton on the Fourth of July. The Young Men's Association of Albany sponsored the celebration in a specially constructed building on the Washington Parade Ground. Invitations were sent out over the signature of Lockwood L. Doty, chief of the Bureau of Military Record. Invitees included all the most prominent officers of the Union army. Winfield Scott sent his regrets, as did Vice Admiral David Farragut. But on the ceremonial stage with the governor, his staff, and several legislators were Ulysses Grant, John Wool, Lew Wallace, Judson Kilpatrick, John Schofield, Daniel Butterfield, and Daniel Sickles, among several other major generals and brigadiers. The only other civilian on the podium was Justice William Campbell of Cherry Valley, which indicated his standing in the political community of Albany and New York State. Butterfield gave the presentation address, in which he stressed union and eschewed revenge. He argued that the South's punishment of economic and social desolation suited the crime: "Then bid the disarmed foe to live amid the scenes of desolation and woe wrought by his treason . . . They are punished. Let them go," he declared.

Governor Fenton accepted the flags with a short speech heavily sprinkled with religion and patriotism. In essence, he said that God favored the Union's side. Using brave Union soldiers, God smote those who promoted "civil discord" and aided the liberators by enfranchising a "downtrodden race." Echoing Lincoln's sentiments at Gettysburg in 1863, Fenton argued that the Northern troops not only preserved the original Constitution but also "have founded [a] constitution and government anew in the principles of eternal justice." The day's principal orator, the Reverend E. H. Chapin, spoke less charitably and arguably in a less "Christian" tone. He held the podium for approximately an hour as he assailed the "malignant treachery and guilty haste" with which the Confederacy tried to negate the Constitution and the Declaration of Independence. Chapin lauded universal suffrage for all men—but only if they had the proper education.

The day concluded with mercifully short remarks by Dan Sickles. Sickles, Fenton, and Butterfield—the representatives of government and the military—sounded the notes of forgiveness and reconciliation, unlike the clergyman Chapin. Sickles called for justice, magnanimity, and charity. He called up the spirit and intention of the country's fallen leader by urging his audience to emulate Lincoln's "considerate and beneficent policy" toward the Southern states. He concluded his remarks with Lincoln's ringing words from his first inaugural address: "The time will come, when the mystic chords of memory, stretching from every battlefield and patriot grave to every living heart and hearthstone throughout the land, shall swell the chorus of the Union, when touched again, as surely as they will be, by the better angels of our nature."[41]

That day, 131 regiments presented their battle flags. Later, an additional 81 surrendered theirs to the state battle flag collection. The 121st gave Capt. Francis E. Lowe the responsibility for depositing its six "relics." Two were national silk flags, both in deplorable condition; one included the words "Salem Church" and "Rappahannock Station"—marking two of their most meaningful engagements. The remaining four were silk guidons mounted on their original staffs, without inscription. One lance lacked its spearhead. Governor Fenton accepted these tokens of war "sadly yet proudly . . . as emblems of heroic endurance," and he promised to treat them with dignity and respect so that future generations would never forget the regiments' dedication and sacrifices.[42]

The captured Confederate colors were shipped express to the secretary of war. With its last official action completed, the 121st as a national and state entity ceased to exist. The men of the 121st were dismissed and were free to return home at their leisure. The three Wood brothers took the train back to Herkimer County and got off at the station in Herkimer. There, they hired a light wagon to take them to Cooperstown, where they arrived at 1:00 in the afternoon. Once in Cooperstown, they began the 3-mile walk to their home in Middlefield. They left their baggage in a Cooperstown store, but Henry clung to the drum he had carried through the war. After they had walked a mile, Henry noticed the dust kicked up by an approaching wagon, and after a while, he realized that his father had driven out to meet them. As the elder Wood drew closer, he recognized his boys and whipped the team to full speed. Once all three had climbed into the wagon and exchanged tearful greetings, Henry Wood remembered, "we saw the light in his eyes, which we are sure had not been there for a long time. It was a gleam of gladness and thankfulness that the boys had come home safe and as well as could be expected under the circumstances. Even the horses looked around as though they understood that something unusual was happening."

The elder Wood had driven to Cooperstown three times that day, not knowing when his boys would finally arrive. He dropped the elder brother, James, off at his home to be united with his wife and family. "We did not remain to see the meeting that was too sacred, but we hurried on home." Henry recalled how many times during the war he had dreamed of home with every detail—the "table set, the white table cloth, and so much good food"—only to awake cold, miserable, hungry, and still tired. Now, Henry's dream had, at long last, come true. When he saw his mother standing near the house just beyond the fence, he jumped out of the wagon before it stopped, hopped the fence, and embraced her once again. As he wrote of the moment nearly seventy years later, he admitted that the "sacred scene" brought tears to his eyes, "and the overflow drops on the paper and blots my writing."

That evening, he played his drum for family and friends until he was exhausted. He fell into bed, the first bed he had slept in in three years. "We appeared to be living in a new world," he wrote. Gone were the noises of other voices and the violent sounds of war. The simple act of sitting in a chair at a table became a meaningful, joyous experience. Henry took his accumulated pay from Uncle Sam and bought a new set of civilian clothes. On the following Sunday, he went to Sunday school with his brother John, where his neighbor Lyman Smith introduced the Wood brothers as heroes. "We were not used to that and hardly knew what to do or say," Henry wrote.[43]

Others went right back to what they were doing when they left home in the heat of August 1862. They returned to the towns and villages of their youth, many going back to the farms and small businesses that had been attended by friends, partners, and families in the interim. Six men who passed through the ranks of the 121st New York State Volunteer Infantry Regiment won the newly instituted Medal of Honor. Andrew Davidson and Delavan Bates earned their medals after leaving the regiment. They were cited for their bravery at the Crater at Petersburg while leading the 30th U.S. Colored Troops on July 30, 1864. Henry Seymour Hall received his honors for two separate actions: for his heroism at Gaines Mill as a member of the 27th New York on June 27, 1862, and for his gallantry at Rappahannock Station with the 121st. All three of these men were awarded their medals in 1891. Warren Dockum and Benjamin Gifford had received their medals almost immediately, on May 10, 1865, for their capture of flags at Sailor's Creek. At the end of 1894, Harris Hawthorne finally received recognition for capturing Custis Lee at Sailor's Creek.

Dockum resembled Beckwith in several respects. He had originally joined the 16th New York, transferring to the 121st after Salem Church. After capturing the Savannah Volunteer Guard's flag, he traveled to Washington to receive the gratitude of Secretary Stanton. He arrived four days after Lincoln's assassination. The city was attempting to maintain control as the president's body lay in state and the authorities tried to track down the assassins. Stanton greeted Dockum and gave him a pass to the city and an introduction to any hotel proprietor who would rent him a room. Four days later, Stanton introduced Dockum to a gathering that included the new president's cabinet, officers and their wives, and "several young girls," and the corps adjutant told his tale of bravery to the assembled group. Dockum never explained why he did not relate the story himself. Perhaps he felt self-conscious about his appearance because he wore the same clothes in which he had traveled to Washington. When the ceremony finished, he accepted a bouquet of flowers, which he gave to his landlord's little girl when he returned to his hotel. The next day, Stanton offered him a thirty-day pass and $100 to travel home to Plattsburg. By the time he returned to Washington, the Union army was preparing for the grand review down Pennsylvania Avenue. Stanton treated Dockum so generously that Dockum felt emboldened to ask him for a seat in the grandstand to see the parade. Stanton agreed. Dockum later joined the 121st for its mustering out at Hall's Hill.[44]

15

Touching Elbows: The Regimental Association

> There is a mystic bond between soldiers, men who have shared battle, privation and hardship together, not to be found in any other association, and nowhere is this bond any stronger than between the men of the 121st New York.
>
> *Dewitt Clinton Beckwith, July 4, 1894*

> There is hardly a member of the 121st regiment but what could relate incidents of their own experience in army life that would interest us very much, and why do we all refrain from doing so?
>
> *Lester Murdock, Company E, September 28, 1881*

> We shall certainly never have any recollections purer and nobler than those which have cemented the soldiers of the Union into one common brotherhood.
>
> *Douglas Campbell, October 10, 1878*

When the war ended, the nation showed little concern for the men who had been exposed to horrendous visions of hell on earth. After World War I, the notion of "shell shock" characterized the trauma of combat; after World War II, "battle fatigue" described the mental stress experienced by the common soldier. "Post-traumatic stress disorder" marked the post-Vietnam era. But in the years following the Civil War, the effect on the human psyche of men killing each other was little understood. Few returnees admitted to any signs of depression or melancholy as they adjusted to civilian life. Many refused to talk about their experiences. Some shared war stories with the males in the family; out of respect for their wives, mothers, and sweethearts, however, they typically held back from discussing such topics with women. John Lovejoy said it well after a leave to his home in Roseboom. He wrote his future wife, Cynthia, that he "could have told a hundred fold more than I did when home, but I dared not for the sake of friends reveal all the horrors."[1]

Many of the 121st survivors were either physically or mentally impaired. Kidder, Cronkite, and Olcott—all from Otsego County and members of the original regiment—endured debilitating wounds. Others tried to return to a semblance of normality. At midwar, in the depth of the 1863–1864 winter, John Hartwell told his wife that scenes of death and destruction and mangled corpses of every shape no longer bothered him. "I seem to be hard against such tender emotions," he wrote, "and could bayonet a man with less feeling than I would have had years ago to kill a favorite cat or dog." He mentioned another person in his company who felt the same way. Hartwell thought he would never agree but told his wife, "We are taught nothing but fight." The loss of sensitivity was incremental. He saw his first dead man after Antietam; he thought himself "quite brave" when he saw masses of dead bodies, and he "soon got used to seeing such scenes."[2]

Cleaveland Campbell, who barely outlived the war, offered a more hopeful judgment of the Union soldier. He described the dignified burial service of a member of the 121st who died of disease after Salem Church. The men in the detail were from every company of the regiment, and they behaved themselves with decorum and sympathy as if they "had been standing in their own village Church yard around the grave of a brother." It "much impressed" him and encouraged him that the war would end successfully and that the character of the Union after the war would be retained.[3]

Clinton Beckwith's admission of his difficult reentry into civilian life was rare. In his reminiscences, he confessed that "for the first few days after I got home, I was very lonesome, things were strange to me . . . but after I got off the blue, I got accustomed to my new way of living." He missed the semblance of structure that his military experience had provided him. He attributed his and his fellow veterans' relatively easy readjustment to their youthful vigor. Slowly, the men of both armies began to reach out to old comrades, to reminisce, to commiserate, and to reconcile across old battle lines. In the process, they shaped and reshaped their own memories. By 1875, with some hesitancy, memories and the attempt to relive the horrid details of war began to slowly leave the dark corners of men's psyches and seek the light of day. At first, they were tentative in the telling. But as the century moved into its last quarter, memories began to fail, and the need for resolution became a powerful force for reunion and reconciliation.

One heartbreaking vignette appeared in the *Herkimer Democrat* in January 1894. Exemplifying the country's gauzy memory thirty years after the war, the story detailed a poignant moment in the Wilderness, where many suffered. It told of the discovery of two dead soldiers, one Union and one Confederate, lying near each other, canteens empty and arms stretched toward one another.

Between them lay a Bible, which surely had prompted them to turn their dying thoughts "to their heavenly father in their last moments, and thus [die] together with no thought of the fierce courage and ardor with which they had previously sought to destroy each other in battle." The Union soldier wore a red cross—he was a member of the 1st Division of the Sixth Corps, the home of the 121st. The dead Confederate's uniform suggested that he belonged to Gordon's Georgia regiment. The two were buried side by side at the National Cemetery at Fredericksburg. The newspaper appended a column-long poem dedicated to the fallen "heroes." It went into excruciating detail about their last moments on earth and their final reconciliation. The final stanza assured everyone that the two did not die in vain:

> Of their dying anguish no human tongue can tell,
> But we buried them together on the field where they fell,
> And united in death, the Blue and the Gray,
> Let us pray will be together on the great judgment day.

At the time the story and poem appeared in the *Herkimer Democrat*, its readers were voraciously consuming Clinton Beckwith's war reminiscences. The story reminded them that the 121st wore the red cross and that the regiment faced Gen. John Gordon's Georgians at the Wilderness. The coincidence of both the story and Beckwith's pieces published at the same time escaped few readers. The story may have been true, but that mattered little. Weariness with Reconstruction and a bonding of whites in the North and South accelerated the momentum toward reconciliation between former enemies. The process of reconciliation became reality as the nation moved beyond Reconstruction and its aftermath. Different reasons and motivations compelled veterans to rejoin their comrades and relive the war, and the "mystic chords of memory" mitigated the bloodletting. Dennis Dewey, who lost his leg and was captured in the Wilderness, recalled later that "50,000 men met there in a death struggle . . . the best soldiers in the world against the best soldiers in the world, for they were brothers." Thirteen years after the war's end, Otsego published a new county history in which it declared the country was united and the people prosperous. "Sectional strife is rapidly passing away, and the same hand strews flowers alike on the graves of the Blue and the Gray," it proclaimed. The history ended with a poem whose last two lines read: "Love and tears for the Blue, / Tears and love for the Gray."[4]

As time erased memories of battlefield horrors, the experiences of war, and the deaths of many friends, veterans' thoughts returned to the prewar notions of glorious combat and noble loss. Wounded at Salem Church, Henry Walker recuperated in Seminary Hospital in Georgetown, Washington, D.C. As he was recovering from his shoulder wound in late summer 1863, he dwelled on his fate, his past year of service, and his future. Despite all the hardships he had faced, he had survived and now took great pleasure in knowing that the worst was behind him. Writing to his sister Sarah in Cooperstown, he began shaping his memories of the conflict that he and his comrades called the "wicked war." He told his sister that "the remembrance of my companions that have fallen brings much sadness and a longing wish that they were with us again. But they were noble and nobly fell in a worthy cause, and I love their memory."[5]

Published reminiscences by major figures such as Ulysses S. Grant's *Memoirs* in the mid-1880s, the publication of *Battles and Leaders* in the same period, and the Victorian penchant for memorializing an event that no one individual quite understood in its entirety encouraged old comrades to gather. As one historian has written, "Out of this milieu of war memorial culture emerged the pseudo-military veteran's organizations." The Grand Army of the Republic (GAR), formed in 1866, hit its peak membership in 1890. The United Confederate Veterans formed in 1889 and crested in 1903 with 85,000 members. Various societies of the old armies of the Confederacy and the Union were organized. The Society of the Army of the Potomac, founded on July 5, 1869, opened its membership to anyone who had served in the Army of the Potomac or in the Tenth Corps and Eighteenth Corps of the Army of the James. Traditional military customs such as dress parades, military courtesy, and titles and ranks, once despised and ridiculed by enlisted men, were reestablished and embraced.

Another less precise rationale motivated Civil War veterans to gather in fellowship. They fought for a noble cause that originally began as a campaign to save the Union and evolved into a moral crusade to free an oppressed people. Those truths needed to be "thundered in the ears of the gross materialism and cynicism" of the postwar era, railed the *Otsego Republican*. As the 121st prepared for its sixth annual meeting in the fall of 1882, the paper ran an insightful editorial entitled "Regimental Reunions: The Lessons They Teach." The *Republican* argued that with "our scurrying and tense life as a people, one might well conclude that power and money were the paramount pursuits of the nation." The new national pastime was avarice; the pursuit of money was a goal unto itself. "These reunions tell of a heroic past to a sordid present," the paper asserted. The reunions restated for all to hear that principles "once had omnipotent sway in American Hearts." The veterans had been willing to fight and die for a noble cause. Their willingness to risk all placed them "apart in the annals of the time to come, as the soldiers of independence were set apart by the people who harvested the first fruits of the revolution."

Despite the "conversion" to the tenets of abolitionism by many of the boys of the 121st during the summer of 1863, there is no evidence they embraced Lincoln's emancipation once they returned home. They went back to the relative isolation and the homogeneous society of upstate New York. And many who returned to their former lives found themselves outside the mainstream of the new Gilded Age.

Instead of focusing on the postwar United States, the associations constantly reminded the contemporary generation that life consisted of more than chasing wealth. These groups became a familiar, orderly, and comfortable oasis from the world's realities. The regimental associations and other military organizations allowed the veterans to associate with colleagues who shared their views, born out of a common experience. The reunions provided a sheltered outlook on a much altered world. As one veteran put it: "Regimental Reunions remind me of Thanksgiving. We meet with those dear to us, but we think of those who can come no more, those whose souls have reached the Homeland. We hope to join them again and it may be soon."[6]

The effort to preserve and shape the war's memory in New York began well before the war ended. As early as December 20, 1862, Governor Morgan proposed the establishment of a bureau of military statistics. In the following two years, the legislature appropriated money for this project and defined its purpose. Morgan wanted to collect information on anyone and anything in New York that played a role in the great Civil War, including towns, cities, and counties across the Empire State. Paper records and physical relics were welcomed and encouraged. In May 1865, the state decided to build the Hall of Military Record, using $75,000 in private contributions and land donated by the city of Albany. For various reasons, the authorities in Albany never built the hall and the relics were relegated to the new state capitol building. While the haggling over the building preoccupied the bureaucrats, the official office of deposit for the relics of the war was shuttled from department to department. The relics eventually ended up in the capital, supported by small appropriations doled out by the legislature each year to complete the task of compiling the state's official war story. In 1909, the collections were located on the second floor of the capitol with the assurance that "all the relics and the colors deposited with the state are placed in airtight cases in the lobby on that floor."[7]

In 1895, State Historian Hugh Hastings sent questionnaires out to veterans across the state asking them to provide as much information as possible for inclusion in the *History of New York in the War of the Rebellion*. Hastings elicited names of officers, lists of battles, details on any and all incidents witnessed by the veterans, names of Medal of Honor recipients, and names of those now in charge of their regimental associations. The papers returned to the state historian offer an important insight into the thinking and memories of the survivors. Nearly every respondent from the 121st referred Hastings back to John Lovejoy, who became the 121st's unofficial historian. Lester Murdock from Hartwick, for instance, recommended Lovejoy to Hastings with this comment:

"History wants simple facts and correct dates and as it is an official history, he [Lovejoy] can boom it and give it such puffs as officers glory in."[8]

With the return of peace, the flags and symbols of warfare were securely retired to archives and museums as vestiges of an earlier time. The overwhelming need to return to a normal civilian life superseded the rush to meet with former comrades. But contrary to recent historians' assertions that the period between 1865 and 1875–1876 was years of "hibernation," there were sporadic attempts to reunite various fighting regiments or groups of regiments on either side of the Mason-Dixon Line. Some regiments tried to establish annual reunions immediately after the war. As early as July 1865, a notice appeared in the *Otsego Republican* announcing a meeting in Cooperstown's Keye's Hotel, "by request of several veterans . . . of the war of 1861–1865," in order to make a respectable appearance in the upcoming Fourth of July celebrations. That Independence Day carried a more significant meaning than many previous Fourths. The residents of Cooperstown, stung by losing their bid to attract the 121st for that year's festivities, were particularly desirous of having a special celebration, since the Fourth had not been commemorated in the village since 1860. The 152nd, prompted by thirty-three former members of the regiment and interested citizens, held a reunion on August 18, 1865, at Seaton's Hotel in Oaksville, a crossroads in Otsego County about 3 miles west of Cooperstown, near Fly Creek. The event was billed as a "social party on the afternoon and evening of the 18th," and A. D. Wiswell's "full band provided the music." Members of other regiments were invited to participate in the "very pleasant affair." That winter, the men of the 1st Regiment of New York Engineers held a reunion at the hotel of John Fields in Schenevus on Friday, December 29. They extended their invitation "to all returned soldiers." And as early as September 2, 1868, the 36th and the 53rd Massachusetts regiments held their reunion in Fitchburg. In December 1874, Cooperstown welcomed Gen. Judson Kilpatrick, who delivered a "graphic" lecture on Sherman's march to the sea and his cavalry's role in the campaign.[9]

If one could point to any single impetus for reunion, it would be the sentiment stirred in the spring of 1876 in response to the upcoming celebration of the nation's centenary. The Fourth of July celebration of the country's hundredth birthday rekindled the dormant patriotic spirit of 1776 and 1861. With a few noted exceptions, between the Fourth of July in 1865 and the Fourth of July in 1876, there had been no universal or organized movement to commemorate or celebrate the war in either Herkimer County or Otsego County. The survivors of the 27th New York originally brigaded with the 121st, the 16th, the 96th Pennsylvania, and the 5th Maine called for a reunion in Binghamton during the first week of May 1876. Cherry Valley, which shared vividly in reminiscences of both the Revolution and the Civil War, held a grand celebration on the Fourth that year. Once again, the Campbell family led the parade and celebrations. Patriarch William Campbell was chosen as the parade's president, and his surviving son, Douglas Campbell, was made chairman for the day. Capt. John E. Hetherington was given the post of parade marshal, and Francis A. Morse was chosen as his assistant. The inclusion of bands from Cooperstown and Fly Creek made it a countywide celebration. The *Otsego County Republican and Democrat* estimated that 6,000 people participated in the day's festivities. Prayers, hymns, patriotic songs, and the usual oratory were followed by a centennial meal in Clinton Hall in the town center. The intense heat wilted the day's featured speaker, the Honorable H. R. Washbon, and prevented him from finishing his extensive speech.

At the meal, participants toasted the Constitution; all the state, national, and local officials; the army and navy; the Union; the state of New York; common schools; "Agriculture, Manufactures and Commerce"; and Washington and Lafayette. They concluded by toasting Cherry Valley and seventy-year-old William Campbell. The toast to their village paid tribute to "[her] Worthy Sons" and referenced the sacrifices made for the "maintenance of the integrity of the Union." Douglas Campbell returned the toast for his father and then launched into a long peroration that recalled the heroes of the Revolution and the antecedent Greek and Roman symbols of democracy. Campbell not only cited the heroic sacrifices of those who went off to war but also paid tribute to the valiant families left behind. "Do you wonder that the descendents of these men," he asked, "love the old hills, baptized with their father's blood?" The Revolutionary heroes "promulgated the Declaration of Independence," and those of the current generation "made it a living actuality." He saw the war as saving the Union, not freeing the slaves, and in his toast, he remembered the "patriotic dead of Otsego who made her history." The day came to an abrupt end when a gale blew the liberty pole down onto a refreshment booth and the crowd went running for shelter. Veterans of all the Civil War regiments of Cherry Valley were present that day. The next year, serious attempts were made to bring everyone together on an annual basis to "touch elbows."[10]

During the war, for ceremonial events such as parades, reviews, and marching in line, every recruit was taught to gently touch the elbow of the soldier on either side, if necessary, in order to keep the ranks in true alignment. "In wheeling or making any change of direction without this touch of elbow and a uniform step both in length and time, there would be no harmony or exactness in the movement." The term *touch elbows* stuck, and after the war, regimental associations used it to indicate the time for another reunion.

For the next fifty years, the members of the 121st New York Regiment met regularly, until the final survivors answered the last call during the 1920s. Over that time, they shaped the memory of the three years they spent in the federal service putting down the rebellion. The monument to the regiment at Gettysburg, erected in the late 1880s, and the very late publication of the official regimental history in 1921 marked the two major accomplishments of the 121st's Regimental Association. In the interim, the members met, enjoyed each other's fellowship, told tall tales, and refought their battles—especially Rappahannock Station and Sailor's Creek.[11]

When the veterans of the 121st finally became serious about holding reunions, they began them in a most peculiar way. The first time the men gathered together, after three years of the most brutal fighting and military campaigning in recent human memory, they staged a sham battle. Other regiments also participated in mock re-creations in local parks, fairgrounds, and large public areas. As early as 1875, talk began about the regiment coming together once again. Emory Upton was serving as commandant at West Point around that time, and the men of the 121st wanted to ensure that he would be present at their first reunion. They invited him, and he politely replied, saying that if the meeting could be held prior to June, he could attend. After that, he intended to embark on his one-year world trip to observe foreign armies as part of his research on the American soldier and the national military establishment.

The regiment's organizers were unable to gather the principals in time for a reunion in 1875 or for the centennial year following. But by 1877, the survivors set a date to meet in Herkimer on August 31. The reunion committee, made up of Andrew Davidson, Marcus Field, and James F. Clark, sent out an invitation on May 16 from Cooperstown. The organizers had chosen the August date to coincide with the fifteenth anniversary of the regiment's departure for the field. They billed the day as a "grand field day and sham battle on the Herkimer County Fair Grounds" to occur under the auspices of the Chismore Post of the GAR of Ilion. Organizers extended another invitation as late as August 20, signed this time by Davidson, D. D. Jackson, and John Kidder, but no one responded. No reasons for a delay were given, but the committee postponed the first reunion further, to September 14, 1877. This time, organizers meant the occasion to coincide with the fifteenth anniversary of the battles of Crampton's Gap and South Mountain. The organizers promised entertainment for everyone, including wheelbarrow racing, sack racing, and greased-pole climbing. "It will be one of the grandest displays of its kind ever witnessed in this county," they boasted. Proceeds were to benefit the Soldiers Home Fund in Bath, New York.

The day of the reunion dawned warm, and it soon heated up. The events went off as planned. Kidder led the Union forces, and Brevet Brig. Gen. John Pembroke Spofford of the 97th New York led the Confederates. The *Otsego Republican and Democrat* reported that the day was a success and that the participants raised nearly $400 for the soldiers' home. The newspaper also portrayed the bizarre beginning of the so-called festivities: "The fun opened by shooting a deserter, which scene was admirably carried out." From there, the

(top left) John Kidder, in a photograph taken around 1890. Kidder returned to Laurens, Otsego County, after the war but eventually took a Republican patronage job as port warden in New York City. Mabie Family Collection. (top right) John M. Lovejoy, who was probably more effective as a member of the 121st Regimental Association than as a soldier. As its secretary he was instrumental in its survival well into the twentieth century. Like many regimental members, he embraced the temperance movement. Mabie Family Collection. (bottom left) With Kidder and Lovejoy, James Cronkite led the campaign to raise funds and construct the monument to the 121st at Gettysburg. He originally intended to write a history of the regiment but never succeeded. Like Kidder, he obtained a patronage job in New York in the Customs Office. From Isaac O. Best, *History of the 121st*. (bottom right) Lt. Francis Lowe, who finished the war as an adjutant. As secretary of the Gettysburg Monument Committee he was chosen as the model for the sculpture atop the 121st's monument at Gettysburg. Author's collection.

celebrations followed an equally peculiar path. Participants drummed a coward out of camp, an ambush squad drilled before enthralled spectators, and a Confederate battery defended a fort that John Kidder and his merry band of attackers handily overwhelmed. The paper described the battle as "not unlike some features of real fights. It included skirmishing, open field fights, charging, storming, flanking and the capture of a rebel fort."

All who attended deemed the reunion a success. The veterans of the 121st juxtaposed the sham battle and its attendant frivolities with the serious concept of establishing an organization to plan and implement yearly reunions. Eighty members voted for officers and to approve the idea of a "volunteer association." The choice of these neutral words differed from the more descriptive names adopted by other organizations. The 77th New York group, for example, called itself the Survivors Association. (That descriptor would have been more appropriate for the 121st's association, given the small number of men who returned to the unit.) Cronkite ran the meeting in 1877, which elected John Kidder as the first president, Andrew Davidson as vice president, and Cronkite and James Smith of Little Falls as secretaries who also acted as treasurers. The group selected Cooperstown for the next year's party. Emory Upton, stationed at Fortress Monroe, sent his regrets once again, but his long letter of apology enumerated the reasons to relive the war. The reunions, he wrote, would give the survivors "an opportunity to exchange greetings and to live over the scenes of former days"; he wished that the first meeting would be "so pleasant" that others would follow, allowing him to attend.[12]

The next year's reunion committee was unsuccessful in luring their former commander as the main attraction. Henry Walker chaired the second annual meeting of the Regimental Association in Cooperstown, on October 3, 1878. By that time, the association had a mailing list of all surviving members of the regiment. The committee placed notices in local papers and invited the 152nd and the 76th New York to join the festivities. The reunion started with a business meeting at 2:00 P.M. in the courthouse. New officers were elected, and someone read a letter from Emory Upton, which probably pleased the members of the 121st but meant little to the 152nd. After the business meeting, John Kidder led survivors down the "principal streets of the village" to Bowne Hall, with the men "executing their movements, marching and wheeling, with so much of their accustomed precision as to surprise the officers themselves." After a hearty lunch, a full dress parade took place and ended in front of the Ballard House, where the Honorable George A. Starkweather, one of the village's oldest residents, gave a short welcome. The sham battle had been dropped from the agenda, never to return. From then on, the officers focused on association business: committees, dues, rules, regulations, military decorum, speeches, toasts, and occasional fireworks.

That evening, Maj. Douglas Campbell regaled the residents and veterans with two hours of soaring oratory. He recounted the grim days leading to war, the response to the call for 300,000 more men, the recruitment of the regiment by Congressman Franchot, and the 121st's glorious deeds in the field. The members of the 121st particularly enjoyed hearing once more about their days of glory and victory. As his father had done on many occasions, Campbell recalled the fabled days of the Revolution when Herkimer and Otsego counties joined together to defeat the enemy in the Mohawk Valley and the "hills of old Otsego." His speech exemplified the conflicted positions of many of his fellow countrymen during this period of national reconciliation. Campbell praised the men and families in the audience for their heroics and sacrifice in preserving the old flag and saving the Union. In his next breath, with tortured logic, he declared: "Even if he wore the Confederate gray instead of the Union blue, my heart warms to the man who, for what he deemed the right, risked his life instead of staying home to talk." He affirmed that "the Union Soldier has always been a friend" to the defeated Confederates. Later, he proclaimed that the war decided if free labor would prevail over slave labor. Even though the former enemies had offered their hands in peace, Campbell reminded his audience that "these men were rebels." In a reference to the resurgence of Southern representatives in the 1878 U.S. Congress, he pointed out that of the forty committees serving in Congress, twenty-four had ex-Confederates as members. "We believe in conciliation and in generosity," he explained, "but while we live, while the graves of our comrades are still green, I do not think that the government . . . should be handed over to the men who with parricidal hands attempted to destroy it." Campbell finished his oration with the hope that the reunions would continue and that they would be permanent. Years later, Emory Upton's first biographer and former instructor at West Point, Peter S. Michie, picked up Campbell's rambling speech and incorporated it in his 1885 publication on Upton's life.[13]

Emory Upton's availability dictated the date and time for the next reunion, the third annual event. Once the local committee secured a firm commitment from him, it announced the reunion would be held on August 22, 1879, at Little Falls. Again, the 121st invited the 152nd to join in the celebration. As a bonus, the committee secured the appearance of their old corps commander, Gen. Henry Slocum. Comrades invited Douglas Campbell to attend and speak again, but a trip to the Scottish Highlands for health purposes prevented his appearance. He promised, though, to drink a dram of scotch to the regiment's health. The program followed the previous year's schedule; there was no consideration of a sham battle. As happened for the grand celebration on July 4, 1865, the town of Little Falls decked itself out in red, white, and blue flags and bunting. Flags were everywhere. By 11:00 A.M., the two regiments were crammed into Skinner's Opera House in Little Falls. The 121st took its seats on the right, the

152nd on the left. When Upton and Slocum were acknowledged, the hall erupted with "three cheers for their old commander." Press reports depicted the scene as "indescribable, hats went up, handkerchiefs were waved, and three cheers with a 'tiger' were given." The old opera house had not witnessed such pandemonium before. Another three cheers were given for General Slocum and three more from the 121st for their old buddies, the 152nd. The latter responded in kind.

The enthusiastic troops called on Upton to say a few words. Earlier in his career, he had admitted to his sister that he was reluctant to speak in public, and now he made a similar confession to the assembled crowd: "To tell you the truth I am very much scared. You know I am no speaker." Standing before them was the same man who courageously led them at Salem Church, Rappahannock Station, and the salient at Spotsylvania, despite being wounded three times during the war. Later, in a separate meeting with only the 121st present, Upton spoke of the importance of West Point and its educational system, which produced professional soldiers such as Grant, Sherman, Sheridan, and Slocum (modestly and obviously omitting himself). He stressed the patriotism of each volunteer—but, he said, "not to these alone, for the most devoted patriot is not made into a soldier by being uniformed." Through West Point and the professional heroes already mentioned, "the soldier was instructed." This point followed from his evolving theories on the professional standing army and its relationship to the volunteer army. His old regiment reminded Upton of a story. He related the tale of the old lady who sent a pair of socks to the Sanitary Commission for a soldier. On the toes, she had pinned a note that read, "Keep the toes toward the enemy." Upton allowed that the 121st never "needed to be reminded of the old lady's injunction, for its members kept their toes toward the enemy." Slocum, recognizing his supporting role to Upton, remained appropriately reserved, deferring to Upton as the hero of the moment. The meeting that day would prove to be Upton's only reunion with his old regiment. Years later, his sister told the association that it was one of the happiest days of his life. "It cheered him very much," she wrote, "and he delighted to tell of it."[14]

The fourth annual reunion failed to live up to the previous year's expectations, but many survivors who were rejuvenated by the celebrities of the previous year attended in Cooperstown on October 8, 1880. It was a glorious autumn day with the leaves in full color; the bright sunlight and crisp air raised spirits. Local railroads offered free and discounted round-trip fares. Some of the attendees traveled down Lake Otsego on the small pleasure boat *Natty Bumppo* and were welcomed by a local band. Generals Grant and Upton were invited, but both graciously declined. Douglas Campbell could not make it either, but in his letter of regret, he noted that he "passed an evening" with Upton, who "spoke very feelingly of the delightful time that he had" the previous year in

Little Falls. "The love of his 'brave old boys' as he called them, gave him great delight." Nearly 200 members of the 152nd and the 121st attended the meeting.

The following year, 1881, the weather mirrored the climate of the reunion. Upton had committed suicide the previous spring. The weather on the day of the meeting turned cold and rainy, deterring many from attending. Originally planned for October 4, the reunion had been postponed by the association to October 18. No more than 75 veterans were able to make it to Richfield Springs in Otsego County. Two years before, the attendees had celebrated their hero and commander, Emory Upton; now, they were lamenting his death. Marcus Casler had also passed away that year. The assembled group sent a resolution to all the local papers expressing their condolences and sorrow at Upton's and Casler's untimely deaths. The regiment adjourned, with plans to meet in Ilion on August 22, 1882—to mark the regiment's twentieth anniversary of marching to the front. A group of New York volunteers from several different regiments met in an impromptu reunion in the spring of that year, hosted by the Galpin Post at Little Falls, and they were honored by the presence of General Slocum, who once again paid homage to his recently deceased personal friend, Emory Upton. The volunteers ended the meeting with the affirmation that they would come together in these reunions as long as "two men remained who belonged to the same regiment."[15]

Throughout the 1880s, the meetings took on a familiar sameness that became comfortable for all. Several old-timers—Davidson, Cronkite, Kidder, Lovejoy, and James Smith—would merely rotate offices until one or the other went on to the "last campfire." For later gatherings, younger survivors were elevated to officer status as the others passed on. The meeting committee ensured that the reunions were moved around to all the major population centers in the two counties. The 1884 meeting in Herkimer hosted more than 800 veterans from the 121st, the 152nd, the 34th, and other units. With family and friends, the number in attendance ballooned to 3,000. Invariably, each village's citizens would attempt to outdo themselves in patriotic decorations. Each occasion featured a prominent speaker after dinner, in a quickly established tradition called "the campfire." A standard round of toasts opened each meeting, with everyone from the "President of the United States" to "Our Fallen Comrades" included. Some of the meetings concluded with fireworks. Occasionally, the activities were interrupted with raucous laughter. At the 1883 meeting, featured speaker Justin D. Fulton, DD, a minister from Brooklyn, described Sheridan's miraculous recovery of victory from defeat in the Shenandoah Valley in 1864. When the good reverend quoted Sheridan as saying on his wild ride, "We shall whip them yet," a salty old 121st vet stood up and rudely corrected him, declaring that Sheridan said, "We'll lick the hell out of 'em yet." When the wild cheering subsided and order was restored, the reverend merely added, "And he did."[16]

At mid-decade, the 121st invited the 5th Maine to join the 152nd, the 34th, and the 81st New York regiments in Little Falls on September 29, 1885. By then, the association's organizational skills had improved to the point that it could afford printed invitations, a printed program, and a printed poem written especially for the occasion by John Tyler of Company G, from Westford. Tyler, an insurance salesman, could boast, as few could, that he had never missed a day due to sickness or wounds during the entire three years in the field. He was promoted to sergeant for his bravery at Cedar Creek, and he was one of the first to cast a vote for Lincoln and, more recently, for President William McKinley. His poem, entitled "The 121st ('Onesters') and the 5th Maine," proclaimed the close bonds between the 121st and the 5th Maine.

Col. Clark S. Edwards, the 5th Maine's commander, and others from the regiment attended the reunion. The 121st's fondness for the 5th Maine was burnished to a high degree after the war, far beyond any feelings of attachment felt during the war. (And when the Reverend George W. Bicknell wrote his history of the 5th Maine in 1871, he made no special mention of his unit's feelings toward the 121st.) The relationship began almost immediately when the 121st joined the Sixth Corps in September 1862. The 5th Maine first took notice of the 121st after the battle of Fredericksburg. It occupied the line on the 121st's right as the troops lay in the Bowling Green Road in December 1862. The 5th Maine's officers were impressed with the 121st's discipline. John Kidder remarked that the "121st N. Y. behaved as cool as any regiment" the 5th had ever seen. As the war years receded, though, the memories of bonding between the two regiments increasingly took on a celebratory flavor. The 121st also shared the brigade with the 95th and 96th Pennsylvania regiments, but it was never as close to those units as it was to the 5th Maine.

The two regiments shared the Reverend Dr. John Adams, originally of the 5th Maine, and every soldier of any religious persuasion easily connected with the good reverend. Delavan Bates remembered a scenario that he incorrectly attributed to Emory Upton. Bates claimed that Upton had ordered the 5th Maine to put the men of the 121st through their paces with the manual of arms, "company drill, and the best methods of camp life." In fact, the incident never occurred, but the affection for the 5th Maine grew exponentially throughout the last quarter of the nineteenth century. In one article, Bates claimed that nine out of ten of the 121st's survivors would have named the 5th Maine as the regiment most remembered of all they fought beside during the war. In another, he enumerated three reasons why the 121st formed a bond with the 5th Maine. First, he cited Upton's use of the 5th Maine to train the 121st because of the extraordinary interest taken by the officers of the 5th Maine in the 121st's welfare. Second, he mentioned the Reverend John Adams. And third and above all, Bates maintained that no matter what the outcome of a battle, the men of the 121st would remember them because "we knew that the 5th Maine would be with us" at the end.[17]

And the 5th Maine returned the admiration in equally liberal amounts. During the first decade of the new century, representatives from that regiment made special trips to be with their former comrades at reunion time, and members of the 121st reciprocated with visits to the 5th Maine's new headquarters building on Peaks Island, Portland, Maine. Former 5th Maine captain George E. Brown and Anna Goodwin, wife of Capt. Lewis E. Goodwin, purchased the land on the south shore of the island in 1887 and gave it to the 5th Maine's survivors' society. They engaged the Portland architects Francis Fassett and Frederick Thompson to design a Queen Anne–style cottage on the island, which eventually became the society's headquarters and is now its museum. The 5th Maine's "beautiful and spacious building with memorial windows" impressed the 121st's Wallace Young. He described the walls covered with the portraits of luminaries of the 5th Maine, living and dead; "conspicuous among the pictures" were Colonel Edwards and Chaplain Adams—"Both noble men." And N. R. Lougee, secretary of the 5th Maine's survivors' association, wrote in 1907 that the men of the regiment had a "warm place in their hearts for the 'onesters'" and that they often spoke of the "grand comradeship between the two regiments when we marched together so long ago with the 'onesters' on our left."[18]

The men in each camp made honorary members of the other regiment's veterans—and they exchanged gifts. The 5th Maine presented a "fine picture of [its] memorial hall" to each member of both regiments. The 121st responded with a black-and-white engraving of its Gettysburg monument. In 1908, Herman Johnson visited the 5th Maine bearing three volumes of *New York at Gettysburg,* "which was appreciated." Purportedly, Col. Clark Edwards, who died on May 3, 1903 (the fortieth anniversary of the battle of Salem Church), remembered his old command and the 121st on his deathbed.[19]

No one really knows when or how the term *onester* originated. Supposedly, it represented a combination of *one* for the 121st and *youngster* and thus referred to the youthful new regiment when it took the field in 1862. There is no evidence that the term was used during the war. It gained currency after the war in reunion circles, particularly after John Tyler wrote his poem "Tribute to the 'Onesters'" and read it at reunion meetings. *Reunion Reports* published the poem several times throughout the many years the regiment met.[20]

The Gettysburg Monument

One of the first calls to memorialize the soldiers of the Civil War in Herkimer and Otsego counties came on June 21, 1865, from the *Cherry Valley Gazette.* The village of Cherry Valley boasted a beautiful new cemetery, and a spot for a memorial had already been chosen by the paper. It attempted to convince its readers that the money to construct the memorial could easily be raised. It envisioned the monument as a tribute to the living and the dead. It reminded all that other communities had gathered subscriptions and that the village "should not delay" in doing the same. "Who will take the matter in hand?" the paper asked.[21]

The impetus for a monument at Gettysburg came from Albany. In May 1886, the state legislature approved a measure to honor all eighty-two New York regiments and batteries that were present at Gettysburg. The legislation authorized a commission of five men, including the state's adjutant general, to research and mark the positions and movements of all the regiments involved in the battle. The state allowed the commission to decide how the regiments would be remembered and how their positions would be marked. The purpose of the 1886 act was merely to establish the whereabouts of each regiment; it did not allow for the design and placement of any memorials. The act also established a staff office in New York City at 31 Cooper Union in anticipation of the volume of paperwork that would be generated.

It took the state three months to get organized and to occupy its new office. Once the commission decided which regiments were present at the battle, secretary of the Monuments Commission George W. Cooney sent a form letter to all the survivors' organizations in September 1886. He asked each to name two "suitable persons" to represent its regiment throughout the process and to send a delegation to Gettysburg in October to attend an organizational meeting with the commission. There and through additional conversations, the committee gleaned information on types of statues, materials and their durability, and a variety of designs. These meetings then informed additional legislation passed by lawmakers in Albany in May 1887 providing for the erection of suitable monuments on the battlefield.

James Cronkite received Cooney's letter of September 1886. He chose Kidder, Beckwith, and Capt. Frank E. Lowe to serve with him. Lowe had joined the 32nd New York as a nineteen-year-old private in August 1862. The following May, after Salem Church and his transfer to Company A in the 121st, he rose from private to sergeant to first lieutenant and finally to adjutant of the regiment. He was severely wounded at Cold Harbor, with either an injury in the abdomen or a "severe gunshot wound" in the back or in the right side and the right leg—depending on the source. He bounced about the medical system from a general hospital in Germantown, Pennsylvania, to Satterlee in Philadelphia. He returned to the regiment and accepted a promotion to adjutant just after Christmas 1864. He mustered out with the regiment. In September 1865, he earned the brevet of captain. Although not an original member of the regiment, he played a role in the monument's design that would gain him long-lasting remembrance.[22]

The commission and the Gettysburg Battlefield Association, a Pennsylvania corporation, were to be the final arbiters of the designs for all monuments submitted by the regiments. The May 1887 legislation gave the New York commission the authority to set strict guidelines for the type of material to be used, the style of lettering, and the wording of all inscriptions. The commissioners were directed to work with the local committees, but local committees were authorized to engage a monument builder and a sculptor. The state appropriated $1,500 for each regimental association for its individual memorial. The state legislature set what appeared to be a realistic goal of July 3, 1888, the twenty-fifth anniversary of the battle's end, for all regiments to erect and dedicate their memorials on the battlefield. The deadline proved too aggressive, however, and several regiments, including the 121st, were unable to meet it.

On July 30, 1887, the 121st regimental committee sent out requests for proposals to designers and sculptors. Initial specifications called for incorporating the state's coat of arms, the Sixth Corps cross, and "a life size medallion likeness in bronze" of Emory Upton. There is no record of any discussion by the committee regarding Upton's inclusion or whether Franchot or Olcott should be honored. The work estimate was to include the cost of other lettering (to be determined later), transportation of the sculpture to the battlefield, and setup at the site. The committee estimated that it would have to raise an additional $500 to $1,000, numbers that would quickly escalate. The committee required a complete proposal from manufacturers by August 23, in time for the annual reunion in Herkimer. In less than a month, four firms provided six legitimate proposals to the regiment's committee.[23]

The Smith Granite Company of Boston submitted two designs; Frederick and Field of Quincy, two; the New England Monument Company, New York, one; and the Monumental Bronze Company of Bridgeport, Connecticut, one. All six were presented to the membership at Herkimer. The four firms hastily prepared preliminary drawings and models for consideration. All six designs were rejected, and the firms were asked to provide additional ideas. With that, a larger permanent committee replaced the temporary committee but featured the same cast of characters. They gave Secretary Clinton Beckwith the responsibility of meeting in Gettysburg with the state commissioners in the near future.

The permanent committee set up headquarters at the Murray Hill Hotel in New York City, where it deliberated throughout the summer and fall of 1887 and nearly the entire year of 1888. In July 1888, on the twenty-fifth anniversary of the battle, instead of erecting their monument as originally planned, Kidder, Lowe, Cronkite, and Beckwith all traveled to the battlefield. Along with the state commissioners, they finally settled on the regiment's exact location on the field on the north slope of Little Round Top.

The committee returned to New York and continued to meet, negotiate, review, and argue before finally deciding on a design and a sculptor. "Competition among the contractors was spirited and that summer and fall were consumed in examining the many designs to be used, and the multitude of details encountered to meet all the requirements of the State Commissioners." The committee petitioned the army's adjutant general, Brig. Gen. R. C. Drum, for the "official" numbers of recruits and casualties and the names and dates of all the battles eligible for recording on the monument. By December 1888, the committee had made all the important decisions, which were reported to the Board of Commissioners. The board approved all on December 12, 1888. Cronkite promised the board that the monument would be in place and dedicated by June or July 1889.[24]

Most significantly, the committee decided how to top off the monument. Clinton Beckwith suggested a "figure of a private soldier fully equipped, standing at 'place rest,' leaning gently on his musket, while intently watching the approach of the enemy and awaiting the order of battle." Beckwith's suggestion was not unique. Other monuments on the field portrayed the alert soldier in all forms of readiness. But the regimental committee easily approved it, probably because it looked very similar to monuments already erected by other units. In order to execute the soldier on the top, the committee needed a model. It turned to one of its own—Frank Lowe—to become the soldier on the sculpture. Once again, Lowe donned the uniform of the private soldier of the late war, complete with all the accoutrements. He assumed the pose for the photographer. From the photo, the sculptor molded a clay maquette and then reproduced it as a life-size bronze "with such perfect fidelity to the original that the likeness has been observed by all his comrades and friends who have seen the monument." Finally, the committee awarded the monument's contract to Frederick and Field of Quincy, one of the original competitors. The committee determined that the monument surmounted by the sculpture would be placed at the center of the regiment's position, with two small stones marking the farthest extent of each flank. When Frederick and Field finished the clay casting, Kidder and Morris Foote went to Quincy to inspect and approve the work.[25]

The committee grossly overestimated the monument's total cost and the attendant ceremonies and memorial publications to accompany the dedication. It erroneously concluded that the association needed to raise a considerable amount of money beyond the $1,500 allotment from the state. As a result, it sent out 2,000 letters over James Cronkite's signature to the "friends of the 121st N.Y. Vols., and to the patriotic people of Otsego and Herkimer Counties," with a plea for a total of $7,000—equivalent to $154,000 in twenty-first-century dollars! It had in hand $2,500, including the state appropriation. The committee suggested that Herkimer County raise $2,000 and Otsego County the remaining $2,500. The committee wanted money in its budget to provide transportation for those who could not afford to travel to the dedication of the monument in July 1888, "if it can be erected in that time." It also wanted to cover the costs of a report, a sketch of the regiment, a photograph of the monument, photos at the dedication, a list of contributors, and a souvenir medallion for each contributor of at least a dollar. Cronkite expected to "make the dedication an event in the history of your counties, one worthy of you, and of the Regiment which you sent forth." Cronkite wrote prophetically that the battlefield would be covered with "such a collection of monuments, as the world has never seen together. We do not expect to erect another memorial to our regiment," he told his supporters. Destined to "stand forever," the 121st's monument, Cronkite guaranteed, would be one of "which your descendants will not be ashamed."[26]

The local newspapers picked up the plea and ran occasional columns through the spring and summer of 1888 and eventually into the next year, tracking the donors and the size of their gifts. Over the next twelve months, donations of all sizes trickled in from friends and survivors. They ranged from $1 to $25, as received from a former regimental nemesis, Maj. Robert P. Wilson. The donations were meaningful to the rank and file. A dollar in 1888 equaled approximately $22 in modern money; Wilson's $25 equated to $550 in current dollars. A letter accompanying Wilson's gift recalled his "fond" connection with the regiment, a sentiment not shared by his colleagues twenty years earlier. Wilson expressed his appreciation at being asked to contribute to the monument fund and pledged his appearance at the dedication if circumstances permitted. A Cooperstown resident, I. K. Williams, sent in $5 with a note saying that he had tried to enlist in 1862; though recruiters had turned him down because of his age, he wanted to remember the heroism of the old 121st.[27]

With donations trickling into headquarters, the Regimental Association sent out another letter in late summer or early fall of 1888, explaining that the monument committee could not meet its deadline because works destined for Gettysburg to a large extent and for other battlefields to a lesser extent had swamped the sculpture and granite companies; they were reported to "have had more orders than they could fill this year." So instead of holding the 1888 reunion in Gettysburg, the association moved the meeting to Worcester and picked the date of October 19. A combination of issues caused the delay in the monument's completion, but it likely was due in large measure to the need to obtain bureaucratic sign-offs at every level together with the inability of the committee to decide what it wanted. More significantly, the committee found itself unable to gauge the final plan's ultimate costs and how much money it really needed to complete the project. With his carriage-manufacturing concern in Laurens, John Kidder was the only member of the committee with a business sense. Charitably, one could also point out that none of the committee members had ever commissioned a work of art, especially a monument they were convinced would stand in perpetuity. Meanwhile, the pledges continued to come in slowly, giving the committee members no confidence that they would have the necessary funds to successfully erect the memorial.

In the spring of 1889, the monument company notified the committee that it could inspect the finished clay maquettes of Upton and Lowe. Kidder and Capt. Morris Foote traveled to Quincy and "pronounced them perfect and satisfactory." Frederick and Field finally shipped the monument to Gettysburg, where they erected it on August 22, 1889, a year after the originally planned date and two months after Cronkite's revised estimate. A few weeks later, Cronkite and Beckwith traveled to the site for the final inspection. There, they concluded that "no more fitting and appropriate monument stands upon that field." They raved about its proportions, its workmanship, and the quality of the materials. They proclaimed the work done on Upton's medallion "as a likeness and in workmanship . . . equal to [General Gouverneur K.] Warren's statue." By then, more than 300 monuments had been erected—all Union. Kidder and Beckwith traveled to Gettysburg in September one more time to ensure that the small details were attended to and the small imperfections were corrected. They pronounced the final product "fitting and appropriate." They never needed the $7,000 they had attempted to raise. In the end, the regiment raised $3,000, which was enough to accomplish nearly all of its goals.[28]

Immediately, the committee members pressed to dedicate the monument on October 10. They planned to include the 5th Maine in the ceremony, but accommodations at the McClellan House and City Hotel in Gettysburg could not be arranged. In another letter over the signatures of Cronkite, Beckwith, Lovejoy, and Kidder, dated September 25, 1889, the committee invited everyone, "comrades and friends" alike, to the festivities. The letter included a program for the day. Elaborate train schedules were established at discount rates from all points of New York and the surrounding areas. The plan called for everyone to assemble on the evening of October 9 for the association's annual reunion. The monument's dedication would be held the next morning at 10:00. Lovejoy followed up with an invitation to the 2nd Connecticut Heavy Artillery. Most survivors were eager to be on hand for the unveiling. Andrew Cowan, Horatio Wright, and Henry Slocum all courteously sent their regrets while taking the opportunity to congratulate the regiment and rekindle fond remembrances of brothers in arms. David Bailey of Roseboom had toiled as a shoemaker and farmer when he enlisted in Douglas Campbell's Company E. Wounded at Salem Church, he survived the war to return home and resume his life and his trade. In October, he received a subpoena to testify before a grand jury the week before the monument's dedication. When he showed up in Cooperstown for his appearance, he petitioned the district attorney to be released so he could attend the dedication. The judge freed him with the words "Go to Gettysburg." He went home "a happy man" and then on to Gettysburg.[29]

The event proved successful and went off as planned, providing the planners a memorable day beyond their fondest hopes. More than 100 members of the regiment and their families attended, many of them having traveled overnight to arrive in Gettysburg early in the morning of October 9. Cronkite brought

121st Regimental Association at the October 9, 1889, dedication of the Gettysburg Monument to the regiment. At left midground is Dewitt Clinton Beckwith standing next to John Kidder. Beckwith holds a top hat, cane, and cigar; Kidder holds a bowler and walking stick. The photograph may have been taken by W. H. Tipton, who took four pictures of the 121st dated October 10, 1889. They were entitled "hats on," "hats off" (perhaps this one), "Survivors Group," and "G.A.R. Band." All four came in two sizes: large and extra large. Tipton's catalogue numbers for the 121st were 784, 785, 786, and 794 respectively. Author's collection.

Lithograph of the 121st Gettysburg Monument, produced by the Frederick Field Quarry in Quincy, Massachusetts, which won the bid to execute the monument over five other designs. The print was presented by the 121st to the Fifth Maine Regimental Association as a token of their regard. Author's collection.

his sons, as did Elias Mather. Kidder's wife and son accompanied him. Thirteen others brought their wives; the rest came as they had in 1863—with each other. Before and after the dedication ceremony, most of them toured the battlefield, visiting all the major historical spots. Even the weather cooperated, providing a colorful autumn day, crisp and cool. The day before, the 66th New York had dedicated its monument, and a few members of their regiment remained to join in with the 121st. After music by the Gettysburg Band and a prayer, Maria Upton Hanford, Emory Upton's sister, unveiled the statue. Another musical selection preceded the Honorable Albert M. Mills of Little Falls, a captain in the 8th New York Cavalry during the war, who delivered the dedication speech. As part of a larger program that included an invocation, an extended poem, and a short recitation of the regiment's history by James Cronkite, Mills kept his address shorter than the nineteenth-century standard would have dictated. Cronkite concluded his remarks with a reference to all the men of the 121st who proved worthy of Otsego and Herkimer counties. They honored "their revolutionary sires," he said, "who like Herkimer, the old hero of Oriskany, fought on even though wounded unto death."[30]

Mills spoke directly and with conviction. He reminded his audience that they were on a great battlefield of the war, not to do battle but "as pilgrims to commemorate deeds and do reverence upon an enchanted field." He saw the struggle waged twenty-five years earlier not as one "to throw off a tyranny or to secure a larger scope of human action" but as a fight to strike down those who would perpetuate slavery. He did not emphasize the Constitution or the Union but the evils of the Southern aristocracy and the godless bondage of one race by another. He viewed the war as the triumph of the Puritan ideals of old New England "over the hordes of Rebellion, the flower and chivalry of the South." Against all odds, he said, the Army of the Potomac had confronted a Copperhead rear action, an inept War Department, Great Britain, a well-trained and well-led Confederate army, the press, and several incompetent leaders to survive and win. He praised the youthful Emory Upton, whom he called the "Model Colonel of the Army." And he pointed out that the boys from Herkimer and Otsego were a far cry from the material available to the government at war's end—"the sordid and unwilling ones of society."

His themes echoed those of the reunion movement. He abhorred the rush to greed, "the false doctrine that license is liberty" and its obverse—communism, where "property is robbery" and "law is oppression," a treacherous conceit "transplanted from the seditious hotbeds of the Old World." With the recent events of the Chicago Haymarket labor riots of 1886 in mind, Mills warned against anarchy, which, insidiously disguised in the "false colors of human rights, comes among us and seeks to be entertained at the hearths and in the homes of our people." He called on the generation that saved the nation to sound the clarion call to action once more. Anarchists and communists were besieging lady liberty; both were far more sinister and amorphous enemies than the Confederate gray backs of a quarter century before. When the ceremonies were concluded and the speeches finished, the veterans clustered around their new monument for large group photographs. The attendees left the next day, most traveling home on the rails that had carried them together to Gettysburg. The weather continued in their favor, and the autumn colors were at their peak. The organizers had managed the occasion to the complete pleasure of the guests.

Although friends and family had pledged enough money, the pledges were slow in being paid. As a result, it took nearly seven years for the Regimental Association to print a report on the day's activities. In October 1895, Cronkite reported that the material was delivered to the printers. A year later, at the end of 1896, a handsome souvenir booklet of some sixty pages finally came off the press: 700 copies in paperback and 300 in hardback. The office of the *Otsego Republican* did the printing for the regiment and turned all 1,000 copies over to John Lovejoy for distribution to those who had donated to the monument fund. The booklet contained a complete history of the monument's origins, the pertinent legislation, and a complete list of donors to the project. It included portraits of Franchot and Upton; Olcott was conspicuous by his absence. Photographs of the monument, front and back, were also incorporated. A photograph of the assembled group of survivors, opposite page 32, preserved for all time their attendance at the monument's dedication. In all, 727 donors contributed to the fund: 162 gifts came from members of the regiment, and 565

Cabinet photograph of the 121st Monument at Gettysburg by Gettysburg photographer W. H. Tipton. Listed in Tipton's 1891 catalogue as number 1146, this view came in cabinet and stereo size. Author's collection.

came from residents and friends of the 121st. Eventually, the regiment raised more money than it needed, so in 1899, John Kidder turned $272.61 over to Herman Johnson, who held it for nine years. When Johnson released it to his successor in 1908, having earned 4 percent interest, it returned $371.62 to the association's treasury. By 1912, the pot had grown to $452.86.[31]

Although the 121st's actions at Salem Church, Rappahannock Station, Spotsylvania, Cedar Creek, and Sailor's Creek are well documented, the regiment placed the one testimonial to its federal service at Gettysburg because, as one veteran put it, "we were there." The fact that the governor appointed the notorious Dan Sickles as the chairman of the New York Monuments Commission, with Henry Slocum as a member, placed pressure on every New York unit that even "thought about being" at Gettysburg to participate in the "monumentation" of the battlefield. The survivors of the 121st recognized that the nation chose Gettysburg "as the grand mausoleum of our patriot dead." General Sickles imposed himself on the process in an effort to ensure that his decision to move his command into harm's way during the battle would be favorably remembered.

Forever, the 121st would be remembered not because it fought at Gettysburg but because it comprised a part of Sedgwick's Sixth Corps, which arrived late on the second day of battle, July 2, 1863. The next day, the regiment would watch the entire, magnificent charge by Pickett, Pettigrew, and Trimble and the 15,000 Confederates in their ill-fated attempt to break the Union line at its center on Cemetery Ridge. No one from the 121st fought in the battle, and (depending on which account one reads) no one was seriously or even slightly wounded. With its new monument, the regiment burnished its memory to perfection.

Reunions: Camp Meetings and Social Clubs

Upton's image grew stronger with his death, and his memory shined brighter as the regiment's regard for him bordered on the idolatrous. Dennis Dewey was one who enhanced Upton's memory at every occasion. In 1909, he remarked during a meeting: "How we loved Upton. He came to us, a boy of 22 years. We thought him to be severe at first but soon learned to love him. We bow the head and drop a tear to Upton's memory." During the early years of the new century, a few members attempted to mobilize an effort to place a statue of Upton in Washington. Erastus Hawks, who had been a corporal in Company F, floated the idea of approaching Congress for an appropriation. The Regimental Association appointed a committee of three to work with Hawks to determine the idea's viability as it unanimously passed a resolution calling on Congress to fund the project. A year later, friends in Washington advised Hawks that "it would be impossible to get action in the matter" during the next session. Hawks vowed to continue the fight, but it faded from the agenda as quickly as it arose.[32]

By the mid-1890s, the Regimental Association had become highly organized. Secretary Lovejoy relished his position as keeper of the lists, and he consistently produced a printed roster of survivors and proceedings—550 copies for $16.50 in 1898. He noted deaths and kept a tight control over the addresses of comrades strung out across the country. Commemorative ribbons were produced for all participants; one year, the association produced a celluloid button with Emory Upton's picture in the center and two ribbons below it. On more than one occasion, the poet laureate of the regiment, John Tyler, read his latest work. The dates of the meetings became more regular: usually they were held in mid- to late August and with the 152nd New York. The association negotiated reduced fares on most of the rail lines to the rotating meeting sites. By 1895, villages were competing for the honor of hosting the heroes of 1861–1865. The routine became predictable: a parade with all the patriotic buntings and flags, speeches, drills, fireworks, one or two large meals provided by the ladies of the village, and a campfire at the end of the day to reminisce. Typically, 100 to 150 people attended. The Regimental Association changed the routine in July 1893, holding its seventeenth annual gathering at Gettysburg on the occasion of the dedication of the New York State monument on the battlefield—the thirtieth anniversary of the battle.

That year also marked the first time a member of the 121st visited and decorated the grave of Emory Upton in Auburn, New York, on Memorial Day—a commemoration that would go on as long as a comrade could travel. The following year, Secretary Lovejoy led a delegation of five members of the 121st to Upton's gravesite at the Fort Hill Cemetery in Auburn. Invariably thereafter, Philip Woodcock would travel to the cemetery every Memorial Day to place a wreath on the grave, and invariably, Upton's sister Sara or his mother-in-law, Cornelia W. Martin, would send a note of thanks to the association.[33]

The grand reunion occurred on June 30, 1897, in Cooperstown. The imposing celebration included the 144th New York from Delaware County along with the 152nd. Residents decorated in patriotic colors, and more than 500 veterans from many different regiments gathered from all over the country. Organizers wanted to hold the reunion on the Fourth of July, but they were able to secure better railroad rates on June 30. To commemorate the occasion, the *Republican* ran a special edition with brief biographies of the principals, accompanied by photographs. Davidson, Cronkite, James Clark, Alonzo Ferguson, John Kidder, James Lovejoy, and John Tyler were featured. Tyler, building his reputation as the 121st's poet laureate, provided yet another poem. The paper reported that "it was a glorious gathering of the Flag's defenders, and comrades touched elbows with one another and fought again the old campaigns, and lived in memory 'on the old camp ground.'" The paper estimated the crowd at more than 4,000 people; 800 veterans and family members were served at two dinner settings. "There were a good many one-armed and one-legged veterans at the Reunion," the *Republican* cheerily reported.

Several veterans sent their regrets. Recovering from pneumonia, Emory Upton's sister, Sara Edwards, enclosed $5 with her letter of regret. Her husband had recently succumbed to the same illness. H. L. Remmel, brother of Caleb and William, contributed a "mite" in memory of his two brothers who had served in the 121st. Delavan Bates, Isaac Best, Allen Lovejoy, General Wright, and Mrs. Cornelia Martin were all invited but sent their regrets. The association noted the recent deaths of comrades. In an ironic commentary on his service and reputation with the regiment, the association discovered that Stephen Valentine, assistant surgeon of the 121st, had died thirty-two years earlier, on April 15, 1865, the day of Lincoln's death, but he "had never been recorded by the association as dead."[34]

The next year, 1898, the nation once again found itself in full battle gear as the Spanish-American War occupied the public's attention. The reunion that year marked the initial recognition by the 121st Regimental Association that white America had truly reunited. The keynote speaker, the pastor of the Congregational Church in West Winfield, proclaimed that, once and for all, "the division line of North and South has been blotted out." In his opinion, the Spanish-American War symbolized the final act in the reconciliation drama. He cited a recent instance in Baltimore where the 10th Massachusetts was pelted with roses instead of rocks as in 1861. "The grey has donned the blue," he exclaimed. "And the flag that once was good enough for only the North is now good enough for every one of our forty-five states." He expressed sorrow that the Union commanders who fought so hard to see this day were now in their graves. "Blessed be this hour if for no other thing," he reasoned. "It has quickened the heart throbs of all alike, and rallied the whole nation around the stars and stripes." When the Spanish-American War was over, veterans of that conflict remained in awe of the boys of 1861 and referred to their own service in Cuba and the Philippines as insignificant compared to that of the Union veterans.[35]

With the dawn of the new century, the list of survivors in the association's annual published roster grew smaller as the list of the deceased grew larger. Participants at each meeting recognized that their numbers were dwindling and that it would not be long until the regiment, the association, and the survivors would be no more. The *Reunion Report* booklets published after every meeting and sent out to all the participants carried lists of surviving and deceased officers and enlisted men "since the War." Every report shaped the collective memory. Upton's name appeared in each report; Olcott escaped mention except under "Officers Deceased," and even then, in the ultimate indignation, the association misspelled his name as Alcott. The association listed the regimental surgeons as well, but always omitted Stephen Valentine.

Recognizing the inevitable, Secretary Cyrus J. Westcott issued a special plea to members to attend the thirty-first annual reunion in 1907, "as we are fast marching down the sunny slope, and not many more times may we look into each other's faces and feel the warm clasp of the hand." With unintended black humor, the association reported in 1904 that comrade Alonzo McNeal decorated the grave of Frank Lowe, who had passed away the year before, and that McNeal intended to do so as long as he lived; in parentheses, the committee noted, "Comrade McNeal has since died." John Lovejoy died in 1900. His replacement, a vigorous Wallace Young, made a concerted effort to track down every former member of the 121st. He wrote to every old soldiers' home and postmasters throughout the country to ensure his lists were current. The association established a resolution committee to acknowledge each comrade's passing and made Philip Woodcock "a permanent committee" of one to place flowers on Upton's grave every Memorial Day.[36]

In the new century, the reunion became a heady mixture of political theater, social club, and old-fashioned religious revival camp meeting. Nearly every talk, speech, reminiscence, and tall tale contained elements of all three genres. The reunions were a means of catharsis for some and an opportunity to spin yarns for others. Dennis Dewey typified the latter. When he was not polishing Upton's memory, he used the stage of the reunions to tell outrageous tales of valor and honor that never happened. He told his stories as gospel, not with tongue in cheek. Dewey had joined the regiment as a sergeant in Company B, from Plainfield. He attained his highest rank of second lieutenant on October 29, 1864, but he was never mustered. The reunion's official rosters consistently listed him as a captain. After the war, he became lost in the bureaucratic maze. He had taken the examination to lead a colored regiment and was eventually accepted. He was to report to the 108th USCT in Tennessee, but could not do so because he was captured and thrown into a Confederate prison. Severely wounded in the Wilderness, Dewey lost his right leg to a Confederate surgeon who probably saved his life. In later years, his description of his last waking moments were worthy of a B movie script for the new motion picture industry. He stated boldly that his "last remembrance of that day was seeing Sergeant W. W. Young as he was blazing away at a terrific speed at the enemy." Dewey claimed that he had been incarcerated in Libby Prison, which normally held only officers. According to his story, the rebels released him three weeks after capturing him, a single amputee ready for duty in the midst of Grant's Overland campaign. He again applied for a commission, and this time, he received it and was mustered as such. Then, for some unknown reason, he promptly resigned. New York State's adjutant general listed him as incarcerated for more than a year and not exchanged until after the war, on April 25, 1865. He was not mustered out with the rest of the regiment at Hall's Hill; he had been released three weeks earlier at Annapolis, on June 12, 1865.

At the 1909 reunion, he told his audience that Henry Galpin's friendly face was the first he encountered when he rejoined the regiment *three weeks* (or *four days* in another version) after serving time in Libby. Because he spoke in the Henry Galpin GAR Post in Little Falls, he told a heartwarming fabrication. He said he had returned as a "sorry looking soldier, wan, emaciated and on rude crutches." He remembered that Galpin gave him a "soldier's welcome back to the land of freedom and plenty." Embellishing further, he claimed that Galpin lent him $10 and told him that when "his ship came in," he could reimburse him. He concluded with ringing appreciation: "There was no better soldier, no grander gentleman, no truer friend than Captain Henry M. Galpin." Three years later, Dewey presented a print of the 121st's Gettysburg Monument to the Galpin Post.[37]

Lester Murdock, another teller of tall tales, claimed that he had been wounded in nearly every battle in which the 121st participated. He boasted that he fired a full complement of forty to sixty rounds of ammunition in many engagements. He said he escaped death at Salem Church and narrowly escaped at Gettysburg when a falling tree nearly killed him. He asserted that rebels captured him at the Wilderness and that in his effort to escape, he took a round in the neck; he supposedly jumped into a hospital wagon but, when the ride proved too jolting, got out and walked back to his regiment. At Spotsylvania, he took credit for killing the rebel who had shot John Kidder in the face. In the Shenandoah Valley, he claimed, two rounds hit him, breaking two ribs; his coffee cup was the only casualty at Cedar Creek. He also said he got an "ugly contusion" on his left leg at Fort Fisher from a spent ball. When asked if he had ever hit anyone with his many shots, he declared that he "killed as many of them as they did of him." He harbored no ill will toward the Confederates. He "knew" that he had fired "a thousand cartridges, marched a thousand miles, and ate as many pounds of hard-tack." He never lost his enthusiasm for the war "as a private of no mean rank." Dewey and Murdock proved to be charming and harmless entertainment for their aging audiences.[38]

Sgt. Wallace W. Young, Dewey's trigger-happy companion, spent nearly a year at Andersonville after his capture at the Wilderness. Contrary to Dewey, he riveted his audience with true and cathartic tales of the suffering at Andersonville that required no embellishment and were amply corroborated. He survived not only Andersonville but also the prison at Florence, South Carolina, where the Confederates moved him with others as Sherman pushed through Georgia. His listeners intently attended to his stories of losing everything but his dignity. After being released, he walked until he caught a ride on a railcar to the Union lines. His clothes hung in tatters from his emaciated body. A comrade threw a Confederate overcoat over him, which he immediately abandoned when he reached friendly lines. He was ashamed, he told his audience, to be seen in the garments of the enemy. He closed with a toast from the prisoners at Andersonville:

Here is to Jeff Davis, old Jeff and the whole darn southern confederacy. May they be set afloat in an open boat, without compass or rudder! May the boat be swallowed by a shark, may the shark be swallowed by a whale, the whale in the devil's belly, the door locked and the key lost, and there may Judas Iscariot hammer Jeff Davis's toes until he whistles the Red, White and Blue and the Star Spangled Banner.[39]

Initially, the veterans met in hotels and village assembly halls. But as the groups grew smaller each year, GAR halls would accommodate them. Local women of the Women's Relief Corps lavished feasts on their heroes of 1861. Sixteen GAR posts opened in Otsego County, ten in Herkimer County. Most of them were incorporated in the 1870s but folded in the 1920s and 1930s. Six of the Otsego posts boasted the names of veterans of the 121st; Herkimer County included four. Herkimer's were named after Henry Galpin, Nelson Wendell, Jonathon Burrell, and Sam Button, who was killed at Spotsylvania Court House. In Otsego County, posts were named after Oneonta native Edwin Farmer, who was killed at Salem Church, as well as John Morton, Egbert Olcott, Emory Upton, Horatio Duroe, and the Hall brothers of Laurens. Two others were named for George Kidder, John's brother in the 152nd New York who was killed at the Wilderness, and Maj. Levi C. Turner. Veterans founded the Turner GAR Post in 1878, and it closed in 1931 with two surviving members. Original members were Davidson, Reuben Bates, Henry Wood, Henry Walker, and nine others.[40]

Not every member of the Regimental Association joined the GAR. Veterans found closer fellowship in the association than in the other veterans' organizations available to them. As the GAR grew in numbers throughout the last quarter of the nineteenth century, its political power became paramount. The Regimental Association never became a political influence except in minor situations on a local level. Regional or national luminaries from the GAR often addressed the association. At the 1912 meeting in Little Falls, the speaker, the department commander of the New York State GAR, Maj. Oscar Smith, scolded the men of the association who were not members of the GAR. Smith recounted that the GAR was responsible for "all pension laws passed." He reminded his audience that it took "weeks and months" of hard work by many veterans to ensure the "last splendid increase" that came about with the "passage of a good bill." The GAR and no one else, "every year since 1868," ensured the enactment of "good laws . . . in the interest of the veteran."[41]

The association remained current with the GAR's goals of seeking pensions for all veterans, ensuring that "proper" history was taught in public schools, and promoting a reverence for the Union. The association and the GAR were similar in many respects: their fraternal leanings, their lack of realistic memories of the confusion and horrors of war, their nostalgic and unrealistic recollections of camp life, their yearly observance of Decoration Day, and more generally their static remembrance of the three or four years of war. Securing an ever escalating financial reward for its members through the government's pension system became one of the GAR's greatest achievements. But the GAR and, for that matter, the 121st Regimental Association never embraced Emory Upton's proposed reforms of the army. Although the 121st revered its former commander, it never weighed in on his reforms and theories as an organization. It remained an insular, reflective institution, relying on reliving the past in nostalgic reveries rather than exercising its political muscle to change the U.S. military. The Grand Army saved the Union and lobbied most effectively for its veterans. The Regimental Association never became a political entity. As far as its members were concerned, the war had ended and the time had come for the volunteer soldier to return to a citizen's life and enjoy the fruits of his labor.[42]

With each passing year, fading memories became enhanced. Erastus L. Hawks pointed out, "As the numbers grow less, with me, the tie that binds us seems stronger and the glorious record of the 121st and the men that composed the regiment grows bright." By 1910, the veterans drove to meetings in automobiles. Little Falls had become a fashionable meeting place for the association since the welcoming home party in 1865. Meetings were held there in 1879, when Slocum and Upton attended, and in 1885, 1894, 1909, and 1912. The last two were held in the Henry Galpin Post. Two years in a row, in 1910 and 1911, the group met at Schuyler Lake, which had no GAR post; however, the women and men of the village entertained them royally, feeding seventy members of the 121st and twenty-three of the 52nd.

The reunions ran well into the 1920s. By then, the vast majority of the members were gone. Their descendants came in their place. Wives, sons, daughters, grandchildren, and widows of those killed in action all made efforts to attend. They bought copies of the regimental history and listened to the heroic stories—now some sixty years old. The association passed on the "past imperfect" to the next generation, to be preserved and, in turn, passed on again. The last documented meeting occurred in 1924. Only nine survivors attended. They all expressed the hope that an adequate number of comrades would be left on earth by 1926 when the fiftieth annual reunion would be held. There is no evidence that that hope was fulfilled or that such a meeting ever occurred.[43]

16

Shaping the Memory: Writing the History

The remembrance of my companions that have fallen brings much sadness and a longing wish that they were with us again. But they were noble and nobly fell in a worthy cause, and I love their memory.

Henry Walker, Company G, August 10, 1863

History wants simple facts and correct dates and as it is an official history, he [Lovejoy] can boom it and give it such puffs as officers glory in.

Lester Murdock, Company E, December 1895

The Regimental Association shaped the ultimate history of the 121st. Its annual reunions became the fuel for the ever-increasing glow of postwar memories. As the older members, mostly officers who had led the regiment during the war, began to die off, they were replaced by the younger men who had served in the ranks. With the older leaders gone, the "youngsters" became freer with the truths as they saw them—or, more important, as they remembered them. They were unhindered and uninhibited in their narration of tales of derring-do. The association provided the forum, for the annual campfire at the end of each meeting encouraged storytelling. The organization did enjoy two major accomplishments: the erection of the Gettysburg Monument and the almost symbolic publication of the regiment's history sixty years after the war's end.

Rappahannock Station

Immediately after the battle of Rappahannock Station, the "second battle" began. That controversy concerned the matter of who got there first with the most and who contributed to the lopsided victory over the larger, entrenched Confederate force. The argument revolved specifically around whether the day was carried by Russell's 3rd Brigade of the Sixth Corps, with the 6th Maine and the 5th Wisconsin supported by the 49th and 119th Pennsylvania, *or* by the Sixth Corps's 2nd Brigade under Emory Upton, with the 5th Maine, the 121st New York, and the 95th and 96th Pennsylvania in reserve. The confusion stemmed from the fact that the troops became purposely intermingled when Lt. John Fish took his detail of two companies from the 121st and joined in on the general assault carried out by the 6th Maine and the 5th Wisconsin. The 121st engaged in both actions—Russell's brigade attack on the left of the fort and Upton's later assault, which took the rifle pits. No one man saw the entire battle. The ensuing arguments in later years were more an indication of the limited knowledge each possessed rather than an accurate account.

A few newspapers carried the story immediately after the battle, but others ignored it as a minor engagement not worth reporting. The Richmond papers were vocal about a Southern loss. Northern newspaper accounts on the Army of the Potomac since Gettysburg were sparse. Meade needed a victory of any sort to regain the upper hand on the rebels and rescue his own military reputation. The news reports that did appear were not well received by the officers and enlisted men of Upton's command. "I am sorry to see that the leading papers do not give the 121st and the 5th [Maine] credit for what was done on the terrible night . . . as they did all of the fighting," John Hartwell wrote his wife. "This is not fair; let those have the honor to whom the honor is due." The 5th Maine and the 121st did not, in fact, do all of the fighting. It just seemed that way.[1]

Within days, John Fish, Cleaveland Campbell, and Emory Upton wrote letters to various newspapers to ensure they told the "true" story of the battle of Rappahannock Station. The lead headline of the November 10, 1863, issue of the *New York Tribune* trumpeted the GREAT BRAVERY OF THE 5TH WISCONSIN AND THE 6TH MAINE. Fish wrote to his brother five days after the encounter. He reacted to the lukewarm reports that placed the 121st "in the fight to some extent." Indeed, Fish told his brother, the men of the 121st were involved "to as great an extent as anybody—and if we don't get the honor of it from some of the papers, we get it here." Emotionally, Fish was flying high. He had performed well in front of his commander, Upton, and more important still, he had survived the battle to enjoy his newly enhanced reputation. Although he was concerned with the glory owed his regiment, he yearned for proper recognition of his own role in the fight as well.

Campbell wrote directly to the *New York Tribune* to set the historical record straight. He chastised the press for its inaccuracies in reporting the "gallant achievements" of the soldiers in the field. He took reporters to task, urging them to "be exact, just and reliable." With an eye to the future, Campbell reminded the editor of the *Tribune* that the historian would "be dependent to great extent upon them for his materials but the men who are making the history look to the press for such a record of their hard earned victories." He complained of the inaccuracies in reporting on what he and his comrades considered one of the signal victories of the war. When Fish discovered that Campbell had composed a letter nearly simultaneously, he immediately forwarded it with his letter to his brother with the hope that he would place both in the *Tribune*. Fish had known nothing of Campbell's independent account until Campbell brought the letter to his tent. Fish implored his brother to get this "true and unexaggerated account" into a daily or weekly issue to "correct many false statements which have made their way into public papers." He also asked him to send copies of the papers once the stories ran. He too complained about the situation with the press: "The great trouble with the newspapers is that they never contain a correct account of any march, skirmish or battle, and one would think to read some articles, that they were written by a crazy man."[2]

Upton assumed that his sister read the various news accounts and learned of his brigade's "astounding success." But he told her that even though there were "many accounts of the battle extant," he would give her "the true version, believing it will interest you all."[3]

The different stories told by the letters home immediately after the battle paled in comparison to the fight that played itself out in the *National Tribune* years later. The *Tribune* started out as a humble veterans' newspaper in 1877. For the next fifty years, it functioned as a lobby for veterans' pensions and benefits and a forum in which veterans could relive the days of 1861–1865. Between 1884 and 1922—a span of thirty-eight years—twenty-four letters and articles entitled "Rappahannock Station" appeared in its pages. In the first two years, 121st veterans John Lovejoy, Joe Round, and Delavan Bates weighed in with their opinions and insights to "correct" the record. Most of the veterans were concerned about the "official historical record," whatever form it took. As Lovejoy pointed out, "I never yet have read an account of that fight in which I thought justice was done to the troops" who made the charge. Capt. A. Boyd Hutchinson, commanding Company C of the 49th Pennsylvania, gave no ground to Upton, who, in his opinion, had arrived too late. He stated that Upton's troops "arrived on our right, it was quite dark and the firing had practically ceased." Bates, for his part, correctly stated that two charges were made, and he proposed that everyone should share the credit.

Bates recognized the *Tribune* as a national repository of Civil War combat history and as a national forum for veterans to provide their views. In a measured statement, he wrote: "If the *National Tribune* is making history—and I believe its columns will be carefully searched by future historians—every comrade should give his views when he knows that others are at fault." Lovejoy responded to Bates's call for comments with a copy of Upton's action report on the battle. J. B. Round, a sergeant in Company B at the time of the battle and now living in Winfield, Kansas, also rebutted Hutchinson at year's end in 1885, and remarkably, he did so again ten years later. In 1895, still contentious but now with ammunition from professional historians, Round revealed that he had read John S. C. Abbott's history of the war published in 1866 and others and did not find mention of the 121st. He felt that he and others from the regiment were duty-bound to set the record straight. Another veteran admitted what others knew—Rappahannock Station was not another Antietam or Gettysburg—but he pointed out that "it was *our* Antietam and Gettysburg." Yet another, now commenting in the twentieth century, urged that someone from the old Sixth Corps should write up the story of Rappahannock Station or, better yet, "some wearer of the old Greek Cross [should] have this action put on canvas. It is worthy of a battle scene." Over the fifty-year period, nearly every unit that participated in the battle weighed in with its particular story or "correction." Each letter drew a response until the veterans died away and the so-called second battle of Rappahannock Station ended in 1922. Upton and Russell were both gone when that second fight broke out, but their names were widely used. The exchanges were lively, never bitter or unfriendly.[4]

Local papers also got into the act. The *Ellsworth (Me.) American* ran a long story on the "forgotten" battle of Rappahannock Station in the fall of 1883; the story had first appeared in the *Milwaukee Sunday Telegraph* and was written by James S. Anderson of Company A, the 5th Wisconsin. A. S. Daggett, a major in the 5th Maine, wrote "Carried by Assault: Work of the Gallant Upton," in the *Otsego Republican* edition of August 12, 1891. Delavan Bates devoted an article on the battle in his contributions to the *Republican,* which Davidson obligingly published on June 27, 1894. And Robert Westbrook, the official historian of the 49th Pennsylvania, essentially toed the party line established by Hutchinson when he summed things up in the regimental history in 1898: "The Fifth Maine and the 121st New York regiments came in from the right and helped gather up the prisoners and they get just as much credit from our Generals as our Brigade does. They deserve some credit, but Russell's brigade did the work, and credit is due us." In the *National Tribune,* Westbrook denied credit to the 5th Maine and the 121st. With faint praise, he wrote that they "assisted us some on the right, and some credit is due them . . . but Russell's brigade stood the brunt of the battle."[5]

Delavan Bates fired his salvos in the *Otsego Republican.* He believed the 121st had never received proper recognition for its role at Rappahannock Station. He cited its "hard fighting" and "deeds of valor that never were recognized as they should have been." He argued that Upton should have received a brevet for Salem Church and a brigadier's star for Rappahannock Station. Bates wrote that he and his comrades of the 121st should have received more credit for their accomplishments. Being placed on Frederick Phisterer's list of 300 fighting regiments in his five-volume history of New York during the war did not convey the regiment's glorious record.[6]

But of all the later accounts, that provided by the 5th Maine's A. S. Daggett stands out as exemplary. Written dispassionately, it most closely mirrors the immediate accounts written by Upton, Campbell, and Fish while the heat of battle was still on them. Daggett maintained that those outside the army and military historians misunderstood or ignored the battle. He mentioned the obvious points—the large number of men overwhelmed by an undersized force; the embarrassment for Lee and his officers; and the fact that on the first try, the attacking troops overran an entrenched position. Daggett's observations informed his precise narration of the confusing and minute movements and details, such as Fish's role in leading a detachment from the 121st and Upton's role in taking the rifle pits. His account, however, did not find its way into the *National Tribune* or the official history of the 5th Maine.

Anderson's article first appeared in regional papers in Milwaukee and in Ellsworth, Maine, in 1883. The *Tribune* reprinted the article with minor changes in 1922, making it one of the last accounts on Rappahannock Station. At the end of the nineteenth century and the beginning of the twentieth, Anderson corresponded with survivors of the battle to obtain their recollections and observations of the fight. Horatio Wright and Andrew Cowan (of Cowan's 1st New York Artillery) responded to him, making corrections and additions to the historical record.[7]

Sailor's Creek

The struggle for the "true" story reached its pinnacle with the retelling of the battle of Sailor's Creek—a controversy that also began immediately after the battle. No one questioned who won the battle. The argument revolved around the burning question of who had captured Gen. George Washington Custis Lee. Simultaneously, the 121st and the 37th Massachusetts claimed the prize. The earliest recorded recognition came on the day of the battle, April 6, 1865, when Lt. Philip Woodcock, Company E, recorded the following in his diary: "We captured two stands of colors" and a number of prisoners from General Ewell's staff, "and General Custis Lee surrendered to us." *Us* went undefined. Did he mean the 121st specifically, the 1st Division, the Sixth Corps, or the Union army in general? Immediately after the fighting, the parties involved in the battle of Sailor's Creek filed their reports, which ended up in the *Official Records of the War of the Rebellion*, published in the 1880s.[8]

On April 7, Capt. Archibald Hopkins, commanding the 37th Massachusetts, claimed that his regiment had captured 360 officers and men and that Pvt. David D. White of Company E from Cheshire, Massachusetts, had received Custis Lee's sword in surrender. The 37th demanded that credit be given to their own

Private White. The regiment actually included three Whites, one of whom was an officer and a second who had been wounded at Opequon Creek the previous September. In his long report of recommendations for meritorious service, General Wheaton mentioned only five enlisted men from the 37th; White's name did not appear in the report. In fact, White's name appeared nowhere in the official records of the battle. As Wheaton's report went up the chain of command, subsequent reports by Hopkins's superiors did not repeat or pick up this detail. Hopkins asserted that his men captured at least one flag; he indicated they took a second as well, "although the capture of it is claimed by another command."

By April 14, Harris Smith Hawthorne of the 121st New York swore out an affidavit attesting to his capture of General Lee. He appeared before Lt. H. E. Hindmarsh, judge advocate of the 1st Division, Sixth Corps, who endorsed his statement. In it, Hawthorne recounted his story. He testified that he never lost sight or control of Lee until he "delivered him to Colonel Olcott" and that he "was one of the men detailed" by Olcott, because of the capture, to conduct Lee to Wheaton's headquarters. Chaplain John Adams, an impeccable, credible witness, attested to Hawthorne's moral character "as a professed Christian" and opined that he was "worthy of confidence, by the uniform consistency of his religious life." He concluded his statement with the assertion that Hawthorne's word was "unimpeachable." Egbert Olcott attached Adams's sworn statement to his official report and affirmed Hindmarsh's endorsement. Additionally, Adams sent off a letter to the editors of the *Otsego Republican* dated April 15, essentially saying the same thing.

Olcott recorded that during the battle, he ordered the regiment to charge the enemy troops, "who were endeavoring to get in the rear of the brigade"; when it did, the rebels retreated in great confusion, and that is when Hawthorne captured Lee. Olcott certified Hawthorne's veracity and, referring to Adams's attached affidavit, acknowledged that "some controversy about the matter" existed. He added further detail by writing that the incident occurred "near the road mentioned where Captain Howland was killed." Olcott stated that the 37th Massachusetts, "farther down the road, near the creek," was fighting desperately "to hold their ground." Gen. Joseph Hamblin, of the 65th New York commanding the 2nd Brigade at Sailor's Creek, picked up Olcott's version and, probably swayed by Adams's statement, repeated the story in his report.[9]

In his official account, Horatio Wright reported that "many general officers were captured by the combined forces of the infantry and cavalry" and that Ewell and Lee surrendered to the Sixth Corps. Wright supported the report of the 1st Division commander, Wheaton, which pointedly noted that "this division took" Ewell and Lee and "several battle flags." Wheaton's long report of April 15, 1865, recommending countless officers and enlisted men for their bravery and meritorious service in the April 2 action around Petersburg and the

April 6 battle of Sailor's Creek, specifically mentioned Hawthorne as Lee's captor. Wheaton also named several officers and enlisted men from the 37th but none in connection with Lee's capture. He did mention Pvt. Dennis Moore of Company K, 2nd Connecticut Heavy Artillery, as "assisting" Hawthorne. Of all the reports filed after the battle, David White was mentioned only in that prepared by Archibald Hopkins, his commanding officer.[10]

A week after the battle, John Lovejoy and John Ingraham wrote letters home. Ingraham specifically said, "Our regiment also captured Maj. Gen. Custis Lee, Gen. Bob Lee's son. Gen. Sheridan captured Lieut. Gen. Ewell." Lovejoy wrote his cousin Cynthia that "a man in Co. F took General Custis Lee prisoner," and to his mother he said, "Our regiment in the last fight lost 9 killed, 17 wounded. Captured 960 prisoners among them Gen. Ewell and Custis Lee and three rebel battle flags." John Kidder, now a major, wrote to his wife on April 10, 1865, stating: "We captured General [George Washington] Custis Lee and two stands of colors and over 1000 prisoners. This the 121st did." Chaplain Adams also mentioned Hawthorne's exploits to a friend, C. A. Lord, Esq., in a letter two weeks after the battle: "Our regiment captured two colors and General Custis Lee (son of General R. F. Lee) was made prisoner by Private H. S. Hawthorne, Company F." Thirty years later, Clinton Beckwith affirmed Hawthorne's standing as Lee's captor: "General Lee was captured by H. S. Hawthorne, of Company F, and turned over to Colonel Olcott."[11]

Perhaps the most damning contemporary evidence came from Brig. Gen. William H. Penrose of the 15th New Jersey Volunteers, who was commanding the 1st Brigade of the 1st Division of the Sixth Corps at Petersburg on April 2. In that fight, two pieces of artillery were captured by his men. As the troops moved forward, they left the two cannon under guard by a few men from the brigade. Shortly, two companies of the 37th Massachusetts came forward and tried to "liberate" the guns from Penrose's 15th New Jersey troops guarding them. The men of the 37th managed to distract the guards, and Penrose complained in his official report that they "drove my guard from the guns claiming them as their capture." His most significant declaration followed: "*As this has occurred once before*, I am not disposed to allow it to pass this time without notice, as *the command is entitled to the credit of the capture*" (italics added). These dismal actions may have been reenacted at Sailor's Creek, where in an enigmatic statement, the 37th commander, Hopkins, wrote in his after-action report that "there were a *few exceptions to the general good behavior of the regiment*, all of which were among the enlisted men, and it is my intention that *they be brought to trial*" (italics added).[12]

The Massachusetts adjutant general, following the common procedure used in other Northern states, issued an annual report for 1865. He recounted the last months of the 37th's history through to its discharge. Considerable coverage was afforded the last dramatic days of the war, but in a very tentative description of Custis Lee's capture, the adjutant general merely said: "Among the prisoners who fell into our hands was Major-General Custis Lee, the son of the commander-in-chief of the rebel armies."[13]

The argument.resonated well into the next century as the 37th Massachusetts continued to pursue credit for the capture. In 1884, the regiment published its official history, and it author, James L. Bowen, credited White with Lee's capture. The men of the 37th had been issued new repeating Spencer rifles, and Bowen wrote dramatically that Custis Lee surrendered his sword "at the muzzle of the Spencer rifle to David White of Company E." Further, he noted that only severe wounds prevented another member of the regiment from capturing the Savannah Guards' flag. The dispute continued into the 1890s. John Lovejoy, now secretary of the 121st's Regimental Association, once again sent Adams's original letter of April 15, 1865, to the editor of the *Otsego Republican*, asking him to reprint it. In his cover letter, Lovejoy explained his role on behalf of the survivors of the regiment and promised "proof, in regard to honors which are now subject to dispute by present writers of War History." The paper reprinted the letter on January 6, 1892.

On September 18, 1897, the *New York Sun* ran a "definitive" article claiming to prove once and for all that Custis Lee had surrendered to Hawthorne. Cooperstown's *Otsego Republican* picked up the story, reprinting it on October 27. Also in 1897, Hawthorne affirmed that Lee had capitulated to him alone at Sailor's Creek, and he referred to Wheaton's first report of the battle action. In a statement reminiscent of General Penrose's incident with the 37th and the capture of Confederate cannon, he further insisted that "*an attempt was made by others to take his prisoner from him*" but that Olcott and Lt. Thomas J. Hassett of Company K "*came to his rescue*" (italics added).[14]

He produced a letter from Lee himself that confirmed he had surrendered to a private "who told him he belonged to the Sixth Corps . . . and was taken to a place where he met an officer." He did not identify the officer, but it may have been Olcott. Joe Heath, who rose to the rank of captain, corroborated Hawthorne's story. The last bit of evidence Hawthorne offered in his defense attacked White's claim that Lee surrendered his sword to White. According to the letter held by Hawthorne, Lee affirmed that Hawthorne had asked him for his arms and that Lee supposedly replied: "I have not as much as a jackknife." Hawthorne arrested an unarmed Custis Lee.[15]

In 1896, Lovejoy, dutifully filling out the New York State questionnaire sent from historian Hugh Hastings's office, recorded that Hawthorne won the Medal of Honor for Lee's capture. In 1901, editors W. F. Beyer and O. F. Keydel published their compendium of Medal of Honor winners, entitled *Deeds of Valor*. They devoted a few paragraphs to Hawthorne's escapade and made no mention of White or the controversy surrounding Lee's capture. They praised Hawthorne, who "greatly distinguished himself in the charge by capturing,

single-handed, General Custis Lee." The editors also praised Olcott, who recognized the importance of the capture by detailing Hawthorne "as one of the
men to conduct the noted rebel general to the headquarters of General
Wheaton."

The last—but probably not the final—word came from Hawthorne's closest
eyewitness, Thomas Hassett. Writing nearly fifty years after the war's end, Hassett remembered the rebel line had wavered and begun to fall back when he noticed that "a Confederate General in command of a division appeared" in the
front of his Company K, accompanied by "one or two orderlies." Hawthorne
saw him and dashed forward in a hail of bullets and "ordered the General to
surrender." As Hassett recalled, "Single handed and alone, Hawthorne brought
his prisoner and his companions to our lines." Custis Lee was captured and held
on the Union line until the battle ended. According to Hassett, Hawthorne
turned Lee over immediately to Sheridan's headquarters.[16]

Best treated Lee's capture equivocally in his official history. He never addressed the issue in a straightforward manner. In his *History of the 121st*, Best relied on Beckwith and Cronkite to speak for him. He quoted Beckwith's account
of Hawthorne capturing the Savannah Guards' flag but not Custis Lee. In a later
narrative entitled "The Siege and Capture of Petersburg," Best credited Sheridan and his cavalry with capturing Fitzhugh Lee, not Custis Lee. The historical evidence weighs heavily in Hawthorne's favor.[17]

Writing the History

The newspaper fights replaying old battles proved to be the warm-up
for the regimental histories of the 121st and other units. After the war, regiments on both sides slowly began to tell their stories. Some produced a finished
product shortly after hostilities ended. Others published their official histories
years later; the 14th New York, for instance, issued its history in 1911 on the fiftieth anniversary of its muster into the service of the United States. The 152nd
New York, the 121st's sister organization from the two counties, managed to
roll out its official chronicle in 1888. By the time the survivors of the 121st produced their history, the world around them had changed completely. By 1921,
the country had experienced two more wars, and the newspapers were counting the dead of World War I. Stories of veterans now related to foreign wars
and foreign battlefields with unfamiliar names. Otsego County lost 73 men during the Spanish-American War and World War I, 68 in the army and 4 in the
navy. In 1862, the veterans of the 121st went to war on foot and on horseback
and in wagons, and they marched hundreds of miles across Maryland and Virginia during the conflict; now, in the 1920s, the R. J. Reynolds tobacco company
placed ads in local papers encouraging the veterans of World War I to "Walk a
Mile for a Camel" cigarette.

(left) Raw recruit Dewitt Clinton Beckwith, the regiment's bad boy, who survived the war unscathed. His story and personality became the heart of the 121st during and much after the war. From Isaac O. Best, *History of the 121st*. (above) Never an official member of the 121st but detailed to Upton's headquarters after transferring from the 16th New York, the Reverend Isaac O. Best became the regiment's official historian. He spent his life after the war as a teacher and temperance preacher. With James Smith and Dewitt Clinton Beckwith, he finally produced a history of the regiment in 1921. From Isaac O. Best, *History of the 121st*.

The need to walk anywhere became largely unnecessary with the introduction of the automobile. A Ford dealership opened in Schenevus—Sam Kelley's village. Richfield Springs, where many of the early war meetings were held, boasted a Buick dealer promoting the "New Buick Four [cylinder] thoroughbred—a pedigree car well worthy of its name." And in Oneonta, the Studebaker dealership advertised the "New Light Six" for $1,335 FOB from South Bend, Indiana. Americans now killed each other with automobiles instead of bullets and bayonets. The National Safety Council estimated that by the end of 1920, there would be 10 million automobiles in the country and that automobiles would fatally injure one person every 35 minutes. In New York State, 1,981 people were accident victims in 1921—an increase of 452 fatalities over the previous year. And Henry Ford, who learned how to make automobiles more efficiently than anyone else, became the richest man in the world, with $180 million in the bank and an annual income of $125 million before paying taxes of $15 million.[18]

At the same time, the motion picture industry was captivating the country. In 1921, Cooperstown residents could pay 17 cents for matinees and 28 cents for evening showings at Smalley's Theater and watch the double feature: *The Mark of Zorro*, starring Douglas Fairbanks, and Norma Talmadge in the provocatively titled *Yes or No?* The Wieting Opera House in Worcester featured Charlie Chaplin in *The Kid*. Warren Harding occupied the White House, and the great Enrico Caruso had just died; Babe Ruth hit fifty-nine home runs that year, and the National League president suspended Tug McGraw, the New York Giants' manager, for using "abusive language" toward an opponent. And the year before, women were given the right to vote. In Ilion and Herkimer, the Remington Company continued to manufacture guns, but since the war had ended, they were not selling nearly as many, so the company diversified into a newer technology—typewriters.

Only thirty years earlier, modern utilities had come to Herkimer County. The village of Little Falls rejoiced in the winter of 1892 when the electric lights were turned on—briefly, as it turned out. School bells, church bells, and mill whistles all proclaimed the arrival of the modern phenomenon until the belt slipped off the dynamo generating the electricity, plunging the village into darkness once again. In that same year, the village of Herkimer planned to install a modern sewer system that would eliminate diseases and the resultant deaths, which had been escalating because of unsanitary conditions. By 1893, 40 manholes, 37 flush tanks, and 15 inspection holes, as well as a pump house and engine, were ready to be installed to move Herkimer's unfiltered "filth" into the Mohawk River.[19]

In the South, Reconstruction came and went. The short-lived African American governance of Southern states had ended years earlier, and Jim Crow now prevailed. In 1922, Mrs. John A. Logan, the widow of General Logan, founder of the Grand Army of the Republic, Virginia, accused the United Confederate Daughters (UCD), who were meeting in Richmond, of rewriting history. The UCD endorsed a new history of the conflict in which Abraham Lincoln was to be held solely responsible for the Civil War. Mrs. Logan called the history a "perversion" of the facts. In the same year, the Confederate Veterans meeting in South Carolina passed a resolution "holding Abraham Lincoln personally responsible for the Civil War and denouncing him for his alleged bloodthirstiness." The *Little Falls Evening Times* denounced the state in a headline that read SHAME ON SOUTH CAROLINA. In both incidents, Northern writers deplored the Southerners' depiction of the sixteenth president. Adopting the GAR mantra, they called for some means of preventing Southerners from "teaching their untruthful doctrines to their children." Along the same line, the paper despaired that the youth of the South would "be taught that John Wilkes Booth is a martyr." The 121st produced its regimental story in this changed world.[20]

There was a good deal of interest in writing the regiment's history. Individually, several of the survivors attempted to leave a lasting chronicle of the 121st's glorious past, depending, of course, on who wrote the tale. Although Isaac Best, Clinton Beckwith, and James Smith eventually produced the regiment's history, others also tried or signaled their intentions to put on paper the historical record of the regiment or their personal experiences. The earliest public thought of producing an official history of the 121st came in newspaper announcements for the impending tenth regimental reunion, to be held at Three Mile Point on Lake Otsego in August 1886. Earlier, one of the most prominent members of the 121st—its last commander, Col. Egbert Olcott—had acknowledged his plan to write a history of the unit a month after the regiment returned home. However, his illness from war wounds and his early death precluded him from accomplishing that goal. There is no evidence that he had even begun writing or that a manuscript in any stage existed. It is also unclear if he planned a personal memoir of his own experiences or a complete regimental history.[21]

Lt. Francis W. Morse from Cherry Valley printed but did not publish his *Personal Experiences in the War of the Great Rebellion from December 1862 to July 1865* in 1866—the earliest known memoir by a member of the regiment. He made it clear that he wrote his memoir "exclusively for the private and indulgent perusal" of his family and not "for my friends." As such, his accounts were not intended for the "criticism of any other person." He admitted that others more qualified than he would write the history of the war. He also admitted to a faulty memory. He relied on a "meager diary" that he had kept for some but not all of his "adventures." He intended to show that he represented his family during the war as a "boy of only eighteen years of age, [engaged] in the great work, so dear to all, of saving the country from ruin." Whereas Dr. Daniel Holt, who left his letters and diaries for all to see after the war, comes off as bombastic in his description of events and florid in his telling of the story, Morse is dry and wry. Writing only a year after the war's end, Morse still confused facts and events such as the sequence of occurrences involved in the raid on Bartlett's headquarters and the raid to eliminate Mosby in the summer of 1863. Because of Morse's desire to keep his memoirs limited to a close circle, it is unknown if Best was aware of that early memoir and if he used it in preparing his own book; at most, we can say that would seem unlikely.[22]

The earliest published source of original materials came from the family of Lt. Adam Clarke Rice of Fairfield, Herkimer County. According to the official roster of the regiment, Rice had originally enlisted in Company C as a sergeant, but his brother indicated that he joined as a private. He barely survived the first year in the field, and his unexpected and rapid death from typhoid fever on September 19, 1863, devastated his family. To assuage their grief, they published

Rice's letters, along with many of his school papers from Fairfield Academy, in 1864. The writings reveal a complex man—haughty, formal, rigid, and decidedly of two different personalities. The early school writings and some of the letters are flowery, rambling, and morose—full of classical allusions meant to impress the reader with his knowledge of ancient scholarship. The other side of Rice reveals a very articulate and precise recorder of events. His letters describing battlefield actions, particularly Salem Church and the retreat from Gettysburg, are detailed, informative, and highly readable, characterized by short sentences filled with visual impact. Although his dream to become a lawyer went unfulfilled, he would have made a very good reporter had the proper tutor forced him to drop the cloying professorial facade he adopted. His ability to witness events and then record them in straightforward terms would have also served him well in the practice of law. His letters leave little doubt of his strong antislavery bias and his passion for a reunited country. Many of them contain predictions of future army movements on both sides, which were invariably wrong. His letters are important for their straight reporting and accurate descriptions.

Thomas J. Hassett of West Winfield, originally a member of the 65th New York who finished the war as a captain in the 121st, also wrote a brief history of the regiment. It was published in the *West Winfield Star* at the end of 1912 and in the first few issues of 1913. Entitled "Initiation into the Ways of Warfare," his writings replayed the war and particularly recapped the battle of Sailor's Creek and the controversy surrounding the 121st's claim to capturing George Washington Custis Lee. His accounts were clouded by poor memory, however; they are full of inaccuracies and misstatements.[23]

Just a few short years after the war, Delavan Bates, one of Captain Kidder's Company I favorites, wrote a long piece about his new home in Aurora, Nebraska, and sent it to his old comrade in arms Andrew Davidson, the editor of the *Otsego Republican*. Davidson and Bates became the best of friends after they received their assignments in the 30th U.S. Colored Regiment. Following the war, Bates migrated to Nebraska. Davidson published his article in the *Republican* on March 22, 1876. Bates wrote in response to several letters he had received from Otsego County residents who expressed interest in his newly adopted state and in moving west. As a booster of the new west, he eagerly described the land, the climate, and the people. He warned that the new immigrants needed a few dollars in their pockets to succeed: "Do not come, however, expecting to make a living by trading jack-knives with the unsophisticated inhabitants." He bore witness to the fact that the inhabitants of Nebraska were sharp, energetic, and "wide awake people from the east." He urged "more of the same kind" to head west.[24]

Bates proved to be prolific in his writings. During the 1870s and 1880s, he continued to send missives home to Otsego County, covering every conceivable topic. In the fall of 1877, he closed his letter from Nebraska noting preparations for the 121st New York's first reunion. He urged the paper to provide a full account of the proceedings. In another piece in 1893, he dealt with "Western Prosperity" and the financial situation facing the western states in the battle over silver and gold as a national monetary standard. By October of that year, he turned to his reminiscences of the war in a piece entitled "The Southern Girls." The following month, with another long essay entitled "The Battle of the Mine Run—Medals of Honor," he began to warm to the subject of his old regiment. Davidson published the essay as he had the others, under the heading "Nebraska Correspondence" or "War Reminiscences." Davidson printed every installment of Bates's reminiscences regularly throughout 1893 and well into 1898 on a monthly and sometimes a bimonthly basis. Bates told the story of his experiences not only with the 121st but also with the 30th USCT. He wrote about Cooper's novels and growing up in Otsego and Leatherstocking country. When he was finished, he had covered such diverse topics as a brief history of the 152nd New York Volunteers, also recruited from Otsego and Herkimer counties; typhoid fever; the Klondike; Ulysses S. Grant; the Spanish-American War; the 51st New York Volunteers; metes and bounds of real estate; and the Badlands, to name just a few.

Best never acknowledged Bates's *Otsego Republican* columns in his history twenty-five years later. He may have been unaware of them. Modern writers who have published on various topics related to the 121st in recent years either have been unaware of Bates's prolific columns or have chosen not to use them. His comrades criticized Bates for not writing of the deeds of other companies in the 121st. He explained that since his responsibilities involved Company I, he felt most comfortable writing about what he knew. "No doubt there were individual cases of daring in all the companies of the regiment," he stated, and "instances of deeds that merited Medals of Honor, but historians appear to be lacking in the regiment." Although Bates's work is a gold mine of information on the 121st, it must, like Best's history, be used with care, as he took liberties with the facts and was hindered by working from memory thirty years after the events he described.[25]

At the tenth annual reunion on Lake Otsego's mellow shores in August 1886, the 121st's Regimental Association gave the task of writing the regiment's history to James W. Cronkite. Twenty-one years had passed since the men had mustered out at Hall's Hill. Cronkite had produced a history of the regiment for D. Hamilton Hurd's *History of Otsego County,* published in 1878, but his position as a deputy collector of the Customs House in New York City made it difficult for him to work toward his goal of amplifying his earlier work and writing the full regimental history. His worthy intentions dragged out for thirteen years, with no results. Initially, he told his comrades that "he wished to make the 'Regimental History' the best one ever written and hoped the 'boys' would be patient." The Regimental Association officers urged everyone to "encourage him by ordering one copy or more." He promised that it would "be completed in the near future." Eventually, though, the regiment's patience wore thin. With the Gettysburg report still unpublished, he asked the "boys" for their forbearance again at the fifteenth annual reunion in 1891. When Cronkite produced nothing throughout the 1890s, the association decided to take another tack. At the 1897 reunion, the group established a committee made up of Kidder, Beckwith, and Davidson "to wait upon Col. J. W. Cronkite, who in 1886 was chosen historian, and request him to complete the regimental history in six months." If he could not complete the project in that period, the association authorized the committee members to ask him to hand over any material he held so that they could write the history "at the earliest possible date."[26]

Cronkite continued to procrastinate, and the committee and the rest of the regiment continued to wait. In 1898, "through the secretary," Cronkite reported to the officers on his lack of progress, information the committee promised would be shared with the entire association. With the lack of progress, the officers disbanded the committee chosen to deal with Cronkite on their behalf. Finally, in 1899, the association gave Cronkite an ultimatum. In a strongly worded resolution, the president and secretary of the association were instructed to write to Cronkite and "ask him to report in writing the status of the history now . . . in his hands, and that if he cannot complete it at an early day that the matter be placed back in the hands of the association for its action." With Cronkite's inability to deliver a completed manuscript and then his death in the summer of 1903, four more years passed, and the 121st's Regimental Association finally looked elsewhere. Outgoing association president Morris Foote, a latecomer who had joined the regiment in March 1865 and thus had minimal experience with the 121st, had turned down the task of helping Cronkite because of an impending yearlong European jaunt. Thereafter, Cronkite's son Romaine turned over to the Regimental Association "all the copy of the history that his father had written."[27]

In 1904, recognizing Bates's and Beckwith's early attempts at a narrative history in the Herkimer and Otsego newspapers, the association appointed Bates, Beckwith, and Herman I. Johnson from Russia, late of Company C, to form a committee to "compile a history" of the regiment. Bates, after writing so extensively from Nebraska about the 121st and a world of other topics, inexplicably declined on the basis that he was too "far away" to help. The fact that the association asked him for help meant that members of the committee were aware of his essays in the *Otsego Republican* during the previous decade. The other two members of the nascent committee, Beckwith and Johnson, demurred as well, stating that pressing business interests would keep them from working on the book. A very frustrated Wallace W. Young, the newly elected secretary of the association, was referring to the Sino-Russian War when he quipped: "The Japs will undoubtedly capture St. Petersburg before the much talked of history of the 121st N. Y. Regt. is published." Nothing ever came of the committee. It is not known if Beckwith ever told the other two of his memoirs written years before, which were serialized in his hometown newspaper.[28]

Finally, in 1911, Cronkite's widow turned "a box of papers" over to the association, prompting consternation that Cronkite had done nothing but gather documents. The officers of the group made a call to set up yet another committee to examine the material. To the relief of many, the association concluded that Secretary C. J. Westcott would be the "committee." He quickly decided that the box of materials was useless—filled only with muster rolls, general orders, a few letters, and some newspaper clippings. Capt. Thomas Hassett bemoaned the lack of regimental history that year at the reunion. He said, "When men feel as proud as we have a right to of our record there should be a history of the regiment so that our children, and children's children, could read it."

The matter of an official history came up for open discussion again in 1912 before the association's dwindling membership. The officers tabled the idea for yet another year on the basis that some members were under the impression it would "cost several thousand dollars." Wallace Young "considered it best to drop the matter." Eventually, in 1920, at the association's forty-fourth annual reunion, the rapidly diminishing membership of the association turned as a last resort to Beckwith, Best, and Smith to produce a regimental history. The three men were picked because they were among the few remaining survivors of the 121st, not for their literary skills. And they accomplished what others could not: they turned out a finished product in one year, a Herculean effort following more than twenty years of aborted attempts. They were able to accomplish the task in such a short time because Beckwith had, in fact, already written most of it. Despite its many inaccuracies and occasionally flawed writing, the work became the regiment's "official" history.[29]

By default, Isaac Oliver Best, the newly ordained Presbyterian minister, became the "official" historian of the 121st. He was not a native of Herkimer or Otsego county, and he was never officially a member of the 121st. But when he was assigned as a clerk to brigade headquarters in 1863, Best found that his post gave him a global perspective over the next two years. More important, he enjoyed direct access to Emory Upton. After the war, he returned to Hamilton College, where he received both his bachelor's and his master's degrees. For a while, he remained in Clinton as the principal of Clinton Grammar School. He became a passionate advocate of Hamilton, where 127 young men he recommended were later admitted for study during the last quarter of the nineteenth century. Best married in 1868, and he taught and preached from 1875 to 1900 off and on through New York and Pennsylvania. He also raised a family of four children. He refused to join any "civic or corporation office," remarking, "Never have been and never want to be." Best remained active in both the 16th and the

121st veterans' organizations. He lectured, wrote, and participated in reunions and remained active with the GAR. He died in 1923, two years after publishing his history.[30]

Best's history, like most celebratory memoirs, was florid, complimentary, uncritical, inaccurate, and sometimes superficial. He attempted to appeal to its primary audience—the survivors and their families. The narrative focused on the heroics and maneuvers of men and armies attendant to great battles, and it minimized the darker side of the war and its effects on the men who fought it. During his time in the service, Best had spent more time on Upton's staff, watching the 121st from afar. He did not get involved with the regiment until well after the war. He resurfaced in 1910 when he sent his regrets in regard to attending the reunion that year at Schuyler Lake. He had reread the history of the regiment published in 1897 in the *Otsego Republican* and had intended to bring to the meeting a copy of Upton's manuscript report of the campaigns in Virginia and in the Shenandoah Valley as well as his farewell to the brigade. He told Secretary Westcott that he prized "these manuscripts very highly, for old times sake"; although he "never served in the ranks of the 121st," he declared his pride in "even a nominal connection with so gallant a regiment." Despite the fact that most of his army experience occurred while serving with the 16th New York and at brigade headquarters, he understood what the 121st "dared and suffered during those strenuous days" of wartime. The following year, in a return visit to Schuyler Lake, the regiment heard Best's credible presentation on the battle of Rappahannock Station, making liberal use of Upton's report on the battle. The officers of the association introduced him as someone who "came in closer touch with Colonel Upton than perhaps any other member of the regiment" and the man who knew "more about General Upton than any other man of the 121st."[31]

That night, Best regaled the assembled veterans and their families with additional stories of the 121st. He unimaginatively entitled his second talk "Reminiscences of the War." He introduced himself as the man with the dog, a reference to the fact that during the war, Best had owned a small mutt who took a liking to Upton and feared the sounds of battle, heading to the rear with the roar of cannon. When Upton was wounded at Cedar Creek, Best's dog comforted him by licking his hand until help arrived. Best spoke fondly of Upton. He finished his short discussion by hinting broadly at his desire to be the regiment's historian. Sometime during the day, a comrade had approached him about the possibility of preparing a history of the regiment. "There is no better way of showing Patriotism than to exemplify it ourselves," he told the veterans. By the end of the reunion, association officers lobbied Best to write the regimental history. The secretary pointedly stated in his report for that year, "It is hoped that at the next reunion some definite steps may be taken in regard to a history of the regiment." Secretary Westcott remained optimistic. He knew that the amount of research and hard work required to produce a respectable history, "even at this late hour," would be worthwhile and "dear to the sons and daughters of our regiment." He urged everyone to cooperate in the effort.[32]

Unfortunately, the call for contributions of photographs and anecdotal material brought scant response, probably because there were few veterans left to respond. And although there were some benefits in using firsthand accounts, sixty-year-old memories limited the book's serious historical intent. In addition, in keeping with the mores of the times, incidents and controversies that could embarrass families and individuals were omitted. And because Best embraced the temperance doctrine, he mentioned drink or drunkenness only when and where it could be roundly denounced and used as an example of folly and degradation. Dr. Valentine was treated lightly, and the unenviable record of desertions and resignations was not met directly. Although not a trained historian, Best worked from veterans' reminiscences, regimental and brigade command reports, diaries of several members of the unit, and all available sources found in mid-nineteenth-century histories that were hastily assembled immediately after the war. He specifically mentioned his sources as Beckwith's "diary," the "notes" of Lt. James H. Smith, James Cronkite's chapters in *The History of Otsego County*, and the diary of Lt. Philip R. Woodcock. His most important source was Clinton Beckwith.

Although Best is listed as the author, Beckwith was really the soul of the official history of the 121st. Best had written three very dry, plodding, and general accounts of the last Shenandoah campaign, the Wilderness campaign, and the siege at Petersburg—all of which were unpublished. Beckwith gave Best carte blanche to use his story, and it is to Best's credit that he acknowledged Beckwith's contribution and his heavy reliance on it. Beckwith was probably too enfeebled to be of much help by that point, for he was admitted to the National Home for Soldiers at Fortress Monroe on May 20, 1921, as a widower. And without Beckwith's input, Best let his temperate and unappealing writing style influence his editorial decisions about which material to use from Beckwith's memoirs. As a result, he ignored Beckwith's joy for life, his flair for a good story, and his youthful embrace of risk taking. Besides, Beckwith liked to take a drink occasionally, and he had written about it. Best ignored the tomfoolery but, to his credit, suppressed his distaste for Beckwith's youthful indiscretions.[33]

Beckwith had entitled his narrative "Three Years with the Colors of a Fighting Regiment of the Army of the Potomac, by a Private Soldier," and it is a lively, colorful, and in many places very entertaining work. As the regiment's sixteen-year-old bad boy, he defied authority, including his father. As the new regiment took the field near Dam No. 4 on the Potomac and he was on picket duty, he went for a swim in the river. "Out of curiosity I went down the bluff across the canal and had a swim in the Potomac," he wrote, "principally, I suppose, because it was against orders." His father truly opposed both of his enlistments, mostly out of love. He feared that his son would be killed because he was too young to be doing a man's job. He surprised his son with a visit in camp after Beckwith received a slight wound at Fredericksburg. He tried to convince him to leave the army while he worked the political machinery to get Clinton out. Beckwith refused, however, and the authorities denied his father's request: "I was not greatly disappointed when [my father] wrote and informed me he feared it could not be accomplished," he wrote in his memoirs.[34]

Taking Beckwith's long passages and connecting them with his own chronological and global account of the regiment, Best wove together a story of the 121st. A thorough reading of the *History of the 121st* leaves one with the impression that Beckwith's original writings existed somewhere, but Best never made clear exactly where Beckwith's work first appeared. As he remarked in one section: "It is very fortunate for the friends of deceased members and survivors of the regiment that he [Beckwith] has written so fully of these important events in the history of the regiment." Beckwith, writing in the third-person voice as the anonymous author of the newspaper articles (until his identity was revealed when the series ended), described his work as the "story of his own army experiences, and of his comrades and the regiment from the enlisted man's viewpoint." Best variously called Beckwith's work a "diary," a "reminiscence," and a "narrative," but a close reading of Beckwith's lengthy quotes indicates that they were all written at least thirty years after the war and were not from a diary.

Beckwith's obituary in 1926 stated that he had published "a few years ago . . . a book entitled 'Three Years With the Colors' and in it set forth much of interest about himself and his regiment in war participation." It revealed that Beckwith's account in his "little book" came from "a diary which [he] kept during his period of service." The obituary gave the impression that Beckwith published his account separately. In fact, the paper's reference was probably to the "official history" published by the regimental association, which bore Best's name as the author. The Beckwith document was clearly not a diary but a much later memoir that may have used his diary as a source. For example, when Beckwith referred to his battle experience at Fredericksburg as something only for the young and the reckless, he noted, "I am speaking for myself and at a distance." And in discussing his comrades, he said, "Only two of those five are now living and the other can speak for himself," to which he added parenthetically, "This was written over twenty years ago."[35]

For years, interested writers and archivists have pursued Beckwith's account. No evidence existed to prove the piece's survival or its publication and what form it took. A stand-alone copy never surfaced, and standard Civil War bibliographies did not list it. Beckwith never produced a book, even though the editors of the *Herkimer Democrat* tried to persuade him to do so. In 1893, however, the editors did convince him to tell his tale in their newspaper. What followed became a marketing masterpiece. Introducing the series on July 5, 1893, the editors coyly admitted that they had talked "an esteemed individual" into giving their readers a view of war not from the general's point of view but from that of "the men in the ranks." They were convinced that their readers were ready for the reminiscences from a private who had served throughout the entire war, but the paper refused to name the author. The series ran from July 5, 1893, to July 4, 1894, in fifty-two separate articles.

As a continuing tease to sell papers, the editors interjected themselves into the story on July 26, 1893, after the first few issues had appeared. In a column summing up community speculation—real or manufactured—the editors congratulated themselves for the buzz surrounding the author's identity. They admitted that the rival *Little Falls Times* had floated Beckwith's name as the author. As some guessed the names of other veterans who were likely candidates, the editors at the *Democrat* obviously enjoyed the gathering notoriety of the series. "Later we will divulge the name of the author, which will occasion much surprise. The articles are complimented on every hand, and proven of great interest to the readers of the *Democrat* and the public," the paper wrote in glowing, unabashedly self-congratulatory terms. And the editors promised to run a picture of the author, taken when he first enlisted. This they did in the middle of the series, with the commentary that their author represented all of the fair-haired boys and men who went off to battle for their country in 1861 and who bled and died for the cause of suppressing the rebellion. They were the men who returned to take "up the pursuits of peace and became our most substantial and patriotic citizens." The *Democrat* welcomed the baited comments from the rival *Herkimer Citizen* over the length of Beckwith's narrative: it had sarcastically observed that a better title might have been "Thirty Years with the Colors" instead of "Three." And anyway, the *Citizen* wrote, "we know it is comrade Beckwith and he tells the story in an interesting way and it will be worthy of the book in which, we understand, the account is finally to be preserved."

The *Democrat*, operating under the maxim that any publicity is good publicity, chided the *Citizen* for the "unwitting appreciation" it now paid to the "popularity and enterprise" of the anonymous piece and the *Democrat*'s own good sense and wisdom in running it. It went on to boast of its increased readership directly attributable to the series and the speculation surrounding the author's identity, even though the *Citizen* had guessed correctly. With the series scheduled to run for another twenty-six weeks, the *Democrat* sarcastically expressed its regret that its "crowded columns" would not allow it to "devote more space to the story, knowing the intense interest with which it is received by some of the comrades of the author."

For his part, Beckwith opened his series with the declaration that he had read several other accounts by veterans in "various books, magazines and papers, all of which were so different from my own, and seemed so unnatural, strained and stilted"; he promised to provide his readers with his own experiences, which were the real thing. In the last article and on the last page, the paper dramatically revealed Beckwith's identity. One week later, in the July 11, 1894, edition, the *Democrat* presented a copy of an ambrotype or carte de visite of Beckwith as a youth of seventeen when he first enlisted (the same one it used in January without identification), together with a contemporary depiction of him with a Vandyke beard.[36]

Beckwith's thirty-year-old memories must be taken carefully. As with most histories or memoirs written years later, the intervening time shaded historical accuracy. For the most part, his work is colorful and entertaining. Privy to every major action of the war after September 1862, Beckwith was never out of action with illness or wounds. But the years between his experience and his telling of the story are significant in terms of how they influenced his memory. As the 121st waited to move forward at Appomattox, Beckwith recorded two conversations that may actually have occurred. What they reveal says more of Reconstruction than of the war. He related two opposing views of what should happen to the Confederates, who the men of the 121st thought were making their last stand. The first man was recorded as saying that the rebs were "damn fools" for thinking they could escape. The Confederacy had collapsed, and they should give up despite what "their fire eating leaders have been pounding into them for years." He went on to say that it would be a "pity to kill so many good soldiers for the sake of satisfying a foolish sentiment that to surrender would forever disgrace them in the eyes of their people at home." Another man reportedly wanted to kill them all because that would even the score—"and besides they won't be around to kick up another war." These were comments more suitable to the "Lost Cause" phenomenon prevalent in the 1890s rather than 1865.[37]

Best's late arrival in the regiment and his tenure at brigade headquarters removed him from the 121st's day-to-day activities. Nevertheless, he had an ideal vantage point from which to act as an impartial observer and thereby evaluate the effectiveness of the officer corps and its standing with superior officers— at a distance. His history is a reworking of his earlier writings on the Army of the Potomac's operations, to which he added his personal views of the 121st from his perspective at brigade headquarters. He folded in Beckwith's memoirs where appropriate. The writers' committee of the Regimental Association, battling the very real passage of time to complete the book, hurried it to the publishers. The last few pages bear evidence of a rushed attempt to beat the ticking clock, with glaring errors and obvious cutting and pasting. With its publication in 1921, the history also served as the Regimental Association's official program, for the last few pages were reflections of all the previous programs and featured a list of surviving members and highlights of those whose whereabouts were known. Best revealed in his foreword that James Cronkite had authored the long unsigned chapter on the regiment in Hurd's *History of Otsego County*, published in 1878. Cronkite's accounts differed in some respects from the Best/Beckwith narrative but in other instances provided corroboration of facts. Since the work was closer in time to actual events, it is a bit more reliable, with a few exceptions. According to Best, Cronkite produced a "condensed sketch of the most important facts connected with the services and exploits of the regiment; but as it may be protected by copyright the facts and not the words, are freely used." Copyright became an issue for Best, as the *Herkimer Democrat* had copyrighted each installment of Beckwith's series.[38]

Lt. James H. Smith's responsibilities as a member of the writers' committee were to find as many photographs as possible and to publish the history in Chicago, where he had moved after the war. (Smith established Victor Photographic Specialties with his sons on Cottage Grove Avenue, a few blocks from Lake Michigan.) Best explained that the emergence of photography during the war and its evolution from daguerreotypes to tintypes to cartes de visite precluded the inclusion of larger photographs in the history. Because the committee members could not locate a "considerable number of photos of the line officers [captains and lieutenants]," they decided to include those of the commanders of the corps, division, brigade, and regiment that were eventually loaned to them. Smith is not among them, and the only two enlisted men pictured in the book are Best and Beckwith. Unfortunately, the delay in publishing the regiment's history handicapped the association's effort to gather photographs of the veterans. John Lovejoy's collection of photos of his comrades remained untapped. Undoubtedly, the committee members were ignorant of its existence, even though the *Republican* reported on it in 1897 after the Cooperstown meeting. The paper wrote of Lovejoy in a biographical sketch: "He has a large collection of historical events of his regiment's services to the field, and many photographs of comrades, which collections he wishes to add to in the future." Moreover, his letters were replete with tantalizing references to photographs. Before the Overland campaign, he recorded that he had sent twenty-one pictures of himself to friends and relatives in Old Otsego. In the field, he carried no less than eight albums, "one for each member of the family." He reserved one album for the "likenesses of one of my soldier friends" belonging to a Massachusetts regiment.[39]

The regimental history's total press run is not known. It is likely that between 300 and 500 copies were printed. The cost of the run is also unknown, as is whether all the costs were recouped with sales to the survivors and their families. After the pages were printed and at the last moment, a strike by the binders at Smith's publishing house held up the finished product. Ultimately, the book was available at $1 per copy ($1.15 mailed), for sale year-round. Its greatest sales occurred at the few remaining annual reunions. Only 59 survivors of the 121st attended the 1899 reunion; 41 sent their regrets, and Secretary John Lovejoy reported there were 13 deaths that year. By 1921, when the committee and the association finally published the history, there were but a handful of survivors left. The Regimental Association appealed to the pride of the survivors' families to market the book. Only 9 of approximately 76 survivors attended the 1924 reunion in Jordanville. Fourteen copies were sold at the meeting; six more were purchased afterward. By then, Best and Smith were gone, and Beckwith was in the National Soldiers' Home in Hampton, Virginia. The 121st had truly passed on. But they ultimately produced their story.

Epilogue
The Survivors of Time

The story of valor is written,— / How they marched, how they fought and they bled; / How few there came back without blemish, / And the many they left with the dead.

John K. Tyler, Company G

The 121st Regiment N.Y. Volunteers was one of the best regiments in the Sixth Corps and in the Army of the Potomac. Its character, discipline and efficiency was equal to any regular regiment.

George Gordon Meade to Ulysses Grant, October 26, 1865

The list is growing smaller, but so the need is greater that you and I should close up the ranks and touch elbows the closer.

Cyrus J. Westcott, Company I, 1912

Once the survivors of the three-year ordeal returned to civilian life and a semblance of reality, they slowly adjusted. Nearly everyone—officers and enlisted men alike—took full advantage of their wartime trials to apply for government pensions. Most were eligible due to horrific wounds and deprivations suffered through three or more years of service. Some found the condition diagnosed as piles to be debilitating beyond the ken of medical science.

The Officers

A month before he died, 1st Lt. Adam Clarke Rice discoursed on the war, the army, and the latest from the front lines. He had nothing but high praise for Emory Upton. The young Rice was impressed with Upton, as were most all the men who came into contact with him. Prophetically, Rice said of Upton in the summer of 1863, "He has the finest prospects as a military man, and *unless his life is beset by more than the ordinary misfortunes of man,* he will yet occupy an exalted position, as he does now in fact, in the esteem of all who know him" (italics added).[1]

Despite his wounds, Upton returned to the fray, joining Wilson's cavalry in the western theater. By the time Lee surrendered, he had served in all three branches of the military. When he wrote his official brigade report for the Overland campaign, he referred to five different time periods during the campaign as "Epochs." Distinct epochs characterized Upton's life and legacy as well. His strict, disciplined childhood and youth in the "Burned Over District" in western New York was followed by equally firm schooling at West Point. He successfully met the intense personal challenges of these two periods, and they prepared him for his Civil War experience. The last epoch, his globe-trotting quest for the perfect army in the postwar years, informed his writings. Each epoch had prepared him for the next. His zealous parents shaped his moral rigidity and sense of duty beyond self. West Point reinforced those qualities and taught him how to lead men. His experiences in all three service branches during wartime served as a laboratory where he learned the limits of human endurance and the sacrifices men made in combat. He grasped the importance of displaying loyalty to his men and understood their need to be protected and cared for as much as humanly possible. When they were called on to respond, they did so out of respect for, not fear of, their leader. Upton also learned that respect flowed in both directions. He was a young man destined for a great future in the military. But as Rice had qualified his remarks, Upton's future was indeed "beset by more than the ordinary misfortunes of man."

With the return of peace and the general reduction of the armed forces, Upton reverted to his permanent rank of captain. His postwar career proved no less illustrious than his service in the war. He became obsessed with the relationship of the armed services to the federal government in the country's defense. His war experience deeply affected him as he struggled to determine the army's level of readiness in peacetime. With William Sherman's encouragement, he traveled widely to observe European and Asian armies. He became enamored with the Prussian army's precision and efficiency. Upton wrote extensively, relying on his war experience to inform his work. Between July 1, 1870, and June 30, 1875, he served as commandant of West Point and as instructor of artillery, infantry, and cavalry tactics. A tour of duty at Fortress Monroe followed that post. He slipped back into command on the West Coast, leading his old unit, the 4th Artillery, as he concurrently held the post of commandant of the Presidio in San Francisco.

On February 19, 1868, Upton had married Emily Norwood Norton from Lake Owasco in central New York. A gentle, modest, and affectionate woman, she suffered from neuralgia. Up to that moment, the only women in Upton's life were his sisters and his mother, but Emily measured up to the high standards those women set. He courted her long distance with letters and in person at home. Unfortunately, their European honeymoon sapped her already weakened condition, and she never fully recovered. Visits to her home in the summer of 1868 and Key West that winter were unhelpful. At Key West, Upton left her to report for duty in Memphis. For the next five months, they communicated only by letter. The next year brought the same routine—a time at home and then Nassau in the winter of 1869. Once again, Upton left her, this time to take a new post at McPherson Barracks in Atlanta. In the spring, he received word that she was failing. She died on March 30, 1870, without him at her side. Many speculated about her death's psychological impact on him. His strict training and ability to suppress the unpleasant may have contributed to his later depression.[2]

In August 1875, Upton took an eighteen-month sojourn to Asia and Europe to study armies on the two continents, a trip that kept him from attending the first two regimental reunions. His fact-finding tour was used to sound the clarion call to American politicians for the reform of a weak U.S. military establishment. He published his findings in 1878 in *The Armies of Asia and Europe*, concluding with fifty-four pages of recommendations, none of which made an impact with politicians and the general public. With no immediate threat to national security on the horizon and a huge ocean on each "flank," policymakers were in no mood to experiment with the country's armed forces. Rebuffed, Upton plunged into a new study of the history of American military policy. He concluded that the armed forces needed tangible technical military reforms and that a major philosophical shift was needed in understanding the relationship between the standing professional army and civilian authority.

Upton's views concerning civilian control of the military created the controversy over which military historians and policymakers have argued since he passed from the scene. His experience with the 121st and the other two branches of the army convinced Upton that the militia's very existence, weighed down by its long traditions, placed the nation's defense in jeopardy. This concept struck at the heart of the volunteer service that had served the nation since George Washington's day. Many interpreted it as Upton's argument for a strong, standing army—a prospect that stoked a uniquely American fear. Upton saw the militia as the weak link in the chain of national defense. He proposed establishing a regular standing army composed of professional soldiers. Remembering his battles with the politicians in Albany during the war, he opposed the Militia Act of 1792, which allowed governors to appoint officers and control and train state militia. He wanted control of the armed services to rest in the hands of professionals and felt the government should have the right to draft men in times of national emergency.

During the 1870s, Upton and a group of Civil War Union luminaries such as Sherman, Grant, Sheridan, and Burnside joined together in a loosely formed faction known as the Veterans and tried to influence legislation in Congress to implement Upton's reforms. By 1875, the army had shrunk to the nearly pre-war level of 25,000 men. Upton's extensive research helped him identify ten weaknesses in the military. He cited (1) undisciplined soldiers and ignorant officers; (2) short, three-month enlistments; (3) voluntary enlistments without the draft; (4) the intrusion of the states into a national situation; (5) confusing militia with volunteers and allowing the states to commission volunteer officers; (6) the bounty; (7) no appreciation of a military education; (8) no regimental depots or territorial recruitment; (9) no postgraduate education for officers; and (10) the assumption of command by the secretary of war.

The last factor allowed the Civil War to drag on too long in his opinion, causing unnecessary deaths and a greater loss of treasure. He came close to blaming Lincoln for the carnage but instead focused his contempt on Stanton, who he (erroneously) believed had prolonged the war. Upton never saw his ideas adopted. With no external threat, with the imperative to subdue the Indians in the West and with a creeping national isolationism, the Veterans' efforts went for naught. When Congress defeated the Burnside Bill of 1879 encompassing many of Upton's theories, he became embittered. He never finished his history. (In 1904, Secretary of War Elihu Root finally recognized Upton's contribution and published a short pamphlet summarizing his main points, entitled *The Epitome of Upton's Military Policy of the United States*.)[3]

Upton's health, physical and mental, now became a major concern. And indeed, his health has long been a topic of speculation, almost as intense as the consideration of his controversial ideas of military reform. There is a tantalizing note in Dr. Daniel Holt's diaries dated July 4, 1864, in the midst of Grant's Overland campaign. The one-line note reads: "Sent for by General Upton to perform a slight surgical operation upon him." Holt never elaborated, but when Upton was a cadet, he had been treated for various skin ailments, including the loss of skin by scratching; "morbus cutis," a genetic skin disease; and on nine different occasions, abscesses on his skin that had to be lanced to release the pus and promote healing. Upton probably called Holt to his tent in 1864 to have him lance a boil.

During his tour at the Presidio, Upton noticed a worsening of his sinus headaches. The previous autumn, in September 1880, he had seen a Philadelphia doctor who cauterized his sinus, a supposedly painful procedure that he claimed caused him little discomfort; his only complaint concerned his need to keep a wad of cotton stuffed up his nose. In San Francisco, his handwriting began to deteriorate, and he became depressed by his inability to finish his treatise on infantry tactics. Modern medical diagnoses based on Upton's symptoms indicate that he probably suffered from a nonmalignant tumor in his sinus (a mucoceal), causing headaches and earaches and a ticking noise in his head, leaving a general feeling of depression. The medical literature is clear that Upton did not have a brain tumor.[4]

Lt. Alexander Dyer, the 4th Artillery's adjutant who had witnessed Upton's anxiety, was the last person to see him alive. On Saturday morning, March 12, 1881, Upton complained to Dyer that he could not think. The following Monday morning, March 14, Upton informed Capt. Henry Hasbrouck of his difficulty in finishing his infantry tactics manual. He complained to Hasbrouck about frequent headaches that were becoming longer and more severe, interfering with his ability to concentrate. He feared for his reputation. His colleagues also noticed that Upton exhibited signs indicating a "loss of memory."

On Monday night, he talked with several people and afterward went directly to his quarters. He did not go right to bed but worked on his tactics manuscript instead. When he could not endure the head pain any further, he removed his coat, vest, and boots and lay on his bed dressed in his uniform. He pulled a blanket up to his knees, and there, at age forty-two, Emory Upton ended his life. He placed his service revolver in his mouth and pulled the trigger—almost as if he were driven by the pain in his head and wished to excise it with a bullet. He had burned most of his writings that night, but three letters survived. One was addressed to his sister Sara; another was written to Lieutenant Dyer, and in it, he termed his tactics manual "a failure." The last letter simply expressed his wish to resign from the service. Sara's letter read: "Since writing to you last Sunday, I have been in no little distress over the revision . . . God only knows how it will eventually end. I know he will lead me to sacrifice myself rather than perpetuate a method which might in the future cost a single man his life." Dyer's letter revealed Upton's surrender to be a perceived failure in his tactics.

The next morning, his orderly knocked on his door to waken him. Receiving no answer, he entered the room and found Upton lying on his back on his bed, clothed in his uniform. His body was cold and stiff, indicating that he had killed himself sometime before midnight. In his fireplace was a stack of burned papers from his desk. He had taken a photograph down from the wall, removed it from the frame, and destroyed it, leaving the frame on the desk. He had compressed a lifetime into twenty years of adulthood: service during the Civil War in all three branches of the army; military research on a worldwide scale; authorship of several manuals and treatises on national military policy; a stint as commandant of West Point after the war; and finally, his service as commander of the Presidio.

Speculation as to the cause of his suicide began immediately. Many inferred that he still mourned his Emily. General Hancock, a close friend, did not believe that Upton would take his own life. Others who knew him were shocked. On Saturday, March 19, more than 3,000 cavalrymen and infantrymen attended his funeral. Flags were set at half-staff as officials moved his body to the wharf for shipment back to New York and his family.

One recent historian has called Upton the "Misunderstood Reformer." A more appropriate description might characterize him as a man well ahead of his time. His philosophy and proposed reforms were not applicable to an isolationist nation. But when foreign winds blew cold as the new century began, his ideas were resurrected by Secretary of War Elihu Root. Many were in place as the United States entered World War I.[5]

Like Upton, Egbert Olcott also was a belated victim of the war and died before his time. As the regiment mustered out at the close of the Civil War, Olcott petitioned to remain as the 121st's highest-ranking officer, a wish the army granted. He also petitioned Horatio Wright, George Meade, and Philip Sheridan to obtain a commission in the Regular Army.

All three endorsed him. Wright wrote glowingly that although Olcott was a young man, he possessed a high intelligence and a good education and exhibited "bravery upon the field." He concluded by saying Olcott "stands amongst the foremost." Meade found him highly qualified "for a position in the regular army." Sheridan responded more coolly, stating only that Olcott served "with distinguished gallantry" during the Shenandoah campaign of 1864. Meade wrote to Grant that "the 121st Regiment N.Y. Volunteers was one of the best regiments in the Sixth Corps and in the army of the Potomac. Its character, discipline and efficiency was equal to any regular regiment." Meade attributed the 121st's high standards to Olcott's leadership, and he echoed Upton, Sedgwick, Wright, and McKenzie in endorsing him. Acknowledging Grant's penchant "to reward real merit" and efficient leadership, Meade concluded that Olcott should be accepted into the Regular Army.[6]

But in the fall of 1872, only seven years after the war's end, Egbert Olcott's father, Horatio, admitted him to King's County Lunatic Asylum in Utica, New York. Cronkite, Kidder, and Frank Morse all certified that the head wound Olcott suffered in the Wilderness had caused his change in behavior and led to his disability. The wound never healed properly, and its effects impaired his ability to function as a normal adult. Remarkably, he fathered two children in the postwar years—Horatio, born in 1871, and Egberta, born in the spring of 1873. One year later, medical authorities transferred him to the state of New York's Asylum for the Insane at Willard, New York. By 1877, he was certified totally disabled, which allowed him to draw $50 per month in a government pension. The surgeons affirmed that Olcott suffered from dementia and presented as a "sullen, filthy" patient. The cold medical assessment concluded, "Insane since October 1872." Doctors testified that he seldom spoke and then only incoherently, and he could not control his bodily functions. They classified the bold officer of the Wilderness and Sailor's Creek as an "imbecile": he was unable to take care of himself, "to dress, and undress himself, [and to] feed himself," and he required constant attendance. He died on February 23, 1882, at age forty-seven.

His autopsy revealed fragments of bone and particles of lead in his brain. The attending coroner could place his thumb in the depression over Olcott's left eye. His family meant to keep his funeral and burial in Cherry Valley private, but when his comrades from the 121st learned of his death, they went to the ceremonies. Those who had been selected originally as pallbearers "gave place to comrades, who bore his remains to their resting place among the heroic and patriotic dead of Cherry Valley." In an ironic turn, his widow, Susan, moved to Yorktown, Virginia, where she lived out the remainder of her life a few miles from the site where her husband had been wounded and captured.[7]

Both Upton and Olcott were tragically affected by their military experiences, albeit in different ways; both were belated victims of the war. Three officers who barely survived the war were the Reverend John Adams, Dr. Daniel Holt, and Maj. Henry Galpin. Adams returned to his native Maine when the war ended, but he never again enjoyed the camaraderie experienced in the two regiments he served during the war. Although he appeared robust, four years of military service had broken his mind and his body. Almost immediately after Adams was discharged, friends and family were alarmed by a serious change in his demeanor and his ability to concentrate. He took ill during the winter of 1865–1866. On April 25, 1866, he died at Northampton Lunatic Hospital, less than a year after returning from the front. His family doctors attributed his death to "typhomania, a type of disease often caused by severe and prolonged exertion." His war duties caused him to succumb to "unnatural symptoms such as nervousness, absent mindedness," and other indications that could directly be linked to his war service. He had turned sixty-four the month before his death.[8]

Holt returned to the Mohawk Valley in the autumn of 1864. He had been gone only twenty-six months, but he lived a lifetime during his war years. Unfortunately, his health continued to deteriorate until he could no longer practice medicine, and in 1867, he applied for a government pension. He exhibited all the characteristic symptoms of tuberculosis, and he knew it. He died on October 15, 1868, almost four years to the day he left his regiment in the Shenandoah Valley. Holt was only forty-seven years old when he died. His wife, Mary Louisa, survived him until 1894.[9]

Holt's replacement, James Kimball, enjoyed his military service. He was transferred to the 65th New York at Hall's Hill. He once said that he would "rather spend the summer in a tent [in Virginia] than in a house anywhere." He rose to the rank of colonel and served as assistant surgeon general in the Medical Corps. He lectured at West Point on physiology, hygiene, and surgical and medical emergencies. Kimball served in the West after the war and during the Spanish-American War at century's end.[10]

Fellow surgeon Edward S. Walker, MD, tendered his resignation from the service at the end of March 1863 and was released on April 1. Suffering from acute diarrhea contracted at White Oak Church, Walker returned to Ilion. He had been on sick leave nearly every day since the regiment left Camp Schuyler, and he was pronounced unfit for duty by his doctors as the chronic diarrhea debilitated him. After the war, he tried to practice medicine, to no avail. He became increasingly dependent on morphine to alleviate his pain. On the night of July 13, 1876, passersby discovered his body in the Erie Canal in the town of German Flats. A coroner's inquest determined that he had overdosed on morphine and that his death, at thirty-nine, could not be attributed to foul play.[11]

Walker's replacement, Surgeon John Ostrander Slocum, mustered out with the regiment at Hall's Hill and returned to upstate New York to resume his private practice. He was never as famous as his brother, Maj. Gen. Henry Warner Slocum. The Slocums descended from English stock, and their forebears ultimately found their way to Delphi Falls, New York, in Onondaga County. The Slocum boys were two of eleven offspring who lived in the family home called "Cheapside." Dr. Slocum settled in Camillus, New York, in 1866, often supporting his brother and his political aspirations. General Slocum became a Democrat. The *Syracuse Journal* accused him of never being comfortable in the Democratic Party. Brother John told the *Otsego Republican* that the general made "the mistake of his life" in 1865 when he left the Republican Party. John remained a loyal Republican and played an active role in the party's functions until his death in 1885.[12]

Sweet-tempered and generous Henry Galpin of Little Falls also succumbed to war wounds and disease. He had married in February 1861. During his wedding trip, which included attending Lincoln's inauguration on March 4, his new bride became ill; she died on his birthday, July 4. Galpin was one of the original Ellsworth's Avengers and was wounded at Malvern Hill a year later, on July 1, 1862. He remarried during the war, in Washington on July 23, 1864. At Bolivar Heights two weeks before the battle of Cedar Creek, he slept on the ground with no shelter or blanket. He contracted a severe cold, which settled in his lungs. Doctors gave him a mid-nineteenth-century diagnosis of "disease of the lungs" or "phthisis," which could cover a multitude of pulmonary ailments including asthma, tuberculosis, emphysema, and even pneumonia. At Cedar Creek, Confederate sharpshooters put minié balls through both his legs. The wounds qualified him for a discharge from the army at Petersburg just before Christmas 1864. He returned to Little Falls and the family stove business but remained a member of the 121st in spirit and heart. He generously welcomed home his former comrades on July 4, 1865, his thirty-first birthday, as they celebrated Independence Day once again. Two years later, he quit the stove business and Little Falls and moved west to Jacksonville, Illinois. He succumbed to his wounds and lung disease nearly ten years to the date of his discharge, in 1874.[13]

The regiment's first commander, Richard Franchot, had returned to civilian life after relinquishing his command to Emory Upton. After only one term in Congress, he went back to the business world, becoming the first president of the Albany and Susquehanna Railroad. He enjoyed a brief association with the Central Pacific Railroad Company. Toward the end of the war, Congress brevetted him as a brigadier general in the U.S. Volunteers. He moved to Schenectady, where he died in 1875 and was buried in Vale Cemetery.[14]

John Kidder and James Cronkite survived the war with terrible wounds, but each man managed to lead as normal a life as possible thereafter. Both played a major role in the Regimental Association. Kidder, like others in his regiment, wrote extensively from the front. His wife bore the brunt of his different moods throughout his three years of service. His low point came immediately after the debacle at Salem Church, when he wanted out. But during the Christmas season of 1863–1864, he talked about staying in the army on a permanent basis. As an immigrant, he became a fervent patriot. Men who deserted "ought to be shot" in his opinion; he could not understand the "miserable cowardly set" up north who refused to support the war and Lincoln. He had no time for the heavy artillery ("I would prefer women with broom handles") and incompetent generals and colonels ("one of those that have more courage than brains"). In his darkest moments, he considered and then rejected the notion of moving to another country. Instead, he decided to "stick with the old ship" or go down with it. His loyalty to his men bordered on the fanatical. As officers around him resigned, he refused to quit. He promised his men he would lead them, and a promise made, to his way of thinking, carried the weight of a contract.

Kidder never returned to wagon making in Laurens. Instead, he perfected his political instincts honed during the war. His congressman, David F. Wilber, secured an appointment for him as port warden of New York Harbor in 1880. He held the position as a Republican appointee until a Democratic administration in 1893 threw him out. With another change in administration in 1896, the Republicans reappointed him. In the intervening three years, Kidder did what generations of public servants have done: he became a consultant to the New York Harbor Board. Who else knew as much as he did after thirteen years on the job? He regained his position by doing just what he had done during the war—lobbying his friends in high places. When he took office the second time, he did so through the efforts of prominent New York City steamship agents, shipping merchants, the surveyors of the Board of Underwriters, twenty-three congressmen, twenty-one state senators, the Republican organization of Otsego, and "other individuals and organizations." His strong marriage allowed Kidder to leave his wife at home in Laurens while he worked in New York City. He lived in Brooklyn with his son George until he retired in 1898. He died in May 1905; his wife survived him for another seventeen years. She never failed to attend a regimental reunion as a member of the Women's Relief Corps.[15]

James Cronkite also spent the rest of his life in government service. In 1872, both houses of Congress passed a private bill allowing him to receive a higher pension as a lieutenant colonel instead of a major. He became the deputy collector at the New York Customs House. With Kidder, he would be the face of the regiment after the war, and he played a large role in executing the 121st's monument at Gettysburg. Cronkite left no explanation as to why he never completed the regiment's official history. He succumbed to Bright's disease in Plainfield, New Jersey, in 1903, halfway through his sixty-second year.[16]

In 1868, Adrian Mather established a wholesale grocery business in Albany, in which his brothers Andrew and Elias joined him. Toward the end of the war, Andrew, with the 20th U.S. Colored Troops in New Orleans, had tried to entice his brothers south to join him in owning and managing a plantation. When Adrian died in 1883, Andrew became the principal owner and manager of the business and eventually a prosperous grocer.[17]

Another merchant and super planner, Alonzo Ferguson, picked up his former life after the war. Credited by his contemporaries for successfully organizing both the 121st and the 152nd New York Volunteers during the hectic summer of 1862, he returned to his roots. He put his management skills to use after the war as a ticket and express agent, an insurance salesman in Cobleskill and then New York City, and finally in a return to his first trade—hardware sales and manufacturing. He passed away in Westwood, New Jersey, in April 1912.[18]

Despite having had his left leg amputated to the thigh, Frank Waite Foote accepted an appointment as a second lieutenant in the Volunteer Reserve Corps, where he served from May 1865 to October 1866. He completed another stint with the 45th U.S. Infantry, Regular Army, in January 1868, when he retired to a position in the U.S. Pension Department. Under a doctor's care, Foote died in Washington on October 1878 from "hemorrhaging lungs," as the 121st held its annual reunion. He left a wife and two children.[19]

Sam Kelley's family disintegrated when the war ended. When his father, Almond Kelley, was discharged from the army in Minnesota at the end of July 1865, he returned home to Schenevus. The elder Kelley remained unscathed physically. But after the war, he applied for a government pension, claiming that his eyesight failed him and he could not find work. Soon, he began to abuse his wife, Mary Anne. She instituted divorce proceedings, which dragged on for several bitter months. The case went all the way to the state supreme court. Almond refused to pay alimony, and she sued for his and Sam's pensions. Mary Anne called Almond a "peculiar man . . . of a sad and ungovernable temper."

Her divorce became final in January 1868. The government rejected her petition for benefits on the basis that Sam did not qualify as her sole support during his army service. Even though she was divorced, the government ruled that her husband qualified as her sole source of support. She appealed the ruling with heart-wrenching, exhaustive letters to New York senator Ira Harris, who petitioned the commissioner of pensions, to whom she also wrote. The commissioner passed her requests on to the White House. In October 1867, after the White House denied her pleas, she wrote directly to the president; he referred her case back to the commissioner of pensions, who rejected her again. No longer able to depend on her husband for support, she became destitute. After her divorce and her unsuccessful attempts to get a government pension, she disappeared from the historical record except for occasional appearances as a member of temperance organizations in and near Schenevus.[20]

Lansing Paine survived his incarceration in Macon, rejoined the 121st, and mustered out with the rest at Hall's Hill. He returned to Garrattsville to work as a clerk and bookkeeper for a lumber mill. He had risen from private to captain by war's end and harbored no further ambitions, unlike his friend Emmet Mather, who Paine predicted would be a colonel if the war lasted until the regiment's muster out in August 1865. Paine contracted rheumatism near Brandy Station and received a pension on that basis. His health began to deteriorate in 1894; a doctor examined him and declared that Paine looked "much older than he gives his age." He died the following year, in the company of his children. His comrades from the 121st attended his services and laid him to rest in the Butternut Valley cemetery. He was only fifty-five years old.[21]

A few veterans of the 121st took advantage of the new Homestead Act, which promised 160 acres in the West to anyone willing to settle on and improve the land. Delavan Bates made a name for himself in Aurora, Nebraska. From his new home, he found time to write his reminiscences of the war, which found their way into the *Otsego Republican*. Actively engaged in community affairs, he held office as mayor, city councilman, and school superintendent. He also served as vice president of the First National Bank. He died in 1918 in an old soldiers' home in Burkett, Nebraska. Quartermaster Theo Sternberg became a lawyer and settled in Kansas. With Bates, he shared the distinction of being an "old Cooperstown boy" who did well in the war, and he later served as a major in the Philippines. When he left Otsego County, he settled in the sparsely populated West. He wrote home, telling all who would listen that "the war built up the West." He saw the land occupied by easterners and southerners. "The stamp of the Union soldier is all over the West," he declared. Others put down roots in the West as well. C. E. Adams, a transfer from the 16th New York after Salem Church, settled in Sacramento and joined the Sumner Post 3 of the GAR. Henry Craske from Little Falls, a member of Company A, stopped in the Midwest, where he joined GAR Post 131 in Rushville, Illinois. James Mc-

Curry settled on the wild prairie of Wright County, Iowa, in 1866. He farmed along the Boone River, where he lived until his death from a stroke on January 27, 1892.[22]

Levi Turner earned a brevet lieutenant colonel commission and then became a colonel in 1865. He died on the job as judge advocate of U.S. Volunteers in Washington at age sixty-one, on March 13, 1867. Struck down "with paralysis" the previous Sunday, he was dead by Wednesday. His family returned his body to Cooperstown in the middle of a cold winter and heavy snows. As the *Otsego Republican* mournfully reported: "There is nothing more sad or sorrowful than a funeral in the midst of winter and a snow storm. It freezes the very fountains of sorrow, and turns the tears of mourners into icicles." His family buried Turner at Lakewood Cemetery near the grave of James Fenimore Cooper.[23]

Although severely wounded at Salem Church, Andrew Davidson escaped the postwar tribulations many of his comrades suffered. He won a Medal of Honor for service at the Crater at Petersburg. After the war, he married and raised three children. He engaged in small business, read the law, and gained admission to the bar in 1873. With a partner, he bought the *Otsego Republican* in 1874, becoming its sole owner ten years later. Davidson turned the paper into a popular vehicle for Republican values and initiatives. The *Republican* also became the unofficial voice of the 121st New York Volunteers. Nearly every request, public announcement, and invitation to an association reunion from the regiment found space in the paper. Bates's articles were premier examples of Davidson's loyalty and his desire to promote the regiment and its exploits. He voted a straight Republican ticket, and the party rewarded his loyalty with an appointment as deputy commissioner of pensions six years later. In 1883, he ran for the state senate and successfully served on several important committees in Albany during his one term. When he died in 1902, Davidson was active as the commandant of the New York State Soldier's and Sailor's Home in Bath.[24]

The Enlisted Men

Enlisted men and officers alike returned home to a different landscape. Many settled back into their former lives, barely missing a beat. Dewitt Clinton Beckwith, at various times a private and a corporal, embodied the human story woven throughout the entire sixty-year history of the 121st New York Volunteer Regiment. He was present at the creation. As an active member of the Regimental Association, he became essential to the success of the regiment's monument at Gettysburg and in executing the regiment's history.

After the war, Beckwith became a devoted Democrat. As a member-delegate of the national Democratic Party, he participated in the 1883 nomination of Grover Cleveland at the national convention. Although he supported the three unsuccessful nominations of William Jennings Bryan, he remained a member of the New York State Democratic Party for twenty-five years and the longest serving at that time. The party nominated him on several occasions for state and local positions, but there is no evidence that he rose any higher in political office than supervisor and later president of the village of Herkimer in 1878 and 1879. In 1894, a fellow Democrat, New York governor Roswell Pettibone Flower (1892–1895), appointed him to be assistant state engineer, with the rank of colonel.

For his work on the 121st's monument at Gettysburg, Flower appointed Beckwith to the New York Monuments Commission, which oversaw many New York monuments on Civil War battlefields. In that capacity, he participated in the design of Brig. Gen. Alexander S. Webb's statue at Gettysburg. Webb had commanded the 2nd Brigade, 2nd Division, Second Corps, which repelled Pickett's charge at the Bloody Angle. Beckwith also played a role in the erection of monuments commemorating Maj. Gen. Abner Doubleday, commander of the 3rd Division, First Corps, and Brig. Gen. John C. Robinson, commander of the 2nd Division, First Corps, at Gettysburg, as well as New York monuments at Knoxville, Vicksburg, Antietam, Lookout Mountain, Chickamauga, and Richmond.

Beckwith joined John V. Quakenbush of Mohawk in a private contractor partnership, as "one of the heaviest operators in this part of the state." The pair won the contract for the construction of the Croton Aqueduct for New York City, the Washington tunnels, and rail-building projects for New York and Boston. They were responsible for the trolley bridge over West Canada Creek, which extended the trolley tracks from Herkimer to Little Falls—another enterprise in which they held a controlling interest. Beckwith remained a citizen of Herkimer throughout his life. As late as September 27, 1919, he received mention in the program as a member of the audience at the Herkimer County Historical Society during a presentation to the society of a Union flag that flew over Libby Prison after the fall of Richmond. The society merely listed him as "Colonel Clinton Beckwith."[25]

When Beckwith began his memoirs in the *Herkimer Democrat*, he found himself in the midst of a brutal struggle for the soul of the Democratic Party in Herkimer County. Distant relative Ezra D. Beckwith vigorously opposed him in the quest to become chair of the Democratic Party in Herkimer County. Ezra, according to the *Herkimer Democrat*, aligned himself with "Sheard's sewer"—meaning the rival Republican newspaper, the *Little Falls Times*, which local mill owner Titus Sheard controlled. The *Democrat*, which threw its support behind Clinton's candidacy for the chairmanship of the Herkimer County Democratic Party, became Clinton's mouthpiece. The *Democrat* blasted the *Times*, calling it "Ezra's personal organ," "Sheard's sewer," and "a liar." Calling Ezra's political patronage tactics "the rankest kind of bunco-ism," the paper likened the "congregation of non-producers" to "geese upon a grass plat—they eat up everything in front of them and kill everything behind them."

The bitter campaign between the two men quickly became personal. One Saturday in September 1893, Ezra approached Clinton at the Allman House, a large brick hotel near the train depot in Herkimer village, and offered his hand in greeting. Clinton refused with the comment, "You will excuse me, but I decline to assist in your fakir game." When Ezra tried to engage Clinton in conversation, Clinton told him that he "had no time to waste with you." The local papers took sides. The *Herkimer Citizen* sided with the *Times* whereas the *Utica Daily Press* and the *Amsterdam Daily Sentinel* congratulated Clinton on his victory. The *Sentinel* called Clinton "adroit" and "more efficient as a political leader than all of them. The gross personal abuse of him did not count with the discerning Democrats of Herkimer County. Long may he wave." A seat as a delegate to the upcoming Democratic National Convention became the prize, which Clinton eventually secured.[26]

Beckwith died on January 30, 1926, in a familiar place: Fortress Monroe in Virginia, in the soldiers' home, Old Point Comfort, after years of failing health. The medical examiner listed a vague diagnosis of "general arteriosclerosis" as the official cause of death. His funeral expenses totaled $525, including his casket at $450. The government allowed $107 toward the burial costs. The mortician sent his body back to Herkimer. Sister Ada Lakeman of Rochester survived him. Beckwith probably contributed little in the way of hands-on labor in the regimental history. There is no evidence that he and Isaac Best corresponded during the history's production. He outlived his coauthors by three years.[27]

His partners in the official history, Best and Smith, went in different directions. Best married after the war, raised four children, became a Presbyterian minister, and embraced the temperance movement. He alternated between preaching and teaching the classics in New York and Pennsylvania. Best based his pension claims on contracting rheumatism at Fredericksburg and Salem Church. He retired sometime after 1910 and was the first of the trio to pass away. He died of a stroke in Cliffside, New Jersey, on March 28, 1923, barely two years after the history's publication, at age eighty-two.

Before the war, James Henry Smith had tilled the land on his Herkimer farm. After the war, he left for the west, settling in Chicago, where he established his photography studio with his sons. He fathered five boys and a girl. He became commander of the Loyal Legion Illinois and a staunch member of the George Thomas Post of the GAR. Smith could not attend the Little Falls meeting of 1912, but he wrote a poignant letter sending his regrets. He penned a heady philosophical rumination. He spoke to the self-sacrifice by many for the common good, leading to the formation of the most powerful nation on earth. As we approach the end of our lives, he wrote, "we may well take cheer in the thought that we have not lived in vain." He believed that his generation was given the privilege to preserve the nation, "the greatest on earth . . . whose future glory is destined to surpass our comprehension." Smith often spoke at veterans' gatherings, and at his last reunion with the 121st in 1920, he narrated a lantern slide show on the country's national parks, illustrated with his own photographs. He drew a pension and disability pay for "exposure" during the Shenandoah campaign. By age sixty-two, he had lost half of his teeth. He succumbed to heart disease in Chicago on December 5, 1923, nine months after Best died.[28]

Others settled back into a routine existence after the war. Charles A. Morehouse, a member of Company C and later the Veteran Reserve Corps, returned to his former profession as a cheese box maker in Herkimer County. Three years after the war, he purchased a cheese box factory, and by 1879, he manufactured 60,000 boxes a year. During the centennial year, he successfully ran for the position of justice of the peace in the town of Russia. Judson A. Chapin, a native of Oneida and a veteran of Company B, had joined the regiment at twenty-four. He had moved to Ilion before the war and found employment as an engineer at the Remington works, a position he returned to in 1869. David Bailey, who served in Company E from Roseboom and was wounded at Salem Church, returned to his life as a shoemaker.[29]

One of the older men to enlist, at thirty-seven, William Murray, a veteran of Company K, reentered civilian life in Butternuts, Otsego County, and resumed his former trade as a cooper. Evidently, he never married and spent the rest of his life as a lonely, bitter man. He died in 1895, and his obituary characterized him as a "quiet, harmless sort of man." The newspaper called him "plain, honest hearted, Bill Murray." With faint praise, the obituary said of him: "Although he had his faults and they were well known, they were always overlooked, and the old saying that 'he was his worst enemy,' would apply very forcibly in his case." But, the paper quickly added, he had no other faults.[30]

Another older man, Reuben Bates (no relation to Delavan Bates), left his farm in Middlefield to enter the service at age thirty-four. Before the war, he had been a mason, a farmer, and a sawyer. He returned to farming. Company K's William Lunn, a twenty-year-old private who had left his farm to join the 121st, also returned to the fields. He married in 1867 and bought his new wife's family farm in Garrattsville. All manner of diseases plagued him throughout the remainder of his life—including recurrent diarrhea, "dropsy," "Sleeping Lethargy," and intermittent biliary fever. In 1879, he suffered a violent attack of "cholera moberus." In the winter of 1896, a wagon accident just outside Morris, New York, killed him. The members of the 121st held him in high esteem, describing him as "a true Christian Soldier." His obituary, written by one of his regimental comrades, was unintentionally humorous. Noting that Lunn had survived all the regiment's battles, his friend wrote of his "burden of sorrow when we think how unaware of any danger and how instantaneous that sleigh tongue pinned him to that tree with such a fatal result."[31]

John Hartwell moved back to Massachusetts immediately after the war and established his profession as a builder and contractor. He never joined the Regimental Association or the GAR. He died two years after his beloved wife, Calista, in 1899. Lester Murdock, who participated in every battle of the war, returned to farming around Hartwick. According to his own account, as furnished to the state historian, he saw Lieutenant Duroe being killed in front of Fort Fisher, Captain Butts "fall" at Spotsylvania, and Ten Eyck Howland perish at Sailor's Creek. He never mentioned Custis Lee's capture. By 1896, as president of the Hartwick Soldier's Monument Association, he played a role in establishing the Horatio Duroe GAR Post; he served as its commander three times.[32]

The new Gilded Age provided opportunities that were unavailable before the war. Erastus Weaver had hoped to attend West Point in the prewar years, but his parents would not allow it. He taught school, married in 1852, and intended to settle in Otsego County when the war broke out. He joined Company K as a sergeant, and Emory Upton promoted him to first lieutenant at Spotsylvania on May 10, 1864. He survived the war and went on to law school, later practicing law in Otsego County. James Clyde started out the war in the 44th New York, where he served four months, and then he took a commission in Company G in the 121st and lasted two months there. He reenlisted in Company E, 76th New York, and finished out the war after being captured at the Wilderness. The authorities exchanged him, and he returned to Otsego County, becoming a practicing physician after he graduated from medical school in New York City. Lt. Charles Bradt, John Hartwell's good friend, also became a doctor and set up a practice in St. Charles, Michigan.[33]

For years after the war, William Remmel's family, particularly his sister, Ada Remmel Benson, tirelessly worked to learn of his fate. Ada tried desperately to accept the notion that he survived the initial federal rout at Cedar Creek but languished in Andersonville, where he died. By 1910, she had admitted that "he probably died there." She remained convinced that his comrades had identified him at the infamous prison on December 16, 1864, in tatters. Frank Mumford, in Company E, was wounded at Cedar Creek. He swore that he and William stood in line together at Andersonville. Mumford said that they were taken first to Libby Prison, where they were held for a month. Supposedly, Mumford tried to talk to him, but Remmel would not engage in conversation. From Mumford, Ada learned that William's head wound healed and the wound in his arm became gangrenous.

Sporadically throughout the remainder of the century, Ada and her family wrote members of Company I and anyone else who would listen to determine what happened to her brother. Adelbert Jaycox told Ada that he "always supposed William was killed at the Battle of Cedar Creek" and coldly added, "Never heard anything different." Treat Young, another Company I soldier imprisoned at Andersonville until he returned to the regiment in November 1864, reported that Remmel was wounded and missing, "but no one knew positively" if he was "killed or taken prisoner." Young never saw Remmel at Andersonville. Young had been wounded at the Wilderness, and a report passed on to his wife and family indicated that he had been killed. Even the church bells tolled, to mark his passing. No one knew differently until he returned from Andersonville. Young advised Ada to pray for guidance and relief from her anxiety.

Another company mate, John Willsey, knew the Remmel brothers and adamantly insisted that William was not taken prisoner, "for he died on the field." Merton Tanner, Cyrus Westcott, E. W. Ostrander, Charles Downing, and Charles Merrill all gently responded to Ada with conflicting reports of her brother's fate. Egbert Olcott referred the Remmel family to Washington, where they received no answers. The Christian Commission, after searching its records, suggested that William might have been wounded and sent to a hospital.

John Kidder responded to the family from New York City in an undated, six-page letter on port warden's stationery (probably in 1888, since he thanked Ada for her $3 contribution to the Gettysburg Monument). He said that the Remmel family should be allowed some pension money. He explained that he had been granted convalescent leave when the regiment reported William "lost" at Cedar Creek. He guessed that father Remmel might be eligible to receive William's last two military payments and any back bounty he was owed. In a postscript, Kidder told the family of William's valor and expressed his "exalted opinion" of him. Kidder's language left no question that he understood William had died at Cedar Creek. In the next decade, on unsigned and undated port warden stationery under the heading "List of men of the 121st who died in the Service (Civil War)," John Kidder recapitulated the war and its toll on the 121st New York. In four categories, he listed the names of those who died from disease, those who were accidentally killed, those who were killed in action, and those who had died since the war's end. For those killed in action, he listed the place and date. Kidder listed Remmel as killed at Cedar Creek on October 19, 1864. He was certain that he had been killed in action and had not languished in Andersonville.[34]

In the spirit of reconciliation, Ada Remmel Benson said she knew that if her brother was still living, "he would cherish towards the southern soldier the same kindly, warm, loving and magnanimous spirit that is cherished by the survivors of the blue and gray." Brother Caleb had joined the 121st in September 1864 at age eighteen. Assigned to Company I, he was badly wounded in the head above the right ear in front of Petersburg at Fort Fisher on April 2, 1865. Joe Heath saw him fall but left him for dead. Caleb recovered, but his wound caused him numbness and other untold maladies for the rest of his life. He married in 1878. After moving to Indiana, he and his new bride lived on his $4-per-month government pension and his earnings as a railroad engineer. He died in 1887.[35]

Robert Bradshaw shared a fate similar to William Remmel's. The former enlisted with Company E as a transfer from the 18th New York after Salem Church, and according to one source, he fell at Spotsylvania Court House on May 10, 1864. Another source indicated that he had died at the Wilderness five days earlier. A conflicting family narrative passed down to later generations insisted that Bradshaw, like Remmel, died at Andersonville on either August 15 or August 24, 1864, and was laid to rest there in grave 6685.[36]

Nearly all the survivors of the 121st suffered in one way or another from their war experiences. Some of them came home to loving families and wives they had not seen for three years. And some of their relationships flowered: John Kidder and John Hartwell are two examples of men who enjoyed marital harmony. Others did not fare so happily. William Barnes had joined the 121st as a nineteen-year-old private from Little Falls. He became a corporal as the year 1865 began and then received a promotion to sergeant. He was wounded at Spotsylvania on May 10, 1864, and again at Hatcher's Run outside Petersburg at the end of March 1865. His wounds qualified him for an honorable discharge. Released from the army in Albany, he returned home and married Alvina Matilda Barnes in 1873. The two of them set up a barbershop in Syracuse; William cut hair, and Alvina worked around the shop to help out. In 1898, Barnes filed for a pension, claiming that Alvina had "cleared out to parts unknown to me." He testified that he had not seen her for twelve years, "and I don't care to see her now. She had no cause of [leaving home. She] had a good home, enough to eat and wear, better than I had my self." Not so, according to Alvina. When she applied for a pension in 1905, she affirmed that William had left her twenty years earlier "and has not returned or did anything for her support since that time." She claimed that William's addiction to drink subjected her to abusive treatment. On one occasion, he threatened to kill her. As a "person of needy circumstances," she maintained that William drove her from their home and then deserted her. William eventually won a pension; Alvina received nothing.[37]

The reunion associations, including the GAR, were for some veterans a means of demonstrating that the common man needed to stand up to the robber barons of the Gilded Age and the wave of capitalism sweeping over the land. One former member of the 121st devoted his life's work to the cause of the common man. Dyer D. Lum of Frankfort was among the more unusual members of the regiment. He had enlisted in the 121st in July 1862 and mustered into Company D on August 23. Born in Geneva, New York, 70 miles from Emory Upton's birthplace in Batavia, he descended from Massachusetts militiamen and Lewis and Arthur Tappan, prominent abolitionists. John Brown and his raid on Harpers Ferry inflamed Lum's sense of justice. The raid became his motivation to join the Union army. The official records listed him as deserting on November 5, 1862, "while on the march" at White Plains as the army headed for Belle Plain and eventually Fredericksburg. The official records also carry the notation that the commanding officer, either Upton or company commander John Fish, ordered him stricken from the rolls as of November 2.[38]

Lum's pension records show that he was captured in Upperville, Virginia, on November 10 and confined to prison in Richmond on November 21. He received a parole from City Point on November 30, 1862. Regimental officers or provosts never pursued him, as the 121st soon became engaged in its first major battle. Lum eventually showed up in Buffalo, New York, reenlisted as a first sergeant, and mustered into Company H of the 14th New York Cavalry. He served for two remarkable years with distinction in the 14th Cavalry, seeing promotions to sergeant major on June 1, 1863, followed by commissions to first lieutenant and adjutant at the end of the year and to captain on August 1, 1864. He finally resigned his commission on April 24, 1865. From 1863 until the war's end, the army and the Department of the Gulf carried the 14th as an element of its command until the regiment merged with the 18th New York Cavalry. It saw duty around Pensacola, Florida, and near New Orleans, Baton Rouge, and other points in Louisiana. By all accounts, Lum served loyally and faithfully.[38]

After the war, Dyer Lum burst onto the national political scene. He moved to Northampton, Massachusetts, in 1873, where he practiced his bookbinding trade. There, he became deeply involved in the anarchist movement as it swept the country in the forefront of labor rights. Later, he joined Wendell Phillips in the reform movement. Lum's admiration for John Brown and his use of force served as a clarion call to Lum, who has been described as a "brilliant writer and a sophisticated intellectual" by modern historians. Between 1885 and his premature death in 1893, Lum "moved toward anarchism [out of] frustration with abolitionism, spiritualism, and labor reform." Anarchism in the United States in the 1880s arose out of two independent sources—indigenous movements and immigrant movements. Lum sought to bring the economic reforms of the "Boston anarchists" and the revolutionary strategy of the "Chicago [Haymarket riots] anarchists" together in a coherent and inspiring movement that laborers could accept and unite around. He joined the Knights of Labor in the 1880s, hoping that an established organization would promote the cause of labor rights for all workers. In October 1880, he resigned his position as assistant secretary of the Greenback Labor Party, accusing the Republican Party of manipulating his organization. A decade later, he joined the American Federation of Labor to continue his work on behalf of the common laborer.[39]

Throughout his short postwar career, Lum wrote countless articles and pamphlets on the subject of anarchism and its role in the American labor movement. After the Haymarket trials, he made his most important contribution to anarchy literature in a pamphlet entitled *Concise History of the Great Trial of the Chicago Anarchists*. The treatise attacked the prosecution's case and became the leading basis of claims for clemency and acquittal for the accused. A jury had convicted seven men of bombing a labor rally in Chicago's Haymarket district in the spring of 1886. Seven policemen died in the blast. The subsequent trial and appeals for clemency captivated the nation that summer. Appeals were entertained throughout the fall. In November 1886, the Illinois governor issued a stay of execution, and for an entire year, defenders tendered one appeal after another. All were heard and rejected, all the way up to the U.S. Supreme Court. With the end of the appeal process, four of the accused were executed on November 11, 1887. Governor Richard J. Olgesby commuted two men's sentences to life in prison. The seventh defendant, Louis Lingg, committed suicide in his cell, cheating the hangman. For years, many believed that the police had assassinated Lingg. Later, in a letter found after his death, Dyer Lum wrote that he had smuggled a cigar to Lingg that had a fulminating cap inside; when lit, it killed Lingg instantly. According to another version of the story, Lingg bit down on the cap, and it exploded in his mouth. Supposedly, Lum knew the identity of the real bomber and took the information to his grave.[40]

In 1875, Lum left his wife of sixteen years and took up with a fellow anarchist, Voltairine de Cleyre, who, like Lum, believed that causes greater than the self were critical to the salvation of the "sacredness of principles." She and Lum believed that the self, or the ego, had to be sublimated for the good of society. Their views consisted of a strange brew of individualism and communism. On April 5, 1893, three months before Governor John P. Altgeld pardoned the executed and incarcerated conspirators, passersby found Lum dead in front of the Summit Hotel at 31 Mott Street in Manhattan. Voltairine insisted he died a suicide, but the official death certificate, dated June 9, gave his cause of death as "fatty degeneration of the heart." In the end, his attempt to meld the two versions of anarchism failed because they were genetically incompatible. Initially labeled as an anarchist, he might more properly be considered an early labor organizer.[41]

During the war, John Kidder's good friend Charles Dean spent time in and out of Union hospitals. Ultimately, he could no longer hide in the bureaucracy. The medical machinery eventually could not cover his "absence without leave," and officials charged him with desertion, an accusation he never had expunged from his record. Even Kidder became a victim of the system after being wounded in the Overland campaign and returned home to recuperate. His medical leave proved insufficient for a full recovery. Through a miscommunication, authorities came dangerously close to charging him with desertion before they assigned him to the Confederate prison camp at Elmira. His intimates in Washington were undoubtedly helpful in clearing his record.

Losing his finger during the battle of the Wilderness, Pvt. Nathan Manzer of Company G became another casualty of the medical bureaucracy during the war. Manzer's doctors first sent him to Campbell Hospital in Washington and from there to his home in Middlefield to recover. When typhoid fever further complicated his rehabilitation at his brother's house in Middlefield, his furlough ran out, and he never returned to his regiment. The attending doctor, E. B. Warren of Elbridge, New York, erroneously reported that he treated Manzer in 1863, not 1864. According to Manzer, Warren's error was the beginning and end of his tribulations because the dates did not correspond to his record in Washington. Compounding his problems, when the war ended, Manzer saw no need to report for a formal discharge and the proper mustering-out procedure. The regiment carried him as a deserter. After the war, he settled in Los Angeles.

For twenty years, Manzer tried to clear his name and prove his loyalty, but more important, he wanted a pension. For years, he petitioned the pension office; for years, the government denied his pleas. He turned to his congressman, William D. Stephenson of Los Angeles, and his senator, Harry S. New, who pledged to help. In May 1913, two months before he died, Manzer wrote directly to President Woodrow Wilson; his daughters wrote to Mrs. Wilson. The year before, Manzer had written a plaintive letter to the 121st's secretary, Cyrus Westcott, who asked members of the association to help Manzer; at seventy-five years of age, Manzer remarked that he could not "possibly be a burden on the Government for a very long period." He never received his pension. Eight years later, led by Stephenson and New, Congress passed a private bill that finally cleared him. The bill became official on February 9, 1921, and Manzer received his honorable discharge. Unfortunately, Manzer had been dead for eight years at that point, and the bill did not include authorization for his wife to petition the government for a widow's pension. Furthermore, the army refused to drop the charge of desertion, claiming that the private bill did not authorize it. His wife began the process once again. The following September, she won a $30-per-month pension for life.[42]

Many of the veterans of the 121st scattered, making a determination of the oldest surviving member nearly impossible. Although their deaths are recorded somewhere, many of their birth dates remained in question, often being off by a year or two at most.

Peter Simmons of Roseboom passed away a few months before his ninety-fourth birthday, on May 31, 1930. He suffered from dementia; from the evidence presented by pension inspectors, he would have been diagnosed with Alzheimer's disease today. An inspector visited Simmons a year before he died. He could not remember his wife's name or his age. His immobility prevented him from using the toilet and from moving from room to room. He took his simple meals of bread and milk alone, in a large first-floor front room of his house, attended by his daughter and granddaughter. His caretakers left Simmons in the house alone only when he "stopped smoking and using matches."

Essentially, he spent the remainder of his life in the same room. The Ottman Funeral Home in Cherry Valley handled the arrangements. It billed the family $273 for its services.[43]

Wounded during the Wilderness campaign, Daniel Harris of Edmeston had enlisted at age twenty-two. He was ninety-seven when he died in Delhi, Otsego County, in 1936. Harris, Henry Cadwell, and Henry Wood were three of the oldest survivors of the regiment. Cadwell and Wood kept up a correspondence in their final years. Henry Wood outlived three wives and probably survived the entire regiment. His third wife, Anna E., whom he married at age seventy-eight, died in 1923. Henry died in Los Angeles on June 13, 1937.[44]

Sometime before 1934 by Henry Cadwell's estimate, he and Wood were the only two left from the regiment. According to Wood, Cadwell "passed away soon after writing this information to me." Drummer boy Henry Wood wrote his memoirs in 1934—nearly seventy years after the war ended. "So far as I know," he stated, "there is not one of the regiment alive except myself." He had survived all the major battles, heat prostration, near drowning, and exhausting marches. In the fall of 1865, he returned to an active social life as he renewed old friendships. That September, he turned twenty, and the next month, he returned to school. One year later, he married Lida Jordan in Cooperstown and settled on a farm in Middlefield. They raised nine children; the last was named Emory Upton Wood. When the farm went under in 1885, he and Lida were forced to move to Kearney, Nebraska, where they lived with their son Fred. They took jobs as cleaning people in a local hotel, working for 40 cents and 30 cents an hour, respectively. Henry became an evangelical minister in his later years. Lida died in Kearney in 1911, and Henry remarried at Hastings, Nebraska, the following year. His brother John died at age fifty in November 1894.[45]

John Lovejoy returned to Roseboom, married his cousin, Cynthia, and named his firstborn Upton. His brother Allen, who had also joined the 121st, spent much of his military life in a hospital or on detached leave in Indiana. At one time, both Lovejoys were in the same hospital at the same time. During the war, John found religion and became a strong temperance advocate. After the war, he became a regular in the 121st's Regimental Association and served as the group's secretary and treasurer. He held the association together during its fund-raising campaign for the Gettysburg Monument.

Two enlisted men in the 121st became general officers in the U.S. Army. George Pennington Borden, born in Fort Wayne, Indiana, in 1844, attended Fairfield Academy and eventually enlisted with the 121st, joining Company C in July 1862. He remained with the regiment only a little more than thirteen months. He left active duty in October 1863 to accept an appointment to West Point. After the war, he went into the Regular Army and rose to the rank of brigadier general before he retired in 1907. He passed away in 1925. The other brigadier was Morris Cooper Foote. Once the war ended, he decided to remain in the service and accepted a commission as a second lieutenant in the 9th U.S. Infantry, Regular Army. He retired in 1903 and died two years later in Geneva, Switzerland.

After the war, former chaplain John Sage joined the weather service. Nineteen-year-old private Delmar Rial Lowell, who lost his right arm at Sailor's Creek, rejoined the army as a chaplain. He attended a Methodist seminary, which ordained him soon after the war ended. He served as the U.S. Army's chaplain from his nomination at age forty-five by the U.S. Senate in 1890 until September 1897. He held the distinction of being the youngest chaplain of the army since the war.[46]

By 1937, all the men from the 121st had passed from the scene. Their story remains incomplete. But the foregoing observations are probably the closest anyone can reasonably and honestly reach in understanding this group of men and the families who shared their world. After the war was over, some merely resumed their lives as they had left them. Others achieved loftier objectives. According to James Cronkite, they all returned from the war with a greater appreciation of what it meant to be an American citizen. Few in the 121st, however, were able to capitalize on the expansion of the American economy or enjoy the fruits of its growth. Most remained the backbone of the national trend: small businessmen and farmers committed to their villages and towns. Those towns and villages in upstate New York sent them forth on their grand, mid-nineteenth-century adventure. They risked everything and were promised only a continuation of a unified country—if they won their battles. They fervently believed they could accomplish that goal.

Acronyms

The following acronyms are used in the notes and bibliography.

ADCWRT   Abner Doubleday Civil War Round Table, Milford, N.Y.
BUL   Binghamton University Library, Binghamton, N.Y.
CHL   Clarke Historical Library, Central Michigan University, Mt. Pleasant, Mich.
CUL   Cornell University Library, Ithaca, N.Y.
CVHA   Cherry Valley Historical Association, Cherry Valley, N.Y.
CWTI   *Civil War Times Illustrated*
DCL   Dartmouth College Library, Dartmouth College, Dartmouth, N.H.
ETSU   East Tennessee State University, Johnson City, Tenn.
F&SNMP   Fredericksburg and Spotsylvania National Military Park,
           Fredericksburg, Va.
GFLG   Gilbertsville Free Library, Gilbertsville, N.Y.
GNMP   Gettysburg National Military Park, Gettysburg, Pa.
HCA   Hamilton College Archives, Clinton, N.Y.
HCHS   Herkimer County Historical Society, Herkimer, N.Y.
HCWRT   Harrisburg Civil War Round Table, Harrisburg, Pa.
HLO   Holland Land Office, Batavia, N.Y.
IHS   Indiana Historical Society, Indianapolis, Ind.
ISL   Indiana State Library, Indianapolis, Ind.
LHC/GFL   Local History Collection, Gilbertsville Free Library, Gilbertsville, N.Y.
MHSM   Military Historical Society of Massachusetts, Boston
           University, Boston, Mass.
MOLLUS   Military Order of the Loyal Legion of the United States
NARA   National Archives and Records Administration, Washington, D.C.
N-YHS   New-York Historical Society, New York, N.Y.
NYSAG   New York State Attorney General's Office, Albany, N.Y.
NYSA-GAR   New York State Archives—Grand Army of the Republic, Albany, N.Y.
NYSHA   New York State Historical Association, Cooperstown, N.Y.
NYSL   New York State Library
NYSL/A   New York State Library Archives, Albany, N.Y.
NYSMM   New York State Military Museum, Saratoga Springs, N.Y.
OHA   Onondaga Historical Association, Syracuse, N.Y.
OR   *The War of the Rebellion: A Compilation of the Official Records of the
           Union and Confederate Armies*
RHFLUM   Raymond H. Fogler Library, University of Maine, Orono, Me.

SC	Special Collections
SHS	Schenectady Historical Society, Schenectady, N.Y.
SUL	Syracuse University Library, Syracuse, N.Y.
SUNY	State University of New York, Binghamton, N.Y.
UAL	University of Arkansas Library, Fayetteville, Ark.
USAGO	United States Adjutant General's Office, Washington
USAMHI	U.S. Army Military History Institute, Carlisle, Pa.
USMA	U.S. Military Academy, Archives and Special Collections, West Point, N.Y.
WFCHS/THL	Winchester-Frederick County Historical Society/ The Handley Library, Winchester, Va.
WLC	William L. Clements Library, University of Michigan, Ann Arbor, Mich.

Notes

Preface and Acknowledgments

1. George Teel, letters, to his wife, April 23, 1864.

Chapter 1. Congressman Franchot Recruits a Regiment

1. James H. Clark, "At Their Country's Call," *Otsego Republican,* February 22, 1893.

2. James Fenimore Cooper, *The Deerslayer* (Rutland, Vt.: Charles E. Tuttle, 1997), 29; James Fenimore Cooper, "The Chronicles of Cooperstown," in *A History of Cooperstown* (Cooperstown, N.Y.: Freeman's Journal, 1929), 42–43; *Otsego Republican,* June 29, 1892.

3. *Otsego Republican,* July 12, 1876.

4. F. W. Beers, *History of Herkimer County, N. Y. with Illustrations Descriptive of Scenery, Private Residences . . . and Portraits of Old Pioneers and Prominent Residents* (New York: F. W. Beers, 1878), 235.

5. George Washington, letter to Marquis de Chastellux, from Princeton, October 12, 1783, cited in Cooper, "Chronicles," 5; Lyman H. Butterfield, "Cooper's Inheritance: The Otsego Country and Its Founders," Papers from the 1951 James Fenimore Cooper Conference, Cooperstown, N.Y., "James Fenimore Cooper—A Re-appraisal," in *New York History* 35, no. 4 (October 1954): 374–411, available at http://external.oneonta.edu/cooper/articles/nyhistory/1954nyhistory-butterfield.html.

6. Beers, *History,* 215; Butterfield, "Cooper's Inheritance," 9.

7. "A Brief History of Herkimer County," available at http://www.rootsweb.ancestry.com/~nyherkim/, accessed on May 1, 2003; "Early Herkimer County History," available at http://www.hopefarm.com/herkimny.htm, accessed on September 19, 2008; 1860 U.S. Census; Beers, *History,* 67, 127, and 137; J. H. French, *Gazetteer of the State of New York Embracing a Comprehensive View of the Geography, Geology, and General History of the State, and a Complete History and Description of Every County, City, Town, Village and Locality* (Syracuse, N.Y.: R. P. Smith, 1860), 150; Sylvea Hollis, "'The Black Man Almost Has Disappeared from Our Country': African American Workers in Cooperstown, New York, 1860–1890," *New York History* 88, no. 1 (2007): 13; John Sawyer, *History of Cherry Valley from 1740 to 1898* (Cherry Valley, N.Y.: Gazette Printers, 1898), 70–71 and 120–121.

8. Hamilton Hurd, *History of Otsego County New York with Illustrations and Biographical Sketches of Some of Its Prominent Men and Pioneers* (Philadelphia: Everts and Fariss, 1878), 23; French, *Gazetteer*, 39, 340–350, and 530–539.

9. Susan Fenimore Cooper, *Rural Hours*, 130, 140–143, 254–255, cited in Alan Taylor, *William Cooper's Town: Power and Persuasion on the Frontier of the Early American Republic* (New York: Alfred A. Knopf, 1995), 396–405.

10. Sawyer, *History of Cherry Valley*, 120.

11. Stewart Mitchell, *Horatio Seymour of New York* (Cambridge, Mass.: Harvard University Press, 1938), 359.

12. Hurd, *History*, 280–282; Nicholas Fox Weber, *The Clarks of Cooperstown* (New York: Alfred A. Knopf, 2007), 18–27 and 33–34.

13. 1860 U.S. Census; *Herkimer County Journal*, February 21, 1861.

14. *Herkimer Democrat*, January 6, 1864, and January 22, 1862; George A. Hardin and Frank H. Willard, *History of Herkimer County, New York* (Syracuse, N.Y.: D. Mason, 1893), 240; George W. Smith, "Newspapers of Herkimer County," in Arthur T. Smith, comp., *Papers Read before the Herkimer County Historical Society during the Years 1896, 1897 and 1898* (Herkimer, N.Y.: Citizens Publishing, 1899), 1:63–75. See a portion of the running feud described in *Freeman's Journal*, August 8, 1862; Cooper, "Chronicles," 45.

15. Daniel Sickles, "Military Affairs in New York, 1861–1865," in *The Union Army: A History of Military Affairs in the Loyal States, 1861–1865—Records of the Regiments in the Union Army—Cyclopedia of Battles—Memoirs of Commanders and Soldiers*, vol. 2, *New York, Maryland, West Virginia and Ohio* (Wilmington, N.C.: Broadfoot Publishing, 1998), 19–20, 21; Thomas Harrold, "Governor Edward Denison Morgan and the Recruitment of the Union Army in New York State," 4–5, available at http://www.albany.edu/nystatehistory/44/gov_recruit.html; Harold Holzer and Hans L. Trefousse, *The Union Preserved: A Guide to the Civil War Records in the New York State Archives* (New York: Fordham University Press and New York State Archives Partnership Trust, 1999), 2–3; Marion H. Brophy, "The Town of Otsego: Home Front, 1861–1865, Compiled from the *Freeman's Journal* and Otsego Town Records," 2, available at http://www.rootsweb.com/~nyotsego/cwotsego.htm; *Freeman's Journal*, May 3 and 10, 1861.

16. *Freeman's Journal*, June 11 and 17, 1861.

17. Martha S. Magill and Bill McKerrow, "Newport, Herkimer County, New York in the Civil War," in *A Glimpse in Passing—Newport, NY, 1791–1991*, Newport Historical Society, 1, available at http://Herkimer.nygenweb.net/Norway/nordic.html; Beverly Crim and Martha S. Magill, "Profile and History of Herkimer County, NY," in *The Gazetteer and Business Directory of Herkimer County, N.Y. 1869–70*, 9, available at http://Herkimer.nygenweb.net/Norway/nordir.html; *Freeman's Journal*, July 25 and August 2, 9, and 16, 1861; Beers, *History*, 81, 84, and 85.

18. *Freeman's Journal*, October 4, 1861.

19. Butterfield, "Cooper's Inheritance," 11; "Franchot, Richard, 1816–1875," in U.S. Congress, ed., *Biographical Directory of the American Congress, 1774–1949* (Washington, D.C.: Government Printing Office, 1950), 1179.

20. *Freeman's Journal*, May 3, 1861.

21. *Freeman's Journal*, May 17, August 16, and September 20, 1861.

22. *Freeman's Journal*, October 4, 11, and 25, 1861.

23. *Cherry Valley Gazette*, January 15, 1862; *Freeman's Journal*, November 22 and 29, 1861; Abram P. Smith, *History of the Seventy-sixth Regiment New York Volunteers, What It Indured and Accomplished, Containing Descriptions of Its Twenty-five Battles, Its Marches, Its Camp and Bivouac Scenes . . .* (Syracuse, N.Y.: Truair, Smith and Miles, 1867), quoted on 76th New York State Volunteer Regiment homepage, available at http://www.bpmlegal.com/76NY/76shaulj.html; also Hurd, *History*, 328.

24. *Freeman's Journal*, November 1, 1861.

25. James A. Rawley, *Edward D. Morgan, 1811–1883: Merchant in Politics* (New York: Columbia University Press, 1955), 167–168; *Freeman's Journal*, July 11, 1862.

26. NYSAG, *Annual Report of the Adjutant General of the State of New York* (Albany, N.Y.: Comstock and Cassidy, 1863), 10–11 (hereafter cited as NYSAG, *Annual Report 1863*); Lincoln's words are also in the *Herkimer County Journal*, July 3, 1862, and Roy Basler, ed., *The Collected Works of Abraham Lincoln* (New Brunswick, N.J.: Rutgers University Press, 1953), 5:297. Lincoln quote is from William B. Hesseltine, *Lincoln and the War Governors* (New York: Alfred A. Knopf, 1948), 200. *Freeman's Journal*, July 4, 1862; NYSAG, *Annual Report 1863*, 10. See Sidney David Brummer, *Political History of New York State during the Period of the Civil War*, vol. 39, pt. 2, *Studies in History, Economics, and Public Law* (New York: Columbia University Press, 1911), 208.

27. Holzer and Trefousse, *Union Preserved*, 3–4; *Herkimer County Journal*, July 10, 1862; *Otsego Republican*, July 26, 1862. All the papers carried Morgan's proclamation, General Order 52, July 7, 1862. Quotes here are from *Freeman's Journal*, July 18, 1862.

28. NYSAG, *Annual Report 1863*, 11. Morgan's hand in recruiting and maintaining "states' rights" was heavy but even. See Harrold, "Governor Edward Denison Morgan," 1–8. *Freeman's Journal*, July 18, 1862; "Enrollment of Persons Liable to Military Duty," Sheriff's copies, Otsego County, NYSHA Research Library, Cooperstown, N.Y.

29. George B. McClellan, Letter to Nathaniel S. Berry, Governor of New Hampshire, July 15, 1862, in Edward W. Sears, ed., *The Civil War Papers of George B. McClellan: Selected Correspondence, 1860–1865* (New York: Da Capo Press, 1992), 359–360.

30. *Freeman's Journal*, July 11 and 25 and August 1, 1862; *Herkimer Democrat*, July 9, 1862; Mather Cleveland, "Diary (Excerpts) of Andrew Adrian Mather, Sheriff of Otsego County, 1861–1863," typed manuscript, entry of July 10, 1862, Manuscript Division, NYSHA Library. Hereafter cited as Mather, "Diary." Despite its call for new regiments, the *Journal* continued to advocate filling the old regiments, reprinting articles from the *New York Times*, the *New York Tribune*, and the *New York Commercial Advertiser*.

31. Beers, *History*, 81; Hesseltine, *Lincoln and the War Governors*, 166; *Albany Atlas Argus*, August 8, 1862; *Freeman's Journal*, August 15, 1862; "The Call to Arms! How to Escape the Draft!" broadside, August 16, 1862, Oswego, N.Y., Manuscript Division, NYSL, Albany. For a complete understanding of the bounty system, the draft, and related issues, see James W. Geary, *We Need Men: The Union Draft in the Civil War* (DeKalb: Northern Illinois University Press, 1991), esp. 1–40.

32. *Herkimer Democrat*, July 16, 1862; *Otsego Republican*, July 26, 1862.

33. *Freeman's Journal*, July 25, 1862; *Herkimer County Journal*, July 17 and 24, 1862; *Herkimer Democrat*, July 23, 1862; "Circular, Cooperstown, N.Y.," dated July 19, 1862, Manuscript Division, NYSHA Library (hereafter cited as NYSHA, "Circular").

34. NYSAG, Special Order No. 349, "Historical Notes on New York Regiments," NYSL,

Albany, 301 (hereafter cited as NYSAG, "Notes"); *Herkimer Democrat*, July 23, 1862; *Cherry Valley Gazette*, July 7, 1862.

35. *Freeman's Journal*, August 8, 15, and 22, 1862; *Otsego Republican*, July 26, 1862; *Cherry Valley Gazette*, July 7, 1862; "Campbell, William W.," in U.S. Congress, ed., *Biographical Directory of the American Congress, 1774–1949* (Washington, D.C.: Government Printing Office, 1950), 944; Douglas Campbell, letter to Cleaveland, August 7, 1864, Campbell-Mumford Papers, Manuscripts Department, N-YHS.

36. *Herkimer County Journal*, August 28, 1862; *Herkimer Democrat*, July 30 and August 6, 1862. The banks in Herkimer County bought the county's bonds as follows: Herkimer County Bank, $9,000; Mohawk Valley Bank, $4,500; Ilion Bank and Winfield Bank, $2,000 each; Frankfort Bank, Newport Bank, and Bollinger Bank, $2,500 each; see *Herkimer County Journal*, July 17, 1862.

37. Silas W. Burt, *My Memoirs of the Military History of the State of New York during the War for the Union, 1861–1865* (Albany, N.Y.: J. B. Lyon, 1902), 98. Also NYSAG, *Annual Report 1863*, 11–12; NYSAG, "Notes," 305; NYSAG, *Annual Report 1863*, 42; "Descriptive List and Account of Pay and Clothing of Corporal Theo. H. Briggs," November 7, 1864, Manuscript Division, NYSHA Library; *Herkimer County Journal*, July 24, 1862.

38. "Directions for Procuring State Bounty," State of New York, Paymaster General's Office, Administration Papers, NYSL/A.

39. *Freeman's Journal*, July 25, 1862; *Cherry Valley Gazette*, July 7, 1862; *Otsego Republican*, July 24, 1862.

40. David P. Krutz, *Distant Drums: Herkimer County, New York in the War of the Rebellion* (Utica, N.Y.: North Country Books, 1997), 49. The *Herkimer Democrat* reported on August 6 that "375 to 400" had been enrolled and had gathered at Camp Schuyler. *Herkimer Democrat*, August 1, 1862; *Otsego Republican*, August 2, 1862; Mather, "Diary," August 4, 1862.

41. Ingraham P. Smith, Letters, letter to his mother, from Middlefield, August 3, 1862, Binghamton University Library, State University of New York Special Collections and Preservation Division, SUNY (hereafter cited as Smith, Letters).

42. Delavan Bates, "Worcester's Quota in the 121st N.Y. Volunteers" and "Petersburg," *Otsego Republican*, February 13 and August 7, 1895; *Cherry Valley Gazette*, July 7, 1862.

Chapter 2. "The Nursery of Soldiers": The Men and Boys from Herkimer and Otsego Counties

1. Turner's obituary, *Otsego Republican*, March 23, 1867; War Department, Adjutant General's Office, General Orders No. 95, August 2, 1862.

2. *Freeman's Journal*, August 8, 1862.

3. Ibid., September 5 and 12 and October 31, 1862, February 6 and August 7, 1863.

4. *Cherry Valley Gazette*, June 30, 1862.

5. *Freeman's Journal*, August 15 and 22 and September 5, 1862; *Oneonta Herald*, September 10, 1862; John Lovejoy, letters to his cousin Cynthia, January 16 and August 9, 1864, private collection; Mather, "Diary," August 4, 8, 14, and 19, 1862.

6. NARA, Pension Records; Francis M. Carran, Letters, private collection; Beers, *Herkimer*, 267.

7. Douglas Campbell, letter to Cleaveland Campbell, August 7, 1864, in the Campbell-Mumford Papers, Manuscripts Department, N-YHS.

8. Henry Walker, Letters, letter to his brother Charles, February 15, 1863, Department of Special Collections, SUL (hereafter cited as Walker, Letters). *Otsego Republican*, September 15, 1897; *1908 Reunion Report*, Dewey Reminiscences, 32; *Cherry Valley Gazette*, July 30, 1862; Douglas Campbell, speech, printed in *Otsego Republican*, October 10, 1878.

9. Dewitt Clinton Beckwith, "Three Years with the Colors of a Fighting Regiment in the Army of the Potomac, by a Private Soldier," *Herkimer Democrat*, July 5, 1893, in fifty-two installments from July 5, 1893, to July 4, 1894. Also NARA, Beckwith Pension Records.

10. French, *Gazetteer*, 125–134.

11. Adam Clarke Rice, *The Letters and Writings of the Late Lieutenant Adam Clarke Rice of the 121st Regiment, N.Y. Volunteers*, compiled and prepared by Charles E. Rice (Little Falls, N.Y.: Journal and Courier Book and Printing Press, 1864), 5.

12. William Remmel Papers, letters and papers, 1862–1924, Manuscript Collection 597, Folders 1 and 13, Special Collections, UAL (hereafter cited as Remmel, Papers). Remmel's letters are replete with mentions of money or the lack of it. In his letter from New York as the train was leaving from Herkimer and Little Falls, he mentions giving more than $75 to different friends to be passed on to his parents; *1910 Reunion Report*, Ada Remmel Benson, letter to C. J. Westcott, August 4, 1910, 14.

13. Rice, *Letters*, 3–5.

14. Samuel Burdett Kelley Papers, March 20 and 26 and April 30, 1860, and March 10, 1861, File 303 2 / 8, Manuscript Division, NYSHA Research Library (hereafter cited as Kelley, Papers).

15. Kelley, Papers, letter to his father, March 10, 1861.

16. NYSAG, February 1, 1864, vol. 1, 7.

17. Kelley, Papers, letter to his father, September 9, 1861, and letter to his sister, Sylvina, October 10, 1861; *Otsego Republican*, September 1, 1862.

18. Beckwith, "Three Years with the Colors," July 5, 12, 19, and 26, 1893.

19. *Otsego Republican*, February 22, 1893.

20. "Class of 1863," *Hamilton Literary Monthly* 2, no. 5 (January 1868): 128. Also Delta Kappa Epsilon Memorial Eulogy, Clinton, N.Y., May 26, 1864. Undated obituary written by Professor Edward North, letter quoted is from his uncle, Henry A. Abbott to Professor Edward North, Hamilton College, June 24, 1864. HCA; NYSAG, 26.

21. *Biographical Review: This Volume Contains Biographical Sketches of the Leading Citizens of Otsego County, New York* (Boston: Biographical Review Publishing, 1893), 467–468. Also Elsie L. Hodgins, Edna L. Barr, and Della S. Kidder, "Kidder Family History: The Story of William Samuel and Mary Elizabeth Kidder," typescript copy, Kidder Papers, private collection; James M. Greiner, *Subdued by the Sword: A Line Officer in the 121st New York Volunteers* (Albany: State University of New York Press, 2003), 1–7; other biographical information on Kidder is in *Otsego Republican*, April 15, 1896.

22. Burt, *My Memoirs*, 56, and E. D. Morgan to S. Humphreys, August 28, 1862, Morgan Papers, NYSL, cited in Rawley, *Morgan*, 162–163, and French, *Gazetteer*, 43–44. According to the state constitution, "Militia officers shall be chosen or appointed, as follows: Captains, subalterns, and non-commissioned officers shall be chosen by the written votes of the members of their respective companies; field officers of regiments and separate

battalions, by the written votes of the commissioned officers of the respective regiments and separate battalions; brigadier generals and brigade inspector, by the field officers of their respective brigades; major generals, brigadier generals, and commanding officers of regiments or separate battalions shall appoint the staff officers to their respective divisions, brigades, regiments, or separate battalions"; *New York State Constitution*, 1822, Article IV, Section 1, and Article XI, Section 2, cited in French, *Gazetteer*, 44.

23. *Freeman's Journal*, July 25, 1862; Isaac O. Best, *History of the 121st New York State Infantry* (Chicago: James H. Smith, 1921), 3; James Cronkite, "Otsego in the Rebellion: The 121st Regiment," in D. Hamilton Hurd, *History of Otsego County, New York* (Philadelphia: Everts and Fariss, 1878), 64.

24. *Herkimer Democrat*, July 23, 1862; Harrold, "Governor Edward Denison Morgan," 5.

25. General Head Quarters, State–New York, Adjutant General's Office, *Special Orders No. 463, Dated August 21, 1862*, and *Special Orders No. 423, Dated August 11, 1862*, SC [Special Collections] 17551, U.S. Army, 121st N.Y. Infantry, Folder 2, NYSL (hereafter cited as SC 17551, NYSL); *Herkimer County Journal*, August 28, 1862. The *Chenango Telegraph* congratulated Sage on his humble gesture and his elevation to chaplain, reported in *Oneonta Herald*, September 10, 1862.

26. NYSAG, *Annual Report, 1893–1905*, 43 vols. (Albany, N.Y.: James B. Lyon, 1894), 46:63 (hereafter cited as NYSAG, *Annual Report, 1893–1905*). Henry Roback, *The Veteran Volunteers of Herkimer and Otsego Counties in the War of the Rebellion Being a History of the 152nd N.Y. Volunteers* (Little Falls, N.Y.: Press of L. C. Childs and Son, 1888), 13–14. Also NYSAG, *Annual Report, 1863*, 742–745.

27. In the autumn of 1863, Capt. John Kidder wrote his wife in great detail about how the 121st had "the post of honor. We are on the extreme right of the line." Kidder, Letters, letters to his wife, October 16, 1863.

28. *Report of the Thirty-fourth Annual Reunion of the 121st New York Volunteers, Held at Schuyler Lake, N.Y., August 10, 1910*, speech by S. J. Galpin to the delegates, 30. (All reunion reports hereafter cited as *Reunion Report*, [date].)

29. *Oneonta Herald*, August 6, 1862; Beers, *History*, 224, 243; Clinton Moon obituary, *Herkimer Democrat*, May 18, 1892.

30. *Freeman's Journal*, August 1, 1862; *Otsego Republican*, September 1, 1862; Douglas Campbell, speech as printed in *Otsego Republican*, October 10, 1878.

31. The *Oneonta Herald*, August 8, 1862, mentioned Wendell's efforts to raise a company for "Franchot's Regiment" and used the occasion to call for all patriotic citizens to rise to the defense of their country; see *Reunion Report, 1909*, Nelson Wendell, letter (to his brother?), February 20, 1863, 14.

32. *Biographical Review*, 416. John de Peyster Douw was Richard Franchot's nephew; see Nicholas Van Vranken Franchot, *Stanislas Pascal Franchot Arrives: A Pageant by Charles Pascal Franchot Including a List of Descendants of Stanislas Pascal Franchot (to December 1, 1940)* (New York: Published privately by Nicholas Van Vranken Franchot, 1940), 82. See also Rufus W. Clark, *The Heroes of Albany: A Memorial of the Patriot-Martyrs of the City and County of Albany . . .* (Albany, N.Y.: John D. Brooks, Publisher, 1866), 384–394.

33. *Biographical Review*, 164.

34. *Special Orders No. 463* in SC 17551, NYSL. Also Frederick Phisterer, *New York in the War of the Rebellion, 1861–1865,* 3rd ed. (Albany, N.Y.: J. B. Lyon, 1912), 3423. "Long Island and New York—Civil War Information," available at http://longislandgeneology.com/civilwar.html; *Freeman's Journal,* October 3, 1862.

35. *Freeman's Journal,* July 25, 1862.

36. "Contract for Land at Camp Schuyler," in Best, *121st,* 2–3. Howard Thomas, in *Boys in Blue from the Adirondack Foothills* (Prospect, N.Y.: Prospect Books, 1960), 94, asserts that the original training ground for the 121st was to be the County Fair Grounds in Herkimer, but there is no evidence for that claim. The contract was agreed to on July 25 but not dated until August 29, 1862. Burt, *My Memoirs,* 105 and 103; and *Oneonta Herald,* August 8, 1862. The *Herkimer Democrat,* August 6, 1862, reported the firm of Lowell, Prescott & Shull doing the "hotel business of Camp Schuyler."

37. *Herkimer County Journal,* August 14, 1862; Best, *121st,* 3.

38. *Cherry Valley Gazette,* August 27, 1862; *Otsego Republican,* September 1, 1862; *Cherry Valley Gazette,* August 9, 1862.

39. *Herkimer County Journal,* July 31, 1862; *Herkimer Democrat,* August 13, 1862; *Chenango Telegraph,* reported in *Oneonta Herald,* September 10, 1862.

40. *Freeman's Journal,* July 25, 1862; Henry Hilton Wood, cited in Mary Wallitt De Young, *Drummer Boy: Henry Hilton Wood and the Civil War* (Spencer City, Iowa: De Young Press, 1990), 6, 8. Also, there is a typewritten copy of Wood's wartime experiences entitled "Experiences during the Civil War" in the NYSMM, Saratoga, N.Y. (hereafter cited as Wood, "Experiences"); Kelley, Papers, letter to his father, August 17, 1862.

41. United States War Department, *The War of the Rebellion: A Compilation of the Official Records of the War of the Union and Confederate Armies* (Washington, D.C.: Government Printing Office, 1880–1901), 128 vols. (hereafter cited as *OR*), ser. 3, vol. 2, 210–211, General Orders No. 75, July 8, 1862.

42. Burt, *My Memoirs,* 108; NYSAG, "Notes," 306.

43. George Teel, Letters, August 29, 1862, private collection (hereafter cited as Teel, Letters); Remmel, Letters, letter to his parents, August 31, 1862; Delavan Bates, "Worcester's Quota in the 121st N.Y. Volunteers," *Otsego Republican,* February 13, 1895.

44. *OR,* ser. 3, vol. 2, 265, 268–269, 364, 385, 393, 406, 413, and 447.

45. Ibid., 496; *Cherry Valley Gazette,* August 27, 1862; Beckwith, "Three Years with the Colors," July 26, 1893.

46. NARA, Books, Special Order No. 423, August 11, 1862, and General Order No. 1, August 25, 1862; NYSAG, "Notes," n.p.; *Otsego Republican,* September 1, 1862.

47. *Herkimer County Journal,* August 28 and September 4, 1862; *Freeman's Journal,* August 22 and September 5, 1862; *Herkimer Democrat,* August 20 and September 3, 1862; *Oneonta Herald,* September 10, 1862. The *Democrat* and the *Herald* both identified the women as "Miss Nancy C. and Miss Nancy Rice."

48. Newspaper account from the files of the NYSMM and Veterans Research Center, NYS Division of Military and Naval Affairs, probably *Herkimer County Journal,* August 1862 (hereafter cited as NYSMM); Remmel, Letters, to his parents, August 31, 1862; Elinas D. Hills, Letters, to his mother and friends, August 31, 1862, private collection (hereafter cited as E. Hills, Letters); *Herkimer County Journal,* September 4, 1862; Samuel D. French, Let-

ters, to his sister, New York City, August 31, 1862, Manuscript Division, NYSHA (hereafter cited as French, Letters).

49. *Albany Journal*, in collections of the NYSMM. All accounts including the exchange of letters in the *Albany Journal* between the officers of the regiment and the captain of the steamer agree it was the *New World*. In his piece entitled "Otsego in the Rebellion" in Hurd's *History of Otsego County* (p. 64), James Cronkite claims it was the *Isaac Newton*. Also Teel, Letters, September 3, 1862; Adelbert Reed, Letters, letter to his parents and friends, September 4, 1862, private collection (hereafter cited as Reed, Letters).

50. Smith, Letters, to his mother from Fort Lincoln, September 5, 1862; Best, *121st*, 7; Delavan Hills, Letters, to his mother and friends, August 31, 1862, private collection (hereafter cited as D. Hills, Letters); Cronkite, *History*, 64.

51. D. Hills, Letters, to his friends, September 3, 1862; Smith, Letters, to his mother from Fort Lincoln, September 5, 1862; John J. Ingraham, *John J. Ingraham's Civil War Letters, 1862–1865* (Frankfort, N.Y.: Phoenix Printing, July 1990), to his father and mother, September 4, 1862, from Fort Lincoln; Andrew Mather, Letters, letter to his brother, September 5, 1862, Rauner Special Collections Library, Archives, Manuscripts, Rare Books, DCL, Hanover, N.H. (hereafter cited as Mather, Letters); Cronkite, *History*, 64; John Lovejoy, "Reminiscences," handwritten memoir in private collection, 2, 3. Ingraham referred to the attack on the 6th Massachusetts State Militia on April 19, 1861, by the citizens of Baltimore. Reed, Letters, to his parents and friends, September 4, 1862; Kelley, Papers, letter to his mother, September 5, 1862; Lyman Herdman, letter to the editor, *Cherry Valley Gazette*, October 15, 1862.

52. NARA, Old Military Records Division, "Regimental Books of the 121st Regiment New York Infantry," Records of the Adjutant General's Office, Record Group 94, Special Order No. 1, Camp Schuyler, August 26, 1862, 2, and General Order No. 1, August 26, 1862 (hereafter cited as NARA, Books).

53. Reed, Letters, to his father, April 25, 1864.

Chapter 3. Stumbling into War

1. *Herkimer County Journal*, September 4, 1862.

2. Lovejoy, "Reminiscences," 3; Cronkite, *History*; Delavan Bates, Letter to his father, September 5, 1862, in private collection (hereafter cited as Bates, Letters); Basler, *Lincoln*, 4:559; Teel, Letters, to his wife, September 3, 1862; French, Letters, September 4, 1862. Dr. Holt placed the arrival of the 121st in Washington on September 2, but all other accounts place it on the first of the month except for that of the official chronicler of the 121st, Isaac O. Best, who wrote that the troops arrived in boxcars on the third of the month; see Best, *121st*, 7.

3. NYSAG, *Rough Abstracts of Expenditures for Salaries and Ordnance, 1863–1866*, 122, 128, 134, 140, 146, 152, and 158, NYSL/A; New York State, *Annual Report of the Commissary General of the State of New York #66* (Albany, N.Y.: Comstock and Cassidy, Printers, 1863), 66 (hereafter cited as NYS, *CG Report 1863*); NYSAG, *Annual Report of the Adjutant General of the State of New York* (Albany, N.Y.: Comstock & Cassidy, Printers, 1863), 085 (hereafter cited as NYSAG, *Report 1863*); New York State, Adjutant General's Office, *Historical Note*

on *New York Regiments*, Manuscript Division, NYSL (hereafter cited as NYSL, *Historical Notes*); Cronkite, *History*, 65; Lovejoy, "Reminiscences," 4.

4. *OR*, ser. 3, vol. 2, 458.

5. *Albany Journal*, quoted in the *Herkimer Democrat*, December 31, 1862.

6. *OR*, ser. 3, vol. 2, 447–448 and 234; Basler, *Lincoln*, Letter to James W. Ripley, April 23, 1862, 4:196–197n.

7. Daniel M. Holt, "Copy of Letters Written by Daniel M. Holt, Assistant Surgeon 121st Regiment N.Y. Vols. 2d Brigade, 1st Division, 6th Corps, Army of the Potomac, to His Wife, while in the Service of the United States, from September 1st, 1862 to October 17th, 1864 at Which Time He Was Discharged from the Service Because of Physical Disability," Manuscript, 1867, HCHS, Herkimer, N.Y. (hereafter Holt, Letters).

8. Holt, Letters, to his wife, September 5, 1862; French, Letters, September 3, 4, and 11, 1862; Kelley, Papers, letter to his mother, September 5, 1862.

9. French, Letters, September 3, 1862; Teel, Letters, September 3, 1862; NYSAG, "Notes," n.p.; Beckwith, "Three Years with the Colors," July 26, 1893; *Herkimer Democrat*, September 17, 1862. Frederick E. Ford, Company C, sent regular reports back to the paper and probably provided this account. At first, the paper refused to identify him, saying only that "we have made arrangements with a young gentleman belonging to Captain Moon's company for a regular correspondence from the 121st regiment. He was one of the best students in the Fairfield Seminary, of good observation, and will furnish all that is of interest relating to the Regiment." Ford also provided accounts to the *Democrat*'s rival, the *Herkimer County Journal*. Mather, Letters, letter to his brother, September 5, 1862.

10. Thomas J. Goss's monograph, *The War within the Union High Command: Politics and Generalship during the Civil War* (Lawrence: University Press of Kansas, 2003), is an excellent argument destroying the stereotypes of political generals versus West Point professionals. Goss argues that in the end, political generals were more important to the success of Lincoln's plans in that they were able to see beyond the battlefield to the political, global implications of military strategy.

11. Galpin's wounding was reported in *Herkimer County Journal*, July 10, 1862; Ezra Stevens, *Early History of the Town of Milford and Other Parts of Otsego County from 1773 to 1903*, available at http://www.rootsweb.com/~nyotsego/histmil.html; *Otsego Republican*, June 12, 1895. At the beginning of 1863, Teel was hospitalized in Harewood Hospital in Washington, suffering from exposure and a lame right hip and leg. He asked that all of his correspondence be forwarded to his in-law, Lewis Cronkite, at the U.S. House of Representatives in Congress; Teel, Letters, to his wife, January 9, 1863, from Harewood Hospital; Delavan Bates, "Nebraska Correspondence," *Otsego Republican*, April 4, 1894.

12. Kidder, Letters, letter to his wife, October 4, 1862; Dean letter to the editor of the *Oneonta Herald*, n.d., cited in Greiner, *Subdued*, 14, in Jerry Reed Collection, Sharon Springs, N.Y.

13. *OR*, ser. 1, vol. 19, pt. 2, Special Order No. 3, Headquarters Washington, September 6, 1862, 197–198; French, Letters, September 11, 1862; NARA, Books, letter Colonel Upton to Lieutenant-Colonel O. D. Greene, AAG, Sixth Corps, November 8, 1862; Remmel, Letters, to his parents, September 14, 1862; Marshall Dye, undated letter to Martha, cited in Alan Sessarego, *Letters Home: A Collection of Original Civil War Soldiers' Letters* (Get-

tysburg, Pa.: Garden Spot Gifts, 1996) (hereafter cited as Dye, *Letters*); Kelley, Papers, letter to his mother, September 18, 1862; Remmel, Letters, to his parents, September 14, 1862.

14. Holt, Letters; also in James M. Greiner, Janet L. Coryell, and James R. Smither, eds., *A Surgeon's Civil War: The Letters and Diary of Daniel M. Holt, M.D.* (Kent, Ohio: Kent State University Press, 1994), 3 and 11. Holt, Letters, to his wife, September 16 and 28, 1862; Lovejoy, "Reminiscences," 4; French, Letters, to his sister, September 11, 1862; Albert Bailey, Letter, to his brother, October 21, 1862, Manuscript Division, NYSHA (hereafter cited as Bailey, Letters); French, Letters, October 5, 1862; John R. Sage, Letter to the editor, *Herkimer County Journal*, October 23, 1862; Edward Wales, Diary, October 31, 1862, Manuscript Division, NYSHA (hereafter cited as Wales, Diary).

15. Beckwith, "Three Years with the Colors," July 26, 1893; Best, *121st*, preface, 2; *Freeman's Journal*, July 24, 1879; Holt, Letters; French, Letters, Darnestown, Maryland, September 11, 1862; Special Orders #3, Headquarters, Washington, September 6, 1862, *OR*, ser. 1, vol. 19, pt. 2, 197–198; also Cronkite, *History*, 65.

16. New York Monuments Commission, *In Memoriam: Henry Warner Slocum, 1862–1894* (Albany, N.Y.: J. Lyon, Printers, 1904), 65–70.

17. Ezra J. Warner, *Generals in Blue: Lives of the Union Commanders* (Baton Rouge: Louisiana State Press, 1964), 451–453 and 23–24; Beckwith, "Three Years with the Colors," August 23, 1893. Both men survived the war; Slocum became a successful millionaire businessman in Brooklyn, and President Grant appointed Bartlett minister to Sweden in his administration. Bartlett eventually held a position for years in the newly invigorated U.S. Patent Office.

18. Beckwith, "Three Years with the Colors," July 26 and August 2 and 9, 1893; Lovejoy, "Reminiscences," 5; John Ripley Adams, *Memorial and Letters of Rev. John R. Adams, Chaplain of the Fifth Maine and the One Hundred and Twenty-first New York Regiments during the War of the Rebellion, Serving from the Beginning to Its Close*, privately printed (Cambridge, Massachusetts, University Press, 1890), to wife, September 14, 1862, 66 (hereafter cited as Adams, *Letters*); A. Reed, Letters, letter to his sister, October 12, 1862, emphasis added.

19. Delavan Bates, "Nebraska Correspondence," *Otsego Republican*, March 6, 1895; Circular Order, Headquarters, 2nd Brigade, Camp near Darnestown, Md., September 9, 1862, in author's collection; Lovejoy, "Reminiscences," 5 and 6.

20. Fred Ford, Letter to the editor, *Herkimer County Journal*, October 16, 1862.

21. Dye, *Letters*; Ingraham, *Letters*, to dear friend, September 22 and 23, 1862, near Williamsport, Md.; Paul Taylor, ed., *Give My Love to All Our Folks: Civil War and Post-war Letters of Clinton DeWitt Staring and Charles E. Staring of Herkimer County, New York* (Mancelona, Mich.: Deep Wood Press, 2007), letter of Charles Staring to his brother, October 30, 1862, 11 (hereafter cited as Staring, *Letters*).

22. Remmel, Letters, to his parents, September 14, 1862; Delavan Bates, "Emory Upton," "The 2nd Brigade, 1st Division, 6th Corps," *Otsego Republican*, December 6, 1893, and March 6, 1895; George Davis, to his wife, September 17, 1862, in author's collection.

23. *Otsego Republican*, September 15, 1897; Lester Murdock wounding, Series #B1706-00 GAR Records, Box 28, f 14, 121st New York Volunteers, NYSA-GAR; Rice, *Letters*, letter to his parents, September 15, 1862; Egbert Olcott, letter to his father Horatio, in the *Otsego Republican*, October 11, 1862. Clinton Beckwith wrote years later that Franchot was adamant that his green unit take the lead in the battle—"Make the charge and do anything

that brave men skilled in war could be asked or depended upon to do"; see Beckwith, "Three Years with the Colors," August 2, 1893.

24. Davis to his wife, September 17, 1862; Holt, Letters, to his wife, November 7, 1862; Teel, Letters, to Mary, September 10 and 21, 1862; Beckwith, "Three Years with the Colors," August 2, 1893; Ingraham, *Letters;* Reed, Letters, letter to his sister, September 17, near Burkettsville.

25. Ingraham, *Letters;* Reed, Letters, letter to his sister, September 17, near Burkettsville; Lovejoy, "Reminiscences," 7; Dye, *Letters;* Rice, *Letters,* to his parents, September 15, 1862; Wood, *Drummer Boy*, 25; Upton, Letters, to his sister, September 27, 1862, Holland Land Office, Batavia, N.Y. (hereafter cited as Upton, Letters).

26. Beckwith, "Three Years with the Colors," August 9, 1893; Captain Edwin Clark, letter dated October 1, 1862, in the *Cherry Valley Gazette,* October 15, 1862; Lyman Herdman, letter dated October 6, *Cherry Valley Gazette,* October 15, 1862; Holt, Letters, to his wife, September 16, 1862.

27. Teel, Letters, to his wife, Mary, September, 21, 1862; Lyman Herdman, letter dated October 6, *Cherry Valley Gazette,* October 15, 1862; *Herkimer Democrat*, September 17, 1862.

28. "Hardtack," letter to the editor, *Herkimer County Journal*, October 23, 1862; J. M. Smith, George Snell, and Joe Heath, letter to the editor, *Herkimer County Journal*, October 2, 1862; Mather, Letters, to his brother, October 13, 1862.

29. Bailey, Letter, letter to his brother, October 21, 1862.

30. Beckwith, "Three Years with the Colors," August 9 and 16, 1893.

31. Maria Porter Brace Kimball, *A Soldier-Doctor of Our Army: James P. Kimball, Late Colonel and Assistant Surgeon-General, U.S. Army* (Boston: Houghton Mifflin, 1917), 6.

32. Lyman Herdman, letter dated October 6, *Cherry Valley Gazette,* October 15, 1862.

33. Holt, Letters, "Introduction." Sgt. James Cronkite wrote, "Many strong constitutions were wrecked, and many brave soldiers, soldiers, stricken with fever and other diseases, lost their lives from exposure during the first week of service," in Best, *121st*, 14; Teel, Letters, to his wife, Mary, September 21, 1862, near Williamsport, Md.; Beckwith, "Three Years with the Colors," July 26, 1893; Lovejoy, "Reminiscences," 6.

34. *Herkimer County Journal*, August 14 and September 11, 1862; Holt, Letters, to wife, September 28, 1862; Kidder, Letters, letter to his wife, October 17, 1862; Cronkite, *History*, 65; Lovejoy, "Reminiscences," 8.

35. *Freeman's Journal*, August 1, 1862, and January 16, 1863; Holt, Letters, to his wife, September 28, 1862; Hurd, *History*, 217. See also Thomas, *Boys in Blue*, 121. Fred Ford, *Herkimer County Journal,* February 5, 1863. Franchot served in the Thirty-seventh Congress from the Nineteenth Congressional District. During the summer recess beginning July 17, 1862, he busily recruited the 121st. After he resigned as commander, Franchot rejoined Congress when its session began on December 1, 1862, and he remained there until it adjourned on March 3, 1863, when he retired from public service. See Phisterer, *New York,* 1:92.

36. *Cherry Valley Gazette,* October 8, 1862. William Remmel wrote his parents that "out of 1146 men that marched out of Camp Schuyler, there are only about 800 men fit for duty. About 250 men are sick. Out of that number, but one has died"; see Remmel, Letters, to his parents, October 8, 1862.

37. Holt, Letters, to his wife, from Bakersville, September 28, 1862.

38. Fred Ford, *Herkimer County Journal,* October 16, 1862; Jonathon Burrell, Letter to

his brother and sister, November 11 and 20, 1862; Beckwith, "Three Years with the Colors," August 23, 1893; Delavan Bates, "War Reminiscences," *Otsego Republican*, May 20, 1896.

39. *Herkimer Democrat*, August 27, 1862; Cronkite, *History*, 65; Phisterer, *New York*, 2273–2274; NYSAG, *Annual Report, 1893–1905*. Also see Phisterer, *New York*, 3430. Clark resigned to be married in Albany, to take over his father's business, and to attend to a civil lawsuit to which he had been a party; Clark, letter to Lieutenant Colonel M. T. McMahon, Adjutant General, Sixth Corps, March 21, 1863, with supporting materials, NARA, Pension Records.

40. NARA, Books, Special Order No. 2, October 2, 1862.

41. Ibid. Special Order No. 3, October 3, 1862; Beckwith, "Three Years with the Colors," August 16, 1863.

42. John F. L. Hartwell, letter to his wife, October 3, 1862, in Ann Hartwell Britton and Thomas J. Reed, eds., *To My Beloved Wife and Boy at Home: The Letters and Diaries of Orderly Sergeant John F. L. Hartwell* (Madison, N.J.: Fairleigh Dickinson University Press, 1997), 29 (hereafter cited as Hartwell, *Letters and Diary*); Ingraham, *Letters*, to Mary Green, October 9, 1862, Camp near Bakersville; Henry Walker, diary entry, October 3, 1862, NARA, Walker Pension Records.

43. Michael Musick, "The Little Regiment: Civil War Units and Commands," *Prologue* (National Archives publication) 27, no. 2 (Summer 1995); A. Reed, Letters, letter to his father, October 26, 1862.

44. NARA, Books, General Order No. 7, October 12, 1862; Bates, Letters, to his mother November 27, 1862, near Hagerstown, Md.; Teel, Letters, to his wife, September 27, 1862, in camp near Williamsport and camp near Bakersville, October 11, 1862.

45. NARA, Books, General Order No. 4, October 11, 1862; Adams, *Letters*, to wife, November 29, 1864, 183.

46. Beckwith, "Three Years with the Colors," August 16, 1863; NARA, Books, Clark to Wilson, October 2, 1862, Clark to Bartlett, October 2, 1862, Special Order No. 11, October 10, Special Order No. 12, October 12, 1862.

47. NARA, Books, Letter, Upton to Lieutenant-Colonel O. D. Greene, Assistant Adjutant General, Sixth Corps; Carran, Letters, to his brother, October 21, 1862; Henry Walker, diary entries, October 19 and 20, NARA, Walker Pension Records.

48. NARA, Charles H. Clark Military Records.

49. Bates, Letters, to his father, August 31, 1863; *Reunion Report, 1909*, Letter, John Sage to C. J. Westcott, August 19, 1909, 9–10.

50. Fred Ford, letter to the editor, *Herkimer County Journal*, October 9, 1862; Remmel, Letters, to his parents, November 15, 1862; Delavan Bates, "Nebraska Correspondence," *Otsego Republican*, April 25, 1894; Cronkite, *History*, 57; French, Letters, October 5, 1862; Wales, Diary, November 23, 27, and 30, 1862; Walker, Letters, to dear friends, March 1 and April 12, 1863.

51. *Freeman's Journal*, August 1, 1862; Beckwith, "Three Years with the Colors," August 23, 1893.

Chapter 4. Emory Upton Takes Command

1. Peter S. Michie, "Reminiscences of Cadet and Army Service," paper read October 4, 1893, in James Grant Wilson and Titus Munson Coan, MD, eds., *Personal Recollections*

of the War of the Rebellion: Addresses Delivered before the New York Commandery MOLLUS, 1883–1891 (New York: New York Commandery, 1891; Wilmington, N.C.: Broadfoot Publishing, 1992), 2:193, citing the 1992 edition.

2. Auspices of the American Council of Learned Societies, *Dictionary of American Biography* (New York: C. Scribner's Sons, 1928–1944), 10:128–129; NARA, Books, Special Order No. 17, October 25, 1862. Campbell's remarks were from a speech given at the regiment's second reunion in 1878 and are quoted in Peter S. Michie, *The Life and Letters of Emory Upton, Colonel of the Fourth Regiment of Artillery, and Brevet Major-General, U.S. Army* (New York: D. Appleton, 1885), 68. Campbell's speech is quoted in its entirety in *Otsego Republican*, October 10, 1878. Upton's request to his sister for a revolver and remarks on the coming war are from the Upton Papers, Holland Land Office Museum, Batavia, N.Y. (hereafter Upton, Papers), letter, April 19, 1861, and letters to his sister, April 25 and November 13, 1861.

3. Kidder, Letters, letter to his wife, October 17, 1862; Burt, *My Memoirs*, 105; *Freeman's Journal*, August 1, 1862; Cronkite, *History*, 66.

4. NARA, Books, Letter, Upton to Platt, December 8, 1862; Upton, Papers, letter to his sister, May 20, 1861; NARA, Letters to the Adjutant General, M1064, Roll 68, #A1339 CB, 1864.

5. Beckwith, "Three Years with the Colors," August 23, 1893; Jonathon Burrell, Letters, New York State Library and Archives (NYSLA) (hereafter cited as Burrell, Letters), to his sister, November 5, 1862.

6. Upton, Papers, letter to his sister, May 20, 1861; Burrell, Letters, to his sister, November 5, 1862; Stephen E. Ambrose, *Upton and the Army* (Baton Rouge: Louisiana State University Press, 1993), 3. Remmel, Letters, to his parents, October 26, 1862; Remmel said that the "companies could hardly muster fit men for duty." Henry Walker, diary entry, Monday, October 27, 1862, NARA, Walker Pension Records.

7. NARA, Books, General Order No. 8, November 12, 1862, General Order No. 16, December 24, 1862, and General Order No. 14, March 12, 1863. All general and special orders are renumbered at the beginning of each year. An order without a date, therefore, is meaningless. Without complaining, Edward Wales noted the twice-a-day drills in his diary on November 12, 1862, and two days later, he reported: "Frosty morning but a fine day drilled two hours in the morning"; on November 25, he noted another "fine day, nothing worthy of note transpired . . . we went through the drills."

8. NARA, Books, General Order No. 34, August 18, 1863, and Special Order No. 33, October 29, 1863; Rice, *Letters*, to his brother Daniel, August 22, 1863.

9. French, Letters, to his sister from White Oak Church, Va., April 11, 1863; NARA, Books, Special Order No. 4, October 3, 1862; Wales, Diary, December 3, 1862, November 11 and 20, and December 2, 1862; NARA, Books, General Order No. 19, March 27, 1863.

10. Bates, Letters, letter to his mother, November 27, 1862, Hagerstown, Md.; Kelley, Papers, letter to his sister from Williamsport, Md., September 27, 1862; Best, *121st*, 29; Remmel, Letters, to his sister Ada, camp near Stafford Court House, Va., November 29, 1862. Remmel said that the only point on which the regiment was discontent was the food—"not because of the small variety, but of the small rations." Lovejoy, "Reminiscences," 9.

11. Burrell, Letters, to his sister Hatt, from Bakersville, Md., November 5 and 15, 1862; Fred Ford, letter to the editor, *Herkimer Journal*, November 27, 1862; *Reunion Report, 1910*, Isaac Best letter to C. J. Westcott, August 8, 1910, 12.

12. Burrell, Letters, to his brother James, December 23, 1862; NARA, Books, General Order No. 9, November 12, 1862; Campbell in the *Otsego Republican*, October 10, 1878.

13. NARA, Books, General Order No. 2, January 2, 1863, near White Oak Church, Va.; Adams, *Letters*, to his wife, January 12, 1865, 195; Wales, Diary, November 15 and 29, 1862.

14. Charles W. Dean, Letter to the *Oneonta Herald*, October 2, 1862, in Best, *121st*, 26; Lovejoy to his mother, November 8, 1862, from Burkettsville, private collection; Kidder, Letters, to his wife, October 4, 1862; Hartwell, *Letters and Diary*, 28, and diary entry of February 25, 1863, 52. Britton and Reed misidentified the victim as Pvt. Orson Olds, Company C, who actually died of typhoid on November 15, 1862, more than a month later and in a different company.

15. Kidder, Letters, to his wife, October 4, 1862; Dye, *Letters*, to Martha, undated, from Bakersville; French, Letters, to his parents, October 5, 1862; Best, *121st*, 28.

16. Mather, "Diary," October 13, 1862, and January 23, 1863; William Herdman, Letters, Manuscript Collection, Cherry Valley Historical Association (CVHA) (hereafter cited as Herdman, Letters), to brother Sperry, March 27, 1863; Rice, *Letters*, letter, Dr. Holt to C. E. Rice, October 8, 1863, 11; Carran, Letters, probably to his mother around November 1, 1862; Rice, *Letters*, letter to his parents, October 19, 1862. On October 30, 1862, Carran wrote home that twelve men had died "since we arrived here only about 5 weeks ago. Only one from our company (B)," and he noted, "There are a great many sick in the regiment. Somewheres about 200 I believe. Some 12 or 14 of our company are in the hospital."

17. Stephen Wolverton, *Soldiers' and Citizens' Album of Biographical Record Containing Personal Sketches of Army Men and Citizens Prominent in Loyalty to the Union; Also a Chronological and Statistical History of the Civil War and a History of the Grand Army of the Republic with Portraits of Soldiers and Prominent Citizens* (Chicago: Grand Army Publishing, 1890), 239, available at http://darciplace.com/darci/soldiers/wolverton-stephen.htm. Wolverton, a descendant of participants in the Revolutionary War and the War of 1812, was born in Montgomery County, New York. He moved around the country, returning to Herkimer County in 1850, where, in turn, he farmed, became a teamster, and sold rags and paper. He was in the flour and feed business in Little Falls in 1861. Upon his discharge, he went back to Little Falls, where he established a dry goods store for a few years, but he returned to Wisconsin in 1876. Two of Wolverton's brothers were in the Confederate army—one of them an owner of twenty slaves and the other a physician. See also *Herkimer County Journal*, January 22, 1863. Cooke survived the war and moved to Iowa afterward. See *Oneonta Herald*, available at http://www.rootsweb.com/~nyotsego/oneontaherald5 .html.

18. Holt, Papers, letter to his wife, November 7, 1862; Burrell, Letters, to his sister, November 14, 1862: "Lieutenant Cameron died last Sunday. He was left at Bakersville when we started on the March." Also see *Herkimer County Journal*, October 23 and November 20, 1862.

19. Henry Walker, diary entry, Sunday, October 26, 1862, NARA, Walker Pension Records; Staring, *Letters*, to his brother, January 6, 1863, 21.

20. Holt, Papers, letter to his wife, September 28, 1862.

21. Ibid., September 19, 1862. Quotation is from U.S. Surgeon General's Office, *The Medical and Surgical History of the War of the Rebellion (1861–1865)*, 3 vols. (Washington, D.C.: Government Printing Office, 1870–1888), vol. 2, pt. 3, 902. Background is from this

3-volume work and from James A. Huston, *The Sinews of War: Army Logistics, 1775–1953* (Washington, D.C.: Office of the Chief of Military History, U.S. Army, 1966), 240–243; Best, *121st*, 21–22; Adams, *Letters,* to his wife, April 10 and October 21, 1864.

22. Adams, *Letters,* to his wife, May 23 and 25, 1863; Holt, Papers, letter to his wife, October 15, 1862.

23. Holt, Papers, letter to his wife, December 8, 1862; Wales, Diary, December 8, 9, 10, and 14, 1862.

24. Rice, *Letters,* to his parents, November 26, 1862.

25. NARA, Books, Letter, Upton to Assistant Adjutant General, Lieutenant Colonel Greene, Left Grand Division, November 20, 1862; Thomas Hyzer, Letter to his wife, September 22 and 23, 1862, from Williamsport, Md., in author's collection; NARA, Books, Letter, Upton to Mrs. Hyzer, November 13, 1862.

26. Best, *121st*, 5; *Freeman's Journal,* August 18, 1865; Burrell, Letters, to his brother and sister, November 11, 1862; Captain Campbell in Michie, *Life and Letters*, 68 and 69; Fred Ford, Letter to *Herkimer County Journal,* November 13, 1862.

27. Upton to Ladies Aid Society, Little Falls, New York, November 26, 1862, *Herkimer County Journal,* December 11, 1862; Holt, Papers, letter to his wife, October 15, 1862; *Oneonta Herald,* December 24, 1862; *Herkimer County Journal,* November 6, 1862. James Cronkite remembered, "Up to this time no shelter had been provided for the men, and to protect themselves from the weather, they were obliged to prepare tents from brushwood, cornstalks, and leaves"; see Cronkite, *History*, 65. Samuel Kelley complained that "habitation which is made of a few rails with some cornstalks for the roof" was the only shelter available to the troops; see Kelley, Papers, letter to his mother, October 3, 1862.

28. French, Letters, from Winter Quarters, White Oak Church, March 1863; Herdman, Letters, to brother Sperry, March 27, 1863.

29. Edgar Jackson Klock, "History of the Town of Schuyler, Herkimer County, New York," typewritten manuscript in the collection of the HCHS, 1930, 310–311; U.S. Census for the Town of Schuyler, 1850, 1855, 1860; NARA, Records of the Office of the Surgeon General (Army), Record Group 112.

30. NYSAG, *Annual Report of the Adjutant-General of the State of New York for the Year 1903*, Serial number 36 (Albany, N.Y.: Oliver A. Quayle, State Legislative Printer) (hereafter cited as NYSAG, *Annual Report, 1903*), 1, 112, and 191; U.S. Adjutant General's Office, *Official Army Register of the Volunteer Force of the United States Army for the Years 1861, '62, '63, '64, '65* (Washington, D.C.: Government Printing Office, 1865), 2:620 (hereafter cited as USAGO, *Official Army Register*); NARA, Books, Clark letter to General Bartlett, October 9, 1862; Holt, Papers, letter to his wife, September 28, 1862, near Bakersville, Md.

31. NARA, Books, Letter, Upton to Bradley, November 15, 1862.

32. Holt, Papers, letter to his wife, January 19, 1863, near White Oak Church, Va.

33. NARA, Books, Letter, Upton to Brigadier General Loring Thomas, Adjutant-General of the Army, January 27, 1863, and List of Commissioned Officers; NYSAG, *Annual Report, 1903*, 191; USAGO, *Official Army Register,* 620; Holt, Papers, letter to his wife, February 8, 1863, near White Oak Church, Va.; NARA, Stephen B. Valentine Pension Records, Special Order No. 354, Army of the Potomac, December 18, 1862, and Special Order No. 37, War Department, January 23, 1863.

34. *Herkimer County Journal*, February 26, 1863.

35. NARA, Elias Mather Military Records, Medical Certificate, June 18, 1863.

36. NARA, Books, Letter, Upton to Thomas, December 27, 1863, and General Order No. 8, February 2, 1863; NYSAG, *Annual Report, 1903*, 189. The *Herkimer County Journal* printed the names with company assignments and hometowns. Upton's message also pointed out that the men had drawn three days of rations and sixty rounds of cartridges.

37. Burrell, Letters, to his brother and sister, November 20, 1862.

38. Wales, Diary, November 15, 1862; Dye, *Letters*, Letter to Martha, undated; NYSAG, *Annual Report, 1863*, 1 and 112; NARA, Books. Indeed, both were listed as deserters on September 25, 1862.

39. Holt, Papers, letter to his wife, November 21, 1862; Records of the Adjutant General's Office, 1780s–1917, 1861–1865 (Record Group 94), General Order No. 95, War Department, Washington, D.C., August 5, 1862.

40. Remmel, Letters, to brother Augustus, February 18, 1863; Burrell, Letters, to his sister, November 15, 1862.

41. Greiner, *Subdued*, 89; *Otsego Republican*, n.d., in the files of the NYSMM, Saratoga; Kidder, Letters, to his wife, August 12, 1863.

42. NYSAG, *Annual Report, 1903*, 36, 98, and 78; Mather, "Diary," December 11, 1863.

43. *Reunion Report, 1910*, reminiscence by Henry Cadwell, 20–21; NARA, Books, Letter, Upton to Major Sprague, Superintendent, General Recruiting Service, Albany, November 10, 1862; NYSAG, *Annual Report, 1903*, 202; "Death of an Old Soldier," obituary of Erastus Weaver, *Otsego Republican*, January 20, 1897.

44. Adams, *Letters*, to his wife, August 11, 1863, 123; Willard Vincent Huntington, "Old Time Notes Relating to Otsego County and the Upper Susquehanna Valley," carbon copy of original notes in the Huntington Library, Oneonta, N.Y., vol. 7, 2125–2426, Manuscript Division, NYSHA; Letter, Mather to Huntington, n.d., 2391–2392, Manuscript Division, NYSHA; Burrell, Letters, to his sister, November 16, 1862.

45. Kidder, Letters, to his wife, October 4 and 19 and November 30, 1862; *Herkimer Democrat*, March 18, 1863.

46. Kidder, Letters, to his wife, October 17, 1862; Remmel, Letters, to his parents, January 18, 1863; NARA, Books, Special Order No. 6, October 4, 1862; Wales, Diary, November 8, 1862.

47. Kidder, Letters, to his wife, January 6, 1863; Delavan Bates, "War Reminiscences, Petersburg," *Otsego Republican*, August 7, 1895.

48. Bates, "War Reminiscences, Petersburg."

49. Burrell, Letters, to his brother and sister, November 11, 1862.

50. Remmel, Letters, to his parents, September 22, 1862, and to his brother, October 20, 1862; Carran, Letters, to his mother, November 10, 1862; Hyzer, letter to his wife, September 22, 1862, in author's collection; Fred Ford, Letter to *Herkimer County Journal*, November 13, 1862.

51. Henry Galpin, letter to the editor, *Herkimer County Journal*, November 20, 1862; Reed, Letters, letter to his parents, November 5, 1862, and to his father, November 13, 1862; Remmel, Letters, letters to his parents, November 8, 1862; Mather, "Diary," September 20 and 22, 1862.

52. French, Letters, to his parents, November 22, 1862; Carran, Letters, to his mother, November 20, 1862.

53. French, Letters, to his parents, November 5 and 22, 1862; Wales, Diary, November 18, 19, and 22, 1862; A. Reed, Letters, November 5, 1862; Remmel, Letters, to his parents, September 14 and 22 and November 29, 1862; Ingraham, *Letters,* to his brother, December 30, 1862, and to his parents, January 1, 1863, in camp near White Oak Church; anonymous letter to the editor, *Herkimer County Journal,* June 4, 1863.

Chapter 5. Desertion, Disarray, and Despair: Winter 1862–1863

1. Several monographs on New York politics inform this section: Sickles, "Military Affairs," 18–29; William B. Weeden, *War Government, Federal and State, in Massachusetts, New York, Pennsylvania and Indiana, 1861–1865* (Boston: Houghton Mifflin, 1906), 224–318; Holzer and Trefousse, *Union Preserved,* 1–13; Brummer, *History,* 201–289; Hesseltine, *Lincoln and the War Governors*; Milledge L. Bonham, "New York and the Civil War," in Alexander C. Flick, ed., *History of the State of New York,* vol. 7, *Modern Party Battles* (New York: Columbia University Press, 1935), 101–135; De Alva Stanwood Alexander, *A Political History of the State of New York* (New York: Henry Holt, 1909), 1–135; Harold Holzer, ed., *The State of the Union: New York and the Civil War* (New York: Fordham University Press and New York State Archives Partnership Trust, 2002), vii–16. Most useful in understanding the impact of the Emancipation Proclamation on Northerners is Allen C. Guelzo, *Lincoln's Emancipation: The End of Slavery in America* (New York: Simon and Schuster, 2004).

2. Guelzo, *Lincoln's Emancipation,* 44–47, 73–75, and 166–169; Brummer, *History,* 201–260; Alexander, *Political History,* 8.

3. Alexander, *Political History,* 28–29 and 40; Bonham, "New York and the Civil War," 113; Hesseltine, *Lincoln and the War Generals,* 269.

4. Seymour quote is from Gerrit Smith, a Seymour opponent, in the *New York Tribune,* January 23, 1863, in Brummer, *History,* 255, and Curtis quote is from Alexander, *Political History,* 52; Holzer and Trefousse, *Union Preserved,* 7.

5. Alexander, *Political History,* 45–47; *Freeman's Journal,* November 14, 21, and 28, 1862; Carran, Letters, William Carran to his brother Frank, November 16, 1862, William Carran to his brother Frank, from Cedar Lake, December 12, 1862, Philenda to Frank, January 23, 1863, and A. J. to Frank, November 16, 1862.

6. Basler, *Lincoln,* 6, Letter to Seymour, March 23, 1863, 145–146.

7. Frank G. Bolles, letter to the editor, *Otsego Republican,* December 2, 1862, in *Freeman's Journal,* December 12, 1862; Burrell, Letters, to his sister, November 7, 1862, and to his brother, February 6, 1863; Carran, Letters, to his mother, November 10, 1863; Fred Ford, letter to the editor, *Herkimer County Journal,* November 27, 1862.

8. *Herkimer County Journal,* December 31, 1863. Stebbins settled in Little Falls from Salisbury, New York, in 1854. See Beers, *History,* 268.

9. *Herkimer County Journal,* November 6, 1862; Rice, *Letters,* to his parents, February 23, 1863, and to his brother Charles, July 30, 1863.

10. Henry Galpin, letter to the editor, *Herkimer County Journal,* November 20, 1862, and January 29, 1863.

11. Holt, Papers, letters to his wife, September 28 and November 21, 1862, April 20, 1863, and October 2, 1864.

12. John Hartwell, letter to the editor, *Herkimer County Journal and Courier*, March 3, 1864.

13. Krutz, *Distant Drums*, 82.

14. James F. Hall, letter to his friend Ent, October 21, 1862, original in the author's collection; Adams, *Letters*, to his wife, January 12, 1863, October 15 and 26 and November 8, 1864; Phillip T. Van Horne, letter to his father, February 22, 1863, in *Otsego Republican*, April 11, 1863; Lansing B. Paine, Letters, to his sister Fan, December 24, 1863, Manuscript Division, NYSHA (hereafter cited as Paine, Letters); NARA, Ten Eyck Howland Pension Records, letter to his father, March 10, 1863; Charles B. West, letter to a friend, Peter Chapin, January 22, 1865, Manuscript Division, NYSHA; Francis W. Morse, *Personal Experiences in the War of the Great Rebellion, from December 1862 to July 1865* (Albany, N.Y.: Printed but not published, 1866), 76–77.

15. *Freeman's Journal*, January 9, 1863.

16. Carran, Letters, Philenda Carran to Frank, February 27, 1863.

17. Burrell, Letters, to his sister, November 7, to his brother, November 9, and to his brother and sister, November 11, 1862.

18. Beckwith, "Three Years with the Colors," August 23 and 30, 1893; Carran, Letters, to his mother, November 10, 1862; *Herkimer County Journal*, November 6, 1862.

19. NARA, Books, Special Order No. 296, October 25, 1862; Headquarters of the Army of the Potomac, cited in Henry Seymour Hall, "Experience in the Peninsular and Antietam Campaigns," paper read before the Kansas Commandery, Military Order of the Loyal Legion of the United States (MOLLUS), January 3, 1894.

20. Anonymous letter to the editor dated November 19, 1862, *Herkimer Democrat*, November 26, 1862; Fred Ford, letter to the editor, *Herkimer County Journal*, November 27, 1862.

21. David A. Ward, "Of Battlefields and Bitter Feuds: The 96th Pennsylvania Volunteers," *Civil War Regiments*, vol. 3, no. 3 (1993), available at http://members.tripod.com/~Jake96th/ward.html. Ingraham, *Letters*, to his parents, December 9, 1862.

22. Mather, "Diary," September 20 and 22, 1862; French, Letters, November 5 and 10, 1862; Beckwith, "Three Years with the Colors," August 30, 1893; Wales, Diary, November 26 and December 3 and 5, 1862.

23. Douglas Campbell, cited in Michie, *Life and Letters*, 68–69; NARA, Douglas Campbell Pension Records.

24. Upton, Papers, letter to his wife, December 7, 1862, 70–71; Lovejoy, "Reminiscences," 11; Ingraham, *Letters*, to his parents, December 9, 1863.

25. *Otsego Republican*, January 17, 1863, and August 31, 1892; Walker, Letters, to his "Friends" in Cooperstown, January 7 and January 22, 1863; *Freeman's Journal*, January 9, 1863.

26. Stephen T. Austin, letters to his brother, Lucius, December 25, 1862, and March 7, 1863, Fredericksburg and Spotsylvania Military National Park, Fredericksburg, Va. (F&SNMP).

27. Teel, Letters, letter to his wife, camp near Belle Plain, Va., December 9, 1862, and January 9, 1863; Remmel, Letters, to his parents, December 5, 1862; Fred Ford, letter to the editor, *Herkimer County Journal*, December 18, 1862. Teel enjoyed his hospital stay. It gave him three square meals a day, a warm bed, clean clothes, and an occasional bath.

For the first time since leaving home, he slept in a bed rather than "on the ground, on brush, on rocks, on rails, and in the mud." He "lived" for breakfast and fresh milk and butter. Olcott's prediction was related by Charles Staring; see Staring, *Letters,* to his brother, December 9, 1862, 13.

28. David J. Eicher, *The Longest Night: A Military History of the Civil War* (New York: Simon and Schuster, 2001), 399.

29. Wales, Diary, Friday, December 12, 1862; A. Reed, Letters, letter to his parents and friends, December 14, 1862; Best, *121st,* 41.

30. Andrew Davidson, letter, *Cherry Valley Gazette,* January 7, 1863; William Farrar Smith, "Franklin's Left Grand Division," in Robert Underwood Johnson and Clarence Clough Buell, eds., *Battles and Leaders of the Civil War* (Edison, N.J.: Castle Edition, 1995), 3:131; Reuben C. Holmes, letter to the editor, *Herkimer County Journal,* February 19, 1863; Hartwell, *Letters and Diary,* letter to his wife, December 17, 1862, 35; Cassius Delavan, Diary, in Greiner, *Subdued,* 27.

31. Charles Dean, letter to the editor dated December 18, 1862, *Freeman's Journal,* December 26, 1862.

32. Elijah H. Hawley to unknown addressee, December 15, 1862, in the *Otsego Republican,* December 27, 1862, and *Oneonta Herald,* December 31, 1862; *Reunion Report, 1908,* Dennis A. Dewey reminiscences, 29–30; Staring, *Letters,* to his brother, December 13, 1862, 14–15.

33. James Longstreet, "The Battle of Fredericksburg," in Robert Underwood Johnson and Clarence Clough Buell, eds., *Battles and Leaders of the Civil War* (Edison, N.J.: Castle Edition, 1995), 3:70–85.

34. Smith, Letters, to his mother, December 13, 1862; Beckwith, "Three Years with the Colors," September 6, 1893.

35. Several members wrote of their experiences at Fredericksburg, including I. P. Smith (Letters, to his mother, December 2 and 12, 1862) and Clinton Beckwith ("Three Years with the Colors," September 13, 1893). Beckwith erroneously reported Oscar, not Edward, as the regiment's first battle casualty. NYSAG, *Annual Report, 1903,* 53 and 175, and NARA, Books, Upton letter to General Thomas, Adjutant General, December 11, 1862, 11, show Edward to be the battle casualty and Oscar the victim of diphtheria. Wales, Diary, December 14, 1862.

36. Kidder, Letters, to his wife, December 14 and 18, 1862; Mather, "Diary," December 20, 1862; Carran, Letters, from his brother, Tommy, December, 28, 1862; Staring, *Letters,* to his brother, December, 13–16, 1862, 17.

37. Chaplain John Sage, letter to the editor, *Herkimer County Journal,* January 8, 1863.

38. NARA, Books, General Order No. 14, December 18, 1862.

39. Davidson, letter, *Cherry Valley Gazette*; Emory Upton to his sister, near White Oak Church, December 23, 1862, HCWRT, USAMHI, Carlisle, Pa.; Kelley, Papers, letter to his mother, December 26, 1862.

Chapter 6. Burnside, Mud, and Hooker

1. Sawyer, *History of Cherry Valley,* 137.

2. D. Hills, Letters, to his mother and friends, August 31, 1862, transcript in author's collection. Hills remarked in his letter: "Tim and I went up on deck and saw many a fine town

and several celebrated spots among which was West-Point and the military academy where Frank Morse is." NARA, Egbert Olcott Pension Records; Morse, *Personal Experiences.*

3. Holt, Papers, letters to his wife, January 12 and 16, 1863. Every history of the Army of the Potomac has covered the Mud March, to a greater or lesser extent. Here, details on the 121st's experiences are drawn largely from Holt, Papers; Carran, Letters; and Morse, *Personal Experiences,* 14–17. The Christmas description is from Merton Tanner, letter to his mother, December 27, 1862, USAMHI. George Rabel's *Fredericksburg, Fredericksburg* (Chapel Hill: University of North Carolina Press, 2002), 408–426, chap. 25, "Mud," provides an excellent overview of the depression, desolation, and near-mutinous frame of mind that pervaded the ranks of the Army of the Potomac immediately after Fredericksburg, during the Mud March, and generally in the months afterward. See also Kenneth P. Williams, *Lincoln Finds a General: A Military Study of the Civil War* (New York: Macmillan, 1957), 2:542–554. Also of use is Frank J. Welcher, *The Union Army, 1861–1865: Organization and Operations,* vol. 1, *The Eastern Theater* (Bloomington: Indiana University Press, 1989).

4. *Reunion Report, 1908,* Dennis A. Dewey reminiscences, 30–32; Chaplain Sage, letter to the editor, *Herkimer County Journal,* January 8, 1863; Beckwith, "Three Years with the Colors," September 30, 1893; *Cherry Valley Gazette,* February 11, 1863.

5. Kidder, Letters, to his wife, January 16, 1863.

6. Morse, *Personal Experiences,* 14–17; Henry Galpin, letter to his sister Abby, January 27, 1863, Clarke Family Papers, Manuscript Department, NYSHA, Library; Carran, Letters, to his mother, January 29, 1863.

7. Carran, Letters, to his mother, January 29, 1863; A. Reed, Letters, letters to his parents and friends, January 28 and 31, 1863; Remmel, Letters, to his brother Augustus, February 18, 1863; Cronkite, *History,* 68; Holt, Papers, letter to his wife, January 27, 1863.

8. Burrell, Letters, to his brother, February 6, 1863; Carran, Letters, to his mother, January 29, 1863.

9. Carran, Letters, to his mother, January 29, 1863; Galpin, letter to his sister, January 27, 1863.

10. Burrell, Letters, to his brother, January 15 and February 5, 1863; Ingraham, *Letters,* Letter to his parents, January 28, 1863; Galpin, letter to his sister; Gen. William B. Franklin, June 1, 1863, in Darius N. Couch, "Sumner's Right Grand Division," in Robert Underwood Johnson and Clarence Clough Buell, eds., *Battles and Leaders of the Civil War* (Edison, N.J.: Castle Edition, 1995), 3:119. Basler, *Lincoln,* letter to Joseph Hooker, January 26, 1863, vi, 48–49.

11. Fred Ford, letter to the editor, *Herkimer County Journal,* December 25, 1862; Reverend John Sage to the editor, *Herkimer County Journal,* January 8, 1863; Remmel, Letters, to his brother Augustus, January 1, 1863; Bates, Letters, to his father, January 10, 1863.

12. Burrell, Letters, to his brother James, December 3, 1862; Tanner, letter to his mother, December 27, 1863, USAMHI. Remmel was convinced that if the 121st had been called into action up on the heights instead of "lying in a road," it would never have survived. Laurin Ingalsbe, letter to his wife, Ann, White Oak Church, January 4, 1863, Abner Doubleday Civil War Round Table, Milford, N.Y.

13. Fred Ford, letter to the editor, *Herkimer Journal,* February 5 and March 5 and 12, 1863.

14. Walker, Letters, to his friends, February 11, 1863.

15. Franklin, June 1, 1863.

16. Burrell, Letters, to his sister, November 13, 1862.

17. Burrell, Letters, to his brother, January 15, 1863; John W. Ballard to his brother and sister, February 2, 1863, Manuscript Department, NYSHA, Research Library. John Kidder wrote to George Teel that seventeen men left the regiment within a few days, including Alonzo Lyon; see Teel, Letters, letter to his wife, January 26, 1863; Henry Galpin, letter to his sister Abby, January 17, 1863, Clarke Family Papers, Manuscript Department, NYSHA, Library.

18. Reuben C. Holmes, letter to the editor, *Herkimer County Journal*, February 19, 1863; *Freeman's Journal*, March 13, 1863; *Herkimer Democrat*, February 19 and March 25, 1863; *Otsego Republican*, March 21, 1863.

19. Basler, *Lincoln*, 6:132–133. "Proclamation Granting Amnesty to Soldiers Absent without Leave," Adjutant General's Office, *General Orders* (not numbered but between No. 57 and No. 58), 1863. In *U.S. Statutes at Large* (13:775–776), this order is listed as "Executive Order No. 1." Kidder, Letters, to his wife, February 25, 1863.

20. *Freeman's Journal*, January 9, 1863; Holt, Papers, letters to his wife, March 7 and April 2, 1863.

21. Reverend John Sage, letter to the editor, *Herkimer County Journal*, March 5, 1863.

22. Hartwell, *Letters and Diary*, diary entry of February 11, 1863, 48; Rice, *Letters*, to his parents, February 23, 1863, 46; Walker, Letters to his friends, March 1, 1863; *Otsego Republican*, March 23, 1863.

23. Quote is from Beckwith, "Three Years with the Colors," September 27, 1893; Hartwell, *Letters and Diary*, diary entry of February 14, 1863, 49. Captain Kidder also referred to the trial but mentioned no one by name; see Kidder, Letters, to his wife, March 19, 1863.

24. NARA, Books, February 19, 1863, General Order No. 40, Transcript of the Court Martial of Barton, Piper, Miller, Gilbert, and Tanner. The numbers vary greatly in regard to how many deserted in mid-January 1863. Ingraham counted fourteen, Holt nineteen; Kidder listed nine from his company alone and seventeen from the entire regiment. Ingraham, *Letters*, letter to his father, January 17, 1863; Holt, Papers, letter to his wife, January 19, 1863; Teel, Letters, to his wife from Harewood Hospital, January 26, 1863; Greiner, *Subdued*, 39.

25. Dean A. Pierce, Diary, February 14, 1863, NYSHA, Library (hereafter cited as Pierce, Diary).

26. Fred Ford, letter to the editor, *Herkimer County Journal*, November 27, 1863; *Herkimer County Journal*, December 4, 11, and 25, 1862, and January 1, February 26, and March 19, 1863.

27. Details on Hooker's reforms are derived from Stephen W. Sears, *Chancellorsville* (Boston: Houghton Mifflin, 1996), 54–82; Warner, *Generals in Blue*, 233–235; Williams, *Lincoln Finds a General*, 547–605. The battle of Chancellorsville is well documented in Sears's book and in Gary Gallagher, ed., *Chancellorsville: The Battle and Its Aftermath* (Chapel Hill: University of North Carolina Press, 1996). Rice, *Letters*, to his brother Charley, June 11, 1863.

28. Bruce Catton, *Glory Road*, 16, cited in Warner, *Generals in Blue*, 233.

29. Herdman, Letters, to his brother, Sperry, March 27, 1863.

30. French, Letters, to his wife, February 11, 1863.

31. A. Reed, Letters, letter to his parents and sister, February 15, 1863; Hartwell, *Letters and Diary,* diary entry of April 15, 1863.

32. Burrell, Letters, to his sister, November 19, 1862, and to his brother and sister, April 24, 1863; Adams, *Letters,* to his wife, January 1, 1863; Remmel, Letters, to his parents, February 16, 1863; Carran, Letters, to his mother, January 29, 1863; *Freeman's Journal,* January 16, 1863. Henry Walker wrote home that "there had been a good deal of complaint and dissatisfaction about not receiving the pay and there were a good many desertions before the last march"; see Walker, Letters, to his brother Charley, February 15, 1863.

33. NARA, Ten Eyck Howland Pension Records, letter to his father, March 10, 1863; A. Reed, Letters, to his parents and sister, February 15, 1863; Fred Ford, letter to the editor, *Herkimer County Journal,* March 3 and 26, 1863.

34. Beckwith, "Three Years with the Colors," October 4, 1893; Isaac Darling, letter to the editor, *Herkimer County Journal,* April 16, 1863.

35. Walker, Letters, to his friends, February 11 and March 1, 1863; Rice, *Letters,* to his brother Charley, April 19, 1863.

36. Remmel, Letters, to his parents, January 18, 1863; Herdman, Letters, to his brother, March 27, 1863.

37. NARA, Books, General Order No. 11, near Stafford Court House, Va., November 25, 1862; NARA, Books, Upton, letter to Charles Evans, assistant adjutant, New York, April 5, 1863; USAGO, *Official Army Register,* 2:619–620.

38. Burrell, Letters, to his sister, November 20, 1862, and to his brother, December 23, 1862; Walker, Letters, to his brother Charley, January 7, 1863; NARA, Sackett Olin Pension Records. After his discharge, Olin returned to farming, lumbering, and ownership of a general store. He died of a stroke in New York City on June 17, 1903.

39. Carran, Letters, letter to Frank from his mother, February 6, 1863; Burrell, Letters, to his brother James, February 6, 1862.

40. Fred Ford, letter to the editor, *Herkimer County Journal,* February 26, 1863; Kidder, Letters, to his wife, February 25, 1863.

41. Hartwell, *Letters and Diary,* diary entries of February 12 and 20 and April 11, 1863.

42. Holt, Papers, letter to his wife, November 20, 1862; Burrell, Letters, to his brother James, January 15, 1863; NYSAG, *Annual Report, 1903,* 27 and 47; Walker, Letters, to his friends, March 1, 1863; *Freeman's Journal,* March 13 and May 8, 1863; Carran, Letters, to his mother, March 8, 1863; NARA, Books, Upton, letter to Charles Evans, assistant adjutant general, April 5, 1863. Cameron and Davis both died at Bakersville, Cameron of typhoid on November 9, 1862, and Davis of an unknown cause on October 20, 1862. Cameron was from Fairfield; Davis was from Otsego.

43. Burrell, Letters, to his brother, December 23, 1862.

44. NARA, Robert P. Wilson Pension Records; Best, *121st,* 68, 103–104; Kidder, Letters, to his wife, undated but probably late May or June 1863. Wilson's grandfather was with Washington at Yorktown when the British surrendered on October 19, 1781. He was in charge of ensuring the safe transfer of twenty-eight British flags to the Americans, and when the Army of the Potomac was near Yorktown in 1862, Robert P. Wilson invited General Bartlett and his staff to tour the old site.

45. Mather, Letters, letter to his brother, September 5, 1862.

46. Kidder, Letters, to his wife, undated, late January, May–June, and June 1, 1863. Also

see Greiner, *Subdued,* 59–61. Galpin quote is in *Reunion Report, 1910,* 31; Holt, Papers, letter to his wife, January 31, 1864. Bates quote is from his "War Reminiscences," *Otsego Republican,* April 17, 1895; NARA, Books, Letter, Mather to Lt. Col. McMahon, AAG, 6th Corps, December 12, 1863.

47. Paine, Letters, December 24, 1863; Mather, Letters, letter to his brother, November 29, 1862.

48. Ingraham, *Letters,* to his brother Lon, June 1, 1863, and Ingraham, letter to the editor, *Herkimer County Journal,* June 4, 1863.

49. Anonymous letter to the editor, *Herkimer County Journal,* April 23, 1863. The letter may have been referring to the new adjutant, Francis Morse, who, although a Cherry Valley native and "the son of the Cherry Valley Morse's," had attended West Point and was described by Henry Walker as "rather young and boyish." Another potential candidate for the author's rage may have been Frank Foote, who became a second lieutenant in Company I on July 23, 1863, with only two years' experience at West Point. Kidder, Letters, to his wife, August 12, 1863.

50. Holt, Papers, letters to his wife, June 5 and 24, 1863.

51. John Slocum, Diary, February 23 and October 16, 1864, Onondaga Historical Society, Syracuse, N.Y. (hereafter cited as Slocum, Diary).

52. Andrew Davidson, letter to the editor dated April 22, 1863, *Otsego Republican,* May 2, 1863; John Bain, letter dated March 10, 1863, *Cherry Valley Gazette,* March 28, 1863; A. Reed, Letters, to his mother, April 9, 1863.

53. NARA, Special Order No. 41, December 22, 1862, Courts Martial Records, KK-493, Burrell; Burrell, Letters, to his brother, January 15, 1863.

54. A. Reed, Letters, to his mother and father, April 9, 1863, and to his mother, January 10, 1863. Reed wrote what many thought: "I hear the boys are enlisting at home very fast. I hope they will fill up the quota this year for it will do considerable towards ending this war if the Rebs hear of the boys enlisting. I guess they will think we are bound to settle this cruel war."

Chapter 7. Chancellorsville and Salem Church

1. Walker, Letters, to his friends, April 27, 1863.

2. Joseph Hooker to Abraham Lincoln, April 27, 1863 in Basler, *Lincoln,* 6:190; Carran, Letters, Richard Turner to "Dear Friend," February 5, 1863.

3. French, Letters, to his sister, April 29, 1863. French transferred to the signal corps that month. Burrell, Letters, to his brother, January 15, 1863; Martin McMahon, "Major-General John Sedgwick," in James Grant Wilson and Titus Munson Coan, MD, eds., *Personal Recollections of the War of the Rebellion: Addresses Delivered before the New York Commandery MOLLUS* (New York: New York Commandery, 1891; Wilmington, N.C.: Broadfoot Publishing, 1992), 2:165, citing the 1992 edition (hereafter cited as McMahon, "Major-General John Sedgwick"); Henry Seymour Hall, "Fredericksburg and Chancellorsville," paper read before the Kansas Commandery, MOLLUS, April 4, 1894, 195 (hereafter cited as Hall, "Fredericksburg").

4. Several official reports were written after the Chancellorsville campaign. One of the best contemporary accounts was provided by 2nd Lt. Marcus Casler of Company H. His

account was first published in the *Herkimer County Journal* and reprinted by the *Cherry Valley Gazette*, May 20, 1863.

5. A. Reed, Letters, to his parents, April 28, 1863; McMahon, "Major-General John Sedgwick," 166–167; Beckwith, "Three Years with the Colors," October 4, 1893.

6. *OR*, ser. 1, vol. 25, pt. 1, 557–562; Rice, *Letters*, to his brother Daniel, August 22, 1863, 112; McMahon, "Major-General John Sedgwick," 170–171.

7. Beckwith, "Three Years with the Colors," October 4, 1893; Remmel, Letters, to his brother Augustus, May 16, 1863. In addition to several official reports by commanders in the field, Remmel's description of the battle of Salem Church is one of the most succinct and descriptive.

8. Beckwith, "Three Years with the Colors," October 4, 1893; McMahon, "Major-General John Sedgwick," 171.

9. Reports of Brigadier General Cadmus M. Wilcox, C. S. Army, commanding brigade, Headquarters Wilcox's Brigade, Near Salem Church, Va., May 10, 1863, *OR*, ser. 1, vol. 25, pt. 1, 854–861 (hereafter cited as *OR*, Wilcox).

10. Ibid., 856–857 and 858; Remmel, Letters, to his brother Augustus, May 16, 1863; Cronkite, "Otsego in the Rebellion," 69; *Reunion Report, 1909*, Dennis A. Dewey reminiscences, 19.

11. Holt, Papers, letter to his wife, October 17, 1863; Report of Brigadier General Joseph J. Bartlett, U.S. Army, commanding Second Brigade, Headquarters, May 11, 1863, 581, and Report of Colonel Emory Upton, Headquarters 121st Regiment New York Volunteers, May 10, 1863, 589, *OR*, ser. 1, vol. 25, pt. 1, chap. 37 (hereafter cited as *OR*, Bartlett, and *OR*, Upton, respectively).

12. *OR*, Bartlett, 581; Cronkite, *History*, 69; *OR*, Wilcox, 858; Beckwith, "Three Years with the Colors," October 11, 1893; Ingraham, *Letters*, to his parents, June 7, 1863; Remmel, Letters, to his brother Augustus, May 16, 1863.

13. Marcus Casler, letter to the editor, *Herkimer County Journal*, in *Cherry Valley Gazette*, May 20, 1863; A. Reed, Letters, to his parents, May 7, 1863.

14. Cronkite, *History*, 69; Morse, *Personal Experiences*, 25–26; Cleaveland Campbell, letter to the editor, *Cherry Valley Gazette*, July 1, 1863; *Reunion Report, 1909*, Dennis A. Dewey reminiscences, 19; Rice, *Letters*, to his brother Charley, May 14, 1863; Herbert, cited in Best, *121st*, 81. Dr. Holt wrote in his diary on July 10, 1864, that the 96th was the "regiment above all others with whom we hate to associate." Both Campbell and Dolphus Sayles of Company D documented Upton's comment on his lack of fear of the devil; Sayles to his father, May 6, 1863, NARA, Dolphus Sayles Pension Records.

15. Morse, *Personal Experiences*, 25–26; Anonymous letter dated May 5, *Herkimer Democrat*, May 13, 1863; *Reunion Report, 1909*, Dennis A. Dewey reminiscences, 19; *OR*, Upton, 589; Beckwith, "Three Years with the Colors," October 18, 1893; *OR*, Wilcox, 859.

16. *OR*, Wilcox, 859; Rice, *Letters*, to his parents from Banks' Ford, May 6, 1863; *OR*, Upton, 589; A. Reed, Letters, to his parents, May 7, 1863; *OR*, Bartlett, 582. Lt. Lansing Paine of Company C described the battle but praised the 121st's bravery under fire; Paine, Letters, letter to his parents, May 4, 1863.

17. Paine, Letters, letter to his parents, May 4, 1863; NYSAG, *Annual Report, 1903*, 18; *OR*, Report of General John Sedgwick, May 15, 1863, ser. 1, vol. 25, pt. 1, chap. 37, 560 (hereafter cited as *OR*, Sedgwick); Mather, "Diary," May 7 and 9, 1863; *Freeman's Journal*,

cited in the *Otsego Republican*, September 7, 1881; Kelley, Papers, letter to his mother, May 5, 1863; Ingraham, *Letters*, to his friend, June 10, 1863; *Otsego Republican*, July 28, 1897; Lester Murdock, New York State Archives–Grand Army of the Republic file; James Cronkite letter to Mrs. Caldwell, published in *Freeman's Journal*, May 22, 1863; *Freeman's Journal*, June 5, 1863; U.S. Surgeon-General's Office, *Medical and Surgical History*, 11:184–185, 297, 298.

18. NARA, Henry Upton Pension Records. Upton ultimately headed west after the war, moving through Illinois, Michigan, and Nebraska. He died in Nebraska on July 29, 1887.

19. Thomas Arnold, letter to Friend Burrell, published in *Herkimer County Journal*, December 18, 1862; NARA, Thomas Arnold Pension Files; Arnold, letter, undated, and letter to Friend Burrell, December 21, 1862, in author's collection. In a letter published in the *Herkimer County Journal*, May 21, 1863, Captain Galpin reported that Arnold's father was with him when he died. Henry Walker reported that Arnold's wife also went to retrieve his body; Walker, Letters, to his friends, May 19, 1863.

20. *Herkimer County Journal*, May 14, 1863; announcement of Fred Ford's death in an undated article, probably from the *Herkimer County Journal*, NYSMM; *The Diary of Miss Alvina Helmer Written at Kast Bridge—March 1915: My Recollections of Eatonville as It Was in 1850*, available at http://www.rootsweb.com/~nyherkim/fairfield/alvina2.html; Rice, *Letters*, to his brother Charley, May 14, 1863. The "Record of Events" for Company G reported that 1st Sgt. John Daniels was shot in the head by a musket ball, that fourteen privates were wounded, and that Joseph Howe succumbed to his wounds; NARA, "Record of Events," Company G, M594–Roll #133.

21. Letter, Emory Upton to Wendell's brother, May 20, 1863, cited in *Freeman's Journal*, June 12, 1863; A. Reed, Letters, to his parents, May 7, 1863; *Reunion Report, 1909*, letter of James Cronkite to Wendell's brother, J. D., May 12, 1863, 15; Fernando W. Wright to his aunt, July 6, 1863, in possession of descendant; Holt, Papers, letter to his wife, May 17, 1863; *Otsego Republican*, May 23, 1863; James Tompkins Jewell, Letter, to his parents, May 7, 1863, as cited in his obituary in (March) 1918, in the Local History Collection/ Gilbertsville Free Library; NARA, "Record of Events," Company F, M594–Roll #133.

22. Roselle G. Firman, letter to Doubleday's brother, published in *Freeman's Journal*, May 15, 1863; *Biographical Review*, 416.

23. Hartwell, *Letters and Diary*, letters to his wife, May 5, 10, and 17 (two letters), 1863, 82–92.

24. Kidder, letter to Delavan Bates's father, Alpheus, May 8, 1863, in Bates, Letters. Also Bates, "Nebraska Correspondence," *Otsego Republican*, January 3 and 17, 1894.

25. Kidder, Letters, to his wife, May 4, 1863; A. Reed, Letters, to his parents, May 7, 1863; Marcus Casler, letter to the editor, *Herkimer County Journal*, in *Cherry Valley Gazette*, May 20, 1863; *Otsego Republican*, May 23, 1863; *Cherry Valley Gazette*, May 20, 1863. The nine men from New Lisbon were enlisted by Andrew Emmet Mather. They were Horatio G. Whitford, James E. Bowe, James Simmons, Ransom Hovey, Thomas Emerson, Isaac Fitch, Sidney Stevens, Adelbert Babcock, and William Chapin. Hurd, *History*, 222; *Oneonta Herald*, May 13, 1863; *Reunion Report, 1909*, Dennis A. Dewey reminiscences, 16.

26. Paine, Letters, letter to his parents, May 4, 1863; NARA, "Records of Events," Entry for Company D, May–June 1863, M594–Roll #133; Wood, *Drummer Boy*, 132; Henry Galpin, letter to the editor, *Herkimer County Journal*, May 6, 1863.

27. 1860 census for the town of Otego, Otsego County, NYSAG, 76. *Reunion Report, 1912*, Dennis A. Dewey reminiscences, 23.

28. Carran, Letters, Frank to his mother, May 25, 1863, Philenda to her grandchildren, June 1 and 3, 1863, Richard Turner to his "friends," August 19, 1863; NARA, Carran Pension and Military Records; Lewis Heard, MD, "Gunshot Wounds of the Hip upon Which Supervened Pyaemia and Rupture of the Liver," *Medical and Surgical Reporter* (Philadelphia) 10, no. 9 (June 27, 1863): 131–133; *New York Times*, May 12, 1863.

29. Beckwith, "Three Years with the Colors," October 18, 1983.

30. Ibid., October 25, 1893.

31. Isaac Darling, letter to the editor, *Herkimer County Journal*, June 4, 1863.

32. Nichols, Obituary, LHC/GFL; entry on Charles Nichols, *Biographical Review*, 785–786.

33. Holt, Papers, letter to his wife, from White Oak Swamp, May 15, 1863, also in Greiner, Coryell, and Smither, *Surgeon's Civil War*, 92–102, and Holt, "In Captivity," *CWTI* 18 (August 1979): 34–39. Holt's capture by General Wilcox is documented. In his subsequent report dated June 5, 1863, Wilcox wrote about the rapidity of the federal retreat over Banks' Ford: "I have heard it stated that the enemy were crossing all night and until broad day next morning. One of the Federal surgeons told me himself that they were crossing until sun-up, but I knew myself that he was mistaken. There was not one of the enemy on this side at Banks' Ford by 12 o'clock at night"; *OR*, Wilcox, 581. James Jewell wrote plainly: "They took our Doctor prisoner"; Jewell, Letter to his parents, May 7, 1863, printed in his obituary, 1918, LHC/GFL. Adam Clarke Rice also wrote that "Dr. Holt, Newton Phelps, and the whole drum corps were taken prisoners"; Rice, *Letters*, to his brother Charley, May 14, 1863. Malcolm Graham, in Company D, writing to his sister after the battle, reported that "the Doctor and part of the drum corps were taken"; Malcolm Graham, letter to his sister, May 10, 1863, transcribed copy in author's collection. Holt never mentioned the drum corps. A local newspaper, probably the *Herkimer County Journal*, published the account of Holt's capture but likely used his letter to his wife, already cited; New York State Military Museum. Holt's story about meeting Lee and Dr. Todd is unsubstantiated. The story of the returned equipment was contained in a letter to his wife, June 19, 1863, and the letter to Robert E. Lee was dated November 7, 1863, both in Holt, Papers.

34. Henry Galpin, letter to the editor, *Herkimer County Journal*, May 20, 1863; Jewell, Letter to his parents, May 7, 1863; *OR*, Wilcox, 583; Michie, *Life and Letters*, 72–73; Bates, "Nebraska Correspondence," *Otsego Republican*, January 3, 1894; Holt, Papers, letter to his wife, May 17, 1863; Paine, Letters, letter to his parents, May 4, 1863; Morse, *Personal Experiences*, 49; Rice, *Letters*, to his brother Charley, May 14, 1863; Best, *121st*, 83.

35. *OR*, Lee's Report to Jefferson Davis, May 5, 1863, ser. 1, vol. 25, pt. 1, 795 (hereafter cited as *OR*, Lee); Rice, *Letters*, to his brother Daniel, August 22, 1863, 113; Beckwith, "Three Years with the Colors," October 25, 1893; Ingraham, *Letters*, to his friend, June 10, 1863; Pierce, Diary, May 5, 1863; Graham, letter to his sister, May 10, 1863.

36. Beckwith, "Three Years with the Colors," November 1, 1893.

37. A. Reed, Letters, letter to his mother, May 7, 9, and 29, 1863; James H. McCurry, Diaries 1863 and 1864, Saturday, May 9, 1863, Gettysburg Military Park, Gettysburg, Pa.

38. *Cherry Valley Gazette*, May 9, 1863; Beckwith, "Three Years with the Colors," November 8, 1893.

39. Remmel, Letters, to his parents, May 19, 1863; Bates, Letters, to his father, June 17, 1863.

40. *New York Times*, May 12, 1863; Walker, Letters, to a friend, May 16, 1863; Mather, "Diary," May 17 and 18, 1863.

41. Holt, Papers, letter to his wife, August 20, 1863.

42. Kidder, Letters, to his wife, June 12, 1863.

43. Upton, Letters to his brother, November 6, 1863, and to his sister, April 10, 1864. Upton's brother Henry was permitted to return to upstate New York. Emory tried to get Henry Walker, also wounded at Salem Church, to escort his brother home. Walker declined because Upton wanted to go through Harrisburg, Pennsylvania, and into Elmira whereas Walker wanted to go home via New York City.

44. Henry S. Hall, "At Gettysburg with the Sixth Corps," paper read before the Kansas Commandery, MOLLUS, November 6, 1896, 251 (hereafter cited as Hall, "At Gettysburg"); Hall, "Fredericksburg," 199; Upton letter to MacMahon, NARA, Regimental Books, April 25, 1863; Remmel, Letters, to his parents, June 1, 1863; Newton M. Curtis, *From Bull Run to Chancellorsville: The Story of the Sixteenth New York Infantry Together with Personal Reminiscences* (New York: G. P. Putnam's Sons, 1906), 302–303 (hereafter cited as Curtis, *From Bull Run*).

45. McCurry, Diaries 1863 and 1864, Sunday, May 3, 1863.

46. Kidder, Letters, to his wife, June 1, 1863; anonymous letter to *Herkimer County Journal*, June 4, 1863; Beckwith, "Three Years with the Colors," October 25, 1893. Delavan Bates wrote years later that was not fair treatment, for "there were plenty men in the ranks of the 121st N. Y. Volunteers well qualified for these positions." There were "so many capable young men in our regiment did not receive higher commissions during such a long period of active service in a regiment with such a brilliant record and such a large death loss"; Bates, "Nebraska Correspondence," *Otsego Republican*, March 6, 1895. Walker's promotion, given on the day of the battle, was delayed by Upton until the new men from the other regiments joined the 121st, entitling the 121st to another furlough; Walker, Letters, to his sister Sarah, May 27, 1863.

47. NYSAG, *Annual Report, 1903*, 1, 2; A. Reed, Letters, to his parents, June 20, 1863.

Chapter 8. After Gettysburg: Becoming Abolitionists, June to October 1863

1. Kelley, Papers, letter to his mother, May 23, 1863. Most useful in understanding the chronology of the 121st and the Sixth Corps are David Ward, "Sedgwick's Foot Cavalry: The March of the Sixth Corps to Gettysburg," *Gettysburg Magazine* 22 (2000): 43–65, and James S. Anderson, "The March of the Sixth Corps to Gettysburg," available at http://www.getttysburgguide.com/march6.html.

2. Eicher, *Longest Night*, 490–491; Anonymous, letter to the *Herkimer County Journal*, June 4, 1863. Eicher maintains that Lee refused aid to his western comrades because of his parochialism and allegiance to his home state and the Army of Northern Virginia. Stephen Sears rebuts Eicher's argument in his *Gettysburg*, calling that line of reasoning the

purview of "Armchair critics"; Stephen W. Sears, *Gettysburg* (Boston: Houghton Mifflin, 2003), 1–17, citation on 12. The gold standard on the battle of Gettysburg remains Edwin B. Coddington, *The Gettysburg Campaign: A Study in Command* (New York: Charles Scribner's Sons, 1968). There is evidence that Lee and Jackson planned an invasion of the North as early as February 1863.

3. A. Reed, Letters, to his parents, June 5, and to his sister, June 7, 1863; "Big Joe, Ding" (Isaac Darling), letter to the editor, *Herkimer County Journal*, April 16, 1863; Teel, Letters, to his wife, June 2, 3, 7, and 14, 1863; Walker, Letters, to his friends, June 4, 1863.

4. Andrew Davidson, letter to the editor dated April 22, 1863, *Otsego Republican,* May 2, 1863; also in *Oneonta Herald,* May 6, 1863.

5. Kelley, Papers, letter to his sister, June 18, 1863; A. Reed, Letters, to his parents, June 20, 1863; Ingraham, *Letters,* to his sister, June 23, 1863.

6. Rice, *Letters,* to his brother Charley, June 11, 1863, 79–81; Remmel, Letters, to his brother Augustus, June 7, 1863; Kelley, Papers, letter to his mother, June 9, 1863; Walker, letters to friends, June 4, 1863. Delavan Bates, writing years later, said although the men were in good spirits, Hooker had not recovered from his defeat at Chancellorsville "and up to June 9th apparently knew not what to do"; Bates, "Nebraska Correspondence," *Otsego Republican*, February 7, 1894. Also Cronkite, *History,* 70.

7. George Collins, *Letters,* to his cousin, June 19, 1863, available at http://www.rootsweb.com/~nyherkim/collins.html (hereafter cited as Collins, *Letters*). Also Ingraham, *Letters,* to his sister, June 23, 1863; Kidder, Letters, to his wife, June 17, 1863; Basler, *Lincoln,* "Proclamation Calling for 100,000 Militia," 6:277–278.

8. Remmel, Letters, to his parents, June 17, 1863; anonymous writer quoted by Bates, "Nebraska Correspondence," *Otsego Republican*, February 7, 1894.

9. *OR,* Hooker to Halleck, June 19, 1863; Collins, *Letters.*

10. Hartwell, *Letters and Diary,* diary entry of June 19, 1863, 103; Remmel, Letters, to his parents, June 17, 1863, and to his brother, June 20, 1863; Teel, Letters, to his wife, June 17, 1863; *OR,* ser. 1, vol. 27, chap. 39, pt. 1, 53–61. As late as October, army rumors anticipated a third Bull Run. Lovejoy, diary entry, October 15, 1863, NYSHA Library.

11. Kelley, Papers, letter to his mother, June 9, 1863; NARA, Dolphus Sayles Pensions Records, letter to his father, June 26, 1863.

12. Beckwith, "Three Years with the Colors," November 15, 1893; A. Reed, Letters, to his parents, June 17 and 20, 1863.

13. *Herkimer Democrat,* June 24, 1863. The *Statesman* is quoted in the *Democrat.*

14. Cronkite, *History,* 71; Lovejoy, "Reminiscences," 22; Rice, *Letters,* to his brother and sister, June 29, 1863, 89–91; Best, *121st,* 89.

15. Meade's report to Halleck, *OR,* ser. 1, vol. 27, chap. 39, pt. 1, 114 (hereafter cited as *OR,* Meade).

16. Ibid.

17. Cronkite, *History,* 71; Horatio Wright's report, *OR,* ser. 1, vol. 27, chap. 39, pt. 1, 665, 666 (hereafter cited as *OR,* Wright).

18. McMahon, "Major-General John Sedgwick," 176–177.

19. *OR,* Upton, 673; Hartwell, *Letters and Diary,* diary entries of June 29 and July 1, 1863, 106; Kelley, Papers, diary entries of June 6–July 3, 1863; Anderson, "March of the Sixth Corps"; Morse, *Personal Experiences,* 33–34.

20. Upton, Letters, to his sister, July 4, 1863; OR, ser. 1, vol. 27, chap. 39, 72 and 116, 671 and 673; Ingraham, Letters, to his parents, July 21, 1863.

21. Cronkite, History, 71; Kidder, Letters, to "Friend (William) Fields," July 22, 1863; Morse, Personal Experiences, 35.

22. Upton, Letters, to his brother, November 6, 1863.

23. Morse, Personal Experiences, 35; Upton, Letters, to his sister, July 4, 1863; Bates, "Nebraska Correspondence," Otsego Republican, March 21, 1894.

24. Beckwith, "Three Years with the Colors," November 22, 1893; Marcus Casler, letter to the editor, Herkimer County Journal, July 8, 1863; Sears, Gettysburg, 437; Cronkite, History, 71; OR, ser. 1, vol. 27, chap. 9, pt. 1, 663; Upton, Letters, to his sister, July 4, 1863. See also Morse, Personal Experiences, 57; Rice, Letters, to Daniel, August 22, 1863, 113.

25. Morse, Personal Experiences, 40.

26. Holt, Letters, to his wife, July 9, 1863; Kidder, Letters, to friend Fields, July 22, 1863; Casler, letter to the editor; Upton, Letters, to his sister, July 4, 1863.

27. OR, Wright, 666; OR, Sedgwick, 663.

28. A. Wilson Greene, Meade's Pursuit of Lee, from Gettysburg to Falling Waters, ed. Gary Gallagher, The Third Day at Gettysburg and Beyond (Chapel Hill: University of North Carolina Press, 1994), 165; Lovejoy, "Reminiscences," 29; Casler, letter to the editor; Rice, Letters, to Charley, July 30, 1863, 94; Morse, Personal Experiences, 40.

29. OR, ser. 1, vol. 27, chap. 39, pt. 1, 79; Holt, Letters, to his wife, June 12 and July 21, 1863.

30. OR, ser. 1, vol. 29, pt. 3, chap. 41, 555; Rice; Letters, to his brother Charley, July 30, 1863; Morse, Personal Experiences, 39–41.

31. OR, ser. 1, vol. 29, pt. 3, 555; Kidder, Letters, to his wife, July 9, 1863; Rice, Letters, to his brother Charley, July 30, 1863.

32. Rice, Letters, to his brother Charley, July 30, 1863; Ingraham, Letters, to his parents, July 11, 1863; Bates, "Nebraska Correspondence," Otsego Republican, April 4, 1894; Lovejoy, "Reminiscences," 31; Bates, Letters, to his mother, March 11, 1864.

33. Cronkite, History, 72; OR, Bartlett, 672.

34. OR, Bartlett, 672; Beckwith, "Three Years with the Colors," November 22, 1893, Kelley, Papers, diary entries of July 7–8, 1863; Best, 121st, 90–91; Remmel, Letters, to his parents, July 17, 1863; Bates, "Nebraska Correspondence," Otsego Republican, April 4 and May 16, 1894; Hance Morgan, Diary, July 14, 1863, Civil War Times Illustrated Collection Archives, USAMHI; Kidder, Letters, to his friend William Fields, July 22, 1863.

35. Hartwell, Letters and Diary, letter to his wife, July 11, 1863, 109; Bailey, Letters, letter to his brother, August 19, 1863, near New Baltimore, Va.; Fred Albert Shannon, The Organization and Administration of the Union Army, 1861–1865 (Cleveland, Ohio: Arthur H. Clark, 1928), 2:188. Henry Walker heard that one of his friends had been drafted and "had cleared out for Canada"; Walker, Letters, to Mrs. Priest, September 12, 1863. Rice, Letters, introduction, 16–18; Teel, Letters, to his wife, September 27, 1863.

36. Leslie M. Harris, In the Shadow of Slavery: African Americans in New York City (Chicago: University of Chicago Press, 2003), 279–288.

37. Lovejoy, "Reminiscences," 31; Casler, letter to the editor, Herkimer County Journal, August 5, 1863; Ingraham, Letters, to his parents, July 17, 1863, and to a friend, July 19, 1863; Kidder, Letters, to his wife, August 12, 1863.

38. Eugene Converse Murdock, *Patriotism Limited, 1862–1865: The Civil War Draft and the Bounty System* (Kent, Ohio: Kent State University Press, 1967), 4; see also 211–214 for commutation statistics and 63–80 for Seymour's motivations. Walker, Letters, to dear friends, September 16, 1863.

39. Marion Brophy, *The Town of Otsego: Home Front, 1861–1865, Compiled from Freeman's Journal/Otsego Town Records,* August 14, 1863–September 2, 1864, available at http://www.rootsweb.com/~nyotsego/cwotesgo.htm.

40. Walker, Letters, to his friends, September 30, 1863; Hartwell, *Letters and Diary,* letter, September 19, 1863; Kidder, Letters, to his wife, February 25, March 1, August 26, and September 27, 1863.

41. Murdock, *Patriotism Limited,* 72; Rice, *Letters,* to his brother Charley, July 30, 1863.

42. Kidder, Letters, to his wife, July 9 and August 12, 1863; A. Reed, Letters, to his wife, July 17, 1863; Teel, Letters, to his wife, June 20, 1863.

43. NARA, Records of the Office of the Judge Advocate General (Army), Court Martial Case Files, 1809–1938, file MM 558, Thomas Jewett, Company D, 5th Maine Infantry. Several men wrote of their experience watching Jewett's execution. Uniformly, they expressed horror, pitying him more than scorning him. Bailey, Letters, letter to his brother, August 19, 1863; Ingraham, *Letters,* to his father, August 15, 1863, near New Baltimore; Report of the Adjutant General of the State of Maine, as cited on *American Civil War Research Database,* available at http://www.civilwardata.com/active/hdsquery.dll?Soldier History?U&185647; Adams, *Letters,* to his wife, August 11 and 15, 1863, 123–125; Holt, Letters, to his wife, August 15, 1863; Morse, *Personal Experiences,* 44; Carran, Letters, Richard Turner to distant friends, August 19, 1863; John Hartwell, letter to the editor, *Herkimer County Journal,* September 4, 1863. Hartwell's letter is signed "F. L."—his two middle initials. He was proud that his letter was printed, and he told his wife, "I have just got the Little Falls Journal [*Herkimer County Journal*] and so my letters signed F. L. Co. C printed Sept. 3rd so if you wish to see it and if you have not—you can borrow a paper but tell no tales, I intend to occasionally write a letter for that paper." He did not say why he wished to remain anonymous; Hartwell, *Letters and Diary,* letter to his wife, September 7, 1863, 123. George W. Bicknell, 5th Maine historian, wrote of the episode in his *History of the Fifth Regiment Maine Volunteers* (Portland, Me.: Hall L. Davis, 1871), 253–255, without naming Jewett as the deserter—mentioning just "one of the members of Company D."

44. Marcus R. Casler, letter to the editor dated August 15, *Herkimer County Journal,* August 27, 1863; Andrew Davidson, letter to the editor dated October 9, 1863, *Otsego Republican,* October 17, 1863.

45. Holt, Letters, to his wife, August 15 and October 9, 1863; Lovejoy, diary entry, September 10, 1863, NYSHA Library; Ingraham, *Letters,* to his brother Oliver, October 9, 1863.

46. Lovejoy, diary entries, August 29 and 31 and September 4 and 7, 1863, NYSHA Library; Bates, Letters, to his father, August 31, 1863.

47. Kelley, Papers, letters to his mother and sister, August 8, September 8, and December 26, 1863, letter from Matilda Sykes to Kelley, September 20, 1863, and letter from Calista to Samuel B. Kelley, December 24, 1863; Hartwell, *Letters and Diary,* letter to his wife, September 29, 1863.

48. Marcus Casler, letter to the editor, *Herkimer County Journal,* July 29, 1863.

49. Hartwell, *Letters and Diary*, letter to his wife, July 22, 1863; Hartwell, letter to the editor, *Herkimer County Journal*, October 8, 1863.

50. Ingraham, *Letters*, to his parents, July 21, 1863; Teel, Letters, to his wife, New Baltimore, September 13, 1863; Rice, *Letters*, to his sister, August 31, 1863; Holt, Letters, to his wife, June 19 and July 24, 1863; Remmel, Letters, to his parents, July 17, 1863; A. Reed, Letters, to his parents, September 30, 1863; Bates, Letters, to his father, July 21, 1863.

51. Kidder, Letters, to his wife, July 9 and August 12, 1863; Casler, letters to the editor, *Herkimer County Journal*, July 29, 1863, and July 27, 1863. Kent Masterson Brown, in *Retreat from Gettysburg: Lee, Logistics and the Pennsylvania Campaign*, estimates the wagon trains with ambulances, artillery batteries, wounded, supplies, livestock, and marching men had to be more than 50 miles long, which illustrated "the extent of foraging that Lee's army had accomplished while in Pennsylvania." See Brown, *Retreat from Gettysburg: Lee, Logistics and the Pennsylvania Campaign* (Chapel Hill: University of North Carolina Press, 2005), 118–120. John Hartwell told his wife, "We have just seen about 3000 head of cattle taken from the rebs at Manassas Gap. They got them in a free state Pa. They were very good to drive them down for us as we can use them to a good advantage"; see Hartwell, *Letters and Diary*, letter to his wife, July 28, 1863.

52. Walker, Letters, to his sister, August 21, 1863; Remmel, Letters, to his parents, September 7, and his brother Augustus, October 17, 1863; *Reunion Report, 1910,* remarks by Henry D. Cadwell, Company D, 20–21; Rice, *Letters*, to his brother Daniel, August 22, 1863, 115.

53. Lovejoy, diary entries, October 11, 1863, NYSHA Library.

54. Ibid., October 25 and 26, 1863, NYSHA Library; Kidder, Letters, to his wife, October 27, 1863; Bates, Letters, to his father, October 30, 1863; Ingraham, *Letters*, to his brothers, October 27, 1863.

55. Casler, letters to the editor, *Herkimer County Journal*, July 29, 1863, and July 27, 1863, emphasis in source; Kidder, Letters, to his wife, August 12, 1863; Rice, *Letters*, to his brother Charley, July 30, 1863, 101.

56. A. Reed, Letters, to his sister, September 25, 1863; Holt, Letters, to his wife, August 25, 1863; Lovejoy, diary entry, September 21, 1863, NYSHA Library; Bates, Letters, to his father, August 31, 1863.

Chapter 9. To Rappahannock Station

1. Upton, Letters, to his sister, August 6, 1863, and to his brother, November 6, 1863.

2. A. Reed, Letters, to his parents and sister, from Berlin, July 17, 1863; Walker, Letters, to his friends, September 18, 1863.

3. Morse, *Personal Experiences*, 43–44, 49; Bates, "Nebraska Correspondence," *Otsego Republican,* October 4, 1893; Ingraham, *Letters*, to his parents, July 26, 1863.

4. Remmel, Letters, to his brother Augustus, October 28, 1863; Walker, Letters, to Mrs. Priest, September 12, 1863; NARA, Egbert Olcott Pension Records, letter, Olcott to E. D. Townsend, Assistant Adjutant General, July 20, 1863; Welcher, *Union Army,* 402; Upton, Letters, to his sister, July 4, 1863.

5. George Teel wrote his wife that Mosby kidnapped one of Upton's aides and hanged

him. Adelbert Reed wrote his family that the guerrillas attacked the federals and, in retaliation, the federals raided a house, finding sixteen guns. The federals took everything usable, broke the rest, and burned the house down. Reed wrote that a rebel woman asked Upton for protection of her property in addition to asking him to take dinner with her. He refused dinner and sent one of his aides, who was captured on his way back to camp by a band of guerrillas and hanged. "Oh if they have [hanged him]," Reed remarked, "then they had better look out for their property"; A. Reed, Letters, to his parents and sister, July 27, 1863. John Ingraham told his parents essentially the same story; Ingraham, Letters, to his parents, July 26, 1863. Upton's aide, Francis Morse, never mentioned the atrocity, and there is no official corroborating evidence; Upton, Letters, to his sister, August 6, 1863. The Upton quote on Jefferson Davis is from Rice, Letters, to his parents, August 15, 1863, 104, and Collins, Letters, to his cousin, September 16, 1863. Also Holt, Letters, to his wife, August 2, 1863; Kidder, Letters, to his wife, August 12, 1863.

6. Beckwith, "Three Years with the Colors," December 6, 1893; Ingraham, Letters, to his brother, August 12, 1863; Morse, Personal Experiences, 45–48; Best, 121st, 95–96; NARA, "Records of Events," reports from all companies except C and K; Kidder, Letters, to his wife, August 12, 1863; A. Reed, Letters, to his parents, August 11, 1863; Andrew Davidson, letter to the editor dated August 11, 1863, Otsego Republican, August 22, 1863; Remmel, Letters, to his brother Caleb, August 12, 1863; John Hartwell, letter to the editor dated August 18, 1863, Herkimer County Journal, September 4, 1863; Hartwell, Letters and Diary, letter to his wife, August 12, 1863.

7. Remmel, Letters, to his brother Augustus, August 10, and to his brother Caleb, August 12, 1863; Rice, Letters, to his parents, August 15, 1863, 105.

8. A. Reed, Letters, to his parents, August 11, 1863; Kelley, Papers, letter to his sister, August 20, 1863; James H. Cox, letter to the editor, Herkimer County Journal, September 17, 1863; Bates, "Nebraska Correspondence," Otsego Republican, October 4, 1893; Walker, Letters, to Mrs. Priest in Cooperstown, September 7, 1863.

9. Collins, Letters, to his cousin, September 16, 1863; Beckwith, "Three Years with the Colors," December 6, 1893; A. Reed, Letters, to his parents, September 4, 1863; Cox, letter to the editor, Herkimer County Journal, September 17, 1863; Bates, "Nebraska Correspondence," Otsego Republican, October 4, 1893; Ingraham, Letters, to his sister Mary, September 7, 1863; Best, 121st, 93–95; Bates, Letters, to his father, September 21, 1863; Morse, Personal Experiences, 44–45.

10. Walker, Letters, to his friends, October 6, 1863.

11. Holt, Letters, to his wife, November 7, 1863.

12. A. Reed, Letters, to his parents, September 4, 1863.

13. Walker, Letters to friends, September 30, 1863; Collins, Letters, to his cousin, November 3, 1863; Best, 121st, 97.

14. Beckwith, "Three Years with the Colors," November 22, 1863; Rice, Letters, to his brother Charley, July 30, 1863, 97, and to his brother Daniel, August 22, 1863, 114.

15. Teel, Letters, to his wife, October 12, 1863; Bates, Letters, to his father, October 15, 1863; Remmel, Letters, to his parents, October 9, 1863; Ingraham, Letters, to his brother, October 9, 1863; Lovejoy, diary entry, October 6 and 7, 1863, NYSHA Library.

16. Lovejoy, diary entry, September 29, 1863, NYSHA Library.

17. Holt, Letters, to his wife, October 17, 1863; Walker, Letters, to his sister, October

20, 1863; A. Reed, Letters, to his parents, September 4, 1863; John Hartwell, letter to the editor, *Herkimer County Journal*, October, 1, 1863.

18. Beckwith, "Three Years with the Colors," November 29, 1893.

19. Walker, Letters, to his friends, September 16, 1863, and to his sister, October 20, 1863; Teel, Letters, to his wife, October 23, 1863.

20. Rice, *Letters*, to his brother Charley, May 14, 1863, 76, to his parents, August 15, 1863, 106, to his brother Daniel, August 22, 1863, 115–116, and introduction, 2–14.

21. Rice, *Letters*, 12; Kidder, Letters, to his wife, September 27, 1863; Pierce, diary entry, August 3 and 4, 1863; A. Reed, Letters, to his parents, July 31, September 30, and October 10, 1863.

22. Mitchell, *Horatio Seymour*, 288–289; Brummer, *History*, 347–354.

23. Paine, Letters, to his sister Fanny, December 24, 1863; Silas E. Pierce, letter to his father, October 21, 1863, in the *Otsego Republican*, October 31, 1863; Carran, Letters, Richard Turner to Thomas Carran, March 16, 1864.

24. Anonymous, letter to the editor dated March 28, 1864, *Otsego Republican*, April 9, 1864; Mitchell, *Horatio Seymour*, 353–354; Kelley, Papers, letter to his mother, November 11, 1863; A. Reed, Letters, to his parents, November 11, 1863; Andrew Davidson, letters of September 21, October 3, and November 7 and 14, 1863, *Otsego Republican;* Kidder, Letters, to his wife, October 14, 1863.

25. Walker, Letters, to dear friends, November 6, 1863; Holt, Letters, to his wife, November 7, 1863; John Fish, letter to his brother, Irvin A. Fish, November 12, 1863, USAMHI, Carlisle, Pa. Also Fish, Letters, in John S. Wilson, "Captain Fish and the 121st New York Volunteers at Rappahannock Station, Virginia," *Military Collector & Historian* (Journal of the Company of Military Historians, Washington, D.C.) 48, no. 3 (Fall 1996): 115–118.

26. Bates, Letters, to his father, October 15, 1863.

27. *Otsego Republican*, November 16, 1863.

28. Meade's report, November 6, 1863, *OR*, ser. 1, vol. 29, pt. 2, chap. 41, 423–424; A. S. Daggett, "The Battle of Rappahannock Station, Va.," in *War Papers Read before the Commandery of the State of Maine*, MOLLUS (Portland, Me.: Lefavor-Tower, 1915), 4:191 (hereafter cited as Daggett, "Battle of Rappahannock Station").

29. Morse, *Personal Experiences*, 51; Mather, Letters, letter to his brother, November 11, 1863; Fish, Letters, in Wilson, "Captain Fish," 116.

30. NARA, Books, Letter, Upton to Captain R. P. Wilson, AAG, 2nd Brigade, Sixth Corps, November 6, 1863, 19–20.

31. *OR*, Sedgwick, 575, Lee to Secretary of War James E. Seddon, November 7, 1863, 609 and 594, and Meade to Halleck, pt. 2, 415; Adams, *Letters*, to his wife, November 12, 1863, 131.

32. Upton, Letters, to his sister, November 15, 1863.

33. Fish, Letters, in Wilson, "Captain Fish," 116–117; *Freeman's Journal*, November 20, 1863; Morse, *Personal Experiences*, 52; Beckwith, "Three Years with the Colors," December 13, 1863; Kidder, Letters, to his wife, November 8, 1863; Mather, Letters, letter to his brother, November 11, 1863.

34. Martin T. McMahon, Brevet Major-General, U.S.V., "From Gettysburg to the Coming of Grant," in Robert Underwood Johnson and Clarence Clough Buel, eds., *Battles and*

Leaders of the Civil War (Edison, N.J.: Castle Edition, 1995), 4:86; Bates, "Nebraska Correspondence," Otsego Republican, June 27, 1894; Best, 121st, 99.

35. Anonymous, letter to the editor, Utica Morning Herald and Daily Gazette, November 16, 1863; Fish, Letters, letter to his brother, November 22, 1863. Captured figures are from Upton, Letters, to his sister, November 15, 1863.

36. Daggett, "Battle of Rappahannock Station," 193.

37. Upton, Letters, to his sister, November 15, 1863; Lt. John Gray, letter to the editor, Herkimer County Journal, November 21, 1863. Gray was promoted to first lieutenant on July 4, 1863, but was not mustered into federal service. Two weeks later, on July 21, he was promoted to captain of the 23rd U.S. Colored Troops, but he was still with the 121st when the battle of Rappahannock Station occurred. Hartwell, Letters and Diary, letter to his wife, February 1, 1864, 194; Morse, Personal Experiences, 54; Mather, Letters, letter to his brother, November 11, 1863.

38. Daggett, "Battle of Rappahannock Station," 195; Upton, Letters, to his sister, November 15, 1863.

39. Beckwith, "Three Years with the Colors," December 13, 1863; Cleaveland J. Campbell, letter to the editor, New York Tribune, November 20, 1863; Fish, Letters, in Wilson, "Captain Fish," 117; Holt, Letters, to his wife, November 9, 1863; Peter Mickel, letter to the editor dated November 10, 1863, Oneonta Herald, November 25, 1863; Upton, Letters, to his sister, November 15, 1863.

40. Teel, Letters, to his wife, November 11, 1863; OR, Upton, 592. The rebel lieutenant's surrender was related by Adelbert Reed to his sister; see A. Reed, Letters, to his sister, November 9, 1863. Mather, Letters, letter to his brother, November 11, 1863; Terry Jones, ed., The Civil War Memoirs of Captain William J. Seymour: Reminiscences of a Louisiana Tiger (Baton Rouge: Louisiana State University Press, 1991), 93–94.

41. Jones, Civil War Memoirs, 2, 4, and 93.

42. Lt. John Gray, letter to the editor, Herkimer County Journal, November 21, 1863.

43. Holt, Letters, to his wife, November 9, 1863; A. Reed, Letters, to his sister, November 9, 1863; Wood, Drummer Boy, 161.

44. Beckwith, "Three Years with the Colors," December 13, 1863; Adams, Letters, to his wife, November 12, 1863, 131–132; Fish, Letter, in Wilson, "Captain Fish," 117; Richmond Enquirer, November 9 and 11, 1863; Charles Cormier, Lt. Colonel, 1st Louisiana Regiment, letters, Tulane University Libraries, Howard-Tilton Memorial Library, November 15, 1863; John McCormick, Company K, 8th Louisiana Regiment, letter, February 26, 1864, Marguerite E. Williams Papers, Southern Historical Collection, University of North Carolina Library; Upton, Letters, to his sister, November 15, 1863.

45. A. Reed, Letters, to his parents, November 11, 1863; Frank Foote, Official Report, Herkimer County Journal, November 21, 1863; Bates, "Nebraska Correspondence," Otsego Republican, June 27, 1894; Bates, Letters, to his father, November 8, 1863; Kidder, Letters, to his wife, November 8, 1863; Morse, Personal Experiences, 55; Cherry Valley Gazette, November 11, 1863; Walker, Letters, to his friends, November 8, 1863; Remmel, Letters, to his parents, November 9, 1863; A. Reed, Letters, to his parents, November 9, 1863; A. J. Merrifield, Company A, 122nd New York, letter to the editor, National Tribune, November 19, 1894; Hartwell, Letters and Diary, letter to his wife, November 15, 1863, Herkimer County Journal, November 14, 1863.

46. Lovejoy, diary entry, November 8, 1863, NYSHA Library; Beckwith, "Three Years with the Colors," December 13, 1893; Bates, Letters, to his father, November 8, 1863; Earl J. Hess, *Field Armies and Fortifications in the Civil War: The Eastern Campaigns, 1861–1864* (Chapel Hill: University of North Carolina Press, 2005), 292–293.

47. NARA, Books, Letter, Major Cronkite to Brigadier General Williams, Assistant Adjutant General, Army of the Potomac, December 27, 1863; Meade's report, *OR*, ser. 1, vol. 29, pt. 1, 591; Phisterer, *New York*, 3428; *Richmond Enquirer*, November 17, 1863.

48. Upton, Letters, to his sister, November 15, 1863; Russell's report, *OR*, ser. 1, vol. 29, pt. 1, 589 and 594; A. Reed, Letters, to his parents, November 9, 1863; Upton, Letters, to his brother, November 13, 1863.

49. Holt, Letters, to his wife, November 9, 1863; Morse, *Personal Experiences*, 56–57; *Portland Advertiser*, November 11, 1863; General Orders No. 101, November 9, 1863, *OR*, ser.1, vol. 29, pt. 1, 576, and Lincoln to Meade, November 9, 1863, pt. 2, 443. Newspaper accounts of the battle were immediate and inaccurate. On November 11, 1863, the *Herkimer Democrat* ran a several-column account of the battle, liberally relying on the *New York Herald*.

50. Beckwith, "Three Years with the Colors," December 20, 1893; *Utica Daily Observer*, November 12, 1863; Letter, General E. D. Townsend, AAG, to General Meade, November 19, 1863, in the author's possession. Townsend acknowledged Stanton's acceptance of Russell's delivery of seven battle flags and one staff and Russell's "gallant" leadership. Supposedly, Russell was not received in Washington by Stanton, who kept Russell cooling his heels all day and ultimately did not see him. Russell left the flags and returned to this command "by the next train." Stanton had the courtesy to thank Russell through Townsend. McMahon, "From Gettysburg," 4:87–88; Morse, *Personal Experiences*, 57.

51. Kidder, Letters, to his wife, December 18, 1863; Upton, Letters, to his sister, November 21, 1863.

52. Gabor Boritt, *The Gettysburg Gospel: The Lincoln Speech That Nobody Knows* (New York: Simon and Schuster, 2006), 126–127 and 165–166.

53. Walker, Letters, to his friends, November 27, 1863.

54. Edwin C. Mason, "Recollections of the Mine Run Campaign," in *Glimpses of the Nation's Struggle: A Series of Papers Read before the Minnesota Commandery MOLLUS* (St. Paul, Minn.: St. Paul Book and Stationery, 1887), 321.

55. Henry Seymour Hall, "Personal Experience as a Staff Officer at Mine Run, and in Albemarle County Raid; and as Commander of the Forty-third Regiment United States Colored Troops through the Wilderness Campaign, and the Mine before Petersburg, Va., from November 7, 1863, to July 30, 1864," paper read before the Kansas Commandery, MOLLUS, 5.

56. Morse, *Personal Experiences*, 61–62; Teel, Letters, to his wife, December 12, 1863; McMahon, "From Gettysburg," 4:91; Carran, Letters, Richard Turner to Thomas Carran, December 12, 1863; Hartwell, *Letters and Diary,* letter to his wife, December 9, 1863, 170.

57, NARA, Beckwith Pension Records.

58. Holt, Letters, to his wife, December 4, 1863.

59. Hartwell, *Letters and Diary,* diary entry of December 1, 1863; Hall, "Personal Experience," 210.

Chapter 10. Winter Quarters, December 15, 1863, to May 4, 1864

1. Clyde C. Webster, "John Minor Botts, Anti-secessionist," 9–37, cited in Greiner, Coryell, and Smither, *Surgeon's Civil War,* 181; Morse, *Personal Experiences,* 64–65.

2. *Reunion Report, 1912,* Capt. T. J. Hassett, 29; James McCurry, Diaries, entries for December 9, 10, and 12, 1863; Paine, Letters, letter to his sister Fanny, December 24, 1863; Ingraham, *Letters,* to Mary Green, March 31, 1864.

3. Holt, Letters, to his wife, December 15, 1863; *Otsego Republican,* quoted in *Cherry Valley Gazette,* April 13, 1864; Bates, "War Reminiscences," *Otsego Republican,* May 20, 1896; Morse, *Personal Experiences,* 64–45.

4. Morse, *Personal Experiences,* 66–68.

5. Ibid., 69–73. James McCurry recorded "a watch presentation to Gen. Bartlett," McCurry, Diaries, entry for December 23, 1863.

6. Dolphus Sayles, Diary, entries for March 7 and 9, 1864, photocopy in author's collection (hereafter cited as Sayles, Diary).

7. Holt, Letters, to his wife, January 24, 1864; Teel, Letters, to his wife, February 23, 1864; Turner, in Carran, Letters, December 27, 1863; Morse, *Personal Experiences,* 71–72; Remmel, Letters, to his brother Augustus, December 30, 1863; George Eaton, letter to the editor, *Little Falls Journal and Courier,* March 3, 1864; Ingraham, *Letters,* to his sister, February 22, 1864.

8. Kidder, Letters, to his wife, November 30, 1862.

9. McMahon, "From Gettysburg to the Coming of Grant," *B&L,* IV, 81–94; John O. Slocum, Diary, entries for January 7, 8, 12, and 19–29, 1864, Onondaga Historical Society, Syracuse, N.Y. (hereafter cited as Slocum, Diary); Thomas J. Hassett, "Initiation into the Ways of Warfare," *West Winfield Star,* November 15, 1912.

10. Teel, Letters, January 23 and February 10, 1864; Smith, Letters, to his sister, March 9, 1864.

11. Kidder, Letters, to his wife, December 5, 1863; Bates, "War Reminiscences," *Otsego Republican,* April 17, 1895; Kelley, Papers, diary entry, March 7, 1864.

12. Holt, Letters, introduction; Bates, "War Reminiscences," *Otsego Republican,* April 3, 1895.

13. Kidder, Letters, to his wife, December 5, 1863; Bates, "War Reminiscences," *Otsego Republican,* April 17, 1895.

14. Walker, Letters, January 4, 1864; Teel, Letters, to his wife, January 24, 1864.

15. Ingraham, *Letters,* to his sister, February 22, 1864. Delavan Bates recalled that Colton received the letter and the children's photographs, not news of their deaths; Bates, "War Reminiscences," *Otsego Republican,* July 17, 1895.

16. Joe Heath, letter to the editor dated December 15, 1864, *Little Falls Journal and Courier,* December 22, 1864.

17. Herdman, Letters, letter to his brother, Sperry, March 8, 1864.

18. Kelley, Papers, letters, Alice Miller to Kelley, October 29 and November 19, 1863, January 4 and 20, February 7 and 17, March 5, and April 10, 1864; Kelley, Papers, diary entries, January 24, 26, and 27, 1864; Kelley, Papers, letters, to his mother, March 19, 1864.

19. Sayles, Diary, entry for April 26, 1864; Kelley, Papers, diary entry, March 7, 1864.

20. Kelley, Papers, letters, Reverend S. H. Synott to Sam Kelley, April 20, 1864; *Otsego Republican*, April 23, 1864; *Unadilla Times*, April 28, 1864.

21. Hartwell, *Letters and Diary*, letter to his wife, September 29 and December 19, 1863, January 11 and March 31, 1864, 171, 187, 212; Hartwell, *Letters and Diary*, diary entries for April 8 and 9, 1864, 214–216.

22. Teel, Letters, to his wife, April 4, 1864; Reed, Letters, to his father, April 15, 1864.

23. Walker, Letters, to his friends, December 1, 1863; Paine, Letters, letter to his sister, Fanny, December 24, 1863.

24. Walker, Letters, to his friends, November 27, 1863.

25. NARA, Books, Court Martial Transcript, February 10 and 11, 1864.

26. NARA, Barney Trainor Pension Records, Letter, Captain Henry Galpin to Captain G. R. Dalton, Assistant Adjutant General, March 16, 1864; NARA, Philip Smith Pension Records.

27. Holt, Letters, diary entries, May 25 and 29 and August 20, 1864.

28. Adams, *Letters*, to his wife, November 3, 1864, 172.

29. Remmel, Letters, to his parents, November 4, 1863; Slocum, Diary, entry for August 27, 1864; Teel, Letters, to his wife, September 27 and October 5, 1863, and March 25, 1864; Morse, *Personal Experiences*, 50; Bates, "War Reminiscences," *Otsego Republican*, August 28, 1895; French, Letters, to his sister, April 29, 1863.

30. Wales, Diary, entry for Thursday, November 27, 1862; Cassius Delavan Diary, November 27, 1862, cited in Greiner, *Subdued*, 103; Holt, Letters, diary entry, Saturday, May 7, 1864; Holt, Letters, to his wife, October 2, 1862; Hartwell, *Letters and Diary*, letter to his wife, December 9, 1863, 170; Beckwith, "Three Years with the Colors," December 6, 1893; Walker, Letters, to his friends, September 30, 1863; Kelley, Papers, diary entries, November 21–22, 1863.

31. Sgt. Lester Baum, letter to the editor, *Herkimer County Journal*, December 31, 1863.

32. NARA, Books, Olcott's Court Martial Transcript, undated but sometime in the month of January 1864; Holt, Letters, to his wife, January 31, 1864; Teel, Letters, to his wife, December 27, 1863, and January 12, 1864; Hartwell, *Letters and Diary*, diary entry of December 25, 1863, and letters to his wife, December 29, 1863, and April 11, 1864, 175–176; Kidder, Letters, to his wife, December 27, 1863; Albert N. Jennings, letter to the editor, *Little Falls Journal and Courier*, January 7, 1864.

33. William Campbell, letter to General Palmer, October 17, 1861, and to Cleaveland, August 23, 1862, Campbell-Mumford Papers, Manuscripts Department, N-YHS (hereafter cited as Campbell, Letters); *Otsego Republican*, June 24, 1865. Palmer reference is in Warner, *Generals in Blue*, 357–358.

34. Bates, "War Reminiscences," *Otsego Republican*, October 30, 1895.

35. The stock sale is in a document in the Campbell-Mumford Papers, Manuscripts Department, N-YHS. Hurd, *History*, 55; *Cherry Valley Gazette*, June 21 and July 12, 1865; Bates, "War Reminiscences," *Otsego Republican*, October 30, 1895, and May 20, 1896.

36. Hall, "Personal Experience," 8.

37. Slocum, Diary, entry for February 1, 1864.

38. Kidder, Letters, Bates to Kidder, March 4 and 17, 1864.

39. Best, *121st*, 113–114; Bates, "Nebraska Correspondence," *Otsego Republican*, October 3, 1894.

40. Campbell, Letters, to Cleaveland, August 7, 1864; Bates, Letters, to his father, November 6, 1864.

41. Teel, Letters, to his wife, November 11, 1863; Walker, Letters, to his friends, December 4, 1863.

42. Kelley, Papers, letters, to his mother, February 2 and 11, 1864, and diary, November 10, 1863.

43. Fish, Letter, in Wilson, "Captain Fish," November 12, 1863, 117.

44. Kidder, Letters, to his wife, December 18 and 27, 1863, and January 7, 1864; NARA, Books, letter, Egbert Olcott to Brigadier General B. Williams, AAG, December 19, 1863, and January 3, 1864.

45. Kidder, Letters, to his wife, January 23, 1864; Teel, Letters, to his wife, February 23, 1864; *Freeman's Journal*, February 19 and 26, 1864. John Hartwell erroneously stated that Pvt. William Whitehead from Company C was a member of the recruiting party; Hartwell, *Letters and Diary*, diary entry for February 12, 1864, 199. NARA, Regimental Books, Special Order No. 11, March 8, 1864, officially authorizing the recruiting trip.

46. Recruiting poster, NYSL Collections; recruiting poster, in author's collection.

47. Fish letter to Kidder, March 30, 1864, John G. Saint Collection; Kidder, Letters, to his wife, April 22 and 24, 1864.

48. Reed, Letters, to his father, April 25, 1864.

49. Delavan Bates, letter to John Kidder, March 4, 1864, John G. Saint Collection; Kidder, Letters, Delavan Bates to John Kidder, March 17, 1864. Norman Herdman wrote his brother simply: "Eg. Olcott is in command of the Regiment, and Lieut. Col. Upton is in command of our Brigade. Frank Morse is a good officer and well liked"; Herdman, Letters, to Sperry, March 8, 1864.

50. Upton, letter to Brigadier General Sprague, Adjutant General, New York, January 28, 1864, in author's collection.

51. Campbell, Letters, John Fish to Cleaveland Campbell, from Frankfort, Herkimer County, March 4, 1864.

52. Hartwell, *Letters and Diary*, diary entries for March 20 and 21, 1864, 209; *Otsego Republican*, quoted in *Cherry Valley Gazette*, April 13, 1864.

53. Upton, Letters, to his sister, April 10, 18, and 25, 1864; Ambrose, *Upton*, 27. Ambrose cites NARA, "Appointment, Commission, and Personnel File of Major General Emory Upton," Records of the War Department, AG's Office.

54. Reed, Letters, to his father, April 30, 1864; Hartwell, *Letters and Diary*, diary entry for April 18, 1864.

55. Holt, Letters, to his wife, January 31 and April 20, 1864.

56. Lovejoy, Letters, to his cousin Cynthia, March 20, 1864, private collection; Hartwell, *Letters and Diary*, diary entry for April 27, 1864; Beckwith, "Three Years with the Colors," January 3, 1864.

57. Oliver Wendell Holmes, *Touched with Fire: Civil War Letters and Diary of Oliver Wendell Holmes, Jr., 1861–1864* (New York: Fordham University Press, 2000), 102.

58. Ingraham, *Letters*, to his brother, February 14, 1864; NARA, Regimental Books, Olcott, letter to BG Sprague, NYSAG, January 11, 1864; Upton endorsement, January 13, 1864, in private collection.

59. Kelley, Papers, letters, to his mother, April 17, 21, and 26, 1864.

60. Morse, *Personal Experiences*, 74–75; Holt, Letters, to his wife, May 3, 1864; Kelley, Papers, letters, to his mother, April 29, 1864; Smith, Letters, to his mother, May 1, 1864.

61. Lovejoy, Letters, to his cousin Cynthia, January 16, April 8, and December 25, 1864, and January 13, 1865.

62. Holt, Letters, to his wife, May 1, 1864; Kidder, Letters, to his wife, May 25, 1864.

63. NARA, Books, General Order No. 4, October 5, 1864, and Special Order No. 5, January 5, 1864. Tanner was discharged April 22, 1864; NARA, Books, Special Order No. 34, May 13, 1865; NARA, Books, Olcott to Brigadier General Sprague, NYSAG, January 11, 1864; Bates, "War Reminiscences," *Otsego Republican*, May 20, 1896; NARA, Books, Special Order No. 18, April 15, 1864. Cpl. Dolphus Sayles's diary has two entries for March 18 and 19, 1864, in which he called Olcott "Daddy." It may be a misinterpretation of Sayles's handwriting or a phrase peculiar to Sayles. No other soldier referred to Olcott as "Daddy."

Chapter 11. Grant's Overland Campaign, May to June 1864

1. Cronkite, "Otsego in the Rebellion," 75; Remmel, Letters, to his parents, April 30, 1864; anonymous letter to the editor, *Little Falls Journal and Courier*, April 14, 1864; NARA, Dolphus Sayles Pension Records, to his father, May 1, 1864.

2. Holt, Papers, diary entries, May 2 and 4, 1864; Herdman, Letters, to his brother, Sperry, March 8, 1864; Slocum, Diary entries, May 1 and May 3, 1864.

3. Slocum, Diary entry, May 4, 1864.

4. Teel, Letters, to his wife, April 23, 1864.

5. Holt, Papers, diary entry, May 5, 1864; Ulysses S. Grant, *Personal Memoirs* (New York: Modern Library, 1999), 405, 413.

6. Holmes, *Touched with Fire*, 104; OR, Upton, 665.

7. Bates, "War Reminiscences," *Otsego Republican*, April 3, 1895; Hartwell, *Letters and Diary*, diary entry, May 5, 1864; Isaac Best, "Through the Wilderness with Grant," Schoff Collection, William L. Clements Library, University of Michigan (hereafter cited as Best, "Through the Wilderness"); Beckwith, "Three Years with the Colors," January 3, 1894.

8. Morse, *Personal Experiences*, 80; John B. Gordon, *Reminiscences of the Civil War* (New York: Scribner's, 1904), 239–242, 1077, 243–249.

9. OR, Upton, 666; Morse, *Personal Experiences*, 80.

10. *Cherry Valley Gazette*, June 15, 1864; Kelley, Papers, letters, to his mother, May 9, 1864, and diary entries, May 6 and 7, 1864; Beckwith, "Three Years with the Colors," January 10, 1894; *New York Tribune*, quoted in *Cherry Valley Gazette*, June 15, 1864.

11. Teel, Letters, to his wife, May 17, 1864; Hartwell, *Letters and Diary*, diary entry, May 6, 1864; Slocum, Diary entry, May 6–9, 1864.

12. McCurry, Diary entry, May 6, 1864.

13. Teel, Letters, to his wife, May 17, 1864; OR, Upton, 666.

14. Kelley, Papers, diary entries, May 9, 13, and 16, 1864.

15. Ibid., May 22, 24, 28, and 30 and June 6, 1864; *Reunion Report 1907*, Dewey reminiscences, 20.

16. Beckwith, "Three Years with the Colors," January 10, 1894; Hartwell, *Letters and Diary*, diary entry, May 7, 1864.

17. Morse, *Personal Experiences*, 82–83.

18. Martin T. McMahon, "The Death of General John Sedgwick," in Robert Underwood Johnson and Clarence Clough Buel, eds., *Battles and Leaders of the Civil War* (Edison, N.J.: Castle Edition, 1995), 4:175; Warner, *Generals in Blue,* 431.

19. Kidder, Letters, to his friend William Fields, July 22, 1863, and to his wife, May 14, 1864.

20. Holt, Papers, diary entry, May 10, 1864.

21. Upton, letter to "my dear Colonel," Fort Monroe, April 18, 1879, MHSM.

22. Beckwith, "Three Years with the Colors," January 24, 1864; *OR,* Upton, 667; Morse, *Personal Experiences,* 85.

23. *OR,* Upton, 667–668; Beckwith, "Three Years with the Colors," January 17, 1894.

24. Morse, *Personal Experiences,* 86.

25. Kidder, Letters, to his wife, May 30, 1864.

26. Hassett, "Initiation," November 15, 1912; *OR,* Upton, 668; Lovejoy, Letters, to his cousin Cynthia, June 27, 1864; Best, *121st,* 127; Kidder, Letters, to his wife, May, 30, 1864; Beckwith, "Three Years with the Colors," January 17, 1894.

27. Kidder, Letters, to his wife, May 30, 1864; Wood, "Experiences"; *OR,* Upton, 668; Gordon Report, in *OR,* ser. 1, vol. 36, pt. 1, 1078 (hereafter cited as *OR,* Gordon).

28. Holt, Papers, diary entry, May 10, 1864; Upton, letter to a Colonel, April 26, 1879, MHSM; Beckwith, "Three Years with the Colors," January 17 and 24, 1894.

29. "Class of 1863," *Hamilton Literary Monthly* 2, no. 5 (January 1868): 128; Delta Kappa Epsilon Memorial Eulogy, Clinton, May 26, 1864; undated obituary of Professor Edward North; letter, Butts's uncle Henry A. Abbott to Professor Edward North, Hamilton College, June 24, 1864; all in Hamilton College Archives; NYSAG, *Annual Report, 1903,* 26.

30. Morse, *Personal Experiences,* 87; Francis W. Foote, letter to his mother published in *Freeman's Journal,* July 29, 1864, and reports in the *Journal,* May 20 and 27, 1864; Beckwith, "Three Years with the Colors," January 24, 1894.

31. *Otsego Republican,* May 21, 1864; Lovejoy, letter to *Cherry Valley Gazette,* March 18, 1886; Slocum, Diary entries, May 10–13, 1864; Joseph Birch's statement, NYSA-GAR; Joe Heath, letter to the editor dated May 13, 1864, *Little Falls Journal and Courier,* May 19, 1864.

32. Sayles, Diary entries, May 8–14, 1864. Internal evidence, his date of rank, company, elimination of all others, his hometown of Frankfort, and his death at Spotsylvania in the NYSAG report indicate that it was Sayles's diary. NARA, Dolphus Sayles Pension Records, letter to his father, June 26, 1863.

33. *Otsego Republican,* April 15, 1865; Herdman, Letters, to Sperry, March 8, 1864.

34. Upton, "letter to my dear Colonel"; Kidder, Letters, to his wife, May 30, 1864. Best wrote after the war—and after he had embraced the temperance movement—that Mott failed to come up because he "was drunk. But for whiskey drinking, I believe the war would have ended a year before it did and certainly the lives of thousands of brave men would have been saved"; Best, "Through the Wilderness."

35. Beckwith, "Three Years with the Colors," January 31, 1894; Grant, *Personal Memoirs,* 2:224–225; Upton, Letters, to his sister, June 7, 1864.

36. Norton Galloway, "Hand to Hand Fighting at Spotsylvania," in Robert Underwood Johnson and Clarence Clough Buel, eds., *Battles and Leaders of the Civil War* (Edison, N.J.: Castle Edition, 1995), 4:170–174, 173; Best, "Through the Wilderness."

37. Oliver Edwards, "Spotsylvania, Va., May 12, 1864," in Edwards Collection, Illinois

State Historical Library, cited in Gordon C. Rhea, *The Battles for Spotsylvania Court House and the Road to Yellow Tavern, May 7–12, 1864* (Baton Rouge: Louisiana State University Press, 1997), 276.

38. Upton, Letters, to Norton Galloway, 95th Pennsylvania, August 31, 1878; Upton, letter to a Colonel, April 26, 1879, MHSM; Galloway, "Hand to Hand Fighting," 171.

39. Beckwith, "Three Years with the Colors," January 31, 1894; Bates, "War Reminiscences," *Otsego Republican*, June 19, 1895; Morse, *Personal Experiences*, 89–90.

40. Bates, "Nebraska Correspondence," *Otsego Republican*, October 3, 1894; Thomas H. Smith, "A Soldier's Story," Gilbertsville Local History Collection, Gilbertsville, N.Y.; Fish, letter to his brother, November 22, 1863, in Wilson, "Captain Fish and the 121st"; Best, "Through the Wilderness"; *Reunion Report, 1911,* Best reminiscences, 25.

41. Morse, *Personal Experiences*, 90–92; Henry Keiser, Diary entry, May 12, 1864, Keiser Papers, Harrisburg Civil War Round Table Collection, USAMHI; Galloway, "Hand to Hand Fighting," 172; Kidder, Letters, to his wife, May 14, 1864.

42. *OR,* Upton, 669; Beckwith, "Three Years with the Colors," January 31, 1894; Upton, Letters, to Norton Galloway, 95th Pennsylvania, August 31, 1878.

43. Best, "Through the Wilderness"; Beckwith, "Three Years with the Colors," January 31, 1894; Theodore Briggs to his wife, May 19, 1864, notes in author's collection; Holt, Papers, diary entry, May 12, 1864.

44. Galloway, "Hand to Hand Fighting,"174; *OR,* Upton, 669; Smith, "Soldiers Story"; Beckwith, "Three Years with the Colors," January 31 and February 7, 1894.

45. A. Reed, Letters, to his parents, May 19, 1864.

46. Teel, Letters, to his wife, May 17, 1864; Kidder, Letters, to his wife, May 14, 22, and 25, 1864.

47. McCurry, Diary entry, May 12, 1864; Kidder, Letters, to his friend Fields, July 22, 1863.

48. *Little Falls Journal and Courier,* n.d., in the collections of the NYSMM; Remmel, Letters, to his brother, May 22, 1864, and to his parents, May 22 and July 21, 1864; Bates, "Nebraska Correspondence," *Otsego Republican,* October 3, 1894; Bates, Letters, to his father, May 16 and 26, 1864; William F. Fox, *Regimental Losses in the American Civil War, 1861–1865* (Albany, N.Y.: Albany Publishing, 1889), 78n. John Lovejoy letter to the *National Tribune,* May 26, 1887. Upton, Letters, to Brayton G. Priest, Theresa, New York, n.d. Edward Johnson, a native of Russia, New York, graduated from Fairfield Seminary prior to attending Hamilton College in the upstate area. He was an exemplary student, admired by classmates and esteemed by his teachers. He joined Company C as a sergeant in the summer of 1862, was promoted to second lieutenant in the winter of 1863–1864, and a few months later was made a first lieutenant.

49. Morse, *Personal Experiences*, 93.

50. Holt, Papers, diary entry May 14, 1864; *OR,* Upton, 669; Beckwith, "Three Years with the Colors," February 7, 1894; Joe Heath, letter to the editor dated May 20, 1864, *Little Falls Journal and Courier,* June 2, 1864; Morse, *Personal Experiences*, 96.

51. Gordon Rhea, *To the North Anna River: Grant and Lee, May 13–25, 1864* (Baton Rouge: Louisiana State University Press, 2000), 243–244.

52. Gordon Rhea, *Cold Harbor* (Baton Rouge: Louisiana State University Press, 2002), 193.

53. Kidder, Letters, James Cronkite to John Kidder, June 5, 1864; Beckwith, "Three Years with the Colors," February 7, 1894.

54. Beckwith, "Three Years with the Colors," February 14, 1894; *OR*, Upton, 669; Welcher, *Union Army*, 1:306–307.

55. Hartwell, *Letters and Diary*, diary entry, June 1, 1864, 235; Cronkite, "Otsego in Rebellion," 75; Teel, Letters, to his wife, June 4, 1864.

56. Hartwell, *Letters and Diary*, diary entry, June 3, 1864, 236, June 3 and 10, 1864, 236 and 238; Adams, *Letters*, to his wife, June 9, 1864; Morse, *Personal Experiences*, 105.

57. Teel, Letters, to his wife, May 17, 1864; Bates, Letters, to his father, May 16, 1864; Slocum, Diary, May 22 and 26 and June 5, 1864; Holt, Papers, to his wife, May 13 and 16 and June 15, 1864.

58. Holt, Papers, June 24, 1864; Slocum, Diary, June 12, 1864; Hartwell, *Letters and Diary*, diary entry, June 13, 1864, 239.

59. *OR*, Upton, 492–493.

60. Frank Foote, a native of Cooperstown and brother of Morris Cooper Foote, enlisted in Warrenton, Virginia, on July 30, 1863, and mustered into Kidder's Company I as a second lieutenant, replacing Delavan Bates. He was promoted on April 19, 1864, before the Overland campaign; was wounded on May 10; and was released in September 1864. Brother Morris was on the staff of Henry Walton Wessels. Foote was a Confederate prisoner along with Wessels at Macon, Georgia. Foote's mother, a strong Unionist, worked tirelessly on behalf of the sick and wounded soldiers. When the *Freeman's Journal* thought that Frank was killed, it reported that she had given both sons to the cause and offered the community's heartfelt sympathy; *Freeman's Journal*, May 20 and 27 and July 29, 1864.

61. Rufus Clark, *The Heroes of Albany: A Memorial of the Patriots of the City and County of Albany* . . . (Albany, N.Y.: John Brooks, Publisher, 1866), 384–368; Kidder, Letters, Cronkite to Kidder, June 7, 1864; Upton letter to Brigadier General J. T. Sprague, New York Adjutant General, March 13, 1863, NARA, Books.

62. Cronkite, "Otsego in the Rebellion," 75; Upton, Letters, to his brother, May 31, 1864, and to his sister, June 4 and 5, 1864.

Chapter 12. To Washington and the Valley

1. Kidder, Letters, to his wife, May 19, June 6 and 24, and July 21, 1864.

2. Ibid., Ann Kidder to Harriett Kidder, July 20, 1864, and John to Harriett, May 25, 1864.

3. Richard Iobst, *Civil War Macon: The History of a Confederate City* (Macon, Ga.: Mercer University Press, 1999), 125–144.

4. Ibid., 135; *OR*, ser. 2, vol. 7, 373, letter of recommendation by Brigadier General William M. Gardner, CSA, Richmond, June 25, 1864; Kelley, Papers, diary entries, May 31, June 2, 3, 4, 5, 6, 10, 26, 27, and 28 and July 4, 1864; Report of Major Thomas Turner, CSA, May 25, 1864, *OR*, ser. 2, vol. 7, 168–169.

5. NARA, Kelley Pension Records, Lansing Paine sworn statement, August 22, 1866; Kelley, Papers, letter, to his mother, June 6, 1864, and diary entries, June 6, 11, and 17, July 3, 6, 18, 22, and 26, and August 3, 1864.

6. Brigadier General John Winder to General S. Cooper, Adjutant and Inspector General, CSA, July 18, 1864, *OR*, ser. 2, vol. 7, 472, and Major General Sam Jones to Cooper, 502; Kelley, Papers, diary entries, August 7, 8, 10, 12, 20, 23, 24, 26, and 28, 1864.

7. Letter, J. McCurdy, Asst. Surgeon, Asst. Medical Director, 14th Army Corps, to Colonel Barnes, Asst. Surgeon General, Washington, D.C., from Youngstown, Ohio, October 1, 1864, *OR*, ser. 2, vol. 7, 908.

8. Kelley Papers, letters, Mrs. Paine of Garrattsville to Mrs. Kelley in Schenevus, September 25, 1864.

9. Campbell, Letters, to his brother Cleaveland, August 7, 1864; Morse, *Personal Experiences*, 112–113.

10. Ingraham, *Letters*, to his brother, June 15, 1864; McCurry, Diary entry, June 19, 1864.

11. Beckwith, "Three Years with the Colors," February 28, 1894; Ingraham, *Letters*, to his brother, June 21, 1864.

12. Slocum, Diary entry, July 4, 1864; Teel, Letters, to his wife, July 13, 1864. The comment about the 96th is from Holt, Papers, letter to his wife, July 13, 1864. Also Beckwith, "Three Years with the Colors," March 14, 1894; Ingraham, *Letters*, to his brother, July 11, 1864; Slocum, Diary entry, July 11, 1864.

13. Holt, Papers, letter to his wife, July 13, 1864; Beckwith, "Three Years with the Colors," March 14, 1894; Lovejoy, Letters, to his cousin Cynthia, July 13 and 15, 1864; Slocum, Diary entry, July 12, 1864.

14. Beckwith, "Three Years with the Colors," March 14 and 21, 1894.

15. Teel, Letters, to his wife, July 13, 1864.

16. Remmel, Letters, to his parents, July 21, 1864.

17. Teel, Letters, to his wife, July 18 and 24, 1864; Ingraham, *Letters*, to Mary Green, July 19, 1864; Hartwell, *Letters and Diary*, letter to his wife, July 19, 1864, 258.

18. Holt, Papers, diary entries, July 24, 26, 29, 30, and 31, 1864, and letter to his wife, July 25, 1864; Slocum, Diary entry, July 19, 1864; McCurry, Diary entries, July 24 and 31, 1864; Beckwith, "Three Years with the Colors," March 21, 1894; Hartwell, *Letters and Diary*, letter to his wife, July 30, 1864, 263.

19. *OR*, ser. 1, vol. 43, pt. 2, Grant to Sheridan, order, August 26, 1864, 202, and Grant to Halleck, September 21, 1864, 103; Holt, Papers, letter to his wife, August 15, 1864.

20. General Orders No. 255, September 12, 1864, War Department, Adjutant General's Office, *OR*, ser. 2, vol. 7, 805; Hartwell, *Letters and Diary*, letter to his wife, August 22, 1864, 275, and diary entries, September 21 and October 10, 1864, 295–296, 287; Holt, Papers, diary entries, Tuesday, August 23, September 10, and October 10, 1864. Beckwith remembered that Olcott returned on August 10. Olcott's orders were dated August 16, 1864, and his Field and Staff Muster Roll Return indicates the date was August 23. The regimental books show he returned August 22. NARA, Regimental Books, letter, Captain Daniel Jackson, commanding the 121st, to Major Thomas M. Vincent, AA General, Washington, October 29, 1864; NARA, Olcott Pension and Military Records; NARA, Special Orders No. 272, Adjutant General's Office, and "Memorandum from Prisoner of War Records."

21. NARA, Regimental Books, General Orders No. 4, October 5, 1864.

22. Ingraham, *Letters*, to his brother Oll, August 1, 1864; Hartwell, *Letters and Diary*, letters to his wife, August 2, 15, and 30 and September 4, 1864, 264, 280; Beckwith, "Three

Years with the Colors," March 21 and 28, 1894; Lovejoy, Letters, to his cousin Cynthia, August 25, 1864; Teel, Letters, to his wife, August 23, 1864.

23. Hartwell, *Letters and Diary*, letter to his wife, August 27, 1864, 278.

24. Holt, Papers, September 16, 1864; NARA, Regimental Books, Letter, Henry Galpin to BG Sprague, Adjutant General, July 4, 1864; Bates, "War Reminiscences," *Otsego Republican*, August 12, 1896, and "Nebraska Correspondence," *Otsego Republican*, March 5, 1895; Adams, *Letters*, Chamberlain letter, undated, 237; Adams, *Letters*, to his wife, October 2 and 5, 1864.

25. Adams, *Letters*, to his wife, January 12, 1865.

26. Ibid., to brother and sister, February 22, 1864, 142, October 2, 158; Holt, Papers, diary entry, October 2, 1864; NARA, Books, General Order No. 3, October 5, 1864, and General Order No. 4, October 5, 1864.

27. Adams, *Letters*, letter to his wife, December 4, 1864.

28. Beckwith, "Three Years with the Colors," April 4, 1894.

29. *OR*, ser. 1, vol. 43, pt. 2, Grant to Sheridan, September 1, 1864, 3; Sheridan to Grant, September 2, 1864, 12; Sheridan to Halleck, September 2, 1864; Augur to Halleck, September 3, 1864, 18; Augur to Sheridan, September 4, 1864, 22.

30. Sheridan to Grant, September 20, 1864, *OR*, ser. 1, vol. 43, pt. 2, 119; Horatio C. King, "The Shenandoah Valley in the Great War," a paper read February 7, 1900, in James Grant Wilson and Titus Munson Coan, M.D., eds., *Personal Recollections of the War of the Rebellion: Addresses Delivered before the New York Commandery, MOLLUS, 1883–1891* (New York: New York Commandery, 1891; repr. Wilmington, N.C.: Broadfoot Publishing, 1992), 3:173 (citation is to the Broadfoot edition).

31. *OR*, Wright, 150; Beckwith, "Three Years with the Colors," March 28 and April 4, 1894; Letter, Sarah Beck to William Ford, in *Little Falls Journal and Courier*, October 27, 1864; Beers, *History*, 244; Teel, Letters, to his wife, September 22, 1864.

32. Adams, *Letters*, to his wife, November 19, 1864, 178.

33. Grant to Sheridan, September 25, 1864, *OR*, ser. 1, vol. 43, pt. 2; Adams, *Letters*, to his wife, September 25, 1864, 156; Hartwell, *Letters and Diary*, letter to his wife, September 21, 1864, 290; Welcher, *Union Army*, "Connecticut Regiments," 1:307; Bates, "Nebraska Correspondence," *Otsego Republican*, April 8, 1896.

34. Morse, *Personal Experiences*, 113–115; Hartwell, *Letters and Diary*, diary entry, Tuesday, November 29, 1864, 315–316; Lovejoy, Letters, to his cousin Cynthia, December 25, 1864. John Slocum recorded in his diary that Upton and Morse came to camp on November 27 and left two days later for the Army of the Cumberland; Slocum, Diary entries, November 27 and 29, 1864.

35. *OR*, ser. 1, vol. 43, pt. 2, Sheridan to Grant, September 19, 1864, 110; Lincoln to Sheridan, September 20, 1864, 117; Stanton to Sheridan, September 20, 1864, 117; Grant to Sheridan, September 20, 1864, 118; Stanton to Stevenson, September 20, 1864, 125.

36. McCurry, Diary entry, September 19, 1864.

37. Beckwith, "Three Years with the Colors," April 4, 1894; *OR*, Wright, 153.

38. *OR*, ser. 1, vol. 43, pt. 2, Sheridan to Grant, September 22, and Grant to Sheridan, September 22, 142; Sheridan to Grant, September 23; Grant to Sheridan, September 23, 152; Forsyth to Torbert, September 23, 156; Stevenson to Stanton, September 23, 158; Stan-

ton to Governor Curtin, September 23; Sheridan to Grant, September 21, 162; Stevenson to Stanton, September 24, 168.

39. Holt, Papers, letters to his wife, September 26 and October 2, 1864; Beckwith, "Three Years with the Colors," April 4 and 11, 1894. Beckwith got his corporal's stripes back on May 1, 1865.

40. Ingraham, *Letters*, to his parents, October 12, 1864.

41. NARA, Regimental Books, Letter, Olcott to BG Sprague, Albany, October 9, 1864.

42. Sheridan's Report on the Shenandoah Campaign, February 3, 1866, *OR*, ser. 1, vol. 43, pt. 1, 40–57, quote on 51 (hereafter cited as *OR*, Sheridan).

43. Joseph Whitehorne, *The Battle of Cedar Creek: A Self Guided Tour* (Washington, D.C.: Government Printing Office, 1992).

44. Ibid.; Beckwith, "Three Years with the Colors," April 11, 1894.

45. Beckwith, "Three Years with the Colors," April 11, 1894.

46. Ibid., April 18, 1894.

47. Olcott's Report, *OR*, ser. 1, vol. 43, pt. 1, 175 (hereafter cited as *OR*, Olcott); Beckwith, "Three Years with the Colors," April 18, 1894; Hartwell, *Letters and Diary*, diary entry, October 19, 1864, 299, and letter to his wife, October 25, 1864, 302–304.

48. Hartwell, *Letters and Diary*, letter to his wife, October 25, 1864, 302–304; *OR*, Sheridan, 52; Ingraham, *Letters*, to his parents, October 23, 1864; Wood, "Experiences"; Beckwith, "Three Years with the Colors," April 25, 1894.

49. *Cherry Valley Gazette*, cited in *Freeman's Journal*, December 23, 1864; Adams, *Letters*, to his wife, November 5 and 7, 1864, 173–174. John Slocum wrote, "Only one line officer remains in the 121st," and "In regiment but one Capt. and one Lieutenant present. It looks lonely enough"; Slocum, Diary entries, October 20 and 23, 1864.

50. Teel, Letters, to his wife, October 26, 1864.

51. Clark, *Heroes*, 384–394.

52. Burrell, Letters, to his brother James, December 23, 1863; NYSAG, *Annual Report, 1903*, 25; *Reunion Report, 1909*, Theodore Sternberg speech, 22–23; Kidder, Letters, to his wife, November 10, 1864.

53. NARA, Henry Galpin Pension and Military Records; *Reunion Report, 1910*, 33.

54. McCurry, Diary entry, October 20, 1864; Remmel, Letters, to his brother, Augustus, October 28, 1863; Hartwell, *Letters and Diary*, diary entry, October 20, 1864, letters to his wife, October 20 and 25, 1864, 300–304.

55. Lester W. Murdock, "Army Incidents," *Otsego Republican*, September 28, 1881; Bates, "Nebraska Correspondence," *Otsego Republican*, March 6, 1895; news item, *Otsego Republican*, February 25, 1865; NYSAG, *Annual Report, 1903*, 92 and 170.

56. *Reunion Report, 1912*, Brandon reminiscences, 19–22.

57. Kidder, Letters, to his wife, November 4, 1864; Parley McIntyre, obituary, February 1916, in the collections of the Gilbertsville Free Library, Gilbertsville, New York. McIntyre died February 13, 1916.

58. Keith S. Bohannon, "'The Fatal Halt' versus 'Bad Conduct': John B. Gordon, Jubal Early and the Battle of Cedar Creek," in Gary W. Gallagher, ed., *The Shenandoah Campaign of 1864* (Chapel Hill: University of North Carolina Press, 2006), 56–84; Horatio C. King, "The Battle of Cedar Creek," a paper read December 3, 1883, in Wilson and Coan, eds.,

Personal Recollections of the War of the Rebellion 1:37; Ingraham, *Letters,* to his parents, October 23, 1864. Early used a battalion to clear the camps of rebel plunderers "and drive the men to their commands." Later, he learned the problem was larger than he first understood it, causing him to send all his "staff officers who could be spared to stop it." See Jubal Early, "Winchester, Fisher's Hill, and Cedar Creek," in Robert Underwood Johnson and Clarence Clough Buel, eds., *Battles and Leaders of the Civil War* (Edison, N.J.: Castle Edition, 1995), 4:528.

59. George Fahey, letter to his mother, November 2, 1864, photocopies of originals in author's collection; Hartwell, *Letters and Diary,* letter to his wife, October 25, 1864, 304.

60. Kidder, Letters, to his wife, October 21, 1864; Holt, Papers, letters to his wife, July 1 and 13, diary entries, July 15 and October 15, 16, 17, 18, 19, 20, and 21, 1864.

61. NARA, Regimental Books, Cronkite to Adjutant General of New York, January 5, 1865; Ingraham, *Letters,* to his parents, November 2, 1864.

Chapter 13. Return to Petersburg, December 1864 to April 1865

1. Slocum, Diary entries, March 4, 1864, and July 29 and August 7, 1864, OHA.

2. Hartwell, *Letters and Diary,* letters to his wife, August 2 and 14, 1864, 264–265, 270; Hartwell, letter to the editor, *Herkimer County Journal and Courier,* March 3, 1864.

3. Teel, Letters, to his wife, September 8 and 22, 1864; Wool to Stanton, September 24, 1864, *OR,* ser. 1, vol. 43, pt. 1, 170; Ingraham, *Letters,* to his father, March 5, to his friend Mary Green, September 18, and to his parents, November 2, 1864; Holt, Papers, letters to his wife, August 1 and September 2, 1864; Adams, *Letters,* to his wife, October 15 and 26, 1864, 166 and 168.

4. *Little Falls Journal and Courier,* October 13, 1864; Peter Mickel, letter to the editor, *Oneonta Herald,* September 21, 1864; Michael Hartford, letter to his sister, November 21, 1864, in author's collection; Mitchell, *Horatio Seymour,* 378; Remmel, Letters, to his parents, October 16, 1864.

5. Slocum, Diary entry, November 8, 1864, OHA; *Cherry Valley Gazette,* cited in *Freeman's Journal,* October 28, 1864; Hesseltine, *Lincoln and the War Governors,* 381; A. Reed, Letters, to his parents, September 9, October 23 and 29, and November 18, 1864; Hartwell, *Letters and Diary,* diary entry, November 8, 1864, 308; Kidder, Letters, to his wife, November 4 and 10, 1864.

6. Ingraham, *Letters,* to his parents, October 23, 1864.

7. Bates, Letters, to his father, November 13, 1864.

8. The *Cherry Valley Gazette* reported that "the 121st is nearly extinct as an organization. Its record has been, from the start, a glorious one." *Freeman's Journal,* November 18, 1864.

9. Hartwell, *Letters and Diary,* diary entry, Saturday, December 3, 1864, 319; Hurd, *History,* 81; Beckwith, "Three Years with the Colors," May 2, 1894; McCurry, Diary entries, December 1–5 and 9, 1864; A. Wilson Greene, *Breaking the Backbone of the Rebellion: The Final Battles of the Petersburg Campaign* (Mason City, Iowa: Savas Publishing, 2000), 55.

10. John Ingraham, letter to the editor, *Little Falls Journal and Courier,* June 23, 1864; Ingraham, *Letters,* to his brother Oll, January 22, 1865.

11. *Freeman's Journal,* December 30, 1864; Kelley, Papers, letters, Cronkite to Kelley,

December 23, 1864; Letter, Cronkite to S. Thomas, Adjutant General, Washington, D.C., December, 24, 1864, NARA, Regimental Books.

12. Kimball, *Soldier-Doctor,* 7–12, 13.

13. Chaplain John Adams, letter to the editor, *Otsego Republican,* November 17, 1864; Lovejoy, Letters, to his cousin Cynthia, January 8, 1865; Horatio Duroe, letter to his father, October 21, 1864, photocopy of original in author's collection.

14. Chaplain Adams was unhappy with Olcott's resignation. When Olcott "concluded to leave," only Adams expressed "great regret." Adams, *Letters,* to his wife, December 14, 1864, and January 6, 1865, 187 and 195; Holt, Papers, diary entry, August 30, 1864.

15. Egbert Olcott, letter to Reuben E. Fenton, January 24, 1865, with endorsement by Gen. Frank Wheaton, January 25, 1865, in private collection; Isaac Bassett, letter to his friend Annie, December 6, 1864, photocopy of letter in author's collection; *Otsego Republican and Democrat,* September 21, 1877; Kidder, Letters, to his wife, January 30, 1865.

16. NARA, Henry Galpin Pension and Military Records.

17. NYSAG, *Annual Report, 1903,* 10; Letter, Cronkite to J. J. Bartlett, December 31, 1864, NARA, Books; Letter, Cronkite to Governor Reuben Fenton, January 2, 1865, NARA, Books.

18. Bates, Letters, to his father, January 15, 1865.

19. Hartwell, *Letters and Diary,* letter to his wife, March 16, 1865, 336–337; Slocum, Diary entry, December 24, 1864, OHA; Lovejoy, Letters, to Cynthia, December 25, 1864.

20. Adams, *Letters,* to his wife, December 31, 1864, 191; Bates, Letters, to his father, January 18, 1865.

21. Beckwith, "Three Years with the Colors," May 9 and 16, 1894.

22. Lovejoy, Letters, to his cousin Cynthia, March 9, 1865.

23. William B. Hesseltine, *Civil War Prisons* (Columbus: Ohio State University Press, 1930), 155, cited in Sister M. Anne Francis Campbell, "Bishop England's Sisterhood, 1829–1929" (PhD diss., Saint Louis University, 1968), 143; Kelley, Papers, diary entries, August 30, September 3, 5, 11, 13, 14, 15, and 24, November 28, 29, and 30, and December 4, 1865.

24. Sam Jones, Major General, to James Seddon, September 7, 1864, *OR,* ser. 2, vol. 7, 782; Chaplain John Adams, letter to the editor dated November 17, 1864, *Otsego Republican,* December 3, 1864; Kelley, Papers, letters, Abbie Howe to Mrs. Kelley, December 4, Sam to his mother and sister, December 16, and Abbie Howe to Mrs. Kelley, December 22, 1864.

25. Kelley, Papers, letters, A. L. Howe to Mrs. Kelley, January 3, Mrs. Kelley to Sylvina, January 17, 20, 21, and 22, 1865; Calista Bailey to Mrs. Kelley, February 23 and March 21, 1863.

26. Kimball, *Soldier-Doctor,* 14.

27. Ibid., 15; Ingraham, *Letters,* to his parents, February 10, 1865; Greene, *Breaking the Backbone,* 143–149.

28. Kimball, *Soldier-Doctor,* 17–18; Bates, "War Reminiscences," *Otsego Republican,* August 12, 1896; Frank Wheaton Report, *OR,* ser. 1, vol. 46, pt. 1, 297–300 (hereafter cited as *OR,* Wheaton); Greene, *Breaking the Backbone,* 149.

29. Bates, "War Reminiscences," *Otsego Republican,* August 12, 1896; Adams, *Letters,* to his wife, March 22, 1865, 212; Kidder, Letters, to his wife, March 12, 1865.

30. Beckwith, "Three Years with the Colors," May 16, 1894, Ingraham, *Letters*, to his parents, March 17, 1865; Woodcock, diary entry March 18, 1865, NYSMM.

31. General Order No. 1, January 8, 1865, NARA, Regimental Books.

32. Ingraham, *Letters*, to Mary Green, February 3, 1865.

33. Bates, Letters, to his father, December 25, 1864, and January 15, 1865; Lovejoy, Letters, to his cousin Cynthia, February 3, 1865.

34. Adams, *Letters*, to his wife, February 28, 1865, 207; Lovejoy, Letters, to his cousin Cynthia, January 23 and March 14, 1865; Ingraham, *Letters*, to his parents, February 23 and 27, 1865.

35. Cronkite, *History*, 82; Ingraham, *Letters*, to his brother Oll, March 27, 1865; Beckwith, "Three Years with the Colors," May 23, 1894; Duroe, letter to his father, October 24, 1864, photocopy in author's collection; NARA, Horatio Duroe Pension Records.

36. Adams, *Letters*, to his wife, March 26, 1865, 213; Hartwell, *Letters and Diary*, letter to his wife, March 26, 1865, 344, and diary entry, March 29, 1865, 345; Beckwith, "Three Years with the Colors," May 23, 1894; Lovejoy, Letters, to his cousin Cynthia, March 27, 1865.

37. Adams, *Letters*, to his wife, April 1, 1865, 214; Hartwell, *Letters and Diary*, diary entry, April 1, 1865, 346; Beckwith, "Three Years with the Colors," May 23, 1894.

38. Adams, *Letters*, to his wife, April 1, 1865, 214; Beckwith, "Three Years with the Colors," May 23, 1894.

39. Adams, letter to the editor dated April 15, 1865, *Otsego Republican*, April 29, 1865; Lovejoy, Letters, to cousin Cynthia, April 15, 1865.

40. Kidder, Letters, to his wife, March 30 and April 10, 1865; *OR*, ser. 1, vol. 46, pt. 1, Olcott's Report, 936, and Wright's Report, 903.

41. Best, William L. Clements Library, University of Michigan, Ann Arbor; Joseph E. Hamblin Report, April 15, 1865, *OR*, ser. 1, vol. 46, pt. 1, 931–932 (hereafter cited as *OR*, Hamblin); *OR*, Wright, 904; Hartwell, *Letters and Diary*, diary entry, April 2, 1865, 347; Greene, *Breaking the Backbone*, 317.

42. *OR*, Hamblin, 932; *OR*, Wheaton, 913; Cronkite, *History*; Adams, *Letters*, letter to the editor, *Otsego Republican*, April 20, 1865, 215; Lovejoy, Letters, to Cynthia, April 15, 1865; Hartwell, *Letters and Diary*, diary entry, April 3, 1865, 347; Ingraham, *Letters*, to his parents, April 28, 1865; Beckwith, "Three Years with the Colors," May 30, 1894; Hassett, "Initiation," December 27, 1912.

43. Hartwell, *Letters and Diary*, diary entry, Monday, April 3, 1865, 347; *OR*, Wright, 905.

44. Hartwell, *Letters and Diary*, diary entry, Wednesday, April 5, 1865, 348; Beckwith, "Three Years with the Colors," May 30, 1894.

45. Beckwith, "Three Years with the Colors," May 30 and June 6, 1894; Hartwell, *Letters and Diary*, diary entry, Thursday, April 6, 1865, 348; *OR*, Wright, 906.

46. Beckwith, "Three Years with the Colors," June 6, 1894; *Freeman's Journal*, May 26, 1865; Lovejoy, Letters, to his cousin, Cynthia, February 26 and April 16, 1865.

47. Hartwell, *Letters and Diary*, diary entry, April 6, 1865, 348; Ingraham, *Letters*, to his parents, April 16, 1865; Lovejoy, Letters, to his mother, April 14, 1864; *Freeman's Journal*, May 26, 1865; *OR*, Wheaton, 916.

48. *OR*, Wright, 905; *OR*, Wheaton, 925; NARA, Benjamin Gifford File; *OR*, Hamblin, 933; Kidder, Letters, to his wife, April 10, 1865.

49. Beckwith, "Three Years with the Colors," June 6, 1894; Adams, *Letters,* to C. A. Lord, Esq., April 20, 1865, 215; Kidder, Letters, to his wife, April 20, 1865.

50. "In Memoriam," *Otsego Republican,* May 20, 1865; "In Memoriam," *Freeman's Journal,* May 26, 1865; Kidder, Letters, to Asa Howland, May 14, 1865, first published in the *Cherry Valley Gazette* and then the *Otsego Republican,* June 17, 1865.

51. *Otsego Republican,* June 17, 1865.

52. Ibid.; *Cherry Valley Gazette,* June 14, 1865; NARA, Ten Eyck Howland Pension Records.

53. Lovejoy, Letters, to his cousin Cynthia, May 5, 10, 14, and 21, 1865, and to his mother, May 4, 1865.

Chapter 14. Lee Surrenders and the War Ends

1. Best, "Siege and Capture of Petersburg," WLC; Beckwith, "Three Years with the Colors," June 6, 1894; Ingraham, *Letters,* to his parents, April 16, 1865.

2. Beckwith, "Three Years with the Colors," June 13, 1894; Hassett, "Initiation," December 27 and February 12, 1913; Kidder, Letters, to his wife, April 10, 1865; Best, *121st,* 220; Ingraham, *Letters,* to his parents, April 16, 1865; Hartwell, *Letters and Diary,* diary entry, Sunday, April 9, 1865, 349; Best, "Siege and Capture of Petersburg," WLC; Lovejoy, Letters, to his cousin Cynthia, April 15, 1865.

3. Kidder, Letters, to his wife, March 30 and April 10, 1865.

4. *Herkimer Democrat,* April 12, 1865.

5. A. Reed, Letters, to his parents, April 14, 1865.

6. Lovejoy, Letters, to his cousin Cynthia, April 16, 1865; Ingraham, *Letters,* to his parents, April 21, 1865; Kidder, Letters, to his wife, April 19 and 25, 1865; Beckwith, "Three Years with the Colors," June 20, 1894; Adams, *Letters,* to his wife, January 6, 1865, 193–194.

7. Best, *121st,* 233 and 238.

8. Wood, "Experiences"; Hartwell, *Letters and Diary,* letter to his wife, April 21, 1865, 351; Adams, *Letters,* to his wife, April 19, 1865, 219; Adams, *Letters,* to C. Lord, Esq., April 20, 1865, 217; Beckwith, "Three Years with the Colors," June 3, 1894; Kidder, Letters, to his wife, April 19, 1865; Ingraham, *Letters,* to his parents, April 21, 1865.

9. A. Reed, Letters, to his parents, April 20, 1865.

10. *Little Falls Journal and Courier,* April 27, 1865.

11. Kimball, *Soldier-Doctor,* 24–26.

12. Lovejoy, Letters, to his cousin Cynthia, May 4, 1865.

13. Ibid.; Luman Baldwin, Letters, to his parents, May 21, 1865; Ingraham, *Letters,* to his parents, May 19, 1865.

14. Joe Heath, letter to the editor, *Little Falls Journal and Courier,* June 22, 1865; Alvan A. Richmond, letter to the editor, *Little Falls Journal and Courier,* June 22, 1865; Lovejoy, Letters, to his cousin Cynthia, May 2 and 4 and June 3, 1865.

15. Ingraham, *Letters,* to his parents, May 5, 1865; Lovejoy, Letters, to his cousin Cynthia, May 2, 4, and 14, 1865.

16. Kidder, Letters, to his wife, April 25 and 29 and May 28, 1865.

17. Kimball, *Soldier-Doctor,* 23–24; Beckwith, "Three Years with the Colors," June 13 and 20, 1894.

18. Beckwith, "Three Years with the Colors," June 20, 1894; Kidder, Letters, to his wife, May 28, 1865.

19. Kidder, Letters, to his wife, May 28, 1865.

20. Ibid., May 21, 1865. Foote was commissioned a first lieutenant in the 121st on March 26, 1865, after serving two and a half years with the 44th New York and the 92nd New York. He escaped from a Confederate prison in Georgia. Along with most of the 121st's officer corps, he was recommended for brevetting, in his case as a captain, for gallant service at Petersburg and Sailor's Creek. Foote's mother was a Cooper, and he was a native of Cooperstown. He remained in the army until he retired in 1903 as a brigadier general two years before his death. His wife lived until the middle of World War II, dying in 1943. He is buried in Arlington Cemetery.

21. Adams, Letters, to his wife, cited in Best, 121st, 224; Wood, "Experiences."

22. Ingraham, Letters, to his parents, June 3, 1865; Lovejoy, Letters, to his cousin Cynthia, May 21 and June 3 and 4, 1865.

23. Hartwell, Letters and Diary, letter to his wife, June 9, 1865, 352.

24. Lovejoy, Letters, to his cousin Cynthia, June 3, 1865.

25. Hassett, "Initiation," December 27, 1912.

26. John Lovejoy, letter to the editor, Cherry Valley Gazette, March 18, 1886; New York Times, June 9, 1865.

27. Joshua Chamberlain, "The Last Review of the Army of the Potomac, May 23, 1865," War Papers Read before the Commandery of the State of Maine, MOLLUS (Portland, Me.: Lefavor-Tower, 1908), 3:330; Wood, "Experiences"; Best, 121st, 225 and 238.

28. Lovejoy, Letters, to his cousin Cynthia, June 10, 12, and 18, 1865; Ingraham, Letters, to his parents, June 6, 1865; Hassett, "Initiation into the Ways of War," West Winfield Star, 1912–1913, February 7, 1913.

29. Beckwith, "Three Years with the Colors," June 21, 1894; Lovejoy, Letters, to his cousin Cynthia, June 30 and July 2, 1865; Albany Evening Journal, July 1, 1865, cited in Freeman's Journal, July 7, 1865; Albany Evening Journal, June 29, 1865; Albany Express, June 29, 1865; Clark, Heroes, 39. Beckwith's recollection of the trip back to the Empire State suffered from a thirty-year distance from the events. John Lovejoy was one of the few men in the regiment who wrote until the bitter end; his last letter was dated July 2, 1865, and was written to his cousin Cynthia. He provided an accurate chronology to Cynthia and, in an earlier letter, to his mother.

30. Kidder, Letters, to his wife, August 27 and September 16, 1863; NARA, Charles Dean Pension File, Dr. P. Croghan, letter to whom it may concern, June 8, 1864, and L. C. Turner, letter to Colonel Hardin, June 13, 1864.

31. Kidder, Letters, to his wife, October 1, 1864.

32. Wood, "Experiences"; New York Monuments Commission for the Battlefields of Gettysburg and Chattanooga, Final Report on the Battlefield of Gettysburg (Albany, N.Y.: J. B. Lyon, 1902), 2:842–843.

33. New York Monuments Commission, Final Report, 843; Freeman's Journal, June 9, 1865; Little Falls Journal and Gazette, quoted in Otsego Republican, June 3, 1865; Otsego Republican, July 1, 1865.

34. Freeman's Journal, July 7, 1865.

35. Beckwith, "Three Years with the Colors," June 27, 1894.

36. The Galpin story is from *Reunion Report, 1912,* reminiscence by D. A. Dewey, 22.

37. *Little Falls Journal and Courier,* July 6, 1865. The paper carried several full pages of coverage on the entire day in Little Falls.

38. *Little Falls Journal and Courier,* August 30, 1865; Beckwith, "Three Years with the Colors," June 27, 1894; Best, *121st,* 228.

39. *Otsego Republican,* July 7, 1897.

40. Ibid., July 1, 1865.

41. New York State Bureau of Military Statistics, *Presentation of Flags of New York Volunteer Regiments and Other Organizations, to His Excellency, Governor Fenton, in Accordance with a Resolution of the Legislature, July 4, 1865* (Albany, N.Y.: Weed, Parsons, 1865), 20–21; Fenton's speech, 24–28; Chapin's speech, 221–244; Sickles's remarks, 243–244.

42. Ibid.; *Otsego Republican,* June 17, 1865.

43. Wood, "Experiences."

44. "Winner of Congressional Medal of Honor in Civil War Wrote Story before Death: Dockum Funeral Held Today; Story of Exploit Is Told," *Colorado Springs Telegraph,* October 5, 1921, available at http://www.homeofheroes.com/news/archives/1921_1005 _dockum.html.

Chapter 15. Touching Elbows: The Regimental Association

1. Lovejoy, Letters, to his cousin Cynthia, April 16, 1865.

2. Hartwell, *Letters and Diary,* letter to his wife, February 1, 1864, 193.

3. Cleaveland Campbell, letter to the editor, *Cherry Valley Gazette,* July 1, 1863.

4. *Herkimer Democrat,* June 27 and January 10, 1894; *Reunion Report, 1907,* Dennis Dewey remarks, 17; Beers, *History,* 97.

5. Walker, Letters, to his sister, August 10, 1863.

6. Gordon Jones, "Gut History: Civil War Reenacting and the Making of the American Past" (PhD diss., Emory University, 2007), 35; *Otsego Republican,* September 13, 1882; *Reunion Report, 1910,* D. C. Hurd speech, 5.

7. Phisterer, *New York,* 1:94–95, 130.

8. NYSA-GAR.

9. *Otsego Republican,* July 1, August 12 and 26, and December 23, 1865; Cooper, "Chronicles," 83.

10. *Otsego Republican and Democrat,* July 12, 1876.

11. Delavan Bates described "touching elbows" in "War Reminiscences," *Otsego Republican,* July 17, 1895.

12. *Otsego Republican and Democrat,* May 16 and 31, August 16, 22, and 30, and September 14 and 21, 1877.

13. *Freeman's Journal,* August 1, 12, 19, and 26 and October 10, 1878, and *Otsego Republican,* September 12 and 19 and October 10, 1878. Campbell's entire speech was in both papers on October 10.

14. *Freeman's Journal,* August 28, 1879; *Otsego Republican,* July 31 and August 7 and 28, 1879; *Reunion Report, 1907,* letter from Sara Upton Edwards to C. J. Westcott, August 27, 1907.

15. *Freeman's Journal,* October 14, 1880; *Otsego Republican,* September 9, 23, and 30 and

October 13, 1880; *Freeman's Journal,* August 28, September 24, and October 10 and 29, 1881; *Otsego Republican,* August 24, September 21, October 5, 12, and 26, 1881, and March 8, 1882.

16. *Otsego Republican,* August 29, 1883.

17. Kidder, Letters, to his wife, December 14, 1862; *Otsego Republican,* July 7, 1896; Bates, "War Reminiscences," *Otsego Republican,* March 6 and April 3, 1895.

18. Bicknell, *History.* The building's history is in the reprint's introduction by Kimberly A. MacIsaac, curator of the Fifth Maine Regiment Community Center, n.p. *Reunion Report, 1907,* description by Wallace W. Young, and Letter, N. R. Lougee to C. J. Westcott, September 1, 1907, 36–37.

19. *Reunion Report, 1908,* 14–16, 46.

20. The thirty-second annual meeting in 1908 was in Oneonta. Tyler's poem was printed in the *Reunion Report, 1908.*

21. *Cherry Valley Gazette,* June 25, 1865.

22. NARA, Francis E. Lowe Pension Records.

23. *Freeman's Journal,* August 5, 1887.

24. Letters, Cronkite to Cooney, December 27, 1888, and Cooney to Cronkite, December 29, 1888, cited in J. W. Cronkite, comp., *Report of the Gettysburg Monument Committee of the 121st New York Volunteers* (Cooperstown, N.Y.: Otsego Republican, n.d. [late 1896]), 17–19, 20–21 (hereafter cited as Cronkite, *Report*).

25. Ibid., 16 and 19.

26. James W. Cronkite, "Letter from the Gettysburg Monument Committee to the friends of the 121st New York volunteers and to the patriotic people of Otsego and Herkimer Counties, New York, January 14, 1888," in ibid., 11–16.

27. *Otsego Republican,* February 8 and 22, April 8 and 25, May 9, 16, and 23, June 8, July 4, September 26, and October 10 and 24, 1888, and *Freeman's Journal,* February 10, September 28, and October 12 and 26, 1888. Wilson's letter appeared on May 16, and Williams's was published on April 25.

28. *Freeman's Journal,* May 17, August 30, and September 20, 1889, and *Otsego Republican,* October 23, 1889; Cronkite, *Report,* 22–24.

29. Letters, John Lovejoy to D. C. Kilbourne, September 25 and 29, 1889, 2nd Connecticut Heavy Artillery, Manuscript Department, New-York State Historical Society. The Bailey story appeared in *Otsego Republican,* October 9, 1889. Also see *Biographical Review, 1893,* 140.

30. *Richfield Springs Mercury,* October 3, 1889; *Freeman's Journal,* October 11, 1889; *Otsego Republican,* October 16 and October 23, 1889; Cronkite, *Report.* Mills's speech was printed in the *Republican* on October 23, 1889, and later in Cronkite's *Report* and the New York Monuments Commission, *Final Report,* 2:830–838. See Cronkite's remarks, entitled "The Regimental Record," in ibid., 830; Cronkite, *Report,* 15. An earlier version appeared in his appeal letter written on January 14, 1888.

31. *Otsego Republican,* December 30, 1896; Cronkite, *Report,* 56–74; *Otsego Republican,* June 23 and July 5, 1893, and September 25, 1895; *Freeman's Journal,* August 29, 1890; *Reunion Report, 1908; Reunion Report, 1912.*

32. *Reunion Report, 1909,* Dewey reminiscence, 4; *Reunion Report, 1907,* letter of Erastus Hawks, September 4, 1907, to C. J. Westcott; *Reunion Report, 1908,* 12 and 22.

33. *Otsego Republican,* June 5, 1895.

34. Ibid., July 7, 1897.

35. *Reunion Report, 1898*, 4; *Reunion Report, 1908*, remarks by Col. Walter Scott of the 1st New York Volunteers, 3. Scott humbly said: "It is hard to talk to you veterans, because I realize my insignificance for I served in a war which was not so significant."

36. *Reunion Report, 1902*, 4; *Reunion Report, 1903*, 25; *Reunion Report, 1904*, 2; *Reunion Report, 1906*, 17; reunion invitation, 1907.

37. *Reunion Report, 1907*; Best, *121st*, 248–249; *Reunion Report, 1909*, Dennis Dewey, Reminiscences, 20; NYSAG, *Annual Report, 1903*, 50; *Reunion Report, 1912*, 16.

38. "A Private," *Otsego Republican*, July 28, 1897; NYSA-GAR, 1895.

39. *Reunion Report, 1908*, 36–37.

40. D. A. Ellis, *Grand Army of the Republic: History of the Order in the U.S. by Counties: Otsego County Posts, Department of New York . . . Together with Valuable Statistics & Miscellaneous Matter* ([Cooperstown, N.Y.?]: Historical Publishing and D. A. Ellis, 1892), available at http://library.morrisville.edu/local_history/sites/gar_post/otsego_gar.html; http://library.morrisville.edu/local_history/sites/gar_post/herk_gar.html.

41. *Reunion Report, 1912*, 25–26.

42. Stuart McConnell, *Glorious Contentment: The Grand Army of the Republic, 1865–1900* (Chapel Hill: University of North Carolina Press, 1992), 177–179, 183.

43. *Reunion Report, 1909*; *Reunion Report, 1910*; *Reunion Report, 1907*; Erastus L. Hawks, letter to C. J. Westcott, September 4, 1907.

Chapter 16. Shaping the Memory: Writing the History

1. Hartwell, *Letters and Diary*, letter to his wife, November 15, 1863.

2. *New York Tribune*, November 10, 1863; Captain John Fish to his brother, November 12 and 22, 1863, and Captain Cleaveland Campbell to the editor of the *New York Tribune*, November 20, 1863, in John S. Wilson, "Captain Fish and the 121st New York Volunteers at Rappahannock Station, Virginia," *Military Collector and Historian: The Journal of the Company of Military Historians* (Washington, D.C.) 48, no. 3 (Fall 1996): 114–120.

3. Upton, Letters, to his sister, November 15, 1863.

4. *National Tribune*, various articles, 1884–1922: John Lovejoy, December 25, 1884; Hutchinson, January 8, 1885; Bates, March 12, 1885; Lovejoy, October 15, 1885; J. B. Round, December 1, 1885, and August 15, 1895; George Lusk, August 19, 1897; W. J. Wray, July 25, 1901.

5. J. S. Anderson, "Load at Will, Load!" *Milwaukee Sunday Telegraph*, cited in *Ellsworth (Me.) American*, October 25, 1883; Bates, "Nebraska Correspondence: Rappahannock Station," *Otsego Republican*, June 27, 1894; A. S. Daggett, "Carried by Assault: Work of the Gallant Upton," *Otsego Republican*, August 12, 1891; Robert S. Westbrook, *History of the 49th Pennsylvania Volunteers* (Altoona, Pa.: Altoona Times, 1898), 168; Westbrook, letter to the *National Tribune*, September 2, 1897.

6. Bates, "Nebraska Correspondence," *Otsego Republican*, June 27, 1894.

7. Letter, Horatio Wright to J. S. Anderson, October 18, 1898, and letter, Andrew Cowan to Anderson, February 3, 1917, USAMHI.

8. Philip Woodcock, photocopy of his diary entry of April 6, 1865, USAMHI.

9. Archibald Hopkins Report, *OR*, ser. 1, vol. 46, pt. 1, 948 (hereafter cited as *OR*, Hop-

kins); Adams, letter to the editor dated April 15, *Otsego Republican*, April 29, 1865; *OR*, Olcott, 937–938; *OR*, Hamblin, 934.

10. *OR*, Wright, 907; *OR*, Wheaton, 915; for Wheaton's long report, see 923–926, esp. "assisting Hawthorne," 925.

11. Ingraham, *Letters*, to his parents, April 16, 1865; Lovejoy, Letters, to his cousin Cynthia, April 15, 1865, and to his mother, April 14, 1865; Kidder, Letters, to his wife, April 10, 1865; Adams, *Letters*, to C. A. Lord, Esq., April 20, 1865; Beckwith, "Three Years with the Colors," June 6, 1894.

12. William H. Penrose Report, April 5, 1865, *OR*, ser. 1, vol. 26, pt. 1, 927 (hereafter cited as *OR*, Penrose); *OR*, Hopkins, 947.

13. Adjutant General of the Commonwealth of Massachusetts, *Annual Report for the Year Ending December 31, 1865* (Public Document No. 7) (Boston: Wright and Porter, State Printers, 1866), 507.

14. James L. Bowen, *History of the Thirty-seventh Regiment Mass. Volunteers* (Holyoke, Mass.: Clark W. Bryan, 1884), 419–420; *Otsego Republican*, January 6, 1892; *New York Sun*, September 19, 1897.

15. *Otsego Republican*, October 27, 1897.

16. NYSA-GAR; W. F. Beyer and O. F. Keydel, eds., *Deeds of Valor: How America's Civil War Heroes Won the Congressional Medal of Honor* (New York: Smithmark Publications, 2000), 530; Hassett, "Initiation," February 7, 1913.

17. Best, *121st*, 215–218; Best, "Siege and Capture of Petersburg," WLC.

18. *Unadilla Times*, May 27 and August 17, 1921; *Otsego Farmer*, April 5 and July 29, 1921; *Herkimer Telegram-Record*, August 24, 1920; *Unadilla Times*, January 13, 1922; *Hartwick Reporter*, October 18, 1922.

19. *Otsego Farmer*, July 21, 1921; *Worcester Times*, August 10, 1921; *Oneonta Star*, July 28, 1921; *Herkimer Democrat*, February 3 and March 16, 1892.

20. *Little Falls Evening Times*, June 24, 1922.

21. *Freeman's Journal*, August 18, 1865, quoted in *Cherry Valley Gazette* (n.d.), stating that Olcott "is writing a history of the organization and military career of this gallant regiment." The announcement of the association's attempt to write a regimental history was printed in the *Journal*, July 17, 1886.

22. Morse, *Personal Experiences*, iii–iv.

23. Hassett, "Initiation," various dates at end of 1912 and early 1913.

24. *Otsego Republican and Democrat*, March 22, 1876.

25. *Otsego Republican and Democrat*, September 21, 1877. Bates wrote voluminously and corrected his errors in his next column. In one piece, he had James Cronkite's watch saving his life at the battle of Funkstown, which he later corrected to the battle of Spotsylvania; *Otsego Republican*, October 3, 1894.

26. The warning was reported in the *Otsego Republican*, July 7, 1897.

27. *Reunion Report, 1898*; *Reunion Report, 1899*; *Reunion Report, 1904*.

28. *Reunion Report, 1904*.

29. Hurd credits Cronkite for the history of the 121st in his *History of Otsego County*, 8. The *Freeman's Journal*, August 11, 1886, reported that Cronkite was authorized to write the official history. The August 29, 1890, *Journal* and the August 13, 1890, *Republican* carried his promise to deliver a manuscript soon. See *Reunion Report, 1898*, 7; the ultimatum

is in the *Otsego Republican,* August 30, 1899; *Reunion Report, 1911,* 15, and Hassett's frustration, 21; *Reunion Report, 1912,* 14–15.

30. "Best, Isaac Oliver, 1841–1923," background note to Best's three essays on deposit with the William Clements Library, University of Michigan, Schoff Civil War Collection, Diaries and Journals, F6.1, pp. 1–3, available at http://www.clements.umich.edu/Web guides/Schoff/B/Best.html (hereafter cited as Best, Background Note). Also see Best, *121st,* v–vii; Best, Background Note, 2; Best, Papers, Hamilton College Library Archives.

31. *Reunion Report, 1910,* Best letter to C. J. Westcott, August 8, 1910, 11–12; *Reunion Report, 1911,* 15–18.

32. *Reunion Report, 1911,* 26, 36–37.

33. NARA, Beckwith Pension Records.

34. Beckwith, "Three Years with the Colors," August 16 and September 27, 1893.

35. Best, *121st,* 65–66 and v and vi.

36. Ibid., 6 and 78, where Beckwith writes of the battle of Salem Church ("More than thirty years have elapsed since the battle of Salem Church"), and 47, on the battle of Fredericksburg. Beckwith's obituary is in the *Herkimer Telegram-Record,* February 9, 1926. Beckwith, "Three Years with the Colors," July 5, 1893, through July 4, 1894. The *Democrat* quotes are from July 29, 1893, and January 10 and 24, 1894.

37. Beckwith, "Three Years with the Colors," June 13, 1894.

38. Best, *121st,* vi.

39. Ibid., 250; *Otsego Republican,* July 7, 1897; Lovejoy, Letters, to Cynthia, March 20, 1864.

Epilogue: The Survivors of Time

1. Rice, *Letters,* to his brother Daniel, August 22, 1863, 115.

2. Michie, *Life and Letters,* 217–235.

3. U.S. War Department, *Emory Upton: The Epitome of Upton's Military Policy of the United States* (Document No. 505) (Washington, D.C.: Government Printing Office, 1916); Stephen Ambrose, "Upton's Military Reforms," *Civil War Times Illustrated* 2, no. 5 (August 1963): 25–30; Andrew J. Bacevich Jr., "Emory Upton: A Centennial Assessment," *Military Review: The Professional Journal of the U.S. Army* 61, no. 12 (1981): 21–28; Richard C. Brown, "General Emory Upton—The Army's Mahan," *Military Affairs: Journal of the American Military Institute* 17 (1953), 125–131; Stephen Ambrose, "Emory Upton and the Armies of Asia and Europe," *Military Affairs* 28, no. 1 (1964): 27–32; Lt. Col. R. M. Cheseldine, Ohio National Guard, "Where Upton Made His Big Mistake," *United States Infantry Association* 36 (March 1930): 279–288. Bacevich argues that Upton was responsible for the concept that American politics or society had no room for the professional soldier.

4. Holt, Papers, diary entry, Tuesday, July 5, 1864; NARA, Record Group 94, Adjutant General's Office, Entry 544, Field Records of Hospitals, 1821–1912, N.Y. Register 609, Cadet Hospital, U.S. Military Academy, West Point, January 1, 1854, to December 29, 1860, 133ff, cited in John M. Hyson Jr., DDS, MS, George E. Sanborn, MD, William H. Mosberg Jr., MD, FACS, and LTC Joseph W. A. Whitehorne, USA, Ret., "The Suicide of General Emory Upton: A Case Report," *Military Medicine* 155, no. 10 (October 1990): 448; Upton,

Letters, to his sister Maria, September 22, 1880, from Philadelphia; "European and American Tactics," *Army Navy Journal* 18 (April 16, 1881): 770.

5. Hyson, "Suicide"; Paul Steiner, MD, "Medical-Military Studies on the Civil War, 12: Brevet Major General Emory Upton, USA," *Military Medicine* (March 1966): 281–289; *Army Navy Journal* 18 (1880–1881): 677, 707, 728, 770–771; Upton, Letters, to his sister, March 13, 1881; "Suicide of General Upton," *Army Navy Journal* 18 (March 19, 1881): 677; "The Late General Upton," *Army Navy Journal* 18 (March 26, 1881): 707; "Honors to General Upton," *Army Navy Journal* 18 (April 2, 1881): 728; David John Fitzpatrick, "Emory Upton: The Misunderstood Reformer" (PhD diss., University of Michigan, 1996); Fitzpatrick, "Emory Upton and the Citizen Soldier," *Journal of Military History* 65, no. 2 (April 2001): 355–389. The *Otsego Republican* carried the same story published by the *Army Navy Journal*, on March 23, 1881, wherein it quoted an article in the *New York Times* with Hancock's reaction.

6. NARA, Microfilm M1064, Roll #197, Letters to the Adjutant General, Olcott Petition to E. D. Townsend, Adjutant General of the U.S. Army, October 28, 1865, including endorsements from Wright, Meade, and Sheridan.

7. *Freeman's Journal*, March 4, 1882, and *Otsego Republican*, March 1, 1882; NARA, Egbert Olcott Military and Pension Records.

8. NARA, John R. Adams Pension Files, letter to whom it may concern by C. K. Bartlett, MD, November 2, 1866, and affidavit by Frederick Robic, MD, April 9, 1869.

9. Griener, Coryell, and Smither, *Surgeons' Civil War*, 270–271.

10. Kimball, *Soldier-Doctor*, 26; Kimball Papers, Hamilton College Library and Archives.

11. NARA, Walker Pension Records.

12. *Syracuse Journal*, cited in *Otsego Republican*, May 30, 1883; *New York Times*, October 30, 1879; Slocum file, OHA.

13. *Reunion Report, 1910*, 29–35; NARA, Henry Galpin Pension and Military Records.

14. Franchot's physical description came from one of his sons—probably Nicholas Van Vranken Franchot, who later was the mayor of Olean, New York. He wrote a cryptic, two-page typewritten "memo" dated Christmas Day 1921 that was tipped into the first few blank pages of a copy of Best's *History of the 121st*. I am indebted to Earl McElfresh of Olean, New York, for providing a photocopy of the memo. See Nicholas Van Vranken Franchot, *Stanislas Pascal Franchot Arrives: A Pageant by Charles Pascal Franchot, Including a List of the Descendants of Stanislas Pascal Franchot (to December 1, 1940)* (Published privately by Nicholas Van Vranken Franchot, December 1940), 86. The Franchot family married well. Descendants include individuals with prominent New York names, such as Van Rensselaer and Huntington. Also see Hurd, *History*, 216–217.

15. Kidder, Letters, to his wife, September 27, 1863; *Otsego Republican*, April 15, 1896; *Reunion Report, 1908*, 45; Harriet's obituary was in the *Hartwick Reporter*, August 9, 1922.

16. NARA, James Cronkite Pension and Military Records, Private Law No. 181, June 10, 1872.

17. Obituary of Adrian O. Mather, *Otsego Republican*, July 25, 1883.

18. NARA, Alonzo Ferguson Pension Records.

19. NARA, Frank Foote Pension Records; obituary of Frank W. Foote, *Otsego Republican*, October 10, 1878.

20. Kelley, Papers, letters to Mary Anne Kelley, August 3, 1867. Responses from Sena-

tor Harris, August 17, 1867, Secretary of the Interior, September 4, 1867, the White House, October 24, 1867, and the Commissioner of Pensions, October 26, 1867, Manuscript Department, NYSHA Library; NARA, Samuel B. Kelley Pension Records.

21. Paine, Letters, to his sister Fanny, December 24, 1863; NARA, Lansing B. Paine Pension Records; obituary, *Otsego Republican*, August 21 and 28, 1895.

22. *Reunion Report, 1909*, Sternberg speech, 21–22; GAR calling cards, in author's collection; NARA, Delavan Bates Pension Records; *Biographical Record and Portrait Album of Wright County, Iowa* (Chicago: Lewis Publishing, 1889), 532–533.

23. *Otsego Republican*, March 23, 1867.

24. Davidson, *Biographical Review*, 362–365; Barbara Lucas, "Capt. Andrew Davidson," available at http://www.rootsweb.com/~nyotsego/davidson.htm; *Otsego Republican*, April 20, 1892, first published in the *American Tribune*, in Indianapolis; *Freeman's Journal*, July 5, 1894, originally published by the *Albany Times-Union* as "A Series of Pen-Portraits, by One Who Knows Them, of the N. Y. State Officials."

25. Best, *121st*, 247–248; George A. Hardin and Frank H. Willard, *History of Herkimer County, New York: Illustrated with Portraits of Many of Its Citizens* (Syracuse, N.Y.: D. Martin, 1893), pt. 1, 222, and pt. 3, 138. Beers, *History*, 260; "Presentation of Historic Flags and World War Relics," in Herkimer County Historical Society, comp., *Papers Read before the Herkimer County Historical Society during the Years May 1914–November 1922*, vol. 5, September 27, 1919 (Published by Herkimer County Historical Society, 1923), 99.

26. *Herkimer Democrat*, September 6, 20, and 27 and October 4 and 11, 1893; Beers, *History*, 260.

27. NARA, Beckwith Pension Records.

28. Best biographical material is from the Schoff Civil War Collection, Diaries and Journals, University of Michigan, William L. Clements Library; Collection Description; NARA, Isaac Best Pension Records; Best, *121st*, 250; NARA, James H. Smith Pension Records; *Reunion Report, 1912*, 43.

29. Beers, *History*, 234, 253.

30. Unknown and undated newspaper obituary, LHC/GFL. The obituary carries this handwritten annotation: "Died May 15, 1887."

31. *Otsego Republican*, March 25, 1896.

32. Hartwell, *Letters and Diary*, Introduction, 14; Lester Murdock, NYSA-GAR records, December 2, 1895; NARA, John Hartwell Pension Records.

33. Obituary of Erastus Weaver, *Otsego Republican*, January 20, 1897; *Biographical Review*, 421; *Reunion Report, 1912*, 48.

34. Remmel, Letters, 1865–1897, letter from Adelbert Jaycox to Ada Benson, February 7, 1897, letter to Ada from Treat Young, January 16, 1907, letter to Caleb from Olcott, August 25, 1865, from Richfield Springs, letter to Caleb from Colonel N. P. Chapman, Judge Advocate, Military Commission, Washington, September 24, 1865, letter to Caleb from William Clayton, Delegate of the Christian Commission, November 16, 1866, from Winchester, West Virginia; *Reunion Report, 1910*, letter from Ada Remmel Benson to C. J. Westcott, August 4, 1910, 15; NARA, William Remmel Military and Pension Records. Kidder's list is in the Manuscript Department of the NYSHA Library, Miscellaneous Manuscripts: "List of men of the 121st who died in the Service (Civil War) handwritten on Stationery of the Board of Port Wardens, New York, 189_."

35. NARA, Caleb Remmel Military and Pension Records. Caleb died of an abscess on August 13, 1887, in Peru, Indiana.

36. See http://www.civilwardata.com/active/hdsquery.dll?SoldierHistory?U&1161 146; http://www.chesco.com/~marys/ancestry/bradshoa.html; NYSAG, *Annual Report, 1903, #36*, 19.

37. NARA, William Barnes Pension Records.

38. James Green, *Death in the Haymarket* (New York: Pantheon Books, 2006), 240–241. NARA, Dyer Lum Military and Pension Records; Frank H. Brooks, "Ideology, Strategy, and Organization: Dyer Lum and the American Anarchist Movement," available at http://www.yo-anarchy.org/labhist93.htm. The article originally appeared in *Labor History* 34, no. 1 (Winter 1993): 57–83.

39. Green, *Death in the Haymarket*, 241; Brooks, "Ideology, Strategy, and Organization"; *Freeman's Journal*, October 7, 1880.

40. Green, *Death in the Haymarket*, 256–257, 264.

41. NARA, Dyer Lum Pension Records; S. E. Parker, "Voltairine de Cleyre: Feminist and Egoist," book review of Paul Avrich's *An American Anarchist: The Life of Voltairine de Cleyre*, available at http://www.blancmange.net/tmh/articles/decleyre.html. Brooks, "Ideology, Strategy, and Organization." Green also maintains that Lum committed suicide; see Green, *Death in the Haymarket*, 292. Lum's death certificate in his pension records in the National Archives does not indicate foul play or suicide.

42. *Reunion Report, 1912*, 44–46; NARA, Nathan Manzer Pension Records.

43. NARA, Peter Simmons Pension Records.

44. NARA, Henry Wood Pension Records.

45. "D. R. Harris, Delhi Veteran, Recalls Meetings with President Lincoln," *Delaware Republican*, February 16, 1929, available at http://freepages.genealogy.rootsweb.com/~kenwark/HHWood/d4244.htm; NARA, Henry Wood Pension Records.

46. See http://www.arlingtoncemetery.net/gpborden.htm and http://arlington cemetery.net/mcfoote.htm; *Otsego Republican*, April 30, 1890.

Bibliography

Manuscripts and Published Primary Sources

Manuscript Collections

Author's Collection

Arnold, Thomas S. Letters. August 1862–December 1863.

Circular Order. Headquarters 2nd Brigade to Colonel Franchot. September 9, 1862.

Davis, G. W. Letter. September 17, 1862.

Drake, George. Letters. Transcripts, January 24, 1864–April 30, 1864.

Galpin, Henry. Pass. October 17, 1862.

Hall, James. Letter. October 21, 1862.

Hartford, Michael. Letter. November 24, 1864.

Howell, Abram. Medical Discharge from Lincoln General Hospital. July 23, 1863. Signed by H. Allen, Assistant Surgeon USA.

Reed, Adelbert. Letters. September 4, 1862–April 20, 1865.

Sheffield, George. Letter. May 28, 1863.

Simmons, Peter. Letter. September 16, 1862.

Smith, Ingraham P. Letter to his sister. April 9, 1864. Photocopy and typewritten transcript.

Teel, George. Letters (73). November 10, 1862–October 26, 1864. Photocopies of transcripts.

"To the Citizens of Herkimer and Otsego Counties! The 121st Reg't, N.Y.V., Your Representative Regiment Asks You for Men." Undated broadside. Circa 1864.

Upton, Emory. Letters. March 13, 1863, and January 28, 1864.

Private Collections

Baldwin, Luman E. Letters. December, 15, 1861, May 6, 1863, and May 21, 1865.

Bassett, Isaac N. Letter. December 6, 1863.

Bates, Delavan. Letters. May 1862–June 1867.

———. Letters. February 17, 1864, and March 4 and 17, 1864. With John S. Kidder Letters.

Carran, F. M., and Richard Turner. Letters. September 11, 1862–March 16, 1864.

Cronkite, James W. Letters. June 7, 1864. With John S. Kidder Letters.

Duroe, Horatio. Letter. October 21, 1864.

Fahey, George. Letters. June 2, 1864, and September 22, 1864. In private collection and in the Allan Tischler Collection, 208 WFCHS/THL; Stewart Bell Jr. Archives, Handley Regional Library, Winchester–Frederick County Historical Society, Winchester, Va.

Graham, Malcolm. Letter. May 12, 1863.

Hills, Elinas D. Letters (5). August 31, 1862–October 14, 1862.

Kidder, Ann Elizabeth Starr. Letters. July 20, 1864–April 6, 1865. With John S. Kidder Letters.

Kidder, H. P. Letters. October 14, 1864. With John S. Kidder Letters.

Kidder, John S. Letters. October 4, 1862–May 28, 1865.

Lovejoy, Allen. Letters. March 1863–June 1865.

Lovejoy, John M. Letters. August 1862–June 1865.

———. Reminiscences. Circa 1887.

Lovejoy, Jonathon. Letters. October 1862–August 1863.

Olcott, Egbert. Letter to Governor Fenton. January 14, 1865, with endorsement.

Sayles, Dolphus. Diary of a Sergeant in Company D. Original and transcript.

Smith, Thomas H. "A Soldier's Story." No date. Four-page manuscript.

Upton, Emory. Endorsement. January 13, 1864.

Wilson, Robert P. Papers.

Woodcock, Philip R. Diary. January 1–April 30, 1865.

Archival Collections

Abner Doubleday Civil War Round Table, Milford, N.Y. (ADCWRT)
  Ingalsbe, Laurin. Letter to his wife. January 4, 1863.

Archives of Appalachia, John Fain Anderson Collection, East Tennessee State University, Johnson City, Tenn. (ETSU)
  Beckwith, Clinton. Newspaper clipping and photograph.

Cherry Valley Historical Association, Cherry Valley, N.Y. (CVHA)
  Ballard, John W. Letter. February 2, 1863.
  Herdman, Norman W. Letters. March 27, 1863, and March 8, 1864.
  Lovejoy, John M. Diary. 1863.

Clarke Historical Library, Central Michigan University, Mt. Pleasant, Mich. (CHL)
  Morgan, Hance. Diary. 1862–1865.

Dartmouth College Library, Dartmouth College, Dartmouth, N.H. (DCL)
  Mather, Andrew E. Letters. September 1862–September 1864.

Fredericksburg and Spotsylvania National Military Park, Fredericksburg, Va. (F&SNMP)
  Austin, Stephen T. Letters. December 25, 1862, March 7, 1863, and October 4, 1864.
  Walker, Henry B. Letters.

Gettysburg National Military Park, Gettysburg, Pa. (GNMP)
  McCurry, James Henry. Diaries. 1863 and 1864.

Gilbertsville Free Library, Gilbertsville, N.Y. (GFLG)
  Local History Collection.

Hamilton College Archives, Clinton, N.Y. (HCA)
  Best, Isaac. Papers.
  Butts, Charles Abbott. Papers.
  Kimball, James P. Papers.

Herkimer County Historical Society, Herkimer, N.Y. (HCHS)

    Holt, Daniel M. "Copy of Letters Written by Daniel M. Holt Assistant Surgeon 121st Regiment N.Y. Vols., 2d Brigade, 1st Div. 6th Corps, Army of the Potomac, to His Wife, While in the Service of the United States, from September 1st, 1862 to October 17th, 1864 at Which Time He Was Discharged from the Service Because of Physical Disability." 1867.

    ———. "Copy of Diary, May 1st 1864 to October 21, 1864." (Handwritten)

    Klock, Edgar Jackson. "History of the Town of Schuyler, Herkimer County, New York." Typed manuscript. 1930.

Holland Land Office, Batavia, N.Y. (HLO)

    Upton, Emory. Letters. 1858–1881.

Military Historical Society of Massachusetts, Boston, Mass. (MHSM)

    Upton, Emory. Letters. April 18 and 26, 1879.

National Archives and Records Administration, Washington, D.C. (NARA)

    Adams, Rev. John. Pension Records.

    Arnold, Thomas. Pension Records.

    Barnes, William H. Pension Records.

    Bates, Delavan. Pension Records.

    Beckwith, Dewitt Clinton. Pension Records.

    Best, Isaac O. Pension Records.

    Burrell, Jonathon. Record Group 153. Records of the Judge Advocate General (Army). KK-493. Special Orders No. 41. December 22, 1862.

    Delavan, Cassius. Pension Records.

    Dockum, Warren. Pension Records.

    Dolliver, Eugene. Pension Records.

    Duroe, Horatio. Pension Records.

    Foote, Frank. Pension Records.

    Galpin, Henry. Pension Records.

    Gould, Jacob. Pension Records.

    Hartwell, John. Pension Records.

    Hawthorne, Harris. Pension Records.

    Herdman, Norman. Pension Records.

    Holt, Daniel. Pension Records.

    Howland, Ten Eyck. Pension Records.

    Jewett, Thomas. Records of the Office of the Judge Advocate General, Army. Court Martial Files, 1809–1980. File no. MM 588. Thomas Jewett, Company D. 5th Maine Infantry.

    Kelley, Samuel Burdett. Pension Records.

    Kidder, John S. Pension and Military Records.

    Letters received by the Commission Branch of the Adjutant General's Office, 1863–1870. Microfilm #1064.

    Lowe, Frank. Pension Records.

    Mann, William. Pension Records.

    Manzer, Nathan. Pension Records.

    Mather, Andrew E. Military and Pension Records.

Mather, Elias. Military and Pension Records.

Merit Rolls of Surgeons and Assistant Surgeons examined by the Army Medical Examining Board. 1862–1865.

Murdock, Lester. Pension Records.

Olin, Sackett. Pension Records.

Paine, Lansing. Military and Pension Records.

Records of the Adjutant General's Office. 1780s–1917, 1861–1865. Record Group 94.

———. Muster Rolls, Returns, Regimental Papers. Volunteer Organizations. Civil War. New York. 121st Infantry. Record Group 94. Box #3260.

Records of the Office of the Chief Surgeon. Correspondence Related to the Army Medical Examination Boards. Surgeons, S–Z. 1862–1863. Record Group 112.

———. Medical Examination Board. Washington, D.C.

———. Indexes for General Correspondence of the Chief Surgeon. 1862–1863. Record Group 112. Entry 9.

Reed, Adelbert. Pension Records.

Regimental Books of the 121st Regiment New York Infantry. Old Military Records Division. Record Group 94.

Remmel, Caleb. Military and Pension Records.

Remmel, William. Military and Pension Records.

Round, Joseph B. Pension Records.

Sayles, Dolphus. Pension Records.

Simmons, Peter. Pension Records.

Smith, James Henry. Pension Records.

Smith, Philip. Pension Records.

Sullivan, Cornelius. Pension Records.

Teel, George. Pension Records.

Trainor, Barney. Pension Records.

Upton, Henry. Pension Records.

Valentine, Stephen B. Military and Pension Records.

———. Surgeon General's Correspondence.

Walker, Henry S. Pension Records.

Wilson, Robert P. Pension Records.

Wood, Henry. Pension Records.

New-York Historical Society, New York, N.Y. (N-YHS)

Campbell-Mumford Papers.

New York State Historical Association, Cooperstown, N.Y. (NYSHA)

Bailey, Albert. Letters. October 21, 1862, and August 19, 1863.

Circular. Cooperstown, N.Y. July 19, 1862.

Clarke Family Papers. 1802–1925.

Cleveland, Mather. "Diary (excerpts) of Andrew Adrian Mather, Sheriff of Otsego County, 1861–1863." (Typewritten)

"Enrollment of Persons Liable to Military Duty." Otsego County. Sheriff's Copies. 21 books. Various dates.

French, Samuel D. Letters. August 31, 1862–April 29, 1863.

Kelley, Samuel Burdett. Papers.

Kelty, Barney. Letter from Unadilla Forks to Commander, Company K. February 18, 1865.

[Kidder, John S.] List of men of the 121st who died in the service (Civil War)—handwritten on stationery of the Board of Port Wardens, New York, 189_. Miscellaneous manuscripts.

Paine, Lansing B. Letters. May 4, 1863, and December 24, 1863.

Pierce, Dean A. Diary. February–December 1863.

Shaul, John D. Papers.

Sheffield, George H. Diary. 1864.

Shepard, Truman. Papers.

Taft, James A. Letter. April 19, 1863.

Wales, Edward. Papers.

West, Charles B. Letter. January 22, 1865.

New York State Library, Albany, N.Y. (NYSL)

Burrell, Jonathon. Letters (17). 1862–1864. #18689.

"The Call to Arms! How to Escape the Draft!" Broadside. August 16, 1862. Oswego, N.Y.

Grand Army of the Republic Papers. New York State Department. 1866–1948. Manuscripts and Special Collections. HH12074.

Morgan, Edwin D. Papers.

New York State. Adjutant General's Office. *Historical Notes on New York Volunteer Regiments, 1861–1865.* 7 vols. Manuscript Division.

———. "Rough Abstract of Expenditures for Salaries and Ordnance, 1863–1866." Unpublished manuscript abstracts.

U.S. Army. 121st New York Infantry Regiment. 1862–1865. 1 Box. SC21123.

New York State Military Museum, Saratoga Springs, N.Y. (NYSMM)

Wood, Henry Hilton. *Experiences during the Civil War.* 1934. Ten typescript pages.

Onondaga Historical Association, Syracuse, N.Y. (OHA)

Slocum, John. Diary. 1864.

———. Cash Account Book. 1864.

Raymond H. Fogler Library, University of Maine, Orono, Maine (RHFLUM)

Lemont, Frank L. Letters. Paul Bean Collection.

State University of New York, Binghamton, N.Y. (SUNY Binghamton)

Smith, Ingraham. Letters. December 1861–May 1865.

Syracuse University Library, Syracuse, N.Y. (SUL)

Walker, Henry B. Letters. January 1863–March 1864.

University of Arkansas Library, Fayetteville, Ark. (UAL)

Remmel, William. Papers. 20 folders. MC 597. Special Collections.

U.S. Army Military History Institute, Carlisle, Pa. (USAMHI)

Campbell, Cleaveland J. Letter. November 20, 1863.

Fish, John D. Letters. November 12 and 22, 1863.

Keiser, Henry. Papers. Harrisburg Civil War Round Table Collection.

Morgan, Hance. Diary. 1862–1865.

Tanner, Merton. Letter. December 27, 1862.

Upton, Emory. Letter. December 23, 1862. *Civil War Times Illustrated (CWTI)* Collection. Also published in *CWTI* 17 (July 1978): 44–45.

U.S. Military Academy, Archives and Special Collections, West Point, N.Y. (USMA) Upton, Emory. Papers.

William L. Clements Library, University of Michigan, Ann Arbor, Mich. (WLC)

Best, Isaac Oliver. "Three Essays: 'Sheridan in the Shenandoah'; 'The Siege and Capture of Petersburg'; and 'Through the Wilderness with Grant.'" Manuscripts in the Schoff Civil War Collection. Diaries and Journals 6:1.

Published Primary Sources

Abstract of General Orders and Proceedings of the Fifty-first Encampment. Department of New York, G.A.R. Held at Saratoga Springs, N.Y., June 26, 27, and 28, 1917. Albany, N.Y.: J. B. Lyon, 1917.

Adams, John Ripley. *Memorial and Letters of Rev. John R. Adams, Chaplain of the Fifth Maine and the One Hundred and Twenty-first New York Regiments during the War of Rebellion, Serving from the Beginning to Its Close.* Cambridge: University Press, privately printed, 1890.

Bates, Samuel P. *History of Pennsylvania Volunteers, 1861–5; Prepared in Compliance with Acts of the Legislature, by Samuel P. Bates.* 6 vols. Harrisburg, Pa.: B. Singerly, State Printer, 1869–1871.

Baxter, J. H., MD. *Statistics, Medical and Anthropological, of the Provost-Marshal-General's Bureau, Derived from Records of the Examination for Military Service in the Armies of the United States during the Late War of the Rebellion, of over a Million Recruits, Drafted Men, Substitutes, and Enrolled Men; Compiled under the Direction of the Secretary of War.* 2 vols. Washington, D.C.: Government Printing Office, 1875.

Beers, F. W. *Atlas of Otsego County, New York.* New York: F. W. Beers, A. P. Ellis, and G. G. Soule, 1868.

Biographical Record and Portrait Album of Wright County, Iowa. Chicago: Lewis Publishing, 1889.

Caynor, William L., Sr., ed. *Without a Scratch: Diary of Corporal William Holmes Morse, Color Bearer of the 5th Maine Infantry.* N.p.: privately printed by the editor, 2007.

Commonwealth of Massachusetts Adjutant General's Office. *Annual Report of the Adjutant-General of the Commonwealth of Massachusetts for the Year Ending December 31, 1865.* Boston: Wright and Potter, State Printers, 1866.

Cronkite, James. *Report of the Gettysburg Monument Committee of the 121st New York Volunteers, Supplemented with Names of the Contributors, and a Brief Sketch of the Regiment.* Cooperstown, N.Y.: Press of the Otsego Republican, 1889.

Cullum, George W. *Biographical Register of the Officers and Graduates of the U.S. Military Academy at West Point, N.Y. from Its Establishment in 1802 to 1890, with the Early History of the United States Military Academy.* 7 vols. Boston: Houghton Mifflin, 1891.

Dye, Marshall. Letter, autumn 1862. In Alan Sessarego, ed., *Letters Home: A Collection of Original Civil War Soldiers' Letters: Antietam, Chancellorsville, Gettysburg.* Gettysburg, Pa.: Garden Spot Gifts, 1996, 4–5.

"European and American Tactics." *Army Navy Journal* 18 (April 16, 1881): 770.

Fisk, Wilbur. *Hard Marching Every Day: The Civil War Letters of Private Wilbur Fisk—Second*

Vermont Volunteers, 1861–1863. Edited by Emil and Ruth Rosenblatt. Lawrence: University Press of Kansas, 1992.

Hartwell, John F. L. *To My Beloved Wife and Boy at Home: The Letters and Diaries of Orderly Sergeant John F. L. Hartwell*. Edited by Ann Hartwell Britton and Thomas J. Reed. Madison, N.J.: Fairleigh Dickinson University Press, 1997.

Heard, Lewis, MD. "Gunshot Wounds of the Hip, upon Which Supervened Pyaemia and Rupture of the Liver." *Medical and Surgical Reporter* (Philadelphia) 10, no. 9, iss. no. 345 (June 27, 1863): 131–133.

Heitman, Francis. *Historical Register and Dictionary of the U.S. Army, 1789–1903*. 2 vols. Washington, D.C.: Government Printing Office, 1903.

Holmes, Oliver Wendell, Jr. *Touched with Fire: Civil War Letters and Diary of Oliver Wendell Holmes, Jr., 1861–1864*. Edited by Mark De Wolfe Howe. New York: Fordham University Press, 2000.

Holt, Daniel M. "In Captivity." *Civil War Times Illustrated* 18 (August 1979): 34–39.

———. *A Surgeon's Civil War: The Letters and Diary of Daniel M. Holt, M.D.* Edited by James M. Greiner, Janet L. Coryell, and James R. Smither. Kent, Ohio: Kent State University Press, 1994.

"Honors to General Upton." *Army Navy Journal* 18 (April 2, 1881): 728.

Huntington, Willard Vincent, comp. "Old Time Notes Relating to Otsego County and the Upper Susquehanna Valley." Carbon copy of original in Huntington Library, Oneonta, N.Y. Vol. 7, 2125–2426. NYSHA.

Ingraham, John James. *Civil War Letters, 1862–1865*. Compiled by Edward C. Ingraham. Copyrighted in 1986 by Edward C. Ingraham, Bethesda, Md., and printed by Phoenix Printing. Frankfort, N.Y.: Dolgeville-Manheim Historical Society, July 1990. (Second printing January 1992).

Kautz, August V. *The Company Clerk; Showing How and When to Make Out All the Returns, Reports, Rolls and Other Papers, and What to Do with Them; How to Keep All the Books, Records, and Accounts Required in the Administration of a Company, Troop, or Battery in the Army of the United States*. Philadelphia: J. B. Lippincott, 1864.

"The Late General Upton." *Army Navy Journal* 18 (March 26, 1881): 707.

Lincoln, Abraham. *The Collected Works of Abraham Lincoln*. 9 vols. Edited by Roy P. Basler. New Brunswick, N.J.: Rutgers University Press, 1953.

Malone, Bartlett Yancey. *Diary*. The James Sprunt Historical Publications Published under the Direction of the North Carolina Historical Society. Vol. 16, no. 2. Chapel Hill: University of North Carolina, 1919. In the collections of the Wilson Library, University of North Carolina, Chapel Hill, N.C.

McClellan, George. *The Civil War Papers of George B. McClellan: Selected Correspondence, 1860–1865*. Edited by Stephen Sears. New York: Da Capo Press, 1992.

Michie, Peter S. *The Life and Letters of Emory Upton, Colonel of the Fourth Regiment of Artillery, and Brevet Major-General, U.S. Army*. New York: D. Appleton, 1885.

Morse, Francis W. *Personal Experiences in the War of the Great Rebellion from December 1862 to July 1865*. Albany, N.Y.: Printed but not published by Munsell, Printer, 1866.

New York Monuments Commission. *In Memoriam: Henry Warner Slocum, 1826–1894*. Albany, N.Y.: J. B. Lyon, Printers, 1904.

New York Monuments Commission for the Battlefields of Gettysburg and Chattanooga.

Final Report on the Battlefield of Gettysburg. 3 vols. Albany, N.Y.: J. B. Lyon, Printers, 1902.

New York State Adjutant General's Office. *Annual Report of the Adjutant General of the State of New York.* 1861–1868. Albany, N.Y.: Various government printers. Also published as Assembly Documents No. 80, 25, 49, 22, 24, and 38.

———. *A Record of the "Commissioned Officers, Non-commissioned Officers and Privates, of the Regiments Which Were Organized in the State of New York and Called into the Service of the United States to Assist in Suppressing the Rebellion Caused by the Secession of Some of the Southern States from the Union, A.D. 1861; As Taken from the Muster-In Rolls on File in the Adjutant General's Office, S.N.Y.* Albany, N.Y.: Comstock and Cassiday, 1864.

———. *Annual Report of the Adjutant General of the State of New York for the Year 1903: Registers of New York Regiments in the War of the Rebellion (Supplementary Volumes to the Annual Reports of the Adjutant General for 1893–1905).* Serial Number 36. Albany, N.Y.: Oliver A. Quayle, State Legislative Printer, 1904.

New York State Bureau of Military Statistics. *Presentation of Flags of New York Volunteer Regiments and Other Organizations, to His Excellency, Governor Fenton, in Accordance with a Resolution of the Legislature, July 4, 1865; Published under Direction of the Chief of Bureau of Military Records.* Albany, N.Y.: Weed, Parsons, and Company, Printers, 1865.

———. *Report of the New York Commission for the Battlefields of Gettysburg, Chattanooga and Antietam for the Year 1915.* March 8, 1916. Albany, N.Y.: J. B. Lyon, Printers, 1916.

New York State Commissary General's Office. *Annual Report (for 1862) of the Commissary General of the State of New York.* Albany, N.Y.: Comstock & Cassiday, Printers, 1863. Also published as Assembly Document No. 66, 1863.

Nichols, B. *Atlas of Herkimer County, New York.* New York: J. Jay Stranahan and Beach Nichols, 1868.

Reed, George E. *A Poetical Description of the Sixth Army Corps Campaign during the Year 1863.* Harrisburg, Pa.: Meyers Printing and Publishing House, n.d.

Remmel, William. *Like Grass before the Scythe: The Life and Death of Sgt. William Remmel, 121st Infantry.* Edited by Robert Patrick Bender. Tuscaloosa: University of Alabama Press, 2007.

Rhodes, Elisha Hunt. *All for the Union: The Civil War Diary and Letters of Elisha Hunt Rhodes.* Edited by Robert Hunt Rhodes. New York: Orion Books, 1991.

Rice, Adam Clarke. *The Letters and Writings of the Late Lieutenant Adam Clarke Rice of the 121st Regiment, N.Y. Volunteers.* Compiled by C. E. Rice. Little Falls, N.Y.: Journal & Courier Book and Printing Press, 1864.

Staring, Charles, and Clinton DeWitt Staring. *Give All My Love to All Our Folks: Civil War and Post-war Letters of Clinton DeWitt Staring and Charles E. Staring of Herkimer County, New York.* Edited by Paul Taylor. Mancelona, Mich.: Deep Wood Press, 2007.

"Suicide of General Upton." *Army Navy Journal* 18 (March 19, 1881): 677.

Twenty-third Annual Circular of Hanover College, Comprising the Catalogue, Course of Study, Etc. Madison, Ind.: Courier Steam Printing, August 1855.

U.S. Adjutant General's Office. *Official Army Register of the Volunteer Force of the United States Army for the Years 1861, '62, '63, '64, '65. Part 2—New York and New Jersey.* Washington, D.C.: Government Printing Office, August 31, 1865.

U.S. Congress. *Biographical Directory of the American Congress: 1774–1949.* Washington, D.C.: Government Printing Office, 1950.

U.S. Congress, Joint Committee on the Conduct of the War. *Report.* Washington, D.C.: Government Printing Office, 1863.

U.S. Surgeon General's Office. *The Medical and Surgical History of the War of the Rebellion (1861–1865).* 6 vols. Washington, D.C.: Government Printing Office, 1870–1988; reprinted in 15 vols., Wilmington, N.C.: Broadfoot Publishing, 1990.

U.S. War Department. *The War of the Rebellion: A Compilation of the Official Records of the Union and Confederate Armies.* 128 vols. Washington, D.C.: Government Printing Office, 1880–1901.

———. *Report of the Gettysburg National Military Park Commission.* Gettysburg, Pa.: Government Printing Office, July 1, 1916.

Newspapers

Albany Express, NYSMM
Albany Weekly Journal, NYSMM
Atlas and Argus, Albany, N.Y., NYSHA
Cherry Valley Gazette, NYSHA, NYSMM
Delaware Republican, Delhi, N.Y., NYSHA
Edmeston Local, NYSHA
Ellsworth (Maine) American, photocopy of October 25, 1883, issue, in author's collection
Evening Times, Little Falls, N.Y., NYSL
Freeman's Journal, NYSHA
Hartwick Reporter, NYSHA
Herkimer County Journal, CUL
Herkimer Democrat, NYSL
Ilion News, NYSL
Little Falls Journal and Courier, CUL
Mercury, Richfield Springs, N.Y., NYSHA
Mohawk Courier, NYSMM
Morris Chronicle, NYSHA
National Tribune, USAMHI
New York Herald, NYSMM
New York Times
New York Tribune, NYSMM
Oneonta Daily Star, NYSHA and NYSL
Oneonta Herald, NYSHA and NYSL
Otsego Farmer, NYSHA and NYSL
Otsego Journal, Gilbertsville, N.Y., NYSHA
Otsego Republican, NYSHA and NYSMM
Republican and Democrat, Cooperstown, N.Y., NYSHA
Telegram Record, Herkimer, N.Y., NYSL
Unadilla Times, NYSHA

Utica Morning Herald and Daily Gazette, NYSMM

Waterville Times, NYSL

West Winfield Star, Courtesy Winfield Town Historian Steve Davis, Winfield, N.Y.

Worcester Times, NYSHA and NYSL

Electronic Sources

Bates, Gen. Delavan. *Collection of Civil War Stories by General Delavan Bates*. NEGenWeb Project, Resource Center, Military. 75 pp. Available at http://www.rootsweb.com/~necivwar/CW/batecnts.html#contents.

———. *The Civil War Letters of Delavan Bates: May 1862–June 1867*. NEGenWeb Project, Resource Center, Military. 63 pp. C 1998–2003 by John G. Saint and Ted and Carole Miller. Transcribed by William S. Saint Jr., 1988. Available at http://www.rootsweb.com/~necivwar/CW/bates/genbate1.html.

Best, Isaac O. *Background Note*. Three essays. William L. Clements Library. University of Michigan. Schoff Civil War Collection. Diaries and Journals F6.1. Available at http://www.clements.umich.ude/Webguides/Schoff/B/Best.html.

Borden, George Pennington. Brigadier General, United States Army. April 1844–April 1925. Available at http://www.arlingtoncemetary.net/gpborden.htm.

Borst, George H. *Selected Papers from the Civil War Pension Application Records of George H. Borst and His Wife Amy Eldredge*. Available at http://www.civilwardata.com/active/hdsquery.dll?SoldierHistory?U&1161080.

Brooks, Frank H. "Ideology, Strategy, and Organization: Dyer Lum and the American Anarchist Movement." Originally published in *Labor History* 34, no. 1 (Winter 1993): 57–83. Available at http://www.yo-anarchy.org/labhist93.htm.

Brophy, Marion H. *The Town of Otsego: Home Front, 1861–1865*. Compiled from the *Freeman's Journal* and Town of Otsego—Civil War Records. Available at http://www.rootsweb.com/~nyotsego/cwotsego.htm.

———. *Otsego Town Minutes, 1864*. Available at http://www.roots.web.com/~nyotsego/Otsego1864.htm.

———. *Town of Otsego: Accounts Audited, 1865–1884/1885, Compiled from Otsego Town Records*. Available at http://www.roots.web.com/~nyotsego/otsegoaccounts.htm.

Butterfield, Lyman H. *Cooper's Inheritance: The Otsego Country and Its Founders*. Papers of the 1951 James Fenimore Cooper Conference, "James Fenimore Cooper—A Reappraisal," Cooperstown, New York. Published in *New York History* 35, no. 4 (October 1954): 374–411. Available at http://external.oneonta.edu/cooper/articles/nyhistory/1954nyhistory-butterfield.html.

Civil War Letters of George W. Collins Co. C. 121st NY Volunteers. Edited by Martha S. Magill, Joan Jones, and Dora and Earl Schwaiger. 1998. 8 pp. Available at http://www.roots.web.com/~nyherkim/collins.html.

Crim, Beverley, and Martha A. Magill. *Profile and History of Herkimer County, NY, "The Gazetteer" and Business Directory of Herkimer County, N.Y., 1869–70*. 1997. Available at http://www.rootsweb.com/~nyherkim/history/herkhist69.html.

Delong, Larry. *Civil War Servicemen Fulfilling the Quotas of the Town of Worcester*. Copied from "The Complete Record Relating to Officers, Soldiers and Seamen Composing the

Quotas of the Troops Furnished to the United States by the Town of Worcester," compiled by Town Clerk Charles Wright, November 28, 1865. Available at http://www.rootsweb.com/~nyotsego/civilwarworcester.htm.

Diary of Miss Alvina Helmer, Written at Kast Bridge—March 1915: "My Recollections of Eatonville as It Was in 1850." Available at http://www.rootsweb.com/~nyherkim/fairfield/alvina2.html.

Directory of the Town of Herkimer, N.Y., 1869–1870. Available at http://www.rootsweb.com/~nyherkim/hertown/herkdir1.html.

Dockum, Warren C. "Dockum Funeral Held Today; Story of Exploit Is Told." Available at http://www.homeofheroes.com/news/archives/1921_1005_dockum.html.

Harrold, Thomas. *Governor Edwin Denison Morgan and the Recruitment of the Union Army in New York State.* Available at http://www.albany.edu/nystatehistory/44/gov_recruit.html.

Huartson–Golladay–Stockwell [family names]. *Trails thru Time—Doranna Glettig.* Huartson Family. Available at http://web0.greatbasin.net/~doranna/Huartson/page2.html.

Krick, Robert. *Fighting at Salem Church.* Available at http://fredericksburg.com/News/FLS/2002/112002/11162002/791010/.

Long Island and New York—Civil War Information. 22 pp. Available at http://longislandgenealogy.com/civilwar.html.

Lunn, William, Jr. *Genealogy.* Available at http://home.att.net/~jslunn/D0005/I524.html.

Magill, Martha S., and Bill McKerrow. "Newport, Herkimer County, New York, in the Civil War." From *A Glimpse in Passing—Newport, NY, 1971–1991.* Newport Historical Society. 1991. 3 pp. Available at http://www.rootsweb.com/~nyherkim/newciv.html.

Remmel, William. *Letter and Papers, 1862–1924 (Predominately 1862–1864).* University of Arkansas, Fayetteville. Description of Manuscript Collection MC 597. 5 pp. Available at http://www.uark.edu/depts/speccoll/findingaids/remmelaid.html.

Sanderson, Irving J. "Obituary." Available at http://www.pastlinks.com/family%20pages/wgz5.html.

Sons of Union Veterans. *Photos from the Past: Joseph W. Lockwood.* Available at http://suvcw.org/past/jcl-1.htm.

Stevens, Ezra. *Early History of the Town of Milford and Other Parts of Otsego Co. from 1773 to 1903.* Electronic text by Joyce Riedinger, October 31, 1998. Three sections. Available at http://www.rootsweb.com/~nyotsego/histmil.htm.

Ward, David. "Of Battlefields and Bitter Feuds: The 96th Pennsylvania Volunteers." *Civil War Regiments* 3, no. 3 (1993). Available at http://members.tripod.com/~Jake96th/ward.html.

Warkentin and Draper Family History. *Henry Hilton and Lida (Judson) Wood.* Available at http://freepages.geneology.rootsweb.com/~kenwark/HHWood/d4244.htm.

Whitaker, Blake. "Changing Generalship and Tactics in the Late 19th Century." Available at http://www.militaryhistoryonline.com/general/articles/generalshipandtactics.aspx.

121st Association Rosters, Proceedings, and Reunion Sources (by date)

Invitation, Veteran's Reunion and Program. Little Falls, N.Y., 1885.

Roster of the 121st N.Y. Volunteer Association and Proceedings at the 15th Reunion. Cooperstown, N.Y.: Otsego Republican Book and Job Printing House, 1891.

Roster of the 121st N.Y. Volunteer Association. Cooperstown, N.Y.: Otsego Republican Book and Job Printing House, 1892.

Roster of the 121st N.Y. Volunteer Association. Cooperstown, N.Y.: Otsego Republican Book and Job Printing House, 1895.

Proceedings of the Nineteenth Annual Reunion of the 121st N.Y. Vol. Association Held at Little Falls, N.Y., Thursday, September 19, 1895. N.p.: publisher unknown, 1895.

Proceedings and Roster of the 22d Annual Reunion of the 121st N.Y. Volunteer Association. Cooperstown, N.Y.: Otsego Republican Book and Job Printing House, 1898.

Proceedings of the 24th Annual Reunion of the 121st N.Y. Vol. Vet. Association. Richmondville, N.Y.: Phoenix Press, 1900.

Report of the 26th Annual Reunion of the 121st N.Y. Vol. Vet. Association. Ilion, N.Y.: Citizen Publishing, Printers, 1902.

Roster of the 121st N.Y. Volunteer Association. Ilion, N.Y.: Citizen Publishing, Printers, 1903.

Notice of the 29th Annual Reunion of the 121st N.Y. Volunteers. Ilion and Herkimer, N.Y.: Citizen Publishing, June 15 and 16, 1904.

Report of the 30th Annual Reunion of the 121st New York Volunteers Held at Worcester, N.Y., Sept. 20, 1906. Oneonta, N.Y.: The Herald, 1906.

Invitation to the Thirty-first Annual Reunion of the 121st N.Y.S. Volunteers at Ilion, New York, September 5, 1907.

Report of the 31st Annual Reunion of the 121st New York Volunteers Held at Ilion, New York, September 5, 1907. Oneonta, N.Y.: The Herald, 1907.

Report of the 32nd Annual Reunion of the 121st New York Volunteers Held at Oneonta, N.Y., August 25, 1908. N.p.: publisher unknown, 1908.

Report of the 33rd Annual Reunion of the 121st New York Volunteers Held at Little Falls, N.Y., August 31, 1909. N.p.: publisher unknown, 1909.

Report of the 34th Annual Reunion of the 121st New York Volunteers Held at Schuyler Lake, N.Y., August 10, 1910. N.p.: publisher unknown, 1910.

Report of the 35th Annual Reunion of the 121st New York Volunteers Held at Schuyler Lake, N.Y., August 9, 1911. N.p.: publisher unknown, 1911.

Report of the 36th Annual Reunion of the 121st New York Volunteers Held at Little Falls, N.Y., August 23, 1912. N.p.: publisher unknown, 1912.

Report of the Forty-first Annual Reunion of the 121st New York Volunteers Held at Cooperstown, N.Y., August 2, 1917. N.p.: publisher unknown, 1917.

Report of the Forty-seventh Annual Reunion of the 121st New York Volunteers Held at Little Falls, N.Y., July 3rd, 1923. N.p.: publisher unknown, 1923.

Report of the Forty-eighth Annual Reunion of the 121st New York Volunteers Held at Jordanville, N.Y., July 9th, 1924. N.p.: publisher unknown, 1924.

Books, Memoirs, and Secondary Sources

Abbott, A. O. *Prison Life in the South: At Richmond, Macon, Savannah, Charleston, Columbia, Charlotte, Raleigh, Goldsborough and Andersonville, during the Years 1864 and 1865.* New York: Harper and Brothers, 1866.

Alexander, De Alva Stanwood. *A Political History of the State of New York.* 3 vols. New York: Henry Holt, 1909.

Ambrose, Stephen E. "Emory Upton and the Armies of Asia and Europe." *Military Affairs* 28, no. 1 (Spring 1964): 27–32.

———. *Upton and the Army.* Baton Rouge: Louisiana State University Press, 1964 and 1992.

———. "Upton's Military Reforms." *Civil War Times Illustrated* 2, no. 5 (August 1963): 24–30.

Anderson, James S. "The March of the Sixth Corps to Gettysburg." In *War Papers: Being Papers Read before the Commandery of the State of Wisconsin MOLLUS.* Vol. 4. Wilmington, N.C.: Broadfoot Publishing, 1993, 77–84.

Anonymous. "Emory Upton Obituary and Eulogy." *Annual Report.* West Point, N.Y.: U.S. Military Academy, Annual Reunion, June 9, 1881.

———. "The Life of Emory Upton." Book review of Michie's *Life and Letters of Emory Upton* in *Science* 6, no. 144 (November 6, 1885): 404.

Anson, Charles H. "Battle of Cedar Creek, October 19th, 1864." In *War Papers: Being Papers Read before the Commandery of the State of Wisconsin MOLLUS.* Vol. 4. Wilmington, N.C.: Broadfoot Publishing, 1993, 355–367.

Bacevich, Major Andrew J., Jr. "Emory Upton: A Centennial Assessment." *Military Review: The Professional Journal of the US Army* 61, no. 12 (December 1981): 21–28.

Bacon, Edwin F. *Otsego County, New York: Geographical and Historical—From the Earliest Settlement to the Present Time with County and Township Maps rrom Original Drawings.* Oneonta, N.Y.: Oneonta Herald, Publishers, 1902.

Barry, Richard. "Emory Upton, Military Genius," *New York Times,* June 16, 1918.

Beckwith, Clinton. "Three Years with the Colors: Of a Fighting Regiment of the Potomac, by a Private Soldier." *Herkimer Democrat,* July 12, 1893–July 4, 1894.

Benton, Nathaniel S. *A History of Herkimer County.* Albany, N.Y.: J. Munsell, 1856.

Best, Isaac O. *History of the 121st New York State Infantry.* Chicago: Lt. Jas. H. Smith, 1921.

Beyer, W. F., and O. F. Keydel, eds. *Deeds of Valor: How America's Civil War Heroes Won the Congressional Medal of Honor.* New York: Smithmark Publishers, 2000. (Originally published in 1901).

Bicknell, George W. *History of the Fifth Regiment Maine Volunteers.* Portland, Maine: Hall L. Davis, 1871.

Biographical Directory of the American Congress: 1774–1949. Compiled under the direction of the Joint Committee on Printing, Congress of the United States. House Document No. 607, 81st Cong., 2d sess. Washington, D.C.: U.S. Government Printing Office, 1950.

Biographical Review: This Volume Contains Biographical Sketches of the Leading Citizens of Otsego County, New York. Boston: Biographical Review Publishing, 1893.

Blight, David. *Race and Reunion: The Civil War in American Memory.* Cambridge, Mass.: Harvard University Press, 2001.

———. *Beyond the Battlefield: Race, Memory, and the American Civil War.* Amherst: University of Massachusetts Press, 2002.

Boatner, Mark Mayo. *The Civil War Dictionary.* New York: David McKay, 1959.

Boritt, Gabor. *The Gettysburg Gospel: The Lincoln Speech That Nobody Knows.* New York: Simon and Schuster, 2006.

Bowen, James L. *History of the Thirty-seventh Regiment Mass. Volunteers, Civil War of 1861–1865, with a Comprehensive Sketch of the Doings of Massachusetts as a State, and of the Principal Campaigns of the War.* Holyoke, Mass.: Clark W. Bryan, Publishers, 1884.

Brown, John Warner. *Stanislas Pascal Franchot (1774–1855)*. N.p.: publisher unknown, n.d. NYSHA.

Brown, Kent Masterson. *Retreat from Gettysburg: Lee, Logistics, and the Pennsylvania Campaign*. Chapel Hill: University of North Carolina Press, 2005.

Brown, Richard C. "General Emory Upton—The Army's Mahan." *Military Affairs: Journal of the American Military Institute* 17 (1953): 125–131.

Brummer, Sidney David. *Political History of New York State during the Period of the Civil War*. Vol. 39 of *Studies in History, Economics and Public Law*, no. 2. Edited by the Faculty of Political Science of Columbia University. New York: Columbia University Press, 1911.

Buell, Thomas B. *The Warrior Generals: Combat Leadership in the Civil War*. New York: Three Rivers Press, 1997.

Burr, George L., supervising ed. *History of Hamilton and Clay Counties, Nebraska*. 2 vols. Chicago: S. J. Clarke Publishing, 1921.

Burt, Silas W. *My Memoirs of the Military History of the State of New York during the War for the Union, 1861–1865*. Albany, N.Y.: J. B. Lyon, 1902.

Butterfield, M. L. "Personal Reminiscences with the Sixth Corps, 1864–5." In *War Papers: Being Papers Read before the Commandery of the State of Wisconsin MOLLUS*. Vol. 4. Wilmington, N.C.: Broadfoot Publishing, 1993, 85–93.

Byers, S. H. M. *What I Saw in Dixie: Of Sixteen Months in Rebel Prisons*. Dansville, N.Y.: Robbins and Porre, Printers, Express Printing House, 1868.

Calkins, Christopher. *Thirty-six Hours before Appomattox: The Battles of Sailor's Creek, High Bridge, Farmville and Cumberland Church, April 6 and 7, 1865*. Farmville, Va.: Farmville Herald, 1980 and 1989.

———. *From Petersburg to Appomattox: A Tour Guide to the Routes of Lee's Withdrawal and Grant's Pursuit, April 2–9, 1865*. Eastern National Park and Monument Association. Farmville, Va.: Farmville Herald, 1983 and 1990.

Campbell, Sister M. Anne Francis, OLM. "Bishop England's Sisterhood, 1829–1929." PhD diss., St. Louis University, 1968.

Cassidy, Robert M. "Prophets or Praetorians? The Uptonian Paradox and the Powell Corollary." *Parameters*, U.S. Army War College (Autumn 2003): 130–143.

Casstevens, Frances H., *"Out of the Mouth of Hell": Civil War Prisons and Escapes*. Jefferson, N.C.: McFarland, 2005.

Chamberlain, Joshua L. "The Last Review of the Army of the Potomac, May 23, 1865." In *War Papers Read before the Commandery of the State of Maine, MOLLUS*. Vol. 3. Portland, Maine: Lefavor-Tower, 1908.

Cheseldine, Lt. Col. R. M. "Where Upton Made His Big Mistake." *Infantry Journal* 36 (March 1931): 279–288.

Clark, Rufus. *The Heroes of Albany: A Memorial of the Patriot-Martyrs of the City and County of Albany Who Sacrificed Their Lives during the Late War in Defence of Our Nation, 1861–1865, with a View of What Was Done in the County to Sustain the United States Government; and Also Brief Histories of the Albany Regiments*. Albany, N.Y.: John D. Brooks, Publisher, 1866.

Colt, Margareta Barton. *Defend the Valley: A Shenandoah Family in the Civil War*. New York: Crown Publishers, 1994.

Cooling, Benjamin Franklin. "The Missing Chapters of Emory Upton: A Note." *Military Affairs* 28 (February 1973): 12–15.

Cooper, James Fenimore. *The Deerslayer.* London: J. M. Dent, 1841; Rutland, Vt.: Charles E. Tuttle; New York: Everyman's Library, 1993.

Craven, Wayne. *The Sculptures of Gettysburg.* Published for the Gettysburg National Military Park. N.p.: Eastern Acorn Press, 1982.

Curtis, Newton Martin. *From Bull Run to Chancellorsville: The Story of the Sixteenth New York Infantry Together with Personal Reminiscences.* New York: G. P. Putnam's Sons, 1906.

Daggett, A. S. "The Battle of Rappannock Station, VA." In *War Papers Read before the Commandery of the State of Maine, MOLLUS.* Vol. 4. Portland, Maine: Lefavor-Tower, 1915.

Desjardin, Thomas A. *These Honored Dead: How Gettysburg Shaped American Memory.* Cambridge Center. Cambridge, Mass.: Da Capo Press, Perseus Books, 2003.

DeYoung, Mary Wallitt, ed. *Drummer Boy: Henry Hilton Wood and the Civil War.* Spencer, Iowa: DeYoung Press, 1990.

Dornbusch, D. E. *Regimental Publications and Personal Narratives of the Civil War: A Checklist.* Vol. 1, *Northern States.* Part 2. New York: New York Public Library, 1961.

Duncan, Captain Louis C. *The Medical Department of the United States Army in the Civil War.* Gaithersburg, Md.: Butternut Press, 1985.

Dyer, Frederick Henry. *A Compendium of the War of the Rebellion.* 3 vols. London: Thomas Yoseloff, 1959.

Edwards, Evelyn. "A Litchfield Family in the Civil War." Unpublished article, June 24, 1987. (On the Carran family).

Eicher, David J. *The Longest Night: A Military History of the Civil War.* New York: Simon and Schuster, 2001.

Ellis, D. A., comp. *Grand Army of the Republic, History of the Order in the U.S. by Counties, Otsego County Posts, Department of New York, Including a Complete Record of Soldiers Surviving and Buried in the County, with Company and Regiment, Together with Valuable Statistics and Miscellaneous Matter.* N.p.: Historical Publishing, 1892.

Esposito, Vincent J., ed. *The West Point Atlas of American Wars.* 2 vols. New York: Frederick A. Praeger, 1959.

Evans, Gen. Clement A., ed. *Confederate Military History Extended Edition: A Library of Confederate States' History in Seventeen Volumes, Written by Distinguished Men of the South.* Reprinted in 19 vols. Wilmington, N.C.: Broadfoot Publishing, 1987.

Fahs, Alice, and Joan Waugh, eds. *The Memory of the Civil War in American Culture.* Chapel Hill: University of North Carolina Press, 2004.

Fairchild, Charles Bryant. *History of the 27th Regiment N.Y. Vols, Being a Record of Its More Than Two Years of Service in the War for the Union, from May 21st, 1861 to May 31st, 1863, with a Complete Roster and Short Sketches of Commanding Officers, Also, a Record of Experience and Suffering of Some of the Comrades in Libby and Other Rebel Prisons; Compiled by C. Fairchild, of Company "D."* Binghamton, N.Y.: Carl and Matthews, Printers, 1888.

Fitzpatrick, David John. "Emory Upton: The Misunderstood Reformer." PhD diss., University of Michigan, 1996.

———. "Emory Upton and the Citizen Soldier." *Journal of Military History* 65, no. 2 (April 2001): 355–389.

Flick, Alexander C., ed. *History of the State of New York.* 10 vols. New York: Columbia University Press, 1933.

Fox, William F. *Regimental Losses in the American Civil War—1861–1865.* Albany, N.Y.: Albany Publishing, 1889.

Franchot, Charles Pascal. *Stanislas Pascal Franchot Arrives: A Pageant.* Published privately by Nicholas Van Vranken Franchot, 1940.

Gallagher, Gary W., ed. *Chancellorsville: The Battle and Its Aftermath.* Chapel Hill: University of North Carolina Press, 1996.

———. *The Wilderness Campaign.* Chapel Hill: University of North Carolina Press, 1997.

Geary, James W. *We Need Men: The Union Draft in the Civil War.* Dekalb: Northern Illinois University Press, 1991.

Glatthaar, Joseph T. *Partners in Command: The Relationships between Leaders in the Civil War.* New York: Free Press, 1994.

Gordon, John B. *Reminiscences of the Civil War.* New York: Charles Scribner's Sons, 1903.

Goss, Thomas, J. *The War within the Union High Command: Politics and Generalship during the Civil War.* Lawrence: University Press of Kansas, 2003.

Grant, Ulysses S. *Personal Memoirs.* 2 vols. New York: Charles L. Webster, 1885.

Green, James. *Death in the Haymarket: A Story of Chicago, the First Labor Movement, and the Bombing That Divided Gilded Age America.* New York: Pantheon, 2006.

Greene, A. Wilson. *Breaking the Backbone of the Rebellion: The Final Battles of the Petersburg Campaign.* Mason City, Iowa: Savas Publishing, 2000.

Greiner, James M. *Subdued by the Sword: A Line Officer in the 121st New York Volunteers.* Albany: State University of New York Press, 2003.

Guelzo, Allen C. *Lincoln's Emancipation Proclamation: The End of Slavery in America.* New York: Simon and Schuster, 2004.

Hagerman, Edward. *The American Civil War and the Origins of Modern Warfare: Ideas, Organization, and Field Command.* Bloomington: Indiana University Press, 1988 and 1992.

Haines, Alanson A. *A History of the 15th Regiment New Jersey Volunteers.* New York: Jenkins & Thomas, Printers, 1883.

Hall, Henry Seymour. "At Gettysburg with the Sixth Corps." November 6, 1896. In *War Talks in Kansas: A Series of Papers Read before the Kansas Commandery MOLLUS.* Kansas City, Kans.: Franklin Hudson Publishing, 1906.

———. "Personal Experience under General McClellan, after Bull Run, Including the Peninsular and Antietam Campaigns from July 27, 1861 to November 10, 1862." January 3, 1894. In *War Talks in Kansas: A Series of Papers Read before the Kansas Commandery MOLLUS.* Kansas City, Kans.: Franklin Hudson Publishing, 1906.

———. "Personal Experience under Generals Burnside and Hooker, in the Battles of Fredericksburg and Chancellorsville, December 11, 12, 13 and 14, 1862, and May 1, 2, 3 and 4, 1863." April 4, 1889. In *War Talks in Kansas: A Series of Papers Read before the Kansas Commandery MOLLUS.* Kansas City, Kans.: Franklin Hudson Publishing, 1906.

———. "Personal Experience as a Staff Officer at Mine Run, and in Albemarle County Raid; and as Commander of the Forty-third Regiment United States Colored Troops through the Wilderness Campaign, and at the Mine before Petersburg, Va., from November 7, 1863, to July 30, 1864." October 3, 1894. In *War Talks in Kansas: A Series of*

Papers Read before the Kansas Commandery MOLLUS. Kansas City, Kans.: Franklin Hudson Publishing, 1906.

Hardin, George A., and Frank H. Willard, eds. *History of Herkimer County, New York—Illustrated with Portraits of Many of Its Citizens*. Syracuse, N.Y.: D. Mason, Publishers, 1893.

Harris, Leslie. *In the Shadow of Slavery: African Americans in New York City, 1626–1863*. Chicago: University of Chicago Press, 2003.

Hathaway, John L. "The Mine Run Movement." In *War Papers Being Read before the Commandery of the State of Wisconsin, MOLLUS*. Vol. 1. Wilmington, N.C.: Broadfoot Publishing, 1993.

Hess, Earl. *The Union Soldier in Battle: Enduring the Ordeal of Combat*. Lawrence: University Press of Kansas, 1997.

———. *Field Armies and Fortification in the Civil War: The Eastern Campaigns, 1861–1864*. Chapel Hill: University of North Carolina Press, 2005.

———. *Trench Warfare under Grant and Lee: Field Fortifications in the Overland Campaign*. Chapel Hill: University of North Carolina Press, 2007.

Hesseltine, William B. *Civil War Prisons*. Columbus: Ohio State University Press, 1930.

———. *Lincoln and the War Governors*. New York: Alfred A. Knopf, 1948.

A History of Cooperstown. Including "The Chronicles of Cooperstown," by James Fenimore Cooper; "The History of Cooperstown: 1839–1886," by Samuel M. Shaw; and "The History of Cooperstown: 1886–1929." Cooperstown, N.Y.: Freeman's Journal, 1929.

History of Herkimer County, N.Y. with Illustrations, Descriptions of Scenery, Private Residences, Public Buildings, Fine Blocks, and Important Manufactories. New York: F. W. Beers, 1879.

History of the Mohawk Valley—Gateway to the West: 1614–1925—Covering the Six Counties of Schenectady, Schoharie, Montgomery, Fulton, Herkimer, and Oneida. Vol. 4. Chicago: S. J. Clarke Publishing, 1925.

Hodgins, Elsie, Edna L. Barr, and Della S. Kidder. "Kidder Family History: The Story of William Samuel and Mary Elizabeth Kidder." Typescript paper. 1961.

Hollis, Sylvia. "'The Black Man Almost Has Disappeared from Our Country': African American Workers in Cooperstown, New York, 1860–1900." *New York History* 88, no. 1 (2007): 13–31.

Holmes, Clay W. "The Elmira Prison Camp." Paper read February 7, 1912. In *Personal Recollections of the War of the Rebellion: Addresses Delivered before the New York Commandery MOLLUS, 1883–1891*. Edited by James Grant Wilson and Titus Munson Coan, MD. New York: The Commandery, 1891; repr., Wilmington, N.C.: Broadfoot Publishing, 1992, 4:351–372.

Holzer, Harold, ed. *The Union Preserved: A Guide to Civil War Records in the New York State Archives*. New York: Fordham University Press and New York State Archives Partnership Trust, 1999.

———. *State of the Union: New York and the Civil War*. New York: Fordham University Press and New York State Archives Partnership Trust, 2002.

Hotchkin, A. *A Concise History of the Town of Maryland from Its First Settlement . . .* Schenevus, N.Y.: Monitor Book and Newspaper Printing, 1876.

Hurd, D. Hamilton. *History of Otsego County, New York, with Illustrations and Biographical*

Sketches of Some of Its Prominent Men and Pioneers. Philadelphia: Everts and Farriss, 1878.

Huston, James A. *The Sinews of War: Army Logistics, 1775–1953.* Washington, D.C.: Office of the Chief of Military History, U.S. Army, 1966.

Hyde, Thomas W. *Following the Greek Cross: Or, Memories of the Sixth Army Corps.* Boston: Houghton Mifflin, 1894.

Hyson, John M., George E. Sanborn, Joseph W. A. Whitehorne, and William H. Mosberg. "The Suicide of General Emory Upton: A Case Report." *Military Medicine* 155, no. 10 (October 1990): 445–452.

Iobst, Richard W. *The Bloody Sixth.* Raleigh: North Carolina Confederate Centennial Commission, 1965.

———. *Civil War Macon: The History of a Confederate City.* Macon, Ga.: Mercer University Press, 1999.

Johnson, Robert Underwood, and Clarence Clough Buel, eds. *Battles and Leaders of the Civil War.* 4 vols. Secaucus, N.J.: Castle, 1887.

Jones, Archer. *Civil War Command and Strategy: The Process of Victory and Defeat.* New York: Free Press, 1992.

Jones, Gordon. "Gut History: Civil War Reenacting and the Making of an American Past." PhD diss., Emory University, 2007.

Keanealy, Thomas. *American Scoundrel: The Life of the Notorious Civil War General Dan Sickles.* New York: Doubleday, 2002.

Kimball, Maria Porter Brace. *A Soldier-Doctor of Our Army: James P. Kimball, Late Colonel and Assistant Surgeon-General, U.S. Army.* Boston: Houghton Mifflin, 1917.

King, Horatio C. "The Battle of Cedar Creek." Paper read at a meeting on December 3, 1883. In *Personal Recollections of the War of the Rebellion: Addresses Delivered before the New York MOLLUS.* Edited by James Grant Wilson and Titus Munson Coan, MD. New York: The Commandery, 1891; repr., Wilmington, N.C.: Broadfoot Publishing, 1992, 1:33–41.

———. "The Shenandoah Valley in the Great War." Paper read at a meeting on February 7, 1900. In *Personal Recollections of the War of the Rebellion: Addresses Delivered before the New York Commandery MOLLUS, 1883–1891.* Edited by James Grant Wilson and Titus Munson Coan, MD. New York: The Commandery, 1891; repr., Wilmington, N.C.: Broadfoot Publishing, 1992, 3:167–176.

Krutz, David P. *Distant Drums: Herkimer County, New York in the War of the Rebellion.* Utica, N.Y.: North Country Books, 1997.

Linderman, Gerald, F. *Embattled Courage: The Experience of Combat in the American Civil War.* New York: Free Press, 1987.

Marvel, William. *Lee's Last Retreat: The Flight to Appomattox.* Chapel Hill: University of North Carolina Press, 2002.

Mason, Edwin C. "Recollections of the Mine Run Campaign." In *Glimpses of the Nation's Struggle: A Series of Papers Read before the Minnesota Commandery MOLLUS.* St. Paul, Minn.: St. Paul Book & Stationery, 1887.

McConnell, Stuart. *Glorious Contentment: The Grand Army of the Republic, 1865–1900.* Chapel Hill: University of North Carolina Press, 1992.

McMahon, Martin T. "Major-General John Sedgwick." In *Personal Recollections of the War of the Rebellion: Addresses Delivered before the New York Commandery of the Loyal Legion of the United States, 1883–1891.* Edited by James Grant Wilson and Titus Munson Coan, MD. New York: The Commandery, 1891; repr., Wilmington, N.C.: Broadfoot Publishing, 1992, 2:159–182.

McPherson, James M. *For Cause and Comrades: Why Men Fought in the Civil War.* New York: Oxford University Press, 1997.

———. *Antietam: The Battle That Changed the Course of the Civil War.* Oxford: Oxford University Press, 2002.

Michie, Peter. "Reminiscences of Cadet and Army Service." Paper read October 4, 1893. In *Personal Recollections of the War of the Rebellion: Addresses Delivered before the New York Commandery MOLLUS, 1883–1891.* Edited by James Grant Wilson and Titus Munson Coan, MD. New York: The Commandery, 1891; repr., Wilmington, N.C.: Broadfoot Publishing, 1992, 2:183–197.

Mitchell, Reid. *The Vacant Chair: The Northern Soldier Leaves Home.* New York: Oxford University Press, 1993.

Mitchell, Stewart. *Horatio Seymour of New York.* Cambridge, Mass.: Harvard University Press, 1938.

Moore, Edward Alexander. *The Story of a Cannoneer under Stonewall Jackson: In Which Is Told the Part Taken by the Rockbridge Artillery in the Army of Northern Virginia.* New York: Neale Publishing, 1907.

Musick, Michael. "The Little Regiment: Civil War Units and Commands." *Prologue* (a publication of the National Archives and Records Administration) 27, no. 2 (Summer 1995): 151–171.

North, Safford E., ed. *Our County and Its People: A Descriptive and Biographical Record of Genesee County, New York.* Boston: Boston History, 1899.

Northcott, Dennis, and Thomas Brooks. *Grand Army of the Republic Department of Illinois Transcription of the Death Rolls, 1879–1947.* St. Louis, Mo.: Northcutt, 2003.

Nosworthy, Brent. *The Bloody Crucible of Courage: Fighting Methods and Combat Experience of the Civil War.* New York: Carroll and Graf Publishers, 2003.

Orcutt, Samuel. *History of the Towns of New Milford and Bridgewater, Connecticut: 1703–1882.* Hartford, Conn.: Case, Lockwood and Brainerd, 1882.

Parker, Maj. John H. *Trained Citizen Soldiery: A Solution of General Upton's Problem.* Menasha, Wisc.: Collegiate Press, George Banta Publishing, 1916.

Phisterer, Frederick. *New York in the War of the Rebellion: 1861 to 1865.* 3rd ed. 5 vols. Albany, N.Y.: J. B. Lyon, State Printers, 1912.

Quiner, E. B. *The Military History of Wisconsin: A Record of the Civil and Military Patriotism of the State in the War for the Union.* Chicago: Clarke, Publishers, 1866.

Rable, George C. *Fredericksburg! Fredericksburg!* Chapel Hill: University of North Carolina Press, 2002.

Rawley, James A. *Edwin D. Morgan, 1811–1883: Merchant in Politics.* New York: Columbia University Press, 1955.

Reed, Thomas B. *A Private in Gray.* Camden, Ark.: publisher unknown, 1905.

Rhea, Gordon C. *The Battle of the Wilderness, May 5–6, 1864.* Baton Rouge: Louisiana State University Press, 1994.

———. *The Battles for Spotsylvania Court House and the Road to Yellow Tavern, May 7–12, 1864.* Baton Rouge: Louisiana State University Press, 1997.

————. *To the North Anna River: Grant and Lee, May 13–25, 1864.* Baton Rouge: Louisiana State University Press, 2000.

————. *Cold Harbor: Grant and Lee, May 26–June 3, 1864.* Baton Rouge: Louisiana State University Press, 2002.

Roback, Henry. *The Veteran Volunteers of Herkimer and Otsego Counties in the War of the Rebellion, Being a History of the 152d N.Y.V., with Scenes, Incidents, etc., Which Occurred in the Ranks of the 34th N.Y., 97th N.Y., 121st N.Y., 2d N.Y., Heavy Artillery, and the 1st and 2nd N.Y. Mounted Rifles; Also the Active Part Performed by the Boys in Blue Who Were Associated with the 152d N.Y.V. in Gen. Hancock's Second Army Corps, during Grant's Campaign, from the Wilderness to the Surrender of Gen. Lee at Appomattox Court House, Va.* Little Falls, N.Y.: L. C. Childs & Son, 1888.

Roe, Alfred S. *The Tenth Regiment, Massachusetts Volunteer Infantry, 1861–1864.* Springfield, Mass.: Tenth Regiment Veteran Association, 1909.

Sabre, G. E. *Nineteen Months a Prisoner of War.* New York: American News Company, 1865.

Sauers, Richard A. *To Care for Him Who Has Borne the Battle: Research Guide to Civil War Material in the National Tribune.* Vol. 1, *1877–1884.* Jackson, Ky.: History Shop Press, 1995.

Sawyer, John. *History of Cherry Valley from 1740 to 1898.* Cherry Valley, N.Y.: Gazette Printers, 1898.

Sears, Stephen. *Chancellorsville.* New York: Houghton Mifflin, 1996.

————. *Gettysburg.* New York: Houghton Mifflin, 2003.

Seymour, William J. *The Civil War Memoirs of Captain William J. Seymour: Reminiscences of a Louisiana Tiger.* Edited and with an introduction by Terry L. Jones. Baton Rouge: Louisiana State University Press, 1991.

Shannon, Fred Albert. *The Organization and Administration of the Union Army, 1861–1865.* 2 vols. Cleveland, Ohio: Arthur H. Clark, 1928.

Shaw, Samuel M. *History of Cooperstown.* Cooperstown, N.Y.: Freeman's Journal, 1929.

Sheridan, Philip H. *Personal Memoirs.* 2 vols. New York: Charles L. Webster, 1888.

Silber, Nina. *The Romance of Reunion: Northerners and the South, 1865–1900.* Chapel Hill: University of North Carolina Press, 1993.

Smith, Abram P. *History of the Seventy-sixth Regiment New York Volunteers, What It Endured and Accomplished, Containing Descriptions of Its Twenty-five Battles, Its Marches, Its Camp and Bivouac Scenes . . .* Syracuse, N.Y.: Truair, Smith and Miles, 1867.

Smith, Arthur T., comp. *Papers Read before the Herkimer County Historical Society during the Years May 1914–November 1922,* vol. 5, paper entitled "Presentation of Historic Flags and World War Relics." Herkimer, N.Y.: Citizens Publishing, 1923.

Smith, George W. "Newspapers of Herkimer County." Paper presented to the Herkimer County Historical Society, December 10, 1898. In *Papers Read before the Herkimer County Historical Society during the Years 1896, 1897 and 1898.* Compiled by Arthur T. Smith. Herkimer, N.Y.: Citizen Publishing, 1899.

Soldiers' and Citizens' Album of Biographical Record Containing Personal Sketches of Army Men and Citizens Prominent in Loyalty to the Union; Also a Chronological and Statistical History of the Civil War and a History of the Grand Army of the Republic with Portraits of Soldiers and Prominent Citizens. Chicago: Grand Army Publishing, 1890.

Steiner, Paul E. "Medical-Military Studies on the Civil War: XII—Brevet Major General Emory Upton, U.S.A." *Military Medicine* 131 (March 1966): 281–289.

————. *Disease in the Civil War: Natural Biological Warfare in 1861–1865.* Springfield, Ill.: Charles C. Thomas Publisher, 1968.

Stevens, George T. *Three Years in the Sixth Corps.* Albany, N.Y.: S. R. Gray, Publisher, 1866.

Swinton, William. *Campaigns of the Army of the Potomac: A Critical History of Operations in Virginia, Maryland and Pennsylvania from the Commencement to the Close of the War, 1861–1865.* New York: Charles B. Richardson, 1866.

Taylor, Alan. *William Cooper's Town: Power and Persuasion on the Frontier of the Early American Republic.* New York: Alfred A. Knopf, 1995.

Thomas, Howard. *Boys in Blue from the Adirondack Foothills.* Prospect, N.Y.: Prospect Books, 1960.

Thompson, Erwin N. "The Presidio of San Francisco: A History from 1846 to 1995." Denver Service Center, National Park Service, Historic Resource Study, July 1997 (NPS-330).

Through the Years in the Town of Franklin 1792–1992. Franklin, N.Y.: Oulehoudt Valley Historical Society, 1995.

Trudeau, Noah Andre. *The Last Citadel: Petersburg, Virginia, June 1864–April 1865.* Baton Rouge: Louisiana State University Press, 1991.

————. *Out of the Storm: The End of the Civil War, April–June 1865.* Baton Rouge: Louisiana State University Press, 1994.

————. *Like Men of War: Black Troops in the Civil War, 1862–1865.* Boston: Little, Brown, 1998.

————. *Bloody Roads South: The Wilderness to Cold Harbor, May–June 1864.* Baton Rouge: Louisiana State University Press, 2000.

The Union Army: A History of Military Affairs in the Loyal States, 1861–1865—Records of the Regiments in the Union Army—Cyclopedia of Battles—Memoirs of Commanders and Soldiers. 8 vols. Wilmington, N.C.: Broadfoot Publishing, 1997. Originally published in 1908 by Federal Publishing.

Upton, Emory. *A New System of Infantry Tactics, Double and Single Rank, Adapted to American Topography and Improved Fire-Arms.* New York: D. Appleton, 1868.

————. *The Armies of Asia and Europe: Embracing Official Reports on the Armies of Japan, China, India, Persia, Italy, Russia, Austria, Germany, France, and England. Accompanied by Letters Descriptive of a Journey from Japan to the Caucasus.* New York: D. Appleton, 1878.

————. *The Military Policy of the United States.* Washington, D.C.: Government Printing Office, 1904.

————. *Epitome of Upton's Military Policy of the United States.* Washington, D.C.: Government Printing Office, 1916.

Walker, Aldace F. "The Old Vermont Brigade." In *Personal Recollections of the War of the Rebellion: Addresses Delivered before the New York Commandery MOLLUS, 1883–1891.* Edited by James Grant Wilson and Titus Munson Coan, MD. New York: The Commandery, 1891; repr., Wilmington, N.C.: Broadfoot Publishing, 1992, 2:316–335.

Walter, John F. "One Hundred and Twenty-first [Regiment] New York Infantry, Middle Village, N.Y." 8-page typescript manuscript, n.d. NYSHA.

Ward, David. "Sedgwick's Foot Cavalry: The March of the Sixth Corps to Gettysburg." *Gettysburg Magazine* 22 (January 2000): 43–65.

Wardell, Bernice. *History of Laurens Township.* Laurens, N.Y.: Bernice Wardell, 1975.

Warner, Ezra J. *Generals in Blue: Lives of the Union Commanders.* Baton Rouge: Louisiana State University Press, 1964.

Weber, Nicholas Fox. *The Clarks of Cooperstown: Their Singer Sewing Machine Fortune, Their Great and Influential Art Collections, Their Forty-Year Feud.* New York: Alfred A. Knopf, 2007.

Weeden, William B. *War Government Federal and State in Massachusetts, New York, Pennsylvania and Indiana, 1861–1865.* Boston: Houghton Mifflin, 1906.

Weigley, Russell. *Towards an American Army: Military Thought from Washington to Marshall.* New York: Columbia University Press, 1962.

———. *The Great Civil War: A Military and Political History, 1861–1865.* Bloomington: Indiana University Press, 2000.

Welcher, Frank J. *The Union Army 1861–1865: Organization and Operations.* Vol. 1, *The Eastern Theater,* and Vol. 2, *The Western Theater.* Bloomington: Indiana University Press, 1989.

Wert, Jeffry D. "Rappahannock Station." *Civil War Times Illustrated* 15 (December 1976): 4–6, 8, and 40–46.

———. *From Winchester to Cedar Creek: The Shenandoah Campaign of 1864.* Carlisle, Pa.: South Mountain Press, Publishers, 1987.

Westbrook, Robert S. *History of the 49th Pennsylvania Volunteers.* Altoona, Pa.: Altoona Times Printing, 1898.

White, Frank Everett. *Sailor's Creek: Major General G. W. Custis Lee, Captured with Controversy.* Lynchburg, Va.: Schroeder Publications, 2008.

Whitehorne, Joseph W. A. *The Battle of Cedar Creek: Self Guided Tour.* Washington, D.C.: U.S. Government Printing Office, 1992.

Williams, Kenneth P. *Lincoln Finds a General: A Military Study of the Civil War.* 5 vols. New York: Macmillan, 1949–1959.

Williams, T. Harry. *Lincoln and His Generals.* New York: Alfred A. Knopf, 1952.

Wilson, John S. "Captain Fish and the 121st New York Volunteers at Rappahannock Station, Virginia." *Military Collector and Historian: Journal of the Company of Military Historians* 48, no. 3 (Fall 1996): 114–120.

Winslow, Richard Elliott, III. *General John Sedgwick: The Story of a Union Corps Commander.* Novarto, Calif.: Presidio Press, 1982.

Index

Army of the Potomac, *continued*
  news accounts of, 137, 436
  and the 121st, 66–69, 104, 108, 194, 251,
    355, 367, 455, 458
  and the Overland campaign, 314, 317,
    318, 277–278, 284–287
  and the siege of Petersburg, 317, 355, 361,
    365–367
  Society of, 407
  See also Hooker, Joseph "Fighting Joe";
    McClellan, George B.; Overland
    campaign
Army of the Shenandoah. *See* Grant, Ulysses
  S.; Shenandoah campaign; Sheridan,
  Philip
Army of Virginia, 20
Army of West Virginia, 329, 339
Arnold, Thomas S., 36, 45, 150, 166 (image),
  171, 172, 505n19
Atlanta
  fall of, 20, 352, 353, 363
  Sherman's march toward, 321, 322, 351
Augur, C. C., 335
Austin, Stephen T., 121
Averell, William Holt, 10, 11, 24, 25

Babcock, H. H., 25
Babcock, Samuel, 332
Babcock, Washington, 174
Bailey, Albert, 66, 73, 205, 211
Bailey, Calista, 212–213, 259, 365
Bailey, David, 423, 472
Bain, John, 157–158
Bakersville (MD), 72, 82, 90, 94, 100, 105,
  494n18, 502n42
Baldwin, Luman, 363, 378, 387
Ballard, John H., 107, 139
Baltimore, 70, 194, 385
  hospitals in, 93, 201, 309, 345, 348
  121st in, 55–56, 153, 394
Baltimore Pike, 195–196
Banks, Nathaniel P., 218–219
Banks' Ford, 161, 164, 176–180, 506n33. *See
  also* Chancellorsville campaign
Barksdale, William, 163, 170
Barlow, Francis, 305
Barnes, Alvina Matilda, 475
Barnes, Elliot, 174
Barnes, William, 475
Barney, Napoleon B., 44
Barr, Charles H., 358
Bartlett, Joseph Jackson "Joe," 131–132, 234,
  490n17
  and the Bartlett affair, 185, 359–360

and Chancellorsville campaign, 161, 165,
  167, 169, 170, 179
at Crampton's Gap, 69–70
and 1863–64 winter quarters, 252–253,
  265
and Johnson's court martial, 142–143
Mosby's attack on headquarters of, 224–
  226
as 2nd Brigade commander, 67–69, 80,
  184, 195, 196, 197, 203–204, 294
Bartlett, Lewis C., 185, 359–360, 384
Bassett, Isaac, 358, 376
Bassett, William, 44, 62, 90, 97
Bates, Delavan, 1, 64, 69, 70, 77, 79, 82, 115,
  154–155, 216, 217, 222 (image), 269,
  356, 351, 356, 359, 468
on Bristoe Station battle, 227
and Chancellorsville campaign, 173–174,
  179, 182
as commander of 30th USCT, 270–271,
  318, 325, 367
on drinking among the 121st, 264, 266
and 1863–1864 winter quarters, 252, 255
and 1865 election, 355
on Fredericksburg, 137
at Gettysburg, 197–198, 202–203
on joining the Army of the Potomac
  (121st's inexperience), 68
on Lincoln's 1864 call for more recruits,
  360–361
and morale, 212
and Mosby's guerrillas, 221, 224
as new recruit, 28, 47, 51–52, 59, 68
on 95th and 96th Pennsylvania regiments,
  255, 256
and 121st's bond with 5th Maine, 417
and the Overland campaign, 288, 292,
  306, 307, 311, 315–316
on plundering, 214–215
post-war writings of, 1, 437, 447–448, 449,
  468, 469, 507n46, 508n6, 531n11,
  534n25
at Rappahannock Station, 237, 243, 244
and the siege of Petersburg, 362
on Upton, 88, 104, 269, 337
Bates, Reuben, 433, 472
Baum, Lester, 265
Beckwith, Dewitt Clinton, 24, 45, 62, 68, 73,
  78, 80, 135, 227, 229, 248, 404, 424
  (image), 444 (image), 490n23, 499n35,
  525n39
at Belle Plain, 121
at Cedar Creek, 342–343, 344–345, 347,
  349

and Chancellorsville campaign, 164, 167,
177, 180–181
on Custis Lee controversy, 441, 443
and 1863–64 winter quarters, 264
and 1864–1865 winter quarters, 367
and 1865 furlough, 362–363
on Franchot, 74–75
at Fredericksburg, 122, 125, 126–127
and Gettysburg, 192, 203
joins Army of the Potomac, 33–35, 53,
66, 68
in Key West, 38–39
and Lincoln's assassination, 385
on McClellan's firing, 117
on morale under Hooker, 148
and 121st Gettysburg Monument, 419,
420–421, 423
and 121st's history, 446, 449–450, 452–457
and the Overland campaign, 288, 289,
290, 293, 298, 299, 301, 302, 308–309,
310, 314, 324
post-war politics of, 469–471
at Rappahannock Station, 237, 244, 245
reenlistment into 121st, 39–40
at Sailor's Creek, 375, 376, 378
and the Shenandoah campaign, 334, 339–
340
and siege of Petersburg, 370, 371–372
on Upton, 83, 279
at war's end, 381, 382, 389–390, 394, 397,
400, 405, 406
Beckwith, Ezra D., 24, 470–471
Belle Island (prison), 174, 214, 291
Belle Plain, 99, 119–122, 158–159, 171, 256,
476
Bennett, Richard, 314, 318
Benson, Ada Remmel, 473–474
Bermuda Hundred, 324
Best, Isaac O., 153, 184, 307, 430, 444
(image)
and Bristoe Station battle, 227
and Chancellorsville campaign, 179–180
death of, 471, 472
and drinking among troops, 264–265,
520n34
at Fredericksburg, 123
on Hooker's firing, 193
and Lee's surrender, 381, 382, 383, 393,
400
and Mosby's raid on Bartlett
headquarters, 225
as 121st official historian, 49, 443, 445–
446, 448, 450–452, 453, 455–457, 488n2
and Overland campaign, 288, 303, 308

and praise for Upton, 89, 128
at Rappahannock Station, 238, 242
and siege/fall of Petersburg, 373
at Spotsylvania, 303, 308
and the Wilderness battle, 288
Bicknell, George W., 163, 417
Birch, Joseph, 302
Birney, David, 305
black soldiers. See U.S. Colored Troops
(USCT)
Bland, Daniel W., 248
the Bloody Angle, 304–311, 470. See also
Overland campaign
Bolles, Frank G., 46, 111
Borden, George Pennington, 479
Botts, John Minor, 250
Bounty Act of 1861, 102
bounty system, 29, 36
and bounty jumpers, 26, 104, 205, 207
and county bank loans, 26, 484n36
to "facilitate enlistments," 24–28, 484n40
and payment to troops, 51
veterans' attitudes toward, 68
Bowe, James, 174, 505n25
Bowen, James L., 386, 442
Bowling Green Road, 124, 127, 161, 163, 417
Boyer, Leonard, 24, 75–76
Bradshaw, Robert, 258, 475
Bradt, Charles M., 44, 151, 473
Brady, Mathew, 20
Bragg, Braxton, 219, 246
Brandon, John, 348, 372, 398
Brandy Station, 189, 192, 246, 255, 280
Briggs, Theodore, 309
Bristoe Station, battle of, 226–227
Brock Road, 286, 287, 292–293, 294
Brooks, William T. H. "Bully"
and Chancellorsville campaign, 161, 164,
165, 167, 169, 184
as 1st division commander, 146, 158
and Johnson court-martial, 143
Brown, John, 95, 331, 475–476
Buford, John, 194, 203, 226, 234
Bull, George, 101
Bull Run, 229, 508n10
first battle of, 16, 20, 21, 34, 38, 56, 67
second battle of, 20–21
Burkeville, 375, 384, 386, 387, 388
Burnside, Ambrose E.
Fredericksburg campaigns, 118, 122–129,
132, 133
lost confidence in, 138–139
as McClellan's replacement, 109, 111,
116–118, 139

fear of, 14, 21, 29, 52
  in New York state, 204–209
  121st views on, 139, 208, 360
  and states' rights, 23–24
  Upton's support for, 219, 460, 461
  v. bounty system, 28
  See also bounty system; Conscription Act
    of 1863; Enrollment Act of 1863
Drake, George, 303
Dry Tortugas Prison, 102, 142–143
Duffy, James N., 289, 305–306
Duroe, Horatio, 263, 340, 358, 370, 433, 473
Dustin, Redford, 372
Dye, Marshall, 65, 69, 71, 91, 100
Dyer, Alexander, 462

Early, Jubal Anderson
  and Chancellorsville, 162, 163, 164, 176–
    177
  and Mine Run, 249
  and rebel plundering, 525–526n58
  in the Shenandoah Valley, 317, 324–329,
    334–336, 338–342, 348–349, 351, 355
  and the Wilderness battle, 289, 291
Eastwood, Wilbur, 243
Eaton, George, 254, 258
Edwards, Clark S., 225, 240, 262, 417, 418
Edwards, Oliver, 306, 337
Edwards, Sara, 430
Edward's Ferry, 191, 192, 193–194
Eighteenth Corps, 313, 315
Eighth Corps, 329, 341, 342, 344
election of 1860, 12–13, 14, 37–38, 92
election of 1865, 351–355
Eleventh Corps, 229
Ellmaker, Peter, 236
Ellsworth American, 438
Ellsworth's Avengers. *See* New York
  Volunteers: 44th regiment (Ellsworth's
  Avengers)
Elmira Prison Camp, 320, 346, 349, 357, 389,
  477
Emancipation Proclamation, 105, 107, 109,
  110, 117, 205
  and 121st views on emancipation, 111–
    116, 216–217
  in the press, 115–116
  See also Lincoln, Abraham; slavery
Emmitsburg (MD), 193, 198, 200, 202, 203
Emmitsburg Pike, 1, 196, 202
Enfield muskets, 60–61, 163–164
Enrollment Act of 1863, 146, 204–206. *See
  also* Conscription Act of 1863; draft;
  recruitment

Erie Canal, 7, 11
Ewell, Richard S., 193, 287, 289, 291, 311,
  439, 440–441

Fahey, George, 319, 349
Fairfield (NY), 26, 36, 45, 54, 79, 92, 171, 201,
  202, 332, 446
Fairfield Academy, 35–36, 46, 53, 92, 112,
  148, 230, 336, 447, 479, 489n9, 521n48
Fairfield Seminary. *See* Fairfield Academy
Falmouth (VA), 122, 130, 133, 134, 161, 186,
  187
Farmer, Edwin, 433
Farr, Andrew Clark, 33
Farragut, David, 352, 400
Fenton, Reuben E., 354, 359, 384, 393, 400,
  401–402
Ferguson, Alonzo, 43, 44, 50, 429, 467
Ferguson, Charles T., 47, 155
Ferraro, Edward, 292
Field, Horace, 258
Field, Marcus, 411
Fields, William C., 24, 25, 41, 183, 272, 310,
  320
Fifth Corps, 65, 66, 253, 355, 360
  chasing Lee, 226
  and Gettysburg, 2–3, 196, 204
  under Meade, 145
  as part of Center Grand Division, 118,
    123
  at Rappahannock Station, 234, 236
  under Warren, 247, 287–288, 292–293,
    295, 304, 311–312, 313, 365–366
Finch, David, 50
Finley General Hospital, 121, 175, 255
Firman, Rosselle, 173
First Corps, 118, 123, 145, 162, 192, 194. *See
  also* Left Grand Division
First Families of Virginia ("FFVs"), 215, 216,
  220
Fish, John D., 153, 155, 185, 216, 233, 257
  (image), 268, 276, 476
  and court-martials, 262–263
  as D Company commander, 45–46, 158
  death at Spotsylvania, 309, 318, 366
  and desertions in Company D, 142
  and drinking among 121st, 264, 265
  and Jewett court-martial, 210
  at Rappahannock Station, 234, 236–238,
    242, 271–272, 436–437, 439
  recruitment efforts, 272, 273–274, 275
  (image)
Fisher, Elisha, 41, 208
Fisher's Hill, 338–339, 340, 352

celebrating the war's end, 383, 398, 400
and Chancellorsville campaign, 175
death of, 465–466
on desertion, 139, 140–141
and 1863–1864 winter quarters, 253
in Ellsworth's Avengers, 63, 153
on emancipation proclamation, 112, 113
and Galpin GAR post, 432, 433
and the Mud March, 134, 136
as 121st officer, 45, 53, 76, 274, 276–277,
330, 358, 360
and Overland campaign, 278, 281, 290,
293, 298, 301, 314, 360
praise for, 72–73
resignation of, 360, 366–367
on slavery, 113
wounding at Cedar Creek, 346, 348, 360
Gano, Nathaniel, 270
GAR. *See* Grand Army of the Republic
(GAR)
Gardner, William, 307
Garrity, James, 241
Gates, John, 33
Gates, William, 25
General Order No. 15, 42, 43, 358
Georgia
4th regiment, 228
18th regiment, 376, 377
German Flats (NY), 6, 12, 45, 47, 48, 98, 140,
465
Germanna Plank Road, 285, 286, 287
Gettysburg
and Army of the Potomac, 188–192, 196,
199–201, 204
battlefield aftermath, 198, 200
casualties, 200–201, 255
military cemetery at, 246
morale after, 213–217
121st at, 2–3, 186, 190, 192–199, 200–204,
213–216, 217
Sixth Corps' march toward, 189–196, 220
South after, 215–216
Gettysburg Battlefield Association, 419–420
Gettysburg Monument Committee, 2–3
Gettysburg National Battlefield Park, 1–2.
See also 121st Gettysburg Monument
Gibbon, John, 123, 125
Gibbs, George C., 321–322
Gifford, Benjamin, 140, 377, 378, 403
Gilbert, George H., 143–144
Gilbert, John H., 25
Godwin, Archibald C., 241
Goodier, William Henry Harrison "Tip," 32,
110, 343, 393

Gordon, John B., 300, 335, 406
at Cedar Creek, 341–344, 348
at Petersburg, 365, 369
and the Wilderness battle, 288–289, 290–291
Gorton, Frank, 47, 155, 185, 259, 265, 300,
311
Gosline, John M., 255
Gould, Jacob, 175
Gould, Orrin, 175
Graham, Homer, 33
Graham, Malcolm, 180, 506n33
Grand Army of the Republic (GAR) posts,
407, 411, 432–434, 445, 468, 471, 473
"Grand March," 228–229
Grant, Ulysses S.
and Hatcher's Run, 361, 366, 373, 475
and Lee's surrender, 382–383
at Lookout Mountain and Missionary
Ridge, 246
and Myers Hill, 311–312
named commander of Union armies, 20
and Opequan Creek, 335–336, 338
and the Overland campaign, 115, 221,
274, 277–278, 280, 282, 284–287, 291,
294–295, 304–305, 313–315, 320
and plan to destroy Lee's army, 285, 309–
310
and the Shenandoah campaign, 324, 328–
329, 334–336, 339–341
and siege and fall of Petersburg, 316, 351,
361–367, 368–374
review of 121st regiment, 278
and Upton promotion, 303–304
Graves, Crosby John, 97–98
Gray, John, 239, 241–242, 244, 270, 514n37
Green, Daniel Webster, 332
Green, Erastus, 101
Gregg, David N., 365, 366

Hagerstown (MD), 92, 94, 125, 203, 204
Haley, Alonzo, 210
Hall, Henry Seymour, 161, 184, 185, 231, 292
appointment to officer board, 118
and 1863–1864 winter quarters, 252, 254,
269
as 43rd USCT commander, 270, 292
at Gaines Mill, 403
at Mine Run, 247, 249
at Rappahannock Station, 240, 242, 244,
403
Halleck, Henry W., 118, 145, 191, 193, 202,
227, 234, 329, 335, 390
Hall's Hill (VA), 388, 391, 392, 394, 403, 432,
448, 464, 465, 468

Hamblin, Joseph E., 334, 337, 370, 372, 373–374, 378, 382, 440
Hamilton College, 40, 73, 184, 357, 450, 521n48
Hancock, Winfield Scott, 118, 287, 292, 304–305, 311, 462
Hanford, Maria Upton, 425
Harcourt, J. W., 55
Harpers Ferry, 95, 220, 319, 327, 331, 475–476
Harper's Weekly, 110
Harrington, N. H. "UHB," 175
Harris, Daniel, 479
Harris, Ira, 277, 468
Hartford, Michael, 128, 354
Hartwell, John, 90, 130, 141, 147, 276–277, 383, 391–392, 405, 436, 475, 510n43, 511n51
  and bitterness after Gettysburg, 213–214
  at Cedar Creek, 343, 344, 347, 349
  and Chancellorsville campaign, 173
  death of, 473
  and 1863–1864 winter quarters, 264, 266–267
  and 1864–1865 winter quarters, 361
  and 1865 election, 352, 354
  on Grant's review of the troops, 278
  on Lincoln's assassination, 385–386
  and low morale, 260, 332
  and Mine Run, 248, 249
  on 121st's "Grand March," 228
  on the 121st's march to Gettysburg, 194
  and the Overland campaign, 288, 290, 293–294, 315, 317, 319
  at Rappahannock Station, 238, 239
  resignation of, 151
  and Sailor's Creek, 375
  and the Shenandoah campaign, 327, 331
  and the siege and fall of Petersburg, 370, 371, 373, 374
  on slavery, 114
  on Upton, 250, 328, 337
  and the war's end, 383, 391–392, 405, 475
Hasbrouck, Henry, 462
Hassett, Thomas, 299, 378, 385, 393, 394, 442, 443, 447, 450
Hassett, William, 348
Hastings, Hugh, 408–409, 442
Hatcher's Run, 361, 366, 373, 475
Hawks, Erastus, 428–429, 434
Hawley, Elijah H., 126
Hawthorne, Harris Smith, 377–378, 403, 440–441, 442–443. *See also* Lee, Custis

Hays, Harry T., 235, 241, 242, 343
Hazel River, 250, 255, 283, 286–287
Hazel Run, 122
Heath, Joe, 33, 72, 258, 318, 388, 474
  and Custis Lee controversy, 442
  at 1864–1865 winter quarters, 367
  and Myers Hill skirmish, 312
  on Spotsylvania casualties, 302
  wounding at Opequan Creek, 336–337
Hendrix, James, 372
Henicker, Henry, 307–308
Herbert, Hilary A., 168, 169, 170, 180–181, 198
Herdman, George, 33, 243
Herdman, Lyman, 33, 72
Herdman, Norman, 33, 96, 146, 148–149, 258, 284, 303, 518n49
Herdman, William, 91
Herkimer County, 8 (map), 79, 110, 116, 156, 336, 394, 445, 446, 472
  and the bounty system, 26, 484n36
  celebration for 121st, 396–400
  and competition for recruits, 25
  deserters from, 140, 142–143
  1864 recruitment efforts in, 273–274, 275 (image)
  GAR posts in, 433
  on news of Lee's surrender, 383
  politics, 12–14, 470–471
  recruits, 16, 19, 24, 28, 32–33, 44–46, 47–48, 91–92, 102–103, 112–113, 494n17
  settlement of, 7, 9, 10–11
  and Valentine affair, 96–98
Herkimer County Historical Society, 470
Herkimer County Journal, 22, 75–76, 92, 151, 199, 503n4, 506n33
  on the bounty system, 26, 81
  on Camp Schuyler, 49
  and Chancellorsville campaign, 179
  deaths reported in, 172
  and 1862 gubernatorial election, 111–112
  and emancipation proclamation, 112
  Fred Ford as 121st's voice in, 144, 171–172
  listed deserters, 140, 496n36
  121st letters to, 213, 214, 265, 510n43
  praise for Franchot, 75
  as pro-Lincoln, 13
  on Upton's appointments, 155–156
  and the Valentine affair, 98
  See also *Little Falls Journal and Courier*
Herkimer Democrat, 72, 117
  on Beckwith candidacy, 470–471
  on Chancellorsville campaign, 169
  on deserters, 103
  on Gettysburg march, 193

on officer elections, 42, 43
and 121st's history, 405–406, 453–454, 456
and opposition to Lincoln, 13
on Rappahannock Station, 515n49
Hetherington, John E., 410
Hill, A. P., 176–177, 193, 227, 287, 311, 365
Hills, Delavan, 55, 56, 499n2
Hindmarsh, H. E., 440
History of the 121st New York Infantry, 49, 443, 453. *See also* Best, Isaac O.
Hogle, Charlie, 347
Hoke, Robert F., 235, 242
Holcomb, Irving
   and bounty system, 27–28
   as Company B captain, 45, 54, 125, 155
   resignation, 150–151, 152
Holmes, Oliver Wendell, 279
Holmes, Reuben, 123, 140
Holt, Daniel M., 74, 114 (image), 61–62, 141, 147, 151, 154, 187, 226, 230, 248–249, 276, 328, 446, 488n2, 504n14
   capture of, 506n33
   and Chancellorsville campaign, 165, 171, 172, 173, 176–180, 182–183
   on Chaplain Adams, 332–333
   death of, 464
   on desertion, 100
   on drinking among 121st, 264
   and 1863–1864 winter quarters, 253, 254, 280
   and 1865 election, 353
   and Gettysburg, 199, 214, 217
   on Jewett execution, 211
   and Mine Run, 248–249
   and Mud March, 135
   on Myers Hill skirmish, 312
   on Olcott court-martial, 266
   as 121st's assistant surgeon, 44, 90, 92, 94, 201, 395, 461
   and the Overland campaign, 278, 281, 283–285, 286, 296, 300, 309, 315, 316, 317
   praise for Olcott, 329–330
   at Rappahannock Station, 242
   resignation of, 90, 157, 349–350, 357
   and the Shenandoah campaign, 326, 328, 339, 341
   and slavery, 112–114, 248–249
   on Slocum appointment, 156–157
   and Valentine affair, 97–98
Hood, John Bell, 123, 126, 361–362
Hooker, Joseph "Fighting Joe," 138, 246
   as Burnside's replacement, 136–137, 144–145, 150

as Center Grand Division leader, 118, 133
and Chancellorsville campaign, 161–165, 168, 176–177, 179–180, 182, 187, 293–294, 508n6
changes implemented by, 145–148, 149, 150, 228
and desertion and dissention, 141–142, 146
at Fort Lincoln, 58–59
Lincoln's firing of, 193
as McClellan's replacement, 199, 228
trailing Lee toward Gettysburg, 188–192
Hopkins, Archibald, 439–440, 441
Hotaling (Houghtaling), Irving W., 90, 183
Howard, Oliver O., 145, 162, 368
Howe, Albion, 177, 272
Howland, Asa, 376, 379–380
Howland, Mote, 380
Howland, Ten Eyck, 115, 147, 216, 376, 377 (image), 379–380, 440, 473
Huartson, George, 32
Huartson, James, 32
Huartson, Robinson, 32
Huartson, William, 32
Hubbell, Fernando, 126
Hurd, D. Hamilton, 448, 456
Hyde, George, 101
Hyzer, Thomas H., 95, 105

Ilion (NY), 9, 10, 12, 28, 39, 98, 122, 332, 383, 416, 445, 465, 472
Ingalsbe, Laurin, 138
Ingraham, John J., 71, 106, 216, 220, 221, 250, 283, 350, 357, 367
   at Belle Plain, 119, 120
   and Chancellorsville campaign, 167–168, 170, 180
   and Copperheads, 188, 206
   and 1863–1864 winter quarters, 251, 254, 258
   and 1865 election, 353, 355
   and Gettysburg, 196
   and Jewett execution, 211, 212
   and Lee's surrender, 383, 387, 388–389, 391, 393
   and Lincoln's assassination, 385–386
   on Lincoln's review of the troops, 78
   and Mosby's raid on Bartlett headquarters, 225
   pessimism of, 136, 327
   and picket duty, 228
   at Rappahannock Station, 202
   at Sailor's Creek, 376
   and the Shenandoah campaign, 331, 340, 344, 349

and 1863–1864 winter quarters, 254
on Fredericksburg, 137
at the front, 69, 104–105, 106
and Gettysburg, 191–192, 204
insubordination of, 103
and the Mud March, 135
as new recruit, 36, 40, 41, 47, 51, 54, 65,
485n12
and the Overland campaign, 284, 310–311
promotion to sergeant, 271
as student, 35, 36, 92
on Upton, 87, 89, 148
Republican Party, 21, 44, 109, 183, 231–232, 352
Republican Radicals, 108, 110, 116
Revolutionary War, 4, 6, 7, 22, 26, 31, 33,
399, 409, 410, 414
Reynolds, John F., 118, 145, 162, 194, 295
Rhode Island, 1st Light Artillery, 343
Rice, Adam Clarke, 36–37, 70, 71, 79, 189,
201, 202, 216, 227, 229
and Chancellorsville, 163, 169, 170, 172, 179
death of, 91, 230–231
and the draft, 205, 208–209
on emancipation proclamation, 112–113
and Gettysburg, 200, 214
on Harpers Ferry, 94–95
on Hooker, 145, 148, 193
on Mosby's guerrillas, 223–224
and 121st's written history, 446–447
on slavery, 217
on Upton, 88, 458–459
Richfield Springs (NY), 10, 24, 27, 45, 48,
416, 444
Richmond (VA), 20, 106, 161, 182, 189, 351,
361, 371, 388
Burnside's plan to capture, 118, 139
fall of, 374, 383, 387
Grant's strategy for, 284, 285, 292, 313,
316, 317, 339
Lee's defense of, 187, 335, 376
Richmond Enquirer, 242
Rider, J. Lafayette, 15–16
Right Grand Division, 118, 122–123, 126,
127. *See also* Army of the Potomac
Robinson, Rufus L., 273
Rodes, Robert, 300, 335–336
Root, Elihu, 461, 463
Rosecrans, William, 187, 218, 226
Round, Joe "J. B.," 437, 438
Russell, David A.
death of, 337, 338
delivers battle flags to Washington, 245,
515n50
at Fredericksburg, 124

at Rappahannock Station, 236–238, 240,
244–245, 254
and "second" Rappahannock Station, 436,
438
at Spotsylvania, 295, 296, 297, 298, 300–
301, 303
Ryder, Anson, 371, 372

Sage, Henry, 92
Sage, John R., 132, 134 (image), 486n25
on deserters, 102
under Franchot, 66
as 121st's chaplain, 44, 81–82, 90, 92, 133,
141, 332
optimism of, 137
post-war years, 480
praise for Upton, 128
Sailor's Creek, 385, 530n20
and Custis Lee controversy, 439–443, 447
121st casualties at, 376, 379–380, 390–391,
473
as the 121st's last battle, 375–377, 378
Salem Church, battle of, 152, 155, 159, 162,
181, 192, 198, 201, 222 (image), 284, 302
desertion at, 209–210
121st regiment at, 119, 165, 167–176, 182–
183, 229, 277, 316 (image), 317, 401,
504n16
121st casualties at, 3, 32, 33, 170–171, 175,
186, 220, 301, 318, 348, 406, 507n43
troops' attitudes after, 213, 244
as Union loss, 182
Upton's praise for 121st at, 219
wounded, 255
See also Chancellorsville campaign
Salient. *See* the Muleshoe (salient)
Sayles, Dolphus, 160, 192, 253, 259, 283,
302–303, 504n14, 519n63
Scott, Winfield, 145, 267, 400
Second Corps, 118, 122–123, 145, 190, 198,
247, 292, 304–305, 315, 375
Sedgwick, John, 132, 188–189, 272, 277
and Chancellorsville campaign, 161–165,
170, 176–177, 179–180
death of, 302
and 1863–64 winter camp, 251, 252–253
and Gettysburg, 195–196, 201–204
at Mine Run, 247
and the Overland campaign, 286–287,
288, 289, 294–295, 302
at Rappahannock Station, 234, 235, 244,
245
as Sixth Corps commander, 145–146, 194,
428

Seminary Ridge, 1, 197, 198, 200
Semmes, Paul, 169
Serrell, Edward S., 18
Seven Days Battles, 16, 20
Seymour, Horatio, 12, 31, 101, 147, 272, 279, 292
  absentee ballot bill veto, 231–232
  and Bartlett affair, 360
  criticism of, 206, 207, 211
  draft riots and, 205–206, 209
  and 1865 presidential election, 353–354
  election of, 108, 109–112, 117, 138
  and opposition to Lincoln's policies, 110–111, 116, 246
  political defeat, 232–233, 353–354
  and Upton, 149–150
Seymour, Truman, 290
Seymour, William Johnson, 241
Shaler, Alexander, 290
Shaul, John D., 19, 23, 28
Shay, George, 377
Shenandoah campaign, 324–350
  Cedar Creek battle, 330–332, 340–349, 360, 366, 376–377, 379
  and Early, 324–329, 334–336, 340–342, 348–349, 355, 526n58
  Fisher's Hill, 338–339, 340, 352
  and Lee's northern movement, 187, 189, 191
  Opequon Creek battle, 330, 335–337, 338–339, 340, 352, 440
  and the Valley's strategic value, 324
  Winchester battle, 335–338
  See also Army of the Shenandoah
Shenandoah River, 341
Sheridan, Philip, 3, 67, 213, 415, 461, 463
  at Cedar Creek, 340–349
  at Cold Harbor, 313
  "legendry ride" of, 344
  praise for Upton at Opequon Creek, 337
  promotion to brigadier general, 338
  at Sailor's Creek, 441
  and the siege of Petersburg, 441, 443
  in the Shenandoah campaign, 3, 20, 328–329, 334–335, 340–342, 344, 349, 416
  victory at Fisher's Hill, 338–339
  victory at Opequon Creek, 335–336, 338
Sherman, James, 377
Sherman, William Tecumseh, 20, 246, 219, 317, 409, 415, 461
  capture of Atlanta, 352
  in Georgia, 302, 321, 322, 341, 351, 361, 368, 432

Johnston's surrender to, 387
  in North Carolina, 368, 384, 386
Shiloh, battle of, 20, 321, 325
Shockley, Charley, 70
Sickles, Daniel, 1–2, 145, 196, 401, 428
Simmons, Peter, 216, 376, 478–479
Singer, Isaac, 12
Sixth Corps, 295, 384, 392–393
  assignment to Army of the Shenandoah, 329
  badge, 114 (image), 146–147, 398
  at Belle Plain, 119
  at Cedar Creek, 341–349
  and Cold Harbor, 313–315
  crossing the Rappahannock, 188–189
  defense of Washington, 326–327
  and Myers Hill skirmish, 311–312
  northern march toward Gettysburg, 189–191
  at Opequon Creek, 335–337, 338
  as part of Burnside's Left Grand Division, 118, 119, 123
  at Sailor's Creek, 375–378
  Sedgwick as commander of, 145–146, 194, 428
  and the siege of Petersburg, 328, 355–356, 365–366, 369–373, 374
  Slocum as commander of, 66–67
  at Spotsylvania, 292–295, 304–307
  three brigades of, 66–67
  Upton as officer in, 85, 97
  Wright as commander of, 279, 295
Skinner, Dolphus I., 172
Skinner, William I., 25, 398
slavery
  and Lee's surrender, 387, 399–400
  121st's views on, 105, 111–116, 215, 216–217, 248–249, 271, 281, 284, 410, 414
  as religious issue, 89
  and states' rights, 108–109
  in upstate New York, 9–10
  Upton's views on, 85
  See also abolition; Emancipation Proclamation
Slocum, Henry W., 66, 69, 270
  and appointment of Upton, 86
  as commander of 1st Division, Sixth Corps, 66, 67
  and 1863–1864 winter quarters, 254
  friendship with Franchot, 82
  at Rappahannock Station, 242
  as Twelfth Corps commander, 145
  and the Wilderness battle, 290

Slocum, John O., 66, 265, 328, 333 (image)
    and Cedar Creek battle, 525n49
    and defense of Washington, 325, 326
    and drinking among recruits, 263–264
    and 1863–1864 winter quarters, 254, 270
    and 1864–1865 winter quarters, 361
    and 1865 election, 352, 354
    as 121st's surgeon, 90, 156–157, 278, 290,
        302, 348, 350, 357
    and the Overland campaign, 284, 285,
        316, 317
    post-war years, 465
    at Rappahannock Station, 242
    at siege of Petersburg, 372
Smith, Albert E., 347–348
Smith, Ingraham, 28, 126, 255, 280–281, 283,
    317
Smith, James H., 452, 456
Smith, Philip, 244, 261, 263
Smith, Thomas, 307, 309
Smith, William "Baldy," 313, 315
Smith, William P., 118
Snell, George H., 44, 72, 398
Snell, Milton, 266
Society of the Army of the Potomac, 407
South Mountain, battle of, 69–70, 202–203,
    301, 411
Special Order No. 463, 43
Spicer, Edward, 125, 127, 164
Spotsylvania, 166 (image), 313, 315–316, 415
    assault on "the bloody angle" at, 304–311,
        470
    assault on the salient (Muleshoe) at, 294,
        295, 296–304
    Lee's army heads toward, 292, 294
    121st at, 3, 119, 292–294, 428, 432
    121st casualties at, 102, 257 (image), 301–
        303, 307, 309–311, 318
    121st troops taken prisoner at, 388
    Upton at, 295, 296–301, 303–304, 305–
        309, 311
    See also Overland campaign
Spotsylvania Court House, 286, 311, 315,
    433, 475
Sprague, John T., 274
Springfield rifles, 60–61
Stanton, Edwin, 11, 31, 131–132, 188, 339,
    403, 515n50
    and desertion, 30, 100
    and election eve furloughs, 354
    on enlistment duration, 185
    and Hooker, 145
    and the "Immortal Six Hundred," 329
    and recruitment needs, 21, 52–53

on Sheridan promotion, 338
    support for Burnside, 139
    weapons issued by, 61
    See also War Department, U.S.
Staring, Charles E., 46, 69, 92–93, 151–152
state militias, 14–15, 16, 19, 21, 24, 41–42,
    460
states' rights, 24, 85, 395–396, 483n28
Stebbins, Jean R. "J. R.," 49, 112, 386
Stephens, Aaron, 174
Sternberg, Theodore, 278, 346, 468
Stevenson, John, 338, 339
Stockley, Charles, 33
Stoneman, George, 146
Story, Albert, 43, 44, 48
Stuart, James Ewell Brown "Jeb," 124, 189,
    250
Sturges, Hezekiah, 24, 31
Sumner, Edwin, 118, 123, 138
Susquehanna River, 5, 11, 193
Sykes, George, 196, 234
Synott, Stephen H., 37, 260, 365
Syracuse Journal, 465

Taft, James, 273
Taney, Roger, 12
Tanner, Albert S., 282
Tanner, Merton, 137–138, 474
Tanner, Milo B., 258
Tanner, N. P., 143
Tappan, Arthur, 475
Tappan, Lewis, 475
Teel, George, 63, 72, 79, 187, 209, 214, 229,
    271, 272–273
    at Belle Plain, 121–122
    and bounty system, 51
    on the draft, 205
    at 1863–1864 winter camp, 253, 254–255,
        263–264, 266
    and 1865 election, 352
    at Fort Stevens, 327
    at Gettysburg, 192
    at Mine Run, 248
    as new recruit, 55, 59, 74
    and the Overland campaign, 290, 291,
        307, 314, 315, 317
    at Rappahannock Station, 240
    and the Shenandoah campaign, 327, 336–
        337
    wounding at Cedar Creek, 345, 348,
        489n11, 498n27
Third Corps, 118, 123, 145, 196, 226
Thomas, Lorenzo, 98, 131–132
Timmerman, Henry, 273